A DICTIONARY OF
Philosophical Quotations

A DICTIONARY OF
Philosophical
Quotations

edited by

A. J. Ayer and Jane O'Grady

BLACKWELL
Reference

Copyright © Blackwell Publishers Ltd, 1992, 1994
Editorial organization © Estate of A.J. Ayer and
Jane O'Grady 1992, 1994
Glossary © Jane O'Grady

First published 1992
First published in USA 1992
First published in paperback (with corrections) 1994
Reprinted 1994, 1995, 1997

Blackwell Publishers Ltd
108 Cowley Road
Oxford OX4 1JF, UK

Blackwell Publishers Inc
350 Main Street
Malden, Massachusetts 02148, USA

All rights reserved. Except for the quotation of short passages for the purposes
of criticism and review, no part of this publication may be reproduced, stored
in a retrieval system, or transmitted, in any form or by any means, electronic,
mechanical, photocopying, recording or otherwise, without the prior permission
of the publisher.

Except in the United States of America, this book is sold subject to the condition
that it shall not, by way of trade or otherwise, be lent, re-sold, hired out, or
otherwise circulated without the publisher's prior consent in any form of binding
or cover other than that in which it is published and without a similar condition
including this condition being imposed on the subsequent purchaser.

British Library Cataloguing in Publication Data
A CIP catalogue record for this book is available from the British Library

Library of Congress Cataloging in Publication Data
A CIP catalogue record for this book is available from the Library of Congress

ISBN 0–631–19478–9 (Pbk)

Typeset in 10 on 12pt Sabon
by Hope Services (Abingdon) Ltd
Printed and bound in Great Britain
by T. J. International Limited, Padstow, Cornwall

This book is printed on acid-free paper

CONTENTS

൫൫൫൫൫൫

PUBLISHER'S NOTE

෨෨෨෨෨෨

At the time of his death in 1989, A. J. Ayer had been working for several months on this dictionary. His idea was to recruit a number of his most distinguished colleagues to assist him in identifying and compiling a range of quotations from many areas of philosophy that each had come across during their professional association with the discipline. The early planning stages of the book benefited from a very clear editorial vision of what the dictionary aimed to do, and no less clear a vision of Ayer's own role as editor. 'You need to cajole, not hector contributors', he wrote, in a lesson to his publisher on editorial manners.

Ayer's literary executors were no less delighted than Blackwell when Jane O'Grady agreed to continue the project and complete the book to Ayer's plan, while nevertheless bringing her own editorial skill and judgement to the final selection and placing of many of the quotations. The Introduction explains her role in more detail but, substantially, this is the volume that A. J. Ayer proposed to Blackwell in 1988.

INTRODUCTION

🔖🔖🔖🔖🔖🔖

A. J. Ayer's suggestion that he should compile a dictionary of philosophical quotations was one of those ideas the excellence of which is attested by puzzlement that it has never been thought of before. In this case, however, there is some reason why, if it had been previously conceived, the idea had not been put into practice. The sort of thing readers expect from a book of quotations is a set of aphoristic utterances which trigger an immediate response of pleasure, agreement, amusement or awe, and which seem 'deep' without requiring to be sounded. But, though incidentally full of stylishness and wit, philosophical thought is not essentially aphoristic, and cannot easily be boiled down into resonant sayings. It consists mainly in intricate, often lengthy, argument, which usually invokes or assumes understanding of the philosophical positions it opposes.

The compiler of philosophical quotations is therefore in a difficult position. To reproduce too many long closely argued passages runs the risk of boring the reader; to produce *only* the conclusions to such arguments would be baffling and frustrating; and it is often misleading, distorting, or impossible to convey an argument in small chunks or in passages full of ellipses. Or where this *can* be done, there is the danger of imposing a certain homogeneousness of quotability, and of replacing ponderousness with pithiness at the cost of losing philosophers' distinctiveness and style. Merely to reproduce their peripheral witticisms would not do justice to them either.

I have used a combination of these various risk-involving methods of quotation, trying to avoid the pitfalls of each. Where possible, in order to supply the necessary presupposed background to the arguments, I have selected quotations which effectively cross-refer to, and complement, one another (Reid attempting to refute Hume, Condillac appreciatively criticizing Locke). This also, I hope, conveys a sense of philosophy as shared and cumulative dispute, rather than just the solitary musing it is often taken to be, and of how philosophers constantly both build on and demolish one another. For readers unused to philosophy there is a

Glossary, in which I have aimed not merely to define the philosophical terms used in the book, but, given the limited space, to set them in the context of the disputes in which they feature, and thus make clear their significance.

Before he died, A. J. Ayer recruited some very able philosophers to contribute quotations on the major philosophers in the book. Of these none perhaps has brought citation to so fine an art as Professor Strawson, who actually managed to represent Kant's weighty, awesome arguments in single sentences or short passages. Justin Broackes was also excellent on the admittedly more fluent and charming Hume, and Christopher Norris was indefatigably cheerful and generous in providing reams of lengthy passages from any Continental philosopher whenever requested. But above all, without the help of my husband, Ted Honderich, especially on contemporary philosophers and on the organizational side of the book, I doubt I could have completed Ayer's enormous task.

As well as these and other major contributors, I was lucky to have occasional little windfalls. J. J. C. Smart, for instance, sent in a quotation from William Lycan which was interestingly similar to an idea he himself had first propounded (a Darwin and Wallace-type coincidence), and Neil Cooper kindly provided many of his own favourite quotations. I must add, though, that none of the major contributors, all of whose work was extremely helpful, can be held responsible for the shortened, lengthened, depleted, supplemented, reordered, or sometimes replaced versions of what they supplied. Some of them may fail to recognize the material they originally produced, or to recognize in the other sense the interpretative slant inevitably put upon it due to the very process of change and supplementation.

For of course another difficulty in this sort of enterprise is how to weigh the claims to representative space of different philosophers (and, within each philosopher's selection, how to do justice to his or her ideas without either producing too superficial a summary of several, or emphasizing one or two at the expense of others) while at the same time providing the occasional taste of their humour and personal history. In the end it seemed impossible satisfactorily to exactly apportion these rival aims, and attempts at encyclopedic balance had to be abandoned. Readers and critics who insist on it may also complain about the amount of space given to contemporary philosophers, and certainly these tend to pall beside dead ones who are more established, or more charming. But since philosophy is not just a matter of venerable figures or of charm but of continuous dispute and living issues, it seemed important to include a good many of them. This in turn, however, produced another possibility for imbalance: high-ranking philosophers, dead and alive, may sometimes be neglected for less distinguished ones where the latters' work seemed more accessibly to express or exemplify a current philosophical preoccupation. Those who object that too much space is given to a philosopher such as Benhabib, for instance, whose writing is not enhanced by being alphabetically adjacent to the stylistically felicitous Benjamin, should bear in mind that she represents an important strand of feminist thinking on ethics and epistemology.

Geographically as well as temporally, the same local perspective has been applied: the selection is confined to the Western tradition, neglecting Eastern, and even Eastern European, philosophy. There was anyway too much immediately to choose from without ranging further afield.

As to sources, the references had necessarily to be brief, and, for this reason and for ease of access, secondary rather than original sources have often been given, though inevitably an occasional citation may refer to an untranslated work, for instance Condillac's *Extrait raisonné*, and the Buridan passage – not unfortunately on the apparently non-existent ass – which I tracked down, via a Rescher article, to where it is quoted by Duhem. I am grateful to Catherine and Jean Gimpel, Aliette Sanford and Anne Diamant for helping me to wrestle with its medieval French and ambiguous ending. My greatest thanks must of course go to editor Caroline Richmond, not just for her excellent work but for saintly patience in putting up with my incessant revising.

*

Had A. J. Ayer lived to carry on the editing of this book, it would obviously be very different. I doubt whether he would have included as much from Derrida or from other Continental philosophicals as I have, being inclined to dismiss that style of philosophy as 'woolly uplift'. In fact, according to the limits he put on respectable philosophy in *Language, Truth and Logic*, many of these quotations would not merit inclusion at all, although he later recanted much of what he said in this young man's book. For, finally, yet another difficulty in compiling philosophical quotations is that, far more than with other subjects or themes, it cannot easily be presupposed what is to count as a quotation of the required type. By its very nature philosophy necessarily involves discussion as to what it actually is, a problem which of course is ultimately undecidable, and usually desultory in comparison with other philosophical issues. But it becomes more pressing whenever, as sporadically happens, a philosopher or school of philosophers insists that one particular method of philosophizing (theirs) is the only correct one, and that the rest of philosophy should be abolished since it is not philosophy at all. Such claims, like that of Ayer himself, have a limited fashion and typically are speedily ousted by assertions that there is not merely a unitary method of correct philosophizing, or simply that the putatively correct one is wrong. In fact, rather than a single subject, philosophy seems to be many, with roots and tendrils in literature, the sciences, sociology and other disciplines, and it would also claim the right to produce constitutive critiques of these. But the undecidability, yet dogmatic assertiveness, about what philosophy is, coupled with the fact that what can count as philosophy is so diffuse and wide-ranging, means that compiling a collection of philosophical quotations is itself a question-begging enterprise, and both more hazardous and personal than the sometimes-assumed objectivity of philosophy would lead one to anticipate. The result may therefore be a book about which everyone will find something to carp – favourite sayings, even favourite philosophers, omitted, Kristeva overbalancing Kuhn, some extracts too pruned, some too lengthy. I hope, though, that the reverse may also be true, that the polyphony of voices – wise, silly, puzzled, dogmatic, humorous, weighty, tragic and elated – speaking through the book, will give readers both inside and outside the subject a sense of its infuriating pleasure.

J. O'G.

LIST OF CONTRIBUTORS

𝕾𝕾𝕾𝕾𝕾𝕾

Major Contributors

Justin Broackes
Alexander Broadie
David Charles
John Cottingham
Simon Critchley
Patrick Gardiner
Anthony Grayling
Stephen Guest
Ted Honderich
Christopher Hookway
Gerard J. Hughes
Michael Inwood
Casimir Lewy
William Newton-Smith
Paul Noordhof
Christopher Norris
Derek Parfit
David Pears
George Pitcher
Stephen Priest
Fred Rosen
Robert Sharpe
John Skorupski
Thomas Sorell
Timothy Sprigge
Peter Strawson

Allen Wood
John Worrall

Other Contributors

Andrew Belsey
James Bogen
Sophie Botros
James Burge
G. A. Cohen
Neil Cooper
Tim Crane
Andrew Edgar
Alastair Hannay
Sarah Hutton
Louis Jacobs
Susan Khin Shaw
Nicola Lacey
Keith Lehrer
David McLellan
Bimal Matilal
Donald Micling
Arthur Miller
Joan O'Grady
Philip Pettit
Alan Ryan
Patricia Ward Scaltsas
J. J. C. Smart
Jonathan Wolff

Acknowledgements

𝔊𝔊𝔊𝔊𝔊𝔊

Every effort has been made to trace all copyright holders of the selections printed in this book. However, if copyright has been infringed, we shall be pleased, on being satisfied as to the owner's title, to make proper acknowledgement in future editions.

American Philosophical Quarterly: William P. Alston. Reprinted with permission.

Analysis: Edmund L. Gettier.

The Aristotelian Society: Errol Bedford, 'Emotions', PAS Vol. LVII, 1956/7, ©1957; Sabina Lovibond, 'True and False Pleasures', PAS Vol. XC, 1989/90, ©1990. Reprinted by courtesy of the Editor of the Aristotelian Society.

Jonathan Bennett: Reprinted by permission of the author.

Simon Blackburn: ©the author.

Blackwell Publishers: G. E. M. Anscombe; Noam Chomsky; René Descartes, *Descartes: Philosophical Letters*; Michèle le Doeuff; Paul Feyerabend; Hartry Field; Gottlob Frege; Martin Heidegger; Karl Jaspers; Anthony Kenny; Saul Kripke; Julia Kristeva; David Lewis; Robert Nozick; Richard Rorty; David Wiggins; Seyla Benhabib. Reprinted with permission of the publisher. Ludwig Wittgenstein. Courtesy of the Wittgenstein Trustees and Blackwell Publishers.

Basic Books Inc.: Robert Nozick.

Bobbs-Merrill Publishers: G. W. F. Hegel, *The Philosophy of History*, in *Reason in History*, copyright Liberal Arts Press Inc., 1953.

Cambridge University Press: G. E. Moore. Reprinted with permission. René Descartes, *The Philosophical Writings I & II*; J. G. Fichte; Thomas Nagel; Friedrich Nietzsche, trs. R. J. Hollingdale; Hilary Putnam; Giambattista Vico; Alfred North Whitehead; Bernard Williams; Richard Wollheim.

David Campbell Publishers Ltd: Gottfried Wilhelm Leibniz, *Leibniz: Philosophical Writing*, Reproduced from the Everyman's Library Edition, 1973, with permission.

University of Chicago Press: Jacques Derrida, *Writing and Difference* (1978). Reprinted with permission.

Noam Chomsky/Praeger: *Knowledge of Language* (Praeger, 1986). Reprinted with permission.

Mrs Margot Cory: George Santayana.

Croom Helm: Auguste Comte, *The Essential Comte* (1974).

Daniel C. Dennett: Reprinted by permission of the author.

Dover Publications Inc.: Arthur Schopenhauer.

Gerald Duckworth & Co Ltd: Alasdair MacIntyre. Reprinted with permission.

University of Notre Dame Press: Alasdair MacIntyre.

Michael Dummett: ©the author.

Dusquesne University Press: Emmanuel Levinas.

Gerald Dworkin: ©the author.

Ronald Dworkin: Reprinted by permission of the author.

Philippa Foot: ©the author.

Michael Frayn: ©Michael Frayn 1962, 1967. Reprinted by permission of the author.

Editions Gallimard: Jean-Paul Sartre, *Being and Nothingness* (1958); *Sketch for a Theory of the Emotions* (1962).

Fundacion José Ortega y Gasset.

Jonathan Glover: ©the author.

Victor Gollancz Ltd: Ernest Gellner, *Words and Things* (1959).

Nelson Goodman: Reprinted by permission of Catherine Z. Elgin for the author.

Hamish Hamilton: Albert Camus, *The Myth of Sisyphus*, trs. Justin O'Brien; *The Rebel*, trs. Anthony Bower.

Stuart Hampshire: Reprinted by permission of the author.

Alastair Hannay: Reprinted by permission of the author.

Harcourt Brace Jovanovich: Noam Chomsky, *Language and Mind*, ©Harcourt Brace Jovanovich 1968, 1972.

Harper Collins Publishers, London: G. E. Moore, *Philosophical Papers* (Allen & Unwin, 1959).

Harper Collins, New York: Robert Paul Wolff; Martin Heidegger. Reprinted with permission.

Harvard University Press: Susanne K. Langer; Willard Quine; Charles Sanders Peirce; John Rawls, *A Theory of Justice*. Reprinted with permission.

Harvester Wheatsheaf: Hélène Cixous, *Sorties*; Michel Foucault, *Power/Knowledge* (1986). Reprinted with permission.

Wm Heinemann: Jürgen Habermas, *Knowledge and Human Interests* (1978); *Legitimation Crisis* (1976).

Acknowledgements

The Johns Hopkins University Press: Jacques Derrida, *Of Grammatology*. Reprinted with permission.

Richard Kearney: ©Richard Kearney 1984.

Jaegwon Kim: ©the author.

Kluwer Academic Publishers: Edmund Husserl; Emmanuel Levinas, *Collected Philosophical Papers* (Martinus Nijhoff, 1987) and *Otherwise Than Being Or Beyond Essence* (Martinus Nijhoff, 1981). Reprinted with permission.

Alfred A. Knopf Inc.: Simone de Beauvoir, *The Second Sex*, trans. H. M. Parshley, copyright 1952 by Alfred A. Knopf Inc. Reprinted by permission of the publisher.

Jacques Lacan see **Alan Sheridan.**

Emmanuel Levinas: *Deconstruction in Context* (Univ. Chicago Press, 1986); *Totality and Infirmity* (Duquesne Univ. Press, 1969); *The Levinas Reader* (Blackwell, 1989); *Difficile Liberté* (Albin Michel, 1976); 'Is Ontology Fundamental' from *Philosophy Today*, Summer 1989.

David Lewis: *Philosophical Papers*, Vol. II. Reprinted by permission of the author.

John McDowell: Reprinted by permission of the author.

Macmillan Publishing Co.: Susanne K. Langer, from *Feeling and Form*, copyright 1953 Charles Scribner's Sons, ©renewed 1981 Susanne K. Langer; from *Problems of Art*, ©1957 Charles Scribner's Sons, ©renewed Leonard Langer. Reprinted with permission.

The University of Massachusetts Press, Amherst: Hélène Cixous, *Sorties*, ©1980 by The University of Massachusetts Press. Reprinted with permission.

The Merlin Press Ltd: Georg Lukács. Reprinted with permission.

Methuen & Co.: Maurice Merleau-Ponty, *The Structure of Behaviour*. Reprinted with permission.

The University of Minnesota Press: Richard Rorty, *Consequences of Pragmatism*.

The MIT Press: Noam Chomsky, *Aspects of the Theory of Syntax*; *Language and Problems of Knowledge*. Reprinted with permission.

Les Editions Nagel S.A.: Jean-Paul Sartre, *Existentialism and Humanism*.

Thomas Nelson & Sons: St Anselm of Canterbury, *Opera Omnia Sanceti Anselm*, ed. Dom Schmitt. Reprinted with permission.

Oxford University Press, Inc.: Thomas Nagel, *The View From Nowhere*, ©1986 by Thomas Nagel. Reprinted by permission.

Oxford University Press: H. L. A. Hart; Shelly Kagan; Sir Isaiah Berlin, *Four Essays on Liberty*; *The Journals of Søren Kierkegaard*; Derek Parfit; Saul Kripke; Thomas Nagel, *The Possibility of Altruism*; W. D. Ross; F. H. Bradley; G. W. F. Hegel, *Encyclopedia, Phenomenology of Spirit, Philosophy of Right*; John Rawls, *A Theory of Justice*; Michael

Slote; J. L. Mackie; Karl Popper, *Objective Knowledge*; Richard M. Hare; Ted Honderich, *A Theory of Determinism . . .*; J. L. Austin; Donald Davidson. All reprinted with permission.

Penguin Books Ltd: Jean-Paul Sartre, *Nausea*, trans. Robert Baldick (Penguin Books, 1963), copyright 1938 by Libraire Gallimard. This translation ©Penguin Books Ltd, 1965. Plato, *Protagoras and Meno*, translated W. K. C. Guthrie (Penguin Classics, 1956), ©1956 W. K. C. Guthrie, *The Republic*, trans. H. D. P. Lee (Penguin Classics, 1955), © H. D. P. Lee, 1953, *Phaedrus and Letters VII and VIII*, trans. Walter Hamilton (Penguin Classics, 1973), ©Walter Hamilton, 1973. Friedrich Nietzsche, *Thus Spake Zarathustra*, trans. R. J. Hollingdale, © R. J. Hollingdale, 1961, 1969, *Twilight of the Idols,* trans. R. J. Hollingdale, translation and translator's note copyright © R. J. Hollingdale, 1968, Introduction copyright © Michael Tanner, 1990, *Beyond Good and Evil*, trans. R. J. Hollingdale, translation, translator's note and commentary copyright © R. J. Hollingdale 1973, 1990, Introduction copyright © Michael Tanner, 1990. Arthur Schopenhauer, *Essays and Aphorisms*, trans. R. J. Hollingdale, translation and introduction copyright © R. J. Hollingdale, 1970. Reprinted by permission.

Penguin USA: Friedrich Nietzsche, from *The Portable Nietzsche* by Walter Kaufman. Copyright 1954 by The Viking Press, renewed ©1982 by Viking Penguin Inc. Used by permission of Viking Penguin, a division of Penguin Books USA Inc.

University of Pennsylvania Press: Karl Jaspers.

Peters Fraser & Dunlop Group Ltd: Rousseau, trans. Maurice Cranston; G. A. Cohen. Reprinted with permission.

D. Z. Phillips: *The Concept of Prayer* (Blackwell, 1981). ©D. Z. Phillips.

Pluto Press: Jürgen Habermas, *Postmodern Culture* (1985).

Sir Karl Popper: *A Pocket Popper*; *The Logic of Scientific Discovery*; *Conjectures and Refutations: The Growth of Scientific Knowledge*. All ©Sir Karl Popper and reprinted with his permission.

Princeton University Press: *Complete Works of Aristotle: Revised Oxford Translation*, ed. Jonathan Barnes, ©1984 by Princeton University Press; Judith Jarvis Thomson; Søren Kierkegaard, *Concluding Unscientific Postscript, Philosophical Fragments, The Sickness Unto Death*, ©renewed 1969 by Princeton University Press; Benedictus Spinoza, *The Collected Works of Spinoza*, ©1985 by Princeton University Press. All reprinted with permission.

Hilary Putnam: *Meaning and the Moral Sciences*. ©the author.

Willard V. Quine: Reprinted by permission of the author.

Anthony Quinton: Reprinted by permission of the author. Also

Acknowledgements

Gottlob Frege, *The Thought: A Logical Inquiry*, trans. A. M. and Marcelle Quinton. Reprinted by permission.

Random House UK Ltd/Penguin USA: Isaiah Berlin, *Russian Thinkers, Concepts & Categories*. Reprinted with permission.

Random House UK Ltd: Simone de Beauvoir, *The Second Sex* (Jonathan Cape Ltd); Gilbert Ryle, *The Concept of Mind* (Hutchinson); Robert Paul Wolff, *A Critique of Pure Tolerance* (Jonathan Cape Ltd); Stuart Hampshire, *Freedom of the Individual* (Chatto, 1972). Reprinted with permission.

Random House UK/Basic Books: Sigmund Freud. Reprinted by permission of the Sigmund Freud Copyrights, The Institute of Psycho-Analysis and The Hogarth Press, from *The Standard Edition of the Complete Psychological Works of Sigmund Freud*, translated and edited by James Strachey.

Random House UK Ltd/Alfred A. Knopf: Stuart Hampshire, *Thought and Action* (1959). Reprinted with permission.

Random House Inc.: Friedrich Nietzsche, *The Gay Science* (Vintage, 1974); *On the Genealogy of Morals* (Vintage, 1969); *Beyond Good and Evil* (Vintage, 1966); *The Will to Power* (Random, 1968); Michel Foucault, *Power/Knowledge* (1986).

Nicholas Rescher: Reprinted by permission of the author.

Janet Radcliffe Richards: Reprinted by permission of the author.

Routledge/Unwin Hyman: Franz Brentano; C. D. Broad, *Lectures on Psychical Research* and *The Mind and Its Place in Nature*; Peter Geach; Jacques Derrida, *Writing and Difference*; Bertrand Russell; Iris Murdoch; Maurice Merleau-Ponty, *Phenomenology of Perception*. Reprinted with permission.

Alan Sheridan: Jacques Lacan, *Four Fundamental Concepts* (Penguin, 1977). Reprinted by permission of the author.

Alan Sheridan/Routledge: Jacques Lacan, *Écrits* (Tavistock, 1977). Reprinted by permission of the author and publisher.

Schocken Books Inc.: Julia Kristeva, *New French Feminisms*.

Sydney Shoemaker: Reprinted by permission of the author.

Peter Singer: *Animal Liberation*, ©the author.

J. J. C. Smart: Reprinted by permission of the author. 'Utilitarianism and Punishment', published in *Israel Law Review* 25 (1991) 360–375.

Sir Peter F. Strawson: Reprinted by permission of the author.

Suhrkamp Verlag: Jürgen Habermas. Reprinted with permission.

Verso/New Left Books, London & New York: P. Feyerabend, *Against Method*; Theodor Adorno, *Minima Moralia*. Reprinted with permission.

Sir Geoffrey and Lady Warnock: Reprinted by permission of the authors.

Richard Wollheim: Reprinted by permission of the author.

A

𝔊𝔊𝔊𝔊𝔊𝔊

PETER ABELARD (1079–1142)

Sin, therefore, is sometimes committed without an evil will. Thus sin **1**
cannot be defined as 'will'. True, you will say, when we sin under
constraint, but not when we sin willingly, for instance, when we will do
something which we know ought not to be done by us. There the evil will
and sin seem to be the same thing. For example, a man sees a woman; his
concupiscence is aroused; his mind is enticed by fleshly lust and stirred to
base desire. This wish, this lascivious longing, what else can it be, you
say, than sin?

I reply: What if that wish may be bridled by the power of temperance?
What if its nature is never to be entirely extinguished but to persist in
struggle and not fully fail even in defeat? . . . It is vicious to give in to our
desires; but not to have any desires at all is impossible for our weak
nature.

The sin, then, consists not in desiring a woman, but in consent to the
desire, and not the wish for whoredom, but the consent to the wish is
damnation.

Abailard's Ethics, trans. J. R. McCallum, pp. 22–3

We call the intention good which is right in itself, but the action is good, **2**
not because it contains within it some good, but because it issues from a
good intention. The same act may be done by the same man at different
times. According to the diversity of his intention, however, this act may
be at one time good, at another bad.

Abailard's Ethics, trans. J. R. McCallum, p. 46

But now that reasons have been presented concerning why things, **3**
whether taken singly or collectively, cannot be called universals, because
they are not predicated of many things, it remains to ascribe universality
in this sense to words alone.

Logica 'Ingredientibus', Philosophische Schriften, ed. B. Geyer, p. 16

THEODOR ADORNO (1903–1969)

1 The more total society becomes, the greater the reification of the mind and the more paradoxical its effort to escape reification on its own. Even the most extreme consciousness of doom threatens to degenerate into idle chatter. Cultural criticism finds itself faced with the final stage of the dialectic of culture and barbarism. To write poetry after Auschwitz is barbaric.
Prisms, trans. Samuel and Shierry Weber, p. 34

2 There is nothing innocuous left. The little pleasures, expressions of life that seemed exempt from the responsibility of thought, not only have an element of defiant silliness, of callous refusal to see, but directly serve their diametrical opposite. Even the blossoming tree lies the moment its bloom is seen without the shadow of terror; even the innocent 'How lovely!' becomes an excuse for an existence outrageously unlovely, and there is no longer beauty or consolation except in the gaze falling on horror, withstanding it, and in unalleviated consciousness of negativity holding fast to the possibility of what is better.
Minima Moralia, trans. E. F. N. Jephcott, p. 25

3 The discovery of genuineness as a last bulwark of individualistic ethics is a reflection of industrial mass-production. Only when countless standardized commodities project, for the sake of profit, the illusion of being unique, does the idea take shape, as their antithesis yet in keeping with the same criteria, that the non-reproducible is the truly genuine. Previously, the question of authenticity was doubtless as little asked of intellectual products as that of originality, a concept unknown in Bach's era.... The ungenuineness of the genuine stems from its need to claim, in a society dominated by exchange, to be what it stands for yet is never able to be.
Minima Moralia, trans. E. F. N. Jephcott, p. 155

4 Among today's adept practitioners, the lie has long since lost its honest function of misrepresenting reality. Nobody believes anybody, everyone is in the know. Lies are told only to convey to someone that one has no need either of him or his good opinion. The lie, once a liberal means of communication, has today become one of the techniques of insolence enabling each individual to spread around him the glacial atmosphere in whose shelter he can thrive.
Minima Moralia, trans. E. F. N. Jephcott, p. 30

5 Had Hegel's philosophy of history embraced this age, Hitler's robot-bombs would have found their place beside the early death of Alexander and similar images, as one of the selected empirical facts by which the

state of the world-spirit manifests itself directly in symbols. Like Fascism itself, the robots career without a subject. Like it they combine utmost technical perfection with total blindness. And like it they arouse mortal terror and are wholly futile. 'I have seen the world spirit', not on horseback, but on wings and without a head, and that refutes, at the same stroke, Hegel's philosophy of history.
Minima Moralia, trans. E. F. N. Jephcott, p. 55

Johnny-Head-in-Air – The relation of knowledge to power is one not 6 only of servility but of truth. Much knowledge, if out of proportion to the disposition of forces, is invalid, however formally correct it may be. If an émigré doctor says: 'For me, Adolf Hitler is a pathological case', his pronouncement may ultimately be confirmed by clinical findings, but its incongruity with the objective calamity visited on the world in the name of that paranoiac renders the diagnosis ridiculous, mere professional preening. Perhaps Hitler is 'in-himself' a pathological case, but certainly not 'for-him'. The vanity and poverty of many of the declarations against Fascism by émigrés is connected with this. People thinking in the forms of free, detached, disinterested appraisal were unable to accommodate within those forms the experience of violence which in reality annuls such thinking. The almost insoluble task is to let neither the power of others, nor our own powerlessness, stupefy us.
Minima Moralia, trans. E. F. N. Jephcott, p. 57*

The prudence that restrains us from venturing too far ahead in a sentence 7 is usually only an agent of social control, and so of stupefaction.
Minima Moralia, trans. E. F. N. Jephcott, p. 86

The assumption that thought profits from the decay of the emotions, or 8 even that it remains unaffected, is itself an expression of the process of stupefaction. The social division of labour recoils on man, however much it may expedite the task exacted from him. The faculties, having developed through interaction, atrophy once they are severed from each other. Nietzsche's aphorism, that 'the degree and kind of a man's sexuality extends to the highest pinnacle of his spirit', has a more than merely psychological application . . .
Minima Moralia, trans. E. F. N. Jephcott, pp. 122–3

. . . the demand for intellectual honesty is itself dishonest. Even if we were 9 for once to comply with the questionable directive that the exposition should exactly reproduce the process of thought, this process would be no more a discursive progression from stage to stage than, conversely, knowledge falls from Heaven. Rather, knowledge comes to us through a network of prejudices, opinions, innervations, self-corrections, presuppositions and exaggerations, in short through the dense, firmly-founded

but by no means uniformly transparent medium of experience. Of this the Cartesian rule that we must address ourselves only to objects, 'to gain clear and indubitable knowledge of which our minds seem sufficient', with all the order and disposition to which the rule refers, gives as false a picture as the opposed but deeply related doctrine of the intuition of essences. If the latter denies logic its rights, which in spite of everything assert themselves in every thought, the former takes logic in its immediacy, in relation to each single intellectual act, and not as mediated by the whole flow of conscious life in the knowing subject. But in this lies also an admission of profound inadequacy. For if honest ideas unfailingly boil down to mere repetition, whether of what was there beforehand or of categorical forms, then the thought which, for the sake of the relation to its object, forgoes the full transparency of its logical genesis, will always incur a certain guilt. It breaks the promise presupposed by the very form of judgement. This inadequacy resembles that of life . . . [Yet] if a life fulfilled its vocation directly, it would miss it.
Minima Moralia, trans. E. F. N. Jephcott, p. 80

10 Properly written texts are like spiders' webs: tight, concentric, transparent, well-spun and firm. They draw into themselves all the creatures of the air. Metaphors flitting hastily through them become their nourishing prey. Subject matter comes winging towards them. The soundness of a conception can be judged by whether it causes one quotation to summon another. Where thought has opened up one cell of reality, it should, without violence by the subject, penetrate the next. It proves its relation to the object as soon as other objects crystallize around it. In the light that it casts on its chosen substance, others begin to glow.
Minima Moralia, trans. E. F. N. Jephcott, p. 87

AHAD HA-AM (Asher Ginzberg) (1856–1927)

1 Wise men weigh the advantages of any course of action against its drawbacks, and move not an inch until they can see what the result of their action will be; but while they are deep in thought, the men with self-confidence 'come and see and conquer'.
Quoted in Leon Simon, *Ahad Ha-Am: A Biography*, p. 39

2 Whoever sets out to persuade men to accept a new idea, or one which seems to be new, not just as an idea, but as a truth that is *felt*, should know beforehand that the human mind is not a blank sheet, on which one can write with ease, and should not therefore grieve or despair when he finds that people do not pay attention to him.
Quoted in Leon Simon, *Ahad Ha-Am: A Biography*, p. 120

JOSEPH ALBO (c.1380–c.1444)

To know God's nature one would have to be God Himself.
Sefer ha-Ikkarim, trans. Louis Jacobs, 2:30

VIRGIL ALDRICH (b. 1903)

I have, most of my philosophical life, been trying to protect appearances against ontological attacks aimed at eliminating them.
The Body of a Person, p. 1

WILLIAM P. ALSTON (b. 1921)

With this background we are in a position to bring out how functionalism can help us to reconcile a degree of univocity with the radical otherness of the divine. The crucial point is . . . that a *functional* concept of X is noncommital as to the intrinsic nature, character, composition or structure of X. In conceiving of X in functional terms we are simply thinking of X in terms of its function (or some of its functions), in terms of the job(s) it is fitted to do. . . . Functionalism is well fitted to bring out a sense in which it might well be true that mental terms (or some of them) apply univocally to human beings and to computers. For . . . [s]ince in saying that S recalled that *p* we are, on the functionalist interpretation, not committing ourselves to whether a neurophysiological, an electronic, or a purely spiritual process was involved, the concept might apply in the same sense to systems of all these sorts. The point is often put by saying that a given functional property or state can have different, even radically different, 'realizations'.

The application to theological predication should be obvious in its main lines. The same functional concept of knowledge that *p*, or of purpose to bring about R, could be applicable to God and to man, even though the realization of that function is radically different, even though what it is to know that *p* is radically different in the two cases. We can preserve the point that the divine life is wholly mysterious to us, that we can form no notion of what it is like to be God, to know or to purpose as God does, while still thinking of God in terms that we understand because they apply to us.
'Functionalism and Theological Language', *American Philosophical Quarterly* (1985), p. 224

LOUIS ALTHUSSER (1918–1990)

. . . what we are dealing with in the opposition science/ideologies 1 concerns the 'break' relationship between a science and the *theoretical* ideology in which the object it gave the knowledge of was 'thought'

before the foundation of the science. This 'break' leaves intact the objective social domain occupied by ideologies (religion, ethics, legal and political ideologies, etc.). In this domain of non-theoretical ideologies, too, there are 'ruptures' and 'breaks', but they are *political* (effects of political practice, of great revolutionary events) and not 'epistemological'.
For Marx, trans. Ben Brewster, p. 13

2   It is impossible to *know* anything about men except on the absolute precondition that the philosophical (theoretical) myth of man is reduced to ashes. So any thought that appeals to Marx for any kind of restoration of a theoretical anthropology or humanism is no more than ashes, *theoretically*. But in practice it could pile up a monument of pre-Marxist ideology that would weigh down on real history and threaten to lead it into blind alleys.
For Marx, trans. Ben Brewster, p. 229

3   . . . in the theatrical world, as in the aesthetic world more generally, ideology is always in essence the site of a competition and a struggle in which the sound and fury of humanity's political and social struggles is faintly or sharply echoed.
For Marx, trans. Ben Brewster, p. 149

4   If the whole social function of ideology could be summed up cynically as a myth (such as Plato's 'beautiful lies' or the techniques of modern advertising) fabricated and manipulated from the outside by the ruling class to fool those it is exploiting, then ideology would disappear with classes. But as we have seen that even in the case of a class society ideology is active on the ruling class itself and contributes to its moulding, to the modification of its attitudes to adapt it to its real conditions of existence (for example, legal freedom) – it is clear that *ideology (as a system of mass representations) is indispensable in any society if men are to be formed, transformed and equipped to respond to the demands of their conditions of existence.*
For Marx, trans. Ben Brewster, p. 235

5   . . . contradiction . . . reveals itself as determined by the structured complexity that assigns it to its role, as – if you will forgive me the astonishing expression – complexly-structurally-unevenly-determined. I must admit, I preferred a shorter term: over-determined.
For Marx, trans. Ben Brewster, p. 209

ANAXAGORAS (*c.*500 BC–*c.*428 BC)

1   Neither is there a smallest part of what is small, but there is always a smaller (for it is impossible that what is should cease to be). Likewise

there is always something larger than what is large.
G. S. Kirk, J. E. Raven and M. Schofield, *The Pre-Socratic Philosophers*, p. 360

In everything there is a portion of everything except Mind.   2
The Pre-Socratic Philosophers, p. 366

How could hair come from what is not hair or flesh from what is not   3
flesh?
The Pre-Socratic Philosophers, p. 369

ANAXIMANDER (c.610 BC–c.547 BC)
Anaximander said that the principle and element of existing things was
the unbounded, . . . and in addition said that motion was eternal.
Quoted by Hippolytus, *The Pre-Socratic Philosophers*, pp. 107, 126

ANAXIMENES (c.585–527 BC)
Anaximenes . . . said that infinite air was the principle, from which the
things that are becoming, and that are, and that shall be, and gods and
things divine, all come into being, and the rest from its products.
Quoted by Hippolytus, *The Pre-Socratic Philosophers*, p. 144

JOHN ANDERSON (1893–1962)

We do not, in fact, step out of the movement of things, ask 'What am I to 1
do' and, having obtained an answer, step in again. All our actions, all our
questionings and answerings, are part of the movement of things, and if
we can work on things, things can work on us – if they can be our
'vehicles', we also can be vehicles; social and other forces can work
through us.
Studies in Empirical Philosophy, p. 241

The general conclusion is that all the objects of science, including minds 2
and goods, are things occurring in space and time . . . and that we can
study them in virtue of the fact that we come into spatial and temporal
relations with them. And therefore all ideals, ultimates, symbols, agencies
and the like are to be rejected, and no such distinction as that of facts and
principles, or facts and values, can be maintained. There are only facts,
i.e. occurrences in space and time.
Studies in Empirical Philosophy, p. 14

We have to recognise *accident*, i.e., the fact that there is no formula, no 3
'principle', which covers all things; that there is no totality or system of
things. And this recognition at once supports a life of 'responsibility and
adventure' and leads to scientific discovery.
Studies in Empirical Philosophy, p. 86

G. E. M. ANSCOMBE (*b.* 1919)

1   Let us suppose that the thought in his mind is 'you silly little twit!' Now here too, it is not enough that these words should occur to him. He has to mean them. This shews once more, that you cannot take any performance (even an interior performance) as itself an act of intention; for if you describe a performance, the fact that it has taken place is not a proof of intention; words for example may occur in somebody's mind without his meaning them. So intention is never a performance in the mind, though in some matters a performance in the mind which is seriously *meant* may make a difference to the correct account of the man's action – e.g., in embracing someone. But the matters in question are necessarily ones in which outward acts are 'significant' in some way.
Intention, p. 49

2   The primitive sign of wanting is *trying to get*: in saying this, we describe the movement of an animal in terms that reach beyond what the animal is now doing. When a dog smells a piece of meat that lies the other side of the door, his trying to get it will be his scratching violently round the edges of the door and snuffling along the bottom of it and so on. Thus there are two features present in wanting; movement towards a thing and knowledge (or at least opinion) that the thing is there. When we consider human action, though it is a great deal more complicated, the same features are present when what is wanted is something that already exists: such as a particular Jersey cow, which is presumed to be on sale in the Hereford market, or a particular woman desired in marriage.
Intention, p. 68

3   'Evil be thou my good' is often thought to be senseless in some way. Now all that concerns us here is that 'What's the good of it?' is something that can be asked until a desirability-characterization has been reached and made intelligible. If then the answer to this question at some stage is 'The good of it is that it is bad', this need not be unintelligible; one can go on to say, 'And what is the good of its being bad?' to which the answer might be condemnation of good as impotent, slavish, and inglorious. Then the good of making evil my good is my intact liberty in the unsubmissiveness of my will. *Bonum est multiplex*: good is multiform, and all that is required for our concept of 'wanting' is that a man should see what he wants under the aspect of some good.
Intention, p. 74

4   . . . it will be said, what *is* unjust is sometimes determined by expected consequences, and certainly that is true. But there are cases where it is not; now if someone says 'I agree, but all this wants a lot of explaining', then he is right, and, what is more, the situation at present is that we

can't do the explaining; we lack the philosophical equipment. But if someone really thinks, *in advance*, that it is open to question whether such an action as procuring the judicial execution of the innocent should be quite excluded from consideration – I do not want to argue with him; he shows a corrupt mind.
'Modern Moral Philosophy', *Philosophy* (1958), p. 16

. . . it is not profitable for us at present to do moral philosophy; . . . it   5
should be laid aside at any rate until we have an adequate philosophy of psychology, in which we are conspicuously lacking.
'Modern Moral Philosophy', *Ethics, Religion and Politics*, p. 26

To have a *law* conception of ethics is to hold that what is needed for   6
conformity with the virtues failure in which is the mark of being bad *qua* man (and not merely, say, *qua* craftsman or logician) – that what is needed for *this*, is required by divine law. Naturally it is not possible to have such a conception unless you believe in God as a law-giver; like Jews, Stoics, and Christians. But if such a conception is dominant for many centuries, and then is given up, it is a natural result that the concepts of 'obligation', of being bound or required as by a law, should remain though they had lost their root; and if the word 'ought' has become invested in certain contexts with the sense of 'obligation' it too will remain to be spoken with a special emphasis and a special feeling in these contexts.
'Modern Moral Philosophy', *Philosophy* (1958), p. 6

ST ANSELM OF CANTERBURY (1033–1109)

Faith seeking understanding   1
Proslogion, Opera Omnia, ed. F. S. Schmitt, I, p. 94

I do not seek to understand so that I may believe, but I believe so that I   2
may understand; and what is more, I believe that 'unless I do believe I shall not understand' (*Isaiah* 7: 9).
Proslogion, Opera Omnia, I, p. 100

If therefore that than which nothing greater can be thought exists in the   3
understanding alone, then this thing than which nothing greater can be thought is something than which a greater can be thought. And this is clearly impossible. Therefore there can be no doubt at all that something than which a greater cannot be thought exists both in the understanding and in reality.
Proslogion, Opera Omnia, I, p. 101

Something than which nothing greater can be thought so truly exists that   4
it is not possible to think of it as not existing. This being is yourself, Lord

our God. Lord my God, you so truly are that it is not possible to think of you as not existing.
Proslogion, Opera Omnia, I, p. 103

5 How can you [God] be omnipotent if you cannot do all things? How can you do all things if you cannot be corrupted, or lie, or make false what is true – which would be to make what exists into non-being – and so forth? If this is so, how can you do all things? Or is it that these things proceed not from power but from powerlessness?
Proslogion, Opera Omnia, I, p. 105

6 Unless I am mistaken therefore, we can define 'truth' as 'rightness perceptible by the mind alone'.
De Veritate, Opera Omnia, I, p. 191

7 Justice, therefore, is rightness of will maintained for its own sake.
De Veritate, Opera Omnia, I, p. 194

8 Since therefore it is certain that all good things, if mutually compared, would be either equally or unequally good, they must all be good by virtue of something which is thought to be the same in the different good things, although different good things sometimes seem to be called good in virtue of different things.
Monologion, Opera Omnia, I, p. 14

9 Furthermore, if truth had a beginning or will have an end, then before truth began it was true that there was no truth, and after it will have ended it will then be true that there will be no truth. And a true thing cannot exist without truth. Therefore truth existed before there was truth, and truth will exist after truth will have ended. This is utterly absurd. Therefore whether truth be said to have a beginning or an end, or be understood not to have a beginning or an end, truth cannot be limited by a beginning and an end.
Monologion, Opera Omnia, I, p. 33

10 Nothing is true except by participating in truth, and hence the truth of something true is in that true thing. But what is said is not in the true proposition, and hence what is said should be called not the *truth* of the proposition, but the *cause* of its truth. For this reason it seems to me that the truth of a proposition should be sought only in the proposition itself.
De Veritate, Opera Omnia, I, p. 177

ANTIPHON (*fl.* mid-5th century)

Many duties imposed by law are hostile to nature.
Quoted in E. Hussey, *The Pre-Socratics*, p. 124

ST THOMAS AQUINAS (c.1225–1274)

All that I have written seems to me like straw compared to what has now 1
been revealed to me.
Quoted in J. A. Weisheipl, Friar Thomas d'Aquino, p. 322

Even if it be granted that everyone understands this name 'God' to signify 2
what is said, viz., 'that than which a greater cannot be thought', it does
not follow that what is signified by the name exists in the nature of
things, but only that it exists in the apprehension of the understanding.
Summa Theologiae, I, Pt. 1, qu. 2, a. 1

Whatever is in motion must be moved by something else. Moreover, this 3
something else, if it too is in motion, must itself be moved by something
else, and that in turn by yet another thing. But this cannot go on forever,
because if it did there would be no first mover and hence no other mover.
For second movers do not move except when moved by a first mover, just
as a stick does not move anything except when moved by a hand. So we
must reach a first mover which is not moved by anything. And this all
men think of as God.
Summa Theologiae, I, Pt. 1, qu. 2, a. 3

It is necessary to assume something which is necessary of itself, and has 4
no cause of its necessity outside itself but is rather the cause of necessity
in other things. And this all men call God.
Summa Theologiae, I, Pt. 1, qu. 2, a. 3

Since we cannot know what God is, but only what He is not, we must 5
consider the ways in which He is not rather than the ways in which He is.
Summa Theologiae, I, Pt. 1, qu. 3, introd.

Thus those words ['good' and 'wise'] when used of God do signify 6
something that God really is, but they do so imperfectly just as creatures
represent Him imperfectly.
Summa Theologiae, I, Pt. 1, qu. 13, a. 2

Words are used of God and creatures in an analogical way. 7
Summa Theologiae, I, Pt. 1, qu. 13, a. 5

Future contingents cannot be certain to us, because we know them *as* 8
future contingents. They can be certain only to God whose understanding is
in eternity above time. In the same way a man going along a road does
not see those who come behind him; but the man who sees the whole
road from a height sees simultaneously all those who are going along the
road.
Summa Theologiae, I, Pt. 1, qu. 14, a. 13

9 Man does not choose of necessity. . . . in all particular goods, the reason can consider an aspect of some good, and the lack of some good, which has the aspect of evil; and in this respect, it can apprehend any single one of such goods as to be chosen or to be avoided. The perfect good alone, which is Happiness, cannot be apprehended by the reason as an evil, or as lacking in any way. Consequently man wills Happiness of necessity, nor can he will not to be happy, or to be unhappy. Now since choice is not of the end, but of the means, . . . it is not of the perfect good, which is Happiness, but of other particular goods. Therefore man chooses not of necessity, but freely.
Summa Theologiae, I, Pt. 1, qu. 13, a. 6

10 There are certain individual goods which have not a necessary connection with happiness, because without them a man can be happy, and to such the will does not adhere of necessity. But there are some things which have a necessary connection with happiness, by means of which things man adheres to God, in Whom alone true happiness consists. Nevertheless, until through the certitude of the Divine Vision, the necessity of such connection be shown, the will does not adhere to God of necessity, nor to those things which are of God. . . . It is therefore clear that the will does not desire of necessity whatever it desires.
Summa Theologiae, I, Pt. 1, qu. 10, a. 2

11 No evil as such can be desirable, either by natural appetite or by conscious will. It is sought indirectly, namely because it is the consequence of some good.
Summa Theologiae, I, Pt. 1a, qu. 19, a. 9

12 Evil denotes the absence of Good. But it is not every absence of good that is called *evil*. For absence of good can be understood either in a privative sense or in a purely negative sense. And absence of good in the latter sense is not evil. . . . Otherwise it would follow that a thing is evil if it lacks the good which belongs to something else. For instance, man would be evil because he lacks the swiftness of a wild goat or the strength of a lion. It is absence of good in the privative sense which is called evil. Thus privation of sight is called blindness.
Summa Theologiae, I, Pt. 1a, qu. 5, a. 48

13 Every act in so far as it has something real about it has something good about it. In so far as it falls short of the full reality that a human act should have, it falls short of goodness, and so is called bad.
Summa Theologiae, I, Pt. 1.2, qu. 18, a. 1

14 Since conscience is the dictate of reason, the application of theory to practice, the inquiry, *whether a will that disobeys an erroneous*

conscience is right, is the same as, *whether a man is obliged to follow a mistaken conscience.*

Now because the object of an act of will is that which is proposed by the conscience, if the will chooses to do what the conscience considers to be wrong, then the will goes out to it in the guise of evil. Hence it should be said that every act of will against conscience, whether the conscience be correct or mistaken, is always bad.
Summa Theologiae, I, Pt. 1a, qu. 19, a. 5

If reason or conscience is mistaken through a voluntary error, whether   15
the error be directly willed or due to negligence, then since it is an error concerning something that the person ought to know about, that error does not excuse; on the contrary the will which follows reason or conscience thus mistaken is bad. But if the error is one which causes involuntariness, arising from ignorance of the circumstances without any negligence involved, then such an error of reason or conscience does excuse, so that the will which follows that mistaken conscience is not bad.
Summa Theologiae, I, Pt. 1.2, qu. 19, a. 6

[Law] is nothing else than an ordinance of reason for the common good,   16
made by the authority who has the care of the community, and promulgated.
Summa Theologiae, I, Pt. 1.2, qu. 90, a. 4

Laws can be unjust because they are contrary to the divine good, for   17
example, the laws of tyrants which promote idolatry or whatever else is against divine law. In no way is it permissible to observe them.
Summa Theologiae, I, Pt. 1.2, qu. 96, a. 4

It is plain that the immateriality of a thing is the reason that it can have   18
knowledge, and the ability to know corresponds to the degree of immateriality. Hence it is said that on account of their materiality plants do not have knowledge. The senses can know because they receive the likenesses of things without the matter. The intellect is even more able to have knowledge because it is more separated from matter and unmixed, as Aristotle says. So since God is immaterial to the highest degree, it follows that He has knowledge to the highest degree.
Summa Theologiae, I, Pt. 1, qu. 14, a. 1

Natural things are intermediate between God's knowledge and ours. For   19
we get our knowledge from natural things of which God, through His knowledge, is the cause.
Summa Theologiae, I, Pt. 1, qu. 14, a. 8

20 Some have said that no intellectual substance can be the form of the body. But because the nature of man seemed to contradict this position, since man seems to be composed of an intellectual soul and of a body, they thought out certain ways by which they could preserve [the unity of] human nature. Plato, therefore, and his followers held that the intellectual soul is not united to the body as form to matter, but only as mover to thing moved, saying that the soul is present in the body as a sailor in a ship. . . . But this can be shown to be impossible. For animals and men are sensible and natural things; and this would not be the case if the body and its parts did not belong to the essence of man and animal.
Summa contra Gentiles, 2, 67

21 The soul is known by its acts. . . . No one perceives that he understands except through the fact that he understands something, for to understand something is prior to understanding that one understands. And so the soul comes to the actual realization of its existence through the fact that it understands and perceives.
De Veritate, 10, 8

HANNAH ARENDT (1906–1975)

1 A complete victory of society will always produce some sort of 'communistic fiction', whose outstanding political characteristic is that it is indeed ruled by an 'invisible hand', namely, by nobody. What we traditionally call state and government give place here to pure admini- stration – a state of affairs which Marx rightly predicted as the 'withering away of the state', though he was wrong when he believed that this victory of society would mean the eventual emergence of the 'realm of freedom'.
The Human Condition, pp. 44–5

2 The connotation of courage, which we now feel to be an indispensible quality of the hero, is in fact already present in a willingness to act and speak at all, to insert one's self into the world and begin a story of one's own.
The Human Condition, p. 186

3 In the face of death, he [Eichmann] had found the cliché used in funeral oratory. Under the gallows, his memory played him the last trick; he was 'elated' and he forgot that this was his own funeral.
   It was as though in those last minutes he was summing up the lesson that this long course in human wickedness had taught us – the lesson of the fearsome, word-and-thought-defying *banality of evil*.
Eichmann in Jerusalem: A Report on the Banality of Evil, p. 252

ARISTOTLE (384 BC–322 BC)

... it would perhaps be thought to be better, indeed to be our duty, for 1
the sake of maintaining the truth even to destroy what touches us closely,
especially as we are philosophers; for, while both are dear, piety requires
us to honour truth above our friends.
Nicomachean Ethics, 1096a

Presumably to say that happiness is the supreme good seems a platitude, 2
and some more distinctive account of it is still required. This might
perhaps be achieved by grasping what is the function of man. . . . Is it
likely that whereas joiners and shoemakers have certain functions or
activities, man as such has none, but has been left by nature a
functionless being?
Nicomachean Ethics, 1097b

The human good turns out to be activity of soul in conformity with 3
excellence, and if there are more than one excellence, in conformity with
the best and most complete.

But we must add 'in a complete life'. For one swallow does not make a
summer, nor does one day; and so too one day, or a short time, does not
make a man blessed and happy.
Nicomachean Ethics, 1098a

Intellectual virtue owes both its birth and its growth to teaching (for 4
which reason it requires experience and time), while moral virtue comes
about as a result of habit. . . . From this fact it is plain that none of the
moral virtues arises in us by nature; for nothing that exists by nature can
form a habit contrary to its nature. The stone, for instance, which by
nature gravitates downwards, cannot be induced through custom to
move upwards, not even if one were to try to train it by throwing it up
ten thousand times. . . . Neither by nature, then, nor contrary to nature
do the virtues arise in us; rather we are furnished by nature with a
capacity for receiving them, and are perfected in them through custom.
Nicomachean Ethics, 1103a

A man is not a good man at all who feels no pleasure in noble actions, 5
just as no one would call that man just who does not feel pleasure in
acting justly . . .
Nicomachean Ethics, 1099a

For a test of the formation of the habits, we must take the pleasure or 6
pain which ensues on acts; for the man who abstains from bodily
pleasures and delights in this very fact is perfected in self-mastery;
whereas he who abstains but is annoyed at doing so is self-indulgent. And
he who stands his ground against danger, either with positive pleasure, or

15

at least without pain, is brave; while he who is pained at doing it is a coward.
Nicomachean Ethics, 1104a

7   Excellence, then, is a state concerned with choice, lying in a mean relative to us, this being determined by reason and in the way in which the man of practical wisdom would determine it. Now it is a mean between two vices, that which depends on excess and that which depends on defect; and again it is a mean because the vices respectively fall short of or exceed what is right in both passions and actions, while excellence both finds and chooses that which is intermediate.
Nicomachean Ethics, 1106b

8   Men are good in one way, but bad in many.
Nicomachean Ethics, 1106b

9   The origin of action – its efficient, not its final cause – is choice, and that of choice is desire and reasoning with a view to an end. This is why choice cannot exist either without thought and intellect or without a moral state; for good action and its opposite cannot exist without a combination of intellect and character. Intellect itself, however, moves nothing, but only the intellect which aims at an end and is practical.
Nicomachean Ethics, 1139a

10 Actions are commonly regarded as involuntary when they are performed (a) under compulsion, (b) as the result of ignorance. An act, it is thought, is done under compulsion when it originates in some external cause of such a nature that the agent or person subject to the compulsion contributes nothing to it. Such a situation is created, for example, when a sea captain is carried out of his course by a contrary wind or by men who have got him in their power. But the case is not always so clear. . . . An involuntary act being one performed under compulsion or as the result of ignorance, a voluntary act would seem to be one of which the origin or efficient cause lies in the agent, he knowing the particular circumstances in which he is acting.
Nicomachean Ethics, 1110a

11 Now, the last proposition both being an opinion about a perceptible object, and being what determines our actions, this a man either has not when he is in the state of passion, or has it in the sense in which having knowledge did not mean knowing but only talking, as a drunken man may utter the verses of Empedocles. And because the last term is not universal nor equally an object of knowledge with the universal term, the position that Socrates sought to establish actually seems to result; for it is not in the presence of what is thought to be knowledge proper that the

passion occurs (nor is it this that is dragged about as a result of the passion), but perceptual knowledge.
Nicomachean Ethics, 1147b

The good person is related to his friend as to himself (for his friend is another self). 12
Nicomachean Ethics, 1166a

The pleasures of creatures different in kind differ in kind, and it is 13 plausible to suppose that those of a single species do not differ. But they too vary to no small extent, in the case of men at least; the same things delight some people and pain others, and are painful and odious to some, and pleasant to and liked by others. This happens, too, in the case of sweet things; the same things do not seem sweet to a man in a fever and a healthy man – nor hot to a weak man and one in good condition. The same happens in other cases. But in all such matters that which appears to the good man is thought to be really so. If this is correct, as it seems to be, and excellence and the good man *qua* good are the measure of each thing, then the true pleasures too will be those that seem to him to be pleasures, and those things will be really pleasant that he enjoys.
Nicomachean Ethics, 1176a

Pleasure completes the activity not as the inherent state does, but as an 14 end which supervenes as the bloom of youth does on those in the flower of their age. So long, then, as both the intelligible or sensible object and the discriminating or contemplative faculty are as they should be, the pleasure will be involved in the activity; for when both the passive and the active factor are unchanged and are related to each other in the same way, the same result naturally follows.
Nicomachean Ethics, 1174b

It is evident that the city-state is a creation of nature, and that man is by 15 nature a political animal.
Politics, 1253a

Now it is evident that that form of government is best in which every 16 man, whoever he is, can act best and live happily.
Politics, 1324a

A city-state is not a mere aggregate of persons, but a union of them 17 sufficing for the purposes of life.
Politics, 1328b

It is thus clear that, just as some are by nature free, others are by nature 18 slaves, and for these latter the condition of slavery is both beneficial and just.
Politics, 1255a

19 The weaker are always anxious for justice and equality. The strong pay no heed to either.
Politics, 1318

20 Rhetoric is useful because things that are true and things that are just have a natural tendency to prevail over their opposites, so that if the decisions of judges are not what they ought to be, the defeat must be due to the speakers themselves, and they must be blamed accordingly.
Rhetoric, 1355a

21 Tragedy is a representation of action that is worthy of serious attention, complete in itself and of some magnitude – bringing about by means of pity and fear the purging of such emotions.
Poetics, 1449b

22 Comedy is an imitation of men worse than the average; worse, however, not as regards any and every sort of fault, but only as regards one particular kind, the ridiculous, which is a species of the ugly. The ridiculous may be defined as a mistake or deformity not productive of pain or harm to others; the mask, for instance, that excites laughter, is something ugly and distorted without causing pain.
Poetics, 1449a

23 A likely impossibility is always preferable to an unconvincing possibility.
Poetics, 1460a

24 The distinction between historian and poet is not in the one writing prose and the other verse – you might put the work of Herodotus into verse, and it would still be a species of history; it consists really in this, that the one describes the thing that has been, and the other a kind of thing that might be. Hence poetry is something more philosophic and of graver import than history, since its statements are of the nature rather of universals, whereas those of history are singulars.
Poetics, 1451b

25 To say of what is that it is not, or of what is not that it is, is false, while to say of what is that it is, and of what is not that it is not, is true.
Metaphysics, 1011

26 Now spoken sounds are symbols of affections in the soul, and written marks symbols of spoken sounds. And just as written marks are not the same for all men, neither are spoken sounds. But what these are in the first place signs of – affections of the soul – are the same for all; and what these affections are likenesses of – actual things – are also the same.
De Interpretatione, 16a

A deduction is an argument in which, certain things being laid down,   27
something other than these necessarily comes about through them. It is a
demonstration, when the premisses from which the deduction starts are
true and primitive, or are such that our knowledge of them has originally
come through premisses which are primitive and true; and it is a
dialectical deduction, if it reasons from reputable opinions.
Topics, 100a

Everything necessarily is or is not, and will be or will not be; but one   28
cannot divide and say that one or the other is necessary. I mean, for
example: it is necessary for there to be or not to be a sea-battle
tomorrow; but it is not necessary for a sea-battle to take place tomorrow,
nor for one not to take place – though it is necessary for one to take place
or not to take place. . . . With these it is necessary for one or the other of
the contradictories to be true or false – not, however, this one or that
one, but as chance has it; or for one to be true *rather* than the other, yet
not *already* true or false.
De Interpretatione, 19a

A *substance* – that which is called a substance most strictly, primarily,   29
and most of all – is that which is neither said of a subject nor in a subject,
e.g., the individual man or the individual horse. The species in which the
things primarily called substances are, are called *secondary substances*, as
also are the genera of these species. For example, the individual man
belongs in a species, man, and animal is a genus of the species; so these –
both man and animal – are called secondary substances.
Categories, 2a

We think we know each thing most fully when we know what it is, e.g.,   30
what man is or what fire is, rather than when we know its quality, its
quantity, or where it is; since we know each of these things also, only
when we know *what* the quantity or the quality *is*.

   And indeed the question which, both now and of old, has always been
raised, and always been the subject of doubt, viz., what being is, is just
the question, what is substance?
Metaphysics, 1028b

Clearly, if people proceed thus in their usual manner of definition and   31
speech, they cannot explain and solve the difficulty of what makes *man*
one and not many: animal plus biped. But if, as we say, one element is
matter and another is form, and one is potentially and the other actually,
the question will no longer be thought a difficulty. For this difficulty is
the same as would arise if 'round bronze' were the definition of cloak; for
this name would be a sign of the definitory formula, so that the question

is, what is the cause of the unity of round and bronze? The difficulty disappears, because the one is matter, the other form.
Metaphysics, 1045a

32 It has been sufficiently pointed out that the objects of mathematics are not substances in a higher sense than bodies are, and that they are not prior to sensibles in being, but only in formula, and that they cannot in any way exist separately. But since they could not exist *in* sensibles either, it is plain that they either do not exist at all or exist in a special way and therefore do not exist without qualification. For 'exist' has many senses.
Metaphysics, 1077b

33 Motion being eternal, the first mover, if there is but one, will be eternal also.
Physics, 259a

34 It is not likely either that fire or earth or any such element should be the reason why things manifest goodness and beauty both in their being and in their coming to be, or that those thinkers [Thales, Anaximenes, Heraclitus] should have supposed it was; nor again could it be right to ascribe so great a matter to spontaneity and luck. When one man [Anaxagoras] said, then, that reason was present – as in animals, so throughout nature – as the cause of the world and of all its order, he seemed like a sober man in contrast with the random talk of his predecessors.
Metaphysics, 984b

35 It is absurd to suppose that purpose is not present because we do not observe the agent deliberating. Art does not deliberate. If the ship-building art were in the wood, it would produce the same results by nature. If, therefore, purpose is present in art, it is present also in nature. The best illustration is a doctor doctoring himself: nature is like that.
Physics, 199b

36 Having already treated of the celestial world, as far as our conjectures could reach, we proceed to treat of animals, without omitting, to the best of our ability, any member of the kingdom, however ignoble. For if some have no graces to charm the sense, yet nature, which fashioned them, gives amazing pleasure in their study to all who can trace links of causation, and are inclined to philosophy. . . . We therefore must not recoil with childish aversion from the examination of the humbler animals. Every realm of nature is marvellous; . . . so we should venture on the study of every kind of animal without distaste; for each and all will reveal to us something natural and something beautiful. Absence of haphazard and conduciveness of everything to an end are to be found in

nature's works in the highest degree, and the end for which those works are put together and produced is a form of the beautiful.
Parts of Animals, 645a

Again, seeing that the whole of nature is in motion, and that nothing is 37 true of what is changing, they [the holders of the Theory of Flux] supposed that it is not possible to speak truly of what is changing in absolutely all respects. For from this belief flowered the most extreme opinion of those I have mentioned – that of those who say they 'Heraclitize', and such as was held by Cratylus, who in the end thought one should say nothing, and only moved his finger, and reproached Heraclitus for saying that you cannot step into the same river twice – for he himself thought you could not do so even once.
Metaphysics, 1010a

The soul is characterised by these capacities: self-nutrition, sensation, 38 thinking and movement.
De Anima, 413b

What is soul? It is substance in the sense which corresponds to the 39 account of a thing. That means that it is what it is to be for a body of the character just assigned. Suppose that a tool, e.g., an axe, were a *natural* body, then being an axe would have been its essence, and so its soul; if this disappeared from it, it would have ceased to be an axe, except in name.
De Anima, 412b

Thought, as we have so far described it, is what it is by virtue of 40 becoming all things, while there is another which is what it is by virtue of making all things: this is a sort of positive state like light; for in a sense light makes potential colours into actual colours.
  Thought in this latter sense is separable, impassible, unmixed, since it is in its essential nature activity.
De Anima, 430a

But how is it that thought is sometimes followed by action, sometimes 41 not; sometimes by movement, sometimes not? What happens seems parallel to the case of thinking and inferring about the immovable objects. There the end is the truth seen (for, when one thinks the two propositions, one thinks and puts together the conclusion), but here the conclusion drawn from two propositions becomes an action.
De Motu, 701a

Why are males usually larger than females? Is it because they are hotter, 42 and heat is productive of growth? Or is it because the male is complete in

all its parts, whereas the female is defective? Or is it because the male takes a long time to attain perfection, the female a short time?
Problems, 891b

D. M. ARMSTRONG (*b.* 1926)

1 The problem of universals has the interesting characteristic that it is almost impossible to explain to the non-philosopher what the fuss is all about. It is truly philosopher's philosophy. Perhaps that should make us suspicious of it. Yet I believe that Plato's instinct was correct when he treated it as the central question in metaphysics.
Profiles, IV, ed. R. J. Bogdan, p. 41

2 I do not think that Hegel's Dialectic has much to tell us about the nature of reality. But I think that human thought often moves in a dialectical way, from thesis to antithesis and then to the synthesis. Perhaps thought about the mind is a case in point. I have already said that classical philosophy has tended to think of the mind as an inner arena of some sort. This we may call the Thesis. Behaviourism moves to the opposite extreme: the mind is seen as outward behaviour. This is the Antithesis. My proposed Synthesis is that the mind is properly conceived as an inner principle, but a principle that is identified in terms of the outward behaviour it is apt for bringing about.
The Nature of Mind, p. 10

3 One of the great problems that must be solved in any attempt to work out a scientific world-view is that of bringing the being who puts forward the world-view *within* the world-view. By treating man, including his mental processes, as a purely physical object, operating according to exactly the same laws as all other physical things, this object is achieved with the greatest possible intellectual economy. The knower differs from the world he knows only in the greater complexity of his physical organization. Man is one with nature.
A Materialist Theory of the Mind, p. 365

4 *Beliefs about particular matters of fact* (including beliefs whose content is an unrestricted existentially quantified proposition) are structures in the mind of the believer which represent or 'map' reality, including the believer's own mind and belief-states. The fundamental representing elements and relations of the map represent the sorts of thing they represent because they spring from capacities of the believer to act selectively towards things of that sort.
Belief, Truth and Knowledge, p. 220

ANTOINE ARNAULD (1612–1694)

I have one further worry, namely how Descartes avoids reasoning in a   1
circle when he says that we are sure that what we clearly and distinctly
perceive is true only because God exists. But we are sure that God exists
only because we clearly and distinctly perceive this. Hence before we are
sure that God exists we ought to be able to be sure that whatever we
perceive clearly and evidently is true.
The Philosophical Writings of Descartes, trans. J. Cottingham, R. Stoothoff and
D. Murdoch, II, p. 150

I call the soul or mind thinking substance. Thinking, knowing and   2
perceiving are all the same thing. I also take the idea of an object and the
perception of an object to be the same thing. Nevertheless, it must be
remarked that this thing, although single, stands in two relations: one to
the soul which it modifies, the other to the thing perceived, in so far as it
exists objectively in the soul.
Des vrais et fausses idées, Oeuvres, XXXVIII, p. 198

MARY ASTELL (1666–1731)

... I found 'Woman', by nature, formed no less capable of all that is good   1
and great than 'Man'; and that the Authority which they have usurped
over us, is from Force, rather than the Law of Nature.
An Essay in Defence of the Female Sex, p. 2

... If Absolute Sovereignty be not necessary in a State how comes it to be   2
so in a Family? or if in a Family why not in a State; since no reason can be
alleg'd for the one that will not hold more strongly for the other. . . . If *all
Men are born free,* how is it that all Women are born slaves? As they
must be if the being subjected to the *inconstant, uncertain, unknown,
arbitrary Will* of Men, be the perfect Condition of Slavery?
Reflections upon Marriage

ST AUGUSTINE (354–430)

But what is time [or, a time]? Who can explain it easily and briefly, or   1
even, when he wants to speak of it, comprehend it in his thought? Yet is
there anything we mention in our talking that is so well known and
familiar? And we certainly understand when we say it, as we understand
when we hear it said by someone else with whom we are talking. So what
is [a] time? If no one asks me, I know; if they ask and I try to explain, I do
not know.
Confessions, Bk 11, Ch. 14, No. 17

2   If the future and the past do exist I want to know where they are. I may not yet be capable of such knowledge, but at least I know that, wherever they are, they are not there as future or past, but as present. For if, wherever they are, they are future, they do not yet exist; if past, they no longer exist. So wherever they are and whatever they are, it is only by being present that they *are*.
Confessions, Bk 11, Ch. 14, No. 18

3   Here is my reply to the person who says, 'What was God doing before he made heaven and earth?' I keep off the facetious reply said to have been given by someone wriggling out of a serious answer, 'He was preparing hell for people who ask awkward questions'. . . . Those who cannot understand why you were idle through countless ages should wake up and pay attention, because the thing they cannot understand is a fiction. How would countless ages have passed if you had not made them, since you are the author and creator of all ages? What times would there have been if they had not been created by you? How could they have passed without ever having been? Therefore since all times are your work, if there was any time before you made heaven and earth, why is it said that you were idle, not at work? You had made time itself; times would not pass before you made them.
Confessions, Bk 11, Ch. 12, No. 14

4   It is not the case . . . that because God foreknew what would be in the power of our wills, there is for that reason nothing in the power of our wills. For He Who foreknew this did not foreknow nothing. . . . If He Who foreknew what would be in the power of our wills did not foreknow nothing, but something, assuredly, even though He did foreknow, there is something in the power of our wills.
City of God, Bk 5, Ch. 10

5   Everyone who observes himself doubting observes a truth, and about that which he observes he is certain; therefore he is certain about a truth. Everyone therefore who doubts whether truth exists has in himself a truth on which not to doubt. . . . Hence one who can doubt at all ought not to doubt about the existence of truth.
De Vera Religione, Ch. 39, No. 73

6   Against these truths the arguments of the Academics are no terror, when they say, 'What if you are deceived?' For if I am deceived, I am. For one who is not, assuredly cannot be deceived; and because of this I am, if I am deceived. Because, therefore, I am if I am deceived, how am I deceived in thinking that I am, when it is certain that I am if I am deceived? Because,

therefore, I who was deceived would be, even if I were deceived, it is beyond doubt that I am not deceived in that I know myself to be.
City of God, Bk 11, Ch. 26

If someone . . . were to ask me what walking is, and I were to attempt to 7
teach him what he asked without a sign, by promptly walking, how am I to guard against his thinking that it is just the *amount* of walking I have done? If he thinks that, he will be mistaken; for he will judge that anyone who walks farther than I have, or less far, has not walked. And what I have said about this one word can be transferred to every word which I had agreed could be exhibited without a sign . . .
De Magistro, Ch. 10, No. 29

God is not the parent of evils. . . . Evils exist by the voluntary sin of the 8
soul to which God gave free choice. If one does not sin by will, one does not sin.
Contra Fortunatum Manichaeum, Acta seu Disputatio, Ch. 20

No one is free to do right who has not been freed from sin and begins to 9
be the servant of justice. And such is true liberty, because he has the joy of right-doing, and at the same time dutiful servitude because he obeys the precept.
Enchiridion, Ch. 9, Sec. 30

Those to whom the apostle allowed bodily intercourse with a single 10
spouse as pardonable on account of their intemperance are on a lower step towards God than the patriarchs who, though each had more than one, aimed in intercourse with them only at the procreation of children, as a wise man aims only at his body's health in food and drink.
De Doctrina Christiana, Bk 3, Ch. 18, No. 27

I have no hope but in your great mercy. Grant what you command and 11
command what you will.
Confessions, Bk 10, Sec. 29

BRUCE AUNE (*b.* 1933)

The goal of our intellectual efforts cannot be a static, polished possession; it can only be further, more successful efforts of the same general kind. In science as in life it is the process, not the terminus, that should concern us – if we are wise.
Rationalism, Empiricism, and Pragmatism, p. 178

J. L. AUSTIN (1911–1960)

I began by drawing your attention, by way of example, to a few simple 1
utterances of the kind known as performatories or performatives. These

have on the face of them the look – or at least the grammatical make-up – of 'statements'; but nevertheless they are seen, when more closely inspected, to be, quite plainly, *not* utterances which could be 'true' or 'false'. Yet to be 'true' or 'false' is traditionally the characteristic mark of a statement. One of our examples was, for instance, the utterance 'I do' (take this woman to be my lawful wedded wife), as uttered in the course of a marriage ceremony. Here we should say that in saying these words we are *doing* something – namely, marrying, rather than *reporting* something, namely *that* we are marrying. And the act of marrying, like, say, the act of betting, is at least *preferably* (though still not *accurately*) to be described as *saying certain words*, rather than as performing a different, inward and spiritual, action of which these words are merely the outward and audible sign. That this is so can perhaps hardly be *proved*, but it is, I should claim, a fact.
How to Do Things With Words, p. 12

2   Care must be taken too to observe the precise position of an adverbial expression in the sentence. This should of course indicate what verb it is being used to modify: but more than that, the position can also affect the *sense* of the expression, i.e., the way in which it modifies that verb. Compare, for example:

a_1 He clumsily trod on the snail.
a_2 Clumsily he trod on the snail.
b_1 He trod clumsily on the snail.
b_2 He trod on the snail clumsily.

Here, in a_1 and a_2 we describe his treading on the creature at all as a piece of clumsiness, incidental, we imply, to his performance of some other action: but with b_1 and b_2 to tread on it is, very likely, his aim or policy, what we criticize is his execution of the feat. Many adverbs, though far from all (not, for example, 'purposely'), are used in these two typically different ways.
Philosophical Papers, p. 198

3   We walk along the cliff, and I feel a sudden impulse to push you over, which I promptly do: I acted on impulse, yet I certainly intended to push you over, and may even have devised a little ruse to achieve it: yet even then I did not act deliberately, for I did not (stop to) ask myself whether to do it or not.
Philosophical Papers, p. 195

4   Words are not (except in their own little corner) facts or things: we need therefore to prise them off the world, to hold them apart from and

against it, so that we can realize their inadequacies and arbitrariness, and can re-look at the world without blinkers.
Philosophical Papers, p. 182

Our common stock of words embodies all the distinctions men have 5
found worth drawing, and the connexions they have found worth marking, in the lifetimes of many generations: these surely are likely to be more numerous, more sound, since they have stood up to the long test of the survival of the fittest, and more subtle, at least in all ordinary and reasonably practical matters, than any that you or I are likely to think up in our arm-chairs of an afternoon – the most favoured alternative method.
Philosophical Papers, p. 182

And it must be added, too, that superstition and error and fantasy of all 6
kinds do become incorporated in ordinary language and even sometimes stand up to the survival test (only, when they do, why should we not detect it?). Certainly, then, ordinary language is *not* the last word: in principle it can everywhere be supplemented and improved upon and superseded. Only remember, it *is* the *first* word.
Philosophical Papers, p. 185

There is a peculiar and intimate relationship between the emotion and 7
the natural manner of venting it, with which, having been angry ourselves, we are acquainted. The ways in which anger is normally manifested are *natural* to anger just as there are tones *naturally* expressive of various emotions (indignation, etc.). There is not normally taken to be such a thing as 'being angry' apart from any impulse, however vague, to vent the anger in the natural way.
Philosophical Papers, p. 108

It seems, does it not, perfectly obvious that every proposition must have a 8
contradictory? Yet it does not turn out so. Suppose that I live in harmony and friendship for four years with a cat: and then it delivers a philippic. We ask ourselves, perhaps, 'Is it a real cat? or is it *not* a real cat?' 'Either it *is*, or it *is not*, but we cannot be sure which.' Now actually, that is not so: *neither* 'It is a real cat' *nor* 'it is not a real cat' fits the facts semantically: each is designed for other situations than this one: you could not say the former of something which delivers philippics, nor yet the latter of something which has behaved as this has for four years.
Philosophical Papers, p. 67

Much, of course, of the amusement, and of the instruction, comes in 9
drawing the coverts of the microglot, in hounding down the minutiae, and to this I can do no more here than incite you. But I owe it to the

subject to say, that it has long afforded me what philosophy is so often thought, and made, barren of – the fun of discovery, the pleasures of co-operation, and the satisfaction of reaching agreement.
Philosophical Papers, p. 175

10 . . . there must be two sets of conventions:

> *Descriptive* conventions correlating the words (= sentences) with the *types* of situation, thing, event, etc., to be found in the world.
> *Demonstrative* conventions correlating the words (= statements) with the *historic* situations, etc., to be found in the world.

A statement is said to be true when the historic state of affairs to which it is correlated by the demonstrative conventions (the one to which it 'refers') is of a type with which the sentence used in making it is correlated by the descriptive conventions.
Philosophical Papers, p. 121

11 Nor does *can* have to be a very special and peculiar verb for *ifs* which are not causal conditional to be found in connexion with it: all kinds of *ifs* are found with all kinds of verbs. Consider for example the *if* in 'There are biscuits on the sideboard if you want them', where the verb is the highly ordinary *are*, but the *if* is more like that in 'I can if I choose' than that in 'I panted if I ran': for we can certainly infer from it that 'There are biscuits on the sideboard whether you want them or not' and that anyway 'There are biscuits on the sideboard', whereas it would be folly to infer that 'If there are no biscuits on the sideboard you do not want them', or to understand the meaning to be that you have only to want biscuits to cause them to be on the sideboard.
Philosophical Papers, p. 210

JOHN AUSTIN (1790–1859)

The existence of law is one thing; its merit or demerit is another.
Province of Jurisprudence Determined, ed. H. L. A. Hart, p. 184

AVICENNA (980–1037)

1 . . . for a body, as body-qua-body, there is no will. Since the will proper to the mover of the body is such that whatever is moved by it is a thing which is in motion due to it, the moved is different from the mover. Thus, the mover of this primary body is neither an intelligent substance nor a natural substance, but is a kind of soul-self. Such a thing we call 'soul-self'.
Metaphysica, ed. P. Morewedge, p. 90

Perhaps you will say, indeed I prove [the existence of] my self through   2
the medium of my action. In that case you will have to have an act to
prove . . . or a movement or some other thing. In the supposition of
suspension in space we isolate you from all that. But as a general
principle, if you prove your act as absolutely an act, you must prove from
it an agent absolutely and not particularly, who is your self definitely. If
you prove that it is an act of yours and you do not prove your self
through it, and if it is part of what is understood from your act in so far
as it is your act, it would then have been proved in the understanding,
before it or at least with it but not through it. Your self is thus not proved
through it.
Quoted in Soheil M. Afnan, *Avicenna: His Life and Work*, p. 151

A. J. AYER (1910–1989)

Like Hume, I divide all genuine propositions into two classes: those   1
which, in his terminology, concern 'relations of ideas', and those which
concern 'matters of fact'. The former class comprises the *a priori*
propositions of logic and pure mathematics, and these I allow to be
necessary and certain only because they are analytic. That is, I maintain
that the reason why these propositions cannot be confuted in experience
is that they do not make any assertion about the empirical world, but
simply record our determination to use symbols in a certain fashion.
Language, Truth and Logic, p. 9

The criterion which we use to test the genuineness of apparent statements   2
of fact is the criterion of verifiability. We say that a sentence is factually
significant to any given person, if, and only if, he knows how to verify the
proposition which it purports to express – that is, if he knows what
observations would lead him, under certain conditions, to accept the
proposition as being true, or reject it as being false. If, on the other hand,
the putative proposition is of such a character that the assumption of its
truth, or falsehood, is consistent with any assumption whatsoever
concerning the nature of his future experience, then, as far as he is
concerned, it is, if not a tautology, a mere pseudo-proposition. The
sentence expressing it may be emotionally significant to him; but it is not
literally significant. . . .

   To make our position clearer, we may formulate it in another way. Let
us call a proposition which records an actual or possible observation an
experiential proposition. Then we may say that it is the mark of a
genuine factual proposition, not that it should be equivalent to an
experiential proposition, or any finite number of experiential propositions,
but simply that some experiential propositions can be deduced from it in

29

conjunction with certain other premises without being deducible from those other premises alone.
Language, Truth and Logic, pp. 16, 20

3 . . . what is important to us is to realize that even the utterances of the metaphysician who is attempting to expound a vision are literally senseless; so that henceforth we may pursue our philosophical researches with as little regard for them as for the more inglorious kind of metaphysics which comes from a failure to understand the workings of our language.
Language, Truth and Logic, p. 29

4 The presence of an ethical symbol in a proposition adds nothing to its factual content. Thus if I say to someone, 'You acted wrongly in stealing that money', I am not stating anything more than if I had simply said, 'You stole that money'. In adding that this action is wrong I am not making any further statement about it. I am simply evincing my moral disapproval of it. It is as if I had said, 'You stole that money', in a peculiar tone of horror, or written it with the addition of some special exclamation marks.
Language, Truth and Logic, p. 110

5 I conclude then that the necessary and sufficient conditions for knowing that something is the case are first that what one is said to know be true, secondly that one be sure of it, and thirdly that one should have the right to be sure. This right may be earned in various ways; but even if one could give a complete description of them it would be a mistake to try to build it into the definition of knowledge, just as it would be a mistake to try to incorporate our actual standards of goodness into a definition of good.
The Problem of Knowledge, p. 34

6 Because of the possibility of illusion, it will not necessarily be true that whenever it seems to me that I am perceiving something, I really am perceiving it. On the other hand, the converse is intended to hold. From the statement that I see the cigarette case it is supposed to follow that it seems to me that I see it. . . .

The next step, continuing with our example, is to convert the sentence 'it now seems to me that I see a cigarette case' into 'I am now seeing a seeming-cigarette case'. And this seeming-cigarette case, which lives only in my present experience, is an example of a sense-datum. Applying this procedure to all cases of perception, whether veridical or delusive, one obtains the result that whenever anyone perceives, or thinks that he perceives, a physical object, he must at least be, in the appropriate sense, perceiving a seeming-object. These seeming-objects are sense-data; and

the conclusion may be more simply expressed by saying that it is always sense-data that are directly perceived.
The Problem of Knowledge, p. 105

Either it is an accident that I choose to act as I do or it is not. If it is an 7 accident, then it is merely a matter of chance that I did not choose otherwise; and if it is merely a matter of chance that I did not choose otherwise, it is surely irrational to hold me morally responsible for choosing as I did. But if it is not an accident that I choose to do one thing rather than another, then presumably there is some causal explanation of my choice: and in that case we are led back to determinism.
Philosophical Essays, p. 275

A point to which Wittgenstein constantly recurs is that the ascription of 8 meaning to a sign is something that needs to be justified: the justification consists in there being some independent test for determining that the sign is being used correctly; independent, that is, of the subject's recognition, or supposed recognition, of the object which he intends the sign to signify. His claim to recognize the object, his belief that it really is the same, is not to be accepted unless it can be backed by further evidence. Apparently, too, this evidence must be public: it must, at least in theory, be accessible to everyone. Merely to check one private sensation by another would not be enough. For if one cannot be trusted to recognize one of them, neither can one be trusted to recognize the other.

But unless there is something that one is allowed to recognize, no test can ever be completed: there will be no justification for the use of any sign at all. I check my memory of the time at which the train is due to leave by visualizing a page of the time-table; and I am required to check this in its turn by looking up the page. But unless I can trust my eyesight at this point, unless I can recognize the figures that I see written down, I am still no better off. It is true that if I distrust my eyesight I have the resource of consulting other people; but then I have to understand their testimony, I have correctly to identify the signs that they make.
The Concept of a Person, p. 41

Can my present view of the table, considered purely in itself as a fleeting 9 visual experience, conceivably guarantee that I am seeing something that is also tangible, or visible to other observers? Can it guarantee even that I am seeing something which exists at any other time than this, let alone something that is made of such and such materials, or endowed with such and such causal properties, or serving such and such a purpose? I think it evident that it cannot. But if these conclusions are not logically guaranteed by the content of my present visual experience, one is surely

entitled to say that they go beyond it, and just this is what I take to be
meant by saying that my judgement that this is a table embodies an
inference. . . .

If I am right on this point, the naive realists are wrong in so far as they
deny that our ordinary judgements of perception are susceptible of
analysis, or deny that they embody inferences which can be made
explicit.
The Central Questions of Philosophy, p. 81

10 What then does *propter hoc* add to *post hoc*? At the factual level, nothing
at all, so long as the conjunction is constant in either case. . . . In nature
one thing just happens after another. Cause and effect have their place
only in our imaginative arrangements and extensions of these primary
facts.
The Central Questions of Philosophy, p. 183

B

ⓢⓢⓢⓢⓢⓢ

FRANCIS BACON (1561–1626)

It is idle to expect any great advancement in science from the   **1**
superinducing and engrafting of new things upon old. We must begin
anew from the very foundations, unless we would revolve for ever in a
circle with mean and contemptible progress.
The Philosophical Works of Francis Bacon, ed. J. M. Robertson, p. 262

Again there is another great and powerful cause why the sciences have   **2**
made but little progress; which is this. It is not possible to run a course
aright when the goal itself has not been rightly placed. Now the true and
lawful goal of the sciences is none other than this: that human life be
endowed with new discoveries and powers. But of this the great majority
have no feeling, but are merely hireling and professorial . . .
The Philosophical Works of Francis Bacon, ed. J. M. Robertson, p. 280

Those who have handled sciences have been either men of experiment or   **3**
men of dogmas. The men of experiment are like the ant; they only collect
and use; the reasoners resemble spiders, who make cobwebs out of their
own substance. But the bee takes the middle course; it gathers its material
from the flowers of the garden and of the field, but transforms and digests
it by a power of its own. Not unlike this is the true business of philosophy
. . .
The Philosophical Works of Francis Bacon, ed. J. M. Robertson, p. 288

What is Truth; said jesting Pilate; And would not stay for an Answer.   **4**
Essays, ed. M. Kiernan, p. 7

It is true, that a little Philosophy inclineth Mans Minde to *Atheisme*; But   **5**
depth in Philosophy, bringeth Mens Mindes about to *Religion* . . .
Essays, p. 51

ROGER BACON (c.1214–c.1292)

For there are two modes of acquiring knowledge, namely by reasoning   **1**
and experience.

Reasoning draws a conclusion and makes us grant the conclusion, but does not make the conclusion certain, nor does it remove doubt.

For if a man who has never seen fire should prove by adequate reasoning that fire burns and injures things and destroys them his mind would not be satisfied thereby nor would he avoid fire until he had placed his hand or some combustible substance in the fire so that he might prove by experience that which reasoning taught.

The Opus Majus of Roger Bacon, trans. Robert Belle Burke, p. 583

2   There are no lectures given in experimental science either at Oxford or at Paris and this is a shameful thing because experimental science is the mistress of the speculative sciences, it alone is able to give us important truths within the confines of the other sciences, which those sciences can learn in no other way.

The Opus Majus of Roger Bacon, trans. Robert Belle Burke, p. 616

ANNETTE BAIER (*b.* 1929)

1   Granted that the men's theories of obligation need supplementation, to have much chance of integrity and coherence, and that the women's hypothetical theories will want to cover obligation as well as love, then what concept brings them together? My tentative answer is – the concept of appropriate trust, oddly neglected in moral theory. This concept also nicely mediates between reason and feeling, those tired old candidates for moral authority, since to trust is neither quite to believe something about the trusted, nor necessarily to feel any emotion towards them – but to have a belief-informed and action-influencing attitude.

'What Do Women Want in a Moral Theory?', *Nous* (1985), p. 53

2   Contract is a device for traders, entrepreneurs, and capitalists, not for children, servants, indentured wives, and slaves. They were the traded, not the traders . . . the liberal morality which takes voluntary agreement as the paradigm source of moral obligation must either exclude the women they expect to continue in their traditional role from the class of moral subjects, or admit internal contradiction in their moral beliefs. Nor does the contradiction vanish once women have equal legal rights with men, as long as they are still expected to take responsibility for any child they conceive voluntarily or nonvoluntarily, either to abort or to bear and either care for or arrange for others to care for.

'Trust and Antitrust', *Ethics* (1986), p. 247

3   What the contractualist makes explicit is a voluntary mutual commitment, and what services each is committed to provide. I have claimed that such explicitness is not only rare in trust relationships, but that many of them must begin inexplicitly and nonvoluntarily and would not do the moral

and social work they do if they covered only what contract does – services that could be pretty exactly spelled out.
'Trust and Antitrust', *Ethics* (1986), p. 257

Men may but women cannot see morality as essentially a matter of 4 keeping to the minimal moral traffic rules, designed to restrict close encounters between autonomous persons to self-chosen ones.
'Trust and Antitrust', *Ethics* (1986), p. 249

. . . a complete moral philosophy would tell us how and why we should 5 act and feel toward others in relationships of shifting and varying power asymmetry and shifting and varying intimacy.
'Trust and Antitrust', *Ethics* (1986), p. 252

MICHAEL BAKUNIN (1814–1876)

Let us therefore trust the eternal Spirit which destroys and annihilates 1 only because it is the unfathomable and eternal source of all life. The passion for destruction is a creative passion too!
Bakunin on Anarchy, ed. S. Dolgoff, p. 57

It is the characteristic of privilege and of every privileged position to kill 2 the hearts and minds of men. The privileged man, whether politically or economically, is a man depraved in mind and heart. That is a social law which admits of no exception, and it is applicable to entire nations as to classes, corporations and individuals. It is the law of equality, the supreme condition of liberty and humanity.
Bakunin on Anarchy, p. 228

All temporal or human authority stems directly from spiritual and/or 3 divine authority. But authority is the negation of freedom. God, or rather the fiction of God, is the consecration and the intellectual and moral source of all slavery on earth, and the freedom of mankind will never be complete until the disastrous and insidious fiction of a heavenly master is annihilated.
Bakunin on Anarchy, p. 238

RENFORD BAMBROUGH (b. 1926)

Philosophers are often too limited in their consideration of a concept 1 because they think primarily or only of the contexts and occasions of the use of the most general word that we have for expressing it. To understand causation is not just to be able to analyse propositions of the form 'A causes B' but to know what we are doing when we speak of cooking, burning, shooting, insulting, disappointing, cutting a cake or a dash or an acquaintance.
'The Scope of Reason: An Epistle to the Persians'

2   To be too much attached to reason is presumably to be more attached to reason than it is reasonable to be; and this way of putting the charge does most of the work of counsel for the defence, as can be shown by setting some parallel cases beside it. . . . When the Hungarian expert in *Pygmalion* finds fault with Eliza Doolittle's speaking of English he condemns it as 'too good' to be genuine; it is too formally perfect to achieve perfection. A work of art that is too perfect is too rigid or too regular or too miniature to be perfect at all. In all these cases we have to do with oblique modes of expression of the attribution of defects. The nature of the defect is in each case expressed as an excess of a good quality, but the excess is a deficiency, and its diagnosis is far from being or involving a suggestion that the quality in question is not a merit.
'The Shape of Ignorance'

ROLAND BARTHES (1915–1980)

1   . . . any semiology postulates a relation between two terms, a signifier and a signified. This relation concerns objects which belong to different categories, and this is why it is not one of equality but one of equivalence. . . . what we grasp is not at all one term after the other, but the correlation which unites them: there are, therefore, the signifier, the signified, and the sign, which is the associative total of the first two terms.
Myth Today, trans. Annette Lavers, p. 121

2   Take a bunch of roses: I use it to *signify* my passion. Do we have here, then, only a signifier and a signified, the roses and my passion? Not even that: to put it accurately, there are here only 'passionified' roses. But on the plane of analysis, we do have three terms; for these roses weighted with passion perfectly and correctly allow themselves to be decomposed into roses and passion: the former and the latter existed before uniting and forming this third object, which is the sign.
Myth Today, trans. Annette Lavers, p. 121

3   The primary evaluation of all texts can come neither from science, for science does not evaluate, nor from ideology . . . Our evaluation can be linked only to a practice, and this practice is that of writing: . . . which texts would I consent to write (to rewrite), to desire, to put forth as a force in this world of mine? What evaluation finds is precisely this value: . . . the *writerly*. Why is the writerly our value? Because the goal of literary work (of literature as work) is to make the reader no longer a consumer, but a producer of the text.
S/Z, trans. Richard Miller, p. 3

4   Our literature is characterized by the pitiless divorce which the literary institution maintains between the producer of the text and its user,

between its owner and its customer, between its author and its reader. This reader is thereby plunged into a kind of idleness – he is intransitive; he is, in short, *serious*: instead of functioning himself, instead of gaining access to the magic of the signifier, to the pleasure of writing, he is left with no more than the poor freedom either to accept or reject the text: reading is nothing more than a *referendum*. Opposite the writerly text, then, is its countervalue, its negative, reactive value: what can be read, but not written: the *readerly*. We call any readerly text a classic text.
S/Z, trans. Richard Miller, p. 4

No sooner has a word been said, somewhere, about the pleasure of the 5
text, than two policemen are ready to jump on you: the political policeman and the psychoanalytical policeman: futility and/or guilt, pleasure is either idle or vain, a class notion or an illusion.
The Pleasure of the Text, A Barthes Reader, ed. S. Sontag, p. 411

In his tale, *Sarrasine*, Balzac, speaking of a castrato disguised as a 6
woman, writes this sentence: 'She was Woman, with her sudden fears, her inexplicable whims, her instinctive fears, her meaningless bravado, her defiance, and her delicious delicacy of feeling.' Who speaks in this way? Is it the hero of the tale, who would prefer not to recognize the castrato hidden beneath the 'woman'? Is it Balzac the man, whose personal experience has provided him with a philosophy of Woman? Is it Balzac the author, professing certain 'literary' ideas about femininity? Is it universal wisdom? Romantic psychology? We can never know, for the good reason that writing is the destruction of every voice, every origin. Writing is that neuter, that composite, that obliquity into which our subject flees, the black-and-white where all identity is lost, beginning with the very identity of the body that writes.
The Rustle of Language, trans. Richard Howard, p. 49

We know now that a text consists not of a line of words, releasing a 7
single 'theological' meaning (the 'message' of the Author-God), but of a multi-dimensional space in which are married and contested several writings, none of which is original: the text is a fabric of quotations, resulting from a thousand sources of culture. . . . the writer can only imitate an ever anterior, never original gesture; his sole power is to mingle writings, to counter some by others, so as never to rely on just one; if he seeks to *express himself*, at least he knows that the interior 'thing' he claims to 'translate' is itself no more than a ready-made lexicon, whose words can be explained only through other words, and this ad infinitum; . . . succeeding the Author, the *scriptor* no longer contains passions, moods, sentiments, impressions, but that immense dictionary from which he draws a writing which will be incessant: life

merely imitates the book, and this book itself is but a tissue of signs, endless imitation, infinitely postponed.

The Rustle of Language, trans. Richard Howard, p. 52

8　Once the Author is distanced, the claim to 'decipher' a text becomes entirely futile. . . . In multiple writing, in effect, everything is to be *disentangled*, but nothing *deciphered*, structure can be followed, 'threaded' (as we say of a run in a stocking) in all its reprises, all its stages, but there is no end to it, no bottom; the space of writing is to be traversed, not pierced; writing constantly posits meaning, but always in order to evaporate it: writing seeks a systematic exemption of meaning. Thereby, literature (it would be better, from now on, to say *writing*), by refusing to assign to the text (and to the world-as-text) a 'secret', i.e., an ultimate meaning, liberates an activity we may call countertheological, properly revolutionary, for to refuse to halt meaning is finally to refuse God and his hypostases, reason, science, the law.

The Rustle of Language, trans. Richard Howard, p. 53

9　What History, our History, allows us today is merely to displace, to vary, to transcend, to repudiate. Just as Einsteinian science compels us to include within the object studied the *relativity of reference points*, so the combined action of Marxism, Freudianism, and structuralism compels us, in literature, to relativize the relations of *scriptor*, reader, and observer (critic). Confronting the *work* – a traditional notion, long since, and still today, conceived in what we might call a Newtonian fashion – there now occurs the demand for a new object, obtained by a shift or a reversal of previous categories. This object is the *Text*.

The Rustle of Language, trans. Richard Howard, p. 56

10　The author is reputed to be the father and the owner of his work; literary science thus teaches us to *respect* the manuscript and the author's declared intentions . . . no vital 'respect' is . . . due to the Text: it can be *broken* (moreover, this is what the Middle Ages did with two nonetheless authoritarian texts: Scripture and Aristotle); the Text can be read without its father's guarantee; the restoration of the intertext paradoxically abolishes inheritance.

The Rustle of Language, trans. Richard Howard, p. 61

11　This mechanism of different 'times', in relation to language, is important. Consider the 'complete' systems (Marxism, Psychoanalysis), *initially* they have an (effective) function of counter-Stupidity: to pass through them is to educate oneself; those who entirely reject one or the other (those who say no, on account of temperament, blindness, stubbornness, to Marxism, to psychoanalysis) nurse, in their den of rejection, a kind of stupidity, of grim opacity. But subsequently these systems themselves

become stupid. Once they 'take', there is stupidity. That is why it is inescapable. One feels like going elsewhere: *Ciao*! *No, thanks*!
The Rustle of Language, trans. Richard Howard, p. 351

SIMONE DE BEAUVOIR (1908–1986)

It is vexing to hear a man say: 'You think thus and so because you are a 1 woman'; but I know that my only defence is to reply: 'I think thus and so because it is true', thereby removing my subjective self from the argument. It would be out of the question to reply: 'And you think thus and so because you are a man', for it is understood that the fact of being a man is no peculiarity. A man is in the right in being a man; it is the woman who is in the wrong. . . . There is an absolute human type, the masculine. . . . Man superbly ignores the fact that his anatomy also includes glands, such as the testicles, and that they secrete hormones. . . . He believes he apprehends objectively.
The Second Sex, trans. H. M. Parshley, p. 15

She appears essentially to the male as a sexual being. . . . She is defined 2 and differentiated with reference to man and not he with reference to her; she is the incidental, the inessential as opposed to the essential. He is the Subject, he is the Absolute – she is the Other.
The Second Sex, trans. H. M. Parshley, p. 16

The most mediocre of males feels himself a demigod as compared with 3 women.
The Second Sex, trans. H. M. Parshley, p. 24

. . . those who are condemned to stagnation are often pronounced happy 4 on the pretext that happiness consists in being at rest. This notion we reject, for our perspective is that of existentialist ethics. Every subject plays his part as such specifically through exploits or projects that serve as a mode of transcendence; he achieves liberty only through a continual reaching out towards other liberties. There is no justification for present existence other than its expansion into an indefinitely open future. Every time transcendence falls back into immanence, stagnation, there is a degradation of existence into the '*en-soi*' – the brutish life of subjection to given conditions – and of liberty into constraint and contingence.
The Second Sex, trans. H. M. Parshley, p. 28

Now, what peculiarly signalizes the situation of woman is that she – a 5 free and autonomous being like all human creatures – nevertheless finds herself living in a world where men compel her to assume the status of the Other. They propose to stabilize her as object and to doom her to immanence since her transcendence is to be overshadowed and for ever

transcended by another ego (*conscience*) which is essential and sovereign. The drama of woman lies in this conflict between the fundamental aspirations of every subject (ego) – who always regards the self as the essential – and the compulsions of a situation in which she is the inessential. How can a human being in woman's situation attain fulfilment? . . . How can independence be recovered in a state of dependency? . . . These are the fundamental questions on which I would fain throw some light. This means that I am interested in the fortunes of the individual as defined not in terms of happiness but in terms of liberty.
The Second Sex, trans. H. M. Parshley, p. 29

6   Man is defined as a human being and woman as a female – whenever she behaves as a human being she is said to imitate the male.
The Second Sex, trans. H. M. Parshley, p. 83

7   One is not born, but rather becomes, a woman. No biological, psychological, or economic fate determines the figure that the human female presents in society; it is civilization as a whole that produces this creature, intermediate between male and eunuch, which is described as feminine.
The Second Sex, trans. H. M. Parshley, p. 295

8   Woman is doomed to immorality, because for her to be moral would mean that she must incarnate a being of superhuman qualities: the 'virtuous woman' of Proverbs, the 'perfect mother', the 'honest woman', and so on. Let her but think, dream, sleep, desire, breathe without permission and she betrays the masculine ideal. This is why many wives let themselves go, 'are themselves', only in the absence of their husbands. On the other hand, the wife does not know her husband; she thinks she perceives his true aspect because she sees him in his daily round of inessential circumstances; but man is first of all what he *does* in the world among other men.
The Second Sex, trans. H. M. Parshley, p. 492

9   I have noted with what disgusted scepticism prostitutes regard the respectable gentlemen who condemn vice in general but view their own personal whims with indulgence; yet they regard the girls who live off their bodies as perverted and debauched, not the males who use them. . . . Woman plays the part of those secret agents who are left to the firing squad if they get caught, and are loaded with rewards if they succeed; it is for her to shoulder all man's immorality.
The Second Sex, trans. H. M. Parshley, p. 624

10   The advantage man enjoys, which makes itself felt from his childhood, is that his vocation as a human being in no way runs counter to his destiny

as a male. . . . He is not divided. Whereas it is required of woman that in order to realize her femininity she must make herself object and prey, which is to say that she must renounce her claims as sovereign subject.
The Second Sex, trans. H. M. Parshley, p. 691

The independent woman – and above all the intellectual, who thinks **11** about her situation – will suffer, as a female, from an inferiority complex; she lacks leisure for such minute beauty care as that of the coquette whose sole aim in life is to be seductive. . . . One does not infallibly stop the surge of a body that is straining towards the world and change it into a statue animated by vague tremors.
The Second Sex, trans. H. M. Parshley, p. 694

For woman to love as man does – that is to say, in liberty, without **12** putting her very *being* in question – she must believe herself his equal and be so in concrete fact.
The Second Sex, trans. H. M. Parshley, p. 705

To be a woman, if not a defect, is at least a peculiarity. **13**
The Second Sex, trans. H. M. Parshley, p. 710

A man would never set out to write a book on the peculiar situation of **14** the human male. But if I wish to define myself, I must first of all say: 'I am a human woman'.
The Second Sex, trans. H. M. Parshley, p. 15

Woman is opaque in her very being; she stands before man not as a **15** subject but as an object paradoxically endued with subjectivity; she takes herself simultaneously as *self* and as *other*, a contradiction that entails baffling consequences.
The Second Sex, trans. H. M. Parshley, p. 727

If the vicious circle is so hard to break, it is because the two sexes are each **16** the victim at once of the other and of itself. Between two adversaries confronting each other in their pure liberty an agreement could be easily reached: the more so as the war profits neither. But the complexity of the whole affair derives from the fact that each camp is giving aid and comfort to the enemy; woman is pursuing a dream of submission, man a dream of identification. Want of authenticity does not pay: each blames the other for the unhappiness he or she has incurred in yielding to the temptations of the easy way.
The Second Sex, trans. H. M. Parshley, p. 728

All oppression creates a state of war. **17**
The Second Sex, trans. H. M. Parshley, p. 726

ERROL BEDFORD (*b.* 1921)

1 The conclusion to be drawn, if I am right, is that being angry is logically prior to feeling angry, and therefore that being angry does not entail feeling angry, and a fortiori does not entail having any other feeling.
'Emotions', *The Philosophy of Mind*, ed. V. Chappell, p. 112

2 . . . I only want to suggest that the traditional answer to the question 'How do we identify our own emotions?' namely, 'By introspection', cannot be correct. It seems to me that there is every reason to believe that we learn about our own emotions essentially in the same way as other people learn about them. Admittedly, it is sometimes the case that we know our own emotions better than anyone else does, but there is no need to explain this as being due to the introspection of feelings. One reason for this is that it is hardly possible for a man to be completely ignorant, as others may be, of the context of his own behavior. Again, thoughts may cross his mind that he does not make public. But the fact that he prefers to keep them to himself is incidental; and if they were known they would only be corroborative evidence, not indispensable evidence of a radically different sort from that which is available to other people.
'Emotions', *The Philosophy of Mind*, p. 113

3 The traditional theory gives the answer that emotion words explain behavior by specifying its cause, i.e., a certain feeling or inner experience. But surely, when we ask what caused someone to do something, we usually neither expect nor receive an answer in terms of feelings. The answer takes the form of a reference to some external circumstance, if that is relevant, or to some thought, memory, observation, etc., that accounts for the action. If we refer to feelings at all, this appears to be a type of explanation that we fall back on as a last resort, because it is unilluminating and only one step removed from saying that the action is unaccountable. What seems to me to be wrong, then, on this score, with the traditional view is that it does not do justice to the explanatory power of emotion words. For the fact is that to know the feeling that may have preceded an action is not to understand it, or to understand it only very imperfectly. One can remember an action that one did many years ago, an action that one no longer understands, and the question 'Why did I do it?' can remain in the face of the clearest recollection of what it felt like to do it. If emotion words merely named some inner experience that preceded or accompanied behavior, to explain behavior by using them would not give the insight that it does.
'Emotions', *The Philosophy of Mind*, p. 124

CLIVE BELL (1881–1964)

That there is a particular kind of emotion provoked by works of visual   1
art, and that this emotion is provoked by every kind of visual art, by
pictures, sculptures, buildings, pots, carvings, textiles, etc., etc., is not
disputed, I think, by anyone capable of feeling it. This emotion is called
the aesthetic emotion; and if we can discover some quality common and
peculiar to all the objects that provoke it, we shall have solved what I
take to be the central problem of aesthetics.
Art, p. 6

What quality is shared by all objects that provoke our aesthetic   2
emotions? What quality is common to Sta. Sophia and the windows at
Chartres, Mexican sculpture, a Persian bowl, Chinese carpets, Giotto's
frescoes at Padua, and the masterpieces of Poussin, Piero della Francesca,
and Cézanne? Only one answer seems possible – significant form. In
each, lines and colours combined in a particular way, certain forms and
relations of forms, stir our aesthetic emotions. These relations and
combinations of lines and colours, these aesthetically moving forms, I
call 'Significant Form'; and 'Significant Form' is the one quality common
to all works of visual art.
Art, p. 8

SEYLA BENHABIB (*b.* 1950)

The transition to modernity does not only privatize the self's relation to   1
the cosmos and to ultimate questions of religion and being. First with
Western modernity the conception of privacy is so enlarged that an
intimate domestic-familial sphere is subsumed under it. Relations of
'kinship, friendship, love, and sex', indeed, as Kohlberg takes them to be,
come to be viewed as spheres of 'personal decision-making'. At the
beginning of modern moral and political theory, however, the 'personal'
nature of the spheres does not mean the recognition of equal, female
autonomy, but rather the removal of gender relations from the sphere of
justice. While the bourgeois male celebrates his transition from conventional to postconventional morality, from socially accepted rules of
justice to their generation in light of the principles of a social contract,
the domestic sphere remains at the conventional level. The sphere of
justice from Hobbes through Locke and Kant is regarded as the domain
where independent, male heads of household transact with one another,
while the domestic-intimate sphere is put beyond the pale of justice and
restricted to the reproductive and affective needs of the bourgeois
paterfamilias. Agnes Heller has named this domain the 'household of the
emotions'. An entire domain of human activity, namely, nurture,

reproduction, love and care, which becomes the woman's lot in the course of the development of modern, bourgeois society, is excluded from moral and political considerations, and relegated to the realm of 'nature'.
Feminism and Critique, p. 83

2   Universalistic moral theories in the Western tradition from Hobbes to Rawls are *substitutionalist*, in the sense that the universalism they defend is defined surreptitiously by identifying the experiences of a specific group of subjects as the paradigmatic case of the human as such. These subjects are invariably white, male adults who are propertied or at least professional. I want to distinguish *substitutionalist* from *interactive* universalism. Interactive universalism . . . regards difference as a starting-point for reflection and action. In this sense 'universality' is a regulative ideal that does not deny our embodied and embedded identity, but aims at developing moral attitudes and encouraging political transformations that can yield a point of view acceptable to all. Universality is not the ideal consensus of fictitiously defined selves, but the concrete process in politics and morals of the struggle of concrete, embodied selves, striving for autonomy.
Feminism and Critique, p. 81

3   The standpoint of the generalized other requires us to view each and every individual as a rational being entitled to the same rights and duties we would want to ascribe to ourselves. In assuming the standpoint, we abstract from the individuality and concrete identity of the other. . . . The moral categories that accompany such interactions are those of right, obligation and entitlement, and the corresponding moral feelings are those of respect, duty, worthiness and dignity.

The standpoint of the concrete other, by contrast, requires us to view each and every rational being as an individual with a concrete history, identity and affective-emotional constitution. . . . each is entitled to expect and to assume from the other forms of behavior through which the other feels recognized and confirmed as a concrete, individual being with specific needs, talents and capacities. . . . The moral categories that accompany such interactions are those of responsibility, bonding and sharing. The corresponding moral feelings are those of love, care and sympathy and solidarity.
Feminism and Critique, p. 87

WALTER BENJAMIN (1892–1940)

1   History is the subject of a structure whose site is not homogeneous, empty time, but time filled by the presence of the now. Thus, to

Robespierre ancient Rome was a past charged with the time of the now which he blasted out of the continuum of history. The French Revolution viewed itself as Rome reincarnate. It evoked ancient Rome the way fashion evokes costumes of the past. Fashion has a flair for the topical, no matter where it stirs in the thickets of long ago; it is a tiger's leap into the past. This jump, however, takes place in an arena where the ruling class gives the commands. The same leap in the open air of history is the dialectical one, which is how Marx understood the revolution.
Illuminations, trans. Harry Zohn, p. 259

A highly embroiled quarter, a network of streets that I had avoided for 2 years, was disentangled at a single stroke when one day a person dear to me moved there. It was as if a searchlight set up at this person's window dissected the area with pencils of light.
One-Way Street and Other Writings, trans. E. Jephcott and K. Shorter, p. 69

In the ruin history has physically merged into the setting. And in this 3 guise history does not assume the form of the process of an eternal life so much as that of irresistible decay.
The Origin of German Tragic Drama, trans. John Osborne, p. 177

JONATHAN BENNETT (*b.* 1930)

It follows from the argument of the preceding section that the possession 1 of a language is necessary for rationality; and it follows from the whole line of argument of this essay that the possession of a language is not sufficient for rationality.
Rationality: An Essay Towards an Analysis, p. 93

In support of my claim that the expression of dated and universal 2 judgments is both necessary and sufficient for rationality, and thus that linguistic capacity is necessary but not sufficient for rationality, I invite consideration of a creature I shall call the Describer. . . . What the Describer does is to describe – accurately, in plain lucid English, *viva voce* – such aspects of its surroundings as a moderately attentive human would be aware of if similarly placed. 'There is a clock on the mantelpiece with a mahogany case and a loud tick; the logs in the grate emit a bluish flame and an acrid smoke; the carpet is soft underfoot; . . .' and so on. . . . The point about the Describer is that it adds nothing to what is before it: everything it tells us is right there in the bit of the world which confronts it, in a way in which this is not true of someone who tells us about the remote past or who generalises. . . . The word 'rational', however, is not my central concern: it will suffice if we can agree that

there is a great gulf between the sorts of competence which are expressed in dated and universal statements and the sorts which are not . . .
Rationality: An Essay Towards an Analysis, p. 94

JEREMY BENTHAM (1748–1832)

1 I recognize, as the *all-comprehensive*, and only right and proper end of Government, the greatest happiness of the members of the community in question: the greatest happiness – of all of them, without exception, in so far as possible: the greatest happiness of the greatest number of them, on every occasion on which the nature of the case renders the provision of an equal quantity of happiness for every one of them impossible: it being rendered so, by its being matter of necessity, to make sacrifice of a portion of the happiness of a few, to the greater happiness of the rest.
Parliamentary Candidate's Proposed Declaration of Principles, p. 7

2 Nature has placed mankind under the governance of two sovereign masters, *pain* and *pleasure*. It is for them alone to point out what we ought to do, as well as to determine what we shall do. On the one hand the standard of right and wrong, on the other the chain of causes and effects, are fastened to their throne. They govern us in all we do, in all we say, in all we think: every effort we can make to throw off our subjection will serve but to demonstrate and confirm it. In words a man may pretend to abjure their empire: but in reality he will remain subject to it all the while. The *principle of utility* recognises this subjection, and assumes it for the foundation of that system, the object of which is to rear the fabric of felicity by the hands of reason and of law. Systems which attempt to question it deal in sounds instead of sense, in caprice instead of reason, in darkness instead of light.
An Introduction to the Principles of Morals and Legislation (Collected Works), p. 11

3 For as to beauty itself, it has not absolute, it has only a relative existence. It depends as much upon the nature of the being in whom the sentiment is produced as on the nature of the being by whom it is produced.
First Principles Preparatory to Constitutional Code (Collected Works), p. 321

4 . . . all inequality that has no special utility to justify it is injustice.
Supply Without Burthen or Escheat Vice Taxation, Jeremy Bentham's Economic Writings, ed. W. Stark, I, p. 329

5 Liberty then is neither more nor less than the absence of coercion. This is the genuine, original and proper sense of the word Liberty. The idea of it is an idea purely negative. It is not any thing that is produced by positive Law. It exists without Law, and not by means of Law.
Bentham Manuscripts, University College London, LXIX, 44

What means *liberty*? What can be concluded from a proposition, one of   6
the terms of which is so vague? What my own meaning is, I know; and I
hope the reader knows it too. *Security* is the political blessing I have in
view: Security as against malefactors, on one hand – security against the
instruments of government, on the other.
Rationale of Judicial Evidence, Works, VII, p. 522

In proportion to the want of happiness resulting from the want of rights,   7
a reason exists for wishing that there were such things as rights. But
reasons for wishing there were such things as rights, are not rights; – a
reason for wishing that a certain right were established, is not that right –
want is not supply – hunger is not bread.

That which has no existence cannot be destroyed – that which cannot
be destroyed cannot require anything to preserve it from destruction.

Natural Rights is simple nonsense: natural and imprescriptible rights,
rhetorical nonsense, – nonsense upon stilts.
'Anarchical Fallacies', *Works*, II, p. 501

As little, under any such notion as that of affording *honour* to the nation,   8
dignity to its functionaries, encouragement to piety, to learning, to arts,
to sciences, and in particular to fine arts, or merely curious sciences or
literary pursuits, – as little, under any such delusive pretence, will I
concur in laying burthens on the comparatively indigent many, for the
amusement of the comparatively opulent few: at their own expense will I
leave them to pursue the gratification of their own tastes.
Constitutional Code (Collected Works), p. 139

I. In all human minds, in howsoever widely different proportions, – *self-*   9
regard, and *sympathy* for others or say *extra-regard*, have place.

II. But, in self-regard even sympathy has its root: and if, in the general
tenour of human conduct, self-regard were not prevalent over sympathy,
– even over sympathy for all others put together, – no such species as the
human could have existence.
Constitutional Code (Collected Works), p. 119

The day has been, I grieve to say in many places it is not yet past, in   10
which the greater part of the species, under the denomination of slaves,
have been treated by the law exactly upon the same footing, as, in
England for example, the inferior races of animals are still. The day *may*
come, when the rest of the animal creation may acquire those rights
which never could have been withholden from them but by the hand of
tyranny. . . . a full-grown horse or dog is beyond comparison a more
rational, as well as a more conversible animal, than an infant of a day, or
a week, or even a month, old. But suppose the case were otherwise, what

would it avail? the question is not, Can they *reason*? nor, Can they *talk*? but, Can they *suffer*?
An Introduction to the Principles of Morals and Legislation (Collected Works), p. 283

11 Greatest happiness *of the greatest number*. Some years have now elapsed since, upon a closer scrutiny, reason altogether incontestable, was found for discarding this appendage.
Deontology (Collected Works), p. 309

12 Publicity is the very soul of justice. It is the keenest spur to exertion, and the surest of all guards against improbity. It keeps the judge himself, while trying, under trial. Under the auspices of publicity, the cause in the court of law, and the appeal to the court of public opinion, are going on at the same time. . . . It is through publicity alone that justice becomes the mother of security.
Draught of a Code for the Organization of the Judicial Establishment in France, Works, IV, p. 316

13 So far as depends upon wealth, – of two persons having unequal fortunes, he who has most wealth must by a legislator be regarded as having most happiness.
    But the quantity of happiness will not go on increasing in anything near the same proportion as the quantity of wealth . . .
    The effect of wealth in the production of happiness goes on diminishing, as the quantity by which the wealth of one man exceeds that of another goes on increasing: in other words, the quantity of happiness produced by a particle of wealth (each particle being of the same magnitude) will be less and less at every particle; the second will produce less than the first, the third than the second, and so on.
'Pannomial Fragments', *Works*, III, p. 228

14 Nothing has been, nothing will be, nothing ever can be done on the subject of Law that deserves the name of Science, till that universal precept of Locke, enforced, exemplified and particularly applied to the moral branch of science by Helvetius, be steadily pursued, 'Define your words'.
'A Comment on the Commentaries' (*Collected Works*), p. 346

15 . . . a regular contribution should be established for the wants of indigence; it being well understood that those only ought to be regarded as indigent, who are in want of necessaries. But from this definition it follows, that the title of the indigent, as indigent, is stronger than the title of the proprietor of a superfluity, as proprietor; since the pain of death, which would finally fall upon the neglected indigent, will always be a greater evil than the pain of disappointed expectation, which falls upon the rich when a limited portion of his superfluity is taken from him.

With regard to the amount of a legal contribution, it ought not to exceed simple necessaries: to exceed this would be to punish industry for the benefit of idleness.
'Principles of the Civil Code', *Works*, I, p. 316

The legislator is not the master of the dispositions of the human heart: he is only their interpreter and their servant. The goodness of his laws depends upon their conformity to the general *expectation*. It is highly necessary, therefore, for him rightly to understand the direction of this expectation, for the purpose of acting in concert with it. Such is the object in view . . .
'Principles of the Civil Code', *Works*, I, p. 322

16

The word *international*, it must be acknowledged, is a new one; though, it is hoped, sufficiently analogous and intelligible. It is calculated to express, in a more significant way, the branch of law which goes commonly under the name of the *law of nations*: an appellation so uncharacteristic, that, were it not for the force of custom, it would seem rather to refer to internal jurisprudence.
An Introduction to the Principles of Morals and Legislation (Collected Works), p. 296

17

'*Whatever is, is right*' – (whatever is – that is to say, whatever, by men in the situation in question, has been done) – being tacitly assumed as a postulate, – the *rectitude* of doing the same thing, on any and every subsequent occasion deemed a similar one, is stated and acted upon, as a necessary consequence. This is called *following precedents*: and this course it is that is constantly held up to view, not only as a safe course, but even as the only safe course: acting, in consequence of all-comprehensive views taken of the same subject, under the guidance of the greatest-happiness principle, being at the same time marked out for a mixture of abhorrence and contempt, under the name of *theory*, and spoken of as an *unsafe* course: that course which, in truth, is the most *opposite* to the only safe one, being thus represented and acted upon as if it were *itself* the only safe one.

18

Thus it is – that, by the comparative blindness of man in each preceding period, the like blindness in each succeeding period is secured: without the trouble or need of reflection, – men, by opulence rendered indolent, and by indolence and self-indulgence doomed to ignorance, follow their leaders – as sheep follow sheep, and geese geese.
Constitutional Code (Collected Works), p. 432

Never, by force or intimidation, never by prohibition or obstruction, will I use any endeavour to prevent my fellow-countrymen, or any of them, from seeking to better their condition in any other part, inhabited or

19

uninhabited, of this globe. In the territory of this State, I behold an asylum to all: a prison to none.
Constitutional Code (Collected Works), p. 144

NICOLAS BERDYAEV (1874–1948)

1   The human spirit is in prison. Prison is what I call this world, the given world of necessity.
The Meaning of the Creative Act, trans. Donald A. Lowrie, p. 11

2   Civilization promises to emancipate man and there can be no dispute that it provides the equipment for emancipation; but it is also the objectification of human existence and, therefore, it brings enslavement with it. Man is made the slave of civilization.
Slavery and Freedom, trans. R. M. French, p. 118

3   Objectification is the ejection of man into the external, it is an exteriorization of him, it is the subjection of him to the conditions of space, time, causality and rationalization.
The Beginning and the End, trans. R. M. French, p. 60

4   The first move was in the direction of objectification. The second move must take the opposite direction, towards primary spiritual experience, towards the existential subject, not towards the 'natural', but towards the reverse of objectified nature, towards spirituality.
Truth and Revelation, trans. R. M. French, p. 67

5   . . . man is not only of this world but of another world; not only of necessity, but of freedom.
The Meaning of the Creative Act, trans. Donald A. Lowrie, p. 61

6   Creativeness in art, like every other form of creative activity, consists in triumph over given, determined, concrete life, it is a victory over the world.
The Beginning and the End, trans. R. M. French, p. 173

7   In art there is liberation. The essential in artistic creativity is victory over the burden of necessity. In art man lives outside himself, outside his burdens, the burden of life. Every creative artistic act is a partial transfiguration of life.
The Meaning of the Creative Act, trans. Donald A. Lowrie, p. 225

8   The divorce of economy from life, the technical interpretation of life, and the fundamental capitalist principle of profit, transform man's economic life into a fiction. The capitalist system is sowing the seeds of its own destruction by sapping the spiritual foundation of man's economic life.
The Meaning of History, trans. George Reavey, p. 219

All the tensions and contradictions in life are, and ought to be, reflected 9
in one's philosophy, and one should not attempt to compose them for the
sake of neat philosophical construction. Philosophy cannot ever be
divorced from the totality of man's spiritual experience, from his
struggles, his insights, his ecstasies, his religious faith and mystical vision.
Dream and Reality, trans. Katherine Lampert, p. 104

My philosophy is a philosophy of existence, . . . that is to say, it gives 10
expression to the problems and wrestlings of man: it is, in this sense, very
close indeed to life.
Dream and Reality, trans. Katherine Lampert, p. 24

HENRI BERGSON (1859–1941)

. . . realism and idealism both go too far, . . . it is a mistake to reduce 1
matter to the perception which we have of it, a mistake also to make of it
a thing able to produce in us perceptions, but in itself of another nature
than they. Matter, in our view, is an aggregate of 'images'. And by
'image' we mean a certain existence which is more than that which the
idealist calls a *representation*, but less than that which the realist calls a
thing, – an existence placed half-way between the 'thing' and the
'representation'. This conception of matter is simply that of common
sense.
Matter and Memory, trans. N. M. Paul and W. Scott Palmer, p. xi

. . . in that continuity of becoming which is reality itself, the present 2
moment is constituted by the quasi-instantaneous section effected by our
perception in the flowing mass; and this section is precisely that which we
call the material world. Our body occupies its centre; it is, in this material
world, that part of which we directly feel the flux; in its actual state the
actuality of our present lies.
Matter and Memory, trans. N. M. Paul and W. Scott Palmer, p. 178

You define the present in an arbitrary manner as *that which is*, whereas 3
the present is simply *what is being made*. Nothing *is* less than the present
moment, if you understand by that the indivisible limit which divides the
past from the future. When we think this present as going to be, it exists
not yet; and when we think it as existing, it is already past.
Matter and Memory, trans. N. M. Paul and W. Scott Palmer, p. 193

Duration is the continuous progress of the past which gnaws into the 4
future and which swells as it advances. And as the past grows without
ceasing, so also there is no limit to its preservation. . . . In its entirety,
probably, it follows us at every instant; all that we have felt, thought and
willed from our earliest infancy is there, leaning over the present which is

about to join it, pressing against the portals of consciousness that would fain leave it outside. The cerebral mechanism is arranged just so as to drive back into the unconscious almost the whole of this past, and to admit beyond the threshold only that which can cast light on the present situation or further the action now being prepared – in short, only that which can give *useful* work. At the most, a few superfluous recollections may succeed in smuggling themselves through the half-open door. These memories, messengers from the unconscious, remind us of what we are dragging behind us unawares.

Creative Evolution, trans. Arthur Mitchell, p. 5

5 Take the flying arrow. At every moment, says Zeno, it is motionless, for it cannot have time to move, that is, to occupy at least two successive positions, unless at least two moments are allowed it. At a given moment, therefore, it is at rest at a given point. Motionless in each point of its course, it is motionless during all the time that it is moving.

Yes, if we suppose that the arrow can ever *be* in a point of its course. Yes again, if the arrow, which is moving, ever coincides with a position, which is motionless. But the arrow never *is* in any point of its course. . . . the trajectory is created in one stroke, although a certain time is required for it; and . . . though we can divide at will the trajectory once created, we cannot divide its creation, which is an act in progress and not a thing. To suppose that the moving body *is* at a point of its course is to cut the course in two by a snip of the scissors at this point, and to substitute two trajectories for the single trajectory which we were first considering. . . . it is to attribute to the course itself of the arrow everything that can be said of the interval that the arrow has traversed, that is to say, to admit *a priori* the absurdity that movement coincides with immobility.

Creative Evolution, trans. Arthur Mitchell, p. 325

6 The mechanistic explanations [of evolution] hold good for the systems that our thought artificially detaches from the whole. But of the whole itself and of the systems which, within this whole, seem to take after it, we cannot admit *a priori* that they are mechanically explicable, for then . . . past, present and future would be open at a glance to a superhuman intellect capable of making the calculation. . . .

But radical finalism is quite as unacceptable, and for the same reason. The doctrine of teleology, in its extreme form, as we find it in Leibniz for example, implies that things and beings merely realize a programme previously arranged. But if there is nothing unforeseen, no invention or creation in the universe, time is useless again. As in the mechanistic hypothesis, here again it is supposed that *all is given*. Finalism thus understood is only inverted mechanism.

Creative Evolution, trans. Arthur Mitchell, p. 39

The whole history of life until man has been that of the effort of   7
consciousness to raise matter, and of the more or less complete
overwhelming of consciousness by the matter which has fallen back on it.
The enterprise was paradoxical, if, indeed, we may speak here otherwise
than by metaphor of enterprise and of effort. It was to create with matter,
which is necessity itself, an instrument of freedom, to make a machine
which should triumph over mechanism, and to use the determinism of
nature to pass through the meshes of the net which this very determinism
had spread. But, everywhere except in man, consciousness has let itself be
caught in the net whose meshes it tried to pass through: it has remained
the captive of the mechanisms it has set up. . . . But man not only
maintains his machine, he succeeds in using it as he pleases. . . .

It is in this quite special sense that man is the 'term' and the 'end' of
evolution.
Creative Evolution, trans. Arthur Mitchell, p. 278

From our point of view, life appears in its entirety as an immense wave   8
. . . which rises, and which is opposed by the descending movement of
matter. . . . this rising wave is consciousness, . . . running through human
generations, subdividing itself into individuals. This subdivision was
vaguely indicated in it, but could not have been made clear without
matter. Thus souls are continually being created, which, nevertheless, in
a certain sense pre-existed. They are nothing else than the little rills into
which the great river of life divides itself, flowing through the body of
humanity. The movement of the stream is distinct from the river bed,
although it must adopt its winding course. Consciousness is distinct from
the organism it animates, although it must undergo its vicissitudes. . . . the
brain underlines at every instant the motor indications of the state of
consciousness; but the interdependence of consciousness and brain is
limited to this; . . . consciousness is essentially free . . .
Creative Evolution, trans. Arthur Mitchell, p. 280

For each of our acts we shall easily find antecedents of which it may in   9
some sort be said to be the mechanical resultant. And it may equally well
be said that each action is the realization of an intention. . . . But if our
action be one that involves the whole of our person and is truly ours, it
could not have been foreseen, even though its antecedents explain it
when once it has been accomplished. . . . Mechanism and finalism are
therefore, here, only external views of our conduct. They extract its
intellectuality. But our conduct slips between them and extends much
further.
Creative Evolution, trans. Arthur Mitchell, p. 49

George Berkeley

10 It is the whole soul, in fact, that gives rise to the free decision, and the act will be so much the freer the more the dynamic series with which it is connected tends to be the fundamental self. . . . But the moments at which we thus grasp ourselves are rare, and that is why we are rarely free.
Time and Free Will, trans. F. L. Pogson, p. 167

GEORGE BERKELEY (1685–1753)

1 We must wth the Mob place certainty in the senses.
Philosophical Commentaries, Works, I, p. 90

2 Upon the whole, I am inclined to think that the far greater part, if not all, of those difficulties which have hitherto amused philosophers, and blocked up the way to knowledge, are entirely owing to our selves. That we have first raised a dust, and then complain, we cannot see.
A Treatise Concerning the Principles of Human Knowledge, Introd., §3

3 Whether others have this wonderful faculty of *abstracting their ideas,* they best can tell: for my self I find indeed I have a faculty of imagining, or representing to my self the ideas of those particular things I have perceived and of variously compounding and dividing them. I can imagine a man with two heads or the upper parts of a man joined to the body of a horse. I can consider the hand, the eye, the nose, each by it self abstracted or separated from the rest of the body. But then whatever hand or eye I imagine, it must have some particular shape and colour. Likewise the idea of man that I frame to my self, must be either of a white, or a black, or a tawny, a straight, or a crooked, a tall, or a low, or a middle-sized man. I cannot by any effort of thought conceive the abstract idea above described.
A Treatise Concerning the Principles of Human Knowledge, Introd., §10

4 Thus much, upon the whole, may be said of all signs: – that they do not always suggest ideas signified to the mind: that when they suggest ideas, they are not general abstract ideas: that they have other uses besides barely standing for and exhibiting ideas, such as raising proper emotions, producing certain dispositions or habits of mind, and directing our actions in pursuit of that happiness which is the ultimate end and design, the primary spring and motive, that sets rational agents at work: that signs may imply or suggest the relations of things; which relations, habitudes or proportions, as they cannot be by us understood but by the help of signs, so being thereby expressed and confuted, they direct and enable us to act with regard to things: that the true end of speech, reason, science, faith, assent, in all its different degrees, is not merely, or principally, or always, the imparting or acquiring of ideas, but rather something of an active operative nature, tending to a conceived good:

which may sometimes be obtained, not only although the ideas marked are not offered to the mind, but even although there should be no possibility of offering or exhibiting any such idea to the mind . . .
Alciphron, Works, III, p. 307

Force, gravity, attraction, and terms of this sort are useful for reasonings   5
and reckonings about motion and bodies in motion, but not for understanding the simple nature of motion itself or for indicating so many distinct qualities. As for attraction, it was certainly introduced by Newton, not as a true, physical quality, but only as a mathematical hypothesis. . . . to be of service to reckoning and mathematical demonstration is one thing, to set forth the nature of things is another.
De Motu, I, §17, *Works*, IV, p. 35

It is evident to any one who takes a survey of the objects of human   6
knowledge, that they are either ideas actually imprinted on the senses, or else such as are perceived by attending to the passions and operations of the mind, or lastly ideas formed by help of memory and imagination, either compounding, dividing, or barely representing those originally perceived in the aforesaid ways. . . . And as several of these are observed to accompany each other, they come to be marked by one name, and so to be reputed as one thing. Thus, for example, a certain colour, taste, smell, figure and consistence having been observed to go together, are accounted one distinct thing, signified by the name *apple*. . . .

But besides all that endless variety of ideas or objects of knowledge, there is likewise something which knows or perceives them, and exercises divers operations, as willing, imagining, remembering about them. This perceiving, active being is what I call *mind, spirit, soul* or *my self*. By which words I do not denote any one of my ideas, but a thing entirely distinct from them, wherein they exist, or, which is the same thing, whereby they are perceived; for the existence of an idea consists in being perceived.
A Treatise Concerning the Principles of Human Knowledge, I, §§1, 2

That neither our thoughts, nor passions, nor ideas formed by the   7
imagination, exist without the mind, is what every body will allow. And it seems no less evident that the various sensations or ideas imprinted on the sense, however blended or combined together (that is, whatever objects they compose) cannot exist otherwise than in a mind perceiving them. I think an intuitive knowledge may be obtained of this, by any one that shall attend to what is meant by the term *exist* when applied to sensible things. The table I write on, I say, exists, that is, I see and feel it; and if I were out of my study I should say it existed, meaning thereby that if I was in my study I might perceive it, or that some other spirit actually

does perceive it. There was an odour, that is, it was smelled; there was a sound, that is to say, it was heard; a colour or figure, and it was perceived by sight or touch. This is all that I can understand by these and the like expressions. For as to what is said of the absolute existence of unthinking things without any relation to their being perceived, that seems perfectly unintelligible. Their *esse* is *percipi*, nor is it possible they should have any existence, out of the minds or thinking things which perceive them.

A Treatise Concerning the Principles of Human Knowledge, I, §3

8   Some truths there are so near and obvious to the mind, that a man need only open his eyes to see them. Such I take this important one to be, to wit, that all the choir of heaven and furniture of the earth, in a word all those bodies which compose the mighty frame of the world, have not any subsistence without a mind, that their being is to be perceived or known; that consequently so long as they are not actually perceived by me, or do not exist in my mind or that of any other created spirit, they must either have no existence at all, or else subsist in the mind of some eternal spirit: it being perfectly unintelligible and involving all the absurdity of abstraction, to attribute to any single part of them an existence independent of a spirit. To be convinced of which, the reader need only reflect and try to separate in his own thoughts the being of a sensible thing from its being perceived.

A Treatise Concerning the Principles of Human Knowledge, I, §6

9   But say you, though the ideas themselves do not exist without the mind, yet there may be things like them whereof they are copies or resemblances, which things exist without the mind, in an unthinking substance. I answer, an idea can be like nothing but an idea; a colour or figure can be like nothing but another colour or figure. If we look but ever so little into our thoughts, we shall find it impossible for us to conceive a likeness except only between our ideas. Again, I ask whether those supposed originals or external things, of which our ideas are the pictures or representations, be themselves perceivable or no? If they are, then they are ideas, and we have gained our point; but if you say they are not, I appeal to anyone whether it be sense, to assert a colour is like something which is invisible; hard or soft, like something which is intangible; and so of the rest.

A Treatise Concerning the Principles of Human Knowledge, I, §8

10   In short, if there were external bodies, it is impossible we should ever come to know it; and if there were not, we might have the very same reasons to think there were that we have now. Suppose, what no one can deny possible, an intelligence, without the help of external bodies, to be affected with the same train of sensations or ideas that you are, imprinted

in the same order and with like vividness in his mind. I ask whether that intelligence hath not all the reason to believe the existence of corporeal substances, represented by his ideas, and exciting them in his mind, that you can possibly have for believing the same thing? Of this there can be no question; which one consideration is enough to make any reasonable person suspect the strength of whatever arguments he may think himself to have, for the existence of bodies without the mind.

A Treatise Concerning the Principles of Human Knowledge, I, §20

But say you, surely there is nothing easier than to imagine trees, for **11** instance, in a park, or books existing in a closet, and no body by to perceive them. I answer, you may so, there is no difficulty in it: but what is all this, I beseech you, more than framing in your mind certain ideas which you call *books* and *trees*, and at the same time omitting to frame the idea of any one that may perceive them? But do not you your self perceive or think of them all the while? This therefore is nothing to the purpose: it only shows you have the power of imagining or forming ideas in your mind; but it doth not shew that you can conceive it possible, the objects of your thought may exist without the mind: to make out this, it is necessary that you conceive them existing unconceived or unthought of, which is a manifest repugnancy.

A Treatise Concerning the Principles of Human Knowledge, I, §23

We perceive a continual succession of ideas, some are anew excited, **12** others are changed or totally disappear. There is therefore some cause of these ideas whereon they depend, and which produces and changes them. That this cause cannot be any quality or idea or combination of ideas, is clear from the preceding section. It must therefore be a substance; but it has been shewn that there is no corporeal or material substance: it remains therefore that the cause of ideas is an incorporeal active substance or spirit.

A Treatise Concerning the Principles of Human Knowledge, I, §26

The ideas of sense are more strong, lively, and distinct than those of the **13** imagination; they have likewise a steadiness, order, and coherence, and are not excited at random, as those which are the effects of human wills often are, but in a regular train or series, the admirable connexion whereof sufficiently testifies the wisdom and benevolence of its Author. Now the set rules or established methods, wherein the mind we depend on excites in us the ideas of sense, are called the *Laws of Nature*: and these we learn by experience, which teaches us that such and such ideas are attended with such and such other ideas, in the ordinary course of things.

A Treatise Concerning the Principles of Human Knowledge, I, §30

14 Seventhly, it will upon this be demanded whether it does not seem absurd to take away natural causes, and ascribe every thing to the immediate operation of spirits? We must no longer say upon these principles that fire heats, or water cools, but that a spirit heats, and so forth. Would not a man be deservedly laughed at, who should talk after this manner? I answer, he would so; in such things we ought to *think with the learned, and speak with the vulgar.* They who to demonstration are convinced of the truth of the Copernican system, do nevertheless say the sun rises, the sun sets, or comes to the meridian: and if they affected a contrary style in common talk, it would without doubt appear very ridiculous. A little reflexion on what is here said will make it manifest, that the common use of language would receive no manner of alteration or disturbance from the admission of our tenets.
A Treatise Concerning the Principles of Human Knowledge, I, §31

15 Colour, figure, motion, extension and the like, considered only as so many *sensations* in the mind, are perfectly known, there being nothing in them which is not perceived. But if they are looked on as notes or images, referred to *things* or *archetypes* existing without the mind, then are we involved all in *scepticism.* We see only the appearances, and not the real qualities of things . . . for aught we know, all we see, hear, and feel, may be only phantom and vain chimera, and not at all agree with the real things, existing in *rerum natura.* All this scepticism follows, from our supposing a difference between *things* and *ideas*, and that the former have a subsistence without the mind, or unperceived. It were easy to dilate on this subject, and shew how the arguments urged by *sceptics* in all ages, depend on the supposition of external objects.
A Treatise Concerning the Principles of Human Knowledge, I, §87

16 I do not pretend to be a setter-up of *new notions.* My endeavours tend only to unite and place in a clearer light that truth, which was before shared between the vulgar and the philosophers: the former being of the opinion, that *those things they immediately perceive are the real things*; and the latter, that *the things immediately perceived, are ideas which exist only in the mind.* Which two notions put together, do in effect constitute the substance of what I advance.
Three Dialogues between Hylas and Philonous, Works, II, p. 262

17 For as we have shewn the doctrine of matter or corporeal substance, to have been the main pillar and support of *scepticism*, so likewise upon the same foundation have been raised all the impious schemes of *atheism* and irreligion. Nay so great a difficulty hath it been thought, to conceive matter produced out of nothing, that the most celebrated among the ancient philosophers, even of these who maintained the being of a God,

have thought matter to be uncreated and coeternal with him. How great a friend material substance hath been to *atheists* in all ages, were needless to relate. All their monstrous systems have so visible and necessary a dependence on it, that when this corner-stone is once removed, the whole fabric cannot choose but fall to the ground; insomuch that it is no longer worth while, to bestow a particular consideration on the absurdities of every wretched sect of *atheists*.
A Treatise Concerning the Principles of Human Knowledge, I, §92

But if we attentively consider the constant regularity, order, and   18
concatenation of natural things, the surprising magnificence, beauty, and perfection of the larger, and the exquisite contrivance of the smaller parts of the creation, together with the exact harmony and correspondence of the whole, but above all, the never enough admired laws of pain and pleasure, and the instincts or natural inclinations, appetites, and passions of animals; I say if we consider all these things, and at the same time attend to the meaning and import of the attributes, one, eternal, infinitely wise, good, and perfect, we shall clearly perceive that they belong to the aforesaid spirit, *who works all in all*, and *by whom all things consist*.
A Treatise Concerning the Principles of Human Knowledge, I, §146

HYLAS. But according to your notions, what difference is there between   19
real things, and chimeras formed by the imagination, or the visions of a dream, since they are all equally in the mind?
PHILONOUS. The ideas formed by the imagination are faint and indistinct; they have besides an entire dependence on the will. But the ideas perceived by sense, that is, real things, are more vivid and clear, and being imprinted on the mind by a spirit distinct from us, have not a like dependence on our will. There is therefore no danger of confounding these with the foregoing: and there is as little of confounding them with the visions of a dream, which are dim, irregular, and confused.
Three Dialogues between Hylas and Philonous, Works, II, p. 235

ISAIAH BERLIN (*b.* 1909)

There is a line among the fragments of the Greek poet Archilochus which   1
says: 'The fox knows many things, but the hedgehog knows one big thing'. Scholars have differed about the correct interpretation of these dark words, which may mean no more than that the fox, for all his cunning, is defeated by the hedgehog's one defence. But, taken figuratively, the words can be made to yield a sense in which they mark one of the deepest differences which divide writers and thinkers, and, it may be, human beings in general.
Russian Thinkers, p. 22

2   'Every man to count for one and no one to count for more than one.' This
    formula, much used by utilitarian philosophers, seems to me to form the
    heart of the doctrine of equality or of equal rights, and has coloured
    much liberal and democratic thought. Like many familiar phrases of
    political philosophy it is vague, ambiguous, and has changed in
    connotation from one thinker and society to another. Nevertheless it
    appears, more than any other formula, to constitute the irreducible
    minimum of the ideal of equality.
    Concepts and Categories: Philosophical Essays, p. 81

3   If social and psychological determinism were established as an accepted
    truth, our world would be transformed more radically than was the
    teleological world of the classical and middle ages by the triumphs of
    mechanistic principles or those of natural selection. Our words – our
    modes of speech and thought – would be transformed in literally
    unimaginable ways; the notions of choice, of responsibility, of freedom,
    are so deeply embedded in our outlook that our new life, as creatures in a
    world genuinely lacking in these concepts, can, I should maintain, be
    conceived by us only with the greatest difficulty. But there is, as yet, no
    need to alarm ourselves unduly.
    Four Essays on Liberty, p. 113

4   The first of these political senses of freedom or liberty (I shall use both
    words to mean the same), which (following much precedent) I shall call
    the 'negative' sense, is involved in the answer to the question 'What is the
    area within which the subject – a person or group of persons – is or
    should be left to do or be what he is able to do or be, without interference
    by other persons?' The second, which I shall call the positive sense, is
    involved in the answer to the question 'What, or who, is the source of
    control or interference that can determine someone to do, or be, this
    rather than that?'
    Four Essays on Liberty, p. 121

5   Pluralism, with the measure of 'negative' liberty that it entails, seems to
    me a truer and more humane ideal than the goals of those who seek in the
    great, disciplined, authoritarian structures the ideal of 'positive' self-
    mastery by classes, or peoples, or the whole of mankind. It is truer,
    because it does, at least, recognize the fact that human goals are many,
    not all of them commensurable, and in perpetual rivalry with one
    another. To assume that all values can be graded on one scale, so that it is
    a mere matter of inspection to determine the highest, seems to me to
    falsify our knowledge that men are free agents, to represent moral
    decision as an operation which a slide-rule could, in principle, perform.
    Four Essays on Liberty, p. 171

'What is an okapi?' is answered easily enough by an act of empirical 6
observation. Similarly 'What is the cube root of 729?' is settled by a piece
of calculation in accordance with accepted rules. But if I ask 'What is
time?', 'What is a number?', 'What is the purpose of human life on
earth?', 'How can I know past facts that are no longer there – no longer
where?', 'Are all men truly brothers?', how do I set about looking for the
answer? . . .

The only common characteristic which all these questions appear to
have is that they cannot be answered either by observation or calculation,
either by inductive methods or deductive; and, as a crucial corollary of
this, that those who ask them are faced with a perplexity from the very
beginning – they do not know where to look for the answers; there are no
dictionaries, encyclopedias, compendia of knowledge, no experts, no
orthodoxies, which can be referred to with confidence as possessing
unquestionable authority or knowledge in these matters. Moreover some
of these questions are distinguished by being general and by dealing with
matters of principle; and others, while not themselves general, very
readily raise or lead to questions of principle.

Such questions tend to be called philosophical.
Concepts and Categories: Philosophical Essays, p. 2

SIMON BLACKBURN (*b.* 1944)

Wittgenstein imagined that the philosopher was like a therapist whose 1
task was to put problems finally to rest, and to cure us of being bewitched
by them. So we are told to stop, to shut off lines of inquiry, not to find
things puzzling nor to seek explanations. This is intellectual suicide.
'Knowledge, Truth and Reliability', *Proc. British Academy* (1984), p. 186

Could it be that, after all, the old pictures and metaphors are important 2
to the disputes, it mattering to us not just that people talk, behave, and
practice intellectually in the same way that we do, but also that they are
haunted by the same ghosts?
'Truth, Realism and the Regulation of Theory', *Midwest Studies*, V, p. 370

Just as the senses constrain what we can believe about the empirical 3
world, so our natures and desires, needs and pleasures, constrain much of
what we can admire and commend, tolerate and work for. There are not
so many livable, unfragmented, developed, consistent, and coherent
systems of attitude. A projectivist, like anyone else, may be sensitive to
the features which make our lives go well or badly; to the need for order,
contracts, sources of stability. If his reflection on these things leads him to
endorse a high Victorian love of promises, rectitude, contracts, conventional sexual behaviour, well and good: there is nothing in his meta-ethic

to suggest otherwise. For instance, a proper respect for promises, the kind of respect which sees them as making requirements, as bounds on conduct, is certainly a good attitude to foster. But it may, for all that, be just that: an attitude.
Spreading the Word, p. 197

4　It might be that there are people who cannot 'put up with' the idea that values have a subjective source: who cannot put up with the idea that the meaning of their life and their activities is ultimately something they confer, and that even critical reflection on how best to confer them conducts itself in the light of other sentiments which must be taken simply as given. But this will be because such people have a defect elsewhere in their sensibilities – one which has taught them that things do not matter unless they matter to God, or throughout infinity, or to a world conceived apart from any particular set of concerns or desires, or whatever. One should not adjust one's metaphysics to pander to such defects.
'Error and the Phenomenology of Value', *Morality and Objectivity*, ed. T. Honderich, p. 10

5　Is it that we projectivists, at the crucial moment when we are about to save the child, throw ourselves on the grenade, walk out into the snow, will think, 'Oh, it's only me and my desires or other conative pressures – forget it'?
'How to be an Ethical Antirealist', *Midwest Studies*, XII, p. 370

6　We all know that unto him that hath shall be given, but is it really better that he should be given a spotless conscience as well?
'Making Ends Meet', *Philosophical Books* (1986), p. 202

NED BLOCK (*b.* 1942)

You ask: What is it that philosophers have called qualitative states? I answer, only half in jest: As Louis Armstrong is said to have said when asked what jazz is, 'If you got to ask, you ain't never gonna get to know.'
'Troubles with Functionalism', *Mind and Cognition*, ed. W. Lycan, p. 453

LAWRENCE A. BLUM (*b.* 1943)

A situation of acting from concern for a friend does not impose on me the obligation to take into account the interests of all the people whom I *might* help at that point in time, and to choose according to some impartial criterion whom to benefit. . . . I cannot just pop over to someone's house who is in need of comfort and comfort him, in the way I can to my friend. . . . The concept of beneficence itself obscures the

particular nature of the ways that we do good for our friends, and encourages the false picture that what we do for our friends we could as well be doing for others, and thus that we choose against others when we choose to do good for our friends.
Friendship, Altruism and Morality, p. 46

I. M. BOCHENSKI (*b.* 1902)

The people make a laughing stock of the philosopher as a person harmlessly absorbed in his ideas, though really he is a terrifying force and his thought has the effect of dynamite. He sticks to his own course, conquers inch by inch, asserts his grip on the masses, until eventually the day dawns when he triumphantly overcomes all obstacles and is free to determine the destiny of mankind – or spread a shroud over its remains. Therefore those who wish to know in what direction they are going would do well to give their attention not to the politicians but to the philosophers, for what they propound today will be the faith of tomorrow.
Contemporary European Philosophy, p. viii

BOETHIUS (*c.*480–*c.*524)

We have found the definition of 'person', namely, 'an individual 1 substance of a rational nature'.
Contra Eutychen, Loeb Classical Library, No. 74, p. 84

Just as you might call a corpse a dead man, but couldn't simply call it a 2 man, so I would agree that the wicked are wicked, but could not agree that they have unqualified existence. A thing exists when it keeps its proper place and preserves its own nature. Anything which departs from this ceases to exist, because its existence depends on the preservation of its nature.
The Consolation of Philosophy, Loeb Classical Library, No. 74, p. 310

'There is nothing that an omnipotent God could not do.' 'No.' 'Then, can 3 God do evil?' 'No.' 'So that evil is nothing, since that is what He cannot do who can do anything.'
The Consolation of Philosophy, p. 290

For just as the knowledge of present things does not impose necessity on 4 the things being done, neither does foreknowledge of future things impose necessity on the things to come.
The Consolation of Philosophy, p. 386

If chance is defined as an event produced by random motion without any 5 causal nexus, I would say that there is no such thing as chance.
The Consolation of Philosophy, p. 366

6   If you think of the infinite recesses of eternity you have little cause to take
    pleasure in any continuation of your name.
    The Consolation of Philosophy, p. 74

SISSELA BOK (*b.* 1934)

How can we single out, then, justifiable lies from all those that their
perpetrators regard as so highly excusable? . . .

Justification must involve more than [the liar's] untested personal steps
of reasoning. To justify is to defend as just, right, or proper, by providing
adequate reasons. It means to hold up to some standard, such as a
religious or legal or moral standard. Such justification requires an
audience: it may be directed to God, or a court of law, or one's peers, or
one's own conscience . . .

I would like to combine this concept of *publicity* with the view of
justification in ethics as being *directed to reasonable persons*, in order to
formulate a workable test for looking at concrete moral choice.
Lying: Moral Choice in Public and Private Life, pp. 90–2

BERNARD BOSANQUET (1848–1923)

1   A mind has its dominant nature, but is no single system equally organised
    throughout. It is rather a construction of such systems, . . . corresponding
    to the totality of social groups as seen from a particular position. . . . If I
    am my own gardener, or my own critic, or my own doctor, does the
    relation of the answering dispositions within my being differ absolutely
    and altogether from what takes place when gardener and master, critic
    and author, patient and doctor, are different persons? . . . If we consider
    my unity with myself at different times as the limiting case, we shall find
    it very hard to establish a difference of principle between the unity of
    what we call one mind and that of all the 'minds' which enter into a
    single social experience.
    The Philosophical Theory of the State, p. 165

2   We find that the essence of human society consists in a common self, a
    life and a will, which belong to and are exercised by the society as such,
    or by the individuals in society as such; it makes no difference which
    expression we choose. The reality of this common self, in the action of
    the political whole, receives the name of the 'general will' . . .
    The Philosophical Theory of the State, p. 93

F. H. BRADLEY (1846–1924)

1   Metaphysics is the finding of bad reasons for what we believe upon
    instinct; but to find these reasons is no less an instinct.
    Appearance and Reality, Preface

64

Motion has from an early time been criticized severely, and it has never 2
been defended with much success.
Appearance and Reality, p. 37

Time is so far from enduring the test of criticism, that at a touch it falls 3
apart and proclaims itself illusory.
Appearance and Reality, p. 183

On the other hand, suppose, for instance, that the lapse of time were 4
ultimately real in our experience, then what on such a view would have
become of our past? . . . If there is not, present in this passing 'now', a
Reality which contains all 'nows' future and past, the whole of our truth
and knowledge must be limited to the 'now' that we perceive. For to
reach a larger universe by transcendence would really be nonsense.
Essays in Truth and Reality, p. 332

Unless thought stands for something that falls beyond mere intelligence, 5
if 'thinking' is not used with some strange implication that never was part
of the meaning of the word, a lingering scruple still forbids us to believe
that reality can ever be purely rational. It may come from a failure in my
metaphysics, or from a weakness of the flesh which continues to blind
me, but the notion that existence could be the same as understanding
strikes as cold and ghost-like as the dreariest materialism. That the glory
of this world in the end is appearance leaves the world more glorious, if
we feel it is a show of some fuller splendour; but the sensuous curtain is a
deception and a cheat, if it hides some colourless movement of atoms,
some spectral woof of impalpable abstractions, or unearthly ballet of
bloodless categories. Though dragged to such conclusions, we can not
embrace them. Our principles may be true, but they are not reality. They
no more *make* that Whole which commands our devotion, than some
shredded dissection of human tatters *is* that warm and breathing beauty
of flesh which our hearts found delightful.
Principles of Logic, p. 590

Nothing is lost to the Absolute, and all appearances have reality. The 6
Nature studied by the observer and by the poet and painter, is in all its
sensible and emotional fullness a very real Nature. It is in most respects
more real than the strict object of physical science. For Nature, as the
world whose real essence lies in primary qualities, has not a high degree
of reality and truth. It is a mere abstraction made and required for a
certain purpose. . . . But the boundary of Nature can hardly be drawn
even at secondary qualities. Or, if we draw it there, we must draw it
arbitrarily, and to suit our convenience. Only on this ground can
psychical life be excluded from Nature, while, regarded otherwise, the
exclusion would not be tenable. And to deny aesthetic qualities in

Nature, or to refuse it those which inspire us with fear or devotion, would once more surely be arbitrary. . . . Our principle, that the abstract is the unreal, moves us steadily upward. It forces us first to rejection of bare primary qualities, and it compels us in the end to credit Nature with our higher emotions. That process can cease only where Nature is quite absorbed into spirit, and at every stage of the process we find increase in reality.

Appearance and Reality, p. 438

7   The way of taking the world which I have found most tenable is to regard it as a single Experience, superior to relations and containing in the fullest sense everything which is. Whether there is any particular matter in this whole which falls outside of any finite centre of feeling, I cannot certainly decide; but the contrary seems perhaps more probable. We have then the Absolute Reality appearing in and to finite centres and uniting them in one experience. We can, I think, understand more or less what, in order for this to be done, such an experience must be. But to comprehend it otherwise is beyond us and even beyond all intelligence. . . . Those for whom philosophy has to explain everything need therefore not trouble themselves with my views.

Appearance and Reality, p. 245

8   If you identify the Absolute with God, that is not the God of religion. If again you separate them, God becomes a finite factor in the Whole. And the effort of religion is to put an end to, and break down, this relation – a relation which, none the less, it essentially presupposes. Hence, short of the Absolute, God cannot rest, and, having reached that goal, he is lost and religion with him.

Appearance and Reality, p. 395

9   The test [of truth] which I advocate is the idea of a whole of knowledge as wide and consistent as may be. In speaking of system I mean always the union of these two aspects, and this is the sense and the only sense in which I'm defending coherence.

Essays in Truth and Reality, p. 202

10   Freedom means *chance*; you are free, because there is no reason which will account for your particular acts, because no one in the world, not even yourself, can possibly say what you will, or will not, do next. You are 'accountable', in short, because you are a wholly 'unaccountable' creature.

Ethical Studies, p. 11

11   In the realized idea which, superior to me, and yet here and now in and by me, affirms itself in a continuous process, we have found the end, we

have found self-realization, duty, and happiness in one – yes, we have found ourselves, when we have found our station and its duties, our function as an organ in the social organism.
Ethical Studies, p. 163

There is nothing better than my station and its duties, nor anything 12
higher or more truly beautiful. It holds and will hold its own against the worship of the 'individual', whatever form that may take.
Ethical Studies, p. 201

It is monstrous to say that for us man has no more right than lower 13
animals or inanimate nature. It is also monstrous to say that these have no right as against him. The covering of a hideous world with the greatest possible number of inferior beings so long as they are human is not the end – even for us.
Unpublished essay on Christian morality, Merton College

If 'Christianity' is to mean the taking the Gospels as our rule of life, then 14
we none of us are Christians and, no matter what we say, we all know we ought not to be.
Unpublished essay on Christian morality, Merton College

To wish to be better than the world is to be already on the threshold of 15
immorality.
Ethical Studies, p. 199

Our pleasure in any one who in some way resembles those we love 16
should warn us that love is in its essence not individual.
Aphorisms, No. 18

The soul's immutable core – if there is one – can hardly be amiable. And 17
to love any one for himself perhaps in the end becomes unmeaning.
Aphorisms, No. 95

The shades nowhere speak without blood, and the ghosts of Metaphysic 18
accept no substitute. They reveal themselves only to that victim whose life they have drained, and, to converse with shadows, he himself must become a shade.
Essays in Truth and Reality, p. 14

FRANZ BRENTANO (1838–1917)

It is a sign of the immature state of psychology that we can scarcely utter 1
a single sentence about mental phenomena which will not be disputed by many people.
Psychology from an Empirical Standpoint, trans. A. C. Rancurello, D. B. Terrell and L. L. McAlister, p. 80

2   Every mental phenomenon is characterized by what the Scholastics of the Middle Ages called the intentional (or mental) inexistence of an object, and what we might call, though not wholly unambiguously, reference to a content, direction toward an object (which is not to be understood here as meaning a thing), or immanent objectivity. Every mental phenomenon includes something as object within itself, although they do not all do so in the same way. In presentation something is presented, in judgement something is affirmed or denied, in love loved, in hate hated, in desire desired and so on.

This intentional in-existence is characteristic exclusively of mental phenomena. No physical phenomenon exhibits anything like it. We can, therefore, define mental phenomena by saying that they are those phenomena which contain an object intentionally within themselves. . . . Our language itself indicates this through the expressions it employs. We say that we are pleased with or about something, that we feel sorrow or grieve about something. Likewise, we say: that pleases me, that hurts me, that makes me feel sorry, etc. Joy and sorrow, like affirmation and negation, love and hate, desire and aversion, clearly follow upon a presentation and are related to that which is presented.

Psychology from an Empirical Standpoint, trans. A. C. Rancurello, D. B. Terrell and L. L. McAlister, p. 88

3   . . . we may consider it established that mental phenomena exhibit no more and no less than a threefold fundamental difference in their reference to a content, or, as we might put it, in their mode of consciousness, and that, in view of this, they fall into three basic classes; the class of *presentations*, the class of *judgements*, and the class of the *phenomena of love and hate*.

Psychology from an Empirical Standpoint, trans. A. C. Rancurello, D. B. Terrell and L. L. McAlister, p. 264

4   We do compare colors which we see with sounds which we hear; indeed, this happens every time we recognize that they are different phenomena. How would this presentation of their difference be possible if the presentations of color and sound belonged to a different reality? . . . Should we, therefore, attribute such a presentation to both of them taken together? . . . it would be like saying that, of course, neither a blind man nor a deaf man could compare colors with sounds, but if one sees and the other hears, the two together can recognize the relationship. . . . Only if sound and color are presented jointly, in one and the same reality, is it conceivable that they can be compared with one another.

Psychology from an Empirical Standpoint, trans. A. C. Rancurello, D. B. Terrell and L. L. McAlister, p. 159

One sees . . . the implication of Lichtenberg's attempt to degrade 5
Descartes' tenet: 'cogito, ergo sum'. This author was of the opinion that,
instead of saying 'I think', we should limit ourselves to saying 'it thinks'.
This conception implies that, in the act of judgement, the relation of
identity between the knower and the known remains unknown. If this
were the case, the possibility of an immediate evidence would vanish.
Quoted in A. C. Rancurello, *A Study of Franz Brentano*, p. 42

Every mental act is conscious; it includes within it a consciousness of 6
itself. Therefore, every mental act, no matter how simple, has a double
object, a primary and a secondary object. The simplest act, for example
the act of hearing, has as its primary object the sound, and for its
secondary object, itself, the mental phenomenon in which the sound is
heard.
Psychology from an Empirical Standpoint, trans. A. C. Rancurello, D. B. Terrell
and L. L. McAlister, p. 153

As for your account of Höfler's comments, I was baffled by the reference 7
to the 'content and immanent object' of thought.
   When I spoke of 'immanent object', I used the qualification 'immanent'
in order to avoid misunderstandings, since many use the unqualified term
'object' to refer to that which is outside the mind. But by an *object* of a
thought I meant what it is that the thought is about, whether or not there
is anything outside the mind corresponding to the thought.
   It has never been my view that the *immanent* object is identical with
'*object of thought*'. What we think about is *the object* or *thing* and not
the 'object of thought'. If, in our thought, we contemplate a horse, our
thought has as its immanent object – not a 'contemplated horse', but a
horse. And strictly speaking only the horse – not the 'contemplated
horse' – can be called an object.
The True and the Evident, trans. R. Chisholm, I. Politzer and K. R. Fischer, p. 77

The 'contemplated horse' considered as object would be the object of 8
introspection which the thinker perceives whenever he forms a correlative
pair consisting of this 'contemplated horse' along with his thinking about
the horse; for correlatives are such that one cannot be perceived or
apprehended without the other. But what are experienced as primary
objects, or what are thought universally as primary objects of reason, are
never themselves the objects of introspection. Had I equated 'object' with
'object of thought', then I would have had to say that the primary
thought relation has no object or content at all. So I protest against this
foolishness that has been dreamed up and attributed to me.
The True and the Evident, trans. R. Chisholm, I. Politzer and K. R. Fischer, p. 78

9   If the 'something' in the expression 'to think about something' really meant only 'something thought about', then the 'something' in 'to reject or deny something' would mean no more nor less than 'something rejected or denied'. But nothing could be more obvious than the fact that, if a man rejects or denies a thing, he does *not* reject or deny it as something rejected or denied; on the contrary, he knows it is something which he himself does reject or deny. If a man denies God, for example, he does not deny a denied God, for this would be to deny that anyone denies God. So the uniform concept which relates to 'something' in the expression 'to think about something' is not the concept of 'something thought about'; rather, it is a concept which is common to God and horse and that which is coloured, and so on and so forth.
    The True and the Evident, trans. R. Chisholm, I. Politzer and K. R. Fischer, p. 96

10 What is meant by the formula *Veritas est adaequatio rei et intellectus* [Truth is the agreement of the thing and the intellect]?It is essential that we have an answer to this question, for we do not concede that, in the strict and proper sense of 'is', there *is* truth. We cannot interpret the 'is' of the formula as having the function that it has in '*A* is' or 'There is an *A*'. Actually what the formula says is no more than this: if *A* is, then whoever accepts or affirms *A* judges correctly; and if *A* is not, then whoever rejects or denies *A* judges correctly. The formula does not at all require that, if there is no *A*, then there has to be something else – the non-being of *A* – to function in its place. *A* itself is the thing with which our judgement is concerned.
        . . . The object of a correct denial or rejection is not something which exists, except in the sense in which one says, improperly, that whatever is thought 'exists in the mind'. . . . The *adaequatio* consists precisely in the fact that the object of the judgement does *not* exist and that the one who judges *denies* its existence.
    The True and the Evident, trans. R. Chisholm, I. Politzer and K. R. Fischer, p. 109

11 And now we have found what we have been looking for. We have arrived at the source of our concepts of the good and the bad, along with that of our concepts of the true and the false. We call a thing *true* when the affirmation relating to it is correct. We call a thing *good* when the love relating to it is correct. In the broadest sense of the term, the good is that which is worthy of love, that which can be loved with a love that is correct.
    The Origin of our Knowledge of Right and Wrong, trans. R. Chisholm and E. H. Schneewind, p. 18

C. D. BROAD (1887–1971)

I do not think that 'Existence' can be defined, but I think that it can be   1
unambiguously described. (*a*) Whatever exists can occur in a proposition
only as a logical subject. Of course the *name* of an existent may appear in
a *sentence* as a grammatical *object* and in other positions too. E.g., in the
sentence 'Smith dislikes Jones' the only grammatical subject is the word
'Smith', and the word 'Jones' counts as a grammatical object. Nevertheless,
the men Smith and Jones are both logical subjects of the proposition for
which this sentence stands. . . . (*b*) A second characteristic which belongs
to all Existents and to no Abstracta is that they are *either* literally and
directly in time; *or*, if time be unreal, have those characteristics, whatever
they may be, which make them appear to human minds to be directly and
literally in time.
The Mind and its Place in Nature, p. 18

. . . the future is simply nothing at all. Nothing has happened to the   2
present by becoming past except that fresh slices of existence have been
added to the total history of the world. The past is thus as real as the
present.
Scientific Thought, p. 66

In the known relevant *normal and abnormal* facts there is nothing to   3
suggest, and much to counter-suggest, the possibility of any kind of
persistence of the psychical aspect of a human being after the death of his
body. . . . The result is naturally a state of hesitation . . . I think I may say
that for my part I should be slightly more annoyed than surprised if I
should find myself in some sense persisting immediately after the death of
my present body. One can only wait and see, or alternately (which is no
less likely) wait and not see.
Lectures on Psychical Research, p. 430

The scientists in question seem to me to confuse the Author of Nature   4
with the Editor of *Nature*; or at any rate to suppose that there can be no
productions of the former which would not be accepted for publication
by the latter. And I see no reason to believe this.
The Mind and its Place in Nature, p. viii

It is worth remembering (though there is nothing that we can do about it)   5
that the world as it really is may easily be a far nastier place than it would
be if scientific materialism were the whole truth and nothing but the truth
about it.
Lectures on Psychical Research, p. 430

Finally I would say that, for me at any rate, the five years which I have   6
spent in wrestling with McTaggart's system and putting the results into

71

writing have been both pleasant and intellectually profitable. I derive a certain satisfaction from reflecting that there is one subject at least about which I probably know more than anyone else in the universe with the possible exception of God (if he exists) and McTaggart (if he survives).
Examination of McTaggart's Philosophy, II, pt. 1, p. lxxiv

7   In the meantime I retire to my well-earned bath chair, from which I shall watch with a fatherly eye the philosophic gambols of my younger friends as they dance to the highly syncopated pipings of Herr Wittgenstein's flute.
The Mind and its Place in Nature, p. viii

L. E. J. BROUWER (1881–1966)

1   . . . the most serious blow for the Kantian theory was the discovery of non-euclidean geometry. . . . However weak the position of intuitionism seemed to be after this period of mathematical development, it has recovered by abandoning Kant's apriority of space but adhering the more resolutely to the apriority of time.
'Intuitionism and Formalism', *Philosophy of Mathematics*, ed. P. Benacerraf and H. Putnam, p. 80

2   The long belief in the universal validity of the principle of the excluded third in mathematics is considered by intuitionism as a phenomenon of history of civilization of the same kind as the old-time belief in the rationality of π or in the rotation of the firmament on an axis passing through the earth. And intuitionism tries to explain the long persistence of this dogma by two facts: firstly the obvious non-contradictority of the principle for an arbitrary single assertion; secondly the practical validity of the whole of classical logic for an extensive group of *simple everyday phenomena*. The latter fact apparently made such a strong impression that the play of thought that classical logic originally was, became a deep-rooted habit of thought which was considered not only as useful but even as aprioristic.
'Consciousness, Philosophy, and Mathematics', *Proceedings of the 10th International Congress of Philosophy* (1948), p. 1247

THOMAS BROWN (1778–1820)

Reid bawled out, We must believe in an outward world; but added in a whisper, We can give no reason for our belief. Hume cries out, We can give no reason for such a notion; and whispers, I own we cannot get rid of it.
Quoted in James Mackintosh, *On the Rise and Progress of Ethical Philosophy*

MARTIN BUBER (1878–1965)

The primary words are not isolated words, but combined words. The one 1
primary word is the combination *I–Thou*. The other primary word is the
combination *I–It*; wherein, without a change in the primary word, one
of the words *He* and *She* can replace *It*. Hence the *I* of man is also
twofold. For the *I* of the primary word *I–Thou* is a different *I* from that
of the primary word *I–It*.
I and Thou, trans. Ronald Gregor Smith, p. 43

When *Thou* is spoken, the speaker has no thing for his object. For where 2
there is a thing, there is another thing. Every *It* is bounded by others; *It*
exists only through being bounded by others. But when *Thou* is spoken,
there is no thing. *Thou* has no bounds.

When *Thou* is spoken, the speaker has no *thing*; he has indeed nothing.
But he takes his stand in relation.
I and Thou, trans. Ronald Gregor Smith, p. 44

. . . the world is not presented to man by experiences alone. These present 3
him only with a world composed of *It* and *He* and *She* and *It* again.

I experience something. If we add 'inner' to 'outer' experiences,
nothing in the situation is changed. We are merely following the
uneternal division that springs from the lust of the human race to whittle
away the secret of death. Inner things or outer things, what are they but
things and things!

I experience something. If we add 'secret' to 'open' experiences,
nothing in the situation is changed. How self-confident is that wisdom
which perceives a closed compartment in things, reserved for the initiate
and manipulated only with the key. O secrecy without a secret! O
accumulation of information! It, always It!
I and Thou, trans. Ronald Gregor Smith, p. 44

But this is the exalted melancholy of our fate, that every *Thou* in our 4
world must become an *It*. . . . Every *Thou* in the world is by its nature
fated to become a thing, or continually to re-enter into the condition of
things.
I and Thou, trans. Ronald Gregor Smith, p. 49

All real living is meeting. 5
I and Thou, trans. Ronald Gregor Smith, p. 46

TYLER BURGE (*b.* 1946)

We now turn to a three-step thought experiment. Suppose first that: 1
    A given person has a large number of attitudes commonly attributed
    with content clauses containing 'arthritis' in oblique occurrence. For

example, he thinks (correctly) that he has had arthritis for years, that
his arthritis in his wrists and fingers is more painful than his arthritis in
his ankles. . . . In addition to these unsurprising attitudes, he thinks
falsely that he has developed arthritis in the thigh.

Generally competent in English, rational and intelligent, the patient
reports to his doctor his fear that his arthritis has now lodged in his thigh.
The doctor replies by telling him that this cannot be so, since arthritis is
specifically an inflammation of joints. Any dictionary could have told
him the same. The patient is surprised, but relinquishes his view and goes
on to ask what might be wrong with his thigh.

The second step of the thought experiment consists of a counterfactual
supposition. We are to conceive of a situation in which the patient
proceeds from birth through the same course of physical events that he
actually does, right to and including the time at which he first reports his
fear to his doctor. Precisely the same things (non-intentionally described)
happen to him. He has the same physiological history, the same diseases,
the same internal physical occurrences. He goes through the same
motions, engages in the same behavior, has the same sensory intake
(physiologically described). His dispositions to respond to stimuli are
explained in physical theory as the effects of the same proximate causes.
All of this extends to his interaction with linguistic expressions. . . . But in
our imagined case, physicians, lexicographers, and informed laymen
apply 'arthritis' not only to arthritis but to various other rheumatoid
ailments. The standard use of the term is to be conceived to encompass
the patient's actual misuse. . . . The final step is an interpretation of the
counterfactual case, or an addition to it as so far described. It is
reasonable to suppose that:

> In the counterfactual situation, the patient lacks some – probably *all* –
> of the attitudes commonly attributed with content clauses containing
> 'arthritis' in oblique occurrence. He lacks the occurrent thoughts or
> beliefs that he has arthritis in the thigh, that he has had arthritis for
> years, that stiffening joints and various sorts of aches are symptoms of
> arthritis, that his father had arthritis, and so on.

'Individualism and the Mental', *Midwest Studies* (1979), p. 77

2   The upshot of these reflections is that the patient's mental contents differ
while his entire physical and non-intentional mental histories, considered
in isolation from their social context, remain the same. (We could have
supposed that he dropped dead at the time he first expressed his fear to
the doctor.) The differences seem to stem from differences 'outside' the
patient considered as an isolated physical organism, causal mechanism,
or seat of consciousness. The difference in his mental contents is
attributable to differences in his social environment.

'Individualism and the Mental', p. 79

. . . the ultimate authority regarding the application, explication, and 3
individuation of a subject's intentional mental events does not derive
solely from the actual motions, behavior, actions, usage, practices,
understanding or even (except trivially) thoughts of any person or social
group. Our conception of mind is responsive to intellectual norms which
provide the permanent possibility of challenge to any actual practices of
individuals or communities that we could envisage.
'Intellectual Norms and Foundations of Mind', *Journal of Philosophy* (1986),
p. 720

JEAN BURIDAN (c.1295–1356)

Is a good distinction made between rational and irrational faculties in
saying: the rational faculty is equally capable of two opposite acts;
whereas the irrational faculty is not; it can produce only one act?

For the will to produce an act of volition, the reason must have already
adjudicated between good and evil. Let us imagine that the intellect sees a
sum of money; . . . the will can decide to take what it judges useful; it can
also decide not to take it because it has judged that to do so would be
unjust and dishonest; it can also remain in abeyance without producing
either the act of willing or the act of not willing . . . Thus intellect is not
enough to determine the will; the will maintains its determinings in its
own freedom.

Let us consider, on the contrary, the sensitive appetite or any non-free
faculty; if this faculty is indifferent to two mutually opposed acts, for
example acceptance or refusal, it will never decide on either act, unless
some other cause determines it. The sensitive appetite of a dog or horse is
therefore determined to act by the judgement of sense alone. As soon as
the horse or dog judges, through the sense with which he is endowed,
that a thing is good, that it suits him, appetite directs him towards this
thing. Indeed, here it can be seen how opposing sensory judgements
sometimes merge. A dog, for example, not having eaten, is starving; he
sees food and desperately wishes to take it; but he also sees his master
holding a stick; he then judges that it would be untoward to take the
meat, and is afraid to do so. But whichever of these two judgements – he
should take this food, or he shouldn't take it – is strongest, will determine
the more powerful act of appetite, which the outward act will, in its turn,
follow.

It seems to me that to account for the difference between the freedom
of our will and the lack of freedom to which the sensitive appetite of the
dog is subject, it would be better to trust to faith than to natural reason.
For it would scarcely be easy to show that our will is wholly indifferent
between two opposite acts; that it, unlike the dog's appetite, can decide

for one or the other alternative without some external factor forcing it.
In Metaphysicam Aristotelis Quaestiones, quoted in P. Duhem, *Études sur Leonard de Vinci*, III, p. 19

EDMUND BURKE (1729–1797)

1 . . . change . . . alters the substance of the objects themselves, and gets rid of all their essential good as well as the accidental evil annexed to them. Change is novelty, and whether it is to operate any one of the effects of reformation at all, or whether it may not contradict the very principle upon which reformation is desired, cannot be certainly known beforehand. Reform is not a change in the substance or in the primary modification of the objects, but a direct application of a remedy to the grievance complained of. So far as that is removed, all is sure. It stops there; and if it fails the substance which underwent the operation, at the very worst, is but where it was.
Letter to a Noble Lord, The Philosophy of Edmund Burke, ed. L. Bredvold

2 Society is indeed a contract. Subordinate contracts for objects of mere occasional interest may be dissolved at pleasure – but the state ought not to be considered as nothing better than a partnership agreement in a trade of pepper and coffee, calico or tobacco, or some other such low concern, to be taken up for a little temporary interest, and to be dissolved by the fancy of the parties. It is to be looked on with other reverence; because it is not a partnership in things subservient only to the gross animal existence of a temporary and perishable nature. It is a partnership in all science; a partnership in all art; a partnership in every virtue, and in all perfection. As the ends of such a partnership cannot be obtained in many generations, it becomes a partnership not only between those who are living, but between those who are living, those who are dead, and those who are to be born. Each contract of each particular state is but a clause in the great primaeval contract of eternal society, linking the lower with the higher natures, connecting the visible and invisible world, according to a fixed compact sanctioned by the inviolable oath which holds all physical and all moral natures, each in their appointed place.
Reflections on the Revolution in France, ed. C. C. O'Brien, p. 194

3 In this choice of inheritance we have given to our frame of polity the image of a relation in blood; binding up the constitution of our country with our dearest domestic ties; adopting our fundamental laws into the bosom of our family affections; keeping inseparable, and cherishing with the warmth of all their combined and mutually reflected charities, our state, our hearths, our sepulchres, and our altars.
Reflections on the Revolution in France, p. 120

The vanity, restlessness, petulance, and spirit of intrigue of several petty **4**
cabals, who attempt to hide their total want of consequence in bustle and
noise, and puffing, and mutual quotation of each other, makes you
imagine that our contemptuous neglect of their abilities is a mark of
general acquiescence in their opinions. No such thing, I assure you.
Because half a dozen grasshoppers under a fern make the field ring with
their importunate chink, whilst thousands of great cattle, reposed
beneath the shadow of the British oak, chew the cud and are silent, pray
do not imagine, that those who make the noise are the only inhabitants of
the field; that, of course, they are many in number; or that, after all, they
are other than the little shrivelled, meagre, hopping, though loud and
troublesome insects of the hour.
Reflections on the Revolution in France, p. 181

I must see with my own eyes, I must, in a manner, touch with my own **5**
hands, not only the fixed but the momentary circumstances, before I
could venture to suggest any political project whatsoever. I must know
the power and disposition to accept, to execute, to persevere. I must see
the means of correcting the plan, where correctives would be wanted. I
must see the things; I must see the men.
Letter to a Member of the National Assembly

The occupation of an hair-dresser, or of a working tallow-chandler, **6**
cannot be a matter of honour to any person – to say nothing of a number
of other more servile employments. Such descriptions of men ought not
to suffer oppression from the state; but the state suffers oppression, if
such as they, either individually or collectively, are permitted to rule.
Reflections on the Revolution in France, ed. C. C. O'Brien, p. 138

WALTER BURLEIGH (1275–c.1344)

Whatever is compatible with the antecedent is compatible with the
consequent, and by 'compatible with something' I mean 'able to be true
along with it'.
De Puritate Artis Logicae, p. 63

MYLES BURNYEAT (b. 1939)

Plato is the model philosopher for those who value integrity above
solutions.
The Theaetetus of Plato, ed. M. Burnyeat, Preface

JOSEPH BUTLER (1692–1752)

Every work, both of nature and of art, is a system: and as every particular **1**
thing, both natural and artificial, is for some use or purpose out of and

beyond itself, one may add to what has been already brought into the idea of a system, its conduciveness to this one or more ends. Let us instance in a watch: suppose the several parts of it taken to pieces, and placed apart from each other: let a man have ever so exact a notion of these several parts, unless he considers the respect and relations which they have to each other, he will not have any thing like the idea of a watch. . . . Thus it is with regard to the inward frame of man. . . . It is from considering the relations which the several appetites and passions in the inward frame have to each other, and, above all, the supremacy of reflection or conscience, that we get the idea of the system or constitution of human nature. And from the idea itself it will as fully appear, that this our nature, *i.e.* constitution, is adapted to virtue, as from the idea of a watch it appears, that its nature, *i.e.* constitution or system, is adapted to measure time. What in fact or event commonly happens, is nothing to this question. Every work of art is apt to be out of order; but this is so far from being according to its system, that let the disorder increase, and it will totally destroy it.
Sermons, Preface

2   . . . nothing can be more evident, than that, exclusive of revelation, man cannot be considered as a creature left by his Maker to act at random, and live at large up to the extent of his natural power, as passion, humour, wilfulness, happen to carry him; which is the condition brute creatures are in; but that, *from his make, constitution, or nature, he is, in the strictest and most proper sense, a law to himself.* He hath the rule of right within: what is wanting is only that he honestly attend to it.
Sermons, no. iii

3   But, allowing that mankind hath the rule of right within himself, yet it may be asked, 'What obligations are we under to attend and follow it?' . . . Your obligation to obey this law, is its being the law of your nature. That your conscience approves of and attests to such a course of action, is itself alone an obligation. Conscience does not only offer itself to show us the way we should walk in, but it likewise carries its own authority with it, that it is our natural guide, the guide assigned us by the Author of our nature . . .
Sermons, no. iii

4   Conscience and self-love, if we understand our true happiness, always lead us the same way. Duty and interest are perfectly coincident; for the most part in this world, but entirely and in every instance if we take in the future, and the whole; this being implied in the notion of a good and perfect administration of things.
Sermons, no. iii

. . . benevolence is not in any respect more at variance with self-love, than   5
any other particular affection whatever, but . . . is, in every respect, at
least as friendly to it.

. . . self-love and benevolence, virtue and interest, are not to be
opposed, but only to be distinguished from each other; in the same way
as virtue and any other particular affection, love of arts, suppose, are to
be distinguished. Every thing is what it is, and not another thing. The
goodness, or badness of actions, does not arise from hence, that the
epithet, interested, or disinterested, may be applied to them, any more
than that any other indifferent epithet, suppose inquisitive or jealous,
may, or may not, be applied to them; not from their being attended with
present or future pleasure or pain, but from their being what they are;
namely, what becomes such creatures as we are, what the state of the case
requires, or the contrary. Or, in other words, we may judge and
determine that an action is morally good or evil, before we so much as
consider, whether it be interested or disinterested.
Sermons, Preface

That all particular appetites and passions are towards *external things*   6
themselves, distinct from the *pleasure arising from them*, is manifested
from hence; that there could not be this pleasure, were it not for that
prior suitableness between the object and the passion: there could be no
enjoyment or delight from one thing more than another, from eating
food more than from swallowing a stone, if there were not an affection or
appetite to one thing more than another.
Sermons, no. xi

C

⬚⬚⬚⬚⬚⬚

ALBERT CAMUS (1913–1960)

1   A world that can be explained even with bad reasons is a familiar world.
But in a universe suddenly divested of illusions and lights, man feels an
alien, a stranger. His exile is without remedy since he is deprived of the
memory of a lost home or the hope of a promised land. This divorce
between man and his life, the actor and his setting, is properly the feeling
of absurdity.
The Myth of Sisyphus, trans. Justin O'Brien, p. 13

2   Man stands face to face with the irrational. He feels within him his
longing for happiness and for reason. The absurd is born of this
confrontation between the human need and the unreasonable silence of
the world.
The Myth of Sisyphus, trans. Justin O'Brien, p. 29

3   To an absurd mind reason is useless and there is nothing beyond reason. . . .
The absurd is lucid reason noting its limits. . . . I don't know whether this
world has a meaning that transcends it. But I know that I do not know
that meaning and that it is impossible for me just now to know it. What
can a meaning outside my condition mean to me? I can understand it
only in human terms.
The Myth of Sisyphus, trans. Justin O'Brien, p. 34

4   The certainty of a God giving a meaning to life far surpasses in
attractiveness the ability to behave badly with impunity. The choice
would not be hard to make. But there is no choice and that is where the
bitterness comes in. The absurd does not liberate; it binds. It does not
authorize all actions. Everything is permitted does not mean that nothing
is forbidden. The absurd merely confers an equivalence on the consequences of those actions.
  . . . If God exists, all depends on him and we can do nothing against his
will. If he does not exist, everything depends on us.
The Myth of Sisyphus, trans. Justin O'Brien, p. 58

His [Sisyphus'] fate belongs to him. His rock is his thing. Likewise, the   5
absurd man, when he contemplates his torment, silences all the idols. In
the universe suddenly restored to its silence, the myriad wondering little
voices of the earth rise up. Unconscious, secret calls, invitations from all
the faces, they are the necessary reverse and price of victory. There is no
sun without shadow, and it is essential to know the night. The absurd
man says yes and his effort will henceforth be unceasing.
The Myth of Sisyphus, trans. Justin O'Brien, p. 98

The sense of the absurd, when one first undertakes to deduce a rule of   6
action from it, makes murder seem a matter of indifference, hence,
permissible. If one believes in nothing, if nothing makes sense, if we can
assert no value whatsoever, everything is permissible and nothing is
important. There is no pro or con; the murderer is neither right nor
wrong. One is free to stoke the crematory fires, or to give one's life to the
care of lepers. Wickedness and virtue are just accident or whim.

We may then decide not to act at all, which comes down to condoning
other people's murder, plus a little fastidious sorrow over human
imperfection. Or we may hit upon tragic dilettantism as a substitute for
action; in this case, human lives become counters in a game. Finally, we
may resolve to undertake some action that is not wholly arbitrary. In this
case, since we have no higher value to direct our action, we shall aim at
efficiency. Since nothing is true or false, good or bad, our principle will
become that of showing ourselves to be the most effective, in other words
the most powerful. And then the world will no longer be divided into the
just and the unjust, but into masters and slaves. Thus, whichever way we
turn in the depths of negation and nihilism, murder has its privileged
position.
The Rebel, trans. Anthony Bower, p. 13

The final conclusion of the absurdist process is, in fact, the rejection of   7
suicide and persistence in that hopeless encounter between human
questioning and the silence of the universe. Suicide would mean the end
of this encounter, and the absurdist position realizes that it could not
endorse suicide without abolishing its own foundations. It would
consider such an outcome running away or being rescued. But it is plain
that absurdist reasoning thereby recognizes human life as the single
necessary good, because it makes possible that confrontation, and
because without life the absurdist wager could not go on. To say that life
is absurd, one must be alive. How can one, without indulging one's desire
for comfort, keep for oneself the exclusive benefits of this argument? The
moment life is recognized as a necessary good, it becomes so for all men.
One cannot find logical consistency in murder, if one denies it in suicide.
The Rebel, trans. Anthony Bower, p. 14

8   The absurdist method, like that of systematic doubt, has wiped the slate clean. It leaves us in a blind alley. But, like the method of doubt, it can, by returning upon itself, disclose a new field· of investigation. Reasoning follows the same reflexive course. I proclaim that I believe in nothing and that everything is absurd, but I cannot doubt the validity of my own proclamation and I am compelled to believe, at least, in my own protest. The first, and only, datum that is furnished me, within absurdist experience, is rebellion.
The Rebel, trans. Anthony Bower, p. 16

9   What is a rebel? A man who says no: but whose refusal does not imply a renunciation. He is also a man who says yes as soon as he begins to think for himself. . . . He rebels because he categorically refuses to submit to conditions that he considers intolerable and also because he is confusedly convinced that his position is justified, or rather, because in his own mind he thinks that he 'has the right to . . .'. Rebellion cannot exist without the feeling that somewhere, in some way, you are justified.
The Rebel, trans. Anthony Bower, p. 19

10 When man submits God to moral judgement, he kills Him in his own heart. And then what is the basis of morality? God is denied in the name of justice but can the idea of justice be understood without the idea of God? Have we not arrived at absurdity? It is absurdity that Nietzsche meets face to face. The better to avoid it, he pushes it to extremities: morality is the final aspect of God which must be destroyed before the period of reconstruction begins. Then God no longer exists and no longer guarantees our existence; man, in order to exist, must decide to act.
The Rebel, trans. Anthony Bower, p. 57

RUDOLF CARNAP (1891–1970)

1   The reader may find it easier to understand the main article if I preface it by some remarks on the general nature of the views held by the Viennese Circle to which I and my friends belong.
   In the first place I want to emphasize that *we are not a philosophical school and that we put forward no philosophical theses whatsoever*. To this the following objection will be made: you reject all philosophical schools *hitherto*, because you fancy your opinions are quite new; but every school shares this illusion, and you are no exception. No, there is this essential difference, must be the answer. Any new philosophical school, though it reject all previous opinions, is bound to answer the old (if perhaps better formulated) questions. But we give no answer to philosophical questions, and instead *reject all philosophical questions*, whether of Metaphysics, Ethics or Epistemology. For our concern is with

Logical Analysis. If that pursuit is still to be called Philosophy let it be so; but it involves excluding from consideration all the traditional problems of Philosophy.
The Unity of Science, trans. M. Black, p. 21

Logic is the last scientific ingredient of Philosophy; its extraction leaves 2 behind only a confusion of non-scientific, pseudo problems.
The Unity of Science, trans. M. Black, p. 22

In formulating the thesis of the unity of Science as the assertion that 3 objects are of a single kind, that states of affairs are of a single kind, we are using the ordinary fashion of speech in terms of 'objects' and 'states of affairs'. The correct formulation replaces 'objects' by 'words' and 'states of affairs' by 'statements', for a philosophical, i.e. a logical, investigation must be an analysis of language. Since the terminology of the analysis of language is unfamiliar we propose to use the more usual mode of speech (which we will call *'material'*) side by side with the correct manner of speaking (which we will call the *'formal'*). The first speaks of 'objects', 'states of affairs', of the 'sense', 'content' or 'meaning' of words, while the second refers only to linguistic forms.
The Unity of Science, trans. M. Black, p. 37

Science is a system of statements based on direct experience, and 4 controlled by experimental verification. Verification in science is not, however, of single statements but of the entire system or a sub-system of such statements.
The Unity of Science, trans. M. Black, p. 42

The present investigations aim to establish a 'constructional system', that 5 is, an epistemic-logical system of objects or concepts. . . .
   Unlike other conceptual systems, a constructional system undertakes more than the division of concepts into various kinds and the investigation of the differences and mutual relations between these kinds. In addition, it attempts a step-by-step derivation or 'construction' of all concepts from certain fundamental concepts, so that a genealogy of concepts results in which each one has its definite place. It is the main thesis of construction theory that all concepts can in this way be derived from a few fundamental concepts, and it is in this respect that it differs from most other ontologies.
The Logical Structure of the World: Pseudo-problems in Philosophy, trans. Rolf A. George, p. 5

We do not here wish to make either a negative or a positive value 6 judgment about faith and intuition (in the non-rational sense). They are areas of life just like poetry and love. Like these latter areas, they can of course become *objects* of science (for there is nothing which could not become an object of science), but, as far as their content is concerned, they are altogether different from science. Those non-rational areas, on the one hand, and science, on the other hand, can neither confirm nor disprove one another.

The Logical Structure of the World: Pseudo-problems in Philosophy, trans. Rolf A. George, p. 293

7 *The problem of mind-body dualism*: are there two essentially different object types? Answer: the physical and the psychological are two different forms of order (analogy: stellar constellations) of the basic elements. There is only one kind of basic element, yet there are not only two, but very many, different ways of ordering them. This is no peculiarity of the empirical world, but holds analytically of any ordered domain.

The Logical Structure of the World: Pseudo-problems in Philosophy, trans. Rolf A. George, p. 299

8 The *self* is the class (not the collection) of the experiences (or autopsychological states). The self does not belong to the expression of the basic experience, but is constructed only on a very high level.

The Logical Structure of the World: Pseudo-problems in Philosophy, trans. Rolf A. George, p. 299

9 By the thesis of realism we shall understand the following two subtheses: 1. the perceived physical things which surround me are not only the content of my perception, but, in addition, they exist in themselves ('reality of the external world'); 2. the bodies of other persons not only exhibit perceivable reactions similar to those of my body, but, in addition, these other persons have consciousness ('reality of the heteropsychological'). The thesis of idealism is identified with the corresponding denials (the second of them however is maintained only by a certain radical idealistic position, namely solipsism): 1. the external world is not itself real, but only the perceptions or representations of it are ('non-reality of the external world'); 2. only my own processes of consciousness are real; the so-called conscious processes of others are merely constructions or even fictions ('non-reality of the heteropsychological'). . . . do these theses express a fact (no matter whether an existent or non-existent one) or are they merely pseudo statements, made with the vain intention of expressing accompanying object representation in the form of statements, as if they were factual representations? We shall find that the latter is indeed the case, so that these theses have no content; they are not statements at all. Hence the question about the correctness of these theses cannot be raised.

The Logical Structure of the World: Pseudo-problems in Philosophy, trans. Rolf A. George, p. 332

The rule 'Do not kill' has grammatically the imperative form and will   10
therefore not be regarded as an assertion. But the value statement 'Killing is evil', although, like the rule, it is merely an expression of a certain wish, has the grammatical form of an assertive proposition. Most philosophers have been deceived by this form into thinking that a value statement is really an assertive proposition, and must be either true or false. Therefore they give reasons for their own value statements and try to disprove those of their opponents. But actually a value statement is nothing else than a command in a misleading grammatical form. It may have effects upon the actions of men, and these effects may either be in accordance with our wishes or not; but it is neither true nor false. It does not assert anything and can neither be proved nor disproved.
Philosophy and Logical Syntax, p. 24

NANCY CARTWRIGHT (*b.* 1945)

Covering-law theorists tend to think that nature is well-regulated; in the extreme, that there is a law to cover every case. I do not. I imagine that natural objects are much like people in societies. Their behaviour is constrained by some specific laws and by a handful of general principles, but it is not determined in detail, even statistically. What happens on most occasions is dictated by no law at all. This is not a metaphysical picture that I urge. My claim is that this picture is as plausible as the alternative. God may have written just a few laws and grown tired. We do not know whether we are in a tidy universe or an untidy one. Whichever universe we are in, the ordinary commonplace activity of giving explanations ought to make sense.
How the Laws of Physics Lie, p. 49

ERNST CASSIRER (1874–1945)

To identify the 'selection' that an electron is able to make from the set of different quantum orbits – in accordance with Bohr's theory – with 'choice' in the ethical sense of that concept would be to succumb to a purely linguistic confusion. For a choice exists only where there are not only different possibilities, but where also a conscious differentiation and a conscious decision is made. To credit the electron with such acts would constitute a severe relapse into anthropomorphism.
Determinism and Indeterminism in Modern Physics, trans. O. T. Benfey, p. 204

RODERICK M. CHISHOLM (*b.* 1931)

Psychological phenomena, according to Brentano, are characterized 'by what the scholastics of the Middle Ages referred to as the intentional (also the mental) inexistence of the object, and what we, although with not quite unambiguous expressions, would call relation to a content, direction upon an object (which is not here to be understood as a reality), or immanent objectivity.' This 'intentional inexistence', Brentano added, is peculiar to what is psychical; things which are merely physical show nothing like it. . . .

These points can be put somewhat more precisely by referring to the language we have used. . . .

First, let us say that a simple declarative sentence is intentional if it uses a substantival expression – a name or a description – in such a way that neither the sentence nor its contradictory implies either that there is or that there isn't anything to which the substantival expression truly applies. 'Diogenes looked for an honest man' is intentional by this criterion. . . .

Secondly, let us say, of any non-compound sentence which contains a propositional clause, that it is intentional provided that neither the sentence nor its contradictory implies either that the propositional clause is true or that it is false. 'James believes there are tigers in India' is intentional by this criterion. . . .

A third mark of intentionality may be described in this way. Suppose there are two names or descriptions which designate the same things and that E is a sentence obtained merely by separating these two names or descriptions by means of 'is identical with' (or 'are identical with' if the first word is plural). Suppose also that A is a sentence using one of those names or descriptions and that B is like A except that, where A uses the one, B uses the other. Let us say that A is intentional if the conjunction of A and E does not imply B.

Perceiving: A Philosophical Study, p. 168

NOAM CHOMSKY (*b.* 1928)

1 Hence, a generative grammar must be a system of rules that can iterate to generate an indefinitely large number of structures. This system of rules can be analyzed into the three major components of a generative grammar: the syntactic, phonological, and semantic components.

The syntactic component specifies an infinite set of abstract formal objects, each of which incorporates all information relevant to a single interpretation of a particular sentence. . . .

The phonological component of a grammar determines the phonetic form of a sentence generated by the syntactic rules. That is, it relates a structure generated by the syntactic component to a phonetically represented signal. The semantic component determines the semantic interpretation of a sentence. That is, it relates a structure generated by the syntactic component to a certain semantic representation. Both the phonological and semantic components are therefore purely interpretive. Each utilizes information provided by the syntactic component. . . . Consequently, the syntactic component of a grammar must specify, for each sentence, a *deep structure* that determines its semantic interpretation and a *surface structure* that determines its phonetic interpretation. The first of these is interpreted by the semantic component; the second, by the phonological component.

Aspects of the Theory of Syntax, p. 15

When we study human language, we are approaching what some might 2 call the 'human essence', the distinctive qualities of mind that are, so far as we know, unique to man and that are inseparable from any critical phase of human existence, personal or social. Hence the fascination of this study, and, no less, its frustration. The frustration arises from the fact that, despite much progress, we remain as incapable as ever before of coming to grips with the core problem of human language, which I take to be this: having mastered a language, one is able to understand an indefinite number of expressions that are new to one's experience, that bear no simple physical resemblance and are in no simple way analogous to the expressions that constitute one's linguistic experience; and one is able, with greater or less facility, to produce such expressions on an appropriate occasion, despite their novelty and independently of detectable stimulus configurations, and to be understood by others who share this still mysterious ability. The normal use of language is, in this sense, a creative activity. This creative aspect of normal language use is one fundamental factor that distinguishes human language from any known system of animal communication.

Language and Mind, p. 100

. . . it is almost universally taken for granted that there exists a problem 3 of explaining the 'evolution' of human language from systems of animal communication. However, a careful look at recent studies of animal communication seems to me to provide little support for these assumptions. Rather, these studies simply bring out even more clearly the extent to which human language appears to be a unique phenomenon, without significant analogue in the animal world.

Language and Mind, p. 66

It may be that the operative principles are not only unknown but even 4 humanly unknowable because of limitations on our own intellectual

capacities, a possibility that cannot be ruled out a priori; our minds are fixed biological systems with their intrinsic scope and limits. We can distinguish in principle between 'problems', which lie within these limits and can be approached by human science with some hope of success, and what we might call 'mysteries', questions that simply lie beyond the reach of our minds, structured and organized as they are, either absolutely beyond those limits or at so far a remove from anything that we can comprehend with requisite facility that they will never be incorporated within explanatory theories intelligible to humans. We may hope that the questions we pursue fall into the domain of 'problems' in this sense, but there is no guarantee that this is so.
Rules and Representations, p. 6

5 ... this theory is now often called 'universal grammar' (UG), adapting a traditional term to a new context of inquiry. UG may be regarded as a characterization of the genetically determined language faculty. One may think of this faculty as a 'language acquisition device', an innate component of the human mind that yields a particular language through interaction with presented experience, a device that converts experience into a system of knowledge attained: knowledge of one or another language.
Knowledge of Language, p. 3

6 ... the language faculty ... has features that are quite unusual, perhaps unique in the biological world. In technical terms it has the property of 'discrete infinity'. To put it simply, each sentence has a fixed number of words ... [and] there is no limit in principle to how many words the sentence may contain. . . . Without this capacity it might have been possible to 'think thoughts' of a certain restricted character, but with the capacity in place, the same conceptual apparatus would be freed for the construction of new thoughts and operations such as inference involving them, and it would be possible to express and interchange these thoughts.
Language and Problems of Knowledge, p. 169

CHRYSIPPUS (c.279 BC–c.206 BC)

1 No particular thing however slight can come into being except in accordance with universal Nature and its rationality (*logos*).
Quoted in Plutarch, *De Stoicorum Repugnantiis*, trans. H. H. Cherniss, p. 547

2 The evil which occurs in terrible disasters has a rationale (*logos*) peculiar to itself; for in a sense it too occurs in accordance with universal reason, and, so to speak, is not without usefulness in relation to the whole. For without it there could be no good.
Quoted in A. A. Long, *Hellenistic Philosophy*, p. 169

There is no possible or more suitable way to approach the subject of 3 good and bad things, the virtues and happiness, than from universal Nature and the management of the universe.
Quoted in Plutarch, *De Stoicorum Repugnantiis*, p. 433

PAUL M. CHURCHLAND (*b.* 1942)

Witches provide another example. Psychosis is a fairly common affliction among humans, and in earlier centuries its victims were standardly seen as cases of demonic possession, as instances of Satan's spirit itself, glaring malevolently out at us from behind the victims' eyes. That witches exist was not a matter of any controversy. One would occasionally see them, in any city or hamlet, engaged in incoherent, paranoid, or even murderous behavior. But observable or not, we eventually decided that witches simply do not exist. We concluded that the concept of a witch is an element in a conceptual framework that misrepresents so badly the phenomena to which it was standardly applied that literal application of the notion should be permanently withdrawn. Modern theories of mental dysfunction led to the elimination of witches from our serious ontology.

The concepts of folk psychology – belief, desire, fear, sensation, pain, joy, and so on – await a similar fate, according to the view at issue. And when neuroscience has matured to the point where the poverty of our current conceptions is apparent to everyone, and the superiority of the new framework is established, we shall then be able to set about *reconceiving* our internal states and activities, within a truly adequate conceptual framework at last.
Matter and Consciousness: A Contemporary Introduction to the Philosophy of Mind, p. 44

CICERO (106 BC–43 BC)

[on the 'idle' argument] If it is fated for you to recover from this illness, 1 you will recover whether or not you call a doctor; similarly if it is fated for you not to recover from this illness, you will not recover whether or not you call a doctor. . . . therefore there is no point in calling a doctor.
De Fato, XII, 28–9, trans. D. Charles

There is nothing so absurd but some philosopher has said it. 2
De Divinatione, II, 58, trans. D. Charles

The good of the people is the chief law. 3
De Legibus, III, 3.8, trans. C. W. Keyes (Loeb edn), p. 467

The fact is that merely holding one's peace about a thing does not 4 constitute concealment, but concealment consists in trying for your own profit to keep others from finding out something that you know, when it is for their interest to know it.

De Officiis, III, 57, trans. W. Miller (Loeb edn), p. 325

HÉLÈNE CIXOUS (*b.* 1937)

1 *Where is she?*
Activity/passivity,
Sun/Moon, Culture/Nature,
Day/Night,
Father/Mother,
Head/heart,
Intelligible/sensitive,
Logos/Pathos. . . .
Man

Woman

. . . The same thread, or double tress leads us, whether we are reading or speaking, through literature, philosophy, criticism, centuries of representation, of reflection.

Thought has always worked by opposition. . . . By dual, *hierarchized oppositions*. . . . Wherever an ordering intervenes, a law organizes the thinkable by (dual, irreconcilable; or mitigable, dialectical) oppositions. And all the couples of oppositions are *couples*. Does all this mean something? Is the fact that logocentrism subjects thought – all of the concepts, the codes, the values – to a two-term system, related to 'the' couple man/woman?

'Sorties', in *New French Feminisms*, ed. E. Marks and I. de Courtivron, p. 90

2 The challenging of this solidarity of logocentrism and phallocentrism has today become insistent enough – the bringing to light of the fate which has been imposed upon woman, of her burial – to threaten the stability of the masculine edifice which passed itself off as eternal-natural. . . . What would become of logocentrism, of the great philosophical systems, of world order in general if the rock upon which they founded their church were to crumble? . . .

Then all the stories would have to be told differently, the future would be incalculable, the historical forces would, will, change hands, bodies; another thinking as yet not thinkable will transform the functioning of all society. Well, we are living through this very period when the conceptual foundation of a millennial culture is in process of being undermined by millions of a species of mole as yet not recognized.

'Sorties', in *New French Feminisms*, p. 92

. . . let us imagine a real liberation of sexuality, that is, a transformation 3
of our relationship to our body (– and to another body). . . . That which
appears as 'feminine' or 'masculine' today would no longer amount to
the same thing. The general logic of difference would no longer fit into
the opposition that still dominates. The difference would be a crowning
display of new differences.

But we are still floundering about – with certain exceptions – in the
Old Order.

'Sorties', in *New French Feminisms*, p. 97

STEPHEN R. L. CLARK (*b.* 1945)

At least for mammals, the primary character of males is that they
reproduce in another, of females that they reproduce in themselves. To
say that Deity is Male is therefore to say that it reproduces its image in
something not-itself, in chaos and the dark. To say that it is Female is to
say that each new being is contained and fed and grows within the
Divine. For the former view, there is a definite division between Creator
and Creation, and the latter may, as it were, stand opposite to God, and
not all its qualities be blamed on God. For the latter view, there is no such
division, no possibility of standing over against Goddess, and whatever is
in the creation is in Her.

The Mysteries of Religion, p. 131

LORRAINE CODE (*b.* 1937)

Privileging these sorts of knowledge claims – 'The book is red', 'The door 1
is open' – is part of the positivist inheritance. The practice derives from
the early empiricist and later positivist conviction that all knowledge,
scientific and 'ordinary', can be broken down into observational 'simples'
that are foundational in providing a basis of certainty for systems of
knowledge constructed on them. . . . In fact knowing other people is at
least as worthy a contender for paradigmatic status as knowledge of
medium-sized everyday objects. . . . An infant learns to respond
cognitively to its caregivers *long before* it can recognize the simplest of
physical objects.

What Can She Know? Feminist Theory and the Construction of Knowledge,
p. 37

Objectivity requires taking subjectivity into account. 2

What Can She Know? Feminist Theory and the Construction of Knowledge,
p. 31

G. A. COHEN (*b.* 1941)

1 . . . we may attribute to Marx, as we cannot to Hegel, not only a *philosophy* of history, but also what deserves to be called a *theory* of history, which is not a reflective construal, from a distance, of what happens, but a contribution to understanding its inner dynamic. Hegel's reading of history as a whole and of particular societies is just that, a *reading*, an interpretation which we may find more or less attractive. But Marx offers not only a reading but also the beginnings of something more rigorous. The concepts of productive power and economic structure (unlike those of consciousness and culture) do not serve only to express a vision. They also assert their candidacy as the leading concepts in a theory of history, a *theory* to the extent that history admits of theoretical treatment, which is neither entirely nor not at all.
Karl Marx's Theory of History: A Defence, p. 27

2 . . . central Marxian explanations are functional, which means, *very roughly*, that the character of what is explained is determined by its effect on what explains it. One reason for so interpreting Marx: if the *direction* of the explanatory tie is as he laid down, then the best account of the *nature* of the tie is that it is a functional one. For production relations profoundly affect productive forces, and superstructures strongly condition foundations. What Marx claims to explain has momentous impact on what he says explains it. Construing his explanations as functional makes for compatibility between the causal power of the explained phenomena and their secondary status in the order of explanation.
Karl Marx's Theory of History: A Defence, p. 278

3 Let us begin with a simple functional explanation. In some industries there is, over a period of time, a marked increase in the median size of the producing units: small workshops grow into, or are replaced by, large factories. The increased scale reduces the costs of producing a given volume of output. It generates economies of scale. If we find that scale grows just when growth in scale would have that effect, and not otherwise, then it is a plausible explanatory hypothesis that scale grows *because* the growth brings economies. Note that we may be justified in proposing this explanation before we know *how* the fact that enlarged scale induces economies explains large scale. We can know that something operated in favour of large scale, because of its cost effectiveness, without knowing what so operated. We may not know whether the increase was deliberately sought by wise managers, or came about through an economic analogue of chance variation and natural selection. We might be able to claim *that* the change is explained by its consequences without being able to say *how* it is so explained.
Karl Marx's Theory of History: A Defence, p. 280

R. G. COLLINGWOOD (1889–1943)

People sometimes talk as if 'selection' were an essential part of every   1
artist's work. This is a mistake. In art proper there is no such thing; the
artist draws what he sees, expresses what he feels, makes a clean breast of
his experience.
The Principles of Art, p. 56

. . . what it is that the artist, as such and essentially, produces . . . is two   2
things. Primarily, it is an 'internal' or 'mental' thing, something (as we
commonly say) 'existing in his head' and there only: something of the
kind which we commonly call an experience. Secondarily, it is a bodily or
perceptible thing (a picture, statue, etc.) whose exact relation to this
'mental' thing will need very careful definition. Of these two things, the
first is obviously not anything that can be called a work of art, if work
means something made in the sense in which a weaver makes cloth. But
since it is the thing which the artist as such primarily produces, I shall
argue that we are entitled to call it 'the work of art proper'. The second
thing, the bodily and perceptible thing, I shall show to be only incidental
to the first. . . . There is no such thing as an *objet d'art* in itself; if we call
any bodily and perceptible thing by that name or an equivalent we do so
only because of the relation in which it stands to the aesthetic experience
which is the 'work of art proper'.
The Principles of Art, p. 37

Until a man has expressed his emotion, he does not yet know what   3
emotion it is. The act of expressing it is therefore an exploration of his
own emotions. He is trying to find out what these emotions are.
The Principles of Art, p. 111

The historian . . . is investigating not mere events (where by a mere event   4
I mean one which has only an outside and no inside) but actions, and an
action is the unity of the outside and inside of an event. He is interested in
the crossing of the Rubicon only in its relation to Republican law, and in
the spilling of Caesar's blood only in its relation to a constitutional
conflict. . . . For history, the object to be discovered is not the mere event,
but the thought expressed in it. . . . All history is the history of thought.
The Idea of History, p. 214

AUGUSTE COMTE (1798–1857)

. . . I believe I have discovered a fundamental law to which [human   1
intelligence] is subjected from an invariable necessity, and which seems to
me to be solidly established, either by rational proof drawn from a
knowledge of our nature, or by the historical test, an attentive

examination of the past. This law is that each of our principal conceptions, each branch of our knowledge, passes successively through three different theoretical states: the theological or fictitious, the metaphysical or abstract, and the scientific or positive.
The Essential Comte, ed. S. Andreski, trans. M. Clarke, p. 19

2   . . . it is the nature of positive philosophy to regard all phenomena as subject to invariable natural *laws*, the discovery of which, and their reduction to the least possible number, is the aim and end of all our efforts, while causes, either first or final, are considered to be absolutely inaccessible, and the search for them meaningless.
The Course in Positive Philosophy, trans. M. Clarke, p. 24

3   Since Bacon, all good intellects have agreed that there is no real knowledge save that which rests on observed facts. In our present advanced age, this principle is evidently incontestible. But . . . if on the one hand every theory must be based on observation, on the other it is equally true that facts cannot be observed without the guidance of some theory. If in contemplating phenomena we had no principles to which to attach them, not only would we find it impossible to combine isolated observations, and therefore to profit from them, but we would not be able to remember them, or, often, even to perceive them.
The Essential Comte, ed. S. Andreski, trans. M. Clarke, p. 21

4   Here then is the great, the only lacuna that must be filled if we are to complete the formation of positive philosophy. The human mind has created celestial and terrestrial physics, mechanics and chemistry, vegetable and animal physics, we might say, but we have still to complete the system of the observational sciences with *social physics*.
The Course in Positive Philosophy, trans. M. Clarke, p. 27

5   . . . the notions of order and of progress must, in social physics, be as strictly indivisible as in biology are those of organisation and of life, from which indeed in the eyes of science they derive.
The Essential Comte, ed. S. Andreski, trans. M. Clarke, p. 127

6   . . . Liberty gives free scope to superiority of all kinds, and especially to moral and mental superiority; so that if a uniform level of Equality is insisted on, freedom of growth is checked. Yet inconsistent as the [Revolution's] motto was, it . . . had, too, a progressive tendency, which partly neutralised its subversive spirit. . . .

But with the adoption of the Republican principle in 1848, the utility of this provisional motto ceased. For the Revolution now entered upon its positive phase; which, indeed, for all philosophical minds, had been already inaugurated by my discovery of the laws of social science. . . . the

motto *Order and Progress* [should be] the principle of all political action
for the future. . . . all Progress implies Liberty.
A General View of Positivism, trans. J. H. Bridges, p. 279

. . . positivism becomes, in the true sense of the word, a religion; the only   7
religion which is real and complete; destined therefore to replace all
imperfect and provisional systems resting on the primitive basis of
theology.
A General View of Positivism, trans. J. H. Bridges, p. 243

Positivists accept, and indeed enlarge, the programme of Communism;   8
but we reject its practical solution . . . The ignorance of the true laws of
social life under which Communists labour is evident in their dangerous
tendency to suppress individuality.
A General View of Positivism, trans. J. H. Bridges, p. 115

Sociology will prove that the equality of the sexes, of which so much is   9
said, is incompatible with all social existence, by showing that each sex
has special and permanent functions . . . the welfare which results being
in no degree injured by the necessary subordination.
The Positive Philosophy of Auguste Comte, trans. H. Martineau, II, ch. 5, p. 112

Green, too, would be the colour of the political flag, common to the   10
whole West. As it is intended to float freely, it does not admit of painting
. . . One side of the flag will have the political and scientific motto, *Order
and Progress*; the other, the moral and esthetic motto, *Live for Others*.
The first will be preferred by men; the other is more specially adapted to
women, who are thus invited to participate in these public manifestations
of social feeling.
A General View of Positivism, trans. J. H. Bridges, p. 286

ÉTIENNE CONDILLAC (1715–1780)

If we had no motivation to be preoccupied with our sensations, the
impressions that objects made on us would pass like shadows, and leave
no trace. After several years, we would be the same as we were at our first
moment, without having acquired any knowledge, and without having
any other faculties than feeling. But the nature of our sensations does not
let us remain enslaved in this lethargy. Since they are necessarily
agreeable or disagreeable, we are involved in seeking the former,
avoiding the latter; and the greater the intensity of difference between
pleasure and pain, the more it occasions action in our souls.
   Thus the privation of an object that we judge necessary for our well-
being, gives us disquiet, that uneasiness we call need, and from which
desires are born. These needs recur according to circumstances, often

95

quite new ones present themselves, and it is in this way that our knowledge and faculties develop.

Locke is the first to have remarked that the uneasiness caused by privation of an object is the principle of our determinations. But he has it that uneasiness arises from desire, and precisely the opposite is true. . . . it is through uneasiness that all the habits of mind and body are born.
Extrait raisonné du Traité des sensations, p. 288

MARQUIS DE CONDORCET (1743–1794)

1   If man can, with almost complete assurance, predict phenomena when he knows their laws, and if, even when he does not, he can still, with great expectation of success, forecast the future on the basis of his experience of the past, why, then, should it be regarded as a fantastic undertaking to sketch, with some pretence to truth, the future destiny of man on the basis of his history?
Sketch for a Historical Picture of the Progress of the Human Mind, in P. Gardiner, *Theories of History*, p. 57

2   Are those differences which have hitherto been seen in every civilized country in respect of the enlightenment, the resources, and the wealth enjoyed by the different classes into which it is divided, is that inequality between men which was aggravated or perhaps produced by the earliest progress of society, are these part of civilization itself, or are they due to the present imperfections of the social art? Will they necessarily decrease and ultimately make way for a real equality, the final end of the social art . . .?

. . . we shall find in the experience of the past, in the observation of the progress that the sciences and civilization have already made, in the analysis of the progress of the human mind and of the development of its faculties, the strongest reasons for believing that nature has set no limit to the realization of our hopes.
Sketch for a Historical Picture of the Progress of the Human Mind, in P. Gardiner, *Theories of History*, p. 57

ANNE CONWAY (1631–1679)

1   [Mathematical Division of Things, is never made in Minima; but Things may be Physically divided into their least parts; as when Concrete Matter is so far divided that it departs into Physical *Monades*, as it was in the first State of its Materiality. . . .] MOREOVER the consideration of this Infinite Divisibility of every thing, into parts always less, is no unnecessary or unprofitable Theory, but a thing of very great moment; *viz.* that thereby may be understood the Reasons and Causes of Things;

and how all Creatures from the highest to the lowest are inseparably united one with another, by means of Subtiler Parts interceding or coming in between, which are the Emanations of one Creature into another, by which also they act one upon another at the greatest distance; and this is the Foundation of all Sympathy and Antipathy which happens in Creatures: And if these things be well understood of any one, he may easily see into the most secret and hidden Causes of Things, which ignorant Men call occult Qualities.

Principles of the Most Ancient and Modern Philosophy Concerning God, Christ and the Creature: that is, concerning Spirit and Matter in General, p. 163
[There is a question about whether the bracketed sentence was inserted by an editor]

In every visible Creature there is a Body and a Spirit, . . . or, *more Active*   2
and more Passive Principle, which may fitly be termed Male and Female, by reason of that Analogy a Husband hath with his Wife. For as the ordinary Generation of Men requires a Conjunction and Co-operation of Male and Female; so also all Generations and Productions whatsoever they be, require an Union, and conformable Operation of those Two Principles, to wit, Spirit and Body; but the Spirit is an Eye or Light beholding its own proper Image, and the Body is a Tenebrosity or Darkness receiving that Image, when the Spirit looks thereinto, as when one sees himself in a Looking-Glass; for certainly he cannot so behold himself in the Transparent Air, nor in any Diaphanous Body, because the reflexion of an Image requires a certain opacity or darkness, which we call a Body: Yet to be a Body is not an Essential property of any Thing; as neither is it a Property of any Thing to be dark; for nothing is so dark that it cannot be made Light; . . . And indeed every Body is a Spirit, and nothing else, neither differs any thing from a Spirit, but in that it is more dark; therefore by how much the thicker and grosser it is become, so much the more remote is it from the degree of a Spirit, so that this distinction is only modal and gradual, not essential or substantial.

Principles of the Most Ancient and Modern Philosophy Concerning God, Christ and the Creature: that is, concerning Spirit and Matter in General, p. 188

From what hath been lately said, and from divers Reactions alledged,   3
That Spirit and Body are originally in their first Substance but one and the same thing, it evidently appears that the Philosophers (so called) which have taught otherwise, whether Ancient or Modern, have generally erred and laid an ill Foundation in the very beginning, whence the whole House and superstructure is so feeble, and indeed so unprofitable, that the whole Edifice and Building must in time decay, from which absurd Foundation have arose very many gross and dangerous Errours, not only in Philosophy, but also in Divinity (so

called) to the great damage of Mankind, hindrance of true Piety, and contempt of God's most Glorious Name . . .
Principles of the Most Ancient and Modern Philosophy Concerning God, Christ and the Creature: that is, concerning Spirit and Matter in General, p. 221

BENEDETTO CROCE (1866–1952)

. . . art is *vision* or *intuition*. The artist produces an image or picture. The person who enjoys art turns his eyes in the direction which the artist has pointed out to him, peers through the hole which has been opened for him, and reproduces in himself the artist's image.
Guide to Aesthetics, trans. Patrick Romanell, p. 8

DON CUPITT (*b.* 1934)

1 Belief in the God of Christian faith is an expression of allegiance to a particular set of values, and the experience of the God of Christian faith is experience of the impact of those values in one's life.
Taking Leave of God, p. 69

2 So it would seem that religion forbids that there should be any extra-religious reality of God. The most we can say is that it is religiously appropriate to think that there may be beyond the God of religion a transcendent divine mystery witnessed to in various ways by the faith of mankind. But we cannot say anything about it. Any possibility of non-religious knowledge of this mystery would weaken the stringency and the saving power of the religious requirement.
Taking Leave of God, p. 96

D

𝕾𝕾𝕾𝕾𝕾𝕾

A. C. DANTO (*b.* 1924)

To see something as art requires something the eye cannot descry – an atmosphere of artistic theory, a knowledge of the history of art: an artworld.

'The Art World', *Journal of Philosophy* (1964), p. 580

DONALD DAVIDSON (*b.* 1917)

It is a feature of physical reality that physical change can be explained by 1
laws that connect it with other changes and conditions physically described. It is a feature of the mental that the attribution of mental phenomena must be responsible to the background of reasons, beliefs and intentions of the individual. There cannot be tight connections between the realms if each is to retain its allegiance to its proper source of evidence.

Essays on Actions and Events, p. 222

Even if someone knew the entire physical history of the world, and every 2
mental event were identical with a physical, it would not follow that he could predict or explain a single mental event (so described, of course).

Essays on Actions and Events, p. 224

The first principle asserts that at least some mental events interact 3
causally with physical events. (We could call this the Principle of Causal Interaction.) . . .

The second principle is that where there is causality, there must be a law: events related as cause and effect fall under strict deterministic laws. (We may term this the Principle of the Nomological Character of Causality.) . . .

The third principle is that there are no strict deterministic laws on the basis of which mental events can be predicted and explained (the Anomalism of the Mental). . . .

. . . from the fact that there can be no strict psychophysical laws, and

99

our other two principles, we can infer the truth of a version of the identity theory, that is, a theory that identifies at least some mental events with physical events.
Essays on Actions and Events, p. 208

4   Anomalous monism shows an ontological bias only in that it allows the possibility that not all events are mental, while insisting that all events are physical. Such a bland monism, unbuttressed by correlating laws or conceptual economies, does not seem to merit the term 'reductionism'; in any case it is not apt to inspire the nothing-but reflex ('Conceiving the *Art of the Fugue* was nothing but a complex neural event', and so forth).
Essays on Actions and Events, p. 214

5   Strange goings on! Jones did it slowly, deliberately, in the bathroom, with a knife, at midnight. What he did was butter a piece of toast. We are too familiar with the language of action to notice at first an anomaly: the 'it' of 'Jones did it slowly, deliberately, . . .' seems to refer to some entity, presumably an action, that is then characterized in a number of ways.
Essays on Actions and Events, p. 105

6   The methodological advice to interpret in a way that optimizes agreement should not be conceived as resting on a charitable assumption about human intelligence that might turn out to be false. If we cannot find a way to interpret the utterances and other behaviour of a creature as revealing a set of beliefs largely consistent and true by our standards, we have no reason to count that creature as rational, as having beliefs, or as saying anything.
Inquiries into Truth and Interpretation, p. 137

7   False beliefs tend to undermine the identification of the subject matter; to undermine, therefore, the validity of a description of the belief as being about that subject. And so, in turn, false beliefs undermine the claim that a connected belief is false. To take an example, how clear are we that the ancients – some ancients – believed that the earth was flat? *This* earth? Well, this earth of ours is part of the solar system, a system partly identified by the fact that it is a gaggle of large, cool, solid bodies circling around a very large, hot star. If someone believes *none* of this about the earth, is it certain that it is the earth that he is thinking about? An answer is not called for. The point is made if this kind of consideration of related beliefs can shake one's confidence that the ancients believed the earth was flat. It isn't that any one false belief necessarily destroys our ability to identify further beliefs, but that the intelligibility of such identifications must depend on a background of largely unmentioned and unquestioned true beliefs. To put it another way: the more things a believer is right

about, the sharper his errors are. Too much mistake simply blurs the focus.

Inquiries into Truth and Interpretation, p. 168

Logical form was invented to contrast with something else that is held to   8
be apparent but mere: the form we are led to assign to sentences by
superficial analogy or traditional grammar. What meets the eye or ear in
language has the charm, complexity, convenience, and deceit of other
conventions of the market place, but underlying it is the solid currency of
a plainer, duller structure, without wit but also without pretence. This
true coin, the deep structure, need never feature directly in the
transactions of real life. As long as we know how to redeem our paper we
can enjoy the benefits of credit.

The image may help explain why the distinction between logical form
and surface grammar can flourish without anyone ever quite explaining
it. But what can we say to someone who wonders whether there is really
any gold in the vaults?

Essays on Actions and Events, p. 137

Conceptual relativism is a heady and exotic doctrine, or would be if we   9
could make good sense of it. The trouble is, as so often in philosophy, it is
hard to improve intelligibility while retaining the excitement.

Inquiries into Truth and Interpretation, p. 183

There is no such thing as a language, not if a language is anything like   10
what many philosophers and linguists have supposed. There is therefore
no such thing to be learned, mastered, or born with. We must give up the
idea of a clearly defined shared structure which language-users acquire
and then apply to cases.

Truth and Interpretation, ed. E. Lepore, p. 46

A theory of meaning (in my mildly perverse sense) is an empirical theory,   11
and its ambition is to account for the workings of a natural language. . . .
The theory reveals nothing new about the conditions under which an
individual sentence is true; it does not make those conditions any clearer
than the sentence itself does. The work of the theory is in relating the
known truth conditions of each sentence to those aspects ('words') of the
sentence that recur in other sentences, and can be assigned identical roles
in other sentences. Empirical power in such a theory depends on success
in recovering the structure of a very complicated ability – the ability to
speak and understand a language. We can tell easily enough when
particular pronouncements of the theory comport with our understanding of the language; this is consistent with a feeble insight into the design
of the machinery of our linguistic accomplishments.

Inquiries into Truth and Interpretation, p. 24

12 Beliefs, desires, and intentions are a condition of language, but language is also a condition for them. On the other hand, being able to attribute beliefs and desires to a creature is certainly a condition of sharing a convention with that creature; while, if I am right, . . . convention is not a condition of language. I suggest, then, that philosophers who make convention a necessary element in language have the matter backwards. The truth is rather that language is a condition for having conventions.
Inquiries into Truth and Interpretation, p. 280

13 The most obvious semantic difference between simile and metaphor is that all similes are true and most metaphors are false. The earth is like a floor, the Assyrian did come down like a wolf on the fold, because everything is like everything. But turn these sentences into metaphors, and you turn them false; the earth is like a floor, but it is not a floor; Tolstoy, grown up, was like an infant, but he wasn't one. We use a simile ordinarily only when we know the corresponding metaphor to be false. We say Mr S. is like a pig because we know he isn't one. If we had used a metaphor and said he was a pig, this would not be because we changed our mind about the facts but because we chose to get the idea across a different way.
Inquiries into Truth and Interpretation, p. 257

WAYNE A. DAVIS (b. 1951)

1 Suppose John wanted to scare away the fish, but had no intention of trying to do so or of manifesting his desire in any way. Suppose he knows, however, that despite his best efforts at concealment, someone else will learn of his desire and push him out of the helicopter, resulting in his scaring away the fish. Then John expected that his desire to scare away the fish would result in his scaring them away, but we could hardly say that he intended to scare away the fish. The causal chain John expected was of the wrong sort. He did not expect his desire to *motivate* him to scare away the fish, or to do anything that would have as a consequence his scaring away the fish, or even to refrain from doing anything that would have as a consequence his not scaring away the fish.
'A Causal Theory of Intending', *American Philosophical Quarterly* (1984), p. 50

2 . . . we obtain a manageable definition: *S intends that p iff S believes that p because he desires that p and believes his desire will motivate him to act in such a way that p.* 'Because' is to be understood here as introducing both the reason *why S* believes that *p* and the reason *for which* he does, i.e., both the explanation and the grounds for his belief.
'A Causal Theory of Intending', p. 51

DEMOCRITUS (*c.*460 BC–400 BC)

By convention are sweet and bitter, hot and cold, by convention is 1
colour; in truth are atoms and the void. . . . In reality we apprehend
nothing for certain, but only as it changes according to the condition of
our body and of the things that impinge on or offer resistance to it.
G. S. Kirk, J. E. Raven and M. Schofield, *The Pre-Socratic Philosophers*, p. 411

The atoms struggle and move in the void because of dissimilarities 2
between them and other differences; and as they move they collide and
become entangled in such a way as to cling in close contact to one
another.
The Pre-Socratic Philosophers, p. 423

There are two forms of knowledge, one legitimate, one bastard. To the 3
bastard belong all the following: sight, hearing, smell, taste, touch. The
other is legitimate, and is separate from this.
The Pre-Socratic Philosophers, p. 412

[The senses reply to comments such as quotation 3 above:] 4
. . . Wretched mind, do you, who get your evidence from us, yet try to
overthrow us? Our overthrow will be your downfall.
The Pre-Socratic Philosophers, p. 411

He who feels any desire to beget a child seems to me better advised to 5
take it from one of his friends; he will then have a child such as he wishes,
for he can choose the kind he wants. . . . But if a man begets his own
child, many are the dangers there; for he must make the best of him
whatever his nature.
G. S. Kirk and J. E. Raven, *The Pre-Socratic Philosophers*, p. 425

DANIEL C. DENNETT (*b.* 1942)

The word 'voice', as it is discovered in its own peculiar environment of 1
contexts, does not fit neatly the physical, non-physical dichotomy that so
upsets the identity theorist, but it is not for that reason a vague or
ambiguous or otherwise unsatisfactory word. This state of affairs should
not lead anyone to become a Cartesian dualist with respect to voices; let
us try not to invent a voice-throat problem to go along with the mind-
body problem.
Content and Consciousness, p. 9

Intentionality . . . serves as a reliable means of detecting exactly where a 2
theory is *in the red* relative to the task of explaining intelligence;
wherever a theory relies on a formulation bearing the logical marks of
intentionality, there a little man is concealed.
Brainstorms, p. 12

103

3   Homunculi are *bogeymen* only if they duplicate *entire* the talents they are
    rung in to explain. If one can get a team or committee of *relatively*
    ignorant, narrow-minded, blind homunculi to produce the intelligent
    behavior of the whole, this is progress.
    Brainstorms, p. 123

4   We are less inclined to strike up the little band in the brain for auditory
    perception than we are to set up the movie screen, so if images can be
    eliminated, mental noises, smells, feels and tastes will go quietly.
    Content and Consciousness, p. 133

5   And to be crass about it, who cares if the little men in one's brain are in
    pain? What matters is whether *I* am in pain. There is no way of adding a
    pain center to the sub-personal level without committing flagrant
    category mistakes, by confusing the personal and sub-personal levels of
    explanation.
    Brainstorms, p. 219

6   Phenomenal space is Mental Image Heaven, but if mental images turn
    out to be *real*, they can reside quite comfortably in the physical space in
    our brains, and if they turn out not to be real, they can reside, with Santa
    Claus, in the logical space of fiction.
    Brainstorms, p. 186

7   This is the true subjectivity of colour qualities: not that they are private,
    internal qualities, but that red things are all and only those things taken
    by normal human beings to be red, regardless of their surface structures
    or reflective capacities.
    Content and Consciousness, p. 141

8   The thesis of determinism carries no implications, of course, about how
    in particular the world will arrange itself, but it sometimes seems as if we
    respond to the prospect of determinism as if it were just such a limiting
    future – as if the pilot in the airplane had just said to us over the intercom
    'I'm afraid we're in for a long stretch of *determinism* just ahead; we'll be
    powerless and *have no room to maneuver*; we'll be very lucky to survive
    intact!'
    Elbow Room: The Varieties of Free Will Worth Wanting, p. 73

9   Only some of the portions of the physical universe have the property of
    being designed to resist their own dissolution, to wage a local campaign
    against the inexorable trend of the Second Law of Thermodynamics. And
    only some of these portions have the further property of being caused to
    have reliable expectations about what will happen next, and hence to
    have the capacity to control things, including themselves. And only some
    of these have the further capacity of significant self-improvement

(through learning). And fewer still have the open-ended capacity (requiring a language of self-description) for 'radical self-evaluation'. These portions of the world are thus loci of self-control, of talent, of decision making. They have projects, interests, and values they create in the course of their own self-evaluation and self-definition. How much less like a domino could a portion of the physical world be?
Elbow Room: The Varieties of Free Will Worth Wanting, p. 100

What spread around the world on July 20, 1969? The belief that a man 10
had stepped on the moon. In no two people was the effect of the receipt of that information the same, and the causal paths eventuating in the state they all had in common were no doubt almost equally various, but the claim that therefore they all had nothing in common – nothing importantly in common – is false, and obviously so.
The Intentional Stance, p. 235

The doctrine of original intentionality is the claim that whereas some of 11
our artifacts may have intentionality derived from us, we have original (or intrinsic) intentionality, utterly underived. Aristotle said that God is the Unmoved Mover, and this doctrine announces that we are Unmeant Meaners.
The Intentional Stance, p. 288

No one wants to learn that one's crusading career is just half of a tempest 12
in a teapot, and so philosophers are typically not eager to accept . . . bland and ecumenical resolutions of their controversies, but it can be reassuring, and even enlightening – if not especially exciting – to remind ourselves of just how much fundamental agreement there is.
The Intentional Stance, p. 340

We are all standing around in each other's data, looking in roughly the 13
same directions for roughly the same things. Priority squabbles may make sense in some disciplines, but in philosophy they tend to take on the air of disputes among sailors about who gets credit for first noticing that the breeze has come up.
The Intentional Stance, p. 350

. . . the brain, as physiology or plain common sense shows us, is just a 14
syntactic engine; all it can do is discriminate its inputs by their structural, temporal, and physical features and let its entirely mechanical activities be governed by these 'syntactic' features of its inputs. That's all brains *can do*. Now how does the brain manage to get semantics from syntax?
'Three Kinds of Intentional Psychology', in *Reduction, Time and Reality*, ed. R. Healey, p. 53

15 . . . it is widely granted these days that dualism is not a serious view to contend with, but rather a cliff over which to push one's opponents . . .
'Current Issues in the Philosophy of Mind', *American Philosophical Quarterly* (1978), p. 252

16 Spiders don't have to think, consciously and deliberately, about how to spin their webs; that is just something that spider brains are designed to get spiders to do. And even beavers, unlike professional human engineers, do not consciously and deliberately plan the structures they build. And finally, *we* (unlike *professional* human storytellers) do not consciously and deliberately figure out what narratives to tell and how to tell them; like spider webs, our tales are *spun by us*; our human consciousness, and our narrative selfhood, is their *product*, not their *source*.
'The Origins of Selves', *Cogito* (1990), p. 168

JACQUES DERRIDA (*b.* 1930)

1 . . . the writer writes *in* a language and *in* a logic whose proper system, laws, and life his discourse by definition cannot dominate absolutely. . . . And the reading must always aim at a certain relationship, unperceived by the writer, between what he commands and what he does not command of the patterns of the language that he uses.
Of Grammatology, trans. G. C. Spivak, p. 158

2 By virtue of its innermost intention, and like all questions about language, structuralism escapes the classical history of ideas which already supposes structuralism's possibility, for the latter naively belongs to the province of language and propounds itself within it.
Writing and Difference, trans. Alan Bass, p. 4

3 We have no language – no syntax and no lexicon – which is foreign to this history; we can pronounce not a single destructive proposition which has not already had to slip into the form, the logic, and the implicit postulations of that which it seeks to contest.
Writing and Difference, trans. Alan Bass, p. 280

4 Only philosophy would seem to wield any authority over its own metaphorical productions. But, on the other hand . . . there is no properly philosophical category to qualify a certain number of tropes that have conditioned the so-called 'fundamental', 'structuring', 'original' philosophical oppositions: they are so many 'metaphors' that would constitute the rubrics of such a tropology, the words 'turn' or 'trope' or 'metaphor' being no exception to the rule. To permit oneself to overlook this *vigil* of philosophy, one would have to posit that the sense aimed at through

these figures is an essence rigorously independent of that which transports it, which is an already philosophical *thesis*, one might even say philosophy's *unique thesis*, the thesis which constitutes the concept of metaphor, the opposition of the proper and the nonproper, of essence and accident, of intuition and discourse, of thought and language, of the intelligible and the sensible.
Margins of Philosophy, trans. Alan Bass, p. 228

We do know that the verb 'to differ' (the Latin verb *differre*) has two   5
seemingly quite distinct meanings . . . But the word 'difference' (with an *e*) could never refer to differing as temporalizing or to difference as *polemos*. It is this loss of sense that the word differance (with an *a*) will have to schematically compensate for. Differance can refer to the whole complex of its meanings at once, for it is immediately and irreducibly multivalent . . .
Speech and Phenomena, trans. D. Allison, p. 136

Differance is what makes the movement of signification possible only if   6
each element that is said to be 'present', appearing on the stage of presence, is related to something other than itself but retains the mark of a past element and already lets itself be hollowed out by the mark of its relation to a future element.
Speech and Phenomena, trans. D. Allison, p. 142

We could thus take up all the coupled oppositions on which philosophy   7
is constructed, and from which our language lives, not in order to see opposition vanish but to see the emergence of a necessity such that one of the terms appears as the differance of the other, the other as 'differed' within the systematic ordering of the same (e.g., the intelligible as differing from the sensible, as sensible differed; the concept as differed-differing intuition, life as differing-differed matter; mind as differed-differing life; culture as differed-differing nature; and all the terms designating what is other than *physis* – *techne*, *nomos*, society, freedom, history, spirit, etc. – as *physis* differed or *physis* differing: *physis in differance*). It is out of the unfolding of this 'same' as differance that the sameness of difference and of repetition is presented in the eternal return.
Speech and Phenomena, trans. D. Allison, p. 148

The conscious text is . . . not a transcription, because there is no text   8
present elsewhere as an unconscious one to be transposed or transported.
. . . The unconscious text is already a weave of pure traces, differences in which meaning and force are united – a text nowhere present, consisting of archives which are *always already* transcriptions. Originary prints. Everything begins with reproduction.
Writing and Difference, trans. Alan Bass, p. 211

9 There are . . . two interpretations of interpretation, of structure, of sign, of play. The one seeks to decipher, dreams of deciphering a truth or an origin which escapes play and the order of the sign, and which lives the necessity of interpretation as an exile. The other, which is no longer turned toward the origin, affirms play and tries to pass beyond man and humanism, the name of man being the name of that being who, throughout the history of metaphysics or of ontotheology – in other words, throughout his entire history – has dreamed of full presence, the reassuring foundation, the origin and the end of play.
Writing and Difference, trans. Alan Bass, p. 292

10 All sentences of the type 'deconstruction is X' or 'deconstruction is not X', *a priori*, miss the point, which is to say that they are at least false. As you know, one of the principal things at stake in what is called in my texts 'deconstruction', is precisely the delimiting of ontology and above all of the third-person present indicative: S is P.
'Letter to a Japanese Friend', in *Derrida and Differance*, ed. D. Wood, p. 3

11 Who is more faithful to reason's call, who hears it with a keener ear . . . the one who offers questions in return and tries to think through the possibility of that summons, or the one who does not want to hear any question about the principle of reason?
'The Principle of Reason', *Diacritics*, XIX, p. 9

12 The passage beyond philosophy does not consist in turning the page of philosophy (which usually amounts to philosophizing badly), but in continuing to read philosophers *in a certain way*.
Writing and Difference, trans. Alan Bass, p. 288

13 To define philosophy as the attempt-to-say-the-hyperbole is to confess – and philosophy is perhaps this gigantic confession – that by virtue of the historical enunciation through which philosophy tranquilizes itself and excludes madness, philosophy also betrays itself (or betrays itself as thought), enters into a crisis and a forgetting of itself that are an essential and necessary period of its movement. I philosophize only in *terror*, but in the *confessed* terror of going mad. . . . But this crisis in which reason is madder than madness – for reason is non-meaning and oblivion – and in which madness is more rational than reason, for it is closer to the wellspring of sense, however silent or murmuring – this crisis has always begun and is interminable.
Writing and Difference, trans. Alan Bass, p. 62

RENÉ DESCARTES (1596–1650)

1 Good sense is the best distributed thing in the world: for everyone thinks himself so well endowed with it that even those who are the hardest to

please in everything else do not usually desire more of it than they possess. In this it is unlikely that everyone is mistaken. It indicates rather that the power of judging well and of distinguishing the true from the false – which is what we properly call 'good sense' or 'reason' – is naturally equal in all men.

Discourse, Philosophical Writings of Descartes, trans. J. Cottingham, R. Stoothoff and D. Murdoch, I, p. 111

At that time I was in Germany, where I had been called by the wars that   2
are not yet ended there. While I was returning to the army from the coronation of the Emperor, the onset of winter detained me in quarters where, finding no conversation to divert me and fortunately having no cares or passions to trouble me, I stayed all day shut up alone in a stove-heated room, where I was completely free to converse with myself about my own thoughts.

Discourse, op. cit., I, p. 116

The first [rule] was never to accept anything as true if I did not have   3
evident knowledge of its truth: that is, carefully to avoid precipitate conclusions and preconceptions, and to include nothing more in my judgements than what presented itself to my mind so clearly and so distinctly that I had no occasion to call it into doubt. The second, to divide each of the difficulties I examined into as many parts as possible and as may be required in order to resolve them better. The third, to direct my thoughts in an orderly manner, by beginning with the simplest and most easily known objects in order to ascend little by little, step by step, to knowledge of the most complex, and by supposing some order even among objects that have no natural order of precedence. And the last, throughout to make enumerations so complete, and reviews so comprehensive, that I could be sure of leaving nothing out.

Discourse, op. cit., I, p. 120

Those long chains composed of very simple and easy reasonings, which   4
geometers customarily use to arrive at their most difficult demonstrations, had given me occasion to suppose that all the things which come within the scope of human knowledge are interconnected in the same way.

Discourse, op. cit., I, p. 120

But immediately I noticed that while I was trying thus to think everything   5
false, it was necessary that I, who was thinking this, was something. And observing that this truth 'I am thinking, therefore I exist' was so firm and sure that all the most extravagant suppositions of the sceptics were incapable of shaking it, I decided that I could accept it without scruple as the first principle of the philosophy I was seeking.

Discourse, op. cit., I, p. 127

6   Next I examined attentively what I was. I saw that while I could pretend that I had no body and that there was no world and no place for me to be in, I could not for all that pretend that I did not exist. From this I knew I was a substance whose whole essence or nature is to think, and which does not require any place, or depend on any material thing, in order to exist. Accordingly this 'I' – that is, the soul by which I am what I am – is entirely distinct from the body, and indeed is easier to know than the body, and would not fail to be whatever it is, even if the body did not exist.
Discourse, op. cit., I, p. 127

7   I have noticed certain laws which God has so established in nature, and of which he has implanted such notions in our minds, that after adequate reflection we cannot doubt that they are exactly observed in everything which exists or occurs in the world.
Discourse, op. cit., I, p. 133

8   This will not seem at all strange to those who know how many kinds of automatons, or moving machines, the skill of man can construct with the use of very few parts, in comparison with the great multitude of bones, muscles, nerves, arteries, veins and all the other parts that are in the body of any animal. For they will regard this body as a machine which, having been made by the hand of God, is incomparably better ordered than any machine that can be devised by man, and contains in itself movements more wonderful than those in any such machine.
Discourse, op. cit., I, p. 140

9   Whereas reason is a universal instrument which can be used in all kinds of situations, bodily organs need some particular disposition for each particular action; hence it is for all practical purposes impossible for a machine to have enough different organs to make it act in all the contingencies of life in the way in which our reason makes us act. . . . This shows not merely that the beasts have less reason than men, but that they have no reason at all.
Discourse, op. cit., I, p. 140

10   When we know how much the beasts differ from us, we understand much better the arguments which prove that our soul is of a nature entirely independent of the body, and consequently that it is not bound to die with it. And since we cannot see any other causes which destroy the soul, we are naturally led to conclude that it is immortal.
Discourse, op. cit., I, p. 141

11   Aristotle's most enthusiastic contemporary followers . . . have an interest in my refraining from publishing the principles of the philosophy I use.

For my principles are so very simple and evident that in publishing them I should, as it were, be opening windows and admitting daylight into that cellar where they have gone down to fight.
Discourse, op. cit., I, p. 147

Some years ago I was struck by the large number of falsehoods that I had   **12**
accepted as true in my childhood, and by the highly doubtful nature of the whole edifice that I had subsequently based on them. I realized that it was necessary, once in the course of my life, to demolish everything completely and start again right from the foundations if I wanted to establish anything at all in the sciences that was stable and likely to last.
First Meditation, op. cit., II, p. 12

How often, asleep at night, am I convinced of just such familiar events –   **13**
that I am here in my dressing-gown, sitting by the fire – when in fact I am lying undressed in bed! . . . As I think about this more carefully, I see plainly that there are never any sure signs by means of which being awake can be distinguished from being asleep. The result is that I begin to feel dazed, and this very feeling only reinforces the notion that I may be asleep.
First Meditation, op. cit., II, p. 13

Since I sometimes believe that others go astray in cases where they think   **14**
they have the most perfect knowledge, how do I know that God has not brought it about that I go wrong every time I add two and three or count the sides of a square?
First Meditation, op. cit., II, p. 14

I will suppose therefore that not God, who is supremely good and the   **15**
source of truth, but rather some malicious demon of the utmost power and cunning has employed all his energies in order to deceive me. I shall think that the sky, the air, the earth, colours, shapes, sounds and all external things are merely the delusions of dreams which he has devised to ensnare my judgement.
First Meditation, op. cit., II, p. 15

But there is a deceiver of supreme power and cunning who is deliberately   **16**
and constantly deceiving me. In that case I too undoubtedly exist, if he is deceiving me; and let him deceive me as much as he can, he will never bring it about that I am nothing so long as I think that I am something. So after considering everything very thoroughly, I must finally conclude that this proposition, *I am, I exist,* is necessarily true whenever it is put forward by me or conceived in my mind.
Second Meditation, op. cit., II, p. 17

17 Thought: this alone is inseparable from me. I am, I exist – that is certain.
But for how long? For as long as I am thinking. For it could be that were I
totally to cease from thinking, I should totally cease to exist. At present I
am not admitting anything except what is necessarily true. I am, then, in
the strict sense only a thing that thinks; that is, I am a mind, or
intelligence, or intellect, or reason – words whose meaning I have been
ignorant of until now. But for all that I am a thing which is real and
which truly exists. But what kind of thing? As I have just said – a
thinking thing.
Second Meditation, op. cit., II, p. 18

18 But what then am I? A thing that thinks. What is that? A thing that
doubts, understands, affirms, denies, is willing, is unwilling, and also
imagines and has sensory perceptions.
Second Meditation, op. cit., II, p. 19

19 So what was it in the wax that I understood with such distinctness?
Evidently none of the features which I arrived at by means of the senses;
for whatever came under taste, smell, sight, touch or hearing has now
altered – yet the wax remains. . . . But what is this wax which is perceived
by the mind alone? It is of course the same wax which I see, which I
touch, which I picture in my imagination, in short the same wax which I
thought it to be from the start. And yet, and here is the point, the
perception I have of it is a case not of vision or touch or imagination –
nor has it ever been, despite previous appearances – but of purely mental
scrutiny.
Second Meditation, op. cit., II, p. 20

20 Now it is manifest by the natural light that there must be at least as much
[reality] in the efficient and total cause as in the effect of that cause. For
where, I ask, could the effect get its reality from, if not from the cause?
And how could the cause give it to the effect unless it possessed it?
Third Meditation, op. cit., II, p. 28

21 And indeed it is no surprise that God, in creating me, should have placed
this idea in me to be, as it were, the mark of the craftsman stamped on his
work – not that the mark need be anything distinct from the work itself.
But the mere fact that God created me is a very strong basis for believing
that I am somehow made in his image and likeness, and that I perceive
that likeness, which includes the idea of God, by the same faculty which
enables me to perceive myself.
Third Meditation, op. cit., II, p. 35

22 If, however, I simply refrain from making a judgement in cases where I
do not perceive the truth with sufficient clarity and distinctness, then it is
clear that I am behaving correctly and avoiding error. But if in such cases

I either affirm or deny, then I am not using my free will correctly. . . . In this incorrect use of free will may be found the privation which constitutes the essence of error.
Fourth Meditation, op. cit., II, p. 41

It is quite evident that existence can no more be separated from the   23
essence of God than the fact that its three angles equal two right angles can be separated from the idea of a triangle, or than the idea of a mountain can be separated from the idea of a valley. Hence it is just as much of a contradiction to think of God (that is, a supremely perfect being) lacking existence (that is, lacking a perfection), as it is to think of a mountain without a valley.
Fifth Meditation, op. cit., II, p. 46

On the one hand I have a clear and distinct idea of myself, in so far as I   24
am simply a thinking non-extended thing; and on the other hand I have a distinct idea of body, in so far as this is simply an extended, non-thinking thing. And accordingly, it is certain that I am really distinct from my body, and can exist without it.
Sixth Meditation, op. cit., II, p. 54

Nature likewise teaches me by these sensations of pain, hunger, thirst,   25
etc., that I am not only lodged in my body as a pilot in a vessel, but that I am besides so intimately conjoined, and as it were intermixed with it, that my mind and body compose a certain unity. For if this were not the case, I should not feel pain when my body is hurt, seeing I am merely a thinking thing, but should perceive the wound by the understanding alone, just as a pilot perceives by sight when any part of his vessel is damaged; and when my body has need of food or drink, I should have a clear knowledge of this, and not be made aware of it by the confused sensations of hunger and thirst: for, in truth, all these sensations of hunger, thirst, pain, etc., are nothing more than certain confused modes of thinking, arising from the union and apparent fusion of mind and body.
Sixth Meditation, trans. John Veitch (Everyman edn), p. 134

There is a great difference between the mind and the body, inasmuch as   26
the body is by its very nature always divisible, while the mind is utterly indivisible. For when I consider the mind, or myself in so far as I am merely a thinking thing, I am unable to distinguish any parts within myself; I understand myself to be something quite single and complete. . . . By contrast, there is no corporeal or extended thing that I can think of which in my thought I cannot easily divide into parts; and this very fact makes me understand that it is divisible.
Sixth Meditation, Philosophical Writings, trans. Cottingham et al., II, p. 59

27 Notwithstanding the immense goodness of God, the nature of man as a combination of mind and body is such that it is bound to mislead him from time to time.
Sixth Meditation, op. cit., II, p. 61

28 When we become aware that we are thinking things, this is a primary notion which is not derived by means of any syllogism. When someone says 'I am thinking, therefore I am, or I exist', he does not deduce existence from thought by means of a syllogism, but recognizes it as something self-evident by a simple intuition of the mind.
Second Set of Replies, op. cit., II, p. 100

29 When I said that we can know nothing for certain until we are aware that God exists, I expressly declared that I was speaking only of knowledge of those conclusions which can be recalled when we are no longer attending to the arguments by means of which we deduced them.
Second Set of Replies, op. cit., II, p. 100

30 Thought. I use this term to include everything that is within us in such a way that we are immediately aware of it. Thus all the operations of the will, the intellect, the imagination and the senses are thoughts.
Second Set of Replies, op. cit., II, p. 113

31 Idea. I understand this term to mean the form of any given thought, immediate perception of which makes me aware of the thought. Hence, whenever I express something in words, and understand what I am saying, this very fact makes it certain that there is within me an idea of what is signified by the words in question.
Second Set of Replies, op. cit., II, p. 113

32 As to the fact that there can be nothing in the mind, in so far as it is a thinking thing, of which it is not aware, this seems to me to be self-evident. For there is nothing that we can understand to be in the mind, regarded in this way, that is not a thought or dependent on a thought. . . . In view of this I do not doubt that the mind begins to think as soon as it is implanted in the body of an infant.
Fourth Set of Replies, op. cit., II, p. 171

33 The nature of matter, or body considered in general, consists not in its being something which is hard or heavy or coloured, or which affects the senses in any way, but simply in its being something which is extended in length, breadth and depth.
Principles of Philosophy, op. cit., I, p. 244

In the bodies we call 'coloured' the colours are nothing other than the various ways in which the bodies receive light and reflect it against our eyes.
Optics, op. cit., I, p. 153

34

If the sense of hearing transmitted to our mind the true image of its object then, instead of making us conceive the sound, it would have to make us conceive the motion of the parts of the air which is then vibrating against our ears. . . . Everyone knows that the ideas of tickling and of pain, which are formed in our mind on the occasion of our being touched by external bodies, bear no resemblance to these bodies. Suppose we pass a feather gently over the lips of a child who is falling asleep, and he feels himself being tickled. Do you think the idea of tickling which he conceives resembles anything present in this feather? . . . I see no reason which compels us to believe that what it is in objects that gives rise to the sensation of light is any more like this sensation than the actions of a feather are like a tickling sensation.
The World, op. cit., I, p. 82

35

There are two facts about the human soul on which depend all things we know of its nature. The first is that it thinks; the second is that it is united to the body and can act and be acted upon along with it. About the second I have said hardly anything.
Letter to Princess Elizabeth, 21 May 1643, *Descartes, Philosophical Letters*, trans. A. Kenny, p. 137

36

It does not seem to me that the human mind is capable of conceiving at the same time the distinction and the union between body and soul, because for this it is necessary to conceive them as a single thing and at the same time to conceive them as two things; and this is absurd. . . . Everyone feels that he is a single person with both body and thought so related by nature that the thought can move the body and feel the things which happen to it.
Letter to Princess Elizabeth, 28 June 1643, p. 142

37

JOHN DEWEY (1859–1952)

Take the case of questions about the past which are intrinsically unanswerable, at least by any means now at our command. What did Brutus eat for his morning meal the day he assassinated Caesar? There are those who call a statement on such a matter a judgment or proposition in a logical sense. It seems to me that at most it is but an esthetic fancy such as may figure in the pages of a historic novelist who wishes to add realistic detail to his romance. . . . Only when the past

1

event which is judged *is a going concern having effects still directly observable are judgment and knowledge possible.*
The Middle Works, 1899–1924, 13, ed. Jo Ann Boydston, p. 42

2 . . . the whole history of science, art and morals proves that the mind that appears *in* individuals is not as such individual mind. The former is in itself a system of belief, recognitions, and ignorances, of acceptances and rejections, of expectancies and appraisals of meanings which have been instituted under the influence of custom and tradition.
The Later Works, 1925–1953, 1, ed. Jo Ann Boydston, p. 170

3 To assume that anything can be known in isolation from its connections with other things is to identify knowing with merely having some object before perception or in feeling, and is thus to lose the key to the traits that distinguish an object as known. . . . The more connections and interactions we ascertain, the more we *know* the object in question.
The Later Works, 1925–1953, 4, ed. Jo Ann Boydston, p. 213

4 Equality does not signify that kind of mathematical or physical equivalence in virtue of which any one element may be substituted for another. It denotes effective regard for whatever is distinctive and unique in each, irrespective of physical and psychological inequalities. It [namely equality] is not a natural possession, but is a fruit of the community when its action is directed by its character as a community.
The Later Works, 1925–1953, 2, ed. Jo Ann Boydston, p. 329

5 . . . the error . . . has unfortunately invaded aesthetic theory – of supposing that the mere giving way to an impulsion, native or habitual, constitutes expression. Such an act is expressive not in itself but only in reflective interpretation on the part of some observer – as the nurse may interpret a sneeze as the sign of an impending cold. As far as the act itself is concerned, it is, if purely impulsive, just a boiling over. While there is no expression, unless there is urge from within outwards, the welling up must be clarified and ordered by taking into itself the values of prior experiences before it can be an act of expression. And these values are not called into play save through objects of the environment that offer resistance to the direct discharge of emotion and impulse. Emotional discharge is a necessary but not a sufficient condition of expression.
Art as Experience, p. 61

6 What is sometimes called an act of self-expression might better be termed one of self-exposure; it discloses character – or lack of character – to others. In itself, it is only a spewing forth.
Art as Experience, p. 62

7 Character is the interpenetration of habits.
Human Nature and Conduct, p. 38

GEORGE DICKIE (*b*. 1936)

A work of art in the classificatory sense is 1) an artifact 2) upon which some person or persons acting on behalf of a certain social institution (the artworld) has conferred the status of candidate for appreciation.
Aesthetics: An Introduction, p. 101

DENIS DIDEROT (1713–1784)

Examine the history of all nations and all centuries and you will always   1
find men subject to three codes: the code of nature, the code of society, and the code of religion; and constrained to infringe upon all three codes in succession, for these codes never were in harmony. The result of this has been that there never was in any country . . . a real man, a real citizen, or a real believer.
Supplément au Voyage de Bougainville, Oeuvres, II

The word *freedom* has no meaning; there are and there can be no free   2
beings. . . . One can no more conceive of a being behaving without a motive than of one arm of a scales moving up or down without the action of a weight.
Letter to Landois, 1756, *Correspondance*, ed. G. Roth and J. Varloot, I, p. 213

Religion is a support that in the end almost always ruins the edifice.   3
Quoted in *Encyclopedia of Philosophy*, ed. P. Edwards, II, p. 402

DIOGENES OF SINOPE (*c*.400 BC–325 BC)

I had rather be mad than delighted.

DIOGENES LAERTIUS (*fl*. 3rd century)

Either all that is held to be good by anyone must be said to be good or not all. But all cannot be said to be good since the same thing is held to be good by one person, for instance pleasure by Epicurus; and bad by another, Antisthenes. The consequence will be that the same thing is both good and bad. But if we do not admit that everything judged to be good by anyone is good, we shall have to distinguish between different opinions. This is impossible owing to the equal weight of arguments on both sides. Therefore that which is really good is unknowable.
Quoted in A. A. Long, *Hellenistic Philosophy*, p. 85

FRED DRETSKE (*b*. 1932)

In the beginning there was information. The word came later. The   1
transition was achieved by the development of organisms with the

capacity for selectively exploiting this information in order to survive and perpetuate their kind.
Knowledge and the Flow of Information, p. vii

2   Knowing is hard, but believing is no piece of cake either. . . . Anyone who believes something *thereby* exhibits the cognitive resources for knowing. There is . . . a gap between belief and knowledge, but it is not one that provides any comfort to the philosophical skeptic. If I may, for dramatic effect, overstate my case, if you can't know it, you can't believe it either.
'The Epistemology of Belief', *Synthèse* (1983), p. 4

3   Beliefs and desires, internal states with meaning, emerge *as* internal states with meaning, *as* mental states, in the learning process wherein is created the conditions that make possible the kind of behavior that internal states with meaning are needed to explain.
Dretske and his Critics, p. 202

PIERRE DUHEM (1861–1916)

1   A physical theory is not an explanation. It is a system of mathematical propositions, deduced from a small number of principles, which aim to represent as simply, as completely, and as exactly as possible a set of experimental laws.
The Aim and Structure of Physical Theory, trans. P. P. Wiener, p. 19

2   But, once again, what the physicist states as the result of an experiment is not the recital of observed facts, but the interpretation and the transposing of these facts into the ideal, abstract, symbolic world created by the theories he regards as established.
The Aim and Structure of Physical Theory, trans. P. P. Wiener, p. 159

3   Any physical law, being approximate, is at the mercy of the progress which, by increasing the precision of experiments, will make the degree of approximation of this law insufficient: the law is essentially provisional. The estimation of its value varies from one physicist to the next, depending on the means of observation at their disposal and the accuracy demanded by their investigations: the law is essentially relative.
The Aim and Structure of Physical Theory, trans. P. P. Wiener, p. 174

4   The laws of physics are therefore provisional in that the symbols they relate are too simple to represent reality completely.
The Aim and Structure of Physical Theory, trans. P. P. Wiener, p. 176

MICHAEL DUMMETT (*b.* 1925)

1   We are, after all, being asked to choose between two metaphors, two pictures. The platonist metaphor assimilates mathematical enquiry to the

investigations of the astronomer: mathematical structures, like galaxies, exist, independently of us, in a realm of reality which we do not inhabit but which those of us who have the skill are capable of observing and reporting on. The constructivist metaphor assimilates mathematical activity to that of the artificer fashioning objects in accordance with the creative power of his imagination. Neither metaphor seems, at first sight, especially apt, nor one more apt than the other: the activities of the mathematician seem strikingly unlike those either of the astronomer or of the artist. What basis can exist for deciding which metaphor is to be preferred?
Truth and Other Enigmas, p. 229

. . . we cannot . . . *first* decide the ontological status of mathematical 2
objects, and then, with that as premiss, deduce the character of mathematical truth or the correct model of meaning for mathematical statements. Rather, we have first to decide on the correct model of meaning – either an intuitionistic one, . . . or a platonistic one, . . . and then one or other picture of the metaphysical character of mathematical reality will force itself on us.
Truth and Other Enigmas, p. 229

Learning language involves learning what justifications are required for 3
sentences of different kinds. In its initial stages, it requires the child to respond to the assertions of others; but, later, also to question what may be asserted, even as a matter of common agreement. Language-learning, on Quine's model, could only be indoctrination, the mere instilling of a propensity to recognize certain sentences as true. If a child, who is still learning his language simultaneously with learning what the world is like, were not to be given an indication of the separate roles of convention and of empirical fact in determining what we say, then he would have to learn all commonly accepted truths involving any given word as part of an extended explanation of the meaning of the word, and could not take any part of this teaching as the communication of information. He could then never be started on the process of learning to question and criticize the things presented to him for acceptance, for he would have no way of knowing what revisions would be possible, or what significance any revision would have.
Frege: Philosophy of Language, p. 622

The conflict between realism and anti-realism is a conflict about the kind 4
of meaning possessed by statements of the disputed class. For the anti-realist, an understanding of such a statement consists in knowing what counts as evidence adequate for the assertion of the statement, and the truth of the statement can consist only in the existence of such evidence.

For the realist, the notion of truth plays a more crucial role in the manner of determining the meaning of the statement. To know the meaning of the statement is to know what it is for the statement to be true: we may in the first place derive such knowledge from learning what is counted as evidence for its truth, but in this case we do so in such a way as to have a conception of the statement's being true even in the absence of such evidence. For this reason, the dispute can arise only for classes of statements for which it is admitted on both sides that there may not exist evidence either for or against a given statement. It is this, therefore, which makes acceptance of the law of excluded middle for statements of a given class a crucial test for whether or not someone takes a realist view of statements of that class. The anti-realist cannot allow that the law of excluded middle is generally valid: the realist may, and characteristically will.

Truth and Other Enigmas, p. 155

5   Since the sentences in question are not in principle decidable, the observations which we imagine as being made are not ones of which we are capable: they are observations which might be made by some being with a different spatio-temporal perspective or whose observational and intellectual powers transcend our own, such powers being modelled on those which we possess, but extended by analogy. . . . but this . . . works only by imputing to us an apprehension of the way in which those sentences might be used by beings very unlike ourselves, and, in so doing, fails to answer the question how we come to be able to assign to our sentences a meaning which is dependent upon a use to which we are unable to put them.

'What is a Theory of Meaning', *in What is a Theory of Meaning?*, ed. G. Evans and J. McDowell, p. 98

ÉMILE DURKHEIM (1858–1917)

1   The first and most basic rule is *to consider social facts as things.*
The Rules of Sociological Method, trans. W. D. Halls, p. 60

2   Anomy, therefore, is a regular and specific factor in suicide in our modern societies; one of the springs from which the annual contingent feeds. So we have here a new type to distinguish from the others. It differs from them in its dependence, not on the way in which individuals are attached to society, but on how it regulates them. Egoistic suicide results from man's no longer finding a basis for existence in life; altruistic suicide, because this basis for existence appears to man situated beyond life itself. The third sort of suicide, the existence of which has just been shown, results from man's activity's lacking regulation and his conse-

quent sufferings. By virtue of its origin we shall assign this last variety the name of *anomic suicide*.
Suicide: A Study in Sociology, trans. J. A. Spaulding and G. Simpson, p. 258

The most barbarous and the most fantastic rites and the strangest myths   3
translate' some human need, some aspect of life, either individual or social. . . . In reality, then, there are no religions which are false. All are true in their own fashion; all answer, though in different ways, to the given conditions of human existence.
The Elementary Forms of Religious Life, trans. Joseph Ward Swain, p. 2

Kant postulates God, since without this hypothesis morality is unintelligible.   4
We postulate a society specifically distinct from individuals, since otherwise morality has no object and duty no roots.
Sociology and Philosophy, trans. D. F. Pocock, p. 51

GERALD DWORKIN (*b.* 1937)

Fitzjames Stephen, the nineteenth-century philosopher of law, stated that   1
'the criminal law stands to the passion of revenge in the same relation as marriage to the sexual appetite.' Unfortunately he died without specifying the relation. Conjecture: greater certainty and less variety.
'A Journal of Mathematical Ethics', *Philosophical Forum* (1982), p. 413

Preoccupation with autonomy . . . leads to the rejection of any use of   2
community and peer pressure to limit the liberty of individuals. This is often defended in the name of Mill – a defense that only charity could attribute to a misreading (since it is obvious that anyone who believes this cannot have read Mill at all).
The Theory and Practice of Autonomy, p. 163

RONALD DWORKIN (*b.* 1931)

Arguments of policy justify a political decision by showing that the   1
decision advances or protects some collective goal of the community as a whole. . . . Arguments of principle justify a political decision by showing that the decision respects or secures some individual or group right.
Taking Rights Seriously, p. 82

We need rights, as a distinct element in political theory, only when some   2
decision that injures some people nevertheless finds *prima facie* support in the claim that it will make the community as a whole better off on some plausible account of where the community's general welfare lies.
A Matter of Principle, p. 371

121

3 A political right is an individuated political aim. An individual has a right to some opportunity or resource or liberty if it counts in favor of a political decision that the decision is likely to advance or protect the state of affairs in which he enjoys the right, even when no other political aim is served and some political aim is disserved thereby, and counts against that decision that it will retard or endanger that state of affairs, even when some other political aim is thereby served.
Taking Rights Seriously, p. 91

4 Constitutional law can make no genuine advance until it isolates the problem of rights against the state and makes that problem part of its own agenda. That argues for a fusion of constitutional law and moral theory, a connection that, incredibly, has yet to take place.
Taking Rights Seriously, p. 149

5 The gravitational force of a precedent may be explained by appeal, not to the wisdom of enforcing enactments, but to the fairness of treating like cases alike. A precedent is the report of an earlier political decision; the very fact of that decision, as a piece of political history, provides some reason for deciding other cases in a similar way in the future.
Taking Rights Seriously, p. 113

6 What is shocking and wrong is not [Lord Devlin's] idea that the community's morality counts, but his idea of what counts as the community's morality.
Taking Rights Seriously, p. 255

E

𝕾𝕾𝕾𝕾𝕾𝕾

A. S. EDDINGTON (1882–1944)

I have settled down to the task of writing these lectures and have drawn up my chairs to my two tables. Two tables! Yes; there are duplicates of every object about me – two tables, two chairs, two pens. . . . One of them has been familiar to me from earliest years. . . . It has extension; it is comparatively permanent; it is coloured; above all it is *substantial*. . . . Table No. 2 is my scientific table. It . . . is mostly emptiness. Sparsely scattered in that emptiness are numerous electric charges rushing about with great speed; but their combined bulk amounts to less than a billionth of the bulk of the table itself. . . . I need not tell you that modern physics has by delicate test and remorseless logic assured me that my second, scientific table is the only one which is really there. . . . On the other hand I need not tell you that modern physics will never succeed in exorcising that first table – strange compound of external nature, mental imagery and inherited prejudice – which lies visible to my eyes and tangible to my grasp.
The Nature of the Physical World, pp. ix–xii

PAUL EDWARDS (*b.* 1923)

Heidegger's . . . *Introduction to Metaphysics* was written in 1935 and   1
compared to what was to follow it is a model of lucidity and concision. . . .
No matter what the starting point of a discussion is in the later works, whether it is a passage from Parmenides, a poem by Hölderlin or a quotation from Nietzsche, the end is always the same: Being '*west*', the Presence presences, Being conceals itself but reveals itself in its very concealment or the other way around, the Appropriation appropriates . . . and of course the basic fact that beings are not Being. In between we get bogus Greek and German etymologies which would prove nothing even if they were not bogus and all kinds of gimmicks including the constant breaking up of German words (what Sheehan had aptly dubbed 'hyphenitis') and the coinage of new words which remain totally

unexplained. As a result we are given huge masses of hideous gibberish which must be unique in the history of philosophy.
'Heidegger's Quest for Being', *Philosophy* (1989), p. 468

2   It is hardly necessary to add that the 'methodological difficulties' which so perplex Heidegger, Macquarrie, Boros and various other phenomenological explorers are altogether spurious. If one first misconceives death as the 'inner state' of the dead person whose dead body is 'the outward aspect' of his death or as the state in which the dead person has sustained the most terrible of all losses, then one is bound to be mystified. One will conclude that such a state is inaccessible to the outside observer who only perceives the 'living dying' and 'the outward aspect'; and it is of course equally inaccessible to the dead person who, being dead, is unable to attend to his deadness. However, there is no justification for thinking about death in this way. If, in agreement with the Heidegger who speaks of death as an utter nullity, we regard it as simply the total absence of experiences and behaviour, the 'methodological difficulties' instantly disappear. My deadness after I have died is no more incomprehensible to me than the fact that I did not exist before I was born or, if you like, before I was conceived. I understand perfectly well what is meant by the statement that I was not yet alive in 1800 although I was not then around to do any phenomenological exploring.
'Heidegger and Death as "Possibility"', *Mind* (1975), p. 566

3   . . . Heidegger will continue to fascinate those hungry for mysticism of the anaemic and purely verbal variety, the 'glossogonous metaphysics' of which his philosophy is such an outstanding example. . . . More sober and rational persons will continue to regard the whole Heidegger phenomenon as a grotesque aberration of the human mind.
'Heidegger's Quest for Being', *Philosophy* (1989), p. 469

ALBERT EINSTEIN (1879–1955)

1   Quantum mechanics is certainly imposing. But an inner voice tells me that it is not yet the real thing. The theory says a lot, but does not really bring us any closer to the secret of the 'old one'. I, at any rate, am convinced that *He* is not playing dice.
The Born–Einstein Letters, trans. I. Born, p. 91

2   I should not want to be forced into abandoning strict causality without defending it more strongly than I have so far. I find the idea quite intolerable that an electron exposed to radiation should choose *of its own free will*, not only its moment to jump off, but also its direction. In

that case I would rather be a cobbler, or even an employee in a gaming-house, than a physicist.
The Born–Einstein Letters, trans. I. Born

In so far as the statements of geometry speak about reality, they are not   3
certain, *and* in so far as they are certain, they do not speak about reality.
Geometry and Experience, p. 3

I think that only daring speculation can lead us further and not   4
accumulation of facts.
Albert Einstein, Michele Besso: Correspondance 1903–1955, p. 464

The whole of science is nothing more than a refinement of everyday   5
thinking.
'Physics and Reality', *Ideas and Opinions*, p. 290

One may say 'the eternal mystery of the world is its comprehensibility'.   6
'Physics and Reality', p. 292

T. S. ELIOT (1888–1965)

No poet, no artist of any art, has his complete meaning alone. His
significance, his appreciation is the appreciation of his relation to the
dead poets and artists. You cannot value him alone; you must set him,
for contrast and comparison, among the dead. I mean this as a principle
of aesthetic, not merely historical, criticism. The necessity that he shall
conform, that he shall cohere, is not one-sided; what happens when a
new work of art is created is something that happens simultaneously to
all the works of art which preceded it. The existing monuments form an
ideal order among themselves, which is modified by the introduction of
the new (the really new) work of art among them.
The Sacred Wood, p. 49

EMPEDOCLES (*c.*490–430 BC)

For I have already been once a boy and a girl, a bush and a bird and a   1
leaping journeying fish.
G. S. Kirk, J. E. Raven and M. Schofield, *The Pre-Socratic Philosophers*, p. 319

The blood around men's hearts is their thought.   2
The Pre-Socratic Philosophers, p. 311

FRIEDRICH ENGELS (1820–1895)

We have the certainty that matter remains eternally the same in all its   1
transformations, that none of its attributes can ever be lost, and
therefore, also, that with the same iron necessity that it will exterminate

on the earth its highest creation, the thinking mind, it must somewhere else and at another time again produce it.
Dialectics of Nature, p. 39

2   Freedom does not consist in the dream of independence from natural laws, but in the knowledge of these laws, and in the possibility this gives of systematically making them work towards definite ends. This holds good in relation both to the laws of external nature and to those which govern the bodily and mental existence of men themselves – two classes of laws which we can separate from each other at most only in thought but not in reality. Freedom of the will therefore means nothing but the capacity to make decisions with knowledge of the subject.
Anti-Dühring: Herr Eugen Dühring's Revolution in Science, p. 157

3   The *freer* a man's judgment is in relation to a definite question, the greater is the *necessity* with which the content of this judgment will be determined; while the uncertainty, founded on ignorance, which seems to make an arbitrary choice among many different and conflicting possible decisions, shows precisely by this that it is not free, that it is controlled by the very object it should itself control. Freedom therefore consists in the control over ourselves and over external nature, a control founded on knowledge of natural necessity; it is therefore necessarily a product of historical development.
Anti-Dühring: Herr Eugen Dühring's Revolution in Science, p. 40

4   . . . it was seen that *all* past history, with the exception of its primitive stages, was the history of class struggles; that these warring classes of society are always the products of the modes of production and of exchange – in a word, of the *economic* conditions of their time; that the economic structure of society always furnishes the real basis, starting from which we can alone work out the ultimate explanation of the whole superstructure of juridical and political institutions as well as of the religious, philosophical, and other ideas of a given historical period.
Socialism: Utopian and Scientific, trans. E. Aveling, *Basic Writings*, p. 88

5   The new tendency, which recognised that the key to the understanding of the whole history of society lies in the history of the development of labour, from the outset addressed itself by preference to the working class and here found the response which it neither sought nor expected from officially recognised science. The German working-class movement is the inheritor of German classical philosophy.
Ludwig Feuerbach and the End of Classical German Philosophy, p. 60

6   With the seizing of the means of production by society, production of commodities is done away with, and, simultaneously, the mastery of the

product over the producer. Anarchy in social production is replaced by plan-conforming, conscious organization. The struggle for individual existence disappears. . . . Only from that time will man himself, with full consciousness, make his own history – only from that time will the social causes set in movement by him have, in the main and in a constantly growing measure, the results intended by him. It is the ascent of man from the kingdom of necessity to the kingdom of freedom.
Anti-Dühring: Herr Eugen Dühring's Revolution in Science, p. 392

The proletariat seizes the public power, and by means of this transforms   7
the socialized means of production, slipping from the hands of the bourgeoisie, into public property. . . . Man, at last the master of his own form of social organization, becomes at the same time the lord over nature, his own master – free.
Socialism: Utopian and Scientific, trans. E. Aveling, *Basic Writings*, p. 111

The state was the official representative of society as a whole; the   8
gathering of it together into a visible embodiment. But it was this only in so far as it was the state of that class which itself represented, for the time being, society as a whole: in ancient times, the state of slave-owning citizens; in the Middle Ages, the feudal lords; in our own time, the bourgeoisie. When at last it becomes the real representative of the whole of society it renders itself unnecessary. As soon as there is no longer any social class to be held in subjection, as soon as class rule and the individual struggle for existence based upon our present anarchy in production, with the collisions and excesses arising from these, are removed, nothing more remains to be repressed, and a special repressive force, a state, is no longer necessary.
Socialism: Utopian and Scientific, trans. E. Aveling, p. 106

The society that will organize production on the basis of a free and equal   9
association of the producers will put the whole machinery of state where it will then belong: into the museum of antiquities, by the side of the spinning wheel and the bronze ax.
The Origin of the Family, Private Property and the State, *Basic Writings*, p. 394

When society, by taking possession of all means of production and using   10
them on a planned basis, has freed itself and all its members from the bondage in which they are now held by these means of production which they themselves have produced but which confront them as an irresistible alien force; when therefore man no longer merely proposes, but also disposes – only then will the last alien force which is still reflected in religion vanish; and with it will also vanish the religious reflection itself, for the simple reason that then there will be nothing left to reflect.
Anti-Dühring: Herr Eugen Dühring's Revolution in Science, p. 439

EPICURUS (341 BC–270 BC)

1   We must not make a pretence of doing philosophy, but really do it; for what we need is not the semblance of health but real health.
Quoted in A. A. Long, *Hellenistic Philosophy*, p. 14

2   We say that pleasure is the starting-point and the end of living blissfully. For we recognize pleasure as a good which is primary and innate. We begin every act of choice and avoidance from pleasure, and it is to pleasure that we return using our experience of pleasure as the criterion of every good thing.
Letter to Menoeceus, *Hellenistic Philosophy*, p. 62

3   When we say that pleasure is the goal we do not mean the pleasures of the dissipated and those which consist in the process of enjoyment . . . but freedom from pain in the body and from disturbance in the mind. For it is not drinking and continuous parties nor sexual pleasures nor the enjoyment of fish and other delicacies of a wealthy table which produce the pleasant life, but sober reasoning which searches out the causes of every act of choice and refusal and which banishes the opinions that give rise to the greatest mental confusion.
Letter to Menoeceus, *Hellenistic Philosophy*, p. 65

4   Moreover we must not suppose that the movement and turning of the heavenly bodies, their eclipses and risings and settings and similar movements are caused by some being which takes charge of them and which controls or will continue to control them, while simultaneously enjoying complete bliss and immortality. For occupation and supervision, anger and favour, are not consistent with sublime happiness. . . . Nor again must we suppose that those things which are merely an aggregate of fire possess sublime happiness and direct these (celestial) movements deliberately and voluntarily.
Letter to Herodotus, *Hellenistic Philosophy*, p. 41

5   That which is sublimely happy and immortal experiences no trouble itself nor does it inflict trouble on anything else, so that it is not affected by passion or partiality. Such things are found only in what is weak.
Principal Doctrines, i, *Hellenistic Philosophy*, p. 41

EUBULIDES (*fl.* 4th century BC)

I say: tell me, do you think that a single grain of wheat is a heap? Thereupon you say: no. Then I say: what do you say about 2 grains? For it is my purpose to ask you questions in succession, and if you do not admit that 2 grains are a heap then I shall ask you about 3 grains. Then I shall proceed to interrogate you further with respect to 4 grains, then 5

and 6 and 7 and 8, and you will assuredly say that none of these makes a heap.
Eubulides' paradox, quoted in Galen, *On Medical Experience*, s. 17, trans. R. Walzer

GARETH EVANS (1946–1980)

. . . there does not seem to me to be anything incoherent in the idea that it may be, for a subject, exactly as though he were thinking about a physical object (say) which he can see, and yet that, precisely because there is no physical object he is seeing, he may fail to have a thought of the kind he supposes himself to have. It is not part of this proposal that his mind is wholly vacant; images and words may clearly pass through it, and various ancillary thoughts may even occur to him. The claim is simply that there is a kind of thought we sometimes have, typically expressed in the form 'This G is F', and we may aim to have a thought of this kind when, in virtue of the absence of any appropriate object, there is no such thought to be had.
The Varieties of Reference, p. 45

F

𒑰𒑰𒑰𒑰𒑰𒑰

EMIL L. FACKENHEIM (b. 1916)

1 I believe that whereas no redeeming voice is heard at Auschwitz a
commanding voice is heard, and that it is being heard with increasing
clarity. *Jews are not permitted to hand Hitler posthumous victories.* Jews
are commanded to survive as Jews, lest their people perish. They are
commanded to remember the victims of Auschwitz, lest their memory
perish. They are forbidden to despair of God, lest Judaism perish. They
are forbidden to despair of the world as the domain of God, lest the
world be handed over to the forces of Auschwitz. For a Jew to break this
commandment would be to do the unthinkable – to respond to Hitler by
doing his work.
Quest for Past and Future, p. 20

2 Man can never escape the ideal or absolute; he can merely exchange one
absolute for another. He can ignore anything beyond his needs only by
making an ideal out of the fulfillment of his needs themselves. In short,
man cannot be an animal; he can only be a philosopher or anthropologist
who asserts that men are animals and ought to live like them. It is not
necessary to point out that this is just to set up another absolute.
Quest for Past and Future, p. 88

JOEL FEINBERG (b. 1936)

Wrongfully prolonged life can be as tragic an error as wrongfully
terminated life. In life's unhappier end games, there can be no 'safe side'
to err on.
Harm to Self, p. 370

JAMES F. FERRIER (1808–1864)

Every question in philosophy is the mask of another question; and all
these masking and masked questions require to be removed and laid
aside, until the ultimate but *truly first* question has been reached. Then,

but not till then, is it possible to decipher and resolve the outside mask, and all those below it, which come before us in the first instance.
Institutes of Metaphysic: The Theory of Knowing and Being, p. 8

LUDWIG FEUERBACH (1804–1872)

Religion is the dream of the human mind. But even in dreams we do not 1 find ourselves in emptiness or in heaven, but on earth in the realm of reality; we only see real things in the entrancing splendour of imagination and caprice instead of seeing them in the simple daylight of reality and necessity. Hence I do nothing more to religion – and to speculative philosophy and theology as well – than to open its eyes . . . i.e., I change the object as it is in the imagination into the object as it is in reality.
The Essence of Christianity, trans. G. Eliot, p. xxxix

He who says no more of me than that I am an atheist, says and knows 2 *nothing* of me. . . . I deny God. But that means for me that I deny the negation of man. In place of the illusory, fantastic, heavenly position of man which in actual life necessarily leads to the degradation of man, I substitute the tangible, actual and consequently also the political and social position of mankind.
Quoted in S. Hook, *From Hegel to Marx*, p. 222

I differ *toto coelo* from those philosophers who pluck out their eyes that 3 they may see better; for *my* thoughts I require the senses, especially sight; . . . I do not generate the object from the thought, but the thought from the object; and I hold *that* alone to be an object which has an existence beyond one's own brain.
The Essence of Christianity, trans. G. Eliot, p. xxxiv

How the philosophers have tortured themselves with the question as to 4 where and with what philosophy begins. . . . Oh, you fools, who open your mouth in sheer wonder over the enigmas of the beginning and yet fail to see that the open mouth is the entrance to the heart of nature: who fail to see that your teeth have long ago cracked the nut upon which you are still breaking your heads. We begin to think with that with which we begin to exist. The *principium essendi* is also the *principium cognoscendi*. But the beginning of existence is nourishment; therefore, food is the beginning of wisdom. The first condition of putting any thing into your head and heart, is to put something into your stomach.
Quoted in S. Hook, *From Hegel to Marx*, p. 269

The doctrine of foods is of great ethical and political significance. Food 5 becomes blood, blood becomes heart and brain, thought and mind stuff. Human fare is the foundation of human culture and thought. Would you

131

improve the people? Give them, instead of declamations against sin, better food. Man is what he eats.
Quoted in D. Hoffding, *History of Modern Philosophy*, II, p. 281

PAUL FEYERABEND (*b.* 1924)

1 The idea of a method that contains firm, unchanging, and absolutely binding principles for conducting the business of science meets considerable difficulty when confronted with the results of historical research. We find then, that there is not a single rule, however plausible, and however firmly grounded in epistemology, that is not violated at some time or other. It becomes evident that such violations are not accidental events, they are not results of insufficient knowledge or of inattention which might have been avoided. On the contrary, we see that they are necessary for progress.
Against Method, p. 21

2 The teaching of standards and their defence never consists merely in putting them before the mind of the student and making them as *clear* as possible. The standards are supposed to have maximal *causal efficacy* as well. This makes it very difficult indeed to distinguish between the *logical force* and the *material effect* of an argument. Just as a well-trained pet will obey his master no matter how great the confusion in which he finds himself, and no matter how urgent the need to adopt new patterns of behaviour, so in the very same way a well-trained rationalist will obey the mental image of *his* master, he will conform to the standards of argumentation he has learned, he will adhere to these standards no matter how great the confusion in which he finds himself, and he will be quite incapable of realizing that what he regards as the 'voice of reason' is but a *causal after-effect* of the training he has received. He will be quite unable to discover that the appeal to reason to which he succumbs so readily is nothing but a *political manoeuvre*.
Against Method, p. 25

3 It is clear, then, that the idea of a fixed method, or of a fixed theory of rationality, rests on too naive a view of man and his social surroundings. To those who look at the rich material provided by history, and who are not intent on impoverishing it in order to please their lower instincts, their craving for intellectual security in the form of clarity, precision, 'objectivity', 'truth', it will become clear that there is only *one* principle that can be defended under *all* stages of human development. It is the principle: *anything goes*.
Against Method, p. 27

There is not a single idea, however absurd and repulsive, that has not a 4
sensible aspect and there is not a single view, however plausible and
humanitarian, that does not encourage and then conceal our stupidity
and our criminal tendencies.
Three Dialogues on Knowledge, p. 50

J. G. FICHTE (1762–1814)

Attend to yourself: turn your attention away from everything that 1
surrounds you and towards your inner life; this is the first demand
that philosophy makes of its disciple. Our concern is not with anything that
lies outside you, but only with yourself.
Science of Knowledge, trans. P. Heath and J. Lachs, p. 6

What sort of philosophy one chooses depends, therefore, on what sort of 2
man one is; for a philosophical system is not a dead piece of furniture
that we can reject or accept as we wish; it is rather a thing animated by
the soul of the person who holds it. A person indolent by nature or dulled
and distorted by mental servitude, learned luxury, and vanity will never
raise himself to the level of idealism.
Science of Knowledge, trans. P. Heath and J. Lachs, p. 16

Our task is to *discover* the primordial, absolutely unconditioned first 3
principle of all human knowledge. . . . It is intended to express that *Act*
which does not and cannot appear among the empirical states of our
consciousness, but rather lies at the basis of all consciousness and alone
makes it possible.
Science of Knowledge, trans. P. Heath and J. Lachs, p. 93

The proposition *A is A* (or A = A, since that is the meaning of the logical 4
copula) is accepted by everyone and that without a moment's thought.
. . . *If* A is posited, it is naturally posited *as* A, as having the predicate
A. But this proposition still tells us nothing as to *whether* it actually is
posited, and hence whether it is posited with any particular predicate.
Yet the proposition 'I am I' is unconditionally and absolutely valid, since
it is equivalent to the proposition X^2; it is valid not merely in form but
also in content. In it the I is posited, not conditionally, but absolutely,
with the predicate of equivalence to itself; hence it really *is* posited, and
the proposition can also be expressed as *I am*. . . .
 Hence it is a ground of explanation of all the facts of empirical
consciousness, that prior to all postulation in the self, the self itself is
posited.
Science of Knowledge, trans. P. Heath and J. Lachs, p. 94

The self posits itself, and by virtue of this mere self-assertion it *exists*; and 5
conversely, the self *exists* and *posits* its own existence by virtue of merely

existing. It is at once the agent and the product of action; . . . and hence the 'I am' expresses an Act . . .
Science of Knowledge, trans. P. Heath and J. Lachs, p. 97

6 As surely as the absolute certainty of the proposition '⌐A is not equal to A' is unconditionally admitted among the facts of empirical consciousness, *so surely is a not-self opposed absolutely to the self.*
Science of Knowledge, trans. P. Heath and J. Lachs, p. 104

7 *In the self I oppose a divisible not-self to the divisible self.*
Science of Knowledge, trans. P. Heath and J. Lachs, p. 110

8 . . . an activity is posited in the not-self by means of a passivity in the self . . . The independent activity in question proceeds from the act of positing; but it is nonpositing that we actually arrive at: hence we may to that extent entitle the latter *an alienation.*
Science of Knowledge, trans. P. Heath and J. Lachs, p. 152

9 . . . we still have the contradiction . . .: if the self posits itself as determined, it is not determined by the not-self; if it is determined by the not-self, it does not posit itself as determined.
Science of Knowledge, trans. P. Heath and J. Lachs, p. 140

10 *The mediacy* of positing . . . is the law of consciousness: *no subject, no object; no object, no subject* . . .
Science of Knowledge, trans. P. Heath and J. Lachs, p. 168

11 . . . the very circumstance which threatened to destroy the possibility of a theory of human cognition becomes the sole condition under which such a theory can be established. . . . Prior to synthesis, the absolute opposites (the finite subjective and the infinite objective) are merely creatures of thought and ideal things, as the term has throughout been employed here. Once they become due for unification through the power of thought, and yet cannot be united, the wavering of the mind, which in this capacity is called imagination, confers reality upon them, since they thereby become intuitable: that is, they acquire reality in general . . .
Science of Knowledge, trans. P. Heath and J. Lachs, p. 201

12 Our doctrine here is therefore that all reality . . . is brought forth solely by the imagination.
Science of Knowledge, trans. P. Heath and J. Lachs, p. 202

HARTRY FIELD (*b.* 1946)

1 I do not propose to reinterpret any part of classical mathematics; instead I propose to show that the mathematics needed for application to the physical world does not include anything which even *prima facie*

contains references to (or quantifications over) abstract entities like numbers, functions, or sets. Towards that part of mathematics which does contain references to (or quantifications over) abstract entities – and this includes virtually all of conventional mathematics – I adopt a fictionalist attitude: that is I see no reason to regard this part of mathematics as *true*.
Science without Numbers, p. 1

Our accounts of primitive reference and of truth are not to be thought of as something that could be given by philosophical reflection prior to scientific information – on the contrary, it seems likely that such things as psychological models of human beings and investigations of neurophysiology will be very relevant to discovering the mechanisms involved in reference. *The reason why accounts of truth and primitive reference are needed is not to tack our conceptual scheme on to reality from the outside; the reason, rather, is that without such accounts our conceptual scheme breaks down from the inside.*
'Tarski's Theory of Truth', *Reference, Truth and Reality*, ed. M. Platts, p. 105

2

A fictionalist needn't (and shouldn't) deny that there is *some* sense in which '2 + 2 = 4' is true; but granting that it is true in some sense does not commit one to finding any interesting translation procedure that makes acceptable mathematical claims into true claims that don't postulate mathematical entities. Rather, the fictionalist can say that the sense in which '2 + 2 = 4' is true is pretty much the same as the sense in which 'Oliver Twist lived in London' is true: the latter is true only in the sense that it is true *according to a certain well-known story*, and the former is true only in that it is true *according to standard mathematics*.
Realism, Mathematics and Modality, pp. 2–3

3

J. N. FINDLAY (1903–1987)

But there are other frames of mind, to which we shouldn't deny the name 'religious', which acquiesce quite readily in the non-existence of their objects. (This non-existence might, in fact, be taken to be the 'real meaning' of saying that religious objects and realities are 'not of this world'.) In such frames of mind we give ourselves over unconditionally and gladly to the task of indefinite approach toward a certain imaginary focus where nothing actually is, and we find this task sufficiently inspiring and satisfying without demanding (absurdly) that there should be something actual at that limit.
'Can God's Existence be Disproved', *New Essays in Philosophical Theology*, p. 56

1

2 We are not, fortunately, in the position of David Hume, that perfect specimen of the pure observer, who in the neurotic seclusion of his own bedroom in France, passively waited for metaphysical visits from his own Ego, the efficacy of causes etc., etc., visits which to an observer so minded never did or could happen.
The Discipline of the Cave, p. 23

T. L. FINE

Too keen an eye for pattern will find it anywhere.
Theories of Probability

JOHN FINNIS (*b.* 1940)

1 . . . law can only be fully understood as it is understood by those who accept it in the way that gives it its most specific mode of operation as a type of reason for acting, viz. those who accept it as a specific type of moral reason for acting. Once one abandons . . . the bad man's concerns as the criterion of relevance in legal philosophy, there proves to be little reason for stopping short of accepting the morally concerned man's concerns as that criterion. . . . Analytical jurisprudence rejoins the programme of philosophizing about human affairs . . .
'Revolutions and Continuity of Law', *Oxford Essays in Jurisprudence*, ed. A. Simpson, p. 74

2 Now besides life, knowledge, play, aesthetic experience, friendship, practical reasonableness, and religion, there are countless objectives and forms of good. But I suggest that these other objectives and forms of good will be found, on analysis, to be ways or combinations of ways of pursuing (not always sensibly) and realizing (not always successfully) one of the seven basic forms of good, or some combination of them.
Natural Law and Natural Rights, p. 90

JERRY FODOR (*b.* 1935)

1 It is a curiosity of the philosophical temperament, this passion for radical solutions. Do you feel a little twinge in your epistemology? Absolute scepticism is the thing to try. Has the logic of confirmation got you down? Probably physics is a fiction. Worried about individuating objects? Don't let anything in but sets. Nobody has yet suggested that the way out of the Liar paradox is to give up talking, but I expect it's only a matter of time. Apparently the rule is: if aspirin doesn't work, try cutting off your head.
'Banish disContent', *Mind and Cognition*, ed. W. Lycan, p. 420

136

One is tempted to transcendental argument: what Kant said to Hume 2
about physical objects holds, mutatis mutandis, for the propositional
attitudes; we can't give them up *because we don't know how to.*
Psychosemantics, p. 9

Reference to a mousetrap may figure largely in your story about what 3
happened to the mouse. And the property of being a mousetrap may be
functionally (hence non-mechanistically) defined. But functional stories
of that kind do not advert to mousetraps with propositional content; to
mousetraps-that-P. Whereas, stories about the causal consequences of
beliefs *do* advert to objects that have propositional content, at least
according to our pretheoretical intuitions about beliefs.
Representations, p. 24

If mental processes are formal, then they have access only to the formal 4
properties of such representations of the environment as the senses
provide. Hence, they have no access to the *semantic* properties of such
representations, including the property of being true, of having referents,
or indeed, the property of being representations of *the environment.* . . .
Only a *naturalistic* psychology will do to specify these facts, because here
we are explicitly in the realm of organism/environment transactions. We
are on the verge of a bland and ecumenical conclusion: that there is room
both for a computational psychology – viewed as a theory of formal
processes defined over mental representations – *and* a naturalistic
psychology, viewed as a theory of the (presumably causal) relations
between representations and the world which fix the semantic interpretations of the former.
Representations, p. 231

. . . acceptance of the computational theory of the mind leads to a sort of 5
methodological solipsism as a part of the research strategy of contemporary cognitive psychology. . . . My point, then, is *of course* not that
solipsism is true; it's just that truth, reference and the rest of the semantic
notions aren't psychological categories. What they are: they're modes of
Dasein. I don't know what *Dasein* is, but I'm sure that there's lots of it
around, and I'm sure that you and I and Cincinnati have all got it. What
more do you want?
Representations, pp. 232, 253

PHILIPPA FOOT (*b.* 1920)

. . . there is no describing the evaluative meaning of 'good', evaluation, 1
commending, or anything of the sort, without fixing the object to which
they are supposed to be attached. Without first laying hands on the
proper object of such things as evaluation, we shall catch in our net either

something quite different such as accepting an order or making a resolution, or else nothing at all.

'Moral Beliefs', *Proceedings of the Aristotelian Society* (1958), p. 112

2   . . . anyone who thinks it would be easy to describe a new virtue connected with clasping the hands three times in an hour should just try. I think he will find that he has to cheat, and suppose that in the community concerned the clasping of hands has been given some special significance, or is thought to have some special effect. The difficulty is obviously connected with the fact that without a special background there is no possibility of answering the question 'What's the point?' It is no good saying that there would be a point in doing the action because the action was a morally good action: the question is how it can be given any such description if we cannot first speak about the point.

'Moral Beliefs', p. 120

3   How exactly the concepts of harm, advantage, benefit, importance, etc., are related to the different moral concepts, such as rightness, obligation, goodness, duty and virtue, is something that needs the most patient investigation, but that they are so related seems undeniable, and it follows that a man cannot make his own personal decision about the considerations which are to count as evidence in morals.

'Moral Arguments', *Mind* (1958), p. 510

4   Is it true, however, to say that justice is not something a man needs in his dealings with his fellows, supposing only that he be strong? Those who think that he can get on perfectly well without being just should be asked to say exactly how such a man is supposed to live. . . . If he lets even a few people see his true attitude he must guard himself against them; if he lets no one into the secret he must always be careful in case the least spontaneity betray him. . . .

   The reason why it seems to some people so impossibly difficult to show that justice is more profitable than injustice is that they consider in isolation particular just acts.

'Moral Beliefs', *Proceedings of the Aristotelian Society* (1958), p. 128

5   Outside moral philosophy we would not think of the cool and prudent, though wicked, man as specifically irrational in his conduct; outside philosophy we also know that there is nothing one can do with a ruthless amoral man except to prevent him from doing too much damage. To say that since his conduct is immoral we can tell him of some reason why he should change it, or that he necessarily has reason to alter his ways, seems yet another case of keeping up a pretence. We speak as if there were an authority in the background to guarantee that wickedness is necessarily foolishness, though the 'binding force' of morality is

supposed to be independent of such an appeal. Would it not be more honest either to change the language or else to recognize that the 'should' of moral judgment is sometimes merely an instrument by which we (for our own very good reasons) try to impose a rule of conduct even on the uncaring man?

'Morality and Art', *Proceedings of the British Academy* (1970), p. 143

Williams thought that the cognitivist must believe that when two ought 6
statements conflict one is necessarily false, and would therefore find himself unable to explain the fact of regret for an unfulfilled obligation such as a promise not kept. It does not seem to have occurred to Williams that his opponent could simply *allow* the truth of 'I ought to do *a*' and 'I ought to do ⌐ *a*' and other consistent propositions whose consistency is easily explicable on a 'because of this . . . , but because of that . . .' basis. And the reason it did not occur to him was, it seems, that he thought the cognitivist was committed to a comparison between moral conflicts and conflicts of belief. But why should the cognitivist ever accept such a comparison? Beliefs that conflict are beliefs that *contradict* each other, either directly or in the context of other beliefs. But the whole point about statements about what is desirable and what ought to be done is (for both) that there is a class of statements which *conflict*, in that they give conflicting guidance for action, but which nevertheless can *both be true*. The strange thing about what Williams wrote in 'Ethical Consistency' is that a great deal of it seems designed to show exactly this: that moral conflict does not imply 'contradiction'. It is as if he himself showed the cognitivist how to avoid the very error he thinks the cognitivist must make.

'Moral Realism and Moral Dilemma', *Journal of Philosophy* (1983)

JOHN FOSTER (*b.* 1941)

Even among philosophers the term 'idealism' is used in a variety of different senses to denote a variety of different positions. In what follows, I shall be concerned with three kinds of idealism, which can be expressed, summarily, by the following three claims:

1) Ultimate contingent reality is wholly mental.
2) Ultimate contingent reality is wholly non-physical.
3) The physical world is the logical product of facts about human sense-experience.

My defence of idealism will be primarily a defence of claims (2) and (3), though I shall also try to show the plausibility of (1).

The Case for Idealism, p. 3

MICHEL FOUCAULT (1926–1984)

1   . . . one's point of reference should not be to the great model of language (*langue*) and signs, but to that of war and battle. The history which bears and determines us has the form of a war rather than that of a language: relations of power, not relations of meaning. History has no 'meaning', though this is not to say that it is absurd or incoherent. . . . 'Dialectic' is a way of evading the always open and hazardous reality of conflict by reducing it to a Hegelian skeleton, and 'semiology' is a way of avoiding its violent, bloody and lethal character by reducing it to the calm Platonic form of language and dialogue.
Power/Knowledge, trans. C. Gordon, L. Marshall, J. Mepham, K. Soper, p. 114

2   Psychiatric internment, the mental normalisation of individuals, and penal institutions have no doubt a fairly limited importance if one is only looking for their economic significance. On the other hand, they are undoubtedly essential to the general functioning of the wheels of power.
Power/Knowledge, trans. C. Gordon, L. Marshall, J. Mepham, K. Soper, p. 116

3   . . . what I would call genealogy . . . is a form of history which can account for the constitution of knowledges, discourses, domains of objects etc., without having to make reference to a subject which is either transcendental in relation to the field of events or runs in its empty sameness throughout the course of history.
Power/Knowledge, trans. C. Gordon, L. Marshall, J. Mepham, K. Soper, p. 117

4   If power were never anything but repressive, if it never did anything but to say no, do you really think one would be brought to obey it? What makes power hold good, what makes it accepted, is simply the fact that it doesn't only weigh on us as a force that says no, but that it traverses and produces things, it induces pleasure, forms knowledge, produces discourse. It needs to be considered as a productive network which runs through the whole social body, much more than as a negative instance whose function is repression.
Power/Knowledge, trans. C. Gordon, L. Marshall, J. Mepham, K. Soper, p. 119

5   . . . the institution of monarchy . . . developed during the Middle Ages against the backdrop of the previously endemic struggles between feudal power agencies. The monarchy presented itself as a referee, a power capable of putting an end to war, violence and pillage and saying no to these struggles and private feuds. . . . political theory has never ceased to be obsessed with the person of the sovereign. Such theories still continue today to busy themselves with the problem of sovereignty. What we need, however, is a political philosophy that isn't erected around the problem of sovereignty, nor therefore around the problems of law and

prohibition. We need to cut off the King's head: in political theory that has still to be done.

Power/Knowledge, trans. C. Gordon, L. Marshall, J. Mepham, K. Soper, p. 121

I would say that the State consists in the codification of a whole number 6
of power relations which render its functioning possible, and that Revolution is a different type of codification of the same relations. This implies that there are many different kinds of revolution, roughly speaking as many kinds as there are possible subversive recodifications of power relations, and further, that one can perfectly well conceive of revolutions which form the basis for the functioning of the State.

Power/Knowledge, trans. C. Gordon, L. Marshall, J. Mepham, K. Soper, p. 122

As soon as one endeavours to detach power with its techniques and 7
procedures from the form of law within which it has been theoretically confined up until now, one is driven to ask the basic question: isn't power simply a form of warlike domination? Shouldn't one therefore conceive all problems of power in terms of relations of war? Isn't power a sort of generalised war which assumes at particular moments the forms of peace and the State? Peace would then be a form of war, and the State a means of waging it.

Power/Knowledge, trans. C. Gordon, L. Marshall, J. Mepham, K. Soper, p. 123

I believe that the political significance of the problem of sex is due to the 8
fact that sex is located at the point of intersection of the discipline of the body and the control of the population.

Power/Knowledge, trans. C. Gordon, L. Marshall, J. Mepham, K. Soper, p. 125

We are at the present experiencing the disappearance of the figure of the 9
'great writer'.

Power/Knowledge, trans. C. Gordon, L. Marshall, J. Mepham, K. Soper, p. 129

. . . truth isn't outside power, or lacking in power: contrary to a myth 10
whose history and functions would repay further study, truth isn't the reward of free spirits, the child of protracted solitude, nor the privilege of those who have succeeded in liberating themselves. Truth is a thing of this world: it is produced only by virtue of multiple forms of constraint. And it induces regular effects of power. Each society has its regime of truth, its 'general politics' of truth: that is, the types of discourse which it accepts and makes function as true; the mechanisms and instances which enable one to distinguish true and false statements, the means by which each is sanctioned; the techniques and procedures accorded value in the acquisition of truth; the status of those who are charged with saying what counts as true.

Power/Knowledge, trans. C. Gordon, L. Marshall, J. Mepham, K. Soper, p. 131

MICHAEL FRAYN (b. 1933)

(According to some sympathisers, the reason why drivers on the motorways failed to slow down in thick fog recently, and so crashed into each other in multiple collisions of up to thirty vehicles, was simply because the authorities had failed to provide illuminated signs explaining that the fog was fog. This is a situation on which Wittgenstein made one or two helpful remarks in a previously unpublished section of 'Philosophical Investigations'.)

694. Someone says, with every sign of bewilderment (wrinkled forehead, widened eyes, an anxious set to the mouth): 'I do not know there is fog on the road unless it is accompanied by an illuminated sign saying "fog".'

When we hear this, we feel dizzy. We experience the sort of sensations that go with meeting an old friend one believed was dead. I want to say: 'But *this* is the man philosophers are always telling us about! This is the man who does not understand – the man who goes on asking for explanations after everything has been explained!'

(A sort of Socratic Oliver Twist. Compare the feelings one would have on meeting Oliver Twist in the flesh. 'And now I want you to meet Oliver Twist.' – 'But . . . !') . . .

699. *Now* the feeling of dizziness vanishes. We feel we want to say: 'Now it seems more like a dull throbbing behind the eyes.'

700. Of course, one is familiar with the experience of seeing something ambiguous. 'Now it is the Taj Mahal – now it is fog.' And one can imagine having a procedural rule that anything ambiguous should be treated as the Taj Mahal unless we see that it is labelled 'fog'.

701. The motorist replies: 'What sort of rule is this? Surely the best guarantee I can have that the fog is fog is if I fail to see the sign saying "fog" because of the fog.' – One can imagine uses for the rule. For example, to lure people to their deaths. . . .

708. If a lion could speak, it would not understand itself.

'Fog-like Sensations', *The Original Michael Frayn*, ed. J. Fenton, p. 67

GOTTLOB FREGE (1848–1925)

1   Now it is plausible to connect with a sign (name, word combination, expression) not only the designated object, which may be called the nominatum of the sign, but also the sense (connotation, meaning) of the sign, in which is contained the manner and context of presentation. Accordingly, in our examples the *nominata* of the expressions 'the point of intersection of a and b' and 'the point of intersection of b and c' would

be the same; – not their senses. The nominata of 'evening star' and 'morning star' are the same but not their senses.

'On Sense and Nominatum', *Readings in Philosophical Analysis*, ed. H. Feigl and W. Sellars, p. 86

The meaning of a proper name is the object itself which we designate by 2 using it; the idea which we have in that case is wholly subjective; in between lies the sense, which is indeed no longer subjective like the idea, but is yet not the object itself. The following analogy will perhaps clarify these relationships. Somebody observes the Moon through a telescope. I compare the Moon itself to the meaning; it is the object of the observation, mediated by the real image projected by the object glass in the interior of the telescope, and by the retinal image of the observer. The former I compare to the sense, the latter is like the idea or experience. The optical image in the telescope is indeed one-sided and dependent upon the stand point of observation, but it is still objective, in as much as it can be used by several observers.

'On Sense and Meaning', *Philosophical Writings*, ed. P. Geach and M. Black, p. 60

Can it not be laid down that truth exists when there is correspondence in 3 a certain respect? But in which? For what would we then have to do to decide whether something were true? We should have to inquire whether it were true that an idea and a reality, perhaps, corresponded in the laid down respect. And then we should be confronted by a question of the same kind and the game could begin again. So the attempt to explain truth as correspondence collapses. And every other attempt to define truth collapses too. For in a definition certain characteristics would have to be stated. And in application to any particular case the question would always arise whether it were true that the characteristics were present. So one goes round in a circle. Consequently, it is probable that the content of the word 'true' is unique and indefinable.

'The Thought: A Logical Inquiry', *Philosophical Logic*, ed. P. Strawson, p. 19

Now these distinctions between a priori and a posteriori, synthetic and 4 analytic, concern, as I see it, not the content of the judgement but the justification for making the judgement. . . . The problem becomes, in fact, that of finding the proof of the proposition, and of following it up right back to the primitive truths. If, in carrying out this process, we come only on general logical laws and on definitions, then the truth is an analytic one, bearing in mind that we must take account also of all propositions upon which the admissibility of any of the definitions depends.

The Foundations of Arithmetic, trans. J. L. Austin, p. 3

5   We deal in arithmetic with objects that do not become known to us as something alien from without, through the intermediary of the senses, but that are given immediately to our reason, which can fully see through them as its very own.

And yet, or rather just because of that, these objects are not subjective figments of the imagination. There is nothing more objective than the laws of arithmetic.

Die Grundlagen der Arithmetik, p. 115, trans. John Worrall

6   I hope I may claim in the present work to have made it probable that the laws of arithmetic are analytic judgements and consequently a priori. Arithmetic thus becomes simply a development of logic, and every proposition of arithmetic a law of logic, albeit a derivative one. To apply arithmetic in the physical sciences is to bring logic to bear on observed facts; calculation becomes deduction.

The Foundations of Arithmetic, trans. J. L. Austin, p. 99

7   In my *Grundlagen der Arithmetik*, I sought to make it plausible that arithmetic is a branch of logic and needs to borrow no evidential basis at all from either experience or intuition. In the present book this will now be proved by deriving, using only logical means, the simplest laws of numbers. But for this to be convincing, considerably higher demands must be placed on the proof procedure than is customary in arithmetic.

Grundgesetze der Arithmetik, I, p. 1, trans. John Worrall

8   Your discovery of the contradiction caused me the greatest surprise and, I would almost say, consternation, since it has shaken the basis on which I intended to build arithmetic. . . . It is all the more serious since, with the loss of my rule V, not only the foundations of my arithmetic, but also the sole possible foundations of arithmetic, seem to vanish.

Letter to Bertrand Russell, *From Frege to Godel*, ed. J. van Heijenoort, p. 127

9   . . . thoughts are neither things of the outer world nor ideas. A third realm must be recognised. What belongs to this corresponds with ideas, in that it cannot be perceived by the senses, but with things, in that it needs no bearer to the contents of whose consciousness to belong. Thus the thought, for example, which we express in the Pythagorean Theorem is timelessly true, true independently of whether anyone takes it to be true. It needs no bearer. It is not true for the first time when it is discovered, but is like a planet which, already before anyone has seen it, has been in interaction with other planets.

'The Thought: A Logical Inquiry', *Philosophical Logic*, ed. P. Strawson, p. 29

SIGMUND FREUD (1856–1939)

Probably but very few people have realized the momentous significance **1**
for science and life of the recognition of unconscious mental processes. It
was not psycho-analysis, however, let us hasten to add, which took this
first step. There are renowned names among the philosophers who may
be cited as its predecessors, above all the great thinker Schopenhauer,
whose unconscious 'Will' is equivalent to the instincts in the mind as seen
by psycho-analysis. It was this same thinker, moreover, who in words of
unforgettable impressiveness admonished mankind of the importance of
their sexual craving, still so depreciated. Psycho-analysis has only this to
its credit, that it has not affirmed these two propositions that are so
wounding to narcissism on an abstract basis . . .
'One of the Difficulties of Psychoanalysis', *Collected Papers*, ed. J. Riviere, IV,
p. 355

In psycho-analysis there is no choice for us but to assert that mental **2**
processes are in themselves unconscious, and to liken the perception of
them by means of consciousness to the perception of the external world
by means of the sense-organs. . . . Just as Kant warned us not to overlook
the fact that our perceptions are subjectively conditioned and must not be
regarded as identical with what is perceived though unknowable, so
psycho-analysis warns us not to equate perceptions by means of
consciousness with the unconscious mental processes which are their
object. Like the physical, the psychical is not necessarily in reality what it
appears to us to be.
The Essentials of Psychoanalysis, ed. A. Freud, p. 147

. . . the ego has voluntary movement at its command. It has the task of **3**
self-preservation. . . . As regards *internal* events, in relation to the id, it
performs that task by gaining control over the demands of the instincts,
by deciding whether they are to be allowed satisfaction, by postponing
that satisfaction to times and circumstances favourable in the external
world or by suppressing their excitations entirely. It is guided in its
activity by consideration of the tensions produced by stimuli, whether
these tensions are present in it or introduced into it.
An Outline of Psychoanalysis, *Works*, trans. James Strachey, XXIII, p. 144

. . . now that we have embarked upon the analysis of the ego we can give **4**
an answer to all those whose moral sense has been shocked and who have
complained that there must surely be a higher nature in man: 'Very true',
we can say, 'and here we have that higher nature, in this ego ideal or
super-ego, the representative of our relation to our parents. When we

were little children we knew these higher natures, we admired them and feared them; and later we took them into ourselves.'
The Essentials of Psychoanalysis, ed. A. Freud, p. 459

5 You will not expect me to have much to tell you that is new about the id apart from its new name. It is the dark, inaccessible part of our personality; what little we know of it we have learnt from our study of the dream-work and of the construction of neurotic symptoms, and most of that is of a negative character and can be described only as a contrast to the ego. We approach the id with analogies: we call it a chaos, a cauldron full of seething excitations. We picture it as being open at its end to somatic influences, and as there taking up into itself instinctual needs which find their psychical expression in it, but we cannot say in what substratum. It is filled with energy reaching it from the instincts, but it has no organization, produces no collective will, but only a striving to bring about the satisfaction of the instinctual needs subject to the observance of the pleasure principle.
The Essentials of Psychoanalysis, p. 498

6 The logical laws of thought do not apply in the id, and this is true above all of the law of contradiction. Contrary impulses exist side by side, without cancelling each other out or diminishing each other: at the most they may converge to form compromises under the dominating economic pressure towards the discharge of energy. . . . There is nothing in the id that corresponds to the idea of time. . . . Wishful impulses which have never passed beyond the id, but impressions, too, which have been sunk into the id by repression, are virtually immortal; after the passage of decades they behave as though they had just occurred.
The Essentials of Psychoanalysis, p. 499

7 We are warned by a proverb against serving two masters at the same time. The poor ego has things even worse: it serves three masters and does what it can to bring their claims and demands into harmony with one another. . . . Its three tyrannical masters are the external world, the super-ego and the id.
New Introductory Lectures on Psychoanalysis, trans. James Strachey, p. 77

8 It is easy to imagine . . . that certain mystical practices may succeed in upsetting the normal relations between the different regions of the mind, so that, for instance, perception may be able to grasp happenings in the depths of the ego and in the id which were otherwise inaccessible to it. It may safely be doubted, however, whether this road will lead us to the ultimate truths from which salvation is to be expected. Nevertheless it may be admitted that the therapeutic efforts of psycho-analysis have chosen a similar line of approach. Its intention is, indeed, to strengthen

the ego, to make it more independent of the super-ego, to widen its field of perception and enlarge its organization, so that it can appropriate fresh portions of the id. Where id was, there ego shall be. It is a work of culture – not unlike the draining of the Zuider Zee.
New Introductory Lectures on Psychoanalysis, trans. James Strachey, p. 79

It may be difficult, too, for many of us, to abandon the belief that there is   **9** an instinct towards perfection at work in human beings, which has brought them to their present high level of intellectual achievement and ethical sublimation and which may be expected to watch over their development into supermen. I have no faith, however, in the existence of any such internal instinct and I cannot see how this benevolent illusion is to be preserved. The present development of human beings requires, as it seems to me, no different explanation from that of animals. What appears in a minority of human individuals as an untiring impulsion towards further perfection can easily be understood as a result of the instinctual repression upon which is based all that is most precious in human civilization.
The Essentials of Psychoanalysis, ed. A. Freud, p. 249

Historians of civilization appear to be at one in assuming that powerful   **10** components are acquired for every kind of cultural achievement by this diversion of sexual instinctual forces from sexual aims and their direction to new ones – a process which deserves the name of 'sublimation'.
Three Essays on the Theory of Sexuality, Works, trans. James Strachey, VII, p. 178

... it often seems that the poet's derisive comment is not unjustified when   **11** he says of the philosopher: 'With his nightcaps and the tatters of his dressing-gown he patches up the gaps in the structure of the universe.'
New Introductory Lectures on Psychoanalysis, trans. James Strachey, p. 161

G

𑀤𑀤𑀤𑀤𑀤

DAVID P. GAUTHIER (b. 1932)

The individual who needs a reason for being moral which is not itself a moral reason cannot have it. There is nothing surprising about this; it would be much more surprising if such reasons could be found. For it is more than apparently paradoxical to suppose that considerations of advantage could ever of themselves justify accepting a real disadvantage.
'Morality and Advantage', *Philosophical Review* (1967), p. 461

PETER GEACH (b. 1916)

1 Only since Descartes has the main problem become: 'How is *cogitatio* related to bodily processes?' ('*cogitatio*' covering, for him, everything 'in the mind', from a toothache to a metaphysical meditation); the old problem was rather: 'How can a being that thinks and judges and decides *also* have sensuous experiences?' It was 'intellectual' acts like judgment, not just *anything* that would now be called 'consciousness', which seemed to Aquinas to be wholly incommensurable with events in the physical world; for him, the 'unbridgeable gulf' was at a different place. The usefulness of historical knowledge in philosophy, here as elsewhere, is that the prejudices of our own period may lose their grip on us if we imaginatively enter into another period, when people's prejudices were different.
Mental Acts, p. 116

2 Psychological judgments have very often been held to be based primarily on the deliverances of an 'inner sense' whereby we are cognizant every one of his own psychical states. . . . The supposed 'inner sense' is compared sometimes to looking ('introspection'), sometimes to feeling. . . . Now could there be, let us say, anger–fear emotion-blindness, as there can be red–green colour-blindness? . . . In regard to colours, we can distinguish between a colour-blind man with a sensory defect and a mentally defective man who is unable to form colour-concepts and learn

the use of colour-words; could we make a similar distinction about emotions? . . .

I chose to set emotion-words and colour-words side by side, because there really is a considerable logical similarity. . . . If in spite of this we find a radical dissimilarity between colour-language and emotion-language, in that we could not apply a term 'emotion-blindness' comparably to 'colour-blindness', then the conclusion we ought to draw is surely that the idea of an introspective 'sense' is an illusion.
Mental Acts, p. 107

ERNEST GELLNER (*b.* 1925)

A cleric who loses his faith abandons his calling, a philosopher who loses   1
his redefines his subject.
Words and Things, p. 259

The new Wittgensteinian vision was to start not from the self, the subject,   2
but from language: doubt presupposes not so much a doubting, thinking self – it presupposes a language in terms of which the doubt could make sense. . . .

What an improvement on Descartes! Instead of 'I think, therefore I am', we get 'We speak, therefore the whole world is, and moreover it is as it has always seemed.' A rich harvest.
Words and Things, p. 154

Linguistic Philosophy confirms everyone in his preferred or older speech   3
habits and their associated world-view. In our period, the conventional world-view tends in fact to be a kind of mitigated naturalism. . . . In a society in whose language and way of life the concept of witchcraft is deeply embedded, on the other hand, the techniques of Linguistic Philosophy would confirm *it* (rather than what *we* now consider naturalism).
Words and Things, p. 125

Of course, Linguistic Philosophy can equally be used to attack religion. It   4
all depends on whether religion is included in the 'everything' which is left as it is, or in the 'philosophy' that is to be exorcized. If the latter, it can be attacked by the usual methods. There is *no* possible rational choice within Linguistic Philosophy between the two approaches. This illustrates the 'magic mirror' theme – one can see just what one pleases.
Words and Things, p. 246

So, by looking at language *games*, we hunt with the empirical-naturalistic   5
hounds; but by accepting their *contents*, we run with the transcendental hares, or any others we care to run with. . . .
Words and Things, p. 167

GERSONIDES (1288–1344)

By means of rational thought we have reached the opinion that God knows in advance only the possibilities open to a man in his freedom, not the particular decisions he will make. . . . It is the opinion of our religion that God never changes . . . and yet we find in the words of the prophets that God does repent over some things. . . . It is impossible to solve this contradiction if we adopt the view that God knows particular things as particulars.

Milhamot ha-Shem, trans. Louis Jacobs, III, 6

EDMUND L. GETTIER (*b.* 1927)

Various attempts have been made in recent years to state necessary and sufficient conditions for someone's knowing a given proposition. The attempts have often been such that they can be stated in a form similar to the following:

(a) S knows that P   *IFF*   (i) P is true,
(ii) S believes that P, and
(iii) S is justified in believing that P. . .

I shall argue that (a) is false in that the conditions stated therein do not constitute a *sufficient* condition for the truth of the proposition that S knows that P. . . .

Suppose that Smith and Jones have applied for a certain job. And suppose that Smith has strong evidence for the following conjunctive proposition:

(d) Jones is the man who will get the job, and Jones has ten coins in his pocket.

Smith's evidence for (d) might be that the president of the company assured him that Jones would in the end be selected, and that he, Smith, had counted the coins in Jones's pocket ten minutes ago. Proposition (d) entails:

(e) The man who will get the job has ten coins in his pocket. Let us suppose that Smith sees the entailment from (d) to (e), and accepts (e) on the grounds of (d), for which he has strong evidence. In this case, Smith is clearly justified in believing that (e) is true.

But imagine, further, that unknown to Smith, he himself, not Jones, will get the job. And, also, unknown to Smith, he himself has ten coins in his pocket. Proposition (e) is then true, though proposition (d), from which Smith inferred (e), is false. In our example, then, all of the following are true: *(i)* (e) is true, *(ii)* Smith believes that (e) is true, and *(iii)* Smith is justified in believing that (e) is true. But it is equally clear

that Smith does not *know* that (e) is true; for (e) is true in virtue of the number of coins in Smith's pocket, while Smith does not know how many coins are in Smith's pocket, and bases his belief in (e) on a count of the coins in Jones's pocket, whom he falsely believes to be the man who will get the job.
'Is Justified True Belief Knowledge?', *Analysis* (1963), p. 121

ARNOLD GEULINCX (1624–1669)

My body moves in various ways in accordance with my will (when I wish   1
to speak, my tongue moves around in my mouth . . . my feet are thrust forward when I desire to walk). But *I* do not make these movements, since I do not know how they are produced. If I am ignorant of how something comes about, I cannot possibly say that it is I who brings it about.
Ethics, Tr. 1, Ch. 2, trans. John Cottingham, p. 32

My will does not produce the motive power to move my limbs. Rather,   2
he who imparted motion to matter, and ordained its laws, shaped my will also; he thus joined together two utterly different things – the movement of matter and the decision of my will in such a way that whenever my will desires some action, the desired bodily movement will occur and vice versa, without there being any causation involved, or any influence of the one upon the other. It is just as if there were two clocks appropriately adjusted with reference to each other and the time of day in such a way that when one struck the hour the other immediately did likewise.
Ethics, Tr. 1, Ch. 2, trans. John Cottingham, p. 211

ANDRÉ GIDE (1869–1951)

Psychological analysis lost all interest for me from the moment that I became aware that men feel what they imagine they feel. From that to thinking they imagine they feel what they feel was a very short step! . . . In the domain of feeling, what is real is indistinguishable from what is imaginary. And if it is sufficient to imagine one loves, in order to love, so it is sufficient to say to oneself that when one loves one imagines one loves, in order to love a little less. . . . But if one is able to say such a thing to oneself, must one not already love a little less?
The Coiners, trans. Dorothy Bussy, p. 58

JONATHAN GLOVER (b. 1941)

The way people do things is partly chosen. But Nietzsche's advice about   1
the cultivation of a style, if too consciously followed, could produce mere

151

affectation. (Nietzsche sometimes seems to have been an eternal first-year undergraduate.)
I: The Philosophy and Psychology of Personal Identity, p. 135

2   On the other hand, not all self-creation involves strenuous efforts of will. It can be a matter of endorsing and encouraging tendencies that are already natural to us. We may be endorsing something which has cost us no effort to produce, but with which we feel an immediate affinity. (I have heard that Picasso, when asked to sign paintings thought to be his, would sign if he liked the painting, even if unsure that it was his work.)
I: The Philosophy and Psychology of Personal Identity, p. 136

3   Imagine a world, produced by utopian adjusters, which took account of the desirability of autonomy and variety. In one place is Sisyphus, contentedly, and of his own choice, rolling stones. Nearby is someone else, hopping about in complicated patterns. There are thousands of such people. They are spending their lives building towers out of marzipan, writing articles about meaning, knitting huge maps of the moon. They are all autonomous, contented and different. Call this world the Human Zoo. Those of us doubtful about the quality of life there have an objection which is not reducible to questions of autonomy and variety.
What Sort of People Should There Be?, p. 163

4   On the whole, the rules of conventional morality are stronger in prohibiting actions than in enjoining them. Not rescuing the drowning child is less frowned on than pushing him in to start with. Even if the conventional rules are not the best ones imaginable, there may still be a case for preserving them rather than setting a precedent which may undermine them. This is an additional reason for not killing someone which may not always apply to taking positive steps to save people.

But these reasons, which have to do with the law and with conventional practices and attitudes, may not always be decisive against killing: the question is whether killing averts a great enough evil to be justified, bearing in mind both the direct objections to killing and the side-effects, including any weakening either of the law or of a desirable common attitude. And, while the conventional revulsion against killing is an additional reason against it, this line of reasoning may not work the other way. The conventional casualness about letting people die from hunger or lack of medical care is something we should be better off without.
Causing Death and Saving Lives, p. 108

KURT GÖDEL (1906–1978)

I don't see any reason why we should have less confidence in this kind of perception, i.e., in mathematical intuition, than in sense perception, which induces us to build up physical theories and to expect that future sense perceptions will agree with them and, moreover, to believe that a question not decidable now has meaning and may be decided in the future.
'What is Cantor's Continuum Problem?', *Philosophy of Mathematics*, ed. P. Benacerraf and H. Putnam, p. 483

ALVIN I. GOLDMAN (*b.* 1938)

A fundamental facet of animate life, both human and infra-human, is   1
telling things apart, distinguishing predator from prey, for example, or a protective habitat from a threatening one. The concept of knowledge has its roots in this kind of cognitive activity.
'Discrimination and Perceptual Knowledge', *Journal of Philosophy* (1976), p. 791

A current time-slice theory makes the justificational status of a belief   2
wholly a function of what is true of the cognizer *at the time* of belief. An historical theory makes the justificational status of a belief depend on its prior history. Since my historical theory emphasizes the reliability of the belief-generating processes, it may be called '*historical reliabilism*'.
'What Is Justified Belief?', *Justification and Knowledge*, ed. G. Pappas, p. 14

NELSON GOODMAN (*b.* 1906)

Any effort in philosophy to make the obscure obvious is likely to be   1
unappealing, for the penalty of failure is confusion while the reward of success is banality. An answer, once found, is dull; and the only remaining interest lies in a further effort to render equally dull what is still obscure enough to be interesting.
The Structure of Appearance, p. xv

Suppose that all emeralds examined before a certain time t are green. At   2
time t, then, our observations support the hypothesis that all emeralds are green; and this is in accord with our definition of confirmation. Our evidence statements assert that emerald a is green, that emerald b is green, and so on; and each confirms the general hypothesis that all emeralds are green. So far, so good.

Now let me introduce another predicate less familiar than 'green'. It is the predicate 'grue' and it applies to all things examined before t just in case they are green but to other things just in case they are blue. Then at time t we have, for each evidence statement asserting that a given emerald

is green, a parallel evidence statement asserting that that emerald is grue. And the statements that emerald *a* is grue, that emerald *b* is grue, and so on, will each confirm the general hypothesis that all emeralds are grue. . . . it is clear that if we simply choose an appropriate predicate, then on the basis of these same observations we shall have equal confirmation, by our definition, for any prediction whatever about other emeralds – or indeed about anything else.
Fact, Fiction and Forecast, p. 73

3   Nothing whatever can be said in support of the assumption that nature will usually follow the simpler theory. . . .

Does this mean, then, that the practice of choosing the simplest surviving theory is quite indefensible? On the contrary, justification is virtually automatic once we admit that we are always faced with making a choice among hypotheses when there is no ground for supposing any of them more likely to be true than any of the rest. . . . The simplest theory is to be chosen not because it is most likely to be true but because it is scientifically the most rewarding among equally likely alternatives. We aim at simplicity and hope for truth.
Problems and Projects, p. 352

4   If I am at all correct, then, the roots of inductive validity are to be found in our use of language. A valid prediction is, admittedly, one that is in agreement with past regularities in what has been observed; but the difficulty has always been to say what constitutes such agreement. The suggestion I have been developing here is that such agreement with regularities in what has been observed is a function of our linguistic practices. Thus the line between valid and invalid predictions (or inductions or projections) is drawn upon the basis of how the world is and has been described and anticipated in words. The problem of induction is not a problem of demonstration but a problem of defining the difference between valid and invalid predictions.
Fact, Fiction and Forecast, p. 77

5   Briefly, then, truth of statements and rightness of descriptions, representations, exemplifications, expressions – of design, drawing, diction, rhythm – is primarily a matter of fit: fit to what is referred to in one way or another, or to other renderings, or to modes and manners of organization. The differences between fitting a version to a world, a world to a version, and a version together or to other versions fade when the role of versions in making the worlds they fit is recognized. And knowing or understanding is seen as ranging beyond the acquiring of true beliefs to the discovering and devising of fit of all sorts.
Ways of Worldmaking, p. 138

If worlds are as much made as found, so also knowing is as much 6
remaking as reporting.
Ways of Worldmaking, p. 22

If a thing can remain the same while its appearance changes, then clearly 7
the real and the apparent are different. But this means not that the real
thing must be something quite separate from its appearances but only
that the real thing comprises many appearances. To say that the same
thing is twice presented is to say that two presentations – two
phenomenal events – are together embraced within a single totality of the
sort we call a thing or object.
The Structure of Appearance, p. 127

Emotion and feeling . . . function cognitively in aesthetic and in much 8
other experience. We do not discern stylistic affinities and differences, for
example, by 'rational analysis' but by sensations, perceptions, feelings,
emotions, sharpened in practice like the eye of a gemologist or the fingers
of an inspector of machined parts. Far from wanting to desensitize
aesthetic experience, I want to sensitize cognition. In art – and I think in
science too – emotion and cognition are interdependent: feeling without
understanding is blind, and understanding without feeling is empty.
Of Mind and Other Matters, p. 7

The plain fact is that a picture, to represent an object, must be a symbol 9
for it, stand for it, refer to it; and that no degree of resemblance is
sufficient to establish the requisite relationship of reference. Nor is
resemblance *necessary* for reference; almost anything may stand for
almost anything else. A picture that represents – like a passage that
describes – an object refers to and, more particularly, *denotes* it.
Denotation is the core of representation and is independent of resemblance.
Languages of Art, p. 5

Briefly, a metaphor is an affair between a predicate with a past and an 10
object that yields while protesting.
Languages of Art, p. 69

Since complete compliance with the score is the only requirement for a 11
genuine instance of a work, the most miserable performance without
actual mistakes does count as such an instance, while the most brilliant
performance with a single wrong note does not. Could we not bring our
theoretical vocabulary into better agreement with common practice and
common sense by allowing some limited degree of deviation in
performances admitted as instances of a work? The practicing musician
or composer usually bristles at the idea that a performance with one

wrong note is not a performance of the given work at all; and ordinary usage surely sanctions overlooking a few wrong notes. But this is one of those cases where ordinary usage gets us quickly into trouble. The innocent-seeming principle that performances differing by just one note are instances of the same work risks the consequence – in view of the transitivity of identity – that all performances whatsoever are of the same work. If we allow the least deviation, all assurance of work-preservation and score-preservation is lost; for by a series of one-note errors of omission, addition, and modification, we can go all the way from Beethoven's *Fifth Symphony* to *Three Blind Mice*.
Languages of Art, p. 186

PAUL GRICE (*b.* 1913)

1   Suppose that A and B are talking about a mutual friend, C, who is now working in a bank. A asks B how C is getting on in his job, and B replies, *Oh quite well, I think; he likes his colleagues, and he hasn't been to prison yet.* . . . It is clear that whatever B implied, suggested, meant in this example, is distinct from what B said, which was simply that C had not been to prison yet. I wish to introduce, as terms of art, the verb *implicate* and the related nouns *implicature* (cf. *implying*) and *implicatum* (cf. *what is implied*).
'Logic and Conversation', *Studies in the Ways of Words*, p. 24

2   We might then formulate a rough general principle which participants will be expected (ceteris paribus) to observe, namely: make your conversational contribution such as is required, at the stage at which it occurs, by the accepted purpose or direction of the talk exchange in which you are engaged. One might label this the Cooperative Principle.
'Logic and Conversation', p. 26

3   At a genteel tea party, A says *Mrs. X is an old bag.* There is a moment of appalled silence, and then B says *The weather has been quite delightful this summer, hasn't it?* B has blatantly refused to make what he says relevant to A's preceding remark. He thereby implicates that A's remark should not be discussed and, perhaps more specifically, that A has committed a social gaffe.
'Logic and Conversation', p. 35

4   Compare the remarks:

(a)   *Miss X sang 'Home Sweet Home'.*
(b)   *Miss X produced a series of sounds that corresponded closely with the score of 'Home Sweet Home'.*
'Logic and Conversation', p. 37

I start, then, by considering the following proposed definition: 5

'U meant something by uttering x' is true iff, for some audience A, U uttered x intending:
   1) A to produce a particular response r
   2) A to think (recognize) that U intends (1)
   3) A to fulfill (1) on the basis of his fulfillment of (2).
'Logic and Conversation', *Studies in the Ways of Words*, p. 92

JAMES GRIFFIN (*b.* 1933)

Are things valuable because desired, or desired because valuable? . . .   1
Desire is not blind. Understanding is not bloodless. Neither is the slave of the other. There is no priority.
Well-Being, pp. 27, 30

A person who utters words, or does acts, of admiration, gratitude, or   2
appreciation only on utilitarian grounds becomes a person without admiration, gratitude, or appreciation. If utilitarianism has no place for desert, desert has no place for utilitarianism either.
Well-Being, p. 259

G. I. GURDJIEFF (1866–1949)

The sole means now for the saving of the beings of the planet Earth   1
would be to implant into their presences a new organ with such properties that every one of these unfortunates during the process of existence should constantly sense and be cognizant of the inevitability of his own death as well as of the death of everyone upon whom his eyes or attention rests.

Only such a sensation and such a cognizance can now destroy the egoism completely crystallized in them that has swallowed up the whole of their Essence and also that tendency to hate others which flows from it – the tendency, namely, which engenders all those mutual relationships existing there, which serve as the chief cause of all their abnormalities unbecoming to three-brained beings and maleficent for them themselves and for the whole of the Universe.
All and Everything, p. 1183

Man is a machine. All his actions, words, thoughts, feelings, opinions   2
and habits are the results of external influences, external impressions. Out of himself a man cannot produce a single thought, a single action. Everything he says, does, thinks, feels – all this happens. To establish this fact for oneself, to be convinced of its truth, means getting rid of a thousand illusions about man, about his being creative and consciously

organising his own life, and so on. But it is one thing to understand with the mind and another thing to feel with one's 'whole mass', to be really convinced that it is so and never forget it.

It is possible to stop being a machine, but for that it is necessary first of all to *know* the machine. A machine, a real machine, does not know itself and cannot know itself. When a machine knows itself it is then no longer a machine, at least, not such a machine as it was before. It already begins to be *responsible* for its actions.

Quoted in P. D. Ouspensky, *In Search of the Miraculous*, p. 19

3   Man has no permanent and unchangeable I. Every thought, every mood, every desire, every sensation says 'I'. And in each case it seems to be taken for granted that this I belongs to the Whole, to the whole man, and that a thought, a desire, or an aversion is expressed by this Whole. In actual fact, there is no foundation whatever for this assumption. Man's every thought and desire appears and lives quite separately and independently of the Whole. And the Whole never expresses itself, for the simple reason that it exists, as such, only physically as a thing, and in the abstract as a concept.

Quoted in P. D. Ouspensky, *In Search of the Miraculous*, p. 59

4   It is necessary to distinguish *consciousness* from the *possibility of consciousness*. We have only the possibility of consciousness and rare flashes of it. Therefore we cannot define what consciousness is. For most people, the chief obstacle in the way of acquiring self-consciousness consists in the fact that they think they possess it. It is evident that a man will not be interested if you tell him that he can acquire by long and difficult work something which, in his opinion, he already has.

Quoted in P. D. Ouspensky, *In Search of the Miraculous*, p.141

H

꧞꧞꧞꧞꧞꧞

JÜRGEN HABERMAS (b. 1929)

From the beginning philosophy has presumed that the autonomy and 1
responsibility posited with the structure of language are not only
anticipated but real. It is pure theory, wanting to derive everything from
itself, that succumbs to unacknowledged external conditions and
becomes ideological. Only when philosophy discovers in the dialectical
course of history the traces of violence that deform repeated attempts at
dialogue and recurrently close off the path to unconstrained communication does it further the process whose suspension it otherwise legitimates:
mankind's evolution toward autonomy and responsibility.
Knowledge and Human Interests, trans. Jeremy J. Shapiro, p. 314

The project of modernity formulated in the 18th century by the 2
philosophers of the Enlightenment consisted in their efforts to develop
objective science, universal morality and law, and autonomous art
according to their inner logic. At the same time, this project intended to
release the cognitive potentials of each of these domains from their
esoteric forms. The Enlightenment philosophers wanted to utilize this
accumulation of specialized culture for the enrichment of everyday life –
that is to say, for the rational organization of everyday social life.
'Modernity', *Postmodern Culture*, ed. H. Foster, p. 9

In his capacity as a participant in argumentation, everyone is on his own 3
and yet embedded in a communication context. This is what Apel means
by an 'ideal community of communication'. In discourse the social bond
of belonging is left intact despite the fact that the consensus required of
all concerned transcends the limits of any actual community. The
agreement made possible by discourse depends on two things: the
individual's inalienable right to say yes or no and his overcoming of his
egocentric viewpoint.
Moral Consciousness and Communicative Action, trans. C. Lenhardt and S. W.
Nicholsen, p. 202

4   The political system takes over tasks of ideology planning (Luhmann). In so doing, maneuvering room is, to be sure, narrowly limited, for the cultural system is peculiarly resistant to administrative control. *There is no administrative production of meaning.* Commercial production and administrative planning of symbols exhausts the normative force of counterfactual validity claims. The procurement of legitimation is self-defeating as soon as the mode of procurement is seen through.
Legitimation Crisis, trans. Thomas McCarthy, p. 70

IAN HACKING (*b*. 1936)

Philosophers long made a mummy of science. When they finally unwrapped the cadaver and saw the remnants of an historical process of becoming and discovering, they created for themselves a crisis of rationality. That happened around 1960.

It was a crisis because it upset our old tradition of thinking that scientific knowledge is the crowning achievement of human reason. Sceptics have always challenged the complacent panorama of cumulative and accumulating human knowledge, but now they took ammunition from the details of history.
Representing and Intervening, p. 1

D. W. HAMLYN (*b*. 1924)
The life-blood of philosophy is argument and counter-argument. Plato and Aristotle thought of this occurring in what they called dialectic – discussion. Today, it might be argued that it is just the same, except that it operates upon a much wider scale, both historically and geographically. Argument and counter-argument in books and journals is the modern version of dialectic.
The Penguin History of Western Philosophy, p. 333

STUART HAMPSHIRE (*b*. 1914)

1   That beings, who are capable of action and observation, are born into, and move among, a world of persisting objects is a logical necessity and not a contingent matter of fact. Anyone who, following Hume, tries to describe the actual experience of beings capable of action, or even their experience in some imaginary world, as merely a succession of sensations at some point contradicts his own hypothesis.
Thought and Action, p. 40

2   . . . the followers of Berkeley, the sense-datum philosophers, have always failed to show that statements identifying physical objects are translatable into statements describing the actual and possible appearances of things.

They have always found that their hypothetical propositions about sense-data could never be equivalent to categorical statements about actual objects, unless the protases of the hypotheticals specify the objective standpoint of the observer. Their mistake has always been not to acknowledge that the standpoint of the observer is one physical fact among others, and that the observer is always a self-moving body among other bodies which he observes and intentionally manipulates.
Thought and Action, p. 49

There remains always the fundamental necessity that we should single   3
out constant objects of reference in order to give sense to every other type of description. It would be impossible to make statements, either true or false, in a language that only tried to record the impressions of the moment. If one was confined to utterances of the form 'Here now red' or 'Here now pain', there would be no method of determining that one so-called statement was incompatible with another, and therefore no method of establishing that any statement was either true or false. 'Here now red and green' would be an empty statement unless there was a means of distinguishing the assertion that the same thing is both red and green, and red and green in the same parts of its surface, from the assertion that both red and green are now visible.
Thought and Action, p. 29

My thesis will be that, no matter what experimental knowledge of the   4
previously unknown causes that determine a man's beliefs is accumulated, that which a man believes, and also that which he aims at and sets himself to achieve, will remain up to him to decide in the light of argument.
Freedom of Mind, p. 3

This stepping-back to review the new possibilities is forced upon me. For   5
once I have the new knowledge, omitting to act to prevent something, which I now know how to prevent and have the means to prevent, amounts to allowing this thing to happen. The knowledge by itself confers the responsibility upon me; having the expectation, together with having the power to alter that which would otherwise occur in the natural course of events, I am immediately exposed to the question – 'What do you intend to do about it?' Even if the newly discovered scientific explanations extended to the most intimate workings of the mind, the knowledge would still have to be put to use by an agent who decides. Suppose that I learn the causes, external to my mind, of my occasional weaknesses of will, of states of hesitation between alternative courses of action, and of my vacillations and changes of mind; these

phenomena of my inner life would become something that I may try to cope with, as I would try to cope with some physical weaknesses.
Freedom of the Individual, p. 89

6   We should look in society not for consensus, but for ineliminable and acceptable conflicts, and for rationally controlled hostilities, as the normal condition of mankind; not only normal, but also the best condition of mankind from the moral point of view, both between states and within states. This was Heraclitus's vision: that life, and liveliness, within the soul and within society, consists in perpetual conflicts between rival impulses and ideals, and that justice presides over the hostilities and finds sufficient compromises to prevent madness in the soul, and civil war or war between peoples. Harmony and inner consensus come with death, when human faces no longer express conflicts but are immobile, composed, and at rest.
Innocence and Experience, p. 189

7   There are two kinds of moral claim – those that, when challenged, are referred to universal needs of human beings and to their reasonable calculations, which should be the same everywhere . . . and those that, when challenged, are referred to the description of a desired and respected way of life, in which those moral claims have been an element thought essential within that way of life. The first kind of moral claim represents moral norms as not unlike norms of good health: the second as not unlike social customs.
'Morality and Convention', *Utilitarianism and Beyond*, ed. A. Sen and B. Williams, p. 156

ALASTAIR HANNAY (*b.* 1932)

1   Perhaps it would be too much to say there is a conspiracy against the mental image. But there is certainly a campaign. . . . Not everyone finds it so strange [as Dennett] that the mental resists being forced into the Procrustean bed of the physical, or is so convinced of the power of the ruler to determine what exists. But if we really do find the image's unmeasurableness . . . so disturbing, we will have to find a better way out of our discomfort than arguing that the image does not exist. Certainly no bump in our understanding will relieve us of *this* potential bulge in our ontology. Concern with ontological trim is a time-honoured source of philosophical energy, but the philosopher's prior commitment is to the maxim that the appearances should first have *their* say before he tries to save them.
'To See a Mental Image', *Mind* (1973), p. 182

The attitude of much physicalism [to consciousness] has been that of new   2
owners to a sitting tenant. They would prefer eviction but, failing that,
are content to dispose of as much of the paraphernalia as possible while
keeping busy in other parts of the house. We should, I think, feel free to
surmise that the current picture of consciousness eking out a sequestered
life as a print-out monitor or raw feeler fails in a quite radical way to
capture the facts.
'The Claims of Consciousness: A Critical Survey', *Inquiry* (1987), p. 397

A . . . factor lending dubious plausibility to prevailing doctrine is the   3
intellectualist assumption that consciousness adds nothing significant to
the hallowed but highly abstract idea of propositional content. . . .
Concentrating the idea of human mentality in the ability to manipulate
sentences in natural languages has clear ideological advantages for those
who aspire to master the principles of the human mind by developing
computer programs capable of processing such languages. . . . It also
helps to make observational accounts of meaning, like Quine's and
Davidson's, look like full-fledged theories of mind. Once propositions are
specified in terms of publicly identifiable truth-conditions there is nothing
more they can 'mean' than states of a common world. What falls through
that net can then be dismissed as psychological incident.
'The Claims of Consciousness: A Critical Survey', p. 422

Without a 'mental' analogue of the pictorial property that allows us to   4
see something when it is perceptually absent one could no more picture
or imagine something to oneself than one could see something represented
without seeing a representation.
'To See a Mental Image', *Mind* (1973), p. 181

Kierkegaard would not have been impressed by Marx's belief that it is . . .   5
the forms of association to which people are bound, and not the people
themselves, that are corrupt. And he would have considered it naïve and
obscurantist to suppose that people have a 'natural' communal capacity,
that all that is required to elicit communality is the replacement of a
corrupting social organization by one that gives a spontaneous sociality
free rein.
Kierkegaard, p. 320

SANDRA HARDING (*b.* 1935)

The radical feminist position holds that the epistemologies, metaphysics,   1
ethics, and politics of the dominant forms of science are androcentric and
mutually supportive; that despite the deeply ingrained Western cultural
belief in science's intrinsic progressiveness, science today serves primarily
regressive social tendencies; and that the social structure of science, many

163

of its applications and technologies, its modes of defining research problems and designing experiments, its ways of constructing and conferring meanings are not only sexist but also racist, classist, and culturally coercive. In their analyses of how gender symbolism, the social division of labor by gender, and the construction of individual gender identity have affected the history and philosophy of science, feminist thinkers have challenged the intellectual and social orders at their very foundations.

The Science Question in Feminism, p. 9

2 . . . central to the notion of masculinity is its rejection of everything that is defined by a culture as feminine and its legitimated control of whatever counts as the feminine. . . . Gender is an *asymmetrical* category of human thought, social organization, and individual identity and behavior.

The Science Question in Feminism, p. 54

RICHARD M. HARE (b. 1919)

1 Thus a complete justification of a decision would consist of a complete account of its effects, together with a complete account of the principles which it observed, and the effects of observing those principles – for, of course, it is the effects (what obeying them in fact consists in) which give content to the principles too. Thus, if pressed to justify a decision completely, we have to give a complete specification of the way of life of which it is a part. This complete specification it is impossible in practice to give; the nearest attempts are those given by the great religions, especially those which can point to historical persons who carried out the way of life in practice. Suppose, however, that we can give it. If the inquirer still goes on asking 'But why *should* I live like that?' then there is no further answer to give him, because we have already, *ex hypothesi*, said everything that could be included in this further answer. We can only ask him to make up his own mind which way he ought to live; for in the end everything rests upon such a decision of principle. He has to decide whether to accept that way of life or not; if he accepts it, then we can proceed to justify the decisions that are based upon it; if he does not accept it, then let him accept some other and try to live by it. The sting is in the last clause.

The Language of Morals, p. 69

2 It is, most fundamentally, because moral judgements are universalizable that we can speak of moral thought as rational (to universalize is to give the reason); and their prescriptivity is very intimately connected with our freedom to form our own moral opinions (only those free to think and act need a prescriptive language).

Freedom and Reason, p. 5

I have been maintaining that the meaning of the word 'ought' and other   3
moral words is such that a person who uses them commits himself
thereby to a universal rule. This is the thesis of universalizability. It is to
be distinguished from *moral* views such as that everybody ought always
to adhere to universal rules and govern all their conduct in accordance
with them, or that one ought not to make exceptions in one's own
favour. The logical thesis has, as we shall see, great potency in moral
arguments; but for that very reason it is most important to make clear
that it is no more than a logical thesis – for otherwise the objection will
be made that a moral principle has been smuggled in disguised as a
logical doctrine.
Freedom and Reason, p. 30

In order to bring out the extraordinary nature of the really fanatical   4
Nazi's desires, let us imagine that we are able to perform on him the
following trick, comparable to another which we shall devise later for a
different sort of racialist. We say to him 'You may not know it, but we
have discovered that you are not the son of your supposed parents, but of
two pure Jews; and the same is true of your wife'; and we produce
apparently cast-iron evidence to support this allegation. Is he at all likely
to say – as he logically *can* say – 'All right then, send me and all my
family to Buchenwald!'?
    . . . our Nazi is unlikely to say this. This is not a matter of logic; he
would not be contradicting himself if he said 'Jews are such an
abomination that I and my whole family, if we were Jews, should be sent
to the gas-chamber.' Our argument, as we are going to develop it, will
rest, not upon logic by itself – though without logic we should never have
got to this point – but upon the fortunate contingent fact that people who
would take this logically possible view, after they had really imagined
themselves in the other man's position, are extremely rare.
Freedom and Reason, p. 171

How often have we not heard people say, 'Unless values are shown to be   5
objective, it will be *right* for everybody to do whatever he *thinks* right'? I
hope that by this time I have made clear to you the confusions which lie
behind this argument. The first confusion is that of supposing that there
is anything to be understood by 'showing values to be objective' (or for
that matter 'subjective'). The second is that of thinking that a view, of
whatever sort, about the logical nature or status or meaning or use of
moral concepts, necessarily commits us to a moral position about what *is*
right or wrong; and in particular, to a moral position as patently absurd
and pernicious as relativism is.
Applications of Moral Philosophy, p. 46

GEOFFREY HARRISON

There is nothing that the relativist, qua relativist, can say either for or against tolerance from a moral point of view. The moment he does this, he ceases to be an observer of morality and becomes a user of a moral system. . . . There is no such thing as a moral judgment made from a morally neutral or 'extramoral' position.

'Relativism and Tolerance', *Ethics* (1976), p. 131

H. L. A. HART (*b.* 1907)

1   At any given moment the life of any society which lives by rules, legal or not, is likely to consist in a tension between those who, on the one hand, accept and voluntarily co-operate in maintaining the rules, and so see their own and other persons' behaviour in terms of the rules, and those who, on the other hand, reject the rules and attend to them only from the external point of view as a sign of possible punishment. One of the difficulties facing any legal theory anxious to do justice to the complexity of the facts is to remember the presence of both these points of view and not to define one of them out of existence.

The Concept of Law, p. 88

2   There are . . . two minimum conditions necessary and sufficient for the existence of a legal system. On the one hand those rules of behaviour which are valid according to the system's ultimate criteria of validity must be generally obeyed, and on the other hand, its rules of recognition specifying the criteria of legal validity and its rules of change and adjudication must be effectively accepted as common public standards of official behaviour by its officials.

The Concept of Law, p. 113

3   What surely is most needed, in order to make men clear sighted in confronting the official abuse of power, is that they should preserve the sense that the certification of something as legally valid is not conclusive of the question of obedience, and that, however great the aura of majesty or authority which the official system may have, its demands must in the end be submitted to a moral scrutiny.

The Concept of Law, p. 206

G. W. F. HEGEL (1770–1831)

1   *The Absolute is Mind* (Spirit) – this is the supreme definition of the Absolute. To find this definition and to grasp its meaning and burden was, we may say, the ultimate purpose of all education and all philosophy: it was the point to which turned the impulse of all religion

and science; and it is this impulse that must explain the history of the world. The word 'Mind' (Spirit) – and some glimpse of its meaning – was found at an early period: and the spirituality of God is the lesson of Christianity. It remains for philosophy in its own element of intelligible unity to get hold of what was thus given as a mental image, and what implicitly is the ultimate reality . . .

Encyclopaedia, trans. W. Wallace, §384

It is natural to suppose that, before philosophy enters upon its subject **2** proper – namely, the actual knowledge of what truly is – it is necessary to come first to an understanding concerning knowledge, which is regarded either as the instrument to get hold of the Absolute, or as the medium through which one discovers it. A certain uneasiness seems justified. . . . For if knowledge is the instrument by which to get hold of absolute Reality, it is obvious that the application of an instrument to anything does *not* leave it as it is for itself, but rather entails in the process, and has in view, a moulding and alteration of it. If, on the other hand, knowledge is not an instrument which we actively employ, but a more or less passive medium through which the light of truth reaches us, then again we do not receive the truth as it is in itself, but only as it exists through and in this medium.

Phenomenology of Spirit, trans. A. V. Miller, p. 46, amended

. . . if the fear of falling into error is the source of a mistrust in Science, **3** which in the absence of any such misgivings gets on with the work itself and actually does know, it is difficult to see why, conversely, a mistrust should not be placed in this mistrust, and why we should not be concerned that this fear of erring is itself the very error.

Phenomenology of Spirit, trans. A. V. Miller, p. 47, amended

[Schelling and his school] subject everything to the Absolute Idea, which **4** seems thus to be recognized in everything, and to have developed into a comprehensive science. But . . . [t]he Idea, which is of course true enough on its own account, never gets any farther than just where it began, as long as the development of it consists in nothing but . . . repetition of the same formula. . . . To pit this single assertion, that 'in the Absolute all is one', against all the distinctions of knowledge, which at least seeks and demands fulfilment – or to palm off one's Absolute as the night in which, as the saying goes, all cows are black – that is knowledge naively reduced to vacuity.

Phenomenology of Spirit, trans. A. V. Miller, p. 8, amended

Kant undertook to examine how far the forms of thought were capable **5** of leading to the knowledge of truth. In particular he demanded a criticism of the faculty of cognition as preliminary to its exercise. That is

a fair demand, if it means that even the forms of thought must be made an object of investigation. Unfortunately there soon creeps in the misconception of already knowing before you know . . .
Encyclopaedia, trans. W. Wallace, §41

6 In every dualistic system, and especially in that of Kant, the fundamental defect makes itself visible in the inconsistency of unifying at one moment what a moment before had been explained to be independent and therefore incapable of unification. . . . It argues an utter want of consistency to say, on the one hand, that the understanding only knows phenomena, and, on the other, assert the absolute character of this knowledge, by such statements as 'Cognition can go no further'; 'Here is the *natural* and absolute limit of human knowledge.' But 'natural' is the wrong word here. The things of nature are limited and are natural things only to such extent as they are not aware of their universal limit, or to such extent as their mode or quality is a limit from our point of view, and not from their own. No one knows, or even feels, that anything is a limit or defect, until he is at the same time above and beyond it. . . . . A very little consideration might show that to call a thing finite or limited proves by implication the very presence of the infinite and unlimited, and that the awareness of limit can only be in so far as the unlimited is *on this side* in consciousness.
Encyclopaedia, trans. W. Wallace, §60

7 The idealism of philosophy consists in nothing else than in recognizing that the finite has no genuine being. Every philosophy is essentially idealism or at least has idealism as its principle, and the question then is only how far this principle is actually carried out. . . . Consequently the opposition of idealistic and realistic philosophy has no significance. A philosophy which ascribed genuine, ultimate, absolute being to finite existence as such, would not deserve the name of philosophy.
The Science of Logic, trans. A. V. Miller, p. 154, amended

8 The common conceptions of God, the Soul, the World, may be supposed to afford thought a firm and fast footing. They do not really do so. . . . In such a sentence as 'God is eternal', we begin with the conception of God, not knowing as yet what he is; to tell us that is the job of the predicate. In logic therefore, where the content is determined in the form of thought alone, it is not merely superfluous to make these categories predicates of propositions in which God, or, still vaguer, the absolute, is the subject, but it would also have the disadvantage of suggesting another criterion than the nature of thought. Besides, the form of the proposition, or, more exactly, judgment, is not suited to express the concrete – and the truth is

concrete – or the speculative. The judgment is by its very form one-sided and, to that extent, false.
Encyclopaedia, trans. W. Wallace, §31, amended

Being itself and the special sub-categories of it which follow, as well as 9
those of logic in general, may be looked upon as definitions of the
Absolute, or metaphysical definitions of God: at least the first and third
category in every triad may . . .

Pure *Being* makes the beginning: because it is on one hand pure
thought, and on the other immediacy itself, simple and indeterminate. . . .
It is possible to define being as 'I = I', as 'Absolute Indifference' or
Identity, and so on. . . .

But this mere Being, as it is mere abstraction, is therefore the absolutely
negative: which, taken similarly immediately, is just *Nothing*. . . .

Nothing, as thus immediate and equal to itself, is also conversely the
same as Being is. The truth of Being and of Nothing is accordingly the
unity of the two: and this unity is *Becoming*.
Encyclopaedia, trans. W. Wallace, §86, amended

In my view, which the developed exposition of the system itself can alone 10
justify, everything depends on grasping and expressing the True, not only
as *Substance*, but equally as *Subject*.
Phenomenology of Spirit, trans. A. V. Miller, p. 9, amended

By the term 'I' I mean myself, a single and altogether determinate person. 11
And yet I really utter nothing peculiar to myself, for everyone else is an 'I'
or 'Ego', and when I call myself 'I', though I indubitably mean the single
person myself, I express a thorough universal. 'I', therefore, is . . . as it
were the ultimate and unanalysable point of consciousness. We may say
'I' and thought are the same, or more definitely, 'I' is thought as a
thinker. What I have in my consciousness is for me. 'I' is the vacuum for
anything and everything. . . . It follows that the 'Ego' is the universal in
which we leave aside all that is particular, and in which at the same time
all the particulars have a latent existence. In other words, it is not a mere
universality and nothing more, but the universality which includes in it
everything.
Encyclopaedia, trans. W. Wallace, §24, amended

The nature of Spirit may be understood by a glance at its direct opposite 12
– Matter. As the essence of Matter is Gravity, so, on the other hand, we
may affirm that the substance, the essence of Spirit is Freedom. . . .
Matter has its essence outside itself; Spirit is Being-within-itself (self-
contained existence). But this, precisely, is Freedom. For if I am
dependent, I refer myself to something else which I am not; I cannot exist
independently of something external. I am free, on the contrary, when

my existence depends upon myself. This self-contained existence of Spirit is none other than self-consciousness – consciousness of one's own being.
Reason in History, trans. R. Hartman, p. 22, amended

13 Self-consciousness is, to begin with, simple being-for-itself, self-equal through the exclusion from itself of everything else. . . . What is 'other' for it is an unessential, negatively characterized object. But the 'other' is also a self-consciousness; one individual makes its appearance in antithesis to another individual. . . . the relation of the two self-consciousnesses is such that they prove themselves and each other through a life-and-death struggle. They must enter into this struggle, for they must bring their certainty of being *for themselves* to the level of objective truth, both in the case of the other and in their own case.
Phenomenology of Spirit, trans. A. V. Miller, p. 113, amended

14 The lord is the consciousness that exists *for itself*, but no longer merely the general notion of existence for self. Rather, it is a consciousness existing *for itself* which is mediated with itself through another consciousness [the bondsman, who] . . . could not get away in the struggle, and for that reason proved himself to be dependent, to have his independence in the shape of thinghood. . . .

In all this, the unessential consciousness is, for the lord, the object which constitutes the *truth* of his certainty of himself. But it is clear that this object does not correspond to its notion, but rather that the object in which the lord has effectively achieved his lordship has in reality turned out to be something quite different from an independent consciousness. What now really confronts him is not an independent consciousness, but a dependent one. He is therefore not assured of *being-for-self* as the truth of himself. On the contrary, his truth is in reality the unessential consciousness and its unessential action.

The *truth* of the independent consciousness is accordingly the servile consciousness of the bondsman. . . . it does in fact contain within itself this truth of pure negativity and being-for-self, for it has experienced this as its own essential nature. . . . its whole being has been seized with dread. . . . Furthermore, [the bondsman's] consciousness is not this dissolution of everything stable merely in principle; in his service he *actually* brings this about. By serving he rids himself of his attachment to natural existence in every single detail; and gets rid of it by working on it. . . . Thus precisely in labour wherein he seemed to have only an alienated existence, the bondsman acquires, through this re-discovery of himself by himself, a 'mind of his own'.
Phenomenology of Spirit, trans. A. V. Miller, p. 115, amended

15 Precisely because the form is as essential to the essence as the essence to itself, absolute reality must not be conceived and expressed as essence

170

alone, i.e. as immediate substance or pure self-contemplation of the divine, but as form also, and in the whole wealth of the developed form. Only then is it grasped and expressed as really actual.

The Truth is the whole. But the whole is nothing other than the essence consummating itself through its development.
Phenomenology of Spirit, trans. A. V. Miller, p. 11, amended

What is rational is actual and what is actual is rational. On this **16** conviction the plain man like the philosopher takes his stand, and from it philosophy starts in its study of the universe of mind as well as the universe of nature. If reflection, feeling, or whatever form subjective consciousness may take, looks upon the present as something vacuous and looks beyond it with the eyes of superior wisdom, it finds itself in a vacuum, and because it is actual only in the present, it is itself mere vacuity. If on the other hand the Idea passes for 'only an Idea', for something represented in an opinion, philosophy rejects such a view and shows that nothing is actual except the Idea. Once that is granted, the great thing is to apprehend in the show of the temporal and transient the substance which is immanent and the eternal which is present.
Philosophy of Right, trans. T. M. Knox, p. 10

The stages in the evolution of the Idea . . . seem to follow each other by **17** accident, and to present merely a number of different and unconnected principles, which the several systems of philosophy carry out in their own way. But it is not so. For these thousands of years the same Architect has directed the work: and that Architect is the one living Mind whose nature is to think, to bring to self-consciousness what it is, and, with its being thus set as object before it, to be at the same time raised above it, and so to reach a higher stage of its own being. The different systems which the history of philosophy presents are therefore not irreconcilable with unity. . . . In philosophy the latest birth of time is the result of all the systems that have preceded it, and must include their principles . . .
Encyclopaedia, trans. W. Wallace, §13, amended

The spectacle of so many and so various systems of philosophy suggests **18** the necessity of defining more exactly the relation of Universal to Particular. When the universal is made a mere form and co-ordinated with the particular, as if it were on the same level, it sinks into a particular itself. Even common sense in everyday matters is above the absurdity of setting a universal *beside* the particulars. Would any one, who wished for fruit, reject cherries, pears, and grapes, on the ground that they were cherries, pears, or grapes, and not fruit? But when philosophy is in question, the excuse of many is that philosophies are so different, and none of them is *the* philosophy – that each is only *a*

philosophy. Such a plea is assumed to justify any amount of contempt for philosophy. And yet cherries too are fruit.
Encyclopaedia, trans. W. Wallace, §13

19   Each of the parts of philosophy is a philosophical whole, a circle rounded and complete in itself. In each of these parts, however, the philosophical Idea is found in a particular specificality or medium. The individual circle, since it is internally a totality, bursts through the limits imposed by its special medium, and gives rise to a wider circle. The whole thus resembles a circle of circles. The Idea appears in each single circle, but, at the same time, the whole Idea is constituted by the system of these peculiar phases, and each is a necessary member of the organization.
Encyclopaedia, trans. W. Wallace, §15, amended

20   The sole thought which philosophy brings to the treatment of history is the simple concept of *Reason*: that Reason is the law of the world and that, therefore, in world history, things have come about rationally. This conviction and insight is a presupposition of history as such; in philosophy itself it is not presupposed. Through its speculative reflection philosophy has *demonstrated* that Reason – and this term may be accepted here without closer examination of its relation to God – is . . . its own exclusive basis of existence and absolute final aim, and also the energising power realising this aim; developing it from potentiality into actuality, from inward source to outward appearance, not only in the Natural but also in the Spiritual Universe, in World History.
Reason in History, trans. R. Hartman, p. 11, amended

21   In everything that is supposed to be scientific, Reason must be awake and reflection applied. To him who looks at the world rationally the world looks rationally back. The relation is mutual.
Reason in History, trans. R. Hartman, p. 13, amended

22   The question of how Reason is determined in itself and what its relation is to the world coincides with the question *What is the ultimate purpose of the world?*
Reason in History, trans. R. Hartman, p. 20, amended

23   In the course of history two factors are important. One is the preservation of a people, a state, of the well-ordered spheres of life. This is the activity of individuals participating in the common effort and helping to bring about its particular manifestations. It is the preservation of ethical life. The other important factor, however, is the decline of a state. The existence of a national spirit is broken when it has used up and exhausted itself. World history, the World Spirit, continues on its course. We cannot deal here with the position of the individuals within the moral

whole and their moral conduct and duty. We are concerned with the
Spirit's development, its progression and ascent to an ever higher concept
of itself. But this development is connected with the degradation,
destruction, annihilation of the preceding mode of actuality which the
concept of the Spirit had evolved. This is the result, on the one hand, of
the inner development of the Idea and, on the other, of the activity of
individuals, who are its agents and bring about its actualization.
Reason in History, trans. R. Hartman, p. 38, amended

The historical men, world-historical individuals, are those who . . . see   **24**
the very truth of their age and their world, the species next in order, so to
speak, which is already formed in the womb of time. It is theirs to know
this new universal, the necessary next stage of their world, to make it
their own aim and put all their energy into it. . . .

In this way the purpose of passion and the purpose of the Idea are one
and the same. . . .

By fulfilling their own great purpose in accordance with the necessity
of the universal Spirit, these world-historical men also satisfy themselves.
These two things belong inseparably together: the cause and its hero.
They must both be satisfied. . . . It is psychological pedantry to make a
separation and, by giving passion the name of addiction, to suspect the
morality of these men. By saying they acted only from morbid craving,
one presents the consequences of their actions as their purposes and
degrades the actions themselves to means. . . . 'No man is a hero to his
own valet', is a well-known proverb; I have added – and Goethe repeated
it two years later – 'but not because the former is no hero, but because
the latter is a valet'.
Reason in History, trans. R. Hartman, p. 39, amended

The hard rind of nature and the common world give the mind more   **25**
trouble in breaking through to the Idea than do the products of art.
Lectures on Aesthetics, trans. B. Bosanquet, p. 16

But if, on the one side, we assign this high position to art, we must no less   **26**
bear in mind, on the other hand, that art is not, either in content or in
form, the supreme and absolute mode of bringing the mind's genuine
interests into consciousness. The form of art is enough to limit it to a
restricted content. Only a certain circle and grade of truth is capable of
being represented in the medium of art.
Lectures on Aesthetics, trans. B. Bosanquet, p. 16

In all these respects art is, and remains for us, a thing of the past. Herein   **27**
it has further lost for us its genuine truth and life, and rather is

transferred into our *ideas* than asserts its former necessity, or assumes its former place, in reality.

Lectures on Aesthetics, trans. B. Bosanquet, p. 19

28 Philosophy is thus the true theodicy, as contrasted with art and religion and the feelings which these call up – a reconciliation of Spirit, of the Spirit which has apprehended itself in its freedom and in the riches of its actuality.

To this point the World-Spirit has come, and each stage has its own form in the true system of philosophy; nothing is lost, all principles are preserved, since philosophy in its final aspect is the totality of forms. . . .

Spirit often seems to have forgotten and lost itself, but inwardly opposed to itself, it is inwardly working ever forward (as Hamlet says of the ghost of his father, 'Well said, old mole! canst work i' the ground so fast?'), until grown strong in itself it bursts asunder the crust of earth which divided it from the sun, its concept, so that the earth crumbles away. At such a time, when the encircling crust, like a soulless decaying tenement, crumbles away, and Spirit displays itself arrayed in new youth, the seven league boots are put on.

Lectures on the History of Philosophy, trans. E. S. Haldane and F. H. Simpson, III, p. 546, amended

29 One word more about giving instruction as to what the world ought to be. Philosophy in any case always comes on the scene too late to give it. As the thought of the world, it appears only when actuality is already there cut and dried after its process of formation has been completed. The teaching of the concept, which is also history's inescapable lesson, is that it is only when actuality is mature that the ideal first appears over against the real and that the ideal apprehends this same real world in its substance and builds it up for itself into the shape of an intellectual realm. When philosophy paints its grey in grey, then has a shape of life grown old. By philosophy's grey in grey it cannot be rejuvenated but only understood. The owl of Minerva spreads its wings only with the falling of the dusk.

Philosophy of Right, trans. T. M. Knox, p. 12

MARTIN HEIDEGGER (1889–1976)

1 Do we in our time have an answer to the question of what we really mean by the word 'being'? Not at all. So it is fitting that we should raise anew *the question of the meaning of Being*. But are we nowadays even perplexed at our inability to understand the expression 'Being'? Not at all. So first of all we must reawaken an understanding for the meaning of this question.

Being and Time, trans. John Macquarrie and Edward Robinson, p. 1

In *Being and Time*, on the basis of the question of the truth of Being, no   2
longer the question of the truth of beings, an attempt is made to
determine the essence of man solely in terms of his relationship to Being.
That essence was described in a firmly delineated sense as *Dasein*.
Nietzsche, Vol. 4: *Nihilism*, trans. Frank A. Capuzzi, p. 141

We are ourselves the entities to be analysed. The Being of any such entity   3
is *in each case mine*. These entities, in their Being, comport themselves
towards their Being. As entities with such Being, they are delivered over
to their own Being. *Being* is that which is an issue for every such entity.
Being and Time, trans. John Macquarrie and Edward Robinson, p. 42

The 'essence' of Dasein lies in its existence.   4
Being and Time, trans. John Macquarrie and Edward Robinson, p. 42

The Nothing nothings.   5
'What is Metaphysics?', *Basic Writings*, ed. D. Krell

In everydayness Dasein can undergo dull 'suffering', sink away in the   6
dullness of it, and evade it by seeking new ways in which its dispersion in
its affairs may be further dispersed. In the moment of vision, indeed, and
often just 'for that moment', existence can even gain the mastery over the
'everyday'; but it can never extinguish it.
Being and Time, trans. John Macquarrie and Edward Robinson, p. 371

Only by the anticipation of death is every accidental and 'provisional'   7
possibility driven out. Only Being-free *for* death, gives Dasein its goal
outright and pushes existence into its finitude. Once one has grasped the
finitude of one's existence, it snatches one back from the endless
multiplicity of possibilities which offer themselves as closest to one –
those of comfortableness, shirking, and taking things lightly – and brings
Dasein into the simplicity of its *fate*. This is how we designate Dasein's
primordial historizing, which lies in authentic resoluteness and in which
Dasein *hands* itself *down* to itself, free for death, in a possibility which it
has inherited and yet has chosen.
Being and Time, trans. John Macquarrie and Edward Robinson, p. 384

Readiness for dread is to say 'Yes!' to the inwardness of things, to fulfil   8
the highest demand which alone touches man to the quick. Man alone of
all beings, when addressed by the voice of Being, experiences the marvel
of all marvels: that what-is *is*.
'What is Metaphysics?', *Existentialism from Dostoevsky to Sartre*, ed. W.
Kaufmann, p. 260

You do not get to philosophy by reading many and multifarious   9
philosophical books, nor by torturing yourself with solving the riddles of

the universe . . . philosophy remains latent in every human existence and need not be first added to it from somewhere else.

The Metaphysical Foundations of Logic, trans. Michael Heim, p. 18

10　So long as man exists, philosophizing of some sort occurs. Philosophy – what we call philosophy – is metaphysics' getting underway, in which philosophy comes to itself and to its explicit tasks. Philosophy gets underway only by a peculiar insertion of our own existence into the fundamental possibilities of Dasein as a whole. For this insertion it is of decisive importance, first, that we allow space for beings as a whole; second, that we release ourselves into the nothing, which is to say, that we liberate ourselves from those idols everyone has and to which he is wont to go cringing; and finally, that we let the sweep of our suspense take its full course so that it swings back into the basic question of metaphysics which the nothing itself compels: why are there beings at all, and why not rather nothing?

'What is Metaphysics?', *Basic Writings*, ed. D. Krell, p. 112

11　Being, as the element of thinking, is abandoned by the technical interpretation of thinking. 'Logic', beginning with the Sophists and Plato, sanctions this explanation. Thinking is judged by a standard that does not measure up to it. Such judgment may be compared to the procedure of trying to evaluate the nature and powers of a fish by seeing how long it can live on dry land. For a long time now, all too long, thinking has been stranded on dry land.

'Letter on Humanism', *Basic Writings*, ed. D. Krell, p. 195

12　Such names as 'logic', 'ethics', and 'physics' begin to flourish only when original thinking has come to an end. During the time of their greatness the Greeks thought without such headings. They did not even call thinking 'philosophy'. Thinking comes to an end when it slips out of its element.

'Letter on Humanism', *Basic Writings*, ed. D. Krell, p. 195

13　When irrationalism, as the counterplay of rationalism, talks about the things to which rationalism is blind, it does so only with a squint.

Being and Time, trans. John Macquarrie and Edward Robinson, p. 136

14　We must avoid uninhibited word-mysticism. Nevertheless, the ultimate business of philosophy is to preserve the *force* of the most elemental words in which Dasein expresses itself, and to keep the common understanding from levelling them off to that unintelligibility which functions in turn as a source of pseudo-problems.

Being and Time, trans. John Macquarrie and Edward Robinson, p. 220

Language is the house of Being. In its home man dwells. Those who think 15
and those who create with words are the guardians of this home.
'Letter on Humanism', *Basic Writings*, ed. D. Krell

Our Western languages are languages of metaphysical thinking, each in 16
its own way. It must remain an open question whether the nature of
Western languages is in itself marked with an exclusive brand of metaphysics, . . . or whether these languages offer other possibilities of utterance
– and that means at the same time of a telling silence.
Identity and Difference, trans. Joan Stambaugh, p. 73

For, strictly speaking, it is language that speaks. Man first speaks when, 17
and only when, he responds to language by listening to its appeal.
'*Poetry, Language, Thought*, trans. Albert Hofstadter, p. 216

The greatness of the discovery of phenomenology lies not in factually 18
obtained results, which can be evaluated and criticized and in these days
have certainly evoked a veritable transformation in questioning and
working, but rather in this: it is the *discovery of the very possibility of
doing research in philosophy*. But a possibility is rightly understood in its
most proper sense only when it continues to be taken as a possibility and
preserved as a possibility. Preserving it as a possibility does not mean,
however, to fix a chance state of research and inquiry as ultimately real
and to allow it to harden; it rather means to keep open the tendency
towards the matters themselves . . .
History of the Concept of Time: Prolegomena, trans. Theodore Kisiel, p. 135

There is no such thing as *the one* phenomenology, and if there could be 19
such a thing it would never become anything like a philosophical
technique. . . . When a method is genuine and provides access to the
objects, it is precisely then that the progress made by following it and the
growing originality of the disclosure will cause the very method that was
used to become necessarily obsolete.
The Basic Problems of Phenomenology, trans. Albert Hofstadter, p. 328

Whatever and however we may try to think, we think within the sphere 20
of tradition. Tradition prevails when it frees us from thinking back to a
thinking forward, which is no longer a planning. Only when we turn
thoughtfully toward what has already been thought, will we be turned to
use for what must still be thought.
Identity and Difference, trans. Joan Stambaugh, p. 41

Hegel at one point mentions the following case to characterise the 21
generality of what is general: someone wants to buy fruit in a store. He
asks for fruit. He is offered apples and pears, he is offered peaches,
cherries, grapes. But he rejects all that is offered. He absolutely wants to

have fruit. What was offered to him in every instance *is* fruit and yet, it turns out, fruit cannot be bought.

It is still infinitely more impossible to represent 'Being' as the general characteristic of particular things. There is Being only in this or that particular historic character: *Phusis, Logos, Hen, Idea, Energeia*, Substantiality, Objectivity, Subjectivity, the Will, the Will to Power, the Will to Will. But these historic forms cannot be found in rows, like apples, pears, peaches, lined up on the counter of historical representational thinking.

Identity and Difference, trans. Joan Stambaugh, p. 66

22 All metaphysics, including its opponent, positivism, speaks the language of Plato.
'The End of Philosophy and the Task of Thinking', *Basic Writings*, ed. D. Krell, p. 386

23 Sartre expresses the basic tenet of existentialism in this way: existence precedes essence. In this statement he is taking *existentia* and *essentia* according to their metaphysical meaning, which from Plato's time on has said that *essentia* precedes *existentia*. Sartre reverses this statement. But the reversal of a metaphysical statement remains a metaphysical statement. With it he stays with metaphysics in oblivion of the truth of Being.
'Letter on Humanism', *Basic Writings*, ed. D. Krell, p. 208

24 Thinking does not overcome metaphysics by climbing still higher, surmounting it, transcending it somehow or other; thinking overcomes metaphysics by climbing back down into the nearness of the nearest.
'Letter on Humanism', *Basic Writings*, ed. D. Krell, p. 231

25 Metaphysics cannot be abolished like an opinion. One can by no means leave it behind as a doctrine no longer believed and represented.
The End of Philosophy, trans. Joan Stambaugh, p.85

26 What is meant by the talk about the end of philosophy? We understand the end of something all too easily in the negative sense as a mere stopping, as the lack of continuation, perhaps even as decline and impotence. In contrast, what we say about the end of philosophy means the completion of metaphysics.
'The End of Philosophy and the Task of Thinking', *Basic Writings*, ed. D. Krell, p. 374

27 The epoch of completed metaphysics stands before its beginning. . . .
The basic form of appearance in which the will to will arranges and calculates itself in the unhistorical element of the world of completed metaphysics can be stringently called 'technology'. This name includes all

the areas of beings which equip the whole of beings: objectified nature, the business of culture, manufactured politics, and the gloss of ideals overlying everything. Thus 'technology' does not signify here the separate area of the production and equipment of machines. . . .

The name 'technology' is understood here in such an essential way that its meaning coincides with the term 'completed metaphysics'.
The End of Philosophy, trans. Joan Stambaugh, p. 93

The unnoticeable law of the earth preserves the earth in the sufficiency of **28** the emerging and perishing of all things in the allotted sphere of the possible which everything follows, and yet nothing knows. The birch tree never oversteps its possibility. The colony of bees dwells in its possibility. It is first the will which arranges itself everywhere in technology that devours the earth in the exhaustion and consumption and change of what is artificial. Technology drives the earth beyond the developed sphere of its possibility into such things which are no longer a possibility and are thus the impossible. The fact that technological plans and measures succeed a great deal in inventions and novelties, piling up upon each other, by no means yields the proof that the conquests of technology make the impossible possible.
The End of Philosophy, trans. Joan Stambaugh, p. 109

No single man, no group of men, no commission of prominent **29** statesmen, scientists, and technicians, no conference of leaders of commerce and industry, can brake or direct the progress of history in the atomic age. No merely human organization is capable of gaining dominion over it.

Is man, then, a defenceless and perplexed victim at the mercy of the irresistable superior power of technology?

. . . We can use technical devices as they ought to be used, and also let them alone as something which does not affect our inner and real core . . . that is, let them alone, as things which are nothing absolute but remain dependent upon something higher. I would call this comportment toward technology which expresses 'yes' and at the same time 'no', by an old word, *releasement toward things*.
Discourse on Thinking, trans. J. E. Anderson and E. H. Freund, p. 52

Man is not the lord of beings. Man is the shepherd of Being. **30**
'Letter on Humanism', *Basic Writings*, ed. D. Krell, p. 221

The end of philosophy proves to be the triumph of the manipulable **31** arrangement of a scientific-technological world and of the social order proper to that world. The end of philosophy means the beginning of the world civilization based upon Western European thinking.

'The End of Philosophy and the Task of Thinking', *Basic Writings*, ed. D. Krell, p. 377

32 Metaphysics is in all its forms and historical stages a unique, but perhaps necessary, fate of the West and the presupposition of its planetary dominance.
The End of Philosophy, trans. Joan Stambaugh, p. 90

33 I saw in the movement that had gained power (the NSDAP [National Socialist German Workers' Party]) the possibility of an inner recollection and renewal of the people and a path that would allow it to discover its historical vocation in the Western world.
'The Rectorate 1933/4, *Review of Metaphysics* (1985), p. 483

34 The will to the essence of the German university is the will to science as will to the historical mission of the German people as a people that knows itself in its state.
'The Self Assertion of the German University', (an address to Freiburg University 1933), *Review of Metaphysics* (1985), p. 471

35 Every nationalism is metaphysically an anthropologism, and as such subjectivism. Nationalism is not overcome through mere internationalism; it is rather expanded and elevated thereby into a system.
'Letter on Humanism', *Basic Writings*, ed. D. Krell, p. 221

36 We are too late for the gods
and too early for Being. Being's poem,
just begun, is man.
Poetry, Language, Thought, trans. Albert Hofstadter, p. 4

37 Is Being a mere word and its meaning a vapor, or does what is designated by the word 'Being' hold within it the historical destiny of the West?
An Introduction to Metaphysics, trans. Ralph Mannheim, p. 42

38 Philosophy will be unable to effect any immediate change in the current state of the world. This is true not only of philosophy but of all purely human reflection and endeavor. Only a god can save us. The only possibility available to us is that by thinking and poetizing we prepare a readiness for the appearance of a god, or for the absence of a god in [our] decline, insofar as in view of the absent god we are in a state of decline.
Heidegger, ed. T. Sheehan, p. 57

VIRGINIA HELD (*b.* 1929)

Frequently in the past various descriptive or normative models have been put forward as appropriate for describing or judging the whole of a society composed of legal and political and economic and personal and

other components. But these models have been derived from consideration or study of some part of a society and then extended, purportedly to take in the whole. For instance, a model of an egoistic society may be constructed by assuming that the self-interested pursuits of much of economic life characterise all social activity. How faulty such a view is can be seen by considering the behavior of a parent sacrificing much for the sake of a child; such behavior simply makes no sense on the egoistic economic model. . . . we should accept the suitability of partial views for partial contexts. We should try to improve the normative thinking we do, and the practice of morality we engage in, in the special domains in which we concentrate our efforts. The efforts of some people should be devoted to seeing these parts in relation to one another, but we should not think that morality demands us all to do so all the time. Too often the attempt to devise moral theories and systems that can encompass all problems leads to so much vagueness, unclarity, grandiosity, and indeterminacy in applying them that these theories and systems are actually applied to almost nothing.
Rights and Goods: Justifying Social Action, p. 4

C. G. HEMPEL (*b.* 1905)

The explanation outlined [above] may be regarded as an argument to the effect that the phenomenon to be explained, *the explanandum phenomenon*, was to be expected in virtue of certain explanatory facts. These fall into two groups: i) particular facts and ii) uniformities expressible by means of general laws. The first group included facts such as these: the tumblers had been immersed in soap suds of a temperature considerably higher than that of the surrounding air; they were put, upside down, on a plate on which a puddle of soapy water had formed that provided a connecting soap film, and so on. The second group of explanatory facts would be expressed by the gas laws and by various other laws concerning the exchange of heat between bodies of different temperature, the elastic behaviour of soap bubbles, and so on. While some of these laws are only hinted at by such phrasings as 'the warming of the trapped air led to an increase in its pressure', and others are not referred to even in this oblique fashion, they are clearly presupposed in the claim that certain stages in the process yielded others as their results.
Aspects of Scientific Explanation, p. 179

The use of theoretical terms in science gives rise to a perplexing problem: why should science resort to the assumption of hypothetical entities when it is interested in establishing predictive and explanatory connections among observables? Would it not be sufficient for the purpose, and much less extravagant at that, to search for a system of general laws

181

mentioning only observables, and thus expressed in terms of the observational vocabulary alone?
Aspects of Scientific Explanation, p. 179

3   The conclusion suggested by these arguments might be called the *paradox of theorizing*. It asserts that if the terms and the general principles of a scientific theory serve their purpose, i.e., if they establish definite connections among observable phenomena, then they can be dispensed with since any chain of laws and interpretative statements establishing such a connection should then be replaceable by a law which directly links observational antecedents to observational consequents.
Aspects of Scientific Explanation, p. 186

HERACLITUS (c.536–470 BC)

1   It is not possible to step into the same river twice.
Quoted in Plato, *Cratylus*, 402A

2   We both step and do not step into the same rivers; we both are and are not.
Quoted in J. E. Barnes, *The Pre-Socratic Philosophers*, p. 66

3   The way up and the way down are one and the same.
G. S. Kirk, J. E. Raven and M. Schofield, *The Pre-Socratic Philosophers*, p. 188

4   The god: day and night, winter and summer, war and peace, satiety and hunger. It alters, as when mingled with perfumes, it gets named according to the pleasure of each one.
Art and Thought of Heraclitus, trans. Charles H. Kahn, p. 276

5   Listening not to me but to the Logos it is wise to agree that all things are one.
G. S. Kirk, J. E. Raven and M. Schofield, *The Pre-Socratic Philosophers*, p. 187

6   Nature loves to hide.
Art and Thought of Heraclitus, p. 105

7   A hidden connexion is stronger than an obvious one.
The Pre-Socratic Philosophers, p. 192

8   You would not find out the boundaries of soul, even by travelling along every path: so deep a measure does it have.
The Pre-Socratic Philosophers, p. 203

9   It is hard to fight with anger; for what it wants it buys at the price of soul.
The Pre-Socratic Philosophers, p. 208

The world order did none of gods or men make, but it always was and is   10
and shall be: an everlasting fire, kindling in measures and going out in
measures.
The Pre-Socratic Philosophers, p. 198

AREND HEYTING (1898–1980)

If 'to exist' does not mean 'to be constructed', it must have some
metaphysical meaning. It cannot be the task of mathematics to
investigate this meaning or to decide whether it is tenable or not. We
have no objection against a mathematician privately admitting any
metaphysical theory he likes, but Brouwer's program entails that we
study mathematics as something simpler, more immediate than metaphysics. In the study of mental mathematical constructions 'to exist' must
be synonymous with 'to be constructed'.
Intuitionism: An Introduction, p. 2

THOMAS HOBBES (1588–1679)

For by art is created that great LEVIATHAN called a COMMON-   1
WEALTH, or STATE, in Latin CIVITAS, which is but an artificial man;
though of greater stature and strength than the natural, for whose
protection and defence it was intended; and in which the *sovereignty* is
an artificial *soul*, as giving life and motion to the whole body; the
magistrates, and other officers of judicature and execution, artificial
joints; *reward* and *punishment*, by which fastened to the seat of
sovereignty every joint and member is moved to perform its duty, are the
nerves, that do the same in the body natural . . .
Leviathan, English Works, 3, p. ix

. . . it is a real unity of them all, in one and the same person, made by   2
covenant of every man with every man, in such manner, as if every man
should say to every man, *I authorize and give up my right of governing
myself, to this man, or to this assembly of men, on this condition, that
thou give up thy right to him, and authorize all his actions in like manner.*
This done, the multitude so united in one person is called a COMMON-
WEALTH, in Latin CIVITAS. This is the generation of that great
LEVIATHAN, or rather, to speak more reverently, of that *mortal god*, to
which we owe under the *immortal God* our peace and defence.
Leviathan, English Works, 3, p. 158

But a man may here object, that the condition of subjects is very   3
miserable; as being obnoxious to the lusts, and other irregular passions
of him, or them that have so unlimited a power in their hands. And
commonly they that live under a monarch, think it the fault of monarchy;

and they that live under the government of democracy, or other sovereign assembly, attribute all the inconvenience to that form of commonwealth; whereas the power in all forms, if they be perfect enough to protect them, is the same: not considering that the estate of man can never be without some incommodity or other; and that the greatest, that in any form of government can possibly happen to the people in general, is scarce sensible, in respect of the miseries, and horrible calamities, that accompany a civil war, or that dissolute condition of masterless men, without subjection to laws, and a coercive power to tie their hands from rapine and revenge . . .
Leviathan, English Works, 3, p. 169

4   Whatsoever therefore is consequent to a time of war, where every man is enemy to every man; the same is consequent to the time, wherein men live without other security, than what their own strength, and their own invention shall furnish them withal. In such a condition, there is no place for industry; because the fruit thereof is uncertain: and consequently no culture of the earth; no navigation, nor use of commodities that may be imported by sea; no commodious building; no instruments of moving, and removing, such things as require much force; no knowledge of the face of the earth; no account of time; no arts; no letters; no society; and which is worst of all, continual fear, and danger of violent death; and the life of man, solitary, poor, nasty, brutish, and short.
Leviathan, English Works, 3, p. 113

5   To this war of every man, against every man, this also is consequent; that nothing can be unjust. The notions of right and wrong, justice and injustice have there no place. Where there is no common power, there is no law: where no law, no injustice. Force, and fraud, are in war the two cardinal virtues. Justice, and injustice, are none of the faculties neither of the body, nor mind. If they were, they might be in a man that were alone in the world, as well as his senses, and passions. They are qualities, that relate to men in society, not in solitude. It is consequent also to the same condition, that there be no propriety, no dominion, no *mine* and *thine* distinct; but only that to be every man's, that he can get; and for so long, as he can keep it.
Leviathan, English Works, 3, p. 113

6   Whosoever therefore holds, that it had been best to have continued in that state in which all things were lawful for all men, he contradicts himself. For every man by natural necessity desires that which is good for him: nor is there any that esteems a war of all against all, which necessarily adheres to such a state, to be good for him. And so it happens, that through fear of each other we think it fit to rid ourselves of this

condition, and to get some fellows; that if there needs must be war, it may not yet be against all men, nor without some helps.
Philosophical Rudiments, English Works, 2, p. 12

... in the mere state of nature, if you have a mind to kill, that state itself 7 affords you a right.
Philosophical Rudiments, English Works, 2, p. 25

... amongst men, there are very many, that think themselves wiser, and 8 abler to govern the public, better than the rest; and these strive to reform and innovate, one this way, another that way; and thereby bring it into distraction and civil war.
Leviathan, English Works, 3, p. 156

... there is no such thing as perpetual tranquillity of mind, while we live 9 here; because life itself is but motion, and can never be without desire, nor without fear, no more than without sense.
Leviathan, English Works, 3, p. 51

For every man is desirous of what is good for him, and shuns what is evil, 10 but chiefly the chiefest of natural evils, which is death; and this he doth by a certain impulsion of nature, no less than that by which a stone moves downward.
Philosophical Rudiments, English Works, 2, p. 3

For all men are by nature provided of notable multiplying glasses, that is, 11 their passions and self-love, through which, every little payment appeareth a great grievance; but are destitute of those prospective glasses, namely moral and civil science, to see far off the miseries that hang over them, and cannot without such payments be avoided.
Leviathan, English Works, 3, p. 170

... he that will do anything for his pleasure, must engage himself to 12 suffer all the pains annexed to it; and these pains, are the natural punishments of those actions, which are the beginning of more harm than good. And hereby it comes to pass that intemperance is naturally punished with diseases; rashness with mischances; injustice with the violence of enemies: pride, with ruin; cowardice, with oppression; negligent government of princes, with rebellion; and rebellion, with slaughter.
Leviathan, English Works, 3, p. 357

For it is with the mysteries of our religion, as with wholesome pills for the 13 sick; which swallowed whole have the virtue to cure; but chewed, are for the most part cast up again without effect.
Leviathan, English Works, 3, p. 360

14 So that the nature of justice, consisteth in keeping of valid covenants: but the validity of covenants begins not but with the constitution of a civil power, sufficient to compel men to keep them; and then it is also that propriety begins.
Leviathan, English Works, 3, p. 131

15 . . . words are wise men's counters, they do but reckon by them; but they are the money of fools, that value them by the authority of an Aristotle, a Cicero, or a Thomas, or any other doctor whatsoever, if but a man.
Leviathan, English Works, 3, p. 25

16 By the advantage of names it is that we are capable of science, which beasts, for want of them, are not; nor man, without the use of them: for a beast misseth not one or two out of her many young ones, for want of those names of order, one, two, three etc., which we call number; so neither would a man, without repeating orally, or mentally, the words of number, know how many pieces of money or other things lie before him.
The Elements of Law, ed. F. Tonnies, p. 19

17 . . . if we do but diligently observe what it is we do when we consider and reason, we shall find, that though all things be still remaining in the world, yet we compute nothing but our own phantasms. For when we calculate the magnitude and motions of heaven or earth, we do not ascend into heaven that we may divide it into parts, or measure the motions thereof, but we do it sitting still in our closets or in the dark.
Elements of Philosophy, English Works, 1, p. 92

18 Seeing then that truth consisteth in the right ordering of names in our affirmations, a man that seeketh precise truth had need to remember what every name he uses stands for, and to place it accordingly, or else he will find himself entangled in words, as a bird in lime twigs, the more he struggles, the more belimed.
Leviathan, English Works, 3, p. 23

19 Method, therefore, in the study of philosophy, *is the shortest way of finding effects by their known causes, or of causes by their known effects.*
Elements of Philosophy, English Works, 1, p. 66

20 . . . words understood are but the seed, and no part of the harvest of philosophy.
Six Lessons to the Professors of Mathematics, English Works, 7, p. 225

21 For it is most true that Cicero saith of them somewhere; that there can be nothing so absurd, but may be found in the books of the philosophers. And the reason is manifest. For there is not one of them begins his ratiocination from the definitions, or explications of the names they are

to use; which is a method that hath been used only in geometry; whose
conclusions have thereby been made indisputable.
Leviathan, English Works, 3, p. 33

... the doctrine of right and wrong, is perpetually disputed, both by the 22
pen and the sword: whereas the doctrine of lines, and figures, is not so;
because men care not, in that subject, what be truth, as a thing that
crosses no man's ambition, profit or lust. For I doubt not, but if it had
been a thing contrary to any man's right of dominion, or to the interest of
men that have dominion, *that the three angles of a triangle, should be
equal to two angles of a square*; that doctrine should have been, if not
disputed, yet by the burning of all books of geometry, suppressed, as far
as he whom it concerned was able.
Leviathan, English Works, 3, p. 33

The world (I mean not the earth only, that denominates lovers of it 23
worldly men, but the *universe*, that is, the whole mass of all things that
are), is corporeal, that is to say, body, and hath the dimensions of
magnitude, namely, length, breadth, and depth: also every part of body,
is likewise body, and hath the like dimensions; and consequently every
part of the universe, is body, and that which is not body, is no part of the
universe: and because the universe is all, that which is no part of it, is
nothing; and consequently *no where*.
Leviathan, English Works, 3, p. 672

To his Lordship's question here: *What I leave God to be?* I answer, I 24
leave him to be a most pure, simple, invisible spirit corporeal.
An Answer to Bishop Bramhall, English Works, 4, p. 313

And I believe that scarce anything can be more absurdly said in natural 25
philosophy, than that which is now called *Aristotle's Metaphysics*; nor
more repugnant to government, than much of that he hath said in his
Politics; nor more ignorantly, than a great part of his *Ethics*.
Leviathan, English Works, 3, p. 669

For ... what *liberty* is; there can no other proof be offered but every 26
man's own experience, by reflection on himself, and remembering what
he useth in his mind, that is, what he himself meaneth when he saith an
action ... is *free*. Now he that reflecteth so on himself, cannot but be
satisfied ... that a *free agent* is he *that can do if he will*, and *forbear if he
will*; and that *liberty* is *the absence of external impediments*. But to those
that out of custom speak not what they conceive, but what they heard,
and are not able, or will not take the pains to consider what they think
when they hear such words, no argument can be sufficient, because

experience and *matter of fact* are not verified by other men's arguments, but by every man's own *sense* and *memory*.
Of Liberty and Necessity, English Works, 4, p. 275

27   The *value*, or WORTH of a man, is as of all things, his price; that is to say, as much so would be given for the use of his power: and therefore is not absolute; but a thing dependent on the need and judgment of another.
Leviathan, English Works, 3, p. 76

TED HONDERICH (*b.* 1933)

1   Each psychoneural pair, which is to say a mental event and a neural event which are a single effect and in a lesser sense a single cause – each such pair is in fact the effect of the initial elements of a certain causal sequence. The initial elements are (i) neural and other bodily elements just prior to the first mental event in the existence of the person in question, and (ii) direct environmental elements then and thereafter.
A Theory of Determinism: The Mind, Neuroscience, and Life Hopes, p. 173

2   Each of us can focus on either of two conflicting sets of propositions, ideas, or images about actions. One set of these things has to do with voluntariness or willingness – in one of several summary definitions, they have to do with action issuing from embraced desires. We can take these propositions as the only essential ones entering into life-hopes, personal feelings, knowledge, and moral matters. If we do this, we may make the intransigent response to determinism, that it does not matter. On the other hand, we can focus on a larger set of propositions and the like about actions. They have to do with both voluntariness and origination. We can take it that only all of these considerations together provide good reasons for life-hopes and so on. If we do this, we may make a different response to determinism – dismay. Neither facts nor logic by themselves, then, force us into either of the two responses. They are in part a matter of the mentioned focusing, the attitudes. What is true, as a matter of logic, is that a determinism is consistent with the first set of considerations and inconsistent with the second. It follows, if determinism is a fact, that the first set of considerations is undisturbed and the second is false. . . . The fundamental mistake of both Compatibilists and Incompatibilists has been to seize on one attitude with respect to the initiation of action, convert it into something else – a single conception of initiation and something presented as a belief – and to ignore another attitude quite as real.
A Theory of Determinism: The Mind, Neuroscience, and Life Hopes, p. 486

We have a clear conception of the connection between a causal   3
circumstance and an effect, got from our experience of the natural world.
On this conception there rests a philosophy of mind and action, free of
ancient and modern mystery. It, or something not fundamentally
different from it, is likely true. It makes our choices and decisions, and
our actions, into certain necessitated events. They cannot then derive
from what is named origination. To be inclined to accept this is to have a
problem of feeling, which one can attempt to resolve by a certain
affirmation. That response first involves the main category of possible
consequences of determinism, which includes life-hopes, personal
feelings, knowledge, moral responsibility, the rightness of actions and the
moral standing of persons. These great things are affected by determinism, but persist, and our lives do not become dark, but remain open to
celebration. This response can also be made with a second category of
possible consequences of determinism, more of the order of necessities
than great things. These have to do with our social lives. It was
Schopenhauer's view, perhaps, that our existence is to be mourned, that
we would decline the gift of life if we could anticipate its nature
beforehand. Nietzsche, in his way also a determinist, said differently, that
we may affirm life. It is Nietzsche with whom we can and must agree.
A Theory of Determinism: The Mind, Neuroscience, and Life Hopes, p. 613

The Principle of Equality . . . is that *our principal end must be to make*   4
well-off those who are badly off, by way of certain policies: increasing
means to well-being and transferring means from the better-off which
will not affect their well-being; transferring means from the better-off
which will affect their well-being, those at the higher levels to be affected
first, and observing a certain limit; reducing the necessity of inequalities.
Violence for Equality: Inquiries in Political Philosophy, p. 54

It may be, then, that neither a commitment to moral necessities nor any   5
proposition about political obligation will allow us to settle the question
of violence with despatch. More generally, and still tentatively, there is
the idea that there may be nothing by way of *doctrine* or *commitment*
which enables us to do so. It may be that we cannot settle our minds by
way of Marx's theory of history and his propositions about terrorism
and revolution, or by way of lawyer-like reflections on what is sometimes
called the rule of law, or by an embracing of liberal values, or by a
politician's reliance on the values of negotiation and compromise, or by
any version of the idea, so refuted by the course of history, or just by its
wars, that those in authority know best. No more needs to be said in
explanation of doctrines and commitments than this: they are all the
supposed means but one of settling the question of violence. That
remaining one is judgement between alternatives. . . .

Which is right, *non-violent action* at a cost of distress D_1 and with a probability P_1 of ending or altering a circumstance M_1 of misery or injustice within the time T_1, or *violence* at a cost of distress D_2 and with a probability P_2 of ending or altering a circumstance M_2 of misery or injustice within the time T_2?

Violence for Equality: Inquiries in Political Philosophy, p. 182

A. M. HONORÉ (b. 1921)

A theory of law is, inter alia, a theory about the appropriate attitudes to obedience and disobedience to certain prescriptions, and it would be less than candid to pretend that such a theory can be morally or politically neutral. Legal theory is a form of practical reason, not a science. In contrast with law-making and law reform, which can in theory be scientific to the same extent as other goal-determined techniques like medicine, legal theory is in the end an elaborate form of exhortation or an elaborate display of commitment.

'Groups, Laws and Obedience', *Oxford Essays in Jurisprudence*, ed. A. Simpson, p. 1

CHRISTOPHER HOOKWAY (b. 1949)

1 . . . sceptical arguments challenge our ability to preserve our rational autonomy while participating in inquiry – or our ability to preserve our rational autonomy while planning actions that rely upon products of our inquiries. The problem of scepticism emerges as a special case of the free will problem.

Scepticism, p. 144

2 Human beings participate in a wide range of activities, from physics to painting, from cognitive psychology to politics. One thing we can look for from philosophy is a clarification of the concepts we use when participating in such activities: how do they enable us to understand our involvement in them? How do they guide the choices and evaluations we make when we vote, visit a gallery, or conduct an experiment? The vocabulary of physics seems wholly unsuited to this kind of self-understanding, and it can thus be argued that . . . what [a physicalist like Quine] misses may somehow be constitutive of human experience – of our ability to think of ourselves as persons. A level of explanation which provides the terms in which we understand our lives and activities has a kind of autonomous validity. For the logician, the task of constructing a calculus which we can use to reflect upon ordinary practices of reasoning is as important as the task of constructing a canonical notation for science.

Quine: Language, Experience and Reality, p. 213

MAX HORKHEIMER (1895–1973)

Good will, solidarity and wretchedness, and the struggle for a better   1
world have now thrown off their religious garb. The attitude of today's
martyrs is no longer patience but action; their goal is no longer their own
immortality in the after-life but the happiness of men who come after
them and for whom they know how to die.
Critical Theory: Selected Essays, trans. Matthew J. O'Connell et al., p. 130

The contradiction between what is requested of man and what can be   2
offered to him has become so striking, the ideology so thin, the
discontents in civilization so great that they must be compensated
through annihilation of those who do not conform, political enemies,
Jews, asocial persons, the insane. The new order of fascism is reason
revealing itself as unreason.
'The End of Reason', *The Essential Frankfurt School Reader*, ed. A. Arato and E.
Gebhardt, p. 46

JENNIFER HORNSBY (*b.* 1951)

To describe an event as a perception (a perceiving of something) is to
describe it in terms of its causes: to describe an event as an action is to
describe it in terms of its effects. The analogy is particularly striking if
one thinks that an action is an event that takes place inside the body and
that the bodily movement₁ required for there to be an action is not itself a
part of that action. We do not think of events of perception as including
the things that we perceive. Perhaps, as I have argued, we should equally
not think of an action as including the movement whose occurrence is a
necessary condition of its having occurred.
Actions, p. 111

GERARD J. HUGHES (*b.* 1934)

Aquinas does indeed refuse what one might term a narrow verificationist
account of the meaning of 'good' when applied to God. To say that God
is good is not simply to say that our world is worth living in, or anything
of that kind. Neither is 'God is good' synonymous with 'God is the cause
of goodness in creatures', if only because God would still be good even
had he never created at all. Goodness is said of God *substantialiter* – that
is to say, God's goodness is neither a property nor an abstraction, but a
subsistent individual. God is whatever it takes to ground the truth of the
fact that he is the cause of goodness in creatures. Of course, we can *say*
that this ground just is 'goodness', thus signalling that it must somehow
resemble goodness in creatures. But though we must use the *word*

191

goodness, we are unable to state in what this resemblance consists. It 'transcends our mode of expression' because God transcends our way of existing. He is not a being among others, let alone the supremely good one among the good of this world.
The Philosophical Assessment of Theology, ed. G. Hughes, p. 47

DAVID HUME (1711–1776)

1 There is no question of importance, whose decision is not compriz'd in the science of man; and there is none, which can be decided with any certainty, before we become acquainted with that science. In pretending therefore to explain the principles of human nature, we in effect propose a compleat system of the sciences, built on a foundation almost entirely new, and the only one upon which they can stand with any security.
A Treatise of Human Nature, ed. L. Selby-Bigge, p. xvi

2 All the perceptions of the human mind resolve themselves into two distinct kinds, which I shall call IMPRESSIONS and IDEAS. The difference betwixt these consists in the degrees of force and liveliness, with which they strike upon the mind, and make their way into our thought or consciousness. Those perceptions, which enter with most force and violence, we may name *impressions*; and under this name I comprehend all our sensations, passions and emotions, as they make their first appearance in the soul. By *ideas* I mean the faint images of these in thinking and reasoning.
A Treatise of Human Nature, p. 1

3 . . . all our simple ideas in their first appearance are deriv'd from simple impressions, which are correspondent to them, and which they exactly represent.
A Treatise of Human Nature, p. 4

4 Whatever has the air of a paradox, and is contrary to the first and most unprejudic'd notions of mankind is often greedily embrac'd by philosophers, as shewing the superiority of their science, which cou'd discover opinions so remote from vulgar conception.
A Treatise of Human Nature, p. 26

5 The idea of time is not deriv'd from a particular impression mix'd up with others, and plainly distinguishable from them; but arises altogether from the manner, in which impressions appear to the mind, without making one of the number. Five notes play'd on a flute give us the impression and idea of time; tho' time be not a sixth impression, which presents itself to the hearing or any other of the senses.
A Treatise of Human Nature, p. 36

Now since nothing is ever present to the mind but perceptions, and since 6
all ideas are deriv'd from something antecedently present to the mind; it
follows, that 'tis impossible for us so much as to conceive or form an idea
of any thing specifically different from ideas and impressions. Let us fix
our attention out of ourselves as much as possible: let us chace our
imagination to the heavens, or to the utmost limits of the universe; we
never really advance a step beyond ourselves, nor can conceive any kind
of existence, but those perceptions, which have appear'd in that narrow
compass. This is the universe of the imagination, nor have we any idea
but what is there produc'd.
A Treatise of Human Nature, p. 67

The only connexion or relation of objects, which can lead us beyond the 7
immediate impressions of our memory and senses, is that of cause and
effect; and that because 'tis the only one, on which we can found a just
inference from one object to another.
A Treatise of Human Nature, p. 89

We have no other notion of cause and effect, but that of certain objects, 8
which have been *always conjoin'd* together, and which in all past
instances have been found inseparable.
A Treatise of Human Nature, p. 93

Thus all probable reasoning is nothing but a species of sensation. 'Tis not 9
solely in poetry and music, we must follow our taste and sentiment, but
likewise in philosophy.
A Treatise of Human Nature, p. 103

Upon the whole, necessity is something, that exists in the mind, not in 10
objects; nor is it possible for us ever to form the most distant idea of it,
consider'd as a quality in bodies. Either we have no idea of necessity, or
necessity is nothing but that determination of the thought to pass from
causes to effects and from effects to causes, according to their experienc'd
union.
A Treatise of Human Nature, p. 165

'Tis a common observation, that the mind has a great propensity to 11
spread itself on external objects, and to conjoin with them any internal
impressions, which they occasion . . .
A Treatise of Human Nature, p. 167

Next to the ridicule of denying an evident truth, is that of taking much 12
pains to defend it; and no truth appears to me more evident, than that
beasts are endow'd with thought and reason as well as men.
A Treatise of Human Nature, p. 176

13 To consider the matter aright, reason is nothing but a wonderful and unintelligible instinct in our souls, which carries us along a certain train of ideas, and endows them with particular qualities, according to their particular situations and relations.
A Treatise of Human Nature, p. 179

14 Our reason must be consider'd as a kind of cause, of which truth is the natural effect; but such-a-one as by the irruption of other causes, and by the inconstancy of our mental powers, may frequently be prevented. By this means all knowledge degenerates into probability . . .
A Treatise of Human Nature, p. 180

15 . . . belief is more properly an act of the sensitive, than of the cogitative part of our natures.
A Treatise of Human Nature, p. 183

16 Thus the sceptic still continues to reason and believe, even tho' he asserts, that he cannot defend his reason by reason; and by the same rule he must assent to the principle concerning the existence of body, tho' he cannot pretend by any arguments of philosophy to maintain its veracity. Nature has not left this to his choice, and has doubtless esteem'd it an affair of too great importance to be trusted to our uncertain reasonings and speculations. We may well ask, *What causes induce us to believe in the existence of body?* but 'tis in vain to ask, *Whether there be body or not?* That is a point, which we must take for granted in all our reasonings.
A Treatise of Human Nature, p. 187

17 . . . philosophy informs us, that every thing, which appears to the mind, is nothing but a perception, and is interrupted, and dependent on the mind; whereas the vulgar confound perceptions and objects, and attribute a distinct continu'd existence to the very things they feel or see.
A Treatise of Human Nature, p. 193

18 . . . the imagination, when set into any train of thinking, is apt to continue, even when its object fails it, and like a galley put in motion by the oars, carries on its course without any new impulse. . . . The same principle makes us easily entertain this opinion of the continu'd existence of body.
A Treatise of Human Nature, p. 198

19 . . . *an object may exist, and yet be no where*: and I assert, that this is not only possible, but that the greatest part of beings do and must exist after this manner. . . . this is evidently the case with all our perceptions and objects, except those of the sight and feeling.
A Treatise of Human Nature, p. 235

The most vulgar philosophy informs us, that no external object can make 20
itself known to the mind immediately, and without the interposition of
an image or perception.
A Treatise of Human Nature, p. 239

For my part, when I enter most intimately into what I call *myself*, I 21
always stumble on some particular perception or other, of heat or cold,
light or shade, love or hatred, pain or pleasure. I never can catch *myself*
at any time without a perception, and never can observe any thing but the
perception. When my perceptions are remov'd for any time, as by sound
sleep; so long am I insensible of *myself*, and may truly be said not to
exist.
A Treatise of Human Nature, p. 252

. . . setting aside some metaphysicians of this kind, I may venture to 22
affirm of the rest of mankind, that they are nothing but a bundle or
collection of different perceptions, which succeed each other with an
inconceivable rapidity, and are in a perpetual flux and movement. . . .
The mind is a kind of theatre, where several perceptions successively
make their appearance; pass, re-pass, glide away, and mingle in an
infinite variety of postures and situations. There is properly no *simplicity*
in it at one time, nor *identity* in different; whatever natural propension
we may have to imagine that simplicity and identity. The comparison of
the theatre must not mislead us. They are the successive perceptions only,
that constitute the mind; nor have we the most distant notion of the
place, where these scenes are represented, or of the materials, of which it
is compos'd.
A Treatise of Human Nature, p. 252

I cannot compare the soul more properly to any thing than to a republic 23
or commonwealth, in which the several members are united by the
reciprocal ties of government and subordination, and give rise to other
persons, who propagate the same republic in the incessant changes of its
parts. And as the same individual republic may not only change its
members, but also its laws and constitutions; in like manner the same
person may vary his character and disposition, as well as his impressions
and ideas, without losing his identity.
A Treatise of Human Nature, p. 261

. . . memory does not so much *produce* as *discover* personal identity, by 24
shewing us the relation of cause and effect among our different
perceptions.
A Treatise of Human Nature, p. 262

25   . . . upon a more strict review of the section concerning *personal identity*, I find myself involv'd in such a labyrinth, that, I must confess, I neither know how to correct my former opinions, nor how to render them consistent.
A Treatise of Human Nature, Appendix, p. 663

26   After the most accurate and exact of my reasonings, I can give no reason why I shou'd assent to it; and feel nothing but a *strong* propensity to consider objects *strongly* in that view, under which they appear to me. . . . The memory, senses, and understanding are, therefore, all of them founded on the imagination, or the vivacity of our ideas.
A Treatise of Human Nature, p. 265

27   . . . the question is, how far we ought to yield to these illusions.
A Treatise of Human Nature, p. 267

28   We have, therefore, no choice left but betwixt a false reason and none at all. For my part, I know not what ought to be done in the present case. I can only observe what is commonly done; which is, that this difficulty is seldom or never thought of; and even where it has once been present to the mind, is quickly forgot, and leaves but a small impression behind it. Very refin'd reflections have little or no influence upon us; and yet we do not, and cannot establish it for a rule, that they ought not to have any influence; which implies a manifest contradiction.
A Treatise of Human Nature, p. 268

29   Most fortunately it happens, that since reason is incapable of dispelling these clouds, nature herself suffices to that purpose, and cures me of this philosophical melancholy and delirium, either by relaxing this bent of mind, or by some avocation, and lively impression of my senses, which obliterate all these chimeras. I dine, I play a game of back-gammon, I converse, and am merry with my friends; and when after three or four hour's amusement, I wou'd return to these speculations, they appear so cold, and strain'd, and ridiculous, that I cannot find in my heart to enter into them any farther.
     Here then I find myself absolutely and necessarily determin'd to live, and talk, and act like other people in the common affairs of life.
A Treatise of Human Nature, p. 269

30   I may, nay I must yield to the current of nature, in submitting to my senses and understanding; and in this blind submission I shew most perfectly my sceptical disposition and principles.
A Treatise of Human Nature, p. 269

If we believe, that fire warms, or water refreshes, 'tis only because it costs   31
us too much pains to think otherwise.
A Treatise of Human Nature, p. 270

Generally speaking, the errors in religion are dangerous; those in   32
philosophy only ridiculous.
A Treatise of Human Nature, p. 272

. . . by the *will*, I mean nothing but *the internal impression we feel and are*   33
conscious of, when we knowingly give rise to any new motion of our
body, or new perception of our mind.
A Treatise of Human Nature, p. 399

According to my definitions, necessity makes an essential part of   34
causation; and consequently liberty, by removing necessity, removes also
causes, and is the very same thing with chance. As chance is commonly
thought to imply a contradiction, and is at least directly contrary to
experience, there are always the same arguments against liberty or free-
will.
A Treatise of Human Nature, p. 407

We speak not strictly and philosophically when we talk of the combat of   35
passion and of reason. Reason is, and ought only to be the slave of the
passions, and can never pretend to any other office than to serve and
obey them.
A Treatise of Human Nature, p. 415

'Tis not contrary to reason to prefer the destruction of the whole world   36
to the scratching of my finger. 'Tis not contrary to reason for me to chuse
my total ruin, to prevent the least uneasiness of an *Indian* or person
wholly unknown to me. 'Tis as little contrary to reason to prefer even my
own acknowledg'd lesser good to my greater, and have a more ardent
affection for the former than the latter. . . . In short, a passion must be
accompany'd with some false judgment, in order to its being unreasonable; and even then 'tis not the passion, properly speaking, which is
unreasonable, but the judgment.
A Treatise of Human Nature, p. 416

Morals excite passions, and produce or prevent actions. Reason of itself   37
is utterly impotent in this particular. The rules of morality, therefore, are
not conclusions of our reason.
A Treatise of Human Nature, p. 457

'Tis one thing to know virtue, and another to conform the will to it.   38
A Treatise of Human Nature, p. 465

39   All beings in the universe, consider'd in themselves, appear entirely loose and independent of each other. 'Tis only by experience we learn their influence and connexion . . .
A Treatise of Human Nature, p. 466

40   Take any action allow'd to be vicious: wilful murder, for instance. Examine it in all lights, and see if you can find that matter of fact, or real existence, which you call *vice*. In which-ever way you take it, you find only certain passions, motives, volitions and thoughts. There is no other matter of fact in the case. The vice entirely escapes you, as long as you consider the object. You never can find it, till you turn your reflexion into your own breast, and find a sentiment of disapprobation, which arises in you, towards this action. Here is a matter of fact; but 'tis the object of feeling, not of reason. It lies in yourself, not in the object. So that when you pronounce any action or character to be vicious, you mean nothing, but that from the constitution of your nature you have a feeling or sentiment of blame from the contemplation of it. Vice and virtue, therefore, may be compar'd to sounds, colours, heat and cold, which, according to modern philosophy, are not qualities in objects, but perceptions in the mind: and this discovery in morals, like that other in physics, is to be regarded as a considerable advancement of the speculative sciences; tho', like that too, it has little or no influence on practice.
A Treatise of Human Nature, p. 468

41   In every system of morality, which I have hitherto met with, I have always remark'd, that the author proceeds for some time in the ordinary way of reasoning, and establishes the being of a God, or makes observations concerning human affairs; when of a sudden I am surpriz'd to find, that instead of the usual copulations of propositions, *is*, and *is not*, I meet with no proposition that is not connected with an *ought*, or an *ought not*. This change is imperceptible; but is, however, of the last consequence. For as this *ought*, or *ought not*, expresses some new relation or affirmation, 'tis necessary that it shou'd be observ'd and explain'd; and at the same time that a reason should be given, for what seems altogether inconceivable, how this new relation can be a deduction from others, which are entirely different from it. But as authors do not commonly use this precaution, I shall presume to recommend it to the readers; and am persuaded, that this small attention wou'd subvert all the vulgar systems of morality, and let us see, that the distinction of vice and virtue is not founded merely on the relations of objects, nor is perceiv'd by reason.
A Treatise of Human Nature, p. 469

Morality, therefore, is more properly felt than judg'd of; tho' this feeling **42** or sentiment is commonly so soft and gentle, that we are apt to confound it with an idea, according to our common custom of taking all things for the same, which have any near resemblance to each other.
A Treatise of Human Nature, p. 470

. . . the actions of each of us have a reference to those of the other, and are **43** perform'd upon the supposition, that something is to be perform'd on the other part. Two men, who pull the oars of a boat, do it by an agreement or convention, tho' they have never given promises to each other.
A Treatise of Human Nature, p. 489

We may begin with considering a-new the nature and force of *sympathy*. **44** The minds of all men are similar in their feelings and operations, nor can any one be actuated by any affection, of which all others are not, in some degree, susceptible. As in strings equally wound up, the motion of one communicates itself to the rest; so all the affections readily pass from one person to another, and beget correspondent movements in every human creature.
A Treatise of Human Nature, p. 575

The only difference betwixt the natural virtues and justice lies in this, that **45** the good, which results from the former, arises from every single act, and is the object of some natural passion: whereas a single act of justice, consider'd in itself, may often be contrary to the public good; and 'tis only the concurrence of mankind, in a general scheme or system of action, which is advantageous.
A Treatise of Human Nature, p. 579

The sentiments of others can never affect us, but by becoming, in some **46** measure, our own . . .
A Treatise of Human Nature, p. 593

If we compare all these circumstances, we shall not doubt, that sympathy **47** is the chief source of moral distinctions . . .
A Treatise of Human Nature, p. 618

All probable arguments are built on the supposition, that there is this **48** conformity betwixt the future and the past, and therefore can never prove it. This conformity is a *matter of fact*, and if it must be proved, will admit of no proof but from experience. But our experience in the past can be a proof of nothing for the future, but upon a supposition, that there is a resemblance betwixt them. This therefore is a point, which can admit of no proof at all, and which we take for granted without any proof.
A Treatise of Human Nature (Abstract), p. 651

49 'Tis not, therefore, reason, which is the guide of life, but custom.
A Treatise of Human Nature (Abstract), p. 652

50 . . . notwithstanding the empire of the imagination, there is a secret tie or union among particular ideas, which causes the mind to conjoin them more frequently together, and makes the one, upon its appearance, introduce the other. . . . These principles of association are reduced to three, *viz. Resemblance*; . . . *Contiguity*; . . . *Causation*; . . . as it is by means of thought only that any thing operates upon our passions, and as these are the only ties of our thought, they are really *to us* the cement of the universe, and all the operations of the mind must, in a great measure, depend on them.
A Treatise of Human Nature (Abstract), p. 661

51 Be a philosopher; but, amidst all your philosophy, be still a man.
An Enquiry concerning Human Understanding, ed. L. Selby-Bigge, p. 9

52 Here, then, is a kind of pre-established harmony between the course of nature and the succession of our ideas; and though the powers and forces, by which the former is governed, be wholly unknown to us; yet our thoughts and conceptions have still, we find, gone on in the same train with the other works of nature. Custom is that principle, by which this correspondence has been effected; so necessary to the subsistence of our species, and the regulation of our conduct, in every circumstance and occurrence of human life.
An Enquiry concerning Human Understanding, p. 54

53 . . . experience only teaches us, how one event constantly follows another; without instructing us in the secret connexion, which binds them together, and renders them inseparable.
An Enquiry concerning Human Understanding, p. 66

54 So that, upon the whole, there appears not, throughout all nature, any one instance of connexion which is conceivable by us. All events seem entirely loose and separate. One event follows another; but we never can observe any ties between them. They seem *conjoined*, but never *connected*. And as we can have no idea of any thing which never appeared to our outward sense or inward sentiment, the necessary conclusion *seems* to be that we have no idea of connexion or power at all, and that these words are absolutely without any meaning, when employed either in philosophical reasonings or common life.

   But there still remains one method of avoiding this conclusion, and one source which we have not yet examined.
An Enquiry concerning Human Understanding, p. 74

. . . we may define a cause to be *an object, followed by another, and*   55
where all the objects similar to the first are followed by objects similar to
the second. Or in other words *where, if the first object had not been, the*
second never had existed. . . . We may . . . form another definition of
cause, and call it, *an object followed by another, and whose appearance*
always conveys the thought to that other.
An Enquiry concerning Human Understanding, p. 76

. . . to proceed in this reconciling project with regard to the question of   56
liberty and necessity; the most contentious question of metaphysics, the
most contentious science; it will not require many words to prove, that
all mankind have ever agreed in the doctrine of liberty as well as in that
of necessity, and that the whole dispute . . . has been hitherto merely
verbal. For what is meant by liberty, when applied to voluntary actions?
We cannot surely mean that actions have so little connexion with
motives, inclinations, and circumstances, that one does not follow with a
certain degree of uniformity from the other, and that one affords no
inference by which we can conclude the existence of the other. For these
are plain and acknowledged matters of fact. By liberty, then, we can only
mean *a power of acting or not acting, according to the determinations of*
the will: that is, if we choose to remain at rest, we may; if we choose to
move, we also may. Now this hypothetical liberty is universally allowed
to belong to every one who is not a prisoner and in chains. Here, then, is
no subject of dispute.
An Enquiry concerning Human Understanding, p. 95

When anyone tells me, that he saw a dead man restored to life, I   57
immediately consider with myself, whether it be more probable, that this
person would either deceive or be deceived, or that the fact, which he
relates, would really have happened. I weigh the one miracle against the
other; and according to the superiority, which I discover, I pronounce my
decision, and always reject the greater miracle. If the falsehood of his
testimony would be more miraculous, than the event which he relates;
then, and not till then, can he pretend to command my belief or opinion.
An Enquiry concerning Human Understanding, p. 115

. . . upon the whole, we may conclude, that the *Christian Religion* not   58
only was at first attended with miracles, but even at this day cannot be
believed by any reasonable person without one.
An Enquiry concerning Human Understanding, p. 131

It is a question of fact, whether the perceptions of the senses be produced   59
by external objects, resembling them; how shall this question be
determined? By experience surely; as all other questions of a like nature.
But here experience is, and must be entirely silent. The mind has never

anything present to it but the perceptions, and cannot possibly reach any experience of their connexion with objects. The supposition of such a connexion is, therefore, without any foundation in reasoning.
An Enquiry concerning Human Understanding, p. 153

60 It seems to me, that the only objects of the abstract sciences or of demonstration are quantity and number. . . .

All other enquiries of men regard only matter of fact and existence. . . .

When we run over libraries, persuaded of these principles, what havoc must we make? If we take in our hand any volume; of divinity or school metaphysics, for instance; let us ask, *Does it contain any abstract reasoning concerning quantity or number?* No. *Does it contain any experimental reasoning concerning matter of fact and existence?* No. Commit it then to the flames; for it can contain nothing but sophistry and illusion.
An Enquiry concerning Human Understanding, p. 163

61 It appears to be matter of fact, that the circumstance of *utility*, in all subjects, is a source of praise and approbation: that it is constantly appealed to in all moral decisions concerning the merit and demerit of actions: that it is the *sole* source of that high regard paid to justice, fidelity, honour, allegiance, and chastity: that it is inseparable from all the other social virtues, humanity, generosity, charity, affability, lenity, mercy, and moderation: and, in a word, that it is a foundation of the chief part of morals, which has a reference to mankind and our fellow-creatures.
An Enquiry concerning the Principles of Morals, ed. L. Selby-Bigge, p. 231

62 A gloomy, hair-brained enthusiast, after his death, may have a place in the calendar; but will scarcely ever be admitted, when alive, into intimacy and society, except by those who are as delirious and dismal as himself.
An Enquiry concerning the Principles of Morals, p. 270

63 . . . what philosophical truths can be more advantageous to society, than those here delivered, which represent virtue in all her genuine and most engaging charms, and make us approach her with ease, familiarity, and affection? . . . She talks not of useless austerities and rigours, suffering and self-denial. . . . The sole trouble which she demands, is that of just calculation, and a steady preference of the greater happiness.
An Enquiry concerning the Principles of Morals, p. 279

64 The hypothesis which we embrace is plain. It maintains that morality is determined by sentiment. It defines virtue to be *whatever mental action or quality gives to a spectator the pleasing sentiment of approbation*; and vice the contrary.
An Enquiry concerning the Principles of Morals, p. 289

Ask a man *why he uses exercise*; he will answer, *because he desires to* 65
keep his health. If you then enquire, *why he desires health*, he will readily
reply, *because sickness is painful*. If you push your enquiries farther, and
desire a reason *why he hates pain*, it is impossible he can ever give any.
This is an ultimate end, and is never referred to any other object.
. . . Something must be desirable on its own account, and because of its
immediate accord or agreement with human sentiment and affection.
An Enquiry concerning the Principles of Morals, p. 293

Never literary attempt was more unfortunate than my Treatise of Human 66
Nature. It fell *dead-born from the press*, without reaching such
distinction, as even to excite a murmur among the zealots.
'My Own Life', *Essays*, ed. E. Miller, p. xxxiv

It would be no crime in me to divert the *Nile* or *Danube* from its course, 67
were I able to effect such purposes. Where then is the crime of turning a
few ounces of blood from their natural chanels!
'Of Suicide', *Essays*, p. 582

. . . the life of man is of no greater importance to the universe than that of 68
an oyster.
'Of Suicide', *Essays*, 583

A man in a fever would not insist on his palate as able to decide 69
concerning flavours; nor would one, affected with the jaundice, pretend
to give a verdict with regard to colours. In each creature, there is a sound
and a defective state; and the former alone can be supposed to afford us a
true standard of taste and sentiment.
'Of the Standard of Taste', *Essays*, p. 233

Good and ill, both natural and moral, are entirely relative to human 70
sentiment and affection.
'The Sceptic', *Essays*, p. 168

How could things have been as they are, were there not an original, 71
inherent principle of order somewhere, in thought or in matter? And it is
very indifferent to which of these we give the preference. Chance has no
place, on any hypothesis, sceptical or religious. Every thing is surely
governed by steady, inviolable laws. And were the inmost essence of
things laid open to us, we should then discover a scene, of which, at
present, we can have no idea. Instead of admiring the order of natural
beings, we should clearly see, that it was absolutely impossible for them,
in the smallest article, ever to admit of any other disposition.
Dialogues concerning Natural Religion, ed. N. Kemp Smith, p. 174

72 Epicurus's questions are yet unanswered. Is he [God] willing to prevent evil, but not able? then is he impotent. Is he able, but not willing? then is he malevolent. Is he both able and willing? whence then is evil?
Dialogues concerning Natural Religion, p. 198

73 Look round this universe. What an immense profusion of beings, animated and organized, sensible and active! You admire this prodigious variety and fecundity. But inspect a little more narrowly these living existences, the only beings worth regarding. How hostile and destructive to each other! How insufficient all of them for their own happiness! How contemptible or odious to the spectator! The whole presents nothing but the idea of a blind nature, impregnated by a great vivifying principle, and pouring forth from her lap, without discernment or parental care, her maimed and abortive children.
Dialogues concerning Natural Religion, p. 211

74 It is, therefore, a just *political* maxim, *that every man must be supposed a knave*, though, at the same time, it appears somewhat strange, that a maxim should be true in *politics* which is false in *fact*.
'The Independency of Parliament', *Essays*, ed. E. Miller, p. 42

EDMUND HUSSERL (1859–1938)

1 Shall I say: only phenomena are truly given to the cognizing subject, he never does and never can break out of the circle of his own mental processes, so that in truth he could only say: I exist, and all that is not-I is mere phenomenon dissolving into phenomenal connections? Am I then to become a solipsist? This is a hard requirement. Shall I, with Hume, reduce all transcendent objectivity to fictions lending themselves to psychological explanation but to no rational justification? But this, too, is a hard requirement. Does not Hume's psychology, along with any psychology, transcend the sphere of immanence? By working with such concepts as habit, human nature, sense-organ, stimulus and the like, is it not working with transcendent existences (and transcendent by its own avowal), while its aim is to degrade to the status of fictions everything that transcends actual 'impressions' and 'ideas'?

But what is the use of invoking the specter of contradictions when / *logic itself is in question* and becomes problematic. *Indeed, the real meaning of logical lawfulness* which natural thinking would not dream of questioning, now becomes *problematic* and *dubious*. Thoughts of a biological order intrude. We are reminded of the modern theory of evolution, according to which man has evolved in the struggle for existence and by natural selection, and with him his intellect too has evolved naturally and along with his intellect all of its characteristic

forms, particularly the logical forms. Accordingly, is it not the case that the logical forms and laws express the accidental peculiarity of the human species, which could have been different and which will be different in the course of future evolution? Cognition is, after all, only *human cognition*, bound up with *human intellectual forms*, and unfit to reach the very nature of things, to reach the things in themselves.
The Idea of Phenomenology, trans. W. P. Alston and G. Nakhnikian, p. 16

Epistemological reflection first brings to light that the sciences of a natural sort are not yet the ultimate science of being. We need a science of being in the absolute sense. This science, which we call *metaphysics*, grows out of a 'critique' of natural cognition in the individual sciences. It is based on what is learned in the general critique of cognition about the essence of cognition and what it is to be an object of cognition of one basic type or other, i.e., in accordance with the different fundamental correlations between cognizing and being an object of cognition.   2

If then we disregard any metaphysical purpose of the critique of cognition and confine ourselves purely to the task *of clarifying the essence of cognition and of being an object of cognition, then this will be phenomenology of cognition and of being an object of cognition* and will be the first and principal part of phenomenology as a whole.
The Idea of Phenomenology, trans. W. P. Alston and G. Nakhnikian, p. 18

. . . [phenomenological] analysis is an analysis of essences and an investigation of the general states of affairs which are to be built up in immediate intuition. Thus the whole investigation is an *a priori* one, though, of course, it is not *a priori* in the sense of mathematical deductions. What distinguishes it from the 'objectivizing' *a priori* sciences is its methods and its goal. *Phenomenology proceeds by 'seeing', clarifying, and determining meaning, and by distinguishing meanings.*   3
The Idea of Phenomenology, trans. W. P. Alston and G. Nakhnikian, p. 46

If we look closer and notice how in the mental process, say of [perceiving] a sound, even after phenomenological reduction, *appearance and that which appears stand in contrast*, and this *in the midst of pure givenness*, hence in the midst of true immanence, then we are taken aback. Perhaps the sound lasts. We have there the patently given unity of the sound and its duration with its temporal phases, the present and the past. On the other hand, when we reflect, the phenomenon of enduring sound, itself a temporal phenomenon, has its own now-phase and past phases. And if one picks out a now-phase of the phenomenon there is not only the objective now of the sound itself, but the now of the sound is but a point in the duration of a sound.   4
The Idea of Phenomenology, trans. W. P. Alston and G. Nakhnikian, p. 8

5 The idea of *phenomenological reduction* acquires a more immediate and more profound determination and a clearer meaning. It means not the exclusion of the genuinely transcendent (perhaps even in some psycho-logico-empirical sense), but the exclusion of the transcendent as such as something to be accepted as existent, i.e., everything that is not evident givenness in its true sense, that is not absolutely given to pure 'seeing'. . . .

Thus the field is now characterized. It is a field of absolute cognitions, within which the ego and the world and God and the mathematical manifolds and whatever else may be a scientifically objective matter are held in abeyance, cognitions which are, therefore, also not dependent on these matters, which are valid in their own right, whether we are sceptics with regard to the others or not. All that remains as it is. The root of the matter, however, is *to grasp the meaning of the absolutely given, the absolute clarity of the given*, which / excludes every meaningful doubt, in a word, *to grasp the absolutely 'seeing' evidence which gets hold of itself.*
The Idea of Phenomenology, trans. W. P. Alston and G. Nakhnikian, p. 7

6 In recent times the longing for a fully alive philosophy has led to many a renaissance. Must not the only fruitful renaissance be the one that reawakens the impulse of the Cartesian *Meditations*: not to adopt their content but, in *not* doing so, to renew with greater intensity the radicalness of their spirit, the radicalness of self-responsibility, to make that radicalness true for the first time by enhancing it to the last degree, / to uncover thereby for the first time the genuine sense of the necessary regress to the ego, and consequently to overcome the hidden but already felt naïveté of earlier philosophizing?
Cartesian Meditations, trans. Dorion Cairns, p. 5

7 It is clear that truth or the true actuality of objects is to be obtained only from *evidence*, and that it is evidence alone by virtue of which an '*actually*' *existing*, true, rightly accepted object of whatever form or kind *has sense for us* – and with all the determinations that for us belong to it under the title of its true nature. Every rightness comes from evidence, therefore from our transcendental subjectivity itself; every imaginable adequation originates as our verification, is our synthesis, has in us its ultimate transcendental basis.
Cartesian Meditations, trans. Dorion Cairns, p. 60

8 . . . the difference between the sense of a psychological, and that of a transcendental-phenomenological, exploration of consciousness is im-measurably profound, though the contents to be described on the one hand and on the other can correspond. In the one case we have data belonging to the world, which is presupposed as existing – that is to say, data taken as psychic components of a man. In the other case the parallel

data, with their like contents, are not taken in this manner, because the whole world, when one is in the phenomenological attitude, is not accepted as actuality, but only as an actuality-phenomenon.
Cartesian Meditations, trans. Dorion Cairns, p. 32

FRANCIS HUTCHESON (1694–1746)

Some strange Love of Simplicity in the Structure of human Nature, or 1 Attachment to some favourite Hypothesis, has engaged many Writers to pass over a great many simple Perceptions, which we may find in ourselves. We have got the number Five fixed for our external Senses, though a larger Number might perhaps as easily be defended. We have Multitudes of Perceptions which have no relation to any external Sensation . . .
An Essay on the Nature and Conduct of the Passions and Affections, s. 431

Do not we find that we often desire the Happiness of others without any 2 . . . selfish Intention? How few have thought upon this part of our Constitution which we call a Publick Sense?
An Essay on the Nature and Conduct of the Passions and Affections, s. 440

The Occasion of the imagined Difficulty in conceiving disinterested 3 Desires, has probably been from the attempting to define this simple Idea, Desire. It is called an uneasy Sensation in the absence of Good. Whereas Desire is as distinct from any Sensation, as the Will is from the Understanding or Senses. This every one must acknowledge, who speaks of desiring to remove Uneasiness or Pain.
An Essay on the Nature and Conduct of the Passions and Affections, s. 441

It is true indeed, that the Actions we approve in others, are generally 4 imagin'd to tend to the natural Good of Mankind, or of some Parts of it. But whence this secret Chain between each Person and Mankind? How is my Interest connected with the most distant Parts of it? . . . If there is no moral Sense, which makes rational Actions appear Beautiful, or Deform'd; if all Approbation be from the Interest of the Approver, 'What's Hecuba to us, or we to Hecuba?'
An Inquiry into the Original of Our Ideas of Beauty and Virtue, II, s. 77

I

𝔊𝔊𝔊𝔊𝔊𝔊

LUCE IRIGARAY (*b.* 1939)

1 Woman? 'Doesn't exist.' She borrows the disguise which she is required
to assume. She mimes the role imposed upon her. The only thing really
expected of her is that she *maintain, without fail, the circulation of
pretense by enveloping herself in femininity.*
'When the Goods Get Together', *New French Feminisms*, ed. E. Marks and I. de
Courtivron, p. 108

2 Women are not, strictly speaking, a class and their dispersion in several
classes makes their political struggle complex and their demands
sometimes contradictory.
'This Sex which is Not One', *New French Feminisms*, p. 105

ARNOLD ISENBERG (1911–1965)

The more radical arguments against critical standards are spread out in
the pages of Croce, Dewey, Richards, Prall, and the great romantic critics
before them. They need not be repeated here. In one way or another they
all attempt to expose the absurdity of presuming to judge a work of art,
the very excuse for whose existence lies in its *difference* from everything
that has gone before, by its degree of *resemblance* to something that has
gone before; and on close inspection they create at least a very strong
doubt as to whether a standard of success or failure in art is either
necessary or possible.
Critical Communication, p. 135

J

𝕾𝕾𝕾𝕾𝕾𝕾

WILLIAM JAMES (1842–1910)

... the tangible fact at the root of all our thought-distinctions, however **1**
subtle, is that there is no one of them so fine as to consist in anything but
a possible difference of practice. To attain perfect clearness in our
thoughts of an object, then, we need only consider what conceivable
effects of a practical kind the object may involve – what sensations we
are to expect from it, and what reactions we must prepare. Our
conception of these effects, whether immediate or remote, is then for us
the whole of our conception of the object, so far as that conception has
positive significance at all.
Pragmatism: A New Way for Some Old Ways of Thinking, p. 46

The pragmatic rule is that the meaning of a concept may always be **2**
found, if not in some sensible particular which it directly designates, then
in some particular difference in the course of human experience which its
being true will make. Test every concept by the question 'What sensible
difference to anybody will its truth make?' and you are in the best
possible position for understanding what it means and for discussing its
importance.
Pragmatism: A New Way for Some Old Ways of Thinking, p. 60

To 'agree' in the widest sense with a reality can only mean to be guided **3**
either straight up to it or into its surroundings, or to be put into such
working touch with it as to handle either it or something connected with
it better than if we disagreed. Better either intellectually or practically.
Pragmatism: A New Way for Some Old Ways of Thinking, p. 212

'The true', to put it very briefly, is only the expedient in the way of our **4**
thinking, just as 'the right' is only the expedient in the way of our
behaving. Expedient in almost any fashion; and expedient in the long run
and on the whole of course; for what meets expediently all the experience
in sight won't necessarily meet all farther experiences equally satisfactorily.
Pragmatism: A New Way for Some Old Ways of Thinking, p. 222

5 Between us and the universe there are no 'rules of the game'. The important thing is that our judgements should be right, not that they should observe a logical etiquette.
Collected Essays and Reviews, p. 10

6 The pursuance of future ends and the choice of means for their attainment are thus the mark and criterion of the presence of mentality in a phenomenon.
The Principles of Psychology, I, p. 8

7 Consciousness, then, does not appear to itself chopped up in bits. Such words as 'chain' or 'train' do not describe it fitly as it presents itself in the first instance. It is nothing jointed; it flows. A 'river' or a 'stream' are the metaphors by which it is most naturally described.
The Principles of Psychology, I, p. 239

8 In a sense, then, it may be truly said that, in one person at least, *the 'Self of selves', when carefully examined, is found to consist mainly of the collection of . . . peculiar motions in the head or between the head and throat. . . .* If the dim portions which I cannot yet define should prove to be like unto these distinct portions in me, and I like other men, *it would follow that our entire feeling of spiritual activity, or what commonly passes by that name, is really a feeling of bodily activities whose exact nature is by most men overlooked.*
The Principles of Psychology, I, p. 301

9 Each thought, out of a multitude of other thoughts of which it may think, is able to distinguish those which belong to its own Ego from those which do not. The former have a warmth and intimacy about them of which the latter are completely devoid, being merely conceived, in a cold and foreign fashion, and not appearing as blood-relatives, bringing their greetings to us from out of the past.
The Principles of Psychology, I, p. 331

10 I might conceivably be as much fascinated, and as primitively so, by the care of my neighbour's body as by the care of my own. I am thus fascinated, by the care of my child's body.
Psychology: Briefer Course, p. 194

11 Everyone assumes that we have direct introspective acquaintance with our thinking activity as such, with our consciousness as something inward and contrasted with the outer objects which it knows. Yet I must confess that for my part I cannot feel sure of this conclusion. Whenever I try to become sensible of my thinking activity as such, what I catch is some bodily fact, an impression coming from my brow, or head, or

throat, or nose. It seems as if consciousness as an inner activity were rather a postulate than a sensibly given fact.
Psychology: Briefer Course, p. 467

My thesis is that if we start with the supposition that there is only one   **12**
primal stuff or material in the world, a stuff of which everything is composed, and if we call that stuff 'pure experience', then knowing can easily be explained as a particular sort of relation towards one another into which portions of pure experience may enter.
Essays in Radical Empiricism, p. 4

Descartes for the first time defined thought as the absolutely unextended,   **13**
and later philosophers have accepted the description as correct. But what possible meaning has it to say that, when we think of a foot-rule or a square yard, extension is not attributable to our thought? Of every extended object the adequate mental picture must have all the extension of the object itself.
Essays in Radical Empiricism, p. 30

On the principles which I am defending, a 'mind' or 'personal   **14**
consciousness' is the name for a series of experiences run together by certain definite transitions, and an objective reality is a series of similar experiences, knit together by different transitions.
Essays in Radical Empiricism, p. 80

Our body itself is the palmary instance of the ambiguous. Sometimes I   **15**
treat my body purely as a part of outer nature. Sometimes, again, I think of it as 'mine', I sort it with the 'me', and then certain local changes and determinations in it pass for spiritual happenings. Its breathing is my 'thinking', its sensorial adjustments are my 'attention', its kinesthetic alterations are my 'efforts', its visceral perturbations are my 'emotions'. The obstinate controversies that have arisen over such statements as these . . . prove how hard it is to decide by bare introspection what it is in experiences that shall make them either spiritual or material.
Essays in Radical Empiricism, p. 153

Nothing shall be admitted as fact, it [i.e., radical empiricism] says, except   **16**
what can be experienced at some definite time by some experient; and for every feature of fact ever so experienced, a definite place must be found somewhere in the final system of reality. In other words: Everything real must be experienceable somewhere, and every kind of thing experienced must somewhere be real.
Essays in Radical Empiricism, p. 160

. . . concepts . . . being thin extracts from perception, are always   **17**
insufficient representatives thereof; and although they yield wide

211

information, must never be treated after the rationalistic fashion, as if they gave a deeper quality of truth. The deeper features of reality are found only in perceptual experience. Here alone do we acquaint ourselves with continuity, or the immersion of one thing in another, here alone with self, with substance, with qualities, with activity in its various modes, with time, with cause, with change, with novelty, with tendency, with freedom. Against all such features of reality the conceptual translation, when candidly and critically followed out, can only raise its *non possumus*, and brand them as unreal or absurd.
Some Problems of Philosophy, Works, VII, p. 54

18   When conceptualism summons life to justify itself in conceptual terms, it is like a challenge addressed in a foreign language to some one who is absorbed in his own business . . .
A Pluralist Universe, p. 291

19   The world of our experience consists at all times of two parts, an objective and a subjective part, of which the former may be incalculably more extensive than the latter, and yet the latter can never be omitted or suppressed. The objective part is the sum total of whatsoever at any given time we may be thinking of, the subjective part is the inner 'state' in which the thinking comes to pass. What we think of may be enormous – the cosmic times and spaces, for example, – whereas the inner state may be the most fugitive and paltry activity of mind. Yet the cosmic objects, so far as the experience yields them, are but ideal pictures of something whose existence we do not inwardly possess but only point at outwardly, while the inner state is our very experience itself; its reality and that of our experience are one. A conscious field plus its object as felt or thought of plus our attitude towards the object plus the sense of a self to whom the attitude belongs – such a concrete bit of personal experience may be a small bit, but it is a solid bit as long as it lasts; not hollow, not a mere abstract element of experience, such as the 'object' is when taken all alone. It is a full fact, even though it be an insignificant fact; it is of the kind to which all realities whatsoever must belong; the motor currents of the world run through the like of it; . . . and any would-be existent that should lack such a feeling or its analogue, would be a piece of reality only half made up.
The Varieties of Religious Experience: A Study in Human Nature, p. 499

20   If this be true, it is absurd for science to say that the egotistic elements of experience should be suppressed. The axis of reality runs solely through the egotistic places, – they are strung upon it like so many beads. To describe the world with all the various feelings of the individual pinch of destiny, all the various spiritual attitudes, left out from the description –

they being as describable as anything else – would be something like offering a printed bill of fare as the equivalent for a solid meal. Religion makes no such blunder.
The Varieties of Religious Experience: A Study in Human Nature, p. 499

... the rigorously impersonal view of science might one day appear as **21** having been a temporarily useful eccentricity rather than the definitively triumphant position which the sectarian scientist at present so confidently announces it to be.
The Varieties of Religious Experience: A Study in Human Nature, p. 501

... that which produces effects within another reality must be termed a **22** reality itself, so I feel as if we had no philosophic excuse for calling the unseen or mystical world unreal.
The Varieties of Religious Experience: A Study in Human Nature, p. 515

... there is a continuum of cosmic consciousness, against which our **23** individuality builds but accidental fences, and into which our several minds plunge as into a mother-sea or reservoir. . . . fitful influences from beyond leak in, showing otherwise unverifiable common connection. . . .

Vast, indeed, and difficult is the inquirer's prospect here, and the most significant data for his purpose will probably be just these dingy little mediumistic facts which the Huxleyan minds of our time find so unworthy of their attention. But when was not the science of the future stirred to its conquering activities by the little rebellious exceptions to the science of the present?
Essays in Religion and Morality, p. 204

Common-sense says, we lose our fortune, are sorry and weep; we meet a **24** bear, are frightened and run; we are insulted by a rival, are angry and strike. The hypothesis here to be defended says that this order of sequence is incorrect, that the one mental state is not immediately induced by the other, that the bodily manifestations must first be interposed between, and that the more rational statement is that we feel sorry because we cry, angry because we strike, afraid because we tremble . . .
The Principles of Psychology, II, p. 449

Among the philosophic cranks of my acquaintance in the past was a lady **25** all the tenets of whose system I have forgotten except one. Had she been born in the Ionian Archipelago some three thousand years ago, that one doctrine would probably have made her name sure of a place in every university curriculum and examination paper. The world, she said, is composed of only two elements, The Thick, namely, and The Thin. No

one can deny the truth of this analysis, as far as it goes . . . and it is nowhere truer than in that part of the world called philosophy.
A Pluralistic Universe, p. 135

26   The history of philosophy is to a great extent that of a certain clash of human temperaments. . . . I will write these traits down in two columns. I think you will practically recognize the two types of mental make-up that I mean if I head the columns by the titles 'tender-minded' and 'tough-minded' respectively.

THE TENDER-MINDED	THE TOUGH-MINDED
Rationalistic (going by 'principles'),	Empiricist (going by 'facts'),
Intellectualistic,	Sensationalistic,
Idealistic,	Materialistic,
Optimistic,	Pessimistic,
Religious	Irreligious
Free-willist,	Fatalistic,
Monistic,	Pluralistic,
Dogmatical	Sceptical

Pragmatism: A New Way for Some Old Ways of Thinking, p. 6

KARL JASPERS (1883–1969)

1   Awakening to myself, in my situation, . . . I must *search for being* if I want to find my real self. But it is not till I fail in this search for intrinsic being that I begin to philosophize.
Philosophy, trans. E. B. Ashton, I, p. 45

2   . . . we ask about *being itself*, which always seems to *recede* from us . . . If I take the content of knowledge already to be reality itself, that which is known leads me, so to speak, along a detour by-passing reality.
Philosophy and Existenz, trans. R. Grabau, p. 18

3   Existenz is the never objectified source of my thoughts and actions. It is that whereof I speak in trains of thought that involve no cognition. It is what relates to itself, and thus to its transcendence. . . . Standing *on the borderline of world and Existenz*, possible Existenz views all existence as more than existence.
Philosophy, I, p. 56

4   The basic difference between mundane and metaphysical meaning is whether, in the relation of the image to that which it represents, the represented thing itself could also be grasped as an object or whether the image is simply an image for something not accessible in any other way.
Philosophy, III, p. 15

Ontology originated as the fusion of all modes of thought into one 5
encompassing thought aglow with being . . . Once ontology is rent,
divided into the methods and contents it had been fusing – thus turning
in fact into the reading of a currently, historically singular cipher script –
the conscious reading of ciphers seems to restore the unity on a new base.
Philosophy, III, p. 143

The objects of the world possess a two-fold transparence: they are 6
manifestations or phenomena of the enveloping reality of the world, and
also relate to transcendence. As phenomena, they reveal the encompassing
reality of the world through their intelligibility; as ciphers, they speak the
polyvalent language of transcendence, a language that is as penetrating as
it is unknowable.
Von der Warheit, trans. S. Samay, p. 108

. . . the point of my existential imagination is to grasp all being as 7
saturated with freedom. To read ciphers means to know about being in a
sense that makes existent being and free being identical, so that in the
deepest view of my imagination there will, so to speak, be neither the one
nor the other, but the ground of both.
Philosophy, III, p. 134

Freedom is the most-used word of our time. What it is seems obvious to 8
all. . . . Yet there is nothing more obscure, more ambiguous, more
abused.
Future of Mankind, trans. E. B. Ashton, p. 85

Today contemplation has advanced so far that we have grown conscious 9
of it as a universal relativism. Everything is valid from a specific,
definable standpoint which I can take, abandon, and change. I need only
to be understandingly at home in every standpoint, without standing on
any. Freedom is the random interchangeability of standpoints.
   The result would be that *I am no longer myself*. When someone wants
to get hold of me I already am someone else. I can defend everything and
refute everything.
Philosophy, I, p. 253

There is either no freedom at all, or it *is* in the very asking about it.   10
Philosophy, II, p. 155

The man who attains true awareness of his freedom gains certainty of 11
God. Freedom and God are inseparable. Why? This I know: in my
freedom I am not through myself but am given to myself; for I can miss
being myself and I cannot force my being free.
The Way to Wisdom, trans. Ralph Mannheim, p. 45

12 The will does not choose between good and evil; it is its choice, rather, that makes it good or evil. The act of choosing either liberates it, as good will, or enchains it as ill will. In neither case is there a choice between two possibilities; my will is its own original freedom or anti-freedom.
Philosophy, II, p. 151

13 I know I am free, and so I admit I am guilty.
Philosophy, II, p. 171

14 The love in this communication is not the blind love which fixes upon one object as readily as another. It is the struggling, clear-sighted love of possible Existenz tackling another possible Existenz, questioning it, challenging it, making demands on it.
Philosophy, II, p. 59

15 What is time, then? As the future, it is possibility; as the past, it is the bond of fidelity; as the present, it is decision.
Philosophy, I, p. 57

16 All forms of the·corporeal world are transitory, [but] for pure existence there is only a passing away of which it has no knowledge. Foundering requires knowledge, and then a reaction to it. . . . Man alone can founder, and this capacity is to him not unequivocal: it challenges him to react to it.
Philosophy, III, p. 192

17 Freedom is only by nature, and it is against nature. . . . This is the antinomy of freedom: to become one with nature will destroy the freedom of an Existenz; to transgress against nature will make it founder in existence.
Philosophy, III, p. 200

18 It is not by revelling in perfection but by suffering, by seeing the grim features of mundane existence, by unconditionally being itself in communication that my possible Existenz can achieve what I cannot plan, what becomes an absurdity when I wish it: in foundering to experience being.
Philosophy, III, p. 208

SAMUEL JOHNSON (1709–1784)

1 After we came out of the church, we stood talking for some time together of Bishop Berkeley's ingenious sophistry to prove the non-existence of matter, and that every thing in the universe is merely ideal. I observed, that though we are satisfied his doctrine is not true, it is impossible to refute it. I never shall forget the alacrity with which Johnson answered,

striking his foot with mighty force against a large stone, till he rebounded from it, 'I refute it *thus*.'
James Boswell, *Boswell's Life of Johnson*, I, p. 471

Being in company with a gentleman who thought fit to maintain Dr. 2
Berkeley's ingenious philosophy, that nothing exists but as perceived by some mind; when the gentleman was going away, Johnson said to him, 'Pray, Sir, don't leave us; for we may perhaps forget to think of you, and then you will cease to exist.'
James Boswell, *Boswell's Life of Johnson*, IV, p. 27

Dr. Johnson shunned to-night any discussion of the perplexed question 3
of fate and free will, which I attempted to agitate: 'Sir (said he), we *know* our will is free, and *there's* an end on't.'
James Boswell, *Boswell's Life of Johnson*, II, p. 82

'If he does really think that there is no distinction between virtue and 4
vice, why, Sir, when he leaves our houses let us count our spoons.'
James Boswell, *Boswell's Life of Johnson*, I, p. 432

To works, however, of which the excellence is not absolute and definite, 5
but gradual and comparative; to works not raised upon principles demonstrative and scientific, but appealing wholly to observation and experience, no other test can be applied than length of duration and continuance of esteem.
Johnson on Shakespeare, *Works*, VII, ed. A. Sherbo, p. 59

K

🔯🔯🔯🔯🔯🔯

SHELLY KAGAN (b. 1954)

1 On the one hand (or so it is thought) morality imposes certain limits on our actions, ruling out various kinds of acts – e.g., harming the innocent – even if greater good might be brought about by an act of the kind in question. Limits of this first kind are imposed *by* morality. But there are also what we might think of as limits imposed *on* morality – for it is typically believed that there are limits to what morality can demand of us. Thus, it is generally held that although morality does sometimes require us to make sacrifices for the sake of others, we are not morally required to make our greatest possible contributions to the overall good. There is a limit to moral requirement.

. . . I will argue that these two fundamental features of ordinary morality cannot be adequately defended.
The Limits of Morality, p. xi

2 If consequentialism is correct there are no limits of the first kind for, in principle, any sort of act at all might be permissible in the right circumstances, provided only that it leads to the best consequences overall. And there are no limits of the second kind, for there is simply no limit to the sacrifices that an agent might be required to make in the pursuit of the greater good. . . .

Most discussion of consequentialism has focused on the first objection – i.e., that it permits too much. This is somewhat surprising, for in practical terms consequentialism may not differ in this area all that much from ordinary morality. Killing the innocent, e.g., will generally not have the best results overall, and so consequentialism and ordinary morality will typically be alike in forbidding it. And in many complex cases it is often unclear what act will lead to the best results, and so unclear whether consequentialism actually diverges in that case from ordinary morality. In contrast, the second objection – which turns on whether there is a limit to the sacrifices that morality can demand of an agent – indicates an area in which consequentialism and ordinary morality

diverge sharply and undeniably. For consequentialism is *far* more demanding than ordinary morality in terms of the sacrifices that must be made for the greater good.
The Limits of Morality, p. x

HORACE MEYER KALLEN (1882–1974)

Philosophy has fallen into the position of a toper whose first drink was taken to save his life and who ever after lived to drink.
William James and Henri Bergson, p. 222

IMMANUEL KANT (1724–1804)

In this enquiry I have made completeness my chief aim, and I venture to assert that there is not a single metaphysical problem which has not been solved, or for the solution of which the key at least has not been supplied.
Critique of Pure Reason, trans. N. Kemp Smith, A xiii

1

Hitherto it has been assumed that all our knowledge must conform to objects. . . . We must therefore make trial whether we may not have more success in the tasks of metaphysics, if we suppose that objects must conform to our knowledge.
Critique of Pure Reason, trans. N. Kemp Smith, B xvi

2

I have therefore found it necessary to deny *knowledge* in order to make room for *faith*.
Critique of Pure Reason, trans. N. Kemp Smith, B xxx

3

Now the proper problem of pure reason is contained in the question: how are *a priori* synthetic judgements possible?
Critique of Pure Reason, trans. N. Kemp Smith, B 19

4

I entitle *transcendental* all knowledge which is occupied not so much with objects as with the mode of our knowledge of objects in so far as this mode of knowledge is to be possible *a priori*.
Critique of Pure Reason, trans. N. Kemp Smith, A 11/12, B 25

5

What here constitutes our subject-matter is not the nature of things, which is inexhaustible, but the understanding which passes judgement on the nature of things; and this understanding, again, only in respect of its *a priori* knowledge.
Critique of Pure Reason, trans. N. Kemp Smith, A 12/13, B 26

6

Without sensibility no object would be given to us, without understanding no object would be thought. Thoughts without content are empty, intuitions without concepts are blind. . . . The understanding can intuit

7

nothing, the senses can think nothing. Only through their union can knowledge arise.
Critique of Pure Reason, trans. N. Kemp Smith, A 51/B 75

8 What objects may be in themselves, and apart from all this receptivity of our sensibility, remains completely unknown to us.
Critique of Pure Reason, trans. N. Kemp Smith, A 42/B 59

9 It is . . . solely from the human standpoint that we can speak of space, of extended things, etc. If we depart from the subjective condition under which alone we can have outer intuition, namely liability to be affected by objects, the representation of space stands for nothing whatsoever.
Critique of Pure Reason, trans. N. Kemp Smith, A 26/B 42

10 Synthesis in general . . . is the mere result of the power of imagination, a blind but indispensable function of the soul, without which we should have no knowledge whatsoever, but of which we are scarcely ever conscious.
Critique of Pure Reason, trans. N. Kemp Smith, A 78/B 103

11 Psychologists have hitherto failed to realise that imagination is a necessary ingredient of perception itself.
Critique of Pure Reason, trans. N. Kemp Smith, A 120

12 Thus the order and regularity in the appearances, which we entitle *nature*, we ourselves introduce.
Critique of Pure Reason, trans. N. Kemp Smith, A 125

13 It must be possible for the 'I think' to accompany all my representations; for otherwise something would be represented in me which could not be thought at all, and that is equivalent to saying that the representation would be impossible, or at least would be nothing to me.
Critique of Pure Reason, trans. N. Kemp Smith, B 131

14 I have no *knowledge* of myself as I am, but merely as I appear to myself.
Critique of Pure Reason, trans. N. Kemp Smith, B 158

15 Deficiency in judgement is just what is ordinarily called stupidity, and for such a failing there is no remedy.
Critique of Pure Reason, trans. N. Kemp Smith, A 134/B 173

16 All our knowledge falls within the bounds of possible experience.
Critique of Pure Reason, trans. N. Kemp Smith, A 146/B 185

17 In all change of appearances substance is permanent; its quantum in nature is neither increased nor diminished.
Critique of Pure Reason, trans. N. Kemp Smith, B 224

All alterations take place in conformity with the law of the connection of   18
cause and effect.
Critique of Pure Reason, trans. N. Kemp Smith, B 232

All substances, in so far as they can be perceived to coexist in space, are   19
in thoroughgoing reciprocity.
Critique of Pure Reason, trans. N. Kemp Smith, B 256

The consciousness of my existence is at the same time an immediate   20
consciousness of the existence of other things outside me.
Critique of Pure Reason, trans. N. Kemp Smith, B 276

Doubtless, indeed, there are intelligible entities corresponding to the   21
sensible entities; there may also be intelligible entities to which our
sensible faculty of intuition has no relation whatsoever; but our concepts
of understanding, being mere forms of thought for our sensible intuition,
could not in the least apply to them.
Critique of Pure Reason, trans. N. Kemp Smith, B 308

Leibniz *intellectualised* appearances, just as Locke . . . *sensualised* all   22
concepts of the understanding. . . . Instead of seeking in understanding
and sensibility two sources of representations which, while quite
different, can supply objectively valid judgements of things only in
conjunction with each other, each of these great men holds to one only of
the two, viewing it as in immediate relation to things in themselves. The
other faculty is then regarded as serving only to confuse or to order the
representations which this selected faculty yields.
Critique of Pure Reason, trans. N. Kemp Smith, A 271/B 327

What the things-in-themselves may be I do not know, nor do I need to   23
know, since a thing can never come before me except in appearance.
Critique of Pure Reason, trans. N. Kemp Smith, A 277/B 333

It is therefore correct to say that the senses do not err – not because they   24
always judge rightly, but because they do not judge at all.
Critique of Pure Reason, trans. N. Kemp Smith, A 293/B 350

I need only remark that it is by no means unusual, upon comparing the   25
thoughts that an author has expressed in regard to his subject, to find
that we understand him better than he has understood himself.
Critique of Pure Reason, trans. N. Kemp Smith, A 314/B 370

The identity of the consciousness of myself at different times is therefore   26
only a formal condition of my thoughts and their coherence, and in no
way proves the numerical identity of my subject.
Critique of Pure Reason, trans. N. Kemp Smith, A 363

27   In order to arrive at the reality of outer objects I have just as little need to resort to inference as I have in regard to the reality of the object of my inner sense, that is, in regard to the reality of my thoughts. For in both cases alike the objects are nothing but representations, the immediate perception (consciousness) of which is at the same time a sufficient proof of their reality.
Critique of Pure Reason, trans. N. Kemp Smith, A 371

28   This 'I' is, however, as little an intuition as it is a concept of any object; it is the mere form of consciousness.
Critique of Pure Reason, trans. N. Kemp Smith, A 382

29   Indeed, it would be a great stumbling-block, or rather would be the one unanswerable objection, to our whole critique, if there were a possibility of proving *a priori* that all thinking beings are in themselves simple substances . . . and that they are conscious of their existence as separate and distinct from all matter.
Critique of Pure Reason, trans. N. Kemp Smith, B 409

30   Appearances are here regarded as given; what reason demands is the absolute completeness of the conditions of their possibility.
Critique of Pure Reason, trans. N. Kemp Smith, A 416/B 443

31   In its empirical meaning, the term 'whole' is always only comparative.
Critique of Pure Reason, trans. N. Kemp Smith, A 483/B 511

32   If the world is a whole existing in itself, it is either finite or infinite. But both alternatives are false. . . . It is therefore also false that the world (the sum of all appearances) is a whole existing in itself. From this it then follows that appearances in general are nothing outside our representations – which is just what is meant by their transcendental ideality.
Critique of Pure Reason, trans. N. Kemp Smith, A 506/B 534

33   The principle of reason is thus properly only a *rule*, prescribing a regress in the series of the conditions of given appearances.
Critique of Pure Reason, trans. N. Kemp Smith, A 508/B 536

34   . . . in the sensible world, this active being must in its actions be independent of, and free from, all such necessity. No action begins *in* this active being itself; but we may yet quite correctly say that the active being *of itself* begins its effects in the sensible world. In so doing, we should not be asserting that the effects in the sensible world can begin of themselves; they are always predetermined through antecedent empirical conditions, though solely through their empirical character (which is no more than the appearance of the intelligible), and so are only possible as a continuation of the series of natural causes. In this way freedom and

nature, in the full sense of these terms, can exist together, without any conflict, in the same actions, according as the actions are referred to their intelligible or to their sensible cause.
Critique of Pure Reason, trans. N. Kemp Smith, A 541/B 569

. . . although we believe that the action is thus determined, we none the   35
less blame the agent, not indeed on account of his unhappy disposition, nor on account of the circumstances that have influenced him, nor even on account of his previous way of life; for we presuppose that we can leave out of consideration what this way of life may have been, that we can regard the past series of conditions as not having occurred and the act as being completely unconditioned by any preceding state, just as if the agent in and by himself began in this action an entirely new series of consequences. Our blame is based on a law of reason whereby we regard reason as a cause that irrespective of all the above-mentioned empirical conditions could have determined, and ought to have determined, the agent to act otherwise. This causality of reason we do not regard as only a co-operating agency, but as complete in itself, even when the sensuous impulses do not favour but are directly opposed to it; the action is ascribed to the agent's intelligible character; in the moment when he utters the lie, the guilt is entirely his. Reason, irrespective of all empirical conditions of the act, is completely free, and the lie is entirely due to its default.
Critique of Pure Reason, trans. N. Kemp Smith, A 554/B 582

All things in the world of sense may be contingent, and so have only an   36
empirically conditioned existence, while yet there may be a non-empirical condition of the whole series; that is, there may exist an unconditionally necessary being.
Critique of Pure Reason, trans. N. Kemp Smith, A 560/B 588

If, on the other hand, we admit, as every reasonable person must, that all   37
existential propositions are synthetic, how can we profess to maintain that the predicate of existence cannot be rejected without contradiction?
. . . 'Being' is obviously not a real predicate.
Critique of Pure Reason, trans. N. Kemp Smith, A 598/B 626

The ideal of the supreme being is nothing but a *regulative principle* of   38
reason, which directs us to look upon all connection in the world *as if* it originated from an all-sufficient necessary cause.
Critique of Pure Reason, trans. N. Kemp Smith, A 619/B 647

Thus the physico-theological proof of the existence of an original or   39
supreme being rests upon the cosmological proof, and the cosmological upon the ontological.
Critique of Pure Reason, trans. N. Kemp Smith, A 630/B 658

40 Moral theology . . . is a conviction of the existence of a supreme being – a conviction which bases itself on moral laws.
Critique of Pure Reason, trans. N. Kemp Smith, A 632/B 660

41 Theoretical knowledge may be defined as knowledge of what *is*, practical knowledge as the representation of what *ought to be*.
Critique of Pure Reason, trans. N. Kemp Smith, A 633/B 661

42 *Philosophical* knowledge is the *knowledge gained by reason from concepts*; mathematical knowledge is the knowledge gained by reason from the *construction* of concepts.
Critique of Pure Reason, trans. N. Kemp Smith, A 713/B 741

43 It is precisely in knowing its limits that philosophy consists.
Critique of Pure Reason, trans. N. Kemp Smith, A 727/B 755

44 The proposition that everything which happens has its cause . . . has the peculiar character that it makes possible the very experience which is its own ground of proof, and that in this experience it must always itself be presupposed.
Critique of Pure Reason, trans. N. Kemp Smith, A 737/B 765

45 Belief in a God and in another world is so interwoven with my moral sentiment that as there is little danger of my losing the latter, there is equally little cause for fear that the former can ever be taken from me.
Critique of Pure Reason, trans. N. Kemp Smith, A 829/B 857

46 Judgement in general is the faculty of thinking the particular as contained under the universal.
Critique of Judgement, trans. J. H. Bernard, p. 17

47 *Taste* is the faculty of judging an object or a method of representing it by an *entirely disinterested* satisfaction or dissatisfaction. The object of such satisfaction is called *beautiful*.
Critique of Judgement, trans. J. H. Bernard, p. 55

48 Consequently the judgement of taste, accompanied with the consciousness of separation from all interest, must claim validity for everyone.
Critique of Judgement, trans. J. H. Bernard, p. 56

49 If we judge objects merely according to concepts, then all representation of beauty is lost. Thus there can be no rule according to which anyone is to be forced to recognise anything as beautiful.
Critique of Judgement, trans. J. H. Bernard, p. 62

50 The excitement of both faculties (imagination and understanding) to indeterminate, but yet, through the stimulus of the given sensation,

harmonious activity, viz. that which belongs to cognition in general, is the sensation whose universal communicability is postulated by the judgement of taste.
Critique of Judgement, trans. J. H. Bernard, p. 66

The *beautiful* is that which pleases universally without a concept. 51
Critique of Judgement, trans. J. H. Bernard, p. 67

A judgement of taste is therefore pure, only so far as no merely empirical 52
satisfaction is mingled with its determining ground. But this always happens if charm or emotion have any share in the judgement by which anything is to be described as beautiful.
Critique of Judgement, trans. J. H. Bernard, p. 73

The judgement is called aesthetical just because its determining ground is 53
not a concept, but the feeling (of internal sense) of that harmony in the play of the mental powers, so far as it can be felt in sensation.
Critique of Judgement, trans. J. H. Bernard, p. 80

There can be no objective rule of taste which shall determine by means of 54
concepts what is beautiful.
Critique of Judgement, trans. J. H. Bernard, p. 84

But the necessity which is thought in an aesthetic judgement can only be 55
called *exemplary*; i.e., a necessity of the assent of *all* to a judgement which is regarded as the example of a universal rule which we cannot state.
Critique of Judgement, trans. J. H. Bernard, p. 91

The *beautiful* is that which without any concept is cognised as the object 56
of a *necessary* satisfaction.
Critique of Judgement, trans. J. H. Bernard, p. 96

The *beautiful* is what pleases in the mere judgement (and therefore not by 57
the medium of sensation in accordance with a concept of the understanding). It follows at once from this that it must please apart from all interest.
   The *sublime* is what pleases immediately through its opposition to the interest of sense.
Critique of Judgement, trans. J. H. Bernard, p. 107

War itself, if it is carried on with order and with a sacred respect for the 58
rights of citizens, has something sublime in it, and makes the disposition of the people who carry it on thus, only the more sublime, the more numerous are the dangers to which they are exposed, and in respect of which they behave with courage.
Critique of Judgement, trans. J. H. Bernard, p. 127

59 In fact a feeling for the sublime in nature cannot well be thought without combining therewith a mental disposition which is akin to the moral.
Critique of Judgement, trans. J. H. Bernard, p. 135

60 We thus see that genius is a *talent* for producing that for which no definite rule can be given; it is not a mere aptitude for what can be learnt by a rule. Hence *originality* must be its first property.
Critique of Judgement, trans. J. H. Bernard, p. 189

61 We say of certain products of which we expect that they should at least in part appear as beautiful art, that they are without *spirit*; although we find nothing to blame in them on the score of taste.
Critique of Judgement, trans. J. H. Bernard, p. 197

62 For beautiful art, therefore, *imagination, understanding, spirit* and *taste* are requisite.
Critique of Judgement, trans. J. H. Bernard, p. 206

63 The arts of *speech* are *rhetoric* and *poetry*. *Rhetoric* is the art of carrying on a serious business of the understanding as if it were a free play of the imagination; *poetry* the art of conducting a free play of the imagination as if it were a serious business of the understanding.
Critique of Judgement, trans. J. H. Bernard, p. 207

64 The Germans are praised in that, when constancy and sustained diligence are demanded, they can go further than other peoples.
Prolegomena to Any Future Metaphysics, trans. P. G. Lucas, p. 153

65 The business of philosophy is not to give rules, but to analyse the private judgments of common reason. Laws themselves arise from the judgments made in particular cases by sound understanding.
Reflexionen zur Anthropologie, trans. P. F. Strawson, AA XV Nr. 436, p. 180

66 In all beautiful art the essential thing is the form.
Critique of Judgement, trans. J. H. Bernard, p. 214

67 Of all the arts *poetry* (which owes its origin almost entirely to genius and will least be guided by precept or example) maintains the first rank.
Critique of Judgement, trans. J. H. Bernard, p. 215

68 Besides, there attaches to music a certain want of urbanity from the fact that, chiefly from the character of its instruments, it extends its influence further than is desired in the neighbourhood.
Critique of Judgement, trans. J. H. Bernard, p. 219

69 Laughter is an affection arising from the sudden transformation of a strained expectation into nothing.
Critique of Judgement, trans. J. H. Bernard, p. 223

Now I say: the beautiful is the symbol of the morally good. 70
Critique of Judgement, trans. J. H. Bernard, p. 250

We are in fact indispensably obliged to ascribe the concept of design to 71
nature if we wish to investigate it, though only in its organised products,
by continuous observation.
Critique of Judgement, trans. J. H. Bernard, p. 310

Skill cannot be developed in the human race except by means of 72
inequality among men; for the great majority provide the necessities of
life, as it were, mechanically, without requiring any art in particular, for
the convenience and leisure of others who work at the less necessary
elements of culture, science and art.
Critique of Judgement, trans. J. H. Bernard, p. 356

It is only as a moral being that man can be a final purpose of creation. 73
Critique of Judgement, trans. J. H. Bernard, p. 371

Faith . . . is the moral attitude of reason as to belief in that which is 74
unattainable by theoretical cognition.
Critique of Judgement, trans. J. H. Bernard, p. 409

It is therefore the moral law, of which we become directly conscious . . . 75
that *first* presents itself to us, and leads directly to the concept of
freedom, inasmuch as reason presents it as a principle of determination
not to be outweighed by any sensible conditions, nay, wholly
independent of them.
Critique of Practical Reason, trans. T. K. Abbott, p. 117

So sharply and clearly marked are the boundaries of morality and self- 76
love that even the commonest eye cannot fail to distinguish whether a
thing belongs to the one or the other.
Critique of Practical Reason, trans. T. K. Abbott, p. 125

Thus the respect for the law is not a motive to morality, but is morality 77
itself subjectively considered as a motive.
Critique of Practical Reason, trans. T. K. Abbott, p. 168

The majesty of duty has nothing to do with the enjoyment of life. 78
Critique of Practical Reason, trans. T. K. Abbott, p. 182

When we attend to the course of conversation in mixed companies, 79
consisting not merely of learned persons and subtle reasoners, but also of
men of business or of women, we observe that besides story-telling and
jesting, another kind of entertainment finds a place in them, namely,
argument; for stories, if they are to have novelty and interest, are soon
exhausted, and jesting is likely to become insipid. Now of all argument

there is none in which persons are more ready to join who find any other subtle discussion tedious, none that brings more liveliness into the company, than that which concerns the *moral worth* of this or that action by which the character of some person is to be made out.
Critique of Practical Reason, trans. T. K. Abbott, p. 251

80 When we can bring any flattering thought of merit into our action, then the motive is already somewhat alloyed with self-love, and has therefore some assistance from the side of sensibility. But to postpone everything to the holiness of duty alone, and to be conscious that we *can* because our own reason recognizes this as its command and says that we *ought* to do it, this is, as it were, to raise ourselves altogether above the world of sense.
Critique of Practical Reason, trans. T. K. Abbott, p. 257

81 Two things fill the mind with ever new and increasing admiration and awe, the oftener and more steadily we reflect on them: *the starry heavens above and the moral law within*.
Critique of Practical Reason, trans. T. K. Abbott, p. 260

82 Nothing can possibly be conceived in the world, or even out of it, which can be called good, without qualification, except a good will.
Fundamental Principles of the Metaphysic of Morals, trans. T. K. Abbott, p. 9

83 The pre-eminent good which we call moral can therefore consist in nothing else than *the conception of law* in itself, *which certainly is only possible in a rational being*, in so far as this conception, and not the expected effect, determines the will.
Fundamental Principles of the Metaphysic of Morals, trans. T. K. Abbott, p. 17

84 We do not need science and philosophy to know what we should do to be honest and good, yea, even wise and virtuous.
Fundamental Principles of the Metaphysic of Morals, trans. T. K. Abbott, p. 20

85 If we attend to the experience of men's conduct, we meet frequent and, as we ourselves allow, just complaints that one cannot find a single certain example of the disposition to act from pure duty. Although many things are done in *conformity* with what *duty* prescribes, it is nevertheless always doubtful whether they are done strictly *from duty*, so as to have moral worth.
Fundamental Principles of the Metaphysic of Morals, trans. T. K. Abbott, p. 23

86 Finally, there is an imperative which commands a certain conduct immediately, without having as its condition any other purpose to be attained by it. This imperative is categorical. It concerns not the matter of the action or its intended result, but its form and the principle of which it

is itself a result; and what is essentially good in it consists in the mental disposition, let the consequence be what it may. This imperative may be called that of morality.
Fundamental Principles of the Metaphysic of Morals, trans. T. K. Abbott, p. 33

The notion of happiness is so indefinite that although every man wishes   87
to attain it yet he never can say definitely and consistently what it is that he really wishes and wills.
Fundamental Principles of the Metaphysic of Morals, trans. T. K. Abbott, p. 35

There is therefore but one categorical imperative, namely this: *act only*   88
on that maxim whereby thou canst at the same time will that it should become a universal law.
Fundamental Principles of the Metaphysic of Morals, trans. T. K. Abbott, p. 38

So act as to treat humanity, whether in thine own person or in that of any   89
other, in every case as an end withal, never as a means only.
Fundamental Principles of the Metaphysic of Morals, trans. T. K. Abbott, p. 47

Now I say that every being that cannot act except *under the idea of*   90
freedom is just for that reason in a practical point of view really free, that is to say, all laws which are inseparably connected with freedom have the same force for him as if his will had been shown to be free in itself by a proof theoretically conclusive.
Fundamental Principles of the Metaphysic of Morals, trans. T. K. Abbott, p. 67

Philosophy must then assume that no real contradiction will be found   91
between freedom and physical necessity of the same human actions, for it cannot give up the conception of nature any more than that of freedom.
Fundamental Principles of the Metaphysic of Morals, trans. T. K. Abbott, p. 76

For there is not the smallest contradiction in saying that *a thing in*   92
appearance (belonging to the world of sense) is subject to certain laws of which the very same *as a thing* or being *in itself* is independent.
Fundamental Principles of the Metaphysic of Morals, trans. T. K. Abbott, p. 77

But reason would overstep all its bounds if it undertook to *explain how*   93
pure reason can be practical, which would be exactly the same problem as to explain *how freedom is possible.*
Fundamental Principles of the Metaphysic of Morals, trans. T. K. Abbott, p. 79

And thus while we do not comprehend the practical unconditional   94
necessity of the moral imperative, yet we comprehend its *incomprehensibility*, and this is all that can be fairly demanded of a philosophy which strives to carry its principles up to the very limit of human reason.
Fundamental Principles of the Metaphysic of Morals, trans. T. K. Abbott, p. 84

95 Metaphysics has to do properly with synthetic propositions *a priori*, and these alone constitute its end.
Prolegomena to Any Future Metaphysics, trans. P. G. Lucas, p. 24

96 From this there flows the following result of all the foregoing researches: 'all synthetic principles *a priori* are nothing more than principles of possible experience' and can never be referred to things in themselves, but only to appearances as objects of experience.
Prolegomena to Any Future Metaphysics, trans. P. G. Lucas, p. 74

97 Criticism is related to ordinary school-metaphysics exactly as *chemistry* to *alchemy*, or as *astronomy* to the divinations of *astrology*.
Prolegomena to Any Future Metaphysics, trans. P. G. Lucas, p. 135

98 How are space, time and that which fills both, the object of sensation, possible in general? The answer is: by means of the quality of our sensibility, according to which it is affected, in its peculiar way, by objects which are in themselves unknown and quite different from those appearances.
Prolegomena to Any Future Metaphysics, trans. P. G. Lucas, p. 79

99 There will always be metaphysics in the world, and what is more in everyone, especially in every thinking man.
Prolegomena to Any Future Metaphysics, trans. P. G. Lucas, p. 136

HANS KELSEN (1881–1973)

1 Law is the primary norm, which stipulates the sanction, and this norm is not contradicted by the delict of the subject, which, on the contrary, is the specific condition of the sanction.
General Theory of Law and State, trans. A. Wedberg, p. 61

2 Legal norms may have any kind of content. There is no kind of human behavior that, because of its nature, could not be made into a legal duty corresponding to a legal right.
General Theory of Law and State, trans. A. Wedberg, p. 113

ANTHONY KENNY (*b.* 1931)

1 What is this thing, the will, that is being claimed to be free? The traditional answer was that the will was a faculty of the mind. Apart from an unexpected revival by the school of Chomsky the psychology of faculties has long been out of fashion. Certainly, if a faculty is thought of as a ghostly operative force in the mysterious medium of the mind, or as a homunculus pulling levers in the signal box of the brain, then faculties are figments of the imagination that will not survive serious reflection.

And it has been a truism since the time of Molière that one does not give a scientific explanation of a phenomenon by assigning it to an appropriate power. None the less there is, I believe, a profound truth in the ancient theory that the will is a faculty of the mind.
Will, Freedom and Power, p. 1

The mind is the capacity to acquire intellectual abilities. Two things must 2 be noticed about this definition. First mind is a capacity, not an activity. Thus it is possible to say that babies have minds even though they do not yet display intellectual activities of the appropriate kind. Secondly, mind is not only a capacity, but a capacity for capacities. Knowledge of a language such as English is itself a capacity or ability: an ability whose exercise is the speaking, understanding, reading of English. To have a mind is to have a capacity at a further remove from actualization: to have the capacity to acquire such abilities as a knowledge of English.
Will, Freedom and Power, p. 2

This two-way ability also was something which interested Aristotle, who 3 drew a sharp distinction between rational powers, such as the ability to speak Greek, and natural powers like the power of fire to burn. If all the necessary conditions for the exercise of a natural power were present, then, he maintained, the power was necessarily exercised: put the wood, appropriately dry, on the fire, and the fire will burn it; there are no two ways about it. Rational powers, however, are essentially, he argued, two-way powers, powers which can be exercised at will: a rational agent, presented with all the necessary external conditions for exercising a power, may choose not to do so. A skilled Germanist at the podium of a hall filled with sharp-eared German speakers may for reasons of his own refuse to speak or may launch into ancient Gaelic.
Will, Freedom and Power, p. 52

The question 'What makes my thoughts *my* thoughts?' has an oddly 4 contemporary ring. It would perhaps be rash to think that contemporary studies have provided an answer to the question; but they have certainly shown one direction in which to look for an answer. My thoughts, surely, are the thoughts which find expression in the words and actions of *my body*.
The Anatomy of the Soul, p. 80

Consider the following case: a man, having written a suicide note, 5 electrocutes himself on a faulty switch while entering the kitchen to put his head in the oven. Such a man does not commit suicide, i.e., does not kill himself voluntarily, but dies by accident. Yet he had the Volition to be dead, by touching the switch he brought it about that he was dead, and it was in his power not to kill himself, for he did not have to touch

the switch. In this case, the man did not *know* that by touching the switch he would bring about his own death. So we must add knowledge to our conditions for voluntary action and say that for A voluntarily to bring it about that *p*, he must know that he is bringing it about that *p*.
Action, Emotion and Will, p. 237

6   It is characteristic of our age to endeavour to replace virtues by technology. That is to say, wherever possible we strive to use methods of physical or social engineering to achieve goals which our ancestors thought attainable only by the training of character. Thus, we try so far as possible to make contraception take the place of chastity, and anaesthetics to take the place of fortitude; we replace resignation by insurance policies and munificence by the Welfare state. It would be idle romanticism to deny that such techniques and institutions are often less painful and more efficient methods of achieving the goods and preventing the evils which unaided virtue once sought to achieve and avoid. But it would be an equal and opposite folly to hope that the take-over of virtue by technology may one day be complete. . .
The Anatomy of the Soul, p. 26

JOHN MAYNARD KEYNES (1883–1946)

Marxian Socialism must always remain a portent to historians of opinion – how a doctrine so illogical and so dull can have exercised so powerful and enduring an influence over the minds of men, and through them, the events of history.
The End of Laissez-Faire, p. 3

SØREN KIERKEGAARD (1813–1855)

1   When the question of truth is raised in an objective manner, reflection is directed objectively to the truth, as an object to which the knower is related. Reflection is not focused upon the relationship, however, but upon the question of whether it is the truth to which the knower is related. If only the object to which he is related is the truth, the subject is accounted to be in the truth. When the question of the truth is raised subjectively, reflection is directed subjectively to the nature of the individual's relationship; if only the mode of this relationship is in the truth, the individual is in the truth even if he should happen to be thus related to what is not true.
Concluding Unscientific Postscript, trans. D. F. Swenson and W. Lowrie, p. 178

2   Subjectivity is the truth. By virtue of the relationship subsisting between the eternal truth and the existing individual, the paradox came into being. Let us now go further, let us suppose that the eternal essential

truth is itself a paradox. How does the paradox come into being? By putting the eternal essential truth into juxtaposition with existence. Hence when we posit such a conjunction within the truth itself, the truth becomes a paradox. The eternal truth has come into being in time: this is the paradox.
Concluding Unscientific Postscript, trans. D. F. Swenson and W. Lowrie, p. 187

The supreme paradox of all thought is the attempt to discover something 3 that thought cannot think.
Philosophical Fragments, trans. D. F. Swenson, p. 46

To answer Kant within the fantastic shadow-play of pure thought is 4 precisely not to answer him. The only thing-in-itself which cannot be thought is existence, and this does not come within the province of thought to think.
Concluding Unscientific Postscript, trans. D. F. Swenson and W. Lowrie, p. 292

If subjectivity is the truth, the conceptual account of truth must include 5 an expression of the antithesis to objectivity, a mark of the fork in the road where the way swings off; that expression will serve at the same time to indicate the tension of the subjective inwardness. Here is such a definition of truth: the truth is an objective uncertainty held fast in an appropriation process of the most passionate inwardness, the highest truth attainable for an *existing* individual.
Concluding Unscientific Postscript, trans. D. F. Swenson and W. Lowrie, p. 182

Belief and doubt are not two forms of knowledge, determinable in 6 continuity with one another, for neither of them is a cognitive act; they are opposite passions.
Philosophical Fragments, trans. D. F. Swenson, p. 105

. . . the opposite of sin is not virtue but faith. 7
The Sickness unto Death, trans. H. V. Hong and E. H. Hong, p. 82

The majority of men are curtailed 'I's; what was planned by nature as a 8 possibility capable of being sharpened into an I is soon dulled into a third person.
The Journals of Søren Kierkegaard, trans. Alexander Dru, p. 533

'The individual' is the category through which, in a religious respect, this 9 age, all history, the human race as a whole, must pass. And he who stood at Thermopylae was not so secure in his position as I who have stood in defence of this narrow defile, 'the individual', with the intent at least of making people take notice of it.
The Point of View for my Work as an Author, trans. W. Lowrie, p. 128

10 The greatest hazard of all, losing one's self, can occur very quietly in the world, as if it were nothing at all. No other loss can occur so quietly; any other loss – an arm, a leg, five dollars, a wife, etc. – is sure to be noticed.
The Sickness unto Death, trans. H. V. Hong and E. H. Hong, p. 32

11 A crowd . . . in its very concept is the untruth, by reason of the fact that it renders the individual completely impenitent and irresponsible, or at least weakens his sense of responsibility by reducing it to a fraction.
The Point of View for my Work as an Author, trans. W. Lowrie, p. 112

12 In relation to their systems most systematisers are like a man who builds an enormous castle and lives in a shack close by; they do not live in their own enormous systematic buildings.
The Journals of Søren Kierkegaard, trans. Alexander Dru, p. 156

13 It is subjectivity that Christianity is concerned with, and it is only in subjectivity that its truth exists, if it exists at all; objectively, Christianity has absolutely no existence.
Concluding Unscientific Postscript, trans. D. F. Swenson and W. Lowrie, p. 116

14 Without risk there is no faith. Faith is precisely the contradiction between the infinite passion of the individual's inwardness and the objective uncertainty. If I am capable of grasping God objectively, I do not believe, but precisely because I cannot do this I must believe. If I wish to preserve myself in faith I must constantly be intent upon holding fast to the objective uncertainty, so as to remain out upon the deep, over seventy thousand fathoms of water, still preserving my faith.
Concluding Unscientific Postscript, trans. D. F. Swenson and W. Lowrie, p. 182

15 The paradox in Christian truth is invariably due to the fact that it is truth as it exists for God. The standard of measure and the end is super-human; and there is only one relationship possible: faith.
The Journals of Søren Kierkegaard, trans. Alexander Dru, p. 376

16 The double-minded one stands at a parting of the ways. Two visions appear: the good and the reward. It is not in his power to bring them into agreement, for [to him] they are fundamentally different from each other.
Purity of Heart is to Will One Thing: Spiritual Preparation for the Office of Confession, trans. Douglas V. Steere, p. 74

17 My either/or does not in the first instance denote the choice between good and evil; it denotes the choice whereby one chooses good *and* evil/ or excludes them. Here the question is under what determinants one would contemplate the whole of existence and would oneself live.
Either/Or, trans. D. F. Swenson and L. M. Swenson, II, p. 173

What the philosophers say about Reality is often as disappointing as a **18**
sign you see in a shop window which reads: Pressing Done Here. If you
brought your clothes to be pressed, you would be fooled; for only the
sign is for sale.
Either/Or, trans. D. F. Swenson and L. M. Swenson, I, p. 31

At every step philosophy sloughs a skin into which creep its worthless **19**
hangers-on.
The Journals of Søren Kierkegaard, trans. Alexander Dru, p. 39

The method which begins by doubting in order to philosophise is just as **20**
suited to its purpose as making a soldier lie down in a heap in order to
teach him to stand up straight.
The Journals of Søren Kierkegaard, trans. Alexander Dru, p. 126

Experience, it is said, makes a man wise. That is very silly talk. If there **21**
were nothing beyond experience it would simply drive him mad.
The Journals of Søren Kierkegaard, trans. Alexander Dru, p. iii

It's quite true what philosophy says, that life must be understood **22**
backwards. But one then forgets the other principle, that it must be lived
forwards. A principle which, the more one thinks it through, precisely
leads to the conclusion that life in time can never properly be understood,
just because no moment can acquire the complete stillness needed to
orient oneself backwards.
Søren Kierkegaard's Papirer, ed. N. Thulstrup, trans. A. Hannay, IV, p. 61

The Two Ways. One is to suffer; the other is to become a professor of the **23**
fact that another suffered. The first is 'the way'; the second goes round
about (the preposition 'about' is so aptly used for lectures and sermons)
and perhaps it ends by going down.
The Journals of Søren Kierkegaard, trans. Alexander Dru, p. 528

The situation of the guilty person travelling through life to eternity is like **24**
that of the murderer who fled the scene of his act – and his crime – on the
express train: alas, just beneath the coach in which he sat ran the
telegraph wires carrying his description and orders for his arrest at the
first station.
The Sickness unto Death, trans. H. V. Hong and E. H. Hong, p. 124

There has been said much that is strange, much that is deplorable, much **25**
that is revolting about Christianity; but the most stupid thing ever said
about it is that it is to a certain degree true.
Concluding Unscientific Postscript, trans. D. F. Swenson and W. Lowrie, p. 205

26 Each age has its own characteristic depravity. Ours is perhaps not pleasure or indulgence or sensuality, but rather a dissolute pantheistic contempt for the individual man.
Concluding Unscientific Postscript, trans. D. F. Swenson and W. Lowrie, p. 317

27 If Hegel had written the whole of his logic and then said, in the preface, that it was merely an experiment in thought in which he had even begged the question in many places, then he would certainly have been the greatest thinker who had ever lived. As it is he is merely comic.
The Journals of Søren Kierkegaard, trans. Alexander Dru, p. 134

28 An eternal happiness is a security for which there is no longer any market value in the speculative nineteenth century; at the very most it may be used by the gentlemen of the clerical profession to swindle rural innocents.
Concluding Unscientific Postscript, trans. D. F. Swenson and W. Lowrie, p. 346

JAEGWON KIM (*b.* 1934)

1 ... Socrates' death is not a cause of Xantippe's widowhood. What then is the cause? The death was caused by Socrates' drinking of hemlock. Could this event be a cause of Xantippe's widowhood? ... by what causal mechanism does the ingestion of hemlock lead to the widowhood? We can trace the causal chain from the hemlock drinking to the death, but no farther; the connection between the death and Xantippe's becoming a widow isn't causal. ...

To rule out Socrates' drinking as a cause of Xantippe's widowhood is to rule out, by implication, any other event that is a cause of the death as a cause of the widowhood. And if neither Socrates' death nor any of its causes is a cause of Xantippe's widowhood, we can only conclude, I think, that this event has no cause.
'Noncausal Connections', *Nous* (1974), p. 42

2 We think of an event as a concrete object (or *n*-tuple of objects) exemplifying a property (or *n*-adic relation) at a time. In this sense of 'event', events include states, conditions, and the like, and not only events narrowly conceived as involving changes. Events, therefore, turn out to be complexes of objects and properties, and also time points and segments. ...
'Causation, Nomic Subsumption, and the Concept of Event', *Journal of Philosophy* (1973), p. 218

3 The delicate task is to find an account that will give the mental a substantial enough causal role to let us avoid 'the great paradox of epiphenomenalism' without infringing upon the closedness of physical

causal systems. I suggest that we view psychophysical causal relations – in fact, all causal relations involving psychological events – as epiphenomenal supervenient causal relations. More specifically, when a mental event M causes a physical event P, this is so because M is supervenient upon a physical event, P*, and P* causes P.
'Epiphenomenal and Supervenient Causation', *Midwest Studies* (1984), p. 267

LESZEK KOLAKOWSKI (*b.* 1927)

According to this [liberal] concept the maximum productive efficiency and consequently the optimum general good is secured within a political framework based on the minimum interference in economic relations. The state has to care about security; welfare and wealth will look after themselves. Marx's anticipated organization of society was exactly the opposite: political government would become superfluous while economic management, 'the administration of things', would exhaust the functions of the public organs. The expression 'withering away of the state' comes from Engels but it fits into Marxian predictions. The question arises: what premises do we have to admit in order to believe that a social organization free from any mediating and coercive power and from any political bodies is practicable? What conditions would make conceiveable a society which can 'administer things' without 'governing people'? **1**
'The Myth of Human Self-Identity', *The Socialist Idea*, ed. L. Kolakowski and S. Hampshire, p. 22

The search for the ultimate foundation is as much an unremovable part of human culture as is the denial of the legitimacy of this search. **2**
Metaphysical Horror, p. 31

AUREL KOLNAI (1900–1973)

Certainly my morality and my moral philosophy are not the same thing; but a doctrine that precludes its professor from really adopting the morality it is meant to supply with philosophical credentials can hardly escape the charge of logical oddness.
Ethics, Value and Reality, p. 21

SAUL KRIPKE (*b.* 1941)

. . . suppose, for example, that '68 + 57' is a computation that I have never performed before. . . . I perform the computation, obtaining, of course, the answer '125'. . . . Now suppose I encounter a bizarre sceptic. This sceptic questions my certainty about my answer, in . . . the 'metalinguistic' sense. Perhaps, he suggests, as I used the term 'plus' in the past, the answer I intended for '68 + 57' should have been '5'! . . . An **1** answer to the sceptic must satisfy two conditions. First it must give an account of what fact it is (about my mental state) that constitutes my meaning plus . . . further . . . it must, in some sense, show how I am justified in giving the answer '125' to '68 + 57'. . . . The sceptical argument . . . remains unanswered. There can be no such thing as meaning anything by any word. Each new application we make is a leap in the dark; any present intention could be interpreted so as to accord with anything we may choose to do.

Wittgenstein on Rules and Private Language, p. 8

2   Wittgenstein's sceptical solution concedes to the sceptic that no 'truth conditions' or 'corresponding facts' in the world exist that make a statement like 'Jones, like many of us, means addition by "+" ' true. Rather we should look at how such assertions are *used*. . . . We have to see under what circumstances attributions of meaning are made and what role these attributions play in our lives. . . . if one person is considered in isolation, the notion of a rule as guiding the person who adopts it can have *no* substantive content. . . . The situation is very different if we widen our gaze from consideration of the rule follower alone and allow ourselves to consider him as interacting with a wider community. Others will then have justification conditions for attributing correct or incorrect rule following to the subject. . . . Any individual who claims to have mastered the concept of addition will be judged by the community to have done so if his particular responses agree with those of the community in enough cases, especially the simple ones. . . . An individual who passes such tests is admitted into the community as an adder; an individual who passes such tests in enough other cases is admitted as a normal speaker of the language and member of the community.

Wittgenstein on Rules and Private Language, p. 86

3   . . . the whole picture given by this theory of how reference is determined seems to be wrong from the fundamentals. It seems to be wrong to think that we give ourselves some properties which somehow qualitatively uniquely pick out an object and determine our reference in that manner. . . . A better picture of what is actually going on . . . might be the following: an initial 'baptism' takes place. Here the object may be named by ostension, or the reference of the name may be fixed by a description. When the name is 'passed from link to link', the receiver of the name must, I think, intend when he learns it to use it with the same reference as the man from whom he heard it.

Naming and Necessity, p. 93

Let's call something a *rigid designator* if in every possible world it 4
designates the same object, a *nonrigid* or *accidental designator* if that is
not the case . . .

One of the intuitive theses I will maintain in these talks is that *names*
are rigid designators. Certainly they seem to satisfy . . . [an] intuitive test
. . . although someone other than the U.S. President in 1970 might have
been the U.S. President in 1970 (e.g., Humphrey might have), no one
other than Nixon might have been Nixon.
Naming and Necessity, p. 48

Given that gold *does* have the atomic number 79, could something be 5
gold without having the atomic number 79? . . . consider a possible world
. . . in which, let us say, fool's gold or iron pyrites was actually found in
. . . the areas which actually contain gold now . . . Would we say . . . that
in that situation gold would not even have been an element (because pyrites
is not an element)? . . . One should *not* say that [this substance] would still
be gold in this possible world though gold would then lack the atomic
number 79. It would be some other stuff. . . . It [is] necessary and not
contingent that gold be an element with atomic number 79.
Naming and Necessity, p. 123

Any necessary truth, whether *a priori* or *a posteriori*, could not have 6
turned out otherwise. In the case of some necessary *a posteriori* truths,
however, we can say that under appropriate qualitatively identical
evidential situations, an appropriate corresponding qualitative statement
might have been false. . . . The inaccurate statement that Hesperus might
have turned out not to be Phosphorus should be replaced by the true
contingency . . . two distinct bodies might have occupied, in the morning
and evening, respectively, the very positions actually occupied by
Hesperus–Phosphorus–Venus.
Naming and Necessity, p. 142

Logical investigations can obviously be a useful tool for philosophy. 7
They must, however, be informed by a sensitivity to the philosophical
significance of the formalism and by a generous admixture of common
sense, as well as a thorough understanding both of the basic concepts and
of the technical details of the formal material used. It should not be
supposed that the formalism can grind out philosophical results in a
manner beyond the capacity of ordinary philosophical reasoning. There
is no mathematical substitute for philosophy.
'Is There a Problem about Substitutional Quantification?', *Truth and Meaning*,
ed. G. Evans and J. McDowell, p. 416

JULIA KRISTEVA (*b.* 1941)

1 . . . we must use 'we are women' as an advertisement or slogan for our demands. On a deeper level, however, a woman cannot 'be'; it is something which does not even belong in the order of *being*. It follows that a feminist practice can only be negative, at odds with what already exists so that we may say 'that's not it' and 'that's still not it.' In 'woman' I see something that cannot be represented, something that is not said, something above and beyond nomenclatures and ideologies.
New French Feminisms, ed. E. Marks and I. de Courtivron, p. 137

2 The question is: 'Who plays God in present-day feminism?' Man? Or Woman – his substitute? As long as any libertarian movement, feminism included, does not analyze its own relationship to power and does not renounce belief in its own identity, it remains capable of being co-opted both by power and an overtly religious or lay spiritualism. Besides, it is spiritualism's last hope.
New French Feminisms, p. 141

3 The solution is infinite, since what is at stake is to move from a patriarchal society, of class and of religion, in other words from pre-history, toward – who knows? In any event, this process involves going through what is repressed in discourse, in reproductive and productive relationships. Call it 'woman' or 'the oppressed social class': it's the same struggle, and you never have one without the other.
New French Feminisms, p. 141

4 Feminism can be but one of capitalism's more advanced needs to rationalize.
New French Feminisms, p. 141

5 The theory of meaning now stands at a crossroad: either it will remain an attempt at formalizing meaning-systems by increasing sophistication of the logico-mathematical tools which enable it to formulate models on the basis of a conception (already rather dated) of meaning as the act of a *transcendental ego*, cut off from its body, its unconscious and also its history; or else it will attune itself to the theory of the speaking subject as a divided subject (conscious/unconscious) and go on to attempt to specify the types of operation characteristic of the two sides of this split. . .
'The System and the Speaking Subject', *The Kristeva Reader*, ed. T. Moi, p. 28

6 The moment of transgression is the key moment in practice: we can speak of practice wherever there is a transgression of systematicity, i.e., a transgression of the unity proper to the *transcendental ego*. The subject of the practice cannot be the transcendental subject, who lacks the shift, the split in logical unity brought about by language which separates out,

within the signifying body, the symbolic order from the workings of the libido . . .
'The System and the Speaking Subject', *The Kristeva Reader*, p. 29

There *is* no subject in the economic rationality of Marxism; there is in 7 Marxist revolution, but the 'founding fathers' have left us no thoughts about it, while the academic Marxologists of today can hardly wait to get rid both of meaning and of the subject in the name of some 'objective' process . . .
'The System and the Speaking Subject', *The Kristeva Reader*, p. 31

THOMAS S. KUHN (*b.* 1922)

As in political revolutions, so in paradigm choice – there is no standard 1 higher than the assent of the relevant community. To discover how scientific revolutions are effected, we shall therefore have to examine not only the impact of nature and of logic, but also the techniques of persuasive argumentation effective within the quite special groups that constitute the community of scientists.
The Structure of Scientific Revolutions, p. 93

In a sense that I am unable to explicate further, the proponents of 2 competing paradigms practice their trades in different worlds. One contains constrained bodies that fall slowly, the other pendulums that repeat their motions again and again. In one, solutions are compounds, in the other mixtures. One is embedded in a flat, the other in a curved, matrix of space. Practicing in different worlds, the two groups of scientists see different things when they look from the same point in the same direction.
The Structure of Scientific Revolutions, p. 149

Can we not account for both science's existence and its success in terms 3 of evolution from the community's state of knowledge at any given time? Does it really help to imagine that there is some one full, objective, true account of nature and that the proper measure of scientific achievement is the extent to which it brings us closer to that ultimate goal? If we can learn to substitute evolution-from-what-we-do-know for evolution-toward-what-we-wish-to-know, a number of vexing problems may vanish in the process.
The Structure of Scientific Revolutions, p. 170

L

𝔊𝔊𝔊𝔊𝔊𝔊

JACQUES LACAN (1901–1981)

1   The child, at an age when he is for a time, however short, outdone by the chimpanzee in instrumental intelligence, can nevertheless already recognize as such his own image in a mirror. This recognition . . . can take place . . . from the age of six months. . . . Unable as yet to walk, or even to stand up, and held tightly as he is by some support, human or artificial (what, in France, we call a 'trotte-bébé'), he nevertheless overcomes, in a flutter of jubilant activity, the obstructions of his support and, fixing his attitude in a slightly leaning-forward position, in order to hold it in his gaze, brings back an instantaneous aspect of the image. . . .

   This jubilant assumption of his specular image by the child at the *infans* stage, still sunk in his motor incapacity and nursling dependence, would seem to exhibit in an exemplary situation the symbolic matrix in which the *I* is precipitated in a primordial form, before it is objectified in the dialectic of identification with the other, and before language restores to it, in the universal, its function as subject. This form . . . situates the agency of the ego, before its social determination, in a fictional direction, which will . . . only rejoin the coming-into-being of the subject asymptotically, whatever the success of the dialectical syntheses by which he must resolve as *I* his discordance with his own reality.
'The Mirror Stage as Formative of the Function of the I as Revealed in Psychoanalytic Experience', *Ecrits*, trans. A. Sheridan, p. 2

2   'I think, therefore I am' (*cogito ergo sum*) is not merely the formula in which is constituted, with the historical high point of reflection on the conditions of science, the link between the transparency of the transcendental subject and his existential affirmation.

   Perhaps I am only object and mechanism (and so nothing more than phenomenon), but assuredly in so far as I think so, I am – absolutely. No doubt philosophers have brought important corrections to this formulation, notably that in that which thinks (*cogitans*), I can never constitute

242

myself as anything but object (*cogitatum*). Nonetheless it remains true that by way of this extreme purification of the transcendental subject, my existential link to its project seems irrefutable, at least in its present form, and that: '*cogito ergo sum*' *ubi cogito, ibi sum*, overcomes this objection.

Of course, this limits me to being there in my being only in so far as I think that I am in my thought; just how far I actually think this concerns only myself and if I say it, interests no one.

'Agency of the Letter in the Unconscious', *Ecrits*, p. 164

It is not a question of knowing whether I speak of myself in a way that   3
conforms to what I am, but rather of knowing whether I am the same as that of which I speak. . . .

. . . the philosophical *cogito* is at the centre of the mirage that renders modern man so sure of being himself even in his uncertainties about himself, and even in the mistrust he has learned to practise against the traps of self-love.

. . . if in the name of 'war is war' and 'a penny's a penny' I decide to be only what I am, how even here can I elude the obvious fact that I am in that very act?

And it is no less true if I take myself to the other, metaphoric pole of the signifying quest, and if I dedicate myself to becoming what I am, to coming into being, I cannot doubt that even if I lose myself in the process, I am in that process. . . .

What one ought to say is: I am not wherever I am the plaything of my thought; I think of what I am where I do not think to think.

'Agency of the Letter in the Unconscious', *Ecrits*, p. 165

How can we be sure that we are not imposters?   4
The Four Fundamental Concepts of Psycho-Analysis, trans. A. Sheridan, p. 263

As a specular mirage, love is essentially deception. It is situated in the   5
field established at the level of the pleasure reference, of that sole signifier necessary to introduce a perspective centred on the Ideal point, capital I, placed somewhere in the Other, from which the Other sees me, in the form I like to be seen.

The Four Fundamental Concepts of Psycho-Analysis, p. 268

. . . I have proved that his [Kant's] theory of consciousness, when he   6
writes of practical reason, is sustained only by giving a specification of the moral law which, looked at more closely, is simply desire in its pure state, that very desire that culminates in the sacrifice, strictly speaking, of everything that is the object of love in one's human tenderness – I would say, not only in the rejection of the pathological object, but also in its sacrifice and murder. That is why I wrote *Kant avec Sade*.

This is the prime example of the eye-opening effect (*désillement*) that

analysis makes possible in relation to the many efforts, even the most noble ones, of traditional ethics.
The Four Fundamental Concepts of Psycho-Analysis, p. 275

IMRE LAKATOS (1922–1974)

Philosophy of science without history of science is empty; history of science without philosophy of science is blind.
Boston Studies in the Philosophy of Science, VIII, p. 91

JULIEN OFFRAY DE LAMETTRIE (1709–1751)

1   Man is a machine so compounded that it is at first impossible to form a clear idea of it, and consequently to define it. That is why all the investigations which the greatest philosophers have conducted *a priori*, that is to say by trying to lift themselves somehow on the wings of their intellect, have proved vain. Thus, it is only *a posteriori* or by seeking to unravel the soul, as it were, via the organs of the body, that one can, I do not say lay bare human nature itself in a demonstrative fashion, but attain to the highest degree of probability possible on this topic. . . .

The soul is, then, an empty symbol of which one has no conception, and which a sound mind could employ only in order to denote that which thinks in us. Given the least principle of movement, animate bodies will possess all they need in order to move, sense, think, repeat, and behave, in a word, all they want of the physical; and of the mental, too, which depends thereon.
The Man-machine, ed. M. Solovine, p. 126

2   If more instruments, more cogwheels, and more springs are required to register the movements of the planets than to denote the hours; if Vaucanson had to employ more art to produce his flutist than his duck, if he had employed still more energy he might have produced a being with the power of speech. . . . The human body is a clock, but an immense one and constructed with so much artifice and skill that if the wheel which turns the second hand should stop, then the minute hand would still turn and continue on its way.
The Man-machine, ed. M. Solovine, p. 129

SUSANNE K. LANGER (1895–1985)

1   . . . what art expresses is *not* actual feeling, but ideas of feeling; as language does not express actual things and events but ideas of them. Art

is expressive through and through – every line, every sound, every gesture; and therefore it is a hundred per cent symbolic. It is not sensuously pleasing and *also* symbolic; the sensuous quality is in the service of its vital import.
Feeling and Form, p. 174

... the forms of feeling and the forms of discursive expression are   2
logically incommensurate, so that any exact concepts of feeling and emotion cannot be projected into the logical form of literal language. Verbal statement ... is almost useless for conveying knowledge about the precise character of the affective life. Crude designations like 'joy', 'sorrow', 'fear' tell us as little about vital experience as general words like 'thing', 'being', or 'place' tell us about the world of our perceptions. Any more precise reference to feeling is usually made by mentioning the circumstance that suggests it – 'a mood of autumn evening', 'a holiday feeling'.
Problems of Art, p. 91

Because the forms of human feeling are much more congruent with   3
musical forms than with the forms of language, music can *reveal* the nature of feelings with a detail and truth that language cannot approach.
Philosophy in a New Key, p. 235

Music, like language, is an articulate form. Its parts not only fuse   4
together to yield a greater entity, but in so doing they maintain some degree of separate existence, and the sensuous character of each element is affected by its function in the complex whole ...

Why, then, is it not a *language* of feeling, as it has often been called? Because its elements are not words – independent associative symbols with a reference fixed by convention. ... Just as music is only loosely and inexactly called a language, so its symbolic function is only loosely called meaning, because the factor of conventional reference is missing from it.
Feeling and Form, p. 179

NICHOLAS LASH (*b.* 1934)

... when we think of the relations between God and the world in terms of cause and effect, we have already 'bound' God into the It-world and made it that much more difficult to take seriously Buber's suggestion that 'the relation to a human being is the proper metaphor for the relation to God'. We have thereby made it more difficult to pray because, under the influence of cause and effect, prayer seems to be a matter of the effect futilely attempting to exert some influence upon its cause.
Easter in Ordinary, p. 225

MICHÈLE LE DOEUFF (b. 1948)

1 The simple fact that philosophical discourse is a discipline is sufficient to show that something is repressed within it. But what is repressed? . . . philosophy creates itself in what it represses . . .
'Women and Philosophy', *French Feminist Thought*, ed. T. Moi, p. 195

2 Today it is possible to think of rationality otherwise than in a hegemonic mode. Possible, but not easy or straightforward. It is what we struggle for, not a historical gain already at our disposal.
'Women and Philosophy', p. 198

3 The irony is that the creative areas in philosophy today do not lie in the region of academic work.
'Women and Philosophy', p. 200

4 Some women say: 'We have been forbidden access to the philosophic realm; rightly understood, this is something positive, and we do not demand any such access; this discourse is riddled with masculine values, and women should not be concerned with it; they must seek their specificity, their own discourse, instead of wanting to share masculine privileges.' We need not always and completely reject a feminism of difference. But when we can see in it the echo of a philosophy, namely Comte's positivism, of the discourse on women produced by a masculine philosophy, we must recognize that this kind of feminism may do the opposite of what it claims, that it may be misled by schemas produced by the very structures against which it is protesting. I shall oppose this mystification by the paradox that a practical application of philosophy is necessary in order to oust and unmask the alienating schemas which philosophy had produced.
'Philosophy and Psychoanalysis', *French Feminist Thought*, p. 182

5 . . . patriarchal societies are fond of tenderly repeating that *woman* is a dear being without reason; and . . . colonialist societies proclaim that the negro, or the savage, is a being without reason. And it is being a little too generous always to credit power with the privilege of reason – just as it shows a somewhat unwarranted complacency in announcing 'rationally' a claim exclusively based on the pleasure it yields.
'Philosophy and Psychoanalysis', p. 197

KEITH LEHRER (b. 1936)

1 The simple theory, though ever seductive, is usually the mistress of error. The queen of truth is a more complicated woman but of better philosophical parts.
Knowledge and Skepticism, p. 152

We are presently ignorant. We had better keep our metaminds open. 2
Metamind, p. 294

When I was young, I thought that any philosopher who abandoned 3
minute analytical method to construct a philosophical system was done
for. But I feel all right.
'Metamental Ascent', *Proceedings of the American Philosophical Association*
(1990), p. 19

There is no exit from the circle of one's beliefs. 4
Knowledge, p. 188

GOTTFRIED WILHELM LEIBNIZ (1646–1716)

All things are understood by God *a priori*, as eternal truths; for he does 1
not need experience, and yet all things are known by him adequately.
We, on the other hand, know scarely anything adequately, and only a few
things *a priori*; most things we know by experience, in the case of which
other principles and other criteria must be applied.
Universal Synthesis and Analysis, Philosophical Writings, ed. G. Parkinson, p. 15

Every true predication has some basis in the nature of things, and when a 2
proposition is not identical, that is, when the predicate is not contained
expressly in the subject, it must be contained in it virtually. This is what
philosophers call *in-esse*, when they say the predicate is 'in' the subject.
The subject-term, therefore, must always include the predicate term, in
such a way that a man who understood the notion of the subject perfectly
would also judge that the predicate belongs in it.
Discourse on Metaphysics, Philosophical Writings, p. 18

No two substances resemble each other entirely and differ *solo numero*, 3
in number alone. What St Thomas asserts about angels or intelligences,
namely that in these cases each individual is an *infima species*, is true of all
substances . . .
Discourse on Metaphysics, Philosophical Writings, p. 19

We must attribute to Adam a notion so complete that everything that can 4
be attributed to Adam can be deduced from it. . . . It follows that he
would not have been our Adam, but another, if different things had
happened to him.
Letter to Antoine Arnauld, *Philosophical Writings*, p. 56

If there were no necessary being, there would be no contingent being; for 5
a reason must be given why contingent things should exist rather than
not exist. But there would be no such reason unless there were a being
which is in itself, that is, a being the reason for whose existence is
contained in its own essence . . .

A Specimen of Discoveries about Marvellous Secrets, Philosophical Writings,
p. 77

6   Either there are no corporeal substances, and bodies are merely
phenomena which are true or consistent with each other, such as a
rainbow or a perfectly coherent dream, or there is in all corporeal
substances something analogous to the soul . . .
A Specimen of Discoveries about Marvellous Secrets, p. 81

' 7   The consideration of an extended mass is not enough in itself; use must
also be made of the notion of *force*, which is fully intelligible, even
though it falls within the province of metaphysics. . . . It is impossible to
find the principles of true unity in matter alone, or in what is merely
passive, since everything in it is but a collection or accumulation of parts
ad infinitum. . . . Therefore to find these real unities, I was constrained to
have recourse to . . . a *real and animated point* or to an atom of
substance, which must embrace some element of form or activity in order
to make a complete being. It was thus necessary to recall and in a manner
to rehabilitate *substantial forms* which are so much decried today.
New System, Philosophical Writings, p. 116

8   By means of the soul or form there is a true unity which corresponds to
what is called the *I* in us.
New System, p. 120

9   I take as an illustration a block of veined marble rather than a wholly
uniform block or blank tablets, that is to say what is called *tabula rasa*.
. . . If there were veins in the stone which marked out the figure of Hercules,
this stone would be more determined thereto, and Hercules would be in
some manner innate in it, although labour would be needed to uncover
these veins. . . . It is in this way that ideas and truths are innate in us, like
natural inclinations and dispositions, natural habits or potentialities . . .
New Essays on Human Understanding, Philosophical Writings, p. 153

10   These minute perceptions . . . constitute that indefinable something, those
tastes, those images of the qualities of the senses, clear in the mass but
confused in the parts, those impressions which surrounding bodies make
on us, which include the infinite, that link which connects every being
with the rest of the universe. It may even be said that as a result of these
minute perceptions the present is big with the future and laden with the
past, that everything is in league together, *sympnoia panta* as Hippocrates
said, and that in the smallest substance eyes as piercing as those of God
could read the whole sequence of things in the universe.
New Essays on Human Understanding, p. 156

It is one of my most important and best verified maxims that *nature* **11**
makes no leaps. This I have called the *law of continuity*.
New Essays on Human Understanding, p. 158

The monad is nothing but a simple substance which enters into **12**
compounds; simple, that is to say, without parts. . . . The monads are the
true atoms of nature and, in a word, the elements of things.
Monadology, Philosophical Writings, p. 179

There is no means of explaining how a monad can be altered or changed **13**
within itself by any other created thing. . . . Monads have no windows by
which anything could come in or go out.
Monadology, p. 179

Suppose there were a machine so constructed as to produce thought, **14**
feeling and perception, we could imagine it increased in size while
retaining the same proportions, so that one might enter as one might a
mill. On going inside we should only see the parts impinging on one
another; we should not see anything that would explain a perception.
The explanation must therefore be sought in a simple substance, and not
in a compound or a machine.
Monadology, p. 181

We may give the name *entelechies* to all created simple substances or **15**
monads. For they have in themselves a certain perfection. . . . there is a
self sufficiency in them which makes them the sources of their internal
actions – incorporeal automata, if I may so put it.
Monadology, p. 181

Our reasonings are founded on two great principles: the *principle of* **16**
contradiction, by virtue of which we judge to be false that which involves
a contradiction, and true that which is opposed or contradictory to the
false; and the *principle of sufficient reason*, by virtue of which we
consider that no fact can be real or existing, and no proposition true
unless there is a sufficient reason why it should be thus and not otherwise,
even though in most cases these reasons cannot be known to us.
Monadology, p. 184

There are two kinds of truths: truths of *reasoning* and truths of *fact*. **17**
Truths of *reasoning* are necessary and their opposite is impossible; those
of *fact* are contingent and their opposite is possible.
Monadology, p. 184

As there is an infinite number of possible universes in the ideas of God, **18**
and as only one can exist, there must be a sufficient reason for God's
choice, to determine him to one rather than to another. And this reason

can only be found in the *fitness*, or in the degrees of perfection, which these worlds contain.
Monadology, p. 187

19   This connection or adaption of all created things with each, and of each with all the rest, means that each simple substance has relations which express all the others, and hence is a perpetual living mirror of the universe.
Monadology, p. 187

20   There is a world of created beings – living things, animals, entelechies, and souls – in the least part of matter. . . . Thus there is nothing waste, nothing sterile, nothing dead in the universe; no chaos, no confusions, save in appearance.
Monadology, p. 190

21   The soul follows its own laws, and the body its own likewise, and they accord by virtue of the *harmony pre-established* among all substances, since they are all representations of one and the same universe.
Monadology, p. 192

22   Everything is regulated in all things once for all with as much order and agreement as possible, since supreme wisdom and goodness cannot act without perfect harmony: the present is big with the future, what is to come could be read in the past, what is distant expressed in what is near. The beauty of the Universe could be learnt in each soul, could one unravel all its folds which develop perceptibly only with time.
Principles of Nature and Grace, Philosophical Writings, p. 201

23   This supreme wisdom, united to a goodness that is no less infinite, cannot but have chosen the best. . . . There would be something to correct in the actions of God if it were possible to do better. . . . So it may be said that if this were not the best of all possible worlds, God would not have created any.
Theodicy, Bk. 1, s. 8

V. I. LENIN (1870–1924)

In one way or another, *all* official and liberal science *defends* wage-slavery, whereas all Marxism has declared relentless war on that slavery. To expect science to be impartial in a wage-slave society is as foolishly naive as to expect impartiality from manufacturers on the question of whether workers' wages ought not to be increased by decreasing the profits of capital.
'The Three Sources and Three Component Parts of Marxism', *Marx Engels Selected Works*, p. 23

GOTTHOLD EPHRAIM LESSING (1729–1781)

What do we lose if freedom be denied us? Something – if it is anything – 1
which we do not need; something which we need neither for our activity
here, nor our happiness hereafter; something whose possession must
make us far more anxious and disturbed than its absence could ever do.
Compulsion and necessity in accordance with which the idea of the best
works, how much more welcome they are to me than that bare capacity
of being able to act in different ways under different circumstances. I
thank the Creator that I must do the best.
Quoted in Henry E. Allison, *Lessing and the Enlightenment*, p. 147

It is not the truth which a man possesses, or believes that he possesses, 2
but the earnest effort which he puts forth to reach the truth, which
constitutes the worth of a man. For it is not by the possession, but by the
search after truth that he enlarges his power, wherein alone consists his
ever-increasing perfection. Possession makes one content, indolent,
proud –
  If God held enclosed in His right hand all truth, and in His left hand
the ever-active striving after truth, although with the condition that I
must forever err, and said to me: choose! I would humbly fall before His
left hand and say: Father give! The pure truth is for Thee alone.
Quoted in Henry E. Allison, *Lessing and the Enlightenment*, p. 135

But if the written tradition of the Christian religion neither can, nor 3
ought to give it inner truth; then it is not from it that the Christian
religion has its inner truth. But if it does not derive its truth from this
tradition, then it does not depend upon it. But if it does not depend upon
it; then it can persist without it. That is all I want.
Quoted in Henry E. Allison, *Lessing and the Enlightenment*, p. 119

What education is to the individual man, revelation is to the whole 4
human race. . . .
  Education gives man nothing which he could not also get from within
himself; it gives him that which he could get from within himself, only
quicker and more easily. In the same way too, revelation gives nothing to
the human race which human reason could not arrive at on its own; only
it has given, and still gives to it, the most important of these things
sooner.
Theological Writings, quoted in *Eighteenth Century Philosophy*, ed. Lewis White
Beck, p. 225

. . . is the human species never to arrive at this highest step of illumination 5
and purity? – Never?
  Never? – Let me not think this blasphemy, All Merciful! Education has

its goal, in the race, no less than in the individual. That which is educated is educated for a purpose. . . .

No! It will come! it will assuredly come! the time of the perfecting, when man, the more convinced his understanding feels about an even better future, will nevertheless not need to borrow motives for his actions from this future; for he will do right because it *is* right, not because arbitrary rewards are set upon it, which formerly were intended simply to fix and strengthen his unsteady gaze in recognizing the inner, better, rewards of well-doing.
Theological Writings, p. 237

EMMANUEL LEVINAS (*b.* 1906)

1   The ethical relation is not grafted on to an antecedent relation of cognition; it is a foundation and not a superstructure.
'Philosophy and the Idea of Infinity', *Collected Philosophical Papers*, p. 56

2   A human being is the sole being which I am unable to encounter without expressing this very encounter to him. In every attitude in regard to the human, there is the salutation, if only in the refusal of the latter.
'Is Ontology Fundamental?', *Philosophy Today* (1989), p. 125

3   The fundamental experience which objective experience itself presumes is the experience of the Other – experience *par excellence*. . . . Moral consciousness is not an experience of values, but access to exterior Being: exterior being *par excellence* is the Other.
'Signature', *Difficile Liberté*, p. 409

4   Access to the face is straightaway ethical.
Ethics and Infinity, trans. R. A. Cohen, p. 85

5   There is first the very uprightness of the face, its upright exposure, without defense. The skin of the face is that which stays most naked, most destitute. It is the most naked, though with a decent nudity. It is the most destitute also: there is an essential poverty in the face; the proof of this is that one tries to mask this poverty by putting on poses, by taking on a countenance. The face is exposed, menaced, as if inviting us to an act of violence. At the same time, the face is what forbids us to kill.
Ethics and Infinity, trans. R. A. Cohen, p. 86

6   Why does the other concern me? What is Hecuba to me? Am I my brother's keeper? These questions have meaning only if one has already supposed that the ego is concerned only with itself, is only a concern for itself. . . . But in the 'prehistory' of the ego posited for itself speaks a responsibility. The self is through and through a hostage, older than the

ego, prior to principles. What is at stake for the self, in its being, is not to be. Beyond egoism and altruism it is the religiosity of the self.
Otherwise than Being or Beyond Essence, p. 117

Ethical subjectivity dispenses with the idealizing subjectivity of ontology, 7 which reduces everything to itself. The ethical 'I' is subjectivity precisely insofar as it kneels before the other, sacrificing its own liberty to the more primordial call of the other. . . . The heteronomy of our response to the human other, or to God as the absolutely other, precedes the autonomy of our subjective freedom. As soon as I acknowledge that it is 'I' who am responsible, I accept that my freedom is anteceded by an obligation to the other.
'Dialogue with Emmanuel Levinas', in Richard Kearney, *Dialogues with Contemporary Continental Thinkers*, p. 63

The subject is a responsibility before being an intentionality. 8
'Humanism and Anarchy', *Collected Philosophical Papers*, p. 134

One has to respond to one's right to be, not by referring to some abstract 9 and anonymous law, or judicial entity, but because of one's fear for the Other. My being-in-the-world or my 'place in the sun', my being at home, have these not also been the usurpation of spaces belonging to the other man whom I have already oppressed or starved, or driven out into a third world; are they not acts of repulsing, excluding, stripping, killing?
'Ethics as First Philosophy', *The Levinas Reader*, p. 82

Politics is opposed to morality, as philosophy to naïveté. 10
Totality and Infinity, p. 21

The end of humanism, of metaphysics, the death of man, the death of 11 God (or death to God!) – these are apocalyptic ideas or slogans of intellectual high society. Like all the manifestations of Parisian taste (or Parisian disgusts), these topics impose themselves with the tyranny of the last word, but become available to anyone and cheapened.
'No Identity', *Collected Philosophical Papers*, p. 141

Indeed in our day there is no end to the end of metaphysics, and the end 12 of metaphysics is our unavowed metaphysics, for no avowal will be its equivalent.
'Humanism and Anarchy', *Collected Philosophical Papers*, p. 129

The existence of God is not a question of an individual soul's uttering 13 logical syllogisms. It cannot be proved. The existence of God is sacred history itself, the sacredness of man's relation to man through which God may pass. God's existence is the story of his revelation in Biblical history.
'Dialogue with Emmanuel Levinas', in Richard Kearney, *Dialogues with Contemporary Continental Thinkers*, p. 18

14 Humanism has to be denounced because it is not sufficiently human.
   Otherwise than Being or Beyond Essence, p. 128

15 What could an entirely rational being speak of with another entirely
   rational being?
   Totality and Infinity, p. 119

16 Art brings into the world the obscurity of fate, but it especially brings the
   irresponsibility that charms as a lightness and grace. It frees. To make or
   to appreciate a novel or a picture is no longer to have to conceptualize, it
   is to renounce the effort of science, philosophy and action. Do not speak,
   do not reflect, admire in silence and in peace, such are the counsels of
   wisdom satisfied before the beautiful. There is something wicked and
   egoist and cowardly in artistic enjoyment. There are times when one can
   be ashamed of it, as of feasting during a plague.
   'Reality and its Shadow', *Collected Philosophical Papers*, p. 12

17 Philosophy is inseparable from scepticism, which follows it like a shadow
   that it chases away by refuting it, only to find it once again under its feet.
   Otherwise than Being or Beyond Essence, p. 168

18 If philosophizing consists in assuring oneself of an absolute origin, the
   philosopher will have to efface the trace of his own footsteps and
   unendingly efface the traces of the effacing of the traces, in an
   interminable movement staying where it is.
   Otherwise than Being or Beyond Essence, p. 20

19 If the essence of philosophy consists in going back from all certainties
   toward a principle, if it lives from critique, the face of the other would be
   the starting point of philosophy. This is a thesis of heteronomy which
   breaks with a very venerable tradition.
   'Philosophy and the Idea of Infinity', *Collected Philosophical Papers*, p. 59

20 Western philosophy coincides with the disclosure of the other where the
   other, in manifesting itself as a being, loses its alterity. From its infancy
   philosophy has been struck with a horror of the other that remains other
   – with an insurmountable allergy.
   'The Trace of the Other', *Deconstruction in Context*, p. 346

21 The best thing about philosophy is that it fails. It is better that philosophy
   fail to totalize meaning for it thereby remains open to the irreducible
   otherness of transcendence.
   'Dialogue with Emmanuel Levinas', in Richard Kearney, *Dialogues with
   Contemporary Continental Thinkers*, p. 63

DAVID LEWIS (*b.* 1941)

A regularity R in the behavior of members of population P when they are 1
agents in a recurrent situation S is a *convention* if and only if, in any
instance of S among members of P,

1) everyone conforms to R
2) everyone expects everyone else to conform to R
3) everyone prefers to conform to R on condition that the others do,
   since S is a co-ordination problem and uniform conformity to R is a
   proper co-ordination equilibrium in S.

Convention, p. 42

'*If kangaroos had no tails, they would topple over*' seems to me to mean 2
something like this: in any possible state of affairs in which kangaroos
have no tails, and which resembles our actual state of affairs as much as
kangaroos having no tails permits it to, the kangaroos topple over. I . . .
give a general analysis of counterfactual conditionals along these lines.

Counterfactuals, p. 1

I believe that there are possible worlds other than the one we happen to 3
inhabit. If an argument is wanted, it is this. It is uncontroversially true
that things might be otherwise than they are. I believe, and so do you,
that things could have been different in countless ways. But what does
this mean? Ordinary language permits the paraphrase: there are many
ways things could have been besides the way they actually are. On the
face of it, this sentence is an existential quantification. It says that there
exist many entities of a certain description, to wit 'ways things could
have been'. . . . I believe permissible paraphrases of what I believe; taking
the paraphrase at its face value, I therefore believe in the existence of
entities that might be called 'ways things could have been'. I prefer to call
them 'possible worlds'.

Counterfactuals, p. 84

Humean Supervenience is named in honour of the great denier of 4
necessary connections. It is the doctrine that all there is to the world is a
vast mosaic of local matters of particular fact, just one little thing after
another. . . . We have geometry: a system of external relations of spatio-
temporal distance between points. Maybe points of spacetime itself,
maybe point-sized bits of matter or aether or fields, maybe both. And at
those points we have local qualities: perfectly natural intrinsic properties
which need nothing bigger than a point at which to be instantiated. For
short: we have an arrangement of qualities. And that is all. There is no
difference without difference in the arrangement of qualities. All else
supervenes on that.

Philosophical Papers, II, p. ix

5 It is not to be demanded that a philosophical theory should agree with anything that the man on the street would insist on offhand, uninformed and therefore uninfluenced by any theoretical gains to be had by changing his mind. (Especially not if, like many men on the streets nowadays, he would rise to the occasion and wax wildly philosophical at the slightest provocation.)
On the Plurality of Worlds, p. 134

GEORG CHRISTOPH LICHTENBERG (1742–1799)

1 My body is that part of the world which can be altered by my thoughts. Even imaginary illnesses can become real. In the rest of the world my hypotheses cannot disturb the order of things.
Aphorisms

2 Our idea of a 'soul' is not unlike the conception of there being a magnet in the earth. It is a mere figure of thought. But to conceive of all things under this form is a device innate in man.
The Reflections of Lichtenberg, trans. Norman Alliston, p. 67

3 After all, is our idea of God anything more than personified incomprehensibility?
The Reflections of Lichtenberg, trans. Norman Alliston, p. 87

4 We are conscious of certain impressions which are involuntary; others – at least, so we believe – depend on ourselves; where is the boundary line? We know of nothing but the existence of our impressions, feelings and thoughts. It thinks, we ought really to say; just as we now say, it thunders. To say *cogito* is too much, if you translate this into 'I think'. Still, to assume or postulate this 'I' is a practical necessity.
The Reflections of Lichtenberg, trans. Norman Alliston, p. 86

5 There is a great difference between believing a thing, and not being able to believe the contrary. I often come to believe in things, without being able to prove them; just as I disbelieve others, without being able to disprove them. What side I take is determined not strictly by logic, but by preponderance.
The Reflections of Lichtenberg, trans. Norman Alliston, p. 69

6 As in dreams we so often take objections of our own for those of another (as for instance in a dispute with someone), it surprises me that the same does not often occur when we are awake. The state of being awake, then, would seem to consist principally in this, that we then draw a sharp and proper distinction between what attaches to ourselves and what to others.
The Reflections of Lichtenberg, trans. Norman Alliston, p. 95

A thinking being recognizing the future more easily than the past would   7
be quite possible. As it is, there is a good deal in the case of insects to lead
us to the conclusion that they are more exercised by the future than the
past. Had animals as good a recollection of the past as they have
presentiment of the future, not a few insects would be superior to
ourselves. It appears, however, as if the capacity of anticipation stood in
inverse ratio to that of remembrance.
The Reflections of Lichtenberg, trans. Norman Alliston, p. 63

We are a great deal more certain that our will is free than that everything   8
that happens is bound to have a cause. This being the case, could we not
for once in a way reverse the argument, and say: our ideas of cause and
effect must be very inaccurate, for were they right, our will could not be
free?
The Reflections of Lichtenberg, trans. Norman Alliston, p. 67

Every moment we do something without being aware of it; facility   9
increases, and in the end a man would get to do everything without
knowing it, and in a literal sense become a rational animal. Thus does
reason gradually approximate to animalism.
The Reflections of Lichtenberg, trans. Norman Alliston, p. 53

Reasons are for the most part only an augmented form of the pretensions   10
by which we seek to defend a course of conduct that we should in any
case have pursued, and to lend it an air of legitimacy and reasonableness.
Nature, it appears, has not cared to let a thing so necessary to her
economy as human conviction depend alone on logical deductions, as
these may so easily be deceptive. The impulse to act, thank Heaven, often
comes to us unawares, before we are half through with proving its need
and utility.
The Reflections of Lichtenberg, trans. Norman Alliston, p. 91

We imagine we are free in our actions, just as in dreaming we deem a   11
place perfectly familiar which we then see doubtless for the first time.
The Reflections of Lichtenberg, trans. Norman Alliston, p. 62

One of the solidest supports of which the Kantian philosophy may boast   12
is the undoubted truth of the observation that we ourselves are as much
something as the objects without us. Whenever, then, anything makes an
impression on us, the effect must depend, not alone on the thing
effecting, but on that also on which the effect is produced. As in the case
of the mechanical impulse both factors are at once active and passive, for
it is impossible for one thing to act on another without the effect as a
whole being a compound one. In this sense a pure *tabula rasa* must, I
should think, be an impossibility, for in every effect the agent undergoes

some modification, and that which passes from it accrues to the patient, and *vice versa*.
The Reflections of Lichtenberg, trans. Norman Alliston, p. 85

13 What am I? What ought I to do? What may I hope and believe? To this everything in philosophy may be reduced. It were to be wished that other things might be thus simplified; at least we ought to try whether everything that we intend to treat of in a book cannot at once be so epitomized.
The Reflections of Lichtenberg, trans. Norman Alliston, p. 75

14 . . . we cannot possibly feel for others, as the expression goes; it is solely for ourselves we feel. This truth sounds harsh, but it is not so if only properly understood. It is neither father nor mother, wife nor child, that we love, but the agreeable emotions which they occasion – something that flatters our pride and self-love. Nor could it possibly be otherwise, and those who deny the fact evidently misunderstand it.
The Reflections of Lichtenberg, trans. Norman Alliston, p. 78

15 When I regard anything first as body and then as spirit, it produces a tremendous parallax. The former might be styled the *somato-centric*, and the latter the *psycho-centric* region of a thing.
The Reflections of Lichtenberg, trans. Norman Alliston, p. 55

16 Contrive what manner of viewing things exterior to the mind we may, it will and must invariably have some trace of the subjective mind in it. It seems to me an extremely unphilosophical idea to conceive of the soul as a thing merely passive; no, it too is a factor in the case. Hence it may be that not a single being in the world really recognizes things as they are. This I should like to call the affinities of the spiritual and corporeal worlds; and I can very well imagine that there might be creatures to whom the universe would be a melody for them to dance to, with Heaven playing the accompaniment.
The Reflections of Lichtenberg, trans. Norman Alliston, p. 75

17 I and myself. *I* feel *myself* – these are two distinct things. Our false philosophy is incorporated in our whole language; we cannot reason without, so to speak, reasoning wrongly. We overlook the fact that speaking, no matter of what, is itself a philosophy.
The Reflections of Lichtenberg, trans. Norman Alliston, p. 75

18 Put it how you will, philosophy is only the art of discrimination. The country bumpkin makes use of all the principles of philosophy, though indirectly, latently, or in combination, as the physicist and chemist would say; the philosopher gives us them pure.
The Reflections of Lichtenberg, trans. Norman Alliston, p. 78

JOSHUA LOTH LIEBMAN (1907–1948)

We human beings not only confront values; we embody them, incarnate them, channel them. We are their transmitters, spectra dancing with their light.
Peace of Mind, p. 154

JOHN LOCKE (1632–1704)

Let us then suppose the Mind to be, as we say, white Paper, void of all   1
Characters, without any *Ideas*; How comes it to be furnished? Whence comes it by that vast store, which the busy and boundless Fancy of Man has painted on it, with an almost endless variety? Whence has it all the materials of Reason and Knowledge? To this I answer, in one word, From *Experience*: In that, all our Knowledge is founded; and from that it ultimately derives it self. Our Observation employ'd either about *external, sensible Objects; or about the internal Operations of our Minds, perceived and reflected on by our selves, is that, which supplies our Understandings with all the materials of thinking.*
An Essay Concerning Human Understanding, Bk. 2, Ch. 1, §2

Whatsoever the Mind perceives in it self, or is the immediate object of   2
Perception, Thought, or Understanding, that I call *Idea*; and the Power to produce any *Idea* in our mind, I call *Quality* of the Subject wherein that power is. Thus a Snow-ball having the power to produce in us the *Ideas* of *White, Cold,* and *Round,* the Powers to produce those *Ideas* in us, as they are in the Snow-ball, I call *Qualities*; and as they are Sensations, or Perceptions, in our Understandings, I call them *Ideas*: which *Ideas*, if I speak of sometimes, as in the things themselves, I would be understood to mean those Qualities in the Objects which produce them in us.
An Essay Concerning Human Understanding, Bk. 2, Ch. 8, §8

. . . the *Ideas of primary Qualities* of Bodies, *are Resemblances* of them,   3
and their Patterns do really exist in the Bodies themselves; but the *Ideas*, produced in us *by* these *Secondary Qualities, have no resemblance* of them at all. There is nothing like our *Ideas*, existing in the Bodies themselves. They are in the Bodies, we denominate from them, only a Power to produce those Sensations in us: And what is Sweet, Blue, or Warm in *Idea*, is but the certain Bulk, Figure, and Motion of the insensible Parts in the Bodies themselves, which we call so.
An Essay Concerning Human Understanding, Bk. 2, Ch. 8, §15

We have as clear a Notion of the Substance of Spirit, as we have of Body;   4
the one being supposed to be (without knowing what it is) the *Substratum* to those simple *Ideas* we have from without; and the other

supposed (with a like ignorance of what it is) to be the *Substratum* to those Operations, which we experiment in our selves within.
An Essay Concerning Human Understanding, Bk. 2, Ch. 23, §5

5 That our *Idea* of Place, is nothing else, but such a relative Position of any thing, as I have before mentioned, I think, is plain, and will be easily admitted, when we consider, that we can have no *Idea* of the Place of the Universe, though we can of all the parts of it; because beyond that, we have not the *Idea* of any fixed, distinct, particular Beings, in reference to which, we can imagine it to have any relation of distance . . .
An Essay Concerning Human Understanding, Bk. 2, Ch. 13, §10

6 The Mind, . . . concluding from what it has so constantly observed to have been, that the like Changes will for the future be made, in the same things, by like Agents, and by the like ways, considers in one thing the possibility of having any of its simple *Ideas* changed, and in another the possibility of making that change; and so comes by that *Idea* which we call *Power*. . . . *Power* thus considered is twofold, viz, as able to make, or able to receive any change: The one may be called *Active*, and the other *Passive Power*.
An Essay Concerning Human Understanding, Bk. 2, Ch. 21, §1

7 The use of Words then being to stand as outward Marks of our internal *Ideas*, and those *Ideas* being taken from particular things, if every particular *Idea* that we take in, should have a distinct Name, Names must be endless. To prevent this, the Mind makes the particular *Ideas*, received from particular Objects, to become general; which is done by considering them as they are in the Mind such Appearances, separate from all other Existences, and the circumstances of real Existence, as Time, Place, or any other concomitant *Ideas*. This is called *ABSTRACTION*, whereby *Ideas* taken from particular Beings, become general Representatives of all of the same kind; and their Names general Names, applicable to whatever exists conformable to such abstract *Ideas*.
An Essay Concerning Human Understanding, Bk. 2, Ch. 11, §9

8 If it may be doubted, Whether *Beasts* compound and enlarge their *Ideas* that way, to any degree: This, I think, I may be positive in, That the power of *Abstracting* is not at all in them; and that the having of general *Ideas*, is that which puts a perfect distinction betwixt Man and Brutes; and is an Excellency which the Faculties of Brutes do by no means attain to.
An Essay Concerning Human Understanding, Bk. 2, Ch. 11, §10

9 . . . that [words] *signify* only Men's peculiar *Ideas*, and that *by a perfectly arbitrary Imposition*, is evident, in that they often fail to excite in others

(even that use the same language) the same *Ideas*, we take them to be the Signs of: And every Man has so inviolable a Liberty, to make Words stand for what *Ideas* he pleases, that no one hath the Power to make others have the same *Ideas* in their Minds, that he has, when they use the same Words, that he does.
An Essay Concerning Human Understanding, Bk. 3, Ch. 2, §8

But as the Mind is wholly Passive in the reception of all its simple *Ideas*, **10** so it exerts several acts of its own, whereby out of its simple *Ideas*, as the Materials and Foundations of the rest, the other are framed. . . . As simple *Ideas* are observed to exist in several Combinations united together; so the Mind has a power to consider several of them united together, as one *Idea*; and that not only as they are united in external Objects, but as it self has join'd them. *Ideas* thus made up of several simple ones put together, I call *Complex*; such as are *Beauty, Gratitude, a Man, an Army, the Universe*; which though complicated of various simple *Ideas*, or *complex Ideas* made up of simple ones, yet are, when the Mind pleases, considered each by it self, as one entire thing, and signified by one name.
An Essay Concerning Human Understanding, Bk. 2, Ch. 12, §1

. . . this whole *mystery* of *Genera* and *Species*, which make such a noise in **11** the Schools, and are, with Justice, so little regarded out of them, is nothing else but abstract *Ideas*, more or less comprehensive, with names annexed to them.
An Essay Concerning Human Understanding, Bk. 3, Ch. 3, §9

. . . only we must take notice, that our complex *Ideas* of Substances, **12** besides all these simple *Ideas* they are made up of, have always the confused *Idea* of *something* to which they belong, and in which they subsist: and therefore when we speak of any sort of Substance, we say it is a *thing* having such or such Qualities . . .
An Essay Concerning Human Understanding, Bk. 2, Ch. 23, §3

. . . the *nominal Essence* of *Gold*, is that complex *Idea* the word *Gold* **13** stands for, let it be, for instance, a Body yellow, of a certain weight, malleable, fusible, and fixed. But the *real Essence* is the constitution of the insensible parts of that Body, on which those Qualities, and all the other Properties of *Gold* depend. How far these two are different, though they are both called *Essence*, is obvious, at first sight, to discover.
An Essay Concerning Human Understanding, Bk. 3, Ch. 6, §2

I presume 'tis not the *Idea* of a thinking or rational Being alone, that **14** makes the *Idea* of a *Man* in most Peoples Sense; but of a Body so and so shaped joined to it; and if that be the *Idea* of a *Man*, the same successive

Body not shifted all at once, must as well as the same immaterial Spirit go to the making of the same *Man*.

This being premised to find wherein *personal Identity* consists, we must consider what *Person* stands for; which, I think, is a thinking intelligent Being, that has reason and reflection, and can consider it self as it self, the same thinking thing in different times and places; which it does only by that consciousness, which is inseparable from thinking, and as it seems to me essential to it. . . . since consciousness always accompanies thinking, and 'tis that, that makes every one to be, what he calls *self*; and thereby distinguishes himself from all other thinking things, in this alone consists *personal Identity*, *i.e.* the sameness of a rational Being: And as far as this consciousness can be extended backwards to any past Action or Thought, so far reaches the Identity of that *Person*; it is the same *self* now it was then; and 'tis by the same *self* with this present one that now reflects on it, that that Action was done.
An Essay Concerning Human Understanding, Bk. 2, Ch. 27, §8

15 . . . that which seems to make the difficulty is this, that this consciousness, being interrupted always by forgetfulness, there being no moment of our Lives wherein we have the whole train of all our past Actions before our Eyes in one view: But even the best Memories losing the sight of one part whilst they are viewing another; and we sometimes, and that the greatest part of our Lives, not reflecting on our past selves, being intent on our present Thoughts, and in sound sleep, having no Thoughts at all, or at least none with that consciousness, which remarks our waking Thoughts. I say, in all these cases, our consciousness being interrupted, and we losing the sight of our past *selves*, doubts are raised whether we are the same thinking thing . . .
An Essay Concerning Human Understanding, Bk. 2, Ch. 27, §10

16 . . . as far as any intelligent Being can repeat the *Idea* of any past Action with the same consciousness it had of it at first, and with the same consciousness it has of any present Action; so far it is the same *personal self*. For it is by the consciousness it has of its present Thoughts and Actions, that it is *self* to it *self* now, and so will be the same *self* as far as the same consciousness can extend to Actions past or to come; and would be by distance of Time, or change of Substance, no more two *Persons* than a Man be two Men, by wearing other Cloaths to Day than he did Yesterday, with a long or short sleep between . . .
An Essay Concerning Human Understanding, Bk. 2, Ch. 27, §10

17 To return then to the Enquiry, *what is it that determines the Will in regard to our Actions?* . . . we shall find, that we being capable but of one determination of the will to one action at once, the present *uneasiness*,

that we are under, does naturally determine the will, in order to that happiness which we all aim at in all our actions: For as much as whilst we are under any *uneasiness*, we cannot apprehend our selves happy, or in the way to it. . . . And therefore that, which of course determines the choice of our *will* to the next action, will always be the removing of pain, as long as we have any left, as the first and necessary step towards happiness.

An Essay Concerning Human Understanding, Bk. 2, Ch. 21, §§31, 36

. . . *Ideas* that in themselves are not at all of kin, come to be so united in some Mens Minds, that 'tis very hard to separate them, they always keep in company, and the one no sooner at any time comes into the Understanding but its Associate appears with it; and if they are more than two which are thus united, the whole gang always inseparable shew themselves together. . . . to this, perhaps, might by justly attributed most of the Sympathies and Antipathies observable in Men, which work as strongly, and produce as regular Effects as if they were Natural, and are therefore called so . . .   **18**

An Essay Concerning Human Understanding, Bk. 2, Ch. 33, §§5, 7

. . . the Mind has a Power, in many cases, to revive Perceptions, which it has once had, with this additional Perception annexed to them, that it has had them before. And in this Sense it is, that our *Ideas* are said to be in our Memories, when indeed, they are actually no where, but only there is an ability in the Mind, when it will, to revive them again; and as it were paint them anew on it self, though some with more, some with less difficulty; some more lively, and others more obscurely.   **19**

An Essay Concerning Human Understanding, Bk. 2, Ch. 10, §2

All the Actions, that we have any *Idea* of, reducing themselves, as has been said, to these two, viz. Thinking and Motion, so far as a Man has a power to think, or not to think; to move or not to move, according to the preference or direction of his own mind, so far is a Man *Free*. Where-ever any performance or forbearance are not equally in a Man's power; where-ever doing or not doing, will not equally follow upon the preference of his mind directing it, there he is not *Free*, though perhaps the Action may be voluntary. . . .   **20**

An Essay Concerning Human Understanding, Bk. 2, Ch. 21, §8

Thus from the Consideration of our selves, and what we infallibly find in our own Constitutions, our Reason leads us to the Knowledge of this certain and evident Truth, That *there is an eternal, most powerful, and most knowing Being*; which whether any one will please to call *God*, it matters not. The thing is evident. . . . If nevertheless any one should be found so senslessly arrogant, as to suppose Man alone knowing and wise,   **21**

but yet the product of mere ignorance and chance; and that all the rest of
the Universe acted only by that blind hap-hazard: I shall leave with him
that very Rational and Emphatical rebuke of *Tully* l. 2. *de leg.* to be
considered at his leisure. 'What can be more sillily arrogant and
misbecoming, than for a Man to think that he has a Mind and
Understanding in him, but yet in all the Universe beside, there is no such
thing?'
An Essay Concerning Human Understanding, Bk. 4, Ch. 10, §6

22   But to conclude, Reason being plain on our side, that Men are naturally
free, and the Examples of History shewing, that the *Governments* of the
World, that were begun in Peace, had their beginning laid on that
foundation, and were *made by the Consent of the People*; There can be
little room for doubt, either where the Right is, or what has been the
Opinion, or Practice of Mankind, about the *first erecting of Governments*.
Two Treatises of Government, ed. P. Laslett, p. 380

23   If Man in the State of Nature be so free, as has been said; If he be
absolute Lord of his own Person and Possessions, equal to the greatest,
and subject to no Body, why will he part with his Freedom? Why will he
give up this Empire, and subject himself to the Dominion and Controul
of any other Power? To which 'tis obvious to Answer, that though in the
state of Nature he hath such a right, yet the Enjoyment of it is very
uncertain, and constantly exposed to the Invasion of others. For all being
Kings as much as he, every Man his Equal, and the greater part no strict
Observers of Equity and Justice, the enjoyment of the property he has in
this state is very unsafe, very unsecure.
Two Treatises of Government, p. 395

24   But though Men when they enter into Society, give up the Equality,
Liberty, and Executive Power they had in the State of Nature, into the
hands of the Society, to be so far disposed of by the Legislative, as the
good of the Society shall require; yet it being only with an intention in
every one the better to preserve himself his Liberty and Property; (For no
rational Creature can be supposed to change his condition with an
intention to be worse) the power of the Society, or *Legislative* constituted
by them, *can never be suppos'd to extend farther than the common good*;
but is obliged to secure every ones Property by providing against those
three defects above-mentioned, that made the State of Nature so unsafe
and uneasie.
Two Treatises of Government, p. 398

25   The Liberty of Man, in Society, is to be under no other Legislative Power,
but that established by consent, in the Common-wealth, nor under the

Dominion of any Will, or Restraint of any Law, but what the Legislative shall enact, according to the trust put in it.
Two Treatises of Government, p. 324

ALFRED LOUCH (*b.* 1927)

In the end, we must reluctantly admit that the terrorist's uncompromising position makes it impossible to treat him or her as other than the enemy – as an outlaw. Except in war we lack the conventions of violent reprisal. And even in war we maintain the minimum conventions of civility; we recognise that our enemies hold other, but still plausible, allegiances. Men and women who blow up supermarkets and glory in their deed have moved beyond the reach of that courtesy. But what it means to treat someone as an outlaw is a matter on which I fear I have no more to say, except to say that it is what we ought to think about.
'The Immorality of Belief', *The Morality of Terrorism*, ed. D. Rappaport and Y. Alexander, p. 274

SABINA LOVIBOND (*b.* 1952)

Where it is a question of communicating some value-attitude which is   1
important or even indispensable for social functioning, the [moral] educator will insist on a certain construction of the learner's experience – will sometimes present certain verbal or gestural forms as the ones that *must* express the learner's response to a given situation (Christmas decorations, pretty! Lavatory humour, appalling! etc.). The status of this 'must' is rather obscure, but it cannot be strictly epistemic. It is not that we find it *incredible* that a child should respond otherwise; it is rather that we shall not be *satisfied* until we get the response we are suggesting. Thus we may continue to press that response on the learner, *as her own response*, in the teeth of the behavioural evidence. This willingness to disregard the evidence is, of course, goal-directed: it aims at making actual what is at present only ideal, namely the spontaneous occurrence in the learner of what we consider to be the appropriate response. . . . At all events, episodes of this kind show – or so I would argue – that in practice our commitment to a first-person epistemic privilege with regard to feelings of pleasure is by no means absolute.
'True and False Pleasures', *Proceedings of the Aristotelian Society* (1989–90), p. 219

. . . if one comes upon a child torturing an animal, it is weak indeed to say   2
'I can see you enjoy doing that, but . . .' (followed by moral rebuke). The didactically correct reaction (though this need not involve any sentimental illusion in the educator's own mind) is, rather, one that *refuses to*

acknowledge any evidence that the experience is enjoyable for the torturer. In that case – putting myself for a moment in the torturer's position – what will (ideally) happen is that, finding the construction of my torturing experience as a pleasurable one universally rejected, I shall lose hermeneutical faith in it: receiving no support within the psychological discourse into which I am being initiated, it will go the way of whatever else in my mental life fails to strike a spark from others, i.e. it will lapse into the category of the *merely* subjective. (And consequently it will become inexpressible . . .)
'True and False Pleasures', p. 220

3   . . . the direction I get from others can do no more than start me off on an essentially autonomous course of development. In the end it is going to be up to me to deal with anything in myself which, to my own critical eye, looks unacceptably 'natural' or primitive.

. . . In the past I could rely on others to observe my behaviour and measure the gap between my actual response to situations, and the evaluatively appropriate response; now I have to do that for myself.
'True and False Pleasures', p. 221

GEORG LUKÁCS (1885–1971)

1   The essence of commodity-structure has often been pointed out. Its basis is that a relation between people takes on the character of a thing and thus acquires a 'phantom objectivity', an autonomy that seems so strictly rational and all-embracing as to conceal every trace of its fundamental nature: the relation between people.
History and Class Consciousness, trans. Rodney Livingstone, p. 83

2   Now class consciousness consists in fact of the appropriate and rational reactions 'imputed' to a particular typical position in the process of production. This consciousness is, therefore, neither the sum nor the average of what is thought or felt by the single individuals who make up the class. And yet the historically significant actions of the class as a whole are determined in the last resort by this consciousness and not by the thought of the individual.
History and Class Consciousness, trans. Rodney Livingstone, p. 51

3   Marx urged us to understand 'the sensuous world', the object, reality, as human sensuous activity. This means that man must become conscious of himself as a social being, as simultaneously the subject and object of the socio-historical process. . . . It was necessary for the proletariat to be born for social reality to become fully conscious.
History and Class Consciousness, trans. Rodney Livingstone, p. 19

And the irony I mean consists in the critic always speaking about the ultimate problems of life, but in a tone which implies that he is only discussing pictures and books, only the inessential and pretty ornaments of real life – and even then not their innermost substance but only their beautiful and useless surface.
Soul and Form, trans. Anna Bostock, p. 9

In the novel . . . ethic – the ethical intention – is visible in the creation of every detail and hence is, in its most concrete content, an effective structural element of the work itself.

Thus, the novel, in contrast to other genres whose existence resides within the finished form, appears as something in process of becoming. That is why, from the artistic viewpoint, the novel is the most hazardous genre, and why it has been described as only half an art by many who equate *having a problematic* with *being problematic*.
The Theory of the Novel, trans. Anna Bostock, p. 72

MARTIN LUTHER (1483–1546)

I greatly longed to understand Paul's Epistle to the Romans and nothing stood in the way but that one expression, 'the justice of God', because I took it to mean that justice whereby God is just and deals justly in punishing the unjust. My situation was that, although an impeccable monk, I stood before God as a sinner troubled in conscience, and I had no confidence that my merit would assuage him. Therefore I did not love a just and angry God, but rather hated and murmured against him. Yet I clung to the dear Paul and had a great yearning to know what he meant.

Night and day I pondered until I saw the connection between the justice of God and the statement that 'the just shall live by his faith'. Then I grasped that the justice of God is that righteousness by which through grace and sheer mercy God justifies us through faith. Thereupon I felt myself to be reborn and to have gone through open doors into paradise. The whole of Scripture took on a new meaning, and whereas before the 'justice of God' had filled me with hate, now it became to me inexpressibly sweet in greater love. This passage of Paul became to me a gate to heaven. . . .
Quoted in Roland Bainton, *Here I Stand*, p. 65

If you have a true faith that Christ is your Saviour, then at once you have a gracious God, for faith leads you in and opens up God's heart and will, that you should see pure grace and overflowing love. This it is to behold God in faith that you should look upon his fatherly, friendly heart, in which there is no anger nor ungraciousness. He who sees God as angry

267

does not see him rightly but looks only on a curtain, as if a dark cloud had been drawn across his face.
Quoted in Roland Bainton, *Here I Stand*, p. 65

WILLIAM G. LYCAN (*b.* 1945)

1   The Homuncular Functionalist sees a human being or any other sentient creature as a kind of corporate entity – as an integrated system of intercommunicating 'departments' that cooperatively go about the business of interpreting the stimuli that impinge on the corporate organism and of producing appropriate behavioral responses. In this model, a psychological description of a human being will consist of a set of flow charts, nested hierarchically. The top or 'master' flowchart will depict the person's immediate subsystems or departments. Each of these will be represented by a black box on the chart, and each of their routes of communicative access to others will be represented by an arrow of some kind or another . . . each of the subsystems will itself be described by a lower level flow chart that breaks it down into its own component departments or agencies. . . . When these more specialised components have been broken down further . . . [the] characterisation will become more recognisably biological although still job-descriptive – and finally neuroanatomical. . . . This leaves it open – indeed positively suggests – that not only we ourselves, but our component homunculi, may have beliefs or at least crude belieflike information-bearing states.
Judgement and Justification, pp. 5, 12

2   It is noteworthy that in this sense of 'impartialism', crass Act Utilitarianism is more strongly impartialist than are views based on respect for the separateness and autonomy of persons: for the Benthamite utilitarian, it does not *in any sense* matter who one is; equality in the sight of the moral law is *total*. . . . Our [Lycan and S. E. Boer] own view is that every person, every individual human being, is a shining, sacred vessel, to be brim-filled with utility.
Knowing Who, p. 194

M

𝔊𝔊𝔊𝔊𝔊𝔊

CATHERINE MACAULAY (GRAHAM) (1731–1791)

For though the doctrine of innate ideas, and innate affections, are in a 1
great measure exploded by the learned, yet few persons reason so clearly
and so accurately on abstract subjects as, through a long chain of
deductions, to bring forth a conclusion which in no respect militates with
their premises. It is a long time before the crowd give up opinions they
have been taught to look upon with respect; and I know many persons
who will follow you willingly through the course of your argument, till
they perceive it tends to the overthrow of some fond prejudice.
Letters on Education with Observations on Religious and Metaphysical Subjects,
p. 203

Power is regarded by all men as the greatest of temporal advantages. The 2
support given to Power, therefore, is an obligation; and, consequently,
the protection given by governors to subjects, a positive duty. The subject
can only be bound to obedience on the considerations of public good; but
the Sovereign, on these considerations, and a thousand others equally
binding, is tied to the exact observance of the laws of that constitution
under which he holds his power.
*An Address to the People of England, Scotland, and Ireland, on the Present
Important Crisis of Affairs*

The virtue of benevolence . . . is of so comprehensive a nature, that it 3
contains the principle of every moral duty.
Letters on Education with Observations on Religious and Metaphysical Subjects,
p. 112

. . . Pope has elegantly said *a perfect woman's but a softer man*. And if we 4
take in the consideration, that there can be but one rule of moral
excellence for beings made of the same materials, organized after the
same manner, and subjected to similar laws of Nature, we must either
agree with Mr. Pope, or we must reverse the proposition, and say, that *a
perfect man is a woman formed after a coarser mold*.

Letters on Education with Observations on Religious and Metaphysical Subjects, p. 204

5 . . . Rousseau . . . sets out with a supposition, that Nature intended the subjection of the one sex to the other; that consequently there must be an inferiority of intellect in the subjected party; but as man is a very imperfect being, and apt to play the capricious tyrant, Nature, to bring things nearer to an equality, bestowed on the woman such attractive graces, and such an insinuating address, as to turn the balance on the other scale. Thus Nature, in a giddy mood, recedes from her purposes, and subjects prerogative to an influence which must produce confusion and disorder in the system of human affairs. Rousseau saw this objection; and in order to obviate it, he has made up a moral person of the union of the two sexes, which, for contradiction and absurdity, outdoes every metaphysical riddle that was ever formed in the schools.
Letters on Education with Observations on Religious and Metaphysical Subjects, p. 205

6 Logic, which is undoubtedly a necessary part of tuition, as it can alone enable us to defend ourselves against the wiles of sophistry, will necessarily make us adepts in the defence of error.
Letters on Education with Observations on Religious and Metaphysical Subjects, p. 168

NEIL MacCORMICK (*b.* 1941)

. . . when we say that law 'embodies' values we are talking metaphorically. What does it mean? Values are only 'embodied' in law in the sense that and to the extent that human beings approve of the laws they have because of the states of affairs they are supposed to secure, being states of affairs which are on some ground deemed just or otherwise good. This need not be articulated at all.
Legal Reasoning and Legal Theory, p. 234

JOHN McDOWELL (*b.* 1940)

1 If the world is, in itself, motivationally inert, and is also the proper province of cognitive equipment, it is inescapable that a strictly cognitive state – a conception of how things are, properly so called – cannot constitute the whole of a reason for acting. But the idea of the world as motivationally inert is not an independent hard datum. It is simply the metaphysical counterpart of the thesis that states of will and cognitive states are distinct existences; which is exactly what is in question. . . . In moral upbringing what one learns is . . . to see situations in a special light,

as constituting reasons for action; this perceptual capacity, once acquired, can be exercised in complex novel circumstances.

'Are Moral Requirements Hypothetical Imperatives?', *Proceedings of the Aristotelian Society* (1978), p. 19

... suppose we say – not at all unnaturally – that an appearance that 2 such-and-such is the case can be *either* a mere appearance *or* the fact that such-and-such is the case making itself perceptually manifest to someone. As before, the object of experience in the deceptive cases is a mere appearance. But we are not to accept that in the non-deceptive cases too the object of experience is a mere appearance, and hence something that falls short of the fact itself. On the contrary, we are to insist that the appearance that is presented to one in those cases is a matter of the fact itself being disclosed to the experiencer. So appearances are no longer conceived as in general intervening between the experiencing subject and the world.

'Criteria, Defeasibility and Knowledge', *Proceedings of the British Academy* (1982), p. 472

Shifting to a secondary-quality analogy renders irrelevant any worry 3 about how something that is brutely *there* could nevertheless stand in an internal relation to some exercise of human sensibility. Values are not brutely there – not there independently of our sensibility – any more than colours are: though, as with colours, this does not stop us supposing that they are there independently of any particular apparent experience of them. As for the epistemology of value, the epistemology of danger is a good model. (Fearfulness is not a secondary quality, although the model is available only after the primary-quality model has been dislodged. A secondary-quality analogy for value experience gives out at certain points, no less than the primary-quality analogy that Mackie attacks.) To drop the primary-quality model in this case is to give up the idea that fearfulness itself, were it real, would need to be intelligible from a standpoint independent of the propensity to fear; the same must go for the relations of rational consequentiality in which fearfulness stands to more straightforward properties of things. Explanations of fear of the sort I envisaged would not only establish, from a different standpoint, that some of its objects are really fearful, but also make plain, case by case, what it is about them that makes them so; this should leave it quite unmysterious how a fear response rationally grounded in awareness (unproblematic, at least for present purposes) of these 'fearful-making characteristics' can be counted as being, or yielding, knowledge that one is confronted by an instance of real fearfulness.

'Values and Secondary Qualities', *Morality and Objectivity*, ed. T. Honderich, p. 120

4   Ironically, when reverence for the authority of phenomenology is carried to the length of making the fact that internal configurations are indistinguishable from the subject's point of view suffice to establish that those configurations are through and through the same, the upshot is to put at risk the most conspicuous phenomenological fact there is. The threat which the Cartesian picture poses to our hold on the world comes out dramatically in this: that within the Cartesian picture there is a serious question about how it can be that experience, conceived from its own point of view, is not blank or blind, but purports to be revelatory of the world we live in.

'Singular Thought and the Extent of Inner Space', *Subject, Thought and Context*, ed. P. Pettit and J. McDowell, p. 152

COLIN McGINN (*b.* 1950)

1   The *philosophical* problem about consciousness and the brain arises from a sense that we are compelled to accept that nature contains miracles – as if the merely metallic lamp of the brain could really spirit into existence the Djin of consciousness. But we do not need to accept this: we can rest secure in the knowledge that some (unknowable) property of the brain makes everything fall into place. What creates the philosophical puzzlement is the assumption that the problem must somehow be scientific but that any science *we* can come up with will represent things as utterly miraculous. And the solution is to recognize that the sense of miracle comes from us and not from the world. There is, in reality, nothing mysterious about how the brain generates consciousness.

The Problem of Consciousness, p. 18

2   Our concepts of the empirical world are fundamentally controlled by the character of our perceptual experience and by the introspective access we enjoy to our own minds. . . . Thus our concepts of consciousness are constrained by the specific form of our own consciousness, so that we cannot form concepts for quite alien forms of consciousness possessed by other actual and possible creatures. Similarly, our concepts of the body, including the brain, are constrained by the way we perceive these physical objects; we have, in particular, to conceive of them as spatial entities essentially similar to other physical objects in space. . . . But now these two forms of conceptual closure operate to prevent us from arriving at concepts for the property or relation that intelligibly links conscious-ness to the brain. For, first, we cannot grasp other forms of consciousness, and so we cannot grasp the theory that explains these other forms: that theory must be general, but *we* must always be parochial in our conception of consciousness. It is as if we were trying for a general theory of light but could only grasp the visible part of the spectrum. And,

second, it is precisely the perceptually controlled conception of the brain that we have which is so hopeless in making consciousness an intelligible result of brain activity. No property we can ascribe to the brain on the basis of how it strikes us perceptually, however inferential the ascription, seems capable of rendering perspicuous how it is that damp grey tissue can be the crucible from which subjective consciousness emerges fully formed. That is why the feeling is so strong in us that there has to be something *magical* about the mind–brain relation.
The Problem of Consciousness, p. 27

. . . this is precisely what externalism affirms about the mind: it is   3
constituted by its relations to distant objects. The characteristic properties of mind – its contentful states – are therefore not like intrinsic primary qualities of material substances, but are rather extrinsic relations that may take as their relata items from elsewhere in space. Neither does the mind seem to have clear (or clearly intelligible) boundaries, according to externalism. Do the distant constituents come within its boundaries, or is it that the boundaries are set somehow by the closer boundaries of the subject? We seem pulled in two directions here. . . . The proper conclusion for an externalist had better not be that the mind is a special kind of miraculous and incomprehensible substance, capable of tricks no regular substance could contrive; it should be, rather, that the mind is *no* sort of substance at all . . .
Mental Content, p. 21

Philosophers, being a verbal breed, have become accustomed to   4
conceiving mental intentionality in linguistic terms, as a kind of inward-directed ventriloquism – a displaced echo of the human voice. . . . The modelling theory abandons this picture entirely. It represents thinking as (sometimes) expressed by language, but not as resting on it, not as issuing from it. The basis of content is more like an engineer's workshop in which no one speaks. There are no volleys of verbal activity occurring in the recesses of your brain, only the production of vastly many practical models. You are not a secret speaker of some hitherto undeciphered language; you are more like the maker of a very sophisticated atlas that covers much more than ordinary geography.
Mental Content, p. 207

ERNST MACH (1838–1916)

Science itself, therefore, may be regarded as a minimal problem, consisting of the completest possible presentment of facts with the *least expenditure of thought*.
The Science of Mechanics: A Critical and Historical Account of Its Development, trans. T. J. McCormack, p. 586

NICOLO MACHIAVELLI (1469–1527)

Thus it is well to seem merciful, faithful, humane, sincere, religious, and also to be so; but you must have the mind so disposed that when it is needful to be otherwise you may be able to change to the opposite qualities. And it must be understood that a prince, and especially a new prince, cannot observe all those things which are considered good in men, being often obliged, in order to maintain the state, to act against faith, against charity, against humanity, and against religion.
The Prince, Ch. 18

ALASDAIR MacINTYRE (*b.* 1929)

1 The hypothesis I wish to advance is that in the actual world which we inhabit, the language of morality is in the same state of grave disorder as the language of natural science in the imaginary world which I have described. What we possess, if this view is true, are the fragments of a conceptual scheme, parts of which now lack those contexts from which their significance derived. We possess indeed simulacra of morality, we continue to use many of the key expressions. But we have – very largely if not entirely – lost our comprehension, both theoretical and practical, of morality.
After Virtue, p. 2

2 The problems of modern moral theory emerge clearly as the product of the failure of the Enlightenment project. On the one hand the individual moral agent, freed from hierarchy and teleology, conceives of himself and is conceived of by moral philosophers as sovereign in his moral authority. On the other hand the inherited, if partially transformed rules of morality have to be found some new status, deprived as they have been of their older teleological character and their even more ancient categorical character as expressions of an ultimately divine law. If such rules cannot be found a new status which will make appeal to them rational, appeal to them will indeed appear as a mere instrument of individual desire and will. Hence there is a pressure to vindicate them either by devising some new teleology or by finding some new categorical status for them. The first project is what lends its importance to utilitarianism; the second to all those attempts to follow Kant in presenting the authority of the appeal to moral rules as grounded in the nature of practical reason. Both attempts, so I shall argue, failed and fail; but in the course of the attempt to make them succeed social as well as intellectual transformations were accomplished.
After Virtue, p. 60

... generally to adopt a stance on the virtues will be to adopt a stance on   3
the narrative character of human life. Why this might be so is easy to
understand.

If a human life is understood as a progress through harms and dangers,
moral and physical, which someone may encounter and overcome in
better and worse ways and with a greater or lesser measure of success, the
virtues will find their place as those qualities the possession and exercise
of which generally tend to success in this enterprise and the vices likewise
as qualities which likewise tend to failure. Each human life will then
embody a story whose shape and form will depend upon what is counted
as a harm and danger and upon how success and failure, progress and its
opposite, are understood and evaluated. To answer these questions will
also explicitly and implicitly be to answer the question as to what the
virtues and vices are. The answer to this linked set of questions given by
the poets of heroic society is not the same as that given by Sophocles; but
the link is the same in both, and it reveals how belief in the virtues being
of a certain kind and belief in human life exhibiting a certain narrative
order are internally connected.
After Virtue, p. 135

... man is in his actions and practice, as well as in his fictions, essentially   4
a story-telling animal. He is not essentially, but becomes through his
history, a teller of stories that aspire to truth. But the key question for
men is not about their own authorship; I can only answer the question
'What am I to do?' if I can answer the prior question, 'Of what story or
stories do I find myself a part?' We enter human society, that is, with one
or more imputed characters – roles into which we have been drafted –
and we have to learn what they are in order to be able to understand how
others respond to us and how our responses to them are apt to be
construed. . . . Deprive children of stories and you leave them unscripted,
anxious stutterers in their actions as in their words. Hence there is no
way to give us an understanding of any society, including our own,
except through the stock of stories which constitute its initial dramatic
resources. Mythology, in its original sense, is at the heart of things. Vico
was right and so was Joyce. And so too of course is that moral tradition
from heroic society to its medieval heirs according to which the telling of
stories has a key part in educating us into the virtues.
After Virtue, p. 201

When Kierkegaard contrasted the ethical and the aesthetic ways of life in   5
Enten-Eller, he argued that the aesthetic life is one [in] which a human
life is dissolved into a series of separate present moments, in which the
unity of a human life disappears from view. By contrast in the ethical life
the commitments and responsibilities to the future springing from the

past episodes in which obligations were conceived and debts assumed unite the present to past and to future in such a way as to make of a human life a unity.
After Virtue, p. 225

6 The Aristotelian tradition has occupied two distinct places in my argument: first, because I have suggested that a great part of modern morality is intelligible only as a set of fragmented survivals from that tradition, and indeed that the inability of modern moral philosophers to carry through their projects of analysis and justification is closely connected with the fact that the concepts with which they work are a combination of fragmented survivals and implausible modern inventions; but in addition to this the rejection of the Aristotelian tradition was a rejection of a quite distinctive kind of morality in which rules, so predominant in modern conceptions of morality, find their place in a larger scheme in which the virtues have a central place; hence the cogency of a Nietzschean rejection and refutation of modern moralities of rules, whether of a utilitarian or of a Kantian kind, did not necessarily extend to the earlier Aristotelian tradition.
After Virtue, p. 239

7 A crucial turning point in that earlier history occurred when men and women of good will turned aside from the task of shoring up the Roman *imperium* and ceased to identify the continuation of civility and moral community with the maintenance of that *imperium*. What they set themselves to achieve instead – often not recognising what they were doing – was the construction of new forms of community within which the moral life could be sustained so that both morality and civility might survive the coming ages of barbarism and darkness. If my account of our moral condition is correct, we ought also to be able to conclude that for some time now we too have reached that turning point. What matters at this stage is the construction of local forms of community within which civility and the intellectual and moral life can be sustained through the new dark ages which are already upon us. And if the tradition of the virtues was able to survive the horrors of the last dark ages, we are not entirely without hope. This time however, the barbarians are not waiting beyond the frontiers; they have already been governing us for quite some time.
After Virtue, p. 244

J. L. MACKIE (1917–1981)

1 Although, on this account, God could not have known what Adam and Eve, or Satan, would do if he created them, he could surely know what

they *might* do: that is compatible even with this extreme libertarianism. If so, he was taking, literally, a hell of a risk when he created Adam and Eve, no less than when he created Satan. Was the freedom to make unforeseeable choices so great a good that it outweighed the risk? This question must be answered not only with reference to the degree of human wickedness that has actually occurred: men might (strange as it may seem) have been much worse than they are, and God (on this account) was accepting that risk too. He would not then be the author of sin in the sense of having knowingly produced it; he could not be accused of malice aforethought; but he would be open to a charge of gross negligence or recklessness.
The Miracle of Theism, p. 175

If we do take statements to be the primary bearers of truth, there seems to 2 be a very simple answer to the question, what is it for them to be true: for a statement to be true is for things to be as they are stated to be.
Truth, Probability and Paradox: Studies in Philosophical Logic, p. 22

The present suggestion, then, is that a statement of the form 'X caused Y' 3 means 'X occurred and Y occurred and Y would not have occurred if X had not', it being understood that when we instantiate 'X' and 'Y' with particular event descriptions we can express the suggested meaning most neatly by going back from the nominalizations to the corresponding clauses or their negations: e.g. 'the striking of the match caused the appearance of the flame' would, on this suggestion, mean 'the match was struck and the flame appeared and the flame would not have appeared if the match had not been struck'.
The Cement of the Universe: A Study of Causation, p. 31

. . . granted that causes are in general sufficient in the circumstances, in 4 this strong sense, as well as necessary in the circumstances, for their effects, while neither relation holds in non-causal sequences, we can still ask whether in calling something a cause we require both of these features or only one, and if so which.

To clear up this problem, let us consider three different shilling-in-the-slot machines, K, L, and M. Each of them professes to supply bars of chocolate. . . L, on the other hand, is an indeterministic machine. It will not, indeed, in normal circumstances produce a bar of chocolate unless a shilling is inserted, but it may fail to produce a bar even when this is done. And such failure is a matter of pure chance.

. . . I put a shilling into L and receive a bar of chocolate. Putting in the shilling was, in the circumstances, necessary for this result. It was also sufficient in the circumstances in the weak sense, but not in the strong, counterfactual, sense. A possible world, with the same laws of working

277

as the actual world, can contain the same circumstances, can lack the result, and yet still contain the inserting of the shilling. The statement, 'Given the circumstances, if the chocolate had not been going to appear, the shilling would not have been inserted' is not now acceptable. But would we say in this case that the inserting of the shilling caused the appearance of the bar of chocolate? I think we would. Our ordinary causal concept seems to require that where the shilling is put in, the mechanism operates, and a bar of chocolate appears, and would not have appeared if the shilling had not been inserted, the insertion of the shilling caused the appearance of the chocolate despite the fact that in the circumstances even given that the shilling was inserted, the chocolate might not have appeared.

The Cement of the Universe: A Study of Causation, p. 40

5   Our problem is that once we have accepted an irreducible distinction between mental and physical facts and properties, and have allowed that physical facts and properties constitute sufficient causes of actions, we seem to be forced to admit that mental facts and properties are epiphenomenal, causally idle; yet this conclusion is itself implausible.

Logic and Knowledge: Selected Papers, I, p. 134

CATHARINE A. MacKINNON (*b.* 1946)

1   Formally, the state is male in that objectivity is its norm. Objectivity is liberal legalism's conception of itself. It legitimates itself by reflecting its view of society, a society it helps make by so seeing it, and calling that view, and that relation rationality. Since rationality is measured by point-of-viewlessness, what counts as reason is that which corresponds to the way things are. Practical rationality, in this approach, means that which can be done without changing anything.

Toward a Feminist Theory of the State, p. 161

2   In conceiving a cognizable injury from the viewpoint of the reasonable rapist, the rape law affirmatively rewards men with acquittals for not comprehending women's point of view on sexual encounters.

Toward a Feminist Theory of the State, p. 182

3   . . . The point of view of a total system emerges as particular only when confronted, in a way it cannot ignore, by a demand from another point of view. This is why epistemology must be controlled for ontological dominance to succeed, and why consciousness raising is subversive. It is also why, when law sides with the powerless, as it occasionally has, it is said to engage in something other than law – politics or policy or personal opinion – and to delegitimate itself. When seemingly ontological conditions are challenged from the collective standpoint of a dissident reality, they

become visible as epistemological. Dominance suddenly appears no longer inevitable. When it loses its ground it loosens its grip.
Toward a Feminist Theory of the State, p. 239

JOHN MACQUARRIE (*b.* 1919)

. . . if God is being and not *a* being, then one can no more say that God *is* than that being *is*. God (or being) *is not* but rather *lets be*. But to let be is more primordial than to be, so that, as has already been said, being 'is' more 'beingful' than any possible being which it lets be; and this justifies us in using such expressions as 'being is', provided we remain aware of their logically 'stretched' character. . . . So it can be asserted that, while to say 'God exists' is strictly inaccurate and may be misleading if it makes us think of him as *some* being or other, yet it is more appropriate to say 'God exists' than 'God does not exist', since God's letting-be is prior to and the condition of the existence of any particular being.
Principles of Christian Theology, p. 108

J. M. E. McTAGGART (1866–1925)

Past, present, and future are incompatible determinations. Every event 1 must be one or the other, but no event can be more than one. If I say that any event is past, that implies that it is neither present nor future, and so with the others. And this exclusiveness is essential to change, and therefore to time. For the only change we can get is from future to present, and from present to past.

The characteristics, therefore, are incompatible. But every event has them all. If *M* is past, it has been present and future. If it is future, it will be present and past. If it is present, it has been future and will be past. Thus all the three characteristics belong to each event. How is this consistent with their being incompatible?
The Nature of Existence, II, Bk. 5, Ch. 33

I believe that nothing that exists can be temporal, and that therefore time 2 is unreal.
The Nature of Existence, II, Bk. 5, Ch. 33

MAIMONIDES (1135–1204)

A great disparity subsists between the knowledge an artificer has of the 1 thing he has made and the knowledge someone else has of the artifact in question.
The Guide of the Perplexed, trans. Shlomo Pines, p. 484

2 Divine providence does not watch in an equal manner over all the individuals of the human species, but providence is graded as their human perfection is graded.
The Guide of the Perplexed, trans. Shlomo Pines, p. 475

3 We are only able to apprehend the fact that He is and cannot apprehend His quiddity. It is consequently impossible that He should have affirmative attributes.
The Guide of the Perplexed, trans. Shlomo Pines, p. 135

JOSEPH DE MAISTRE (1754–1821)

1 Monsieur Rousseau says that man is born free, but is everywhere in chains. That is like saying that sheep are born carnivores, but are everywhere herbivores.
Attribd, but see I. Berlin, *The Crooked Timber of Humanity*, p. 125

2 The Constitution of 1795, just like its predecessors, was made for *man*. But there is no such thing as *man* in the world. In the course of my life I have seen Frenchmen, Italians, Russians etc.; I know, too, thanks to Montesquieu, *that one can be a Persian*. But as for *man*, I declare that I have never met him in my life; if he exists, he is unknown to me.
Oeuvres complètes de Joseph de Maistre, I, 74

NORMAN MALCOLM (1911–1990)

1 Religion is a form of life; it is language embedded in action – what Wittgenstein calls a 'language-game'. Science is another. Neither stands in need of justification, the one no more than the other.
'The Groundlessness of Belief', *Reason and Religion*, ed. S. Brown, p. 156

2 I was inclined at one time to think of this result as amounting to a proof that dreaming is not a mental activity or a mental phenomenon or a conscious experience. But now I reject that inclination. For one thing, the phrases 'mental activity', 'mental phenomenon', 'conscious experience', are so vague that I should not have known what I was asserting. . . . What I say instead is that if anyone holds that dreams are identical with, or composed of, thoughts, impressions, feelings, images, and so on (here one may supply whatever other mental nouns one likes, except 'dreams'), occurring in sleep, then his view is false.
Dreaming, p. 52

NICOLAS MALEBRANCHE (1638–1715)

1 God communicates His power to creatures and unites them among themselves solely by virtue of the fact that He makes their modalities

occasional causes of effects which He produces Himself – occasional causes, I say, which determine the efficacy of His volitions in consequence of general laws that He has prescribed for Himself, so as to make His conduct bear the character of His attributes and spread throughout His work the uniformity of action necessary to bind together all the parts that compose it and to extricate it from the confusion and irregularity of a kind of chaos in which minds could never understand anything.
Dialogues on Metaphysics, trans. W. Doney, p. 157

A true cause as I understand it is one such that the mind perceives a   2
necessary connection between it and its effect. Now the mind perceives a necessary connection between the will of an infinitely perfect being and its effects. Therefore, it is only God who is the true cause and who truly has the power to move bodies.
Search After Truth and Elucidations, ed. T. Lennon and P. Olscamp, p. 450

GABRIEL MARCEL (1889–1973)

In the *Journal Métaphysique* I had already begun to state the following   1
problem, which seems at first to be of a purely psychological order. How, I asked, is it possible to identify a feeling which we have for the first time? Experience shows that such an identification is often extremely difficult. (Love may appear in such disconcerting shapes as to prevent those who feel it from suspecting its real nature.) I observed that an identification of this sort can be realised in proportion as the feeling can be compared with something I *have*, in the sense that I *have* a cold or the measles. In that case, it can be limited, defined and intellectualised. So far as this can be done, I can form some idea of it and compare it with the previous notion I may have had about this feeling in general. . . . On the other hand, I went on to say, in proportion as my feeling cannot be isolated, and so distinguished, I am less sure of being able to recognise it. But is there not really a sort of emotional woof running across the warp of the feeling I *have*? and is it not consubstantial with what I *am*, and that to such a degree that I cannot really set it before myself and so form a conception of it? This is how I got my first glimpse of something which, though it was not a clear-cut distinction, was at least a sort of scale of subtle differences, an imperceptible shading-off from a feeling I have to a feeling I am. Hence this note written on March 16th, 1933:
    'Everything really comes down to the distinction between what we have and what we are. . . .'
Being and Having, p. 154

In principle, what we *have* are things (or what can be compared to things,   2
precisely in so far as this comparison is possible). I can only *have*, in the

281

strict sense of the word, something whose existence is, up to a certain point, independent of me. In other words, what I have is added to me. . . .

Here, then, is one approach, but it is not the only one. I cannot, for instance, concentrate my attention on what is properly called *my* body – as distinct from the body-as-object considered by physiologists – without coming once more upon this almost impenetrable notion of having. And yet, can I, with real accuracy, say that my body is something which I have? In the first place, can my body as such be called a thing? If I treat it as a thing, what is this 'I' which so treats it? 'In the last analysis,' I wrote in the *Journal Métaphysique*, 'we end up with the formula: my body is (an object), I am – nothing. Idealism has one further resource: it can declare that I am the act which posits the objective reality of my body. But is not this a mere sleight-of-hand? I fear so. The difference between this sort of idealism and pure materialism amounts almost to nothing.'
Being and Having, p. 155

3   Surely killing ourselves is disposing of our bodies (or lives) as though they are something we *have*, as though they are things. And surely this is an implicit admission that we belong to ourselves? But almost unfathomable perplexities then assail us: what is the self? What is this mysterious relation between the self and ourself?
Being and Having, p. 156

4   . . . the moment I treat my body as an object of scientific knowledge, I banish myself to infinity.
Being and Having, p. 12

5   Not only do we have a right to assert that others exist, but I should be inclined to contend that existence can be attributed only to others, and in virtue of their otherness, and that I cannot think of myself as existing except in so far as I conceive of myself as not being the others: and so as other than them. I would go so far as to say that it is of the essence of the Other that he exists. I cannot think of him as other without thinking of him as existing. Doubt only arises when his otherness is, so to say, expunged from my mind.

I would go so far as to ask if the *cogito* (whose incurable ambiguity can never be too clearly exposed) does not really mean: 'when I think, I am standing back from myself, I am raising myself up before myself as other, and I therefore appear as existent.' Such a conception as this is radically opposed to the idealism which defines the self as self-consciousness. Would it be absurd to say that the self in so far as it is self-consciousness is only *subexistent*? It only exists in so far as it treats itself as being for another, with reference to another; and therefore in so far as it recognises that it eludes itself.

People will say: '. . . nothing will stop *the others* from being *my thought of the others*. And then the problem has merely shifted its ground.' But . . . [i]f you posit the primacy of subject-object – the primacy of the category subject-object – or of the act by which the subject sets up objects somehow or other within itself, the existence of others becomes unthinkable. And so does any existence whatever; there is no doubt of that.
Being and Having, p. 104

When I treat another as a Thou and no longer as a He, does this 6 difference of treatment qualify me alone and my attitude to this other, or can I say that by treating him as a Thou I pierce more deeply into him and apprehend his being or his essence more directly?

Here again we must be careful. If by 'piercing more deeply' or 'apprehending his essence more directly', we mean reaching a more exact knowledge, a knowledge that is in some sense more objective, then we must certainly reply 'No'. In this respect, if we cling to a mode of objective definition, it will always be in our power to say that the Thou is an illusion. But notice that the term *essence* is itself extremely ambiguous; by essence we can understand either a nature or a freedom. It is perhaps of my essence *qua* freedom to be able to conform myself *or not* to my essence *qua* nature. *It may be of my essence to be able not to be what I am*; in plain words, to be able to betray myself. Essence *qua* nature is not what I reach in the Thou. In fact if I treat the Thou as a He, I reduce the other to being only nature; an animated object which works in some ways and not in others. If, on the contrary, I treat the other as Thou, I treat him and apprehend him *qua* freedom. I apprehend him *qua* freedom because he *is* also freedom, and is not only nature. What is more, I help him, in a sense, to be freed, I collaborate with his freedom. The formula sounds paradoxical and self-contradictory, but love is always proving it true.
Being and Having, p. 106

HERBERT MARCUSE (1898–1979)

However, the freedom attained by Descartes' *ego cogito*, Leibniz's 1 monad, Kant's transcendental ego, Fichte's subject of original activity, and Hegel's world-spirit is not the freedom of pleasurable possession with which the Aristotelian God moved in his own happiness. It is rather the freedom of interminable, arduous labour.
Negations, p. 139

The turn from the liberalist to the total-authoritarian state occurs within 2 the framework of a single social order. With regard to the unity of this economic base, we can say it is liberalism that 'produces' the total-authoritarian state out of itself, as its own consummation at a more advanced stage of development. The total-authoritarian state brings with it the organization and theory of society that correspond to the monopolistic stage of capitalism.

Negations, p. 19

3 We can tentatively define 'aesthetic form' as the result of the transformation of a given content (actual or historical, personal or social fact) into a self-contained whole: a poem, play, novel, etc. The work is thus 'taken out' of the constant process of reality and assumes a significance and truth of its own. The aesthetic transformation is achieved through a reshaping of language, perception, and understanding so that they reveal the essence of reality in its appearance: the repressed potentialities of man and nature. The work of art thus re-presents reality while accusing it.

The Aesthetic Dimension, p. 8

4 This essay examines the idea of tolerance in our advanced industrial society. The conclusion reached is that the realization of the objective of tolerance would call for intolerance toward prevailing policies, attitudes, opinions, and the extension of tolerance to policies, attitudes, and opinions which are outlawed or suppressed. In other words, today tolerance appears again as what it was in its origins, at the beginning of the modern period – a partisan goal, a subversive liberating notion and practice. Conversely, what is proclaimed and practised as tolerance today, is in many of its most effective manifestations serving the cause of oppression.

'Repressive Tolerance', *Critical Sociology*, ed. P. Connerton, p. 301

KARL MARX (1818–1883)

1 The philosophers have only *interpreted* the world differently, what matters is to *change* it.

'Theses on Feuerbach', *Marx Engels Werke*, 3: 7, trans. A. Wood

2 The chief defect of all previous materialism (including Feuerbach's) is that the object, actuality, sensuousness is conceived only in the form of the *object or perception*, but not as *sensuous human activity, practice* [*Praxis*], not subjectively. Hence in opposition to materialism the *active* side was developed by idealism – but only abstractly since idealism naturally does not know actual, sensuous activity as such. . . .

The question whether human thinking can reach objective truth – is not a question of theory but a *practical* question. In practice man must prove the truth, that is, actuality and power, this-sidedness of his

thinking. The dispute about the actuality or non-actuality of thinking – thinking isolated from practice – is a purely *scholastic* question.
Writings of the Young Marx on Philosophy and Society, ed. and trans. L. Easton and K. Guddart, p. 400

Religion is the sigh of the oppressed creature, the heárt of a heartless 3 world, just as it is the spirit of spiritless conditions. It is the *opium* of the people.
   To abolish religion as the *illusory* happiness of the people is to demand their *real* happiness.
'Toward a Critique of Hegel's Philosophy of Right', *Marx Engels Werke*, 1: 378, trans. A. Wood

In total contrast to German philosophy, which descends from heaven to 4 earth, here it is a matter of ascending from earth to heaven; that is to say, not of setting out from what people say, imagine, conceive nor from human beings as narrated, thought of, imagined, conceived, in order to arrive at human beings in the flesh; but of setting out from real, active human beings, and on the basis of their real life process demonstrating the development of the ideological reflexes and echoes of this life process. The phantoms formed in the brains of human beings are also, necessarily, sublimates of their material life process, which is empirically verifiable and bound to material premises. Morality, religion, metaphysics, and all the rest of ideology as well as the forms of consciousness corresponding to these, thus no longer retain the semblance of independence. They have no history, no development; but human beings, developing their material production and their material intercourse, alter along with this their actual world, also their thinking and the products of their thinking. It is not consciousness that determines life, but life that determines consciousness.
The German Ideology, Marx Engels Werke, 3: 26, trans. A. Wood

To be radical is to grasp the root of the matter. But for the human being 5 the root is the human being himself. The criticism of religion ends with the teaching that *the human being is the highest being for the human being,* hence with the *categorical imperative to overthrow all relations* in which the human being is a degraded, enslaved, forsaken, despicable being.
'Toward a Critique of Hegel's Philosophy of Right', *Marx Engels Werke*, 1: 385, trans. A. Wood

The worker becomes all the poorer the more wealth he produces, the 6 more his production increases in power and extent. The worker becomes a cheaper commodity the more commodities he produces. The *increase in value* of the world of things is directly proportional to the *decrease in value* of the human world. Labour not only produces commodities. It also produces itself and the worker as a *commodity*, and indeed in the same proportion as it produces commodities in general.

'Economic and Philosophical Manuscripts', *Marx Engels Werke*, 1: 511, trans. A. Wood

7   Private property has made us so stupid and one-sided that an object is *ours* only when we have it – when it exists for us as capital, or when it is directly possessed. . . . In the place of *all* physical and mental senses there has therefore come to be the sheer alienation of *all* these senses, the sense of *having*. The human being had to be reduced to this absolute poverty in order that he might yield his inner wealth to the outer world. . . .

The overcoming of private property means the complete *emancipation* of all human senses and qualities, but it means this emancipation precisely because these senses and qualities have become *human* both subjectively and objectively. The eye has become a *human* eye, just as its *object* has become a social, *human* object derived from and for the human being. The senses have therefore become *theoreticians* immediately in their *practice*. They try to relate themselves to their *subject matter* for its own sake, but the subject matter itself is an *objective human* relation to itself and to the human being, and vice versa. Need or satisfaction have thus lost their *egoistic* nature, and nature has lost its mere *utility* by use becoming *human* use.

'Economic and Philosophical Manuscripts', *Marx Engels Werke*, 1: 540, trans. A. Wood

8   And, finally, the division of labour offers us the first example of the fact that, as long as the human being remains in naturally evolved society, that is, as long as a cleavage exists between the particular and the common interest, as long, therefore, as activity is not voluntarily but naturally divided, the human being's own deed becomes an alien power opposed to him, which enslaves him instead of being controlled by him. For as soon as the division of labour comes into being, each human being has a particular, exclusive sphere of activity, which is forced upon him and from which he cannot escape. He is a hunter, a fisherman, a shepherd, or a critical critic, and must remain so if he does not want to lose his means of livelihood; whereas in communist society, where nobody has one exclusive sphere of activity but each can become accomplished in any branch he wishes, society regulates the general production and thus makes it possible for me to do one thing today and another tomorrow, to hunt in the morning, fish in the afternoon, rear cattle in the evening, criticize after dinner, just as I have a mind, without ever becoming hunter, fisherman, shepherd or critic.

The German Ideology, *Marx Engels Werke*, 3: 32, trans. A. Wood

In modern times the philosophy of enjoyment arose with the decline of 9
feudalism and with the transformation of the feudal landed nobility into
the pleasure-loving and extravagant nobles of the court under the
absolute monarchy. . . . Of course it was possible to discover the
connection between the kinds of enjoyment open to individuals at any
particular time and the class relations in which they live, the conditions
of production and intercourse which give rise to these relations, the
narrowness of the hitherto existing forms of enjoyment, which were
outside the actual content of the life of people and in contradiction to it,
the connection between every philosophy of enjoyment and the
enjoyment actually present and the hypocrisy of such a philosophy which
treated of all individuals without distinction – it was possible to discover
all this only when it became possible to criticize the conditions of
production and intercourse in the hitherto existing world, i.e. when the
contradiction between the bourgeoisie and the proletariat had given rise
to communist and socialist views. This broke the staff of all morality,
whether the morality of asceticism or of enjoyment.
The German Ideology, Marx Engels Werke, 3: 403, trans. A. Wood

Economists have a singular method of procedure. There are only two 10
kinds of institutions for them, artificial and natural. The institutions of
feudalism are artificial institutions, those of the bourgeoisie are natural
institutions. . . . Feudalism also had its proletariat – serfdom, which
contained all the germs of the bourgeoisie. Feudal production also had
two antagonistic elements which are likewise designated by the name of
the *good side* and the *bad side* of feudalism, irrespective of the fact that it
is always the bad side that in the end triumphs over the good side. It is the
bad side that produces the movement which makes history, by bringing
the struggle to life.
The Poverty of Philosophy, Marx Oeuvres, 1: 88, trans. A. Wood

The history of all hitherto existing society is the history of class struggles. 11
Manifesto of the Communist Party, Marx Engels Collected Works, 6: 482

The bourgeoisie, wherever it has got the upper hand, has put an end to all 12
feudal, patriarchal, idyllic relations. It has pitilessly torn asunder the
motley feudal ties that bound man to his 'natural superiors', and has left
remaining no other nexus between man and man than naked self-interest,
than callous 'cash payment'. It has drowned the most heavenly ecstasies
of religious fervor, of chivalrous enthusiasm, of philistine sentimentalism,
in the icy water of egotistical calculation. It has resolved personal worth
into exchange value, and in place of the numberless indefeasible
chartered freedoms, has set up that single unconscionable freedom – Free

Trade. In one word, for exploitation, veiled by religious and political illusions, it has substituted naked, shameless, direct, brutal exploitation . . .
Manifesto of the Communist Party, 6: 486

13 What the bourgeoisie produces above all is its own gravediggers. Its fall and the victory of the proletariat are equally inevitable.
Manifesto of the Communist Party, 6: 496

14 You are horrified at our intending to do away with private property. But in your existing society, private property is already done away with for nine-tenths of the population: its existence for the few is due solely to its non-existence in the hands of those nine-tenths. You reproach us, therefore, with intending to do away with a form of property, the necessary condition for whose existence is the non-existence of any property for the immense majority of society.

In one word, you reproach us with intending to do away with *your* property. Precisely so; that is just what we intend.
Manifesto of the Communist Party, 6: 500

15 When, in the course of development, class distinctions have disappeared, and all production has been concentrated in the hands of a vast association of the whole nation, the public power will lose its political character. Political power, properly so called, is merely the organized power of one class for oppressing another. If the proletariat during its contest with the bourgeoisie is compelled, by the force of circumstances, to organize itself as a class, if, by means of a revolution, it makes itself the ruling class, and, as such, sweeps away by force all the old conditions of production, then it will, along with these conditions, have swept away the conditions for the existence of class antagonisms and of classes generally, and will thereby have abolished its own supremacy as a class.

In place of the old bourgeois society, with its classes and class antagonisms, we shall have an association, in which the free development of each is the condition for the free development of all.
Manifesto of the Communist Party, 6: 505

16 The Communists disdain to conceal their views and aims. They openly declare that their ends can be attained only by the forcible overthrow of all existing conditions. Let the ruling classes tremble at a Communistic revolution. The proletarians have nothing to lose but their chains. They have a world to win.
     WORKING MEN OF ALL COUNTRIES, UNITE!
Manifesto of the Communist Party, 6: 519

17 Human beings make their own history, but they do not make it just as they please; they do not make it under circumstances chosen by

themselves, but under circumstances directly encountered, given and transmitted from the past. The tradition of all the dead generations weighs like a nightmare on the brain of the living. And just when they seem engaged in revolutionising themselves and things, in creating something that has never yet existed, precisely in such periods of revolutionary crisis they anxiously conjure up the spirits of the past to their service and borrow from them names, battle-cries and costumes in order to present the new scene of world history in this time-honoured disguise and this borrowed language.

The Eighteenth Brumaire of Louis Bonaparte, Marx Engels Werke, 8: 115, trans. A. Wood

Upon the different forms of property, upon the social conditions of   **18** existence, there rises an entire superstructure of different and distinctly formed sentiments, illusions, modes of thought and views of life. The entire class creates and forms them out of its material foundations and out of the corresponding social relations. The single individual, to whom they are transmitted through tradition and upbringing, may imagine that they form the starting point of his activity. . . . Thus the Tories of England long imagined that they were enthusiastic about monarchy, the church and the beauties of the old English Constitution, until the day of danger wrung from them the confession that they are enthusiastic only about *ground rent*.

The Eighteenth Brumaire of Louis Bonaparte, Marx Engels Werke, 8: 139, trans. A. Wood

What is society, whatever its form may be? The product of men's   **19** reciprocal activities. Are men free to choose this or that form of society? Not at all. Presuppose a particular state of development of men's faculties, and you will have a corresponding form of commerce and consumption. Presuppose a certain stage of development of production, commerce and consumption, and you will have a corresponding form of social constitution, a corresponding organization of the family, estates or classes, in a word, a corresponding civil society. Presuppose such a civil society, and you will have a corresponding political state, which is nothing but the official expression of civil society . . .

Letter to P. V. Annenkov, *Marx Oeuvres*, 1: 1439, trans. A. Wood

The capitalist mode of appropriation, which springs from the capitalist   **20** mode of production, produces capitalist private property. This is the first negation of individual private property, as founded on the proprietor's own labour. But capitalist production begets, with the inexorability of a natural process, its own negation. It is the negation of the negation. This does not re-establish private property, but it does establish individual property on the basis of the achievements of the capitalist era: namely, co-operation and the possession in common of the land and the means of production produced by labour itself.

The transformation of scattered private property resting on the personal labour of the individuals themselves into capitalist private property is naturally an incomparably more protracted, violent and difficult process than the transformation of capitalist private property, which in fact already rests on the carrying on of production by society, into social property. In the former case, it was a matter of the expropriation of the mass of the people by a few usurpers; but in this case, we have the expropriation of a few usurpers by the mass of the people.

Capital, Marx Engels Werke, 23: 791, trans. A. Wood

21 He [Adam Smith] is right, of course, that in its historical forms as slave-labour, serf-labour and wage-labour, labour always appears as repulsive, always as *external, forced labour*; and non-labour by contrast as 'freedom and happiness'. This holds doubly for this contradictory labour and for labour which has not yet created the subjective and objective conditions in which labour becomes attractive work, the individual's self-actualization; this in no way means that it becomes mere fun or amusement, as Fourier, naive as a grisette, conceives it. Really free working, e.g., composing, is at the same time precisely the most damned serious, intense exertion.

Grundrisse der Kritik der politischen Okonomie, p. 504, trans. A. Wood

22 In the social production of their existence, human beings necessarily enter into determinate relations, independent of their will, relations of production, corresponding to a given stage of development of their material productive powers. The totality of these relations of production constitutes the economic structure of society, the real foundation on which rises a legal and political superstructure and to which correspond determinate forms of social consciousness. The mode of production of material life conditions the general process of social, political and spiritual life. It is not the consciousness of human beings which determines their existence, but their social existence determines their consciousness. At a certain stage of development, the material productive powers of society come into conflict with the existing relations of production or – this merely expresses the same thing in terms of right – with the property relations in the framework of which they have thus far operated. From forms of development of the productive powers these relations turn into their fetters. Then begins an era of social revolution.

The changes in the economic foundation lead sooner or later to the transformation of the whole immense superstructure.
Toward a Critique of Political Economy, Marx Engels Werke, 13: 9, trans. A. Wood

No social formation is ever destroyed before all the productive powers   23
for which it is sufficient have developed, and new superior relations of production never replace older ones before the material conditions for their existence have matured within the womb of the old society. Humankind thus inevitably sets itself only such tasks as it is able to solve, since closer examination will always show that the problem itself arises only when the material conditions for its solution are already present or at least in the course of formation. In broad outline, the asiatic, ancient, feudal and modern bourgeois modes of production may be designated as epochs marking progress in the economic development of society. The bourgeois relations of production are the last antagonistic form of the social process of production – antagonistic not in the sense of individual antagonism but of an antagonism arising from the individuals' social conditions of existence – but the productive powers developing within bourgeois society create also the material conditions for a solution of this antagonism. This social formation accordingly brings the prehistory of human society to a close.
Toward a Critique of Political Economy, 13: 10, trans. A. Wood

What is mysterious in the commodity form consists in the fact that the   24
commodity reflects back to human beings the social characteristics of their labour as objective characteristics of the products of labour themselves, as socially natural properties of these things. Thus it also reflects the social relation of the producers to the sum total of labour as a social relation between objects, a relation which exists apart from and external to the producers. Through this substitution, the products of labour become commodities, sensible things which are at the same time supersensible or social. Similarly, the impression made by a thing on the optic nerve is perceived not as a subjective excitation of that nerve but as the objective form of a thing outside the eye. In the act of seeing, of course, light is really transmitted from one thing, the external object, to another thing, the eye. This is a physical relation between physical things. In contrast, the commodity form and the value relation of the products of labour within which it appears, have absolutely no connection with the physical nature of the commodity and the real relations arising out of this. It is nothing but the definite social relation between human beings themselves which assumes for them the fantastic form of a relation between things. Thus in order to find an analogy we must fly to the misty region of the religious world. There the products of the human brain

appear endowed with their own life, as self-dependent shapes standing in relation to human beings. Thus it is in the world of commodities with the products of the human hand. I call this the fetishism which attaches to the products of labour as soon as they are produced as commodities, and which is therefore inseparable from the production of commodities.

Capital, Marx Engels Werke, 23: 86, trans. A. Wood

25 The value of labour power and its valorization in the process of labour are thus two different magnitudes. The capitalist had his eye on this difference in value when he purchased the labour power. The decisive thing was the specific use value of this commodity, that of being a source of value and producing more value than it itself has. This is the specific service the capitalist expects from it. And what he experiences is in accord with the eternal laws of commodity exchange. In fact the seller of labour power, like the seller of any other commodity, realizes its exchange value and alienates its use value. He cannot receive the one without parting with the other. The use value of labour power, labour itself, belongs to its seller as little as the use value of oil belongs to the oil merchant. The possessor of money has paid for a day's worth of labour; hence the use of a whole day's labour belongs to him during that day. The circumstance that it costs only a half day's labour to get a day's labour power, even though the labour power can work for a whole day, that therefore the value created by its use during one day is twice as much as its own value for that day – this is a piece of good luck for the buyer, but no injustice at all to the seller.

Capital, 23: 208, trans. A. Wood

26 What is a 'just' distribution?

Does not the bourgeoisie claim that the present system of distribution is 'just'? And given the present mode of production is it not, in fact, the only 'just' system of distribution? Are economic relations regulated by conceptions of right or is not the opposite the case, that relations of right spring from economic ones?

'Critique of the Gotha Program', *Marx Engels Werke*, 19: 18, trans. A. Wood

27 Right can never be higher than the economic structure of society and the cultural development conditioned by it.

In a higher phase of communist society, when the enslaving subjugation of individuals to the division of labour and thereby the opposition between intellectual and physical labour have disappeared; when labour is no longer just a means to life but has itself become the primary need of life; when the all-round development of individuals has also increased their productive powers and all the springs of co-operative wealth flow more abundantly – only then can society wholly cross the narrow

horizon of bourgeois right and inscribe on its banner: *from each according to his abilities, to each according to his needs!*
'Critique of the Gotha Program', 19: 21, trans. A. Wood

F. MAUTHNER (1849–1923)

If Aristotle had spoken Chinese or Dacotan, he would have had to adopt an entirely different Logic, or at any rate an entirely different theory of categories.
Beitrage zu einer Kritik der Sprache, III, p. 4

ALEXIUS MEINONG (1853–1920)

. . . objects are such that their nature either allows them, as it were, to exist and to be perceived or prohibits it, so that, if they have being at all, this being cannot be *existence*, but only *subsistence* in a sense which has to be explained further. For example, it cannot be doubted that the difference between red and green has being, but this difference does not exist, it merely subsists. Similarly, the number of books in a library does not exist in addition to the books; the number of diagonals of a polygon exists, if that is possible, even less. But we must acknowledge, surely, that each of these numbers subsists. 1
'Zur Gegenstandstheorie', quoted in R. Grossman, *Meinong*, p. 226

Being (in the narrower sense), as already mentioned, can be existence, but also subsistence: the sun exists, equality – and, similarly, any other ideal entity – cannot exist, but can only subsist. Existence itself, too, does not exist (and similarly, any other objective), but can only subsist. What exists, also subsists; what does not subsist, does not exist either. 2
'Zur Gegenstandstheorie', quoted in *Meinong*, p. 228

An absurd object like the round square carries in itself the guarantee of its non-being in every sense, an ideal object like inequality carries in itself the guarantee of its non-existence. . . . The object is by nature beyond being (*ausserseiend*), although one of its two objectives of being, its being or non-being, subsists in any case. 3
Gesammelte Abhandlungen, quoted in *Meinong*, p. 117

But existential assertions also, as language has them at its disposal, can easily cloud the issue rather than throw light on it; especially, when they occur in a form like 'Water exists' and thus create the impression, by means of a superficial analogy to judgments of so-being like 'The water murmurs', that existence is, as it were, a piece of an object like murmurs; but existence is nothing more than the objective. 4
Über die Erfahrungsgrundlagen unseres Wissens, quoted in *Meinong*, p. 247

D. H. MELLOR (*b.* 1938)

1 We all rely, and believe we should rely, more on well-attested laws or theories than on new or refuted ones. A century of electromagnetic theory has transformed radio from the merest speculation to the firmest of facts. A modern Moore could as well have appealed to radio waves as to hands to show the existence of the external world. No contractor whose transmitter fails can get away in court with a Popperian defence of its failure as merely demonstrating the scientifically falsifiable character of the bold conjectures underlying its design.
'The Popper Phenomenon', *Philosophy* (1977), p. 196

2 Dispositions are as shameful in many eyes as pregnant spinsters used to be – ideally to be explained away, or entitled by a shotgun wedding to take the name of some decently real categorical property. It is time to remove this lingering Victorian prejudice. Dispositions, like unmarried mothers, can manage on their own.
'In Defense of Dispositions', *Philosophical Review* (1974), p. 157

3 Appeals to rationality are mostly bluff. There is no good theory of what it is nor of how to recognise it. How, for instance, can we know it is rational to think that a pain-killing drug will work if we can't know that it *will* work? But if we can know that, why not act on that knowledge? Because it is harder to come by? And here the rationalist faces a dilemma. If we can be wrong about rationalist reasons, they are apt to become as objective and hard to know as objective ones; if we can't, because they are whatever we think they are, they become subjective.
'Objective Decision Making', *Social Theory and Practice* (1983), p. 289

MAURICE MERLEAU-PONTY (1908–1961)

1 The most important accomplishment of phenomenology is, without a doubt, to have joined extreme subjectivism and extreme objectivism in its notion of the world or of rationality.
Phenomenology of Perception, trans. Colin Smith, p. xix

2 Phenomenology . . . is a transcendental philosophy which places in abeyance the assertions arising out of the natural attitude, the better to understand them; but it is also a philosophy for which the world is always 'already there' before reflection begins – as an inalienable presence; and all its efforts are concentrated upon re-achieving a direct and primitive contact with the world, and endowing that contact with a philosophical status.
Phenomenology of Perception, trans. Colin Smith, p. vii

Husserl's first directive to phenomenology, in its early stages, to be a 3
'descriptive psychology', or to return to the 'things themselves', is from
the start a foreswearing of science. . . . we must begin by reawakening the
basic experience of the world of which science is the second-order
expression.
Phenomenology of Perception, trans. Colin Smith, p. viii

To return to things themselves . . . is absolutely distinct from the idealist 4
return to consciousness, and the demand for a pure description excludes
equally the procedure of analytical reflection on the one hand, and that of
scientific explanation on the other. Descartes and particularly Kant
detached the subject, or consciousness, by showing that I could not
possibly apprehend anything as existing unless I first of all experienced
myself as existing in the act of apprehending it. They presented
consciousness, the absolute certainty of my existence for myself, as the
condition of there being anything at all . . . Thus reflection is carried off
by itself and installs itself in an impregnable subjectivity, as yet
untouched by being and time. But this is very ingenuous, or at least it is
an incomplete form of reflection which loses sight of its own beginning.
When I begin to reflect my reflection bears upon an unreflective
experience; moreover my reflection cannot be unaware of itself as an
event, and so it appears to itself in the light of a truly creative act, of a
changed structure of consciousness, and yet it has to recognize, as having
priority over its own operations, the world which is given to the subject
because the subject is given to himself. The real has to be described, not
constructed or formed. Which means that I cannot put perception into
the same category as the syntheses represented by judgements, acts or
predications. . . . it is not even an act, a deliberate taking up of a position;
it is the background from which all acts stand out, and is presupposed by
them. The world is not an object such that I have in my possession the
law of its making; it is the natural setting of, and field for, all my
thoughts and all my explicit perceptions. Truth does not 'inhabit' only
'the inner man', or more accurately, there is no inner man, man is in the
world, and only in the world does he know himself.
Phenomenology of Perception, trans. Colin Smith, p. ix

The world is not what I think, but what I live through. 5
Phenomenology of Perception, trans. Colin Smith, p. xvi

We must not, therefore, wonder whether we really perceive a world, we 6
must instead say: the world is what we perceive. . . . To seek the essence
of perception is to declare that perception is, not presumed true, but
defined as access to truth.
Phenomenology of Perception, trans. Colin Smith, p. xvi

7   Our perception ends in objects, and the object once constituted appears as the reason for all the experiences of it which we have had or could have. For example, I see the next-door house from a certain angle, but it would be seen differently from the right bank of the Seine, or from the inside, or again from an aeroplane: the house *itself* is none of these appearances; it is, as Leibnitz said, the flat projection of these perspectives and of all possible perspectives, that is, the perspectiveless position from which all can be derived, the house seen from nowhere. But what do these words mean? Is not to see always to see from somewhere? . . . We must try to understand how vision can be brought into being from somewhere without being enclosed in its perspective.
    Phenomenology of Perception, trans. Colin Smith, p. 67

8   The house *has its* water pipes, *its* floor, perhaps its cracks which are insidiously spreading in the thickness of its ceilings. We never see them, but it *has them* along with its chimneys and windows which we can see. We shall forget our present perception of the house . . . But we still believe that there is a truth about the past; we base our memory on the world's vast Memory, in which the house has its place as it really was on that day, and which guarantees its *being* at this moment. Taken in itself — and as an object it demands to be taken thus — the object has nothing cryptic about it; it is completely displayed and its parts co-exist while our gaze runs from one to another, its present does not cancel its past, nor will its future cancel its present. The positing of the object therefore makes us go beyond the limits of our actual experience which is brought up against and halted by an alien being, with the result that finally experience believes that it extracts all its own teaching from the object. It is this *ek-stase* of experience which causes all perception to be perception of something.
    Phenomenology of Perception, trans. Colin Smith, p. 70

9   In its descriptions of the body from the point of view of the self, classical psychology was already wont to attribute to it 'characteristics' incompatible with the status of an object. In the first place it was stated that my body is distinguishable from the table or the lamp in that I can turn away from the latter whereas my body is constantly perceived. It is therefore an object which does not leave me. But in that case is it still an object?
    Phenomenology of Perception, trans. Colin Smith, p. 90

10 I observe external objects with my body, I handle them, examine them, walk round them, but my body itself is a thing which I do not observe: in order to be able to do so, I should need the use of a second body which itself would be unobservable.
    Phenomenology of Perception, trans. Colin Smith, p. 91

My head is presented to my sight only to the extent of my nose end and 11 the boundaries of my eye-sockets. I can see my eyes in three mirrors, but they are the eyes of someone observing, and I have the utmost difficulty in catching my living glance when a mirror in the street unexpectedly reflects my image back at me.
Phenomenology of Perception, trans. Colin Smith, p. 91

When I press my two hands together, it is not a matter of two sensations 12 felt together as one perceives two objects placed side by side, but of an ambiguous set-up in which both hands can alternate the rôles of 'touching' and being 'touched'. . . . in this bundle of bones and muscles which my right hand presents to my left, I can anticipate for an instant the integument or incarnation of that other right hand, alive and mobile, which I thrust towards things in order to explore them. The body catches itself from the outside engaged in a cognitive process; it tries to touch itself while being touched . . .
Phenomenology of Perception, trans. Colin Smith, p. 93

. . . we could not accept any of the materialistic models to represent the 13 relations of the soul and body – but neither could we accept the mentalistic models, for example, the Cartesian metaphor of the artisan and his tool. An organ cannot be compared to an instrument, as if it existed and could be conceived apart from integral functioning, nor the mind to an artisan who uses it: this would be to return to a wholly external relation like that of the pilot and his ship which was rightly rejected by Descartes. The mind does not use the body, but realizes itself through it while at the same time transferring the body outside of physical space. . . . at the same time and reciprocally . . . a mind . . . *comes into the world.*
The Structure of Behaviour, trans. Alden L. Fisher, p. 208

There is always a duality which reappears at one level or another: hunger 14 or thirst prevents thought or feelings; the properly sexual dialectic ordinarily reveals itself through a passion; integration is never absolute and it always fails – at a higher level in the writer, at a lower level in the aphasic. . . .

But it is not a duality of substances; or, in other words, the notions of soul and body must be relativized: there is the body as mass of chemical components in interaction, the body as dialectic of living being and its biological milieu, and the body as dialectic of social subject and his group; even all our habits are an impalpable body for the ego of each moment. Each of these degrees is soul with respect to the preceding one, body with respect to the following one. The body in general is an ensemble of paths already traced, of powers already constituted; the

body is the acquired dialectical soil upon which a higher 'formation' is accomplished, and the soul is the meaning which is then established.
The Structure of Behaviour, trans. Alden L. Fisher, p. 210

15 Man taken as a concrete being is not a psyche joined to an organism, but the movement to and fro of existence which at one time allows itself to take corporeal form and at others moves towards personal acts.
Phenomenology of Perception, trans. Colin Smith, p. 88

16 Again, it is clear that no causal relationship is conceivable between the subject and his body, his world or his society. Only at the cost of losing the basis of all my certainties can I question what is conveyed to me by my presence to myself. Now the moment I turn to myself in order to describe myself, I have a glimpse of an anonymous flux, a comprehensive project in which there are so far no 'states of consciousness', nor, *a fortiori*, qualifications of any sort. For myself I am neither 'jealous', nor 'inquisitive', nor 'hunchbacked', nor 'a civil servant'. It is often a matter of surprise that the cripple or the invalid can put up with himself. The reason is that such people are not for themselves deformed or at death's door. Until the final coma, the dying man is inhabited by a consciousness, he is all that he sees, and enjoys this much of an outlet.
Phenomenology of Perception, trans. Colin Smith, p. 434

17 Even what are called obstacles to freedom are in reality deployed by it. An unclimbable rock face, a large or small, vertical or slanting rock, are things which have no meaning for anyone who is not intending to surmount them, for a subject whose projects do not carve out such determinate forms from the uniform mass of the *in itself* and cause an orientated world to arise – a significance in things. There is, then, ultimately nothing that can set limits to freedom, except those limits that freedom itself has set in the form of its various initiatives, so that the subject has simply the external world that he gives himself.
Phenomenology of Perception, trans. Colin Smith, p. 436

18 The rationalist's dilemma: either the free act is possible, or it is not – either the event originates in me or is imposed on me from outside, does not apply to our relations with the world and with our past. Our freedom does not destroy our situation, but gears itself to it: as long as we are alive, our situation is open, which implies both that it calls up specially favoured modes of resolution, and also that it is powerless to bring one into being by itself.
Phenomenology of Perception, trans. Colin Smith, p. 442

19 What is then liberty? To be born is at once to be born in the world and to the world. The world is already constituted, but never completely. Under

the first rapport, we are solicited, under the second, we are open to an infinity of possibilities. But this analysis is still abstract, because we exist under these two relations at once. There is therefore never determinism and never absolute choice; I am never a thing and never naked consciousness.
Phenomenology of Perception, trans. Colin Smith, p. 453

Time presupposes a view of time. It is, therefore, not like a river, not a 20
flowing substance. The fact that the metaphor based on this comparison has persisted from the time of Heraclitus to our own day is explained by our surreptitiously putting into the river a witness of its course.
Phenomenology of Perception, trans. Colin Smith, p. 411

The existence of other people is a difficulty and an outrage for objective 21
thought. . . . another person would seem to stand before me as an *in-itself* and yet to exist *for himself*, thus requiring of me, in order to be perceived, a contradictory operation, since I ought both to distinguish him from myself, and therefore place him in the world of objects, and think of him as a consciousness, that is, the sort of being with no outside and no parts, to which I have access merely because that being is myself, and because the thinker and the thought about are amalgamated in him. . . .

But we have in fact learned to shed doubt upon objective thought, and have made contact, on the hither side of scientific representations of the world and the body, with an experience of the body and the world which these scientific approaches do not successfully embrace. . . . If my consciousness has a body, why should other bodies not 'have' consciousnesses?
Phenomenology of Perception, trans. Colin Smith, p. 349

As Scheler so rightly declares, reasoning by analogy presupposes what it 22
is called on to explain. The other consciousness can be deduced only if the emotional expressions of others are compared and identified with mine, and precise correlations recognized between my physical behaviour and my 'psychic events'. Now the perception of others is anterior to, and the condition of, such observations, the observations do not constitute the perception. A baby of fifteen months opens its mouth if I playfully take one of its fingers between my teeth and pretend to bite it. And yet it has scarcely looked at its face in a glass, and its teeth are not in any case like mine. The fact is that its own mouth and teeth, as it feels them from the inside, are immediately, for it, an apparatus to bite with, and my jaw, as the baby sees it from the outside, is immediately, for it, capable of the same intentions. 'Biting' has immediately, for it, an intersubjective significance. It perceives its intentions in its body, and my body with its own, and thereby my intentions in its own body. . . . The other can be

evident to me because I am not transparent for myself, and because my subjectivity draws its body in its wake.
Phenomenology of Perception, trans. Colin Smith, p. 352

23 In reality, the other is not shut up inside my perspective of the world, because this perspective itself has no definite limits, because it slips spontaneously into the other's, and because both are brought together in the one single world in which we all participate as anonymous subjects of perception.
Phenomenology of Perception, trans. Colin Smith, p. 353

24 I enter into a pact with the other, having resolved to live in an interworld in which I accord as much place to others as to myself. But this interworld is still a project of mine, and it would be hypocritical to pretend that I seek the welfare of another *as if it were mine*, since this very attachment to another's interest still has its source in me. . . . There is here a solipsism rooted in living experience and quite insurmountable.
Phenomenology of Perception, trans. Colin Smith, p. 357

25 It is true that I do not feel that I am the constituting agent either of the natural or of the cultural world. . . . Yet the fact remains that I am the one by whom they are experienced, . . . the indeclinable *I* . . . Consciousnesses present themselves with the absurdity of a multiple solipsism . . .
Phenomenology of Perception, trans. Colin Smith, p. 358

26 I can evolve a solipsist philosophy but, in doing so, I assume the existence of a community of men endowed with speech, and I address myself to it. . . . The other transforms me into an object and denies me, I transform him into an object and deny him, it is asserted [by Sartre]. In fact the other's gaze transforms me into an object, and mine him, only if both of us withdraw into the core of our thinking nature, if we both make ourselves into an inhuman gaze, if each of us feels his actions to be not taken up and understood, but observed as if they were an insect's. This is what happens, for instance, when I fall under the gaze of a stranger. But even then, the objectification of each by the other's gaze is felt as unbearable only because it takes the place of possible communication. A dog's gaze directed towards me causes me no embarrassment.
Phenomenology of Perception, trans. Colin Smith, p. 360

27 Solipsism would be strictly true only of someone who managed to be tacitly aware of his existence without being or doing anything, which is impossible, since existing is being in and of the world. The philosopher cannot fail to draw others with him into his reflective retreat, because in the uncertainty of the world, he has for ever learned to treat them as *consorts*, and because all his knowledge is built on this datum of opinion.
Phenomenology of Perception, trans. Colin Smith, p. 361

MARY MIDGLEY (*b.* 1919)

The 'stranger' or 'outsider' of Camus's novel is indeed a kind of alien. But 1
he is so because he is an emotional cripple, someone apparently incapable
of sharing human feelings – though it struck me even when I first read the
book that he didn't seem to try very hard. He can be no sort of an ideal
for others. If people without his handicap imitate him, they lose the really
excellent and central point of Existentialism; the acceptance of responsibility for being as we have made ourselves, the refusal to make bogus
excuses.
Beast and Man, p. 199

It used to be supposed that animals roamed wildly and unpredictably 2
over the earth, and that fixed routine was an artificial interference
imposed on man by that unnatural thing, society. Far from which, studies
of territorial behaviour show that fixed and regular movement patterns
are almost universal. Migrant birds and other long-distance travelers,
retrace their journeys exactly; . . . ritual and ceremonial clothe the
lightest interactions of all social creatures. Greetings, bows, and tactful
turnings away are of the first importance; unexpected gestures cause
alarm and are signs of some serious disturbance. Happiness centers on
habit. In fact, the human commuter on the 8:45, far from being in any
way biologically exceptional, is a most natural phenomenon, whereas
someone who seriously thought to live without routine would be flying in
the face of nature far more radically than the most rigid puritan or
Trappist. The normal pattern of development in conduct, as in art,
proceeds through modest variations on a theme. The Libertarian way of
talking is, however, very deep-rooted today. As I have remarked, we tend
to think of ourselves as *prisoners* of our culture, as being *limited* by it,
'indoctrinated' or 'brainwashed' as people often say, as though taking in
the way of life around us were no more natural than the process
undergone by Pavlov's dogs.
    But how would we manage without a culture?
Beast and Man, p. 289

JOHN STUART MILL (1806–1873)

The only proof capable of being given that an object is visible is that 1
people actually see it. The only proof that a sound is audible is that
people hear it: and so of the other sources of our experience. In like
manner, I apprehend, the sole evidence it is possible to produce that
anything is desirable is that people do actually desire it.
Utilitarianism, Collected Works, X, p. 234

2   . . . desiring a thing and finding it pleasant, aversion to it and thinking of
     it as painful, are phenomena entirely inseparable, or rather two parts of
     the same phenomenon; in strictness of language, two different modes of
     naming the same psychological fact . . . to desire anything, except in
     proportion as the idea of it is pleasant, is a physical and metaphysical
     impossibility.
     Utilitarianism, p. 237

3   It is better to be a human being dissatisfied than a pig satisfied; better to
     be Socrates dissatisfied than a fool satisfied. And if the fool, or the pig, is
     of a different opinion, it is because they only know their own side of the
     question.
     Utilitarianism, p. 212

4   May it not be the fact that mankind, who after all are made up of single
     human beings, obtain a greater sum of happiness when each pursues his
     own, under the rules and conditions required by the good of the rest,
     than when each makes the good of the rest his only object, and allows
     himself no personal pleasures not indispensable to the preservation of his
     faculties? The regimen of a blockaded town should be cheerfully
     submitted to when high purposes require it, but is it the ideal perfection
     of human existence?
     Auguste Comte and Positivism, Collected Works, X, p. 337

5   I regard utility as the ultimate appeal on all ethical questions; but it must
     be utility in the largest sense, grounded on the permanent interests of a
     man as a progressive being.
     On Liberty, Collected Works, XVIII, p. 224

6   He [Bentham] was a boy to the last. Self-consciousness, that daemon of
     the men of genius of our time, from Wordsworth to Byron, from Goethe
     to Chateaubriand, and to which this age owes so much both of its
     cheerful and its mournful wisdom, never was awakened in him. How
     much of human nature slumbered in him he knew not, neither can we
     know. He had never been made alive to the unseen influences which were
     acting on himself, nor consequently on his fellow-creatures. Other ages
     and other nations were a blank to him for purposes of instruction. He
     measured them but by one standard; their knowledge of facts, and their
     capability to take correct views of utility, and merge all other objects in
     it.
     'Bentham', *Collected Works*, X, p. 82

7   The object of this essay is to assert one very simple principle as entitled to
     govern absolutely the dealings of society with the individual in the way of
     compulsion and control, whether the means used be physical coercion in

the form of legal penalties, or the moral coercion of public opinion. That principle is, that the sole end for which mankind are warranted, individually or collectively, in interfering with the liberty of action of any of their number, is self-protection . . . the only purpose for which power can be rightfully exercised over any member of a civilised community, against his will, is to prevent harm to others. His own good, either physical or moral, is not a sufficient warrant. He cannot rightfully be compelled to do or forbear because it will be better for him to do so, because it will make him happier, because, in the opinion of others, to do so would be wise, or even right. . . . The only part of the conduct of any one, for which he is amenable to society, is that which concerns others. In the part which merely concerns himself, his independence is, of right, absolute. Over himself, over his own body and mind, the individual is sovereign.
On Liberty, p. 223

Protection . . . against the tyranny of the magistrate is not enough: there 8 needs protection also against the tyranny of the prevailing opinion and feeling; against the tendency of society to impose, by other means than civil penalties, its own ideas and practices as rules of conduct on those who dissent from them.
On Liberty, p. 220

As it is useful that while mankind are imperfect there should be different 9 opinions; so is it that there should be different experiments of living.
On Liberty, p. 260

Complete liberty of contradicting and disproving our opinion is the very 10 condition which justifies us in assuming its truth for purposes of action; and on no other terms can a being with human faculties have any rational assurance of being right.
On Liberty, p. 231

The beliefs which we have most warrant for have no safeguard to rest on, 11 but a standing invitation to the whole world to prove them unfounded. If the challenge is not accepted, or is accepted and the attempt fails, we are far enough from certainty still; but we have done the best that the existing state of human reason admits of; we have neglected nothing that could give the truth a chance of reaching us: if the lists are kept open, we may hope that if there be a better truth, it will be found when the human mind is capable of receiving it; and in the meantime we may rely on having attained such approach to truth as is possible in our own day. This is the amount of certainty attainable by a fallible being, and this the sole way of attaining it.
On Liberty, p. 232

12   It is not by wearing down into uniformity all that is individual in themselves, but by cultivating it and calling it forth, within the limits imposed by the rights and interests of others, that human beings become a noble and beautiful object of contemplation.
On Liberty, p. 266

13   Instead of the function of governing, for which it is radically unfit, the proper office of a representative assembly is to watch and control the government: to throw the light of publicity on its acts: to compel a full exposition and justification of all of them which any one considers questionable; to censure them if found condemnable, and if the men who compose the government abuse their trust, or fulfil it in a manner which conflicts with the deliberate sense of the nation, to expel them from office and either expressly or virtually appoint their successors.
Representative Government (Everyman edn), p. 239

14   The Conservatives, as being by the law of their existence the stupidest party . . .
Representative Government, p. 261

15   Despotism is a legitimate mode of government in dealing with barbarians, provided the end be their improvement, and the means justified by actually effecting that end. Liberty, as a principle, has no application to any state of things anterior to the time when mankind have become capable of being improved by free and equal discussion.
On Liberty, p. 224

16   I will call no being good who is not what I mean when I apply that epithet to my fellow-creatures; and if such a being can sentence me to hell for not so calling him, to hell I will go.
Examination of Sir William Hamilton's Philosophy, Collected Works, IX, p. 103

17   So long as an opinion is strongly rooted in the feelings, it gains rather than loses in stability by having a preponderating weight of argument against it. For if it were accepted as a result of argument, the refutation of the argument might shake the solidity of the conviction; but when it rests solely on feeling, the worse it fares in argumentative contest, the more persuaded its adherents are that their feeling must have some deeper ground, which the arguments do not reach . . .
The Subjection of Women, Three Essays, ed. R. Wollheim, p. 427

18   In the first place, the opinion in favour of the present system, which entirely subordinates the weaker sex to the stronger, rests upon theory only; for there never has been trial made of any other: so that experience, in the sense in which it is vulgarly opposed to theory, cannot be pretended to have pronounced any verdict. And in the second place, the

adoption of this system of inequality never was the result of deliberation, or forethought, or any social ideas, or any notion whatever of what conduced to the benefit of humanity or the good order of society. It arose simply from the fact that from the very earliest twilight of human society, every woman . . . was found in a state of bondage to some man. . . . the slavery of the male sex has, in all the countries of Christian Europe at least (though, in one of them, only within the last few years) been at length abolished, and that of the female sex has been gradually changed into a milder form of dependence. But this dependence, as it exists at present, . . . has not lost the taint of its brutal origin. No presumption in its favour, therefore, can be drawn from the fact of its existence.
The Subjection of Women, p. 431

Men do not want solely the obedience of women, they want their 19 sentiments. . . . They have therefore put everything in practice to enslave their minds. The masters of all other slaves rely, for maintaining obedience, on fear; either fear of themselves, or religious fears. The masters of women wanted more than simple obedience, and they turned the whole force of education to effect their purpose. All women are brought up from the very earliest years in the belief that their ideal of character is the very opposite to that of men; not self-will, and government by self-control, but submission, and yielding to the control of others. . . . Can it be doubted that any of the other yokes which mankind have succeeded in breaking would have subsisted till now if the same means had existed, and had been as sedulously used, to bow down their minds to it? . . . would not serfs and seigneurs, plebeians and patricians, have been as broadly distinguished at this day as men and women are? and would not all but a thinker here and there have believed the distinction to be a fundamental and unalterable fact in human nature?
The Subjection of Women, p. 443

Whether the institution to be defended is slavery, political absolutism, or 20 the absolutism of the head of a family, we are always expected to judge of it from its best instances; and we are presented with pictures of loving exercise of authority on one side, loving submission to it on the other – superior wisdom ordering all things for the greatest good of the dependants, and surrounded by their smiles and benedictions. All this would be very much to the purpose if any one pretended that there are no such things as good men. Who doubts that there may be great goodness, and great happiness, and great affection, under the absolute government of a good man? Meanwhile, laws and institutions require to be adapted, not to good men, but to bad.
The Subjection of Women, p. 466

21　The notion that truths external to the human mind may be known by intuition or consciousness, independently of observation and experience, is, I am persuaded, in these times, the great intellectual support of false doctrines and bad institutions. By the aid of this theory, every inveterate belief and every intense feeling, of which the origin is not remembered, is enabled to dispense with the obligation of justifying itself by reason, and is erected into its own all-sufficient voucher and justification. There never was such an instrument devised for consecrating all deep-seated prejudices. And the chief strength of this false philosophy in morals, politics, and religion lies in the appeal which it is accustomed to make to the evidence of mathematics and of the cognate branches of physical science. To expel it from these, is to drive it from its stronghold . . .
Autobiography, Collected Works, I, p. 233

22　. . . the most scientific proceeding can be no more than an improved form of that which was primitively pursued by the human understanding, while undirected by science. When mankind first formed the idea of studying phenomena according to a stricter and surer method than that which they had in the first instance adopted, they did not, conformably to the well-meant but impracticable precept of Descartes, set out from the supposition that nothing had been already ascertained. . . . The first scientific inquirers assumed [various] known truths, and set out from them to discover others . . . it is impossible to frame any scientific method of induction, or test of the correctness of inductions, unless on the hypothesis that some inductions deserving of reliance have been already made.
A System of Logic, Collected Works, VII, p. 318

23　We are constantly told that the uniformity of the course of nature cannot itself be an induction, since every inductive reasoning assumes it, and the premise must have been known before the conclusion. Those who argue in this manner can never have directed their attention to the continual process of giving and taking, in respect of certainty, which reciprocally goes on between this great premise and the narrower truths of experience; the effect of which is, that, though originally a generalization from the more obvious of the narrower truths, it ends by having a fulness of certainty which overflows upon these, and raises the proof of them to a higher level . . .
Examination of Sir William Hamilton's Philosophy, p. 482

24　What is called explaining one law of nature by another, is but substituting one mystery for another; and does nothing to render the general course of nature other than mysterious: we can no more assign a *why* for the more extensive laws than for the partial ones. The explanation may substitute a mystery which has become familiar, and

has grown to *seem* not mysterious, for one which is still strange. And this is the meaning of explanation, in common parlance. But the process with which we are here concerned often does the very contrary: it resolves a phenomenon with which we are familiar, into one of which we previously knew little or nothing . . .
A System of Logic, p. 471

Matter . . . may be defined, a Permanent Possibility of Sensation. If I am   25
asked whether I believe in matter, I ask whether the questioner accepts this definition of it. If he does, I believe in matter: and so do all Berkelians. In any other sense than this, I do not. But I affirm with confidence that this conception of Matter includes the whole meaning attached to it by the common world, apart from philosophical, and sometimes from theological, theories.
Examination of Sir William Hamilton's Philosophy, p. 183

The laws of the phenomena of society are, and can be, nothing but the   26
laws of the actions and passions of human beings united together in the social state. Men, however, in a state of society, are still men; their actions and passions are obedient to the laws of individual human nature. Men are not, when brought together, converted into another kind of substance, with different properties; as hydrogen and oxygen are different from water, or as hydrogen, oxygen, carbon, and azote are different from nerves, muscles, and tendons. Human beings in society have no properties but those which are derived from, and may be resolved into, the laws of the nature of individual man.
A System of Logic, p. 879

The modern mind is, what the ancient mind was not, brooding and self-   27
conscious; and its meditative self-consciousness has discovered depths in the human soul which the Greeks and Romans did not dream of, and would not have understood. But what they had got to express, they expressed in a manner which few even of the greatest moderns have attempted to rival.
Inaugural Address, Collected Works, XXI, p. 230

. . . speculative philosophy, which to the superficial appears a thing so   28
remote from the business of life and the outward interests of men, is in reality the thing on earth which most influences them, and in the long run overbears every other influence save those which it must itself obey.
'Bentham', *Collected Works*, X, p. 77

I have been toiling through Stirling's *Secret of Hegel*. It is right to learn   29
what Hegel is and one learns it only too well from Stirling's book. I say too well because I found by actual experience of Hegel that conversancy

with him tends to deprave one's intellect. . . . For some time after I had
finished the book all such words as *reflection, development, evolution,*
etc., gave me a sort of sickening feeling which I have not yet entirely got
rid of.
Letter to Alexander Bain, *Collected Works,* XVI, p. 132

RUTH GARRETT MILLIKAN (*b.* 1933)

1 . . . if we as realists understand ontology the right way, we do not have to
claim that mapping the world with sentences requires that the world be
'cut up' in a way that somehow 'gets things right'. The realist need only
give an account of objective *identity* or selfsameness, which is something
quite other than Nature's preferred classification system or Nature's
preferred way of carving parts out of wholes or her preferred way of
grouping things into unities.
Language, Thought and Other Biological Categories, p. 13

2 Wilfrid Sellars taught us that truth and meaning and even 'representing' .
. . are all entangled in the 'logical order', and that the logical order is part
of the *normative* order. Meaning and truth cannot be naturalized
without a theory that naturalizes norms generally. Sellars followed
Wittgenstein, grounding his theory of norms in community. An
alternative, some of us have argued, is to ground the needed norms in
evolutionary biology – to let Darwinian natural purposes set the
standards against which failures, untruths, incorrectnesses, etc. are
measured.
Meaning in Mind: Fodor and his Critics, p. 151

3 It follows that 'normal conditions' must not be read as having anything
to do with what is typical or average or even, in many cases, at all
common. . . . For example, very few wild seeds land in conditions normal
for their growth and development, and the protective colorings of
caterpillars seldom actually succeed in preventing them from being eaten.
. . . (If normal conditions for proper functioning, hence survival and
proliferation, were a statistical norm, imagine how many rabbits there
would be in the world.)
'Biosemantics', *Journal of Philosophy* (1989), p. 285

HERMANN MINKOWSKI (1864–1909)

Henceforth space by itself, and time by itself, are doomed to fade away
into mere shadows, and only a kind of union of the two will preserve an
independent reality.
Problems of Space and Time, p. 297

BASIL MITCHELL (*b.* 1917)

There is not in point of fact any warrant in logic for proceeding from the theological doctrine of justification by faith alone to the epistemological doctrine that faith admits of no rational support. The former insists that man cannot earn salvation by good works and is part of the teaching of traditional Christian theism (which has received especial emphasis in the Lutheran tradition); the latter claims that traditional Christian theism, of which this theological doctrine is a part, must be accepted without question by an existential choice for which no reason can or need be given. They are entirely distinct and it is an evident *non sequitur* to suppose that the one follows from the other.
The Justification of Religious Belief, p. 141

G. E. MOORE (1873–1958)

The hypothesis that disagreement about the meaning of good is 1 disagreement with regard to the correct analysis of a given whole, may be most plainly seen to be incorrect by consideration of the fact that, whatever definition be offered, it may be always asked, with significance, of the complex so defined, whether it is itself good. To take, for instance, one of the more plausible, because one of the more complicated, of such proposed definitions, it may easily be thought, at first sight, that to be good may mean to be that which we desire to desire. Thus if we apply this definition to a particular instance and say 'When we think that A is good, we are thinking that A is one of the things which we desire to desire', our proposition may seem quite plausible. But, if we carry the investigation further, and ask ourselves 'Is it good to desire to desire A?' it is apparent, on a little reflection, that this question is itself as intelligible, as the original question 'Is A good?' – that we are, in fact, now asking for exactly the same information about the desire to desire A, for which we formerly asked with regard to A itself.

. . . whoever will attentively consider with himself what is actually before his mind when he asks the question 'Is pleasure (or whatever it may be) after all good?' can easily satisfy himself that he is not merely wondering whether pleasure is pleasant. And if he will try this experiment with each suggested definition in succession, he may become expert enough to recognise that in every case he has before his mind a unique object, with regard to the connection of which with any other object, a distinct question may be asked.
Principia Ethica, p. 15

If, when one man says, 'This action is right', and another answers, 'No, it 2 is not right', each of them is always merely making an assertion about *his*

309

own feelings, it plainly follows that there is never really any difference of opinion between them: the one of them is never really contradicting what the other is asserting. They are no more contradicting one another than if, when one had said, 'I like sugar', the other had answered, 'I *don't* like sugar.' . . . It is surely plain matter of fact that when I assert an action to be wrong, and another man asserts it to be right, there sometimes is a real difference of opinion between us: he sometimes is denying the very thing which I am asserting. But, if this is so, then it cannot possibly be the case that each of us is merely making a judgment about his own feelings; since two such judgments never can contradict one another.
Ethics, p. 100

3   . . . the assertion 'I am morally bound to perform this action' is identical with the assertion 'This action will produce the greatest possible amount of good in the Universe' . . .
Principia Ethica, p. 147

4   The value of a whole must not be assumed to be the same as the sum of the values of its parts.
Principia Ethica, p. 28

5   No one, probably, who has asked himself the question, has ever doubted that personal affection and the appreciation of what is beautiful in Art or Nature, are good in themselves; nor, if we consider strictly what things are worth having *purely for their own sakes*, does it appear probable that any one will think that anything else has *nearly* so great a value as the things which are included under these two heads. . . . That it is only for the sake of these things – in order that as much of them as possible may at some time exist – that any one can be justified in performing any public or private duty; that they are the *raison d'être* of virtue; that it is they – these complex wholes *themselves*, and not any constituent or characteristic of them – that form the rational ultimate end of human action and the sole criterion of social progress: these appear to be truths which have been generally overlooked.

   . . . personal affections and aesthetic enjoyments include *all* the greatest, and *by far* the greatest, goods we can imagine. . . . All the things, which I have meant to include under the above descriptions, are highly complex *organic unities*; and in discussing the consequences, which follow from this fact, and the elements of which they are composed, I may hope at the same time both to confirm and to define my position.
Principia Ethica, p. 188

6   If we are told that the existence of blue is inconceivable apart from the existence of the sensation the speaker *probably* means to convey to us, by this ambiguous expression, that is a self-contradictory error. For we can

and must conceive the existence of blue as something quite distinct from the existence of the sensation. We can and must conceive that blue might exist and yet the sensation of blue not exist. For my own part I not only conceive this, but conceive it to be true.

'The Refutation of Idealism', *Philosophical Studies*, p. 18

Two things only seem to me to be quite certain about the analysis of such   7
propositions [as 'This is a hand', 'That is the sun', 'This is a dog'] . . . namely that whenever I know, or judge, such a proposition to be true, (1) there is always some *sense-datum* about which the proposition in question is a proposition – some sense-datum which is *a* subject (and, in a certain sense, the principal or ultimate subject) of the proposition in question, and (2) that, nevertheless, *what* I am knowing or judging to be true about this sense-datum is not (in general) that it is *itself* a hand, or a dog, or the sun, etc., etc., as the case may be.

Some philosophers have I think doubted whether there are any such things as other philosophers have meant by 'sense-data' or 'sensa'. . . . I therefore define the term in such a way that it is an open question whether the sense-datum which I now see in looking at my hand and which is a sense-datum of my hand is or is not identical with that part of its surface which I am now actually seeing.

'A Defence of Common Sense', *Philosophical Papers*, p. 54

It seems to me that, so far from its being true, as Kant declares to be his   8
opinion, that there is only one possible proof of the existence of things outside of us, namely the one which he has given, I can now give a large number of different proofs, each of which is a perfectly rigorous proof; and that at many other times I have been in a position to give many others. I can prove now, for instance, that two human hands exist. How? By holding up my two hands, and saying, as I make a certain gesture with the right hand, 'Here is one hand', and adding, as I make a certain gesture with the left, 'and here is another'. And if, by doing this, I have proved *ipso facto* the existence of external things, you will all see that I can also do it now in numbers of other ways: there is no need to multiply examples.

'Proof of an External World', *Philosophical Papers*, p. 145

Suppose we use . . . another way . . . of expressing the very same   9
statement . . . and say: 'To be a brother is the same thing as to be a male sibling.' The paradox arises from the fact that, *if* this statement is true, then it seems as if it must be the case that you would be making exactly the same statement if you said: 'To be a brother is the same thing as to be a brother.' But it is obvious that these two statements are *not* the same; and obvious also that nobody would say that by asserting 'To be a

brother is to be a brother' you were giving an analysis of the concept 'brother'.

The Philosophy of G. E. Moore, ed. A. Schilpp, p. 665

10 Have 'All tame tigers exist' and 'Most tame tigers exist' any meaning at all? Certainly they have not a clear meaning, as have 'All tame tigers growl' and 'Most tame tigers growl'. They are puzzling expressions, which certainly do not carry their meaning, if they have any, on the face of them. That this is so indicates, I think, that there is some important difference between the usage of 'exist' with which we are concerned, and the usage of such words as 'growl' or 'scratch'; but it does not make clear just what the difference is.

'Is Existence a Predicate?', *Philosophical Papers*, p. 117

11 Let us imagine one world exceedingly beautiful. Imagine it as beautiful as you can; put into it whatever on this earth you most admire – mountains, rivers, the sea; trees, and sunsets, stars and moon. Imagine these all combined in the most exquisite proportions, so that no one thing jars against another, but each contributes to increase the beauty of the whole. And then imagine the ugliest world you can possibly conceive. Imagine it simply one heap of filth, containing everything that is most disgusting to us, for whatever reason, and the whole, as far as may be, without one redeeming feature. Such a pair of worlds we are entitled to compare: they fall within Prof. Sidgwick's meaning, and the comparison is highly relevant to it. The only thing we are not entitled to imagine is that any human being ever has or ever, by any possibility, *can*, live in either, can ever see and enjoy the beauty of the one or hate the foulness of the other. Well, even so, supposing them quite apart from any possible contemplation by human beings; still, is it irrational to hold that it is better that the beautiful world should exist, than the one which is ugly? Would it not be well, in any case, to do what we could to produce it rather than the other? Certainly I cannot help thinking that it would; and I hope that some may agree with me in this extreme instance.

Principia Ethica, p. 83

12 What, for instance, is the sense in which I could have walked a mile in twenty minutes this morning, though I did not? There is one suggestion, which is very obvious: namely, that what I mean is simply after all that I could, *if* I had chosen; or (to avoid a possible complication) perhaps we had better say 'that I *should*, *if* I had chosen'. In other words, the suggestion is that we often use the phrase 'I *could*' simply and solely as a short way of saying 'I *should*, if I had chosen'. . . .

There is, therefore, much reason to think that when we say that we *could* have done a thing which we did not do, we *often* mean merely that

we *should* have done it, *if* we had chosen. And if so, then it is quite certain that, in *this* sense, we often really *could* have done what we did not do, and that this fact is in no way inconsistent with the principle that everything has a cause. And for my part I must confess that I cannot feel certain that this may not be *all* that we usually mean and understand by the assertion that we have Free Will.
Ethics, p. 211

IRIS MURDOCH (*b.* 1919)

I want now to go on to argue that the view I am suggesting offers a more   **1** satisfactory account of human freedom than does the existentialist view. I have classified together as existentialist both philosophers such as Sartre who claim the title, and philosophers such as Hampshire, Hare, Ayer, who do not. Characteristic of both is the identification of the true person with the empty choosing will, and the corresponding emphasis upon the idea of movement rather than vision. This emphasis will go with the anti-naturalistic bias of existentialism. There is no point in talking of 'moral seeing' since there is nothing *morally* to see. There is no moral vision. There is only the ordinary world which is seen with ordinary vision, and there is the will that moves within it. What may be called the Kantian wing and the Surrealist wing of existentialism may be distinguished by the degree of their interest in *reasons* for action, which diminishes to nothing at the Surrealist end.
The Sovereignty of Good, p. 35

Such transformations as these are cases of seeing the order of the world in   **2** the light of the Good and revisiting the true, or more true, conceptions of that which we formerly misconceived. Freedom, we find out, is not an inconsequential chucking of one's weight about, it is the disciplined overcoming of self. Humility is not a peculiar habit of self-effacement, rather like having an inaudible voice, it is selfless respect for reality and one of the most difficult and central of all virtues.
The Sovereignty of Good, p. 95

A genuine mysteriousness attaches to the idea of goodness and the Good.   **3** This is a mystery with several aspects. The indefinability of Good is connected with the unsystematic and inexhaustible variety of the world and the pointlessness of virtue. In this respect there is a special link between the concept of Good and the ideas of Death and Chance. (One might say that Chance is really a subdivision of Death. It is certainly our most effective *memento mori*.) A genuine sense of mortality enables us to see virtue as the only thing of worth; and it is impossible to limit and foresee the ways in which it will be required of us.
The Sovereignty of Good, p. 99

N

𝔊𝔊𝔊𝔊𝔊𝔊

THOMAS NAGEL (b. 1937)

1   Any reductionist program has to be based on an analysis of what is to be reduced. If the analysis leaves something out, the problem will be falsely posed. It is useless to base the defense of materialism on any analysis of mental phenomena that fails to deal explicitly with their subjective character. . . . If physicalism is to be defended, the phenomenological features must themselves be given a physical account. But when we examine their subjective character it seems that such a result is impossible. The reason is that every subjective phenomenon is essentially connected with a single point of view, and it seems inevitable that an objective, physical theory will abandon that point of view.
'What is it Like to be a Bat?', *Mortal Questions*, p. 167

2   Conscious experience is a widespread phenomenon. It occurs at many levels of animal life, though we cannot be sure of its presence in the simpler organisms, and it is very difficult to say in general what provides evidence of it. . . . No doubt it occurs in countless forms totally unimaginable to us, on other planets in other solar systems throughout the universe. But no matter how the form may vary, the fact that an organism has conscious experience *at all* means, basically, that there is something it is like to *be* that organism. . . . something it is like *for* the organism. . . . There is a sense in which phenomenological facts are perfectly objective: one person can know or say of another what the quality of the other's experience is. They are subjective, however, in the sense that even this objective ascription of experience is possible only for someone sufficiently similar to the object of ascription to be able to adopt his point of view. The more different from oneself the other experiencer is, the less success one can expect with this enterprise.
'What is it Like to be a Bat?', *Mortal Questions*, p. 166

3   If the facts of experience – facts about what it is like *for* the experiencing organism – are accessible only from one point of view, then it is a

mystery how the true character of experiences could be revealed in the physical operation of that organism. The latter is a domain of objective facts *par excellence* – the kind that can be observed and understood from many points of view and by individuals with differing perceptual systems.
'What is it Like to be a Bat?', *Mortal Questions*, p. 172

It certainly seems that I can believe that reality extends beyond the reach 4 of possible human thought, since this would be closely analogous to something which is not only possibly but actually the case. There are plenty of ordinary human beings who constitutionally lack the capacity to conceive of some of the things that others know about. . . . People with a permanent mental age of nine cannot come to understand Maxwell's equations or the general theory of relativity or Gödel's theorem. We can elaborate the analogy by imagining first that there are higher beings, related to us as we are related to the nine-year-olds, and capable of understanding aspects of the world that are beyond our comprehension. Then they would be able to say of us, as we can say of the others, that there are certain things about the world that we cannot even conceive. And now we need only imagine that the world is just the same, except that these higher beings do not exist. Then what they could say if they did exist remains true. So it appears that the existence of unreachable aspects of reality is independent of their conceivability by any actual mind.
The View from Nowhere, p. 95

If the theories of historical captivity or grammatical delusion are not true, 5 why have some philosophers felt themselves cured of their metaphysical problems by these forms of therapy? My counterdiagnosis is that a lot of philosophers are sick of the subject and glad to be rid of its problems. Most of us find it hopeless some of the time, but some react to its intractability by welcoming the suggestion that the enterprise is misconceived and the problems unreal. This makes them receptive not only to scientism but to deflationary metaphilosophical theories like positivism and pragmatism, which offer to raise us above the old battles.
The View from Nowhere, p. 11

I shall attempt to explain altruism, like prudence, as a rational 6 requirement on action. Just as it became clear in the earlier discussion that prudence is not fundamental, but derives from the requirement that reasons be timelessly formulable, so it will turn out that altruism is not fundamental, but derives from something more general: a formal principle which can be specified without mentioning the interests of others at all.
The Possibility of Altruism, p. 87

OTTO NEURATH (1882–1945)

1 What is originally given to us is our *ordinary natural language* with a stock of imprecise, unanalyzed terms. We start by purifying this language of metaphysical elements and so reach the *physicalistic ordinary language*. In accomplishing this we may find it very useful to draw up a list of proscribed words.

There is also the *physicalistic language of advanced science* which we can so construct that it is free from metaphysical elements from the start. We can use this language only for special sciences, indeed only for parts of them.

'Protocol Sentences', trans. George Schick, in *Logical Positivism*, ed. A. J. Ayer, p. 200

2 We believe that every word of the physicalistic ordinary language will prove to be replaceable by terms taken from the language of advanced science, just as one may also formulate the terms of the language of advanced science with the help of the terms of ordinary language. Only the latter is a very unfamiliar proceeding, and sometimes not easy. Einstein's theories are expressible (somehow) in the language of the Bantus – but not those of Heidegger, unless linguistic abuses to which the German language lends itself are introduced into Bantu. A physicist must, in principle, be able to satisfy the demand of the talented writer who insisted that: 'One ought to be able to make the outlines of any rigorously scientific thesis comprehensible in his own terms to a hackney-coach-driver.'

'Protocol Sentences', trans. George Schick, in *Logical Positivism*, ed. A. J. Ayer, p. 200

3 We are like sailors who must rebuild their ship on the open sea, never able to dismantle it in dry-dock and to reconstruct it there out of the best materials. Only the metaphysical elements can be allowed to vanish without trace. Vague linguistic conglomerations always remain in one way or another as components of the ship. If vagueness is diminished at one point, it may well be increased at another.

'Protocol Sentences', trans. George Schick, in *Logical Positivism*, ed. A. J. Ayer, p. 201

4 The 'moral sciences', the 'psychical world', the world of the 'categorical imperative', the realm of *Einfühlung* . . . the realm of *Verstehen* . . . these are more or less interpenetrating, often mutually substitutable expressions. Some authors prefer one group of meaningless phrases, some another, some combine and accumulate them.

'Sociology and Physicalism', in *Logical Positivism*, ed. A. J. Ayer, p. 295

FRIEDRICH NIETZSCHE (1844–1900)

Have you not heard of that madman who lit a lantern in the bright 1
morning hours, ran to the market place, and cried incessantly: 'I seek
God! I seek God!' . . . 'Whither is God?' he cried; 'I will tell you. *We have
killed him* – you and I. All of us are his murderers. But how did we do
this? . . . Who gave us the sponge to wipe away the entire horizon? . . .
God is dead. God remains dead. And we have killed him. . . . There has
never been a greater deed; and whoever is born after us – for the sake of
this deed he will belong to a higher history than all history hitherto'.
The Gay Science, trans. Walter Kaufmann, s. 125

After Buddha was dead, his shadow was still shown for centuries in a 2
cave – a tremendous, gruesome shadow. God is dead; but given the way
of men, there may still be caves for thousands of years in which his
shadow will be shown. – And we – we still have to vanquish his shadow,
too.
The Gay Science, trans. Walter Kaufmann, s. 108

We have arranged for ourselves a world in which we can live – by 3
positing bodies, lines, planes, causes and effects, motion and rest, form
and content; without these articles of faith nobody now could endure
life. But that does not prove them. Life is no argument. The conditions of
life might include error.
The Gay Science, trans. Walter Kaufmann, s. 121

The reasons for which 'this' world has been characterized as 'apparent' 4
are the very reasons which indicate its reality; any other kind of reality is
absolutely indemonstrable.
Twilight of the Idols, trans. Walter Kaufmann, ch. 3, s. 6

. . . it is high time to replace the Kantian question, 'How are synthetic 5
judgements *a priori* possible?' by another question, 'Why is belief in such
judgements *necessary*?' – and to comprehend that such judgements must
be *believed* to be true, for the sake of the preservation of creatures like
ourselves; though they might, of course, be *false* judgements for all that!
Beyond Good and Evil, trans. Walter Kaufmann, s. 11

What then is truth? A mobile army of metaphors, metonyms, and 6
anthropomorphisms – in short, a sum of human relations, which have
been enhanced, transposed, and embellished poetically and rhetorically,
and which after long use seem firm, canonical, and obligatory to a
people: truths are illusions about which one has forgotten that this is
what they are; metaphors which are worn out and without sensuous
power; coins which have lost their pictures and now matter only as
metal, no longer as coins.

317

'On Truth and Lie in an Extra-Moral Sense', trans. Walter Kaufmann, *The Portable Nietzsche*, p. 46

7   There are no facts, only interpretations.
    Nachlass, ed. K. Schlechta, trans. A. Danto

8   Henceforth, my dear philosophers, let us be on guard against the dangerous old conceptual fiction that posited a 'pure, will-less, painless, timeless knowing subject'; let us guard against the snares of such contradictory concepts as 'pure reason', 'absolute spirituality', 'knowledge in itself': these always demand that we should think of an eye that is completely unthinkable, an eye turned in no particular direction, in which the active and interpreting forces, through which alone seeing becomes seeing *something*, are supposed to be lacking; these always demand of the eye an absurdity and a nonsense. There is *only* a perspective seeing, *only* a perspective 'knowing'; and the *more* emotions we allow to speak about one thing, the *more* eyes, different eyes, we can use to observe one thing, the more complete will our 'concept' of this thing, our 'objectivity', be.
    On the Genealogy of Morals, trans. Kaufmann and Hollingdale, e. III, s. 12, amended

9   Physicists believe in a 'true world' in their own fashion . . . But they are in error. The atom they posit is inferred according to the logic of the perspectivism of consciousness – and is therefore itself a subjective fiction. This world picture they sketch differs in no essential way from the subjective world picture: it is only construed with more extended sense, but with *our* senses nonetheless.
    The Will to Power, trans. Walter Kaufmann, s. 636

10 Subject, object, a doer added to the doing, the doing separated from that which it does: let us not forget that this is mere semiotics and nothing real. Mechanistic theory as a theory of motion is already a translation into the sense language of man.
    The Will to Power, trans. Walter Kaufmann, s. 634

11 How should explanation be at all possible when we make everything into an image, *our* image! . . . Cause and effect: such a duality probably never occurs – in reality there lies before us a continuum out of which we isolate a couple of pieces . . .
    The Gay Science, trans. Walter Kaufmann, s. 112

12 We believed ourselves to be causal agents in the act of willing; we at least thought we were there *catching causality in the act.* . . . causality had, on the basis of will, been firmly established as a given fact, as *empiricism.* – Meanwhile we have thought better. Today we do not believe a word of it.

The 'inner world' is full of phantoms and false lights: the will is one of them.
Twilight of the Idols, trans. R. J. Hollingdale, ch. 6, s. 3

What are man's truths ultimately? Merely his *irrefutable* errors.   13
The Gay Science, trans. Walter Kaufmann, s. 265

I also maintain the phenomenality of the *inner* world: everything of   14
which we become *conscious* is, through and through, merely arranged,
simplified, schematized, interpreted. The actual situation behind inner
perception, the causal uniting between thoughts, feelings, desires, and
between subject and object, is absolutely concealed from us, and is
perhaps a pure fancy. This 'apparent inner world' is manipulated with
just the same forms and procedures as 'the external world'. We never hit
upon 'facts'.
Nachlass, ed. K. Schlechta, trans. A. Danto, p. 673

. . . a thought comes when 'it' wishes, and not when 'I' wish, so that it is a   15
falsification of the facts of the case to say that the subject 'I' is the
condition of the predicate 'think'. *It* thinks: but that this 'it' is precisely
the famous old 'ego' is, to put it mildly, only a superstition, an assertion,
and assuredly not an 'immediate certainty'. . . . Even the 'it' contains an
interpretation of the process, and does not belong to the process itself.
One infers here according to the grammatical habit: 'thinking is an
activity; every activity requires an agent; consequently –'.
Beyond Good and Evil, trans. Walter Kaufmann, s. 17

But now observe the strangest thing of all about the will – about this so   16
complex thing for which people have only *one* word: inasmuch as in the
given circumstances we at the same time command *and* obey, and as the
side which obeys know the sensations of constraint, compulsion,
pressure, resistance, motion which usually begin immediately after the
act of will; inasmuch as, on the other hand, we are in the habit of
disregarding and deceiving ourselves over this duality by means of the
synthetic concept 'I'; so a whole chain of erroneous conclusions . . . has
become attached to the will as such . . . 'Freedom of will' – is the
expression for that complex condition of pleasure of the person who
wills, who commands and at the same time identifies himself with the
executor of the command – who as such also enjoys the triumph over
resistances involved but who thinks it was his will itself which overcame
these resistances. He who wills adds in this way the sensations of pleasure
of the successful executive agents, the serviceable 'under-wills' or under-
souls – for our body is only a social structure composed of many souls –
to his sensations of pleasure as commander. *L'effet, c'est moi* . . .
Beyond Good and Evil, trans. R. J. Hollingdale, s. 19

17 People are accustomed to consider the goal (purposes, vocations, etc.) as the *driving force*, in keeping with a very ancient error; but it is merely the *directing* force – one has mistaken the helmsman for the steam. And not even always the helmsman, the directing force.
The Gay Science, trans. Walter Kaufmann, s. 360

18 Thoughts are the shadows of our feelings – always darker, emptier, and simpler.
The Gay Science, trans. Walter Kaufmann, s. 179

19 Granted that nothing is 'given' as real except our world of desires and passions, that we can rise or sink to no other 'reality' than the reality of our drives – for thinking is only the relationship of these drives to one another – : is it not permitted to make the experiment and ask the question whether this which is given does not *suffice* for an understanding even of the so-called mechanical (or 'material') world? I do not mean as a deception, an 'appearance', an 'idea' (in the Berkeleyan and Schopen-haueran sense), but as possessing the same degree of reality as our emotions themselves – . . . enough, one must venture the hypothesis that wherever 'effects' are recognized, will is operating upon will – and that all mechanical occurrences, in so far as a force is active in them, are force of will, effects of will. – Granted finally that one succeeded in explaining our entire instinctual life as the development and ramification of *one* basic form of will – . . . The world seen from within, the world described and defined according to its 'intelligible character' – it would be 'will to power' and nothing else. –
Beyond Good and Evil, trans. R. J. Hollingdale, s. 36

20 When one speaks of *humanity*, the idea is fundamental that this is something that *separates* and distinguishes man from nature. In reality, however, there is no such separation: 'natural' qualities and those called properly 'human' are indivisibly grown together. Man, in his highest and most noble capacities, is wholly nature and embodies its uncanny dual character. Those of his abilities which are awesome and considered inhuman are perhaps the fertile soil out of which alone all humanity . . . can grow.
Homer's Contest, trans. Walter Kaufmann, p. 369

21 [Anything which] is a living and not a dying body . . . will have to be an incarnate will to power, it will strive to grow, spread, seize, become predominant – not from any morality or immorality but because it is *living* and because life simply *is* will to power. . . . 'Exploitation' . . . belongs to the *essence* of what lives, as a basic organic function; it is a consequence of the will to power, which is after all the will of life.
Beyond Good and Evil, trans. Walter Kaufmann, s. 259

'Truth' is therefore not something there, that might be found or 22
discovered – but something that must be created and that gives a name to
a process, or rather to a will to overcome that has in itself no end –
introducing truth, as a *processus in infinitum*, an active determining – not
a becoming-conscious of something that is in itself firm and determined.
The Will to Power, trans. Walter Kaufmann, s. 522

All philosophers have the common failing of starting out from man as he 23
is now and thinking they can reach their goal through an analysis of him.
They involuntarily think of 'man' as an *aeterna veritas*, as something that
remains constant in the midst of all flux, as a sure measure of things.
Everything the philosopher has declared about man is, however, at
bottom no more than a testimony as to the man of a *very limited* period
of time. Lack of historical sense is the family failing of all philosophers.
Human, All Too Human, trans. R. J. Hollingdale, s. 2

I teach you the Superman. Man is something that should be overcome. 24
Thus Spoke Zarathustra, trans. R. J. Hollingdale, p. 41

Man is a rope, tied between beast and Superman – a rope over an abyss. 25
Thus Spoke Zarathustra, trans. R. J. Hollingdale, p. 43

All instincts that do not discharge themselves outwardly *turn inward* – 26
this is what I call the *internalisation* of man: thus it was that man first
developed what was later called his 'soul'. The entire inner world,
originally as thin as if it were stretched between two membranes,
expanded and extended itself, acquired depth, breadth and height, in the
same measure as the outward discharge was *inhibited*.
On the Genealogy of Morals, trans. Kaufmann and Hollingdale, e. II, s. 16

Truth as Circe. Error has transformed animals into men; could truth be 27
capable of transforming man again into an animal?
Human, All Too Human, trans. R. J. Hollingdale, s. 519

For to translate man back into nature; to master the many vain and 28
fanciful interpretations and secondary meanings which have been
hitherto scribbled and daubed over that eternal basic text *homo natura*;
to confront man henceforth with man in the way in which, hardened by
the discipline of science, man today confronts the *rest* of nature, with
dauntless Oedipus eyes and stopped-up Odysseus ears, deaf to the siren
songs of old metaphysical bird-catchers who have all too long been
piping to him 'you are more! you are higher! you are of a different
origin!' – that may be a strange and extravagant task but it is a *task* –
who would deny that?
Beyond Good and Evil, trans. R. J. Hollingdale, s. 230

29 If one is to pursue physiology with a good conscience one is compelled to insist that the sense-organs are *not* phenomena in idealist philosophy's sense: for if they were they could not be causes! . . . What? and others even go so far as to say that the external world is the work of our organs? But then our body, as a piece of this external world, would be the work of our organs! But then our organs themselves would be – the work of our organs! This, it seems to me, is a complete *reductio ad absurdum* . . .
Beyond Good and Evil, trans. R. J. Hollingdale, s. 15, amended

30 Change, mutation, becoming in general, were formerly taken as proof of mere appearance, as a sign that there must be something that led us astray. Today, on the contrary, we regard ourselves as somehow entangled in error, *necessitated* to error, to precisely the extent that our prejudice in favour of reason compels us to posit unity, identity, duration, substance, cause, materiality, being. . . .
It is no different in this case than with the movements of the sun: there our eye is the constant advocate of error, here it is our language. Language belongs in its origin to the age of the most rudimentary form of psychology.
Twilight of the Idols, trans. R. J. Hollingdale, ch. 3, s. 5, amended

31 Every word is a prejudice.
The Wanderer and his Shadow, trans. R. J. Hollingdale, s. 55

32 What is originality? *To see* something that has no name as yet and hence cannot be mentioned although it stares us all in the face. The way men usually are, it takes a name to make something visible for them.
The Gay Science, trans. Walter Kaufmann, s. 261

33 The human being inventing signs is at the same time the human being who becomes ever more keenly conscious of himself. It was only as a social animal that man acquired self-consciousness . . .
The Gay Science, trans. Walter Kaufmann, s. 354

34 We could think, feel, will, remember; we could likewise 'act' in every sense of the word; and yet none of this would need to 'come into consciousness' (to put it metaphorically).
The Gay Science, trans. Walter Kaufmann, s. 354

35 'I have done that', says my memory. 'I cannot have done that', says my pride, and remains inexorable. Eventually – memory yields.
Beyond Good and Evil, trans. Walter Kaufmann, s. 68

36 There is *master morality* and *slave morality* – . . . when it is the rulers who determine the concept 'good', . . . the antithesis 'good' and 'bad' means the same thing as 'noble' and 'despicable' – the antithesis 'good'

and '*evil*' originates elsewhere. . . . The noble type of man feels *himself* to be the determiner of values, he does not need to be approved of, he judges 'what harms me is harmful in itself'. . . . The slave is suspicious of the virtues of the powerful: he is sceptical and mistrustful, *keenly* mistrustful, of everything 'good' that is honoured among them – he would like to convince himself that happiness itself is not genuine among them. On the other hand, those qualities which serve to make easier the existence of the suffering will be brought into prominence and flooded with light: here it is that pity, the kind and helping hand, the warm heart, patience, industriousness, humility, friendliness come into honour – for here these are the most useful qualities and virtually the only means of enduring the burden of existence. Slave morality is essentially the morality of utility.
Beyond Good and Evil, trans. R. J. Hollingdale, s. 260

. . . your love of your neighbour is your bad love of yourselves.   37
Thus Spoke Zarathustra, trans. R. J. Hollingdale, p. 86

Over one man *necessity* stands in the shape of his passions, over another   38
as the habit of hearing and obeying, over a third as a logical conscience, over a fourth as caprice and a mischievous pleasure in escapades. These four will, however, seek the *freedom* of their will precisely where each of them is most firmly fettered: it is as if the silkworm sought the freedom of its will in spinning. How does this happen? Evidently because each considers himself most free where his *feeling of living* is greatest.
The Wanderer and his Shadow, trans. R. J. Hollingdale, s. 9

An experience in the social-political realm has been falsely transferred to   39
the farthest metaphysical domain: in the former the strong man is also the free man, . . . while the subjected man, the slave, lives dull and oppressed. – The theory of freedom of will is an invention of the *ruling* classes.
The Wanderer and his Shadow, trans. R. J. Hollingdale, s. 9

If only those actions are moral . . . which are performed out of freedom of   40
will, then there are no moral actions.
Dawn, trans. Richard Schacht, s. 148

Whatever has *value* in our world now does not have value in itself,   41
according to its nature – nature is always value-less, but has been *given* value at some time, as a present – and it was *we* who gave and bestowed it.
The Gay Science, trans. Walter Kaufmann, s. 301

My demand upon the philosopher is known, that he take his stand   42
beyond good and evil and leave the illusion of moral judgement *beneath*

323

himself. This demand follows from an insight which I was the first to formulate: that *there are altogether no moral facts.*
Twilight of the Idols, trans. Walter Kaufmann, ch. 7, s. 1

43 Moral sensibilities are nowadays at such cross-purposes that to one man a morality is proved by its utility, while to another its utility refutes it.
Daybreak, trans. R. J. Hollingdale, p. 226

44 Not to perpetrate cowardice against one's own acts! Not to leave them in the lurch afterward! The bite of conscience is indecent.
Twilight of the Idols, trans. Walter Kaufmann, ch. 1, s. 10

45 To our strongest drive, the tyrant in us, not only our reason bows but also our conscience.
Beyond Good and Evil, trans. Walter Kaufmann, s. 158

46 *The greatest weight.* – What, if some day or night a demon were to steal after you into your loneliest loneliness and say to you: 'This life as you now live it and have lived it, you will have to live once more and innumerable times more; and there will be nothing new in it, but every pain and every joy and every thought and sigh and everything unutterably small or great in your life will have to return to you, all in the same succession and sequence – even this spider and this moonlight between the trees, and even this moment and I myself. The eternal hourglass of existence is turned upside down again and again, and you with it, speck of dust!'
Would you not throw yourself down and gnash your teeth and curse the demon who spoke thus? . . . Or how well disposed would you have to become to yourself and to life *to crave nothing more fervently* than this ultimate eternal confirmation and seal?
The Gay Science, trans. Walter Kaufmann, s. 341

47 . . . a circular movement of absolutely identical series is thus demonstrated: the world as a circular movement that has already repeated itself infinitely often and plays its game *in infinitum.*
The Will to Power, trans. Walter Kaufmann and R. J. Hollingdale, s. 1066

48 I mistrust all systematizers and I avoid them. The will to a system is a lack of integrity.
Twilight of the Idols, trans. Walter Kaufmann, ch. 1, s. 26

49 Art raises its head when religions relax their hold.
Human, All Too Human, trans. R. J. Hollingdale, s. 150

50 Art makes the sight of life bearable by laying over it the veil of unclear thinking.
Human, All Too Human, trans. R. J. Hollingdale, s. 151

The profundity of the tragic artist lies in this, that his aesthetic instinct 51
surveys the more remote consequences, that he does not halt shortsightedly
at what is closest at hand, that he affirms the large-scale economy which
justifies the terrifying, the evil, the questionable – and more than merely
justifies them.
The Will to Power, trans. Walter Kaufmann, s. 852

Only artists . . . have taught us the art of viewing ourselves as heroes – 52
from a distance, and, as it were, simplified and transfigured. . . . Only in
this way we deal with some base details in ourselves. Without this art we
would be nothing but foreground and live entirely in the spell of that
perspective which makes what is closest at hand and most vulgar appear
as if it were vast, and reality itself.
The Gay Science, trans. Walter Kaufmann, s. 78

The word 'Dionysian' means: an urge to unity, a reaching out beyond 53
personality, the everyday, society, reality, across the abyss of transitoriness: a passionate-painful overflowing into darker, fuller, more floating
states. . . .

The word 'Apollinian' means: the urge to perfect self-sufficiency, to the
typical 'individual', to all that simplifies, distinguishes, makes strong,
clear, unambiguous, typical: freedom under law.

The further development of art is as necessarily tied to these two
natural artistic powers as the further development of man is to that
between the sexes. Plenitude of power and moderation.
The Will to Power, trans. Walter Kaufmann, s. 1050

Of this foundation of all existence – the Dionysian basic ground of the 54
world – not one whit more may enter the consciousness of the human
individual than can be overcome again by this Apollinian power of
transfiguration.
The Birth of Tragedy, trans. Walter Kaufmann, p. 25

Kant, like all philosophers, instead of viewing the aesthetic issue from the 55
side of the artist, envisaged art and beauty solely from the 'spectator's'
point of view, and so, without himself realizing it, smuggled the
'spectator' into the concept of beauty. . . . 'That is beautiful', Kant
proclaims, 'which gives us disinterested pleasure'. Disinterested! . . .
When our aestheticians tirelessly rehearse, in support of Kant's view, that
the spell of beauty enables us to view even *nude* female statues
'disinterestedly' we may be allowed to laugh a little at their expense. The
experiences of artists in this delicate matter are rather more 'interesting'. . .
On the Genealogy of Morals, trans. Kaufmann and Hollingdale, e. III, s. 6

Whoever despises himself still respects himself as one who despises. 56
Beyond Good and Evil, trans. Walter Kaufmann, s. 78

57 The degree and kind of a man's sexuality reach up into the ultimate pinnacle of his spirit.
Beyond Good and Evil, trans. Walter Kaufmann, s. 75

58 All psychology so far has got stuck in moral prejudices and fears; it has not dared to descend into the depths.
Beyond Good and Evil, trans. Walter Kaufmann, s. 23

59 Gradually it has become clear to me what every great philosophy so far has been: namely, the personal confession of its author and a kind of involuntary and unconscious memoir; also that the moral (or immoral) intentions in every philosophy constituted the real germ of life from which the whole plant has grown.
Beyond Good and Evil, trans. Walter Kaufmann, s. 6

60 To live alone one must be a beast or a god, says Aristotle. Leaving out the third case: one must be both – a philosopher.
Twilight of the Idols, trans. Walter Kaufmann, ch. 1, s. 3

61 Philosophy, as I have so far understood and lived it, means living voluntarily among ice and high mountains – seeking out everything strange and questionable in existence, everything so far placed under a ban by morality.
Ecce Homo, trans. Walter Kaufmann, Preface, s. 3

62 Those thinkers in whom all stars move in cyclic orbits are not the most profound. Whoever looks into himself as into vast space and carries galaxies in himself, also knows how irregular all galaxies are; they lead into the chaos and labyrinth of existence.
The Gay Science, trans. Walter Kaufmann, s. 322

63 I tell you: one must have chaos in one, to give birth to a dancing star.
Thus Spoke Zarathustra, trans. R. J. Hollingdale, p. 46

NOVALIS (1772–1801)

1 Precisely because we are philosophers we need not bother ourselves about issues. We have the principle, that is enough; the rest can be left for commoner brains.
The Disciples at Sais and other Fragments, trans. F. V. M. T. and U.C.B., p. 68

2 Activity is the only reality.
The Disciples at Sais and other Fragments, p. 69

3 A Realist is an Idealist who knows nothing of himself.
The Disciples at Sais and other Fragments, p. 78

P. H. NOWELL-SMITH (*b.* 1914)

A man can, therefore, question the morality of his own principles and try 1
to change them; but he cannot do so while applying them or if he has no
pro-attitude towards making the change. Whether or not he can change
them if these logical conditions are satisfied is an empirical question, to
which the only answer is: 'Sometimes. He may not always succeed; but
he can always try.'
Ethics, p. 313

What sort of principles a man adopts will, in the end, depend on his 2
vision of the Good Life, his conception of the sort of world that he
desires, so far as it rests with him, to create. Indeed his moral principles
just *are* this conception. The conception can be altered; perhaps he meets
someone whose character, conduct, or arguments reveal to him new
virtues that he has never even contemplated; or he may do something
uncharacteristic and against his principles without choosing to do it and,
in doing it, discover how good it is. Moral values, like other values, are
sometimes discovered accidentally. But the one thing he cannot do is to
try to alter his conception of the Good Life; for it is ultimately by
reference to this conception that all his choices are made. And the fact
that he cannot choose to alter this conception neither shields him from
blame nor disqualifies him from admiration.
Ethics, p. 313

ROBERT NOZICK (*b.* 1938)

Individuals have rights, and there are things no person or group may do 1
to them (without violating their rights). So strong and far-reaching are
these rights that they raise the question of what, if anything, the state and
its officials may do. . . . Our main conclusions about the state are that a
minimal state, limited to the narrow functions of protection against
force, theft, fraud, enforcement of contracts, and so on, is justified; that
any more extensive state will violate persons' rights not to be forced to do
certain things, and is unjustified; and that the minimal state is inspiring as
well as right.
Anarchy, State, and Utopia, p. ix

It is not clear how those holding alternative conceptions of distributive 2
justice can reject the entitlement conception of justice in holdings. For
suppose a distribution favored by one of these non-entitlement conceptions
is realized. Let us suppose it is your favorite one and let us call this
distribution D1; perhaps everyone has an equal share, perhaps shares
vary in accordance with some dimension you treasure. Now suppose that
Wilt Chamberlain is greatly in demand by basketball teams, being a great

327

gate attraction. (Also suppose contracts run only for a year, with players being free agents.) He signs the following sort of contract with a team: in each home game, twenty-five cents from the price of each ticket of admission goes to him. . . . Let us suppose that in one season one million persons attend his home games, and Wilt Chamberlain winds up with $250,000, a much larger sum than the average income and larger even than anyone else has. Is he entitled to this income? Is this new distribution D2, unjust? If so, why? . . . If D1 was a just distribution, and people voluntarily moved from it to D2, transferring parts of their shares they were given under D1 (what was it for if not to do something with?), isn't D2 also just?

Anarchy, State, and Utopia, p. 160

3   The socialist society would have to forbid capitalist acts between consenting adults.
Anarchy, State, and Utopia, p. 163

4   Why does mixing one's labor with something make one the owner of it? Perhaps because one owns one's labor, and so one comes to own a previously unowned thing that becomes permeated with what one owns. Ownership seeps over into the rest. But why isn't mixing what I own with what I don't own a way of losing what I own rather than a way of gaining what I don't? If I own a can of tomato juice and spill it in the sea so that its molecules (made radioactive, so I can check this) mingle evenly throughout the sea, do I thereby come to own the sea, or have I foolishly dissipated my tomato juice?
Anarchy, State and Utopia, p. 174

5   A person knows that *p* when he not only does truly believe it, but also would truly believe it and wouldn't falsely believe it. He not only actually has a true belief, he subjunctively has one. It is true that *p* and he believes it; if it weren't true he wouldn't believe it, and if it were true he would believe it. To know that *p* is to be someone who would believe it if it were true, and who wouldn't believe it if it were false.

It will be useful to have a term for this situation when a person's belief is thus subjunctively connected to the fact. Let us say of [such] a person . . . [that] his belief *tracks* the truth that *p*.
Philosophical Explanations, p. 178

6   Why are philosophers intent on forcing others to believe things? Is that a nice way to behave towards someone?
Philosophical Explanations, p. 5

O

𝕲𝕲𝕲𝕲𝕲𝕲

OCKHAM *See* WILLIAM OF OCKHAM

ONORA O'NEILL (*b.* 1941)

Situations have no unique descriptions. What we see under one true description as an urgent crisis or problem, may appear under another as mere and trivial routine. Ways of reasoning that assume that 'the facts' of human situations can be uncontroversially stated are likely to be dominated by established and often by establishment views. Without a critical account of the selection of minor premises, ethical reasoning may avoid formalism only to become hostage to local ideology. This is not an idle worry. Writing in applied ethics has to work with some account of the topics to be handled. Neither the selection of topics nor their description is neutrally given. Could any of us demonstrate that contemporary applied ethics is more than the scholasticism of a liberal tradition?
'Abstraction, Idealization and Ideology in Ethics', *Moral Philosophy and Contemporary Problems*, ed. J. D. Evans, p. 65

JOSÉ ORTEGA Y GASSET (1883–1955)

We must learn to free ourselves from the traditional idea which would   1
have reality always consist in some *thing*, be it physical or mental.
'In Search of Goethe from Within', *The Worlds of Existentialism*, ed. M. Friedman, p. 118

Philosophy has always gone astray by giving the name of 'I' to the most   2
unlikely things but never to the thing you call 'I' in your daily life.
'In Search of Goethe from Within', p. 118

Life is an operation which is done in a forward direction. One lives   3
toward the future, because to live consists inexorably in *doing*, in each individual life *making* itself.
'In Search of Goethe from Within', p. 117

4 The soul . . . remains as much *outside* the *I* which you are, as the landscape remains outside your body.
'In Search of Goethe from Within', p. 118

5 Your soul is the closest to you, but it is not you yourself.
'In Search of Goethe from Within', p. 118

6 You are no *thing*, you are simply the person who has to live *with* things, *among* things, the person who has to live, not *any* life but a *particular* life.
'In Search of Goethe from Within', p. 118

7 There is no abstract living.
'In Search of Goethe from Within', p. 118

8 We must get over the error which makes us think that a man's life takes place inside himself.
'In Search of Goethe from Within', p. 118

9 This unity of dramatic dynamism between the two elements, the I and the world – is life.
'In Search of Goethe from Within', p. 119

10 Nothing so saps the profound resources of a life as finding life too easy.
'In Search of Goethe from Within', p. 122

11 Life is our reaction to the basic insecurity which constitutes its substance.
'In Search of Goethe from Within', p. 121

BRIAN O'SHAUGHNESSY (*b.* 1925)

1 What I wish to say is, that the solipsist tendencies of twentieth-century thought, and the resultant exacerbation of the problem of other minds, can cause us to exaggerate the *epistemological* significance of the fact that psychological phenomena generally manifest their presence in bodily action. The fact that they tend to cause phenomena that are accessible and intelligible to the consciousness of others may be emphasised; while that they tend to cause phenomena that advance life may be disregarded. And yet the fundamental emphasis, in my opinion, is to be placed upon the latter rather than the former property of the psychological. . . . Before we are predators, prey, lovers, parents, and suckling infants, let alone fellow citizens, we are living creatures actively embedded in the world.
The Will, I, p. xl

2 . . . trying to move a limb is a unique psychological event simply in being *standardly* a causally sufficient condition of a physical change; for all other examples of causal power on the part of the mental, like the power

of an erotic thought to affect the pulse, are either merely typical or haphazard powers. But even more important is the fact that trying is *in essence* normally a causally sufficient condition of bodily change. For in this we find the material for demonstrating that trying to move a limb is the psychological 'pineal gland'.

The Will, II, p. 352

P. D. OUSPENSKY (1878–1947)

The dispute between the theory of a predestined future and the theory of 1 a free future is an endless dispute. This is so because both theories are too literal, too rigid, too material, and the one excludes the other. . . . These opposites are both equally wrong because the truth lies in a unification of these two opposite understandings into one whole. At any given moment all the future of the world is predestined and existing – *provided no new factor comes in*. And a new factor can only come in from the side of *consciousness* and the will resulting from it.

Tertium Organum, trans. E. Kadloubovsky and P. D. Ouspensky, p. 30

Philosophy is based on speculation, on logic, on thought, on the synthesis 2 of what we know and on the analysis of what we do not know. Philosophy must include within its confines the whole content of science, religion and art. But where can such a philosophy be found? All that we know in our times by the name of philosophy is not philosophy, but merely 'critical literature' or the expression of personal opinions, mainly with the aim of overthrowing and destroying other personal opinions. Or, which is still worse, philosophy is nothing but self-satisfied dialectic surrounding itself with an impenetrable barrier of terminology unintelligible to the uninitiated and solving for itself all the problems of the universe without any possibility of proving these explanations or making them intelligible to ordinary mortals.

A New Model of the Universe, p. 25

The whole of our positive science – physics, chemistry and biology – is 3 based on hypotheses contradictory to Kant's propositions. . . . positivist philosophy appears to consider Kant's view erroneous and assumes that scientific experience acquaints us with the very substance of things, with the true causes of our sensations, or, if it does not yet do that, it may succeed in doing so later. 'Positivists' believe in the very thing the possibility of which Kant denied, namely in the comprehension of the true essence of things through the study of phenomena.

Tertium Organum, trans. E. Kadloubovsky and P. D. Ouspensky, p. 8

Religious revelation, philosophical thought, scientific investigation all 4 converge on the problem of time and all come to the same view of it –

time does not exist. There is no perpetual and eternal appearance and disappearance of phenomena. Everything exists always. There is only one eternal present. The world is a world of infinite possibilities. Our mind follows the development of possibilities always in one direction only. But in fact every moment contains a very large number of possibilities, and all of them are actualised.

A New Model of the Universe, p. 138

P

🔊🔊🔊🔊🔊

GIOVANNI PAPINI (1881–1956)

There are pages of Hegel which have in the field of thought the same effect that the sonnets of Mallarmé have in the field of poetry. They are instruments of evocation and of indefinite, sentimental suggestiveness – and they are nothing more. That does not lessen their value; it may even increase it. But verbal narcotics and hypnotic formulas are not to be imposed on us as truths.
Four and Twenty Minds, trans. E. H. Wilkins, p. 113

DEREK PARFIT (*b.* 1943)

The Harmless Torturers. In the Bad Old Days, each torturer inflicted   1
severe pain on one victim. Things have now changed. Each of the thousand torturers presses a button, thereby turning the switch once on each of the thousand instruments. The victims suffer the same severe pain. But none of the torturers makes any victim's pain perceptibly worse.
Reasons and Persons, p. 80

It is not enough to ask, 'Will my act harm other people?' Even if the   2
answer is No, my act may still be wrong, *because* of its effects on other people. I should ask, 'Will my act be one of a set of acts that will *together* harm other people?' The answer may be Yes. And the harm to others may be great. If this is so, I may be acting *very* wrongly, like the Harmless Torturers.
Reasons and Persons, p. 86

At the beginning of my story, the Scanner destroys my brain and body.   3
My blueprint is beamed to Mars, where another machine makes an organic *Replica* of me. My Replica thinks that he is me, and he seems to remember living my life up to the moment when I pressed the green button. In every other way, both physically and psychologically, my

Replica is just like me. If he returned to Earth, everyone would think that he was me.

Simple Teletransportation, as just described, is a common feature in science fiction. And it is believed, by some readers of this fiction, merely to be the fastest way of travelling. They believe that my Replica *would* be *me*. Other science fiction readers, and some of the characters in this fiction, take a different view. They believe that, when I press the green button, I die. My Replica is *someone else*, who has been made to be exactly like me. . . . As I shall argue later, I ought to regard having a Replica as being about as good as ordinary survival.

Reasons and Persons, p. 200

4   *My Division.* My body is fatally injured, as are the brains of my two brothers. My brain is divided, and each half is successfully transplanted into the body of one of my brothers. Each of the resulting people believes that he is me, seems to remember living my life, has my character, and is in every other way psychologically continuous with me. And he has a body that is very like mine. . . .

It may help to state, in advance, what I believe this case to show. It provides a further argument against the view that we are separately existing entities. But the main conclusion to be drawn is that *personal identity is not what matters.*

Reasons and Persons, p. 254

5   *How Timeless Greets Good News.* Timeless is in hospital for a painful operation, that will be followed by induced amnesia. He wakes up, with no particular memories of the previous day. He asks his nurse when and for how long he will have to endure this painful operation. As before, the nurse knows the facts about two patients, but is unsure which he is. In either case, however, his operation needed to be unusually long, lasting a full ten hours. The nurse knows that one of the following is true. Either he did suffer yesterday for ten hours, or he will suffer later today for ten hours.

Timeless is plunged in gloom. He had hoped for a shorter operation.

When the nurse returns, she exclaims 'Good News! You are the one who suffered yesterday'.

Timeless is just as glum. 'Why is that good news?', he asks. 'My ordeal is just as painful, and just as long. And it is just as much a part of my life. Why should it make a difference to me now that my ordeal is in the past?'
. . .

Is Timeless making a mistake? Ought he to be relieved? Most of us would answer Yes. But it is hard to explain why, without begging the question.

Reasons and Persons, p. 177

If it was put forward on its own, it would be difficult to accept the view 6
that personal identity is not what matters. But I believe that, when we
consider the case of division, this difficulty disappears. When we see *why*
neither resulting person will be me, I believe that, on reflection, we can
also see that this does not matter, or matters only a little.
Reasons and Persons, p. 263

It may help to add these remarks. On the Reductionist View, my 7
continued existence just involves physical and psychological continuity.
On the Non-Reductionist View, it involves a further fact. It is natural to
believe in this further fact, and to believe that, compared with the
continuities, it is a *deep* fact, and is the fact that really matters. When I
fear that, in Teletransportation, *I* shall not get to Mars, my fear is that
the abnormal cause may fail to produce this further fact. As I have
argued, there is no such fact.
Reasons and Persons, p. 279

The truth is very different from what we are inclined to believe. Even if 8
we are not aware of this, most of us are Non-Reductionists. . . .
   Is the truth depressing? Some may find it so. But I find it liberating, and
consoling. When I believed that my existence was such a further fact, I
seemed imprisoned in myself. My life seemed like a glass tunnel, through
which I was moving faster every year, and at the end of which there was
darkness. When I changed my view, the walls of my glass tunnel
disappeared. I now live in the open air. There is still a difference between
my life and the lives of other people. But the difference is less. Other
people are closer. I am less concerned about the rest of my own life, and
more concerned about the lives of others.
Reasons and Persons, p. 281

Each counts for one. That is why more count for more. 9
'Innumerate Ethics', *Philosophy and Public Affairs* (1978), p. 301

PARMENIDES (*c.*515–*c.*480 BC)

Come now, and I will tell thee – and do thou hearken and carry my word 1
away – the only ways of enquiry that can be thought of. The one way,
that it *is* and cannot not-be, is the path of Persuasion, for it attends upon
Truth; the other, that it *is-not* and needs must not-be, that I tell thee is a
path altogether unthinkable. For thou couldst not know that which is-
not (that is impossible) nor utter it.
G. S. Kirk, J. E. Raven and M. Schofield, *The Pre-Socratic Philosophers*, p. 244

You will not find thinking apart from what is . . .; for there is not, nor 2
shall be, anything else besides what is, since Fate fettered it to be entire

and immovable. Therefore all these are mere names which mortals laid down believing them to be true – coming into being and perishing, being and not being, change of place and variation of bright colour.

The Pre-Socratic Philosophers, p. 252

BLAISE PASCAL (1623–1662)

1   Man is only a reed, the weakest in nature, but he is a thinking reed. There is no need for the whole universe to take up arms to crush him: a vapour, a drop of water is enough to kill him. But even if the universe were to crush him, man would still be nobler than his slayer, because he knows that he is dying and the advantage the universe has over him. The universe knows none of this.

   Thus all our dignity consists in thought. It is on thought that we must depend for our recovery, not on space and time, which we could never fill. Let us then strive to think well; that is the basic principle of morality.

   Pensées, trans. A. J. Krailsheimer, No. 200, p. 95

2   If there is a God, he is infinitely beyond our comprehension, since, being indivisible and without limits, he bears no relation to us. We are therefore incapable of knowing either what he is or whether he is. That being so, who would dare to attempt an answer to the question? Certainly not we, who bear no relation to him.

   Who then will condemn Christians for being unable to give rational grounds for their belief, professing as they do a religion for which they cannot give rational grounds? They declare that it is a folly, *stultitiam*, in expounding it to the world, and then you complain that they do not prove it. . . . Let us then examine this point, and let us say: 'Either God is or he is not.' But to which view shall we be inclined? Reason cannot decide this question. Infinite chaos separates us. At the far end of this infinite distance a coin is being spun which will come down heads or tails. How will you wager? Reason cannot make you choose either, reason cannot prove either wrong.

   . . . 'the right thing is not to wager at all.'

   Yes, but you must wager. There is no choice, you are already committed. Which will you choose then? Let us see: since a choice must be made, let us see which offers you the least interest. You have two things to lose: the true and the good; and two things to stake: your reason and your will, your knowledge and your happiness; and your nature has two things to avoid: error and wretchedness. Since you must necessarily choose, your reason is no more affronted by choosing one rather than the other. That is one point cleared up. But your happiness? Let us weigh up the gain and the loss involved in calling heads that God

exists. Let us assess the two cases: if you win you win everything, if you lose you lose nothing. Do not hesitate then; wager that he does exist.
Pensées, trans. A. J. Krailsheimer, No. 418, p. 150

. . . here there is an infinity of infinitely happy life to be won, one chance 3 of winning against a finite number of chances of losing, and what you are staking is finite. That leaves no choice; wherever there is infinity, and where there are not infinite chances of losing against that of winning, there is no room for hesitation, you must give everything. And thus, since you are obliged to play, you must be renouncing reason if you hoard your life rather than risk it for an infinite gain, just as likely to occur as a loss amounting to nothing.
Pensées, trans. A. J. Krailsheimer, No. 418, p. 151

'. . . my hands are tied and my lips are sealed; I am being forced to wager 4 and I am not free; I am being held fast and I am so made that I cannot believe. What do you want me to do then?' – 'That is true, but at least get it into your head that, if you are unable to believe, it is because of your passions, since reason impels you to believe and yet you cannot do so. Concentrate then not on convincing yourself by multiplying proofs of God's existence but by diminishing your passions. . . .'
Pensées, trans. A. J. Krailsheimer, No. 418, p. 152

A given man lives a life free from boredom by gambling a small sum 5 every day. Give him every morning the money he might win that day, but on condition that he does not gamble, and you will make him unhappy. It might be argued that what he wants is the entertainment of gaming and not the winnings. Make him play then for nothing; his interest will not be fired and he will become bored, so it is not just entertainment he wants. A half-hearted entertainment without excitement will bore him. He must have excitement, he must delude himself into imagining that he would be happy to win what he would not want as a gift if it meant giving up gambling. He must create some target for his passions and then arouse his desire, anger, fear, for this object he has created, just like children taking fright at a face they have daubed themselves.
Pensées, trans. A. J. Krailsheimer, No. 136, p. 70

JOHN PASSMORE (*b.* 1914)

The concept of imaginativeness has been greatly damaged by those who 1 confuse it with mere fancy. They have supposed that in order to be imaginative one must break not only with routines but with the restraints imposed by the very character of an enterprise and its relationship to the social and political world surrounding it. They have condemned application, conscientiousness, carefulness, as obstacles to imaginative-

ness whereas in fact they are characteristics of which the imaginative person has particular need if he is not to collapse into fantasy.
Philosophy of Teaching, p. 158

2 Social scientists can no more predict everything that many people would like them to predict than a physicist can predict, for all his theoretical advantages, when and where a feather will land when it drops from the Sydney Harbour Bridge.
'Predictability: Some Closing Observations', *Limits to Prediction*, ed. R. Kern and G. Lowenthal, p. 163

CHRISTOPHER PEACOCKE (*b.* 1950)

Nothing is more fundamental to understanding the content of psychological states than sense experience. . . . My claim [is] that concepts of sensation are indispensable to the description of the nature of any experience. This claim stands in opposition to the view that, while sensations may occur when a subject is asked to concentrate in a particular way on his own experience, or may occur as by-products of perception, they are not to be found in the mainstream of normal human experience, and certainly not in visual experience.
Sense and Content: Experience, Thought and their Relations, p. 4

C. S. PEIRCE (1839–1914)

1 Consider what effect, which might conceivably have practical bearing, we conceive the object of our conception to have. Then our conception of those effects is the whole of our conception of the object.
Collected Papers, 5, §402

2 If you look into a textbook of chemistry for a definition of *lithium*, you may be told that it is that element whose atomic weight is 7 very nearly. But if the author has a more logical mind he will tell you that if you search among minerals that are vitreous, translucent, grey or white, very hard, brittle, and insoluble, for one which imparts a crimson tinge to an unluminous flame, this mineral being triturated with lime or witherite rats-bane, and then fused, can be partly dissolved in muriatic acid; and if this solution be evaporated, and the residue be extracted with sulphuric acid, and duly purified, it can be converted by ordinary methods into a chloride, which being obtained in the solid state, fused, and electrolyzed with half a dozen powerful cells, will yield a globule of a pinkish silvery metal that will float on gasolene; and the material of *that* is a specimen of lithium. The peculiarity of this definition – or rather this precept that is more serviceable than a definition – is that it tells you what the word

lithium denotes by prescribing what you are to *do* in order to gain a perceptual acquaintance with the object of the word.
Collected Papers, 2, §330

It is . . . easy to be certain. One has only to be sufficiently vague. 3
Collected Papers, 4, §237

The opinion which is fated to be ultimately agreed to by all who 4
investigate is what we mean by truth and the object represented by this
opinion is the real.
Collected Papers, 5, §407

And what do we mean by the real? It is a conception which we must first 5
have had when we discovered that there was an unreal, an illusion; that
is, when we first corrected ourselves. Now the distinction for which alone
this fact logically called, was between an *ens* relative to private inward
idiosyncrasy, and an *ens* such as would stand in the long run. The real,
then, is that which, sooner or later, information and reasoning would
finally result in, and which is therefore independent of the vagaries of you
and me. Thus, the very origin of the conception of reality shows that this
conception involves the notion of an unlimited COMMUNITY, without
definite limits and capable of a definite increase of knowledge.
Collected Papers, 5, §311

There are Real things, whose characters are entirely independent of our 6
opinions about them; those realities affect our sense according to regular
laws, and, though our sensations are as different as our relations to the
objects, yet, by taking advantage of the laws of perception, we can
ascertain by reasoning how things really are; and any man, if he have
sufficient experience and reason enough about it, will be led to the one
true conclusion.
Collected Papers, 5, §384

. . . to call an argument illogical, or a proposition false, is a special kind of 7
moral judgement.
Collected Papers, 8, §191

Truth, the conditions of which the logician endeavours to analyze, and 8
which is the goal of the reasoner's aspirations, is nothing but a phase of
the *summum bonum* which forms the subject of pure Ethics.
Collected Papers, 1, §576

. . . it seems to me that while in esthetic enjoyment we attend to the 9
totality of Feeling – and especially to the total resultant Quality of
Feeling presented in the work of art we are contemplating – yet it is a sort

of intellectual sympathy, a sense that here is a Feeling that one can comprehend, a reasonable feeling.
Collected Papers, 5, §113

10 The most logical way of reasoning is the method which while reaching some conclusion will the most ensure us against surprise, or, if you please, the method which while leading us as seldom as possible into surprise, produces the maximum of expectation, or again, which leads us by the shortest cut to the maximum of expectation and the minimum of surprise.
Reason's Conscience, Annotated Catalogue, ed. R. Robin, No. 693

11 Nothing is *vital* for science; nothing can be. Its accepted propositions, therefore, are but opinions at most; and the whole list is provisional. The scientific man is not in the least wedded to his conclusions. He risks nothing upon them. He stands ready to abandon one or all as soon as experience opposes them.
Collected Papers, 1, §635

12 I look at a black stove. There is a direct sensation of blackness. But if I judge the stove to be black, I am comparing this experience with previous experiences. I am comparing the sensation with a familiar idea derived from familiar black objects. When I say to myself that the stove *is* black, I am making a little theory to account for the look of it.
Reason's Conscience, No. 403

13 I define a Sign as anything which is so determined by something else, called its Object, and so determines an effect upon a person, which effect I call its interpretant, that the latter is thereby mediately determined by the former.
Semiotic and Significs, ed. C. Hardwick, p. 81

14 One and the same proposition may be affirmed, denied, judged, doubted, inwardly inquired into, put as a question, wished, asked for, effectively commanded, taught, or merely expressed and does not thereby become a different proposition.
The New Elements of Mathematics, ed. C. Eisle, IV, p. 248

15 The capital error of Hegel which permeates his whole system in every part of it is that he almost altogether ignores the Outward Clash. . . . this direct consciousness of hitting and getting hit enters into all cognition and serves to make it mean something real.
Collected Papers, 8, §41

16 . . . abductive inference shades into perceptual judgment without any sharp line of demarcation between them; or, in other words, our first

premisses, the perceptual judgments, are to be regarded as an extreme case of abductive inferences, from which they differ in being absolutely beyond criticism. The abductive suggestion comes to us in a flash. It is an act of *insight*, although of extremely fallible insight. It is true that the different elements of the hypothesis were in our minds before; but it is the idea of putting together what we had never before dreamed of putting together which flashes the new suggestion before our contemplation.
Collected Papers, 5, §181

Science presupposes that we have a capacity for 'guessing' right. We shall   17
do better to abandon the whole attempt to learn the truth however urgent may be our need of ascertaining it, unless we can trust to the human mind's having such a power of guessing right that before very many hypotheses shall have been tried, intelligent guessing may be expected to lead us to the one which will support all tests, leaving the vast majority of possible hypotheses unexamined.
Collected Papers, 6, §530

. . . the word ['pragmatism'] begins to be met with occasionally in the   18
literary journals, where it gets abused in the merciless way that words have to expect when they fall into literary clutches. . . . So then, the writer, finding his bantling 'pragmatism' so promoted, feels that it is time to kiss his child good-bye and relinquish it to its higher destiny; while to serve the precise purpose of expressing the original definition, he begs to announce the birth of the word 'pragmaticism', which is ugly enough to be safe from kidnappers.
Collected Papers, 5, §414

PELAGIUS (*c.*360–*c.*431)

No one knows the extent of our powers better than He who gave us those powers. . . . And He who is righteous has not will to command anything impossible; neither would He who is holy condemn a man for what he cannot help.
Epistle to Demetriades, Patrologia Latina, 33, col. 1110

D. Z. PHILLIPS (*b.* 1934)

Medical treatment has failed and a child is dying. Religious parents pray,   1
'O God, let her live'. What does this amount to? The parents . . . seek something to sustain them which does not depend on the way things go, namely, the love of God. If the child recovers, the recovery *occasions* the prayer of thanksgiving. If one thinks in terms of causing God to save the child, one is nearer the example of non-religious parents who pray 'O God, save our child' where the thought behind the prayer is that God

could save the child if He wanted to. The prayer is an attempt at influencing the divine will. In short, one is back in the realm of superstition. It is true that love of God's will can be found in whatever happens, but the prayer of petition is best understood, not as an attempt at influencing the way things go, but as an expression of, and a request for, devotion to God through the way things go.

The Concept of Prayer, p. 120

2 Hick claims that 'for me, the "existence of God" consists in man's use – his spontaneous and committed use – of theistic language'. These words are puzzling. Clearly a man's commitment to God shows itself in the language he uses, not only about God, but about the world and his general behaviour. That he is able to have such a commitment depends on there being a shared language and shared practices in which he can partake. But if Hick is saying that for me commitment to God *means* commitment to language, the results would obviously be absurd. I do not think 'I believe in the language almighty' would strike a responsive chord in many and I certainly would not recognize it as an account of religious belief.

'Postscript', *Reason and Religion*, ed. S. Brown, p. 134

D. Z. PHILLIPS (*b.* 1934) and H. O. MOUNCE (*b.* 1939)

1 One's condemnation of a particular lie occurs within a way of life in which it is taken for granted that a lie is something to be condemned. The agreement in the way of life forms the background against which the particular judgement has its sense. Without such an agreement it would be impossible, not only to agree with a particular moral opinion, but also to disagree with it. Disagreement in morals, as in everything else, can occur only among people who, sharing a way of life, hold certain things in common which they do not consider to be in dispute.

Moral Practices, p. 70

2 The error of relativism, as it is traditionally conceived, may be stated in general terms by saying that relativists treat moral judgements as if they were statements about certain of the conditions on which they depend for their sense. Protagoras, having supposed correctly that moral judgements depend on some kind of agreement in judgement, goes on to assume that moral judgements are statements about that agreement. He assumes that to call something morally right is merely to say that this is what the majority agree to call right, whereas, in fact, an agreement in judgement, though a necessary condition for making a particular moral judgement, is not what the particular judgement itself refers to.

Moral Practices, p. 71

PHILOLAUS (*fl.* 5th century BC)

And all things that can be known contain number; without this nothing could be thought or known.

G. S. Kirk, J. E. Raven and M. Schofield, *The Pre-Socratic Philosophers*, p. 326

MAX PLANCK (1858–1947)

. . . a new scientific truth does not triumph by convincing its opponents and making them see the light, but rather because its opponents eventually die, and a new generation grows up that is familiar with it.

Scientific Autobiography, trans. F. Gaynor, p. 33

ALVIN PLANTINGA (*b.* 1932)

And the interesting fact here is this: it is possible that every creaturely essence – every essence including the property of being created by God – suffers from transworld depravity. But now suppose this is true. Now God can create a world containing moral good only by creating significantly free persons. And, since every person is the instantiation of an essence, He can create significantly free persons only by instantiating some essences. But if every essence suffers from transworld depravity, then no matter which essences God instantiates, the resulting persons, if free with respect to morally significant actions, would always perform at least some wrong actions. If every essence suffers from transworld depravity, then it was beyond the power of God Himself to create a world containing moral good but no moral evil.

God, Freedom and Evil, p. 53

PLATO (*c.*428 BC–347 BC)

Philosophy begins in wonder.   1
Theaetetus, 155D

SOCRATES: The ideal society we have described can never grow into a   2
reality or see the light of day, and there will be no end to the troubles of states, or indeed of humanity itself, till philosophers become kings in this world, or till those we now call kings and rulers really and truly become philosophers.
The Republic, trans. H. D. P. Lee, 473C10

SOCRATES: Unless Polus can show Socrates that he was wrong and prove   3
that orators and dictators do what they really will, how can they be said to enjoy great power in a state?
POLUS: This fellow –
SOC.: Says that they don't do what they really will. Prove me wrong.

POL.: Didn't you admit just now that they do what seems best to them?
SOC.: Certainly; I don't retract it.
POL.: Then don't they do what they will?
SOC.: No.
POL.: Although they do what they please?
SOC.: Yes.
POL.: What you say is monstrous and outrageous, Socrates.
Gorgias, trans. Walter Hamilton, 467

4 SOCRATES: We agree that what is holy is loved by the gods because it is holy, and not holy because it is loved by the gods.
Euthyphro, 10D

5 'Do you think . . . that a man would be living well who passed his life in pain and vexation?'
'No.'
'But if he lived it out to the end with enjoyment, you would count him as having lived well?'
'Yes.'
'Then to live pleasurably is good, to live painfully bad?'
'Yes, if one's pleasure is in what is honourable.'
'What's this, Protagoras? Surely you don't follow the common opinion that some pleasures are bad and some pains good? I mean to say, in so far as they are pleasant, are they not also good, leaving aside any consequence that they may entail? And in the same way pains, in so far as they are painful, are bad.'
Protagoras, trans. W. K. C. Guthrie, 351B

6 The absurdity of this will become evident if we stop using all these names together – pleasant, painful, good and evil – and since they have turned out to be only two, call them by only two names – first of all good and evil, and only at a different stage pleasure and pain. Having agreed on this, suppose we now say that a man does evil though he recognizes it as evil. Why? Because he is overcome. By what? We can no longer say 'by pleasure', because it has changed its name to good. 'Overcome' we say. 'By what?' we are asked. 'By the good', I suppose we shall say. I fear that if our questioner is ill-mannered, he will laugh and retort: 'What ridiculous nonsense, for a man to do evil, knowing it is evil and that he ought not to do it, because he is overcome by good. Am I to suppose that the good in you is or is not a match for the evil?' Clearly we shall reply that the good is not a match; otherwise the man whom we speak of as being overcome by pleasure would not have done wrong. 'And in what way' he may say, 'does good fail to be a match for evil, or evil for good? Is it not by being greater or smaller, more or less than the other?' . . .

Having noted this result, suppose we reinstate the names pleasant and painful for the same phenomena . . . So, like an expert in weighing, put the pleasures together and the pains together, set both the near and distant in the balance, and say which is the greater quantity. In weighing pleasures against pleasures, one must always choose the greater and the more; in weighing pains against pains, the smaller and the less: whereas in weighing pleasures against pains, if the pleasures exceed the pains, whether the distant, the near or vice versa, one must take the course which brings those pleasures; but if the pains outweigh the pleasures, avoid it.

Protagoras, 355B

SOCRATES: To prefer evil to good is not in human nature; and when a   7
man is compelled to choose one of two evils, no one will choose the
greater when he may have the less.

Protagoras, 358C

SOCRATES: It appears to me that the conjunction of memory with   8
sensations, together with the feelings attendant upon them, may be said
almost to write words in our souls; and when the inscribing feeling writes
what is true, then true opinion and true propositions spring up in us;
while when the scribe within us writes what is false, the result is false.
PROTARCHUS: That certainly seems to me right, and I approve of the way
you put it.
SOC.: Then please give your approval to another artist, who is busy at the
same time in the chambers of the soul. . . . The painter, who, after the
scribe has done his work, draws images in the soul of the things he has
described.
PROT.: How do we make out that he in his turn acts, and when?
SOC.: When we have got those opinions or assertions clear of the act of
sight, or other sense, and as it were see in ourselves images of what we
previously opined or asserted; – is not this a common mental
phenomenon? . . . Now may we say that what is written in the minds of
the good is as a rule a true communication, since they are dear to the
gods, while with the evil the opposite is generally the case?
PROT.: Certainly. . . .
SOC.: The bad, then, delight for the most part in false pleasures, the good
in true ones.

Philebus trans. B. Jowett, 39A, amended

SOCRATES: The reason why pleasures appear greater and more intense   9
when compared with something painful, or pains appear so by being
compared with pleasures, is found in the pleasures and pains *per se*,
according as we pass from a distant to a close observation of them. . . .

And suppose you part off from pleasures and pains the element which makes them appear to be greater or less than they really are: you will acknowledge the subtracted portion to be an illusion, and refrain from saying that such pleasure or pain as is felt in respect of it is real or true.
Philebus, trans. B. Jowett, 42A–C, amended

10 As I said at the beginning of this tale, I divided each soul into three – two horses and a charioteer; and one of the horses was good and the other bad . . . The right-hand horse is upright and cleanly made; he has a lofty neck and an aquiline nose; his colour is white, and his eyes dark; he is a lover of honour and modesty and temperance, and the follower of true glory; he needs no touch of the whip, but is guided by word and admonition only. The other is a crooked lumbering animal, put together anyhow; he has a short thick neck; he is flat-faced and of a dark colour, with grey eyes and blood-red complexion; the mate of insolence and pride, shag-eared and deaf, hardly yielding to whip and spur.
Phaedrus, 253C

11 We shall conclude that a man is just in the same way that a state is just. And we have surely not forgotten that justice in the state meant that each of the three elements within it [businessmen, auxiliaries and governors] was doing the work of its own class. . . . Then we must remember that each of us will be just, and do his duty, only if each part of him is performing its proper function. . . . So it will be the business of reason to rule, having the ability and foresight to act for the whole, while the spirited principle ought to act as its subordinate and ally. . . . When these two elements have been nurtured and trained to know their own true functions, they must be set in command over appetite, which forms the greater part of each man's soul and is by nature insatiable. They must keep watch in case this part, by battening on bodily pleasures, grows so large and powerful that it no longer keeps to its own work, but tries to enslave the others and unrightfully usurp dominion, thus overturning the whole life of man.
The Republic, 441C

12 'So whenever soul takes possession of a body, it always brings life with it?'
'Yes, it does.'
'Is there an opposite to life, or not?'
'Yes, there is.'
'What?'
'Death.'
'Does it follow, then, from our earlier agreement, that soul will never admit the opposite of that which accompanies it?'

'Most definitely,' said Cebes. . . .
'Very good. And what do we call that which does not admit death?'
'Immortal.'
'And soul does not admit death?'
'No.'
'So soul is immortal.'
'Yes, it is immortal.'
'Well', said Socrates, 'can we say that that has been proved? What do you think?'
'Most completely, Socrates.'
Phaedo, trans. Hugh Tredennick, 105D

'You know', I continued, 'our ideal state has many excellent features, 13 especially our rule not on any account to admit the poetry of dramatic representation. Now that we have distinguished the various elements in the soul, we can see even more clearly how essential it is to exclude it. . . . Such poetry seems to be injurious to minds which do not possess the antidote in a knowledge of its real nature. . . . It is at the third remove from reality, nothing more than semblances, easy to produce with no knowledge of the truth.'
The Republic, 595A

When I do not know what something essentially is, how can I know what 14 its properties are? How, if I knew nothing at all of Meno, could I tell if he was fair or the opposite of fair; rich and noble, or the reverse of rich and noble?
Meno, trans. W. K. C. Guthrie, 71B1

SOCRATES: And so of the virtues, however many and different they may 15 be, they have all a common nature which makes them virtues; and on this he who would answer the question 'What is virtue?' would do well to have his eye fixed; do you understand?
Meno, 72C5

SOCRATES: The result of our discussion appears to me to be singular. For 16 if the argument had a human voice, that voice would be heard laughing at us and saying: 'Protagoras and Socrates, you are strange beings; there are you, Socrates, who were saying that virtue cannot be taught, contradicting yourself now by your attempt to prove that all things are knowledge, including justice, and temperance, and courage, – which tends to show that virtue can certainly be taught. . . .'
Protagoras, 361AB

SOCRATES: And this is the line which the learned call the diagonal. And if 17 this is the proper name, then you, Meno's slave, are prepared to affirm that the double space is the square of the diagonal?

BOY: Certainly, Socrates.

SOC.: What do you say of him, Meno? Were not all these answers given out of his own head?

MENO: Yes, they were all his own.

SOC.: And yet, as we were just now saying, he did not know?

MENO: True.

SOC.: But still he had in him those notions of his – had he not?

MENO: Yes.

SOC.: Then he who does not know may still have true notions of that which he does not know?

MENO: He has.

SOC.: And at present these notions have just been stirred up in him, as in a dream; but if he were frequently asked the same questions, in different forms, he would know as well as anyone at last?

Meno, 85C

18   MENO: And I am certain that no one ever did teach him.

SOCRATES: And yet he has the knowledge?

MENO: The fact, Socrates, is undeniable.

SOC.: But if he did not acquire the knowledge in this life, then he must have had and learned it at some other time?

MENO: Clearly he must.

SOC.: Which must have been the time when he was not a man?

MENO: Yes.

SOC.: And if there have been always true thoughts in him, both at the time when he was and was not a man, which only need to be awakened into knowledge by putting questions to him, his soul must have always possessed this knowledge, for he always either was or was not a man?

MENO: Obviously.

SOC.: And if the truth of all things always existed in the soul, then the soul is immortal.

Meno, 86A

19   SOCRATES: If I can assign names as well as pictures to objects, the right assignment of them we may call truth, and the wrong assignment of them falsehood. Now if there be such a wrong assignment of names, there may also be a wrong or inappropriate assignment of verbs; and if of names and verbs then of the sentences, which are made up of them. What do you say, Cratylus?

CRATYLUS: I agree; and think that what you say is very true.

SOC.: And further, primitive nouns may be compared to pictures, and in pictures you may either give all the appropriate colours and figures, or you may not give them all – some may be wanting; or there may be too many or too much of them – may there not?

CRAT.: Very true.

Cratylus, trans. H. N. Fowler, 431BC

SOCRATES: What is the function of names, and what good do they 20 accomplish?

CRATYLUS: I think, Socrates, their function is to instruct, and this is the simple truth, that he who knows the names knows also the things named.

SOC.: I suppose, Cratylus, you mean that when anyone knows the nature of the name – and its nature is that of the thing – he will know the thing also, since it is like the name, and the science of all things which are like each other is one and the same. It is, I fancy, on this ground that you say whoever knows names will know things also. . . . Do you think that he who has discovered the names has discovered also the things named; or do you think inquiry and discovery demand another method, and this belongs to instruction?

CRA.: I most certainly think inquiry and discovery follow this same method and in the same way.

SOC.: Let us consider the matter, Cratylus. Do you not see that he who in his inquiry after things follows names and examines into the meaning of each one runs great risks of being deceived?

CRA.: How so?

SOC.: Clearly he who first gave names, gave such names as agreed with his conception of the nature of things. That is our view, is it not?

CRA.: Yes.

SOC.: Then if his conception was incorrect, and he gave the names according to his conception, what do you suppose will happen to us who follow him? Can we help being deceived?

Cratylus, 435D

I had a dream, and I heard in my dream that the primeval letters or 21 elements out of which you and I and all other things are compounded have no reason or explanation; you can only name them, but no predicate can be either affirmed or denied of them, for in the one case existence in the other non-existence is already implied, neither of which must be added, if you mean to speak of this or that thing by itself alone. . . . None of these primeval elements can be defined; they can only be named, for they have nothing but a name, and the things which are compounded of them, as they are complex, are expressed by a combination of names, for the combination of names is the essence of a definition.

Theaetetus, 201B

22   SOCRATES: When a person at the time of learning writes the name of
Theaetetus, and thinks that he ought to write and does write *Th* and *e*;
but, again, meaning to write the name of Theodorus, thinks that he ought
to write and does write *T* and *e* – can we suppose that he knows the first
syllables of your two names?

THEAETETUS: We have already admitted that such a one has not yet
attained knowledge.

SOC.: And in like manner he may enumerate without knowing them the
second and third and fourth syllables of your name?

THEAET.: He may.

SOC.: And in that case, when he knows the order of the letters and can
write them out correctly, he has right opinion?

THEAET.: Clearly.

SOC.: But although we admit that he has right opinion, he will still be
without knowledge?

THEAET.: Yes.

SOC.: And yet he will have explanation, as well as right opinion, for he
knew the order of the letters when he wrote; and this we admit to be
explanation.

THEAET.: True.

SOC.: Then, my friend, there is such a thing as right opinion united with
definition or explanation, which does not as yet attain to the exactness of
knowledge.

Theaetetus, 207B

23   Next, said I, here is a parable to illustrate the degrees in which our nature
may be enlightened or unenlightened. Imagine the condition of men
living in a sort of cavernous chamber underground, with an entrance
open to the light and a long passage all down the cave. Here they have
been from childhood, chained by the leg and also by the neck, so that
they cannot move and can see only what is in front of them, because the
chains will not let them turn their heads. At some distance higher up is
the light of a fire burning behind them; and between the prisoners and the
fire is a track with a parapet built along it, like the screen at a puppet-
show, which hides the performers while they show their puppets over the
top.

I see, said he.

Now behind this parapet imagine persons carrying along various
artificial objects, including figures of men and animals in wood or stone
or other materials, which project above the parapet. Naturally, some of
these persons will be talking, others silent.

It is a strange picture, he said, and a strange sort of prisoners.

Like ourselves, I replied; for in the first place prisoners so confined

would have seen nothing of themselves or of one another, except the
shadows thrown by the fire-light on the wall of the Cave facing them,
would they?

Not if all their lives they had been prevented from moving their heads.

And they would have seen as little of the objects carried past.

Of course.

Now, if they could talk to one another, would they not suppose that
their words referred only to those passing shadows which they saw?

Necessarily.

And suppose their prison had an echo from the wall facing them?
When one of the people crossing behind them spoke, they could only
suppose that the sound came from the shadow passing before their eyes.

No doubt.

In every way, then, such prisoners would recognize as reality nothing
but the shadows of those artificial objects.

Inevitably.

The Republic, trans. Francis Cornford, 514A

Wherever you turn, there is nothing . . . which is a single thing, in itself;   24
all things are coming into being relatively to something. The verb 'to be'
must be totally abolished – though indeed we have been led by habit and
ignorance into using it ourselves more than once, even in what we have
just been saying.

Theaetetus, 157B

SOCRATES: I seem to have a vision of Heraclitus repeating wise traditions   25
of antiquity as old as the reign of Cronos and Rhea, and of which Homer
also spoke.

HERMOGENES: How do you mean?

SOCRATES: Heraclitus is supposed to say that all things are in flux and
nothing at rest; he compares the universe to the current of a river, saying
that you cannot step into the same stream twice.

Cratylus, 402A

Since, then, these things never, any of them, appear as the same things,   26
which form of them can one maintain to be this, as being whatever it is,
and not something else, without being ashamed of oneself? . . . For they
escape and do not wait to be referred to as 'this' or 'that' . . . or by any
expression that displays them as existent things.

Timaeus, 49B

STRANGER: When you speak of Movement and Rest, these are things   27
completely opposed to one another, aren't they?

THEAETETUS: Of course.

STR.: At the same time you say of both and of each severally, that they are real?

THEAET.: I do.

STR.: And when you admit that they are real, do you mean that either or both are in movement?

THEAET.: Certainly not.

STR.: Then, perhaps, by saying both are real you mean they are both at rest?

THEAET.: No, how could I?

STR.: So, then, you conceive of reality (realness) as a third thing over and above these two; and when you speak of both as being real, you mean that you are taking both movement and rest together as embraced by reality and fixing your attention on their common association with reality?

THEAET.: It does seem as if we discerned reality as a third thing, when we say that movement and rest are real.

STR.: So reality is not motion and rest 'both at once', but something distinct from them.

The Sophist, trans. Francis Cornford, 250

28 THEAETETUS: Whenever we use the expression 'not Beautiful', the thing we mean is precisely that which is different from the nature of the Beautiful. . . .

STRANGER: May we not say that the *existence* of the not-Beautiful is constituted by its being marked off from a single definite Kind among existing things and again set in contrast with something that exists?

THEAET.: Yes.

STR.: So it appears that the not-Beautiful is an instance of something that exists being set in contrast to something that exists.

THEAET.: Perfectly.

STR.: What then? On this showing has the not-Beautiful any less claim than the Beautiful to be a thing that exists?

The Sophist, 257D

29 STRANGER: We have advanced to a further point, and shown him more than he [Parmenides] forbad us to investigate.

THEAETETUS: How is that?

STR.: Why, because he says – 'Not-being never is, and do thou keep thy thoughts from this way of enquiry.'

THEAET.: Yes, he says so.

STR.: Whereas, we have not only proved that things which are not are, but we have shown what form of being not-being is; for we have shown that the nature of the other is, and is distributed over all things which are

related to each other, and whenever one part is contrasted with being something, this is what we have ventured to call not-being.
The Sophist, 258D

Well, is it your wish that we should pursue our usual course in the outset   30
of our investigation? We have, I believe, been in the habit of assuming the existence, in each instance, of some one Form, which includes the numerous particular things to which we apply the same name. Do you understand, or not?
  I do understand.
The Republic, 596AB

I imagine that the way in which you are led to assume one Form of each   31
kind is as follows: – You see a number of great objects, and when you look at them there seems to you to be one and the same Form (or nature) in them all; hence you conceive of greatness as one.
  Very true, said Socrates.
  And if you go on and allow your mind in like manner to embrace in one view the Form of greatness and of great things which are not the Form, and to compare them, will not another greatness arise, which will appear to be the source of all these?
  It would seem so.
  Then another Form of greatness now comes into view over and above absolute greatness, and the individuals which partake of it; and then another, over and above all these, by virtue of which they will all be great, and so each Form instead of being one will be infinitely multiplied.
Parmenides, 131E

PARMENIDES: If a man . . . does away with Forms of things and will not   32
admit that every individual thing has its own determinate Form which is always one and the same, he will have nothing on which his mind can rest; and so he will utterly destroy the power of reasoning, as you seem to me to have particularly noted.
SOCRATES: Very true.
Parmenides, 135A

'Suppose that when you see something you say to yourself "This thing   33
which I can see has a tendency to be like something else, but it falls short and cannot be really like it, only a poor imitation"; don't you agree with me that anyone who receives that impression must in fact have previous knowledge of that thing which he says that the other resembles, but inadequately?'
  'Certainly he must.' . . .
  'Then we must have had some previous knowledge of equality before

353

the time when we first saw equal things and realized that they were striving after equality, but fell short of it.'

'That is so.'

'And at the same time we are agreed also upon this point, that we have not and could not have acquired this notion of equality except by sight or touch or one of the other senses. . . . So before we began to see and hear and use our other senses we must somewhere have acquired the knowledge that there is such a thing as absolute equality . . . So we must have obtained it before birth.'

'So it seems.'

'Then if we obtained it before our birth, and possessed it when we were born, we had knowledge, both before and at the moment of birth, not only of equality and relative magnitudes, but of . . . absolute beauty, goodness, uprightness, holiness, and, as I maintain, all those characteristics which we designate in our discussions by the term "absolute".'

Phaedo, 73D

34 If this is true, then, we must conclude that education is not what it is said to be by some, who profess to put into a soul knowledge that was not there before – rather as if they could put sight into blind eyes. On the contrary, our argument indicates that this is a capacity which is innate in each man's soul, and that the faculty by which he learns is like an eye which cannot be turned from darkness to light unless the whole body is turned; in the same way the entire soul must be turned away from this world of change until its eye can bear to look straight at reality, and at the brightest of all realities which we have called the Good.

The Republic, 518B

35 The true lover of knowledge naturally strives for truth, and is not content with common opinion, but soars with undimmed and unwearied passion till he grasps the essential nature of things.

The Republic, 490A

36 DIOTIMA: The true order of going, or being led, to the things of love is to begin with the beautiful things on earth and to mount upwards for the sake of the other beauty, using these as steps only, and from one going on to two, and from two to all beautiful bodies, and from beautiful bodies to beautiful practices, and then to beautiful thoughts until he comes to understand absolute beauty, and know what the essence of beauty is.

Symposium, 211BC

37 But those who are capable of reaching to the independent contemplation of abstract beauty will be rare exceptions, will they not?

They will indeed.

Therefore if a man recognizes the existence of beautiful things, but disbelieves in abstract beauty, and has not the power to follow should another lead the way to the knowledge of it, is his life, think you, a dreaming or a waking one? Just consider. Is it not dreaming when a person, whether asleep or awake, mistakes the likeness of anything for the real thing of which it is a likeness?

I confess I should say that a person in that predicament was dreaming.
The Republic, 476CD

PLOTINUS (c.205–270)

Those divinely possessed and inspired have at least the knowledge that   1
they hold some greater thing within them, though they cannot tell what it is; from the movements that stir them and the utterances that come from them they perceive the power, not themselves, that moves them: in the same way, it must be, we stand towards the Supreme when we hold *nous* pure; we know the Divine Mind within, that which gives Being and all else of that order: but we know, too, that other, know that it is none of these, but a nobler principle than anything we know as Being; fuller and greater; above reason, mind, and feeling; conferring these powers, not to be confounded with them.
Enneads, V, 3.14, trans. W. K. C. Guthrie

Many times it has happened: Lifted out of the body into myself;   2
becoming external to all other things and self-encentred; beholding a marvellous beauty; then, more than ever, assured of community with the loftiest order; enacting the noblest life, acquiring identity with the divine; stationing within It by having attained that activity; poised above whatsoever in the Intellectual is less than the Supreme: yet, there comes the moment of descent from intellection to reasoning, and after that sojourn in the divine, I ask myself how it happens that I can now be descending, and how did the Soul ever enter into my body, the Soul which even within the body, is the high thing it has shown itself to be.
Enneads, IV, 8.1, trans. W. K. C. Guthrie

HENRI POINCARÉ (1854–1912)

Logic, which alone can give certainty, is the instrument of demon-   1
stration; intuition is the instrument of invention.
The Value of Science, trans. G. B. Halsted, p. 23

Experiment is the sole source of truth.   2
Science and Hypothesis, p. 140

And yet – strange contradictions for those who believe in time – geologic   3
history shows us that life is only a short episode between two eternities of

death, and that, even in this episode, conscious thought has lasted and will last only a moment. Thought is only a gleam in the midst of a long night. But it is this gleam which is everything.
The Value of Science, trans. G. B. Halsted, p. 142

4   It is often said that experiments should be made without preconceived ideas. That is impossible.
Science and Hypothesis, p. 143

5   The very possibility of mathematical science seems an insoluble contradiction. If this science is only deductive in appearance, from whence is derived that perfect rigour which is challenged by none? If, on the contrary, all the propositions which it enunciates may be derived in order by the rules of formal logic, how is it that mathematics is not reduced to a gigantic tautology?
Science and Hypothesis, p. 1

KARL POPPER (*b.* 1902)

1   The history of science, like the history of all human ideas, is a history of irresponsible dreams, of obstinacy, and of error. But science is one of the very few human activities – perhaps the only one – in which errors are systematically criticized and fairly often, in time, corrected. This is why we can say that, in science, we often learn from our mistakes, and why we can speak clearly and sensibly about making progress there.
Conjectures and Refutations, p. 216

2   There is reality behind the world as it appears to us, possibly a many-layered reality, of which the appearances are the outermost layers. What the great scientist does is boldly to guess, daringly to conjecture, what these inner realities are like. This is akin to myth making. . . . The boldness can be gauged by the distance between the world of appearance and the conjectured reality, the explanatory hypotheses.
'Replies to my Critics', *The Philosophy of Karl Popper*, ed. P. A. Schilpp, p. 980

3   But there is another, a special kind of boldness – *the boldness of predicting* aspects of the world of appearance which so far have been overlooked but which it must possess if the conjectured reality is (more or less) right, if the explanatory hypotheses are (approximately) true. It is this more specific kind of boldness which I have usually in mind when I speak of bold scientific conjectures. It is the boldness of a conjecture which takes real risk – the risk of being tested, and refuted; the risk of clashing with reality.

   Thus my proposal was, and is, that it is this second boldness, together with the readiness to look out for tests and refutations, which

distinguishes 'empirical' science from non-science, and especially from pre-scientific myths and metaphysics.
'Replies to my Critics', p. 980

In so far as a scientific statement speaks about reality, it must be falsifiable: 4
and in so far as it is not falsifiable, it does not speak about reality.
The Logic of Scientific Discovery, p. 314

We can never make absolutely certain that our theory is not lost. All we 5
can do is to search for the falsity content of our best theory. We do so by
trying to refute our theory; that is, by trying to test it severely in the light of
all our objective knowledge and all our ingenuity. It is, of course, always
possible that the theory may be false even if it passes all these tests; this is
allowed for by our search for verisimilitude. *But if it passes all these tests
then we may have good reason to conjecture that our theory, which as we
know has a greater truth content than its predecessor, may have no greater
falsity content.* And if we fail to refute the new theory, especially in fields in
which its predecessor has been refuted, then we can claim this as one of the
objective reasons for *the conjecture that the new theory is a better
approximation to truth than the old theory.*
Objective Knowledge, p. 81

In other words, the logical problem of induction arises from (*a*) Hume's 6
discovery (so well expressed by Born) that it is impossible to justify a law
by observation or experiment, since it 'transcends experience'; (*b*) the fact
that science proposes and uses laws 'everywhere and all the time'. (Like
Hume, Born is struck by the 'scanty material', i.e. the few observed
instances upon which the law may be based.) To this we have to add (*c*) *the
principle of empiricism* which asserts that in science, only observation and
experiment may decide upon the *acceptance or rejection* of scientific
statements, including laws and theories. . . . in fact the principles (*a*) to (*c*)
do not clash. We can see this the moment we realize that the acceptance by
science of a law or of a theory is *tentative only*; which is to say that all laws
and theories are conjectures, or tentative *hypotheses* (a position which I
have sometimes called 'hypotheticism'); and that we may reject a law or
theory on the basis of new evidence, without necessarily discarding the old
evidence which originally led us to accept it. . . .
Thus the problem of induction is solved.
Conjectures and Refutations, p. 54

H. H. PRICE (1899–1984)

Where we consider the world around us, we cannot help noticing that
there is a great deal of recurrence or repetition in it. The same colour recurs
over and over again in ever so many things. Shapes repeat themselves

likewise. Over and over again we notice oblong-shaped things, hollow things, bulgy things. Hoots, thuds, bangs, rustlings occur again and again.
Thinking and Experience, p. 7

H. A. PRICHARD (1871–1947)

1 Suppose we ask ourselves whether our sense that we ought to pay our debts or to tell the truth arises from our recognition that in doing so we should be originating something good, e.g. material comfort in A or true belief in B, i.e. suppose we ask ourselves whether it is this aspect of the action which leads to our recognition that we ought to do it. We at once and without hesitation answer 'no'.
Moral Obligation, p. 4

2 This apprehension is immediate, in precisely the same sense in which a mathematical apprehension is immediate, e.g. the apprehension that this three-sided figure, in virtue of its being three-sided, must have three angles. Both apprehensions are immediate in the sense that, in both, insight into the nature of the subject directly leads us to recognize its possession of the predicate; and it is only stating this fact from the other side to say that in both cases the fact apprehended is self-evident.
Moral Obligation, p. 8

3 Suppose we come genuinely to doubt whether we ought to pay our debts, owing to a genuine doubt whether our previous conviction that we ought to do so is true, a doubt which can, in fact, only arise if we fail to remember the real nature of what we now call our past conviction. The only remedy lies in actually getting into a situation which occasions the obligation, or if our imagination be strong enough in imagining ourselves in that situation, and then letting our moral capacities of thinking do their work.
Moral Obligation, p. 16

4 In no case whatever, where we think of ourselves as having brought about something directly, do we think that our activity was that of bringing about that something. On the contrary we think of the activity as having been of another sort, and mean by saying that we brought about directly what we did, that this activity of another sort had the change in question as a direct effect.
'Duty and Ignorance of Fact', British Academy lecture, 1932

PROTAGORAS (c.485 BC–c.420 BC)

1 Man is the measure of all things.
Quoted in E. Hussey, *The Pre-Socratics*, p. 109

Concerning the gods I have no means of knowing either that they exist or   2
that they do not exist nor what sort of form they have. There are many
reasons why knowledge on this subject is impossible, owing to lack of
knowledge and shortness of human life.
Quoted in E. Hussey, *The Pre-Socratics*, p. 109

PIERRE-JOSEPH PROUDHON (1809–1865)

If I had to answer the question 'What is slavery?' and if I were to answer in   1
one word, 'Murder', I would immediately be understood. I would not need
to use a lengthy argument to demonstrate that the power to deprive a man
of his thoughts, his will and his personality is a power of life and death, and
that to enslave a man is to murder him. Why then, to the question 'What is
property?' may I not likewise reply 'theft', without knowing that I am
certain to be misunderstood, even though the second proposition is simply
a transformation of the first?
What is Property?, *Selected Writings*, ed. S. Edwards, p. 124

Thus it is clear that property in itself owes allegiance to no particular form   2
of government, and is bound by no dynastic or legal ties. Its politics may be
summed up in a single word: exploitation, or even anarchy. It is the most
formidable enemy and most treacherous ally of any form of power. In
short, in its relation to the State it is governed by only one principle, one
sentiment, one concern: self-interest, or egoism. . . .

   This is why all governments, all utopias and all Churches distrust
property, not to mention Lycurgus and Plato, who banned property – like
poetry – from their republics, or the Caesars, popular leaders who
conquered only to obtain property, and attacked the civil rights of citizens
as soon as they had become dictators. . . .

   In the light of all these facts we can conclude that property is the greatest
existing revolutionary force, with an unequaled capacity for setting itself
against authority. . . .
The Theory of Property, *Selected Writings*, p. 134

If one force is to compel respect from another force, each must be   3
independent of the other. They must be two distinct forces, not one. If,
therefore, the citizen is to count for anything in the State, personal
freedom is not enough. His individuality, like that of the State, must be
founded on something material over which he must have sovereign
possession, just as the State has sovereign possession over public
property. Private property provides this foundation.
The Theory of Property, p. 135

In my *System of Economic Contradictions*, I reiterated and confirmed my   4
first definition of property and then added another, quite contrary one

based on considerations of quite a different kind. But this neither destroyed nor was destroyed by my first argument. This new definition was: property is liberty. Property is theft; property is liberty: these two propositions stand side by side in my *System of Economic Contradictions* and each is shown to be true.

The Theory of Property, p. 140

HILARY PUTNAM (*b.* 1926)

1 For the purpose of the following science-fiction examples, we shall suppose that somewhere in the galaxy there is a planet we shall call Twin Earth. Twin Earth is very much like Earth; in fact, people on Twin Earth even speak *English*. In fact, apart from the differences we shall specify in our science-fiction examples, the reader may suppose that Twin Earth is *exactly* like Earth. He may even suppose that he has a *Doppelgänger* – an identical copy – on Twin Earth, if he wishes, although my stories will not depend on this. . . .

We will now suppose that molybdenum is as common on Twin Earth as aluminum is on Earth, and that aluminum is as rare on Twin Earth as molybdenum is on Earth. In particular, we shall assume that 'aluminum' pots and pans are made of molybdenum on Twin Earth. Finally, we shall assume that the words 'aluminum' and 'molybdenum' are *switched* on Twin Earth: 'aluminum' is the name of *molybdenum* and 'molybdenum' is the name of *aluminum*. . . .

If $Oscar_1$ and $Oscar_2$ are standard speakers of Earthian English and Twin Earthian English respectively, and neither is chemically or metallurgically sophisticated, then there may be no difference at all in their psychological state when they use the word 'aluminum'; nevertheless we have to say that 'aluminum' has the extension *aluminum* in the idiolect of $Oscar_1$ and the extension *molybdenum* in the idiolect of $Oscar_2$. . . .

Cut the pie any way you like, 'meanings' just ain't in the *head*!

'The Meaning of "Meaning"', *Mind, Language and Reality*, p. 223

2 According to functionalism, the behaviour of, say, a computing machine is not explained by the physics and chemistry of the computing machine. It is explained by the machine's *program*. Of course, that program is realized in a particular physics and chemistry, and could, perhaps, be deduced from that physics and chemistry. But that does not make the program a physical or chemical property of the machine; it is an abstract property of the machine. Similarly, I believe that the psychological properties of human beings are not physical and chemical properties of

human beings, although they may be realized by physical and chemical properties of human beings.
'Philosophy of Language and the Rest of Philosophy', *Mind, Language and Reality*, p. xiii

I have reviewed a succession of failures: failures to show that we *must* say   3
that robots are conscious, failures to show that we *must* say they are not, failures to show that we *must* say that we can't tell. I have concluded from these failures that there is no correct answer to the question: is Oscar conscious? Robots may indeed have (or lack) properties unknown to physics and undetectable by us; but not the slightest reason has been offered to show that they do, as the ROBOT analogy demonstrates. It is reasonable, then, to conclude that the question that titles this paper calls for a decision and not for a discovery. If we are to make a decision, it seems preferable to me to extend our concept so that robots *are* conscious.
'Robots', *Mind, Language and Reality*, p. 407

The Greek dramatists, Freudian psychology, and the Russian novel are   4
all supposed by these thinkers to embody *knowledge – knowledge about man*. Thus they both do and do not conflict with science. They conflict with science in the sense of representing a rival kind of knowledge, and thereby contest the claim of science to monopolize reliable knowledge. But it is a rival *kind* of knowledge, and hence inaccessible to scientific testing. If we add the claim that this rival kind of knowledge is somehow 'higher' or more important than scientific knowledge, we have a full-blown obscurantist position – not the position of the serious student or critic of literature, to be sure, but the position of the religion of literature.
Meaning and the Moral Sciences, p. 89

In the late 1920s, about 1928, the Vienna Circle announced the first of   5
what were to be a series of formulations of an empiricist meaning criterion: *the meaning of a sentence is its method of verification*. A. J. Ayer's *Language, Truth and Logic* spread the new message to the English-speaking philosophical world: *untestable statements are cognitively meaningless*. A statement must either be (*a*) analytic (logically true, or logically false to be more precise) or (*b*) empirically testable, or (*c*) *nonsense*, i.e., not a real statement at all, but only a pseudo-statement. Notice that this was already a change from the first formulation.

An obvious rejoinder was to say that the logical positivist criterion of significance was *self-refuting*: for the criterion itself is neither (*a*) analytic (unless, perhaps, it is analytically *false*!), nor (*b*) empirically testable. Strangely enough this criticism had very little impact on the logical positivists and did little to impede the growth of their movement. I want to suggest that the neglect of this particular philosophical gambit was a great mistake; that the gambit is not only correct, but contains a deep lesson. . . .

'Logical Positivism is Self-Refuting', *Realism and Reason*, p. 184

6   . . . the propositional attitudes (and especially belief and desire) are [considered] part of a body of superstition called 'folk psychology' (by Stephen Stich and by Paul and Patricia Churchland, for example). . . . Their whole argument turns on the following inference: if the instances of X do not have something in common which is *scientifically* describable (where the paradigm science is neurobiology in the case of the Churchlands, and computer science in the case of Stich), then X is a 'mythological' entity. There is, however, no attempt to apply this attitude *consistently*. For example: suppose these philosophers are right, and there are no such things as *desires* or *purposes*. What makes various things all members of the class Chair is that they are portable *seats for one person* (with a back). Being a *seat for one person* is just being *manufactured for the purpose of being sat upon by one person at a time*. If there are no 'purposes', then it is 'mythology' that all chairs have something in common. So not only are there no such things as beliefs, if this view is right; there are no such things as chairs!

Representation and Reality, p. 58

7   The incoherence of the attempts to turn the world views of either physics or history into secular theologies have not yet been entirely exposed, but the process is, I hope, well under way. As philosophers, we seem caught between our desire for integration and our recognition of the difficulty. I don't know what the solution to this tension will look like. But Etienne Gilson was right when he wrote that 'Philosophy always buries its undertakers.'

'Beyond Historicism', *Realism and Reason*, p. 303

Q

𝔊𝔊𝔊𝔊𝔊𝔊

WILLARD V. O. QUINE (b. 1908)

A curious thing about the ontological problem is its simplicity. It can be   1
put in three Anglo-Saxon monosyllables: 'What is there?' It can be
answered, moreover, in a word – 'Everything'.
From a Logical Point of View, p. 1

To be is to be the value of a variable. There are no ultimate philosophical   2
problems concerning terms and their references, but only concerning
variables and their values; and there are no ultimate philosophical
problems concerning existence except insofar as existence is expressed by
the quantifier '($\exists x$)'.
Methods of Logic, p. 224

The totality of our so-called knowledge or beliefs, from the most casual   3
matters of geography and history to the profoundest laws of atomic
physics or even of pure mathematics and logic, is a man-made fabric,
which impinges on experience only along the edges. Or, to change the
figure, total science is like a field of force whose boundary conditions are
experience. A conflict with experience at the periphery occasions
readjustments in the interior of the field. Truth values have to be
redistributed over some of our statements. Re-evaluation of some
statements entails re-evaluation of others, because of their logical
interconnections – the logical laws being in turn simply certain further
statements of the system, certain further elements in the field. Having re-
evaluated one statement we must re-evaluate some others, which may be
statements logically connected with the first or may be statements of
logical connections themselves. But the total field is so underdetermined
by its boundary conditions, experience, that there is much latitude of
choice as to what statements to re-evaluate in the light of any single
contrary experience. No particular experiences are linked with any
particular statements in the interior of the field except indirectly through
considerations of equilibrium affecting the field as a whole.
From a Logical Point of View, p. 43

4   . . . it becomes folly to seek a boundary between synthetic statements, which hold contingently on experience, and analytic statements, which hold come what may. Any statement can be held true come what may, if we make drastic enough adjustments elsewhere in the system. Even a statement very close to the periphery can be held true in the face of recalcitrant experience by pleading hallucination or by amending certain statements of the kind called logical laws. Conversely, by the same token, no statement is immune to revision. Revision even of the logical law of the excluded middle has been proposed as a means of simplifying quantum mechanics . . .
From a Logical Point of View, p. 43

5   As an empiricist I continue to think of the conceptual scheme of science as a tool, ultimately, for predicting future experience in the light of past experience. Physical objects are conceptually imported into the situation as convenient intermediaries – not by definition in terms of experience, but simply as irreducible posits comparable, epistemologically, to the gods of Homer. . . . Moreover, the abstract entities which are the substance of mathematics – ultimately classes and classes of classes and so on up – are another posit in the same spirit. Epistemologically these are myths on the same footing with physical objects and gods, neither better nor worse except for differences in the degree to which they expedite our dealings with sense experiences.
From a Logical Point of View, p. 44

6   Our acceptance of an ontology is, I think, similar in principle to our acceptance of a scientific theory, say a system of physics; we adopt, at least insofar as we are reasonable, the simplest conceptual scheme into which the disordered fragments of raw experience can be fitted and arranged.
From a Logical Point of View, p. 16

7   The quest of a simplest, clearest overall pattern of canonical notation is not to be distinguished from a quest for ultimate categories, a limning of the most general traits of reality.
Word and Object, p. 161

8   Our talk of external things, our very notion of things, is just a conceptual apparatus that helps us to foresee and control the triggering of our sensory receptors in the light of previous triggering of our sensory receptors.
Theories and Things, p. 1

9   More objects are wanted, certainly, than just bodies and substances. We need all sorts of parts or portions of substances. For lack of a natural

stopping place, the natural course at this point is to admit as an object the material content of any portion of space-time, however irregular and discontinuous and heterogeneous. This is the generalization of the primitive and ill-defined category of bodies to what I call physical objects.
Theories and Things, p. 10

Physics investigates the essential nature of the world, and biology 10
describes a local bump. Psychology, human psychology, describes a bump on the bump.
Theories and Things, p. 93

One man's antinomy is another man's falsidical paradox, give or take a 11
couple of thousand years.
The Ways of Paradox, p. 11

One man's antinomy can be another man's veridical paradox, and one 12
man's veridical paradox can be another man's platitude.
The Ways of Paradox, p. 14

Irrefragability, thy name is mathematics. 13
The Ways of Paradox, p. 25

The lore of our fathers is a fabric of sentences. . . . It is a pale gray lore, 14
black with fact and white with convention. But I have found no substantial reasons for concluding that there are any quite black threads in it, or any white ones.
The Ways of Paradox, p. 132

Entification begins at arm's length; the points of condensation in the 15
primordial conceptual scheme are things glimpsed, not glimpses.
Word and Object, p. 1

Epistemology is best looked upon, then, as an enterprise within natural 16
science. Cartesian doubt is not the way to begin. Retaining our present beliefs about nature, we can still ask how we have arrived at them.
'The Nature of Natural Knowledge', *Mind and Language*, ed. S. Guttenplan, p. 68

. . . my position is a naturalistic one; I see philosophy not as an *a priori* 17
propaedeutic or groundwork for science, but as continuous with science. I see philosophy and science as in the same boat – a boat which, to revert to Neurath's figure as I so often do, we can rebuild only at sea while staying afloat in it. There is no external vantage point, no first philosophy.
Ontological Relativity and Other Essays, p. 126

18 In psychology one may or may not be a behaviorist, but in linguistics one has no choice. Each of us learns his language by observing other people's verbal behavior and having his own faltering verbal behavior observed and reinforced or corrected by others. We depend strictly on overt behavior. As long as our command of our language fits all external checkpoints, where our utterance or our reaction to someone's utterance can be appraised in the light of some shared situation, so long all is well.
Pursuit of Truth, p. 37

19 Two translators might develop independent manuals of translation, both of them compatible with all speech behaviour, and yet one manual would offer translations that the other translator would reject. My position was that either manual could be useful, but as to which was right and which wrong there was no fact of the matter.
'Facts of the Matter', *Essays on the Philosophy of W. V. Quine*, ed. R. Shahan and C. Swoyer, p. 167

20 Manuals for translating one language into another can be set up in divergent ways, all compatible with the totality of speech dispositions, yet incompatible with one another. In countless places they will diverge in giving, as their respective translations of a sentence of the one language, sentences of the other language which stand to each other in no plausible sort of equivalence however loose.
Word and Object, p. 27

21 Brentano's thesis of the irreducibility of intentional idioms is of a piece with the thesis of indeterminacy of translation.
    One may accept the Brentano thesis either as showing the indispensability of intentional idioms and the importance of an autonomous science of intention or as showing the baselessness of intentional idioms and the emptiness of the science of intention. My attitude, unlike Brentano's, is the second.
Word and Object, p. 221

22 I have been accused of denying consciousness, but I am not conscious of having done so. Consciousness is to me a mystery, and not one to be dismissed. We know what it is like to be conscious, but not how to put it into satisfactory scientific terms. Whatever it precisely may be, consciousness is a state of the body, a state of nerves.
Quiddities: An Intermittently Philosophical Dictionary, p. 132

23 The line that I am urging as today's conventional wisdom is not a denial of consciousness. It is often called, with more reason, a repudiation of mind. It is indeed a repudiation of mind as a second substance, over and above body. It can be described less harshly as an identification of mind

with some of the faculties, states, and activities of the body. Mental states and events are a special subclass of the states and events of the human or animal body.
Quiddities: An Intermittently Philosophical Dictionary, p. 133

ANTHONY QUINTON (*b.* 1925)

The fundamental reason for thinking that there is more to a thing than its 1 properties is that by their nature properties are general. They can apply to many, to an indefinitely large number, of individual instances, whether or not they do in fact.
The Nature of Things, p. 12

I conclude from the first stage of this argument, a little untidily, that the 2 only type of persons whom we can readily conceive are embodied and that the circumstances in which disembodied existence is conceivable are at once marginal and susceptible of a less uneconomical interpretation.
The Nature of Things, p. 101

The idea of the soul, as a pure ego or mental substance, persists 3 tenaciously in philosophy. I have argued that it cannot satisfactorily discharge the various tasks for which it has been recruited. The body, with marginal, speculative and dependent exceptions, is all that is required to individuate experiences and to supply them with an owner. An unobservable mental substance cannot individuate and provides a merely formal, because wholly inscrutable, solution to the problem of ownership. It is equally, and even more obviously, inept as an explanation of the identity of a person through time, which rests, not on the body, but on the complex of a person's character and memories, related by continuity.
The Nature of Things, p. 103

The pursuit of an understanding of fundamental conservative principles 4 is made difficult by the anti-theoretical tendency of conservatives generally. It seems perverse to look for organized and articulate theory in writings that are throughout concerned with the dangerous unreliability of abstract theoretical constructions . . .
The Politics of Imperfection, p. 12

What I have been arguing so far is that there is a persisting tradition of 5 thought about government and society in England, whose leading principles are those of traditionalism, organicism (in an unassuming, factual form) and political scepticism. These principles are variously involved with and dependent on the idea of human imperfection, intellectual, moral or both.
The Politics of Imperfection, p. 22

R

𝕤𝕤𝕤𝕤𝕤𝕤

FRANK RAMSEY (1903–1930)

1   . . . I am following the great school of mathematical logicians who, in virtue of a series of startling definitions, have saved mathematics from the sceptics, and provided a rigid demonstration of its propositions. Only so can we preserve it from the Bolshevik menace of Brouwer and Weyl.
The Foundations of Mathematics, p. 56

2   The chief danger to our philosophy, apart from laziness and wooliness, is *scholasticism*, the essence of which is treating what is vague as if it were precise and trying to fit it into an exact logical category.
The Foundations of Mathematics, p. 269

3   Theology and Absolute Ethics are two famous subjects which we have realized to have no real objects.
The Foundations of Mathematics, p. 289

4   But before we proceed further with the analysis of judgment, it is necessary to say something about truth and falsehood, in order to show that there is really no separate problem of truth but merely a linguistic muddle. Truth and falsity are ascribed primarily to propositions. The proposition to which they are ascribed may be either explicitly given or described. Suppose first that it is explicitly given; then it is evident that 'It is true that Caesar was murdered' means no more than that Caesar was murdered, and 'It is false that Caesar was murdered' means that Caesar was not murdered. They are phrases which we sometimes use for emphasis or for stylistic reasons, or to indicate the position occupied by the statement in our argument.
Foundations, ed. D. H. Mellor, p. 44

JOHN RAWLS (*b.* 1921)

1   My aim is to present a conception of justice which generalizes and carries to a higher level of abstraction the familiar theory of the social contract

as found, say, in Locke, Rousseau, and Kant. In order to do this we are not to think of the original contract as one to enter a particular society or to set up a particular form of government. Rather, the guiding idea is that the principles of justice for the basic structure of society are the object of the original agreement.
A Theory of Justice, p. 11

This original position is not, of course, thought of as an actual historical   2
state of affairs, much less as a primitive condition of culture. It is understood as a purely hypothetical situation characterized so as to lead to a certain conception of justice. Among the essential features of this situation is that no one knows his place in society, his class position or social status, nor does any one know his fortune in the distribution of natural assets and abilities, his intelligence, strength, and the like. . . . The principles of justice are chosen behind a veil of ignorance.
A Theory of Justice, p. 12

We shall want to say that certain principles of justice are justified because   3
they would be agreed to in an initial situation of equality. I have emphasized that this original position is purely hypothetical. It is natural to ask why, if this agreement is never actually entered into, we should take any interest in these principles, moral or otherwise. The answer is that the conditions embodied in the description of the original position are ones that we do in fact accept. Or if we do not, then perhaps we can be persuaded to do so by philosophical reflection.
A Theory of Justice, p. 21

The idea of the original position is to set up a fair procedure so that any   4
principles agreed to will be just. The aim is to use the notion of pure procedural justice as a basis of theory. Somehow we must nullify the effects of specific contingencies which put men at odds and tempt them to exploit social and natural circumstances to their own advantage. . . . I assume that the parties are situated behind a veil of ignorance. They do not know how the various alternatives will affect their own particular case and they are obliged to evaluate principles solely on the basis of general considerations.
A Theory of Justice, p. 136

First Principle   5
Each person is to have an equal right to the most extensive total system of equal basic liberties compatible with a similar system of liberty for all.
Second Principle
Social and economic inequalities are to be arranged so that they are both:

(a) to the greatest benefit of the least advantaged, consistent with the just savings principle, and

(b) attached to offices and positions open to all under conditions of fair equality of opportunity.

First Priority Rule (The Priority of Liberty)

The principles of justice are to be ranked in lexical order and therefore liberty can be restricted only for the sake of liberty. . . .

Second Priority Rule (The Priority of Justice over Efficiency and Welfare)

The second principle of justice is lexically prior to the principle of efficiency and to that of maximizing the sum of advantages; and fair opportunity is prior to the difference principle.

A Theory of Justice, p. 302

6 The two principles mentioned seem to be a fair agreement on the basis of which those better endowed, or more fortunate in their social position, neither of which we can be said to deserve, could expect the willing cooperation of others when some workable scheme is a necessary condition of the welfare of all. Once we decide to look for a conception of justice that nullifies the accidents of natural endowment and the contingencies of social circumstance as counters in quest for political and economic advantage, we are led to these principles. They express the result of leaving aside those aspects of the social world that seem arbitrary from a moral point of view.

A Theory of Justice, p. 15

7 The perspective of eternity is not a perspective from a certain place beyond the world, nor the point of view of a transcendent being; rather it is a certain form of thought and feeling that rational persons can adopt within the world. And having done so, they can, whatever their generation, bring together into one scheme all individual perspectives and arrive together at regulative principles that can be affirmed by everyone as he lives by them, each from his own standpoint. Purity of heart, if one could attain it, would be to see clearly and to act with grace and self-command from this point of view.

A Theory of Justice, p. 587

JOSEPH RAZ (*b.* 1939)

1 The rule of law is essentially a negative value. The law inevitably creates a great danger of arbitrary power – the rule of law is designed to minimise the danger created by the law itself. Similarly, the law may be unstable, obscure, retrospective, etc., and thus infringe people's freedom and dignity. The rule of law is designed to prevent this danger as well. Thus the rule of law is a negative virtue in two senses: conformity to it

does not cause good except through avoiding evil and the evil which is avoided is evil which could only have been caused by the law itself.
The Authority of Law, p. 224

An anarchist can be not only a law teacher, but also a lawyer. As a lawyer 2 he adopts and expresses a professional point of view, the point of view of legal science, as Kelsen calls it, which does not commit him, and is understood not to commit him to the view that the law is just.
The Authority of Law, p. 142

HANS REICHENBACH (1891–1953)

The picture of scientific method drafted by modern philosophy is very 1 different from traditional conceptions. Gone is the ideal of a universe whose course follows strict rules, a predetermined cosmos that unwinds itself like an unwinding clock. Gone is the ideal of the scientist who knows the absolute truth. The happenings of nature are like rolling dice rather than like revolving stars; they are controlled by probability laws, not by causality, and *the scientist resembles a gambler more than a prophet*. He can tell you only his best posits – he never knows beforehand whether they will come true. He is a better gambler, though, than the man at the green table, because his statistical methods are superior. And his goal is staked higher – the goal of foretelling the rolling dice of the cosmos.
The Rise of Scientific Philosophy, p. 251

There are more things in heaven and earth than are dreamt of in your 2 philosophy, my dear logician.
The Rise of Scientific Philosophy, p. 251

THOMAS REID (1710–1796)

If [my mind] is, indeed, what the *Treatise of Human Nature* makes it, I 1 find I have been only in an enchanted castle, imposed upon by spectres and apparitions. . . . I see myself, and the whole frame of Nature, shrink into fleeting ideas, which, like Epicurus's atoms, dance about in emptiness. . . . Descartes no sooner began to dig in this mine than scepticism was ready to break in upon him. He did what he could to shut it out. Malebranche and Locke, who dug deeper, found the difficulty of keeping out this enemy still to increase; but they laboured honestly in the design. Then Berkeley, who carried on the work, despairing of securing all, bethought himself on an expedient. By giving up the material world, which he thought might be spared without loss, and even with advantage, he hoped by an impregnable partition to secure the world of

spirits. But, alas! the *Treatise of Human Nature* wantonly sapped the foundation of this partition, and drowned all in one universal deluge.
An Inquiry into the Human Mind, Works, ed. W. Hamilton, p. 103

2 If a plain man, uninstructed in philosophy, has faith to receive these mysteries, how great must be his astonishment! He is brought into a new world, where everything he sees, tastes, or touches, is an idea – a fleeting kind of being which he can conjure into existence, or can annihilate in the twinkling of an eye.

   After his mind is somewhat composed, it will be natural for him to ask his philosophical instructor: Pray, Sir, are there then no substantial and permanent beings called the sun and moon, which continue to exist whether we think of them or not? . . .
Essays on the Intellectual Powers of Man, Works, ed. W. Hamilton, p. 299

3 To what purpose is it for philosophy to decide against common sense in this or any other matter? The belief of a material world is older, and of more authority, than any principles of philosophy. It declines the tribunal of reason, and laughs at all the artillery of the logician.
An Inquiry into the Human Mind, p. 127

4 Reason, says the sceptic, is the only judge of truth, and you ought to throw off every opinion and every belief that is not grounded on reason. Why, sir, should I believe the faculty of reason more than that of perception? – they both came out of the same shop, and were made by the same artist; and if he puts one piece of false ware into my hands, what should hinder him from putting another?
An Inquiry into the Human Mind, p. 183

5 Let us suppose, for a moment, that it is the real table we see: must not this real table seem to diminish as we remove farther from it? It is demonstrable that it must. How then can this apparent diminution be an argument that it is not the real table? When that which must happen to the real table, as we remove farther from it, does actually happen to the table we see, it is absurd to conclude from this that it is not the real table we see. It is evident, therefore, that this ingenious author [Hume] has imposed upon himself by confounding real magnitude with apparent magnitude, and that his argument is a mere sophism.
An Inquiry into the Human Mind, p. 304

6 Methinks, therefore, it were better to make a virtue of necessity; and, since we cannot get rid of the vulgar notion and belief of an external world, to reconcile our reason to it as well as we can; for, if Reason should stomach and fret ever so much at this yoke, she cannot throw it

off; if she will not be the servant of Common Sense, she must be her slave.
An Inquiry into the Human Mind, p. 127

I know of no author before Mr Hume, who maintained that we have no 7 other notion of a cause but that it is something prior to the effect, which has been found by experience to be constantly followed by the effect.

. . . It follows from this definition of a cause, that night is the cause of day, and day the cause of night. For no two things have more constantly followed each other since the beginning of the world.
Of Arguments for Necessity, Works, p. 627

The laws of nature are the rules according to which the effects are 8 produced; but there must be a cause which operates according to these rules. The rules of navigation never navigated a ship; the rules of architecture never built a house.
Of Arguments for Necessity, p. 527

If a philosopher should undertake to account for the force of gunpowder 9 in the discharge of a musket, and then tell us gravely that the cause of this phaenomenon is the drawing of the trigger, we should not be much wiser by this account. As little are we instructed in the cause of memory, by being told that it is caused by a certain impression on the brain. For, supposing that impression on the brain were as necessary to memory as the drawing of the trigger is to the discharge of the musket, we are still as ignorant as we were how memory is produced; so that, if the cause of memory, assigned by this theory, did really exist, it does not in any degree account for memory.
An Inquiry into the Human Mind, p. 354

To say that an object which I see with perfect indifference makes an 10 impression upon my mind, is not, as I apprehend, good English . . . it is evident from the manner in which this phrase is used by modern philosophers that they . . . think that the object perceived acts upon the mind in some way similar to that in which one body acts upon another.
. . . The impression upon the mind is conceived to be something wherein the mind is altogether passive. . . . But this is a hypothesis which contradicts the common sense of mankind. When I look upon the wall of my room, the wall does not act at all, nor is capable of acting: the perceiving it is an act or operation in me.
Essays on the Powers of the Human Mind, p. 254

There is indeed nothing more ridiculous than to imagine that any motion 11 or modification of matter should produce thought.
An Inquiry into the Human Mind, p. 253

12 If one should tell of a telescope so exactly made as to have the power of seeing; of a whispering gallery that had the power of hearing; of a cabinet so nicely framed as to have the power of memory; or of a machine so delicate as to feel pain when it was touched – such absurdities are so shocking to common sense that they would not find belief even among savages; yet it is the same absurdity to think that the impressions of external objects upon the machine of our bodies can be the real efficient cause of thought and perception.
An Inquiry into the Human Mind, p. 253

13 Perception, as we here understand it, hath always an object distinct from the act by which it is perceived; an object which may exist whether it be perceived or not. I perceive a tree that grows before my window; there is here an object which is perceived, and an act of the mind by which it is perceived; and these two are not only distinguishable, but they are extremely unlike in their natures.
An Inquiry into the Human Mind, p. 182

14 Thus, *I feel a pain*; *I see a tree*: the first denoteth a sensation, the last a perception. The grammatical analysis of both expressions is the same: for both consist of an active verb and an object. But, if we attend to the things signified by these expressions, we shall find that, in the first, the distinction between the act and the object is not real but grammatical; in the second, the distinction is not only grammatical but real.

The form of the expression, *I feel pain*, might seem to imply that the feeling is something distinct from the pain felt; yet, in reality, there is no distinction. As *thinking a thought* is an expression which could signify no more than *thinking*, so *feeling a pain* signifies no more than *being pained*. What we have said of pain is applicable to every other mere sensation.
An Inquiry into the Human Mind, p. 183

15 Suppose that such a man [a plain one] meets with a modern philosopher, and wants to be informed what smell in plants is. The philosopher tells him that there is no smell in plants, nor in anything but in the mind; that it is impossible there can be smell but in a mind; and that all this hath been demonstrated by modern philosophy. The plain man will, no doubt, be apt to think him merry . . .
An Inquiry into the Human Mind, p. 112

16 It is genius, and not the want of it, that adulterates philosophy, and fills it with error and false theory.
An Inquiry into the Human Mind, p. 99

The weakness of human reason makes men prone, when they leave one 17
extreme to rush into the opposite . . . from ascribing active power to all
things to conclude all things to be carried on by necessity.
An Inquiry into the Human Mind, p. 605

Men are often led into error by *the love of simplicity, which disposes us* 18
to reduce things to few principles, and to conceive a greater simplicity in
nature than there really is.
An Inquiry into the Human Mind, p. 470

This natural conviction of our acting freely, which is acknowledged by 19
many who hold the doctrine of necessity, ought to throw the whole
burden of proof upon that side; for, by this, the side of liberty has what
lawyers call a *jus quaesitum*, or a right of ancient possession, which
ought to stand good till it be overturned. If it cannot be proven that we
always act from necessity, there is no need of arguments on the other side
to convince us that we are free agents.
An Inquiry into the Human Mind, p. 620

Suppose a brave officer to have been flogged when a boy at school, for 20
robbing an orchard, to have taken a standard from the enemy in his first
campaign, and to have been made a general in advanced life: Suppose
also, which must be admitted to be possible, that, when he took the
standard, he was conscious of his having been flogged at school, and that
when made a general he was conscious of his taking the standard, but
had absolutely lost the consciousness of his flogging.

These things being supposed, it follows, from Mr. Locke's doctrine,
that he who was flogged at school is the same person who took the
standard, and that he who took the standard is the same person who was
made a general. Whence it follows, if there be any truth in logic, that the
general is the same person with him who was flogged at school. But the
general's consciousness does not reach so far back as his flogging –
therefore, according to Mr. Locke's doctrine, he is not the person who
was flogged. Therefore, the general is, and at the same time is not the
same person with him who was flogged at school.
An Inquiry into the Human Mind, p. 351

NICHOLAS RESCHER (*b.* 1928)

Present-day science cannot speak for future science: it is in principle 1
impossible to make any secure inferences from the substance of science at
one time about its substance at a significantly different time. The
prospect of future scientific revolutions can never be precluded. We

cannot say with unblinking confidence what sorts of resources and conceptions the science of the future will or will not use.
The Limits of Science, p. 102

2   We cannot satisfactorily monitor the adequacy and completeness of our science by its ability to effect 'all things possible', because science alone can inform us about what actually is possible. As science grows and develops, it poses new issues of power and control, reformulating and reshaping those demands whose realization represents 'control over nature'. For science itself brings new possibilities to light.
Baffling Phenomena and Other Studies in the Philosophy of Knowledge and Valuation, p. 215

3   Sceptics from antiquity onward have always said, 'Forget about those abstruse theoretical issues; focus on your practical needs.' They overlook the crucial fact that an intellectual accommodation to the world is itself one of our deepest practical needs – that in a position of ignorance or cognitive dissonance we cannot function satisfactorily. We are creatures for whom intellectual comfort is no less crucial than physical comfort. The human condition is such that we are going to have some view (after all, scepticism itself is just one such). The question is simply whether we are going to have one that is well thought out or not.
The Strife of Systems: An Essay on the Grounds and Implications of Philosophical Diversity, p. 249

4   In philosophy we . . . cannot rise above the battle of the schools. The proliferation of points of view is inherent in the enterprise. We cannot attain a 'position of reason' outside the arena of controversy.
The Strife of Systems: An Essay on the Grounds and Implications of Philosophical Diversity, p. 160

5   While ideals are, in a way, mere fictions, they nevertheless direct and canalize our thought and action. To be sure, an ideal is not a goal we can expect to attain. But it serves to set a direction in which we can strive. Ideals are irrealities, but they are irrealities that condition the nature of the real through their influence on human thought and action. Stalin's cynical question 'But how many divisions has the Pope?' betokens the Soviet *Realpolitiker* rather than the Marxist ideologue. (How many soldiers did Marx command?)
Ethical Idealism: An Inquiry into the Nature and Function of Ideals, p. 133

6   Reason itself . . . demands that we recognize the limited place of the virtues of cognition, inquiry, and the cerebral side of life. An adequate account of rationality must rightly stress its importance and primacy

while recognizing that the intellectual virtues are only limited components of the good life.
Human Interests: Reflections on Philosophical Anthropology, p. 191

One cannot properly appreciate the human realities so long as one labors 7 under the adolescent delusion that people get the fates they deserve.
Human Interests: Reflections on Philosophical Anthropology, p. 101

I. A. RICHARDS (1893–1979) and C. K. OGDEN (1889–1957)

'Good' is alleged to stand for a unique, unanalyzable concept . . . [which] is the subject matter of ethics. This peculiar ethical use of 'good' is, we suggest, a purely emotive use. When so used the word stands for nothing whatever. . . . Thus, when we so use it in the sentence 'This is good', we merely refer to *this*, and the addition of 'is good' makes no difference whatever to our reference . . . it serves only as an emotive sign expressing our attitude to *this*, and perhaps evoking similar attitudes in other persons, or inciting them to actions of one kind or another.
The Meaning of Meaning, p. 125

JANET RADCLIFFE RICHARDS (b. 1944)

Feminism is not concerned with a group of people it wants to benefit, but 1 a type of injustice it wants to eliminate.
The Sceptical Feminist, p. 5

It seems most unlikely that so much effort would have been put into 2 making women artificially dependent on men if they had been naturally so.
The Sceptical Feminist, p. 145

The only conceivable reason for a rule or practice excluding women is its 3 perpetrators' thinking that without such a rule women would have to be let in.
The Sceptical Feminist, p. 102

Many men are far more oppressed than many women, and any feminist 4 who was determined to support women in all situations would certainly encounter some where her support of women against men would increase the level of injustice in the world.
The Sceptical Feminist, p. 8

Men may have had their own very good reasons for bringing women up 5 to servitude, but the soul of a servant is not an attractive thing, and one of the most infuriating aspects of women's constricted upbringing is that it has made them less attractive, even in the eyes of their constrictors,

than they should have been. Man has twisted and pruned woman out of all recognition and *then not liked the results*.
The Sceptical Feminist, p. 156

6 Radical feminism cannot go in for a simple rejection of everything which happens to have male fingerprints on it, because to do that is to accept part of the legacy of patriarchy, by conceding that the traditional packages must be left intact, to be accepted or rejected as wholes. It is to *accept* that if certain things exist at all, they must take the form they have always taken: one oppressive to women. But that is not in the least radical. What is necessary is to insist on *splitting up the packages,* looking at the good and bad aspects of tradition and keeping what is good wherever we can. That is the radical thing to do, even though it may produce policies which look reformist to the casual glance.
The Sceptical Feminist, p. 289

RICHARD RORTY (b. 1931)

1 It is pictures rather than propositions, metaphors rather than statements, which determine most of our philosophical convictions. The picture which holds traditional philosophy captive is that of the mind as a great mirror, containing various representations – some accurate, some not – and capable of being studied by pure, non-empirical methods. Without the notion of the mind as mirror, the notion of knowledge as accuracy of representation would not have suggested itself. Without this latter notion, the strategy common to Descartes and Kant – getting more accurate representations by inspecting, repairing, and polishing the mirror, so to speak – would not have made sense. Without this strategy in mind, recent claims that philosophy could consist of 'conceptual analysis' or 'phenomenological analysis' or 'explication of meanings' or examination of 'the logic of our language' or of 'the structure of the constituting activity of consciousness' would not have made sense.
Philosophy and the Mirror of Nature, p. 12

2 If we have a Deweyan conception of knowledge, as what we are justified in believing, then we will not imagine that there are enduring constraints on what can count as knowledge, since we will see 'justification' as a social phenomenon rather than a transaction between 'the knowing subject' and 'reality'. If we have a Wittgensteinian notion of language as tool rather than mirror, we will not look for necessary conditions of the possibility of linguistic representation. If we have a Heideggerian conception of philosophy, we will see the attempt to make the nature of the knowing subject a source of necessary truths as one more self-

deceptive attempt to substitute a 'technical' and determinate question for that openness to strangeness which initially tempted us to begin thinking.
Philosophy and the Mirror of Nature, p. 9

Whichever happens, however, there is no danger of philosophy's 'coming 3 to an end'. Religion did not come to an end in the Enlightenment, nor painting in Impressionism. . . . For even if problems about representation look as obsolete to our descendants as problems about hylomorphism look to us, people will still read Plato, Aristotle, Descartes, Kant, Hegel, Wittgenstein, and Heidegger. . . . The only point on which I would insist is that philosophers' moral concern should be with continuing the conversation of the West, rather than with insisting upon a place for the traditional problems of modern philosophy within that conversation.
Philosophy and the Mirror of Nature, p. 394

The self-image of a philosopher – his identification of himself as such 4 (rather than as, perhaps, an historian or a mathematician or a poet) – depends almost entirely upon how he sees the history of philosophy. It depends upon which figures he imitates, and which episodes and movements he disregards. So a new account of the history of philosophy is a challenge which cannot be ignored.
Consequences of Pragmatism, p. 41

If we have Dewey's picture of what has happened in the intellectual 5 history of the West, we shall have a certain quite specific account of Heidegger's role in this history; he will appear as a final decadent echo of Platonic and Christian otherworldliness. If we have Heidegger's perception, conversely, we shall have a quite specific picture of Dewey; he will appear as an exceptionally naive and provincial nihilist.
Consequences of Pragmatism, p. 41

I think that analytic philosophy culminates in Quine, the later Wittgenstein, 6 Sellars, and Davidson – which is to say that it transcends and cancels itself.
Consequences of Pragmatism, p. xviii

As usual with pithy little formulae, the Derridean claim that 'There is 7 nothing outside the text' is right about what it implicitly denies and wrong about what it explicitly asserts. The *only* force of saying that texts do not refer to non-texts is just the old pragmatist chestnut that any specification of a referent is going to be in some vocabulary. Thus one is really comparing two descriptions of a thing rather than a description with the thing-in-itself. This chestnut, in turn, is just an expanded form of Kant's slogan that 'Intuitions without concepts are blind', which, in turn, was just a sophisticated restatement of Berkeley's ingenuous remark that

'nothing can be like an idea except an idea'. These are all merely misleading ways of saying that we shall not see reality plain, unmasked, naked to our gaze.
Consequences of Pragmatism, p. 154

8 The philosophers' own scholastic little definitions of 'philosophy' are merely polemical devices – intended to exclude from the field of honor those whose pedigrees are unfamiliar. We can pick out 'the philosophers' in the contemporary intellectual world only by noting who is commenting on a certain sequence of historical figures. All that 'philosophy' as a name for a sector of culture means is 'talk about Plato, Augustine, Descartes, Kant, Hegel, Frege, Russell . . . and that lot'. Philosophy is best seen as a kind of writing. It is delimited, as is any literary genre, not by form or matter, but by tradition – a family romance involving, e.g., Father Parmenides, honest old Uncle Kant, and bad brother Derrida.
Consequences of Pragmatism, p. 92

FRANZ ROSENZWEIG (1886–1929)

Yea is the beginning. Nay cannot be the beginning for it could only be a Nay of the Nought. This, however, would presuppose a negatable Nought, a Nay, therefore, that had already decided on a Yea. Therefore Yea is the beginning.
The Star of Redemption, trans. William W. Hallo, p. 16

W. D. ROSS (1877–1971)

1 . . . [that] 'right' means 'productive of so and so' . . . cannot with any plausibility be maintained. . . . When a plain man fulfils a promise because he thinks he ought to do so, it seems clear that he does so with no thought of its total consequences, still less with any opinion that these are likely to be the best possible. He thinks in fact much more of the past than of the future. What makes him think it right to act in a certain way is the fact that he has promised to do so – that and, usually, nothing more.
The Right and the Good, ch. 2

2 Suppose . . . that the fulfilment of a promise to A would produce 1,000 units of good for him, but that by doing some other act I could produce 1,001 units of good for B, to whom I have made no promise, the other consequences of the two acts being of equal value; should we really think it self-evident that it was our duty to do the second act and not the first? I think not. . . . The co-extensiveness of the right and the optimific is, then, not self-evident.
The Right and the Good, ch. 2

... the theory of 'ideal utilitarianism' ... says, in effect, that the only 3 morally significant relation in which my neighbours stand to me is that of being possible beneficiaries by my action. ... But they may also stand to me in the relation of promisee to promiser, of creditor to debtor, of wife to husband, ... and the like; and each of these relations is the foundation of a *prima facie* duty, which is more or less incumbent on me according to the circumstances of the case. When I am in a situation, as perhaps I always am, in which more than one of these *prima facie* duties is incumbent on me, what I have to do is to study the situation as fully as I can until I form the considered opinion (it is never more) that in the circumstances one of them is more incumbent than any other; then I am bound to think that to do this *prima facie* duty is my duty *sans phrase* in the situation.
The Right and the Good, ch. 2

... no act is ever, in virtue of falling under some general description, 4 necessarily actually right ... moral acts often (as every one knows) and indeed always (on reflection we must admit) have different characteristics that tend to make them at the same time *prima facie* right and *prima facie* wrong; there is probably no act, for instance, which does good to anyone without doing harm to someone else, and *vice versa*.
The Right and the Good, ch. 2

That an act, *qua* fulfilling a promise, or *qua* effecting a just distribution 5 of good, ... is *prima facie* right, is self-evident ... just as a mathematical axiom, or the validity of a form of inference, is evident. The moral order expressed in these propositions is just as much part of the fundamental nature of the universe (and, we may add, of any possible universe in which there were moral agents at all) as is the spatial or numerical structure expressed in the axioms of geometry or arithmetic. ... In both cases we are dealing with propositions that cannot be proved, but that just as certainly need no proof.
The Right and the Good, ch. 2

It would be a mistake to found a natural science on 'what we really think' 6 ... opinions are interpretations, and often misinterpretations, of sense-experience; and the man of science must appeal from these to sense-experience itself, which furnishes his real data. In ethics no such appeal is possible. ... the moral convictions of thoughtful and well-educated people are the data of ethics just as sense-perceptions are the data of a natural science.
The Right and the Good, ch. 2

JEAN-JACQUES ROUSSEAU (1712–1778)

1 Man was born free, and he is everywhere in chains. Those who think themselves the masters of others are indeed greater slaves than they. How did this transformation come about? I do not know. How can it be made legitimate? That question I believe I can answer.
The Social Contract, trans. Maurice Cranston, p. 49

2 . . . wandering in the forest, I sought for and found there the image of the primitive ages of which I boldly traced the history. I confounded the pitiful lies of men; I dared to unveil their nature; to follow the progress of time, and the things by which it has been disfigured; and comparing the man of art with the natural man, to show them, in their pretended improvement, the real source of all their misery.
Confessions, p. 312

3 The fundamental principle of all morals, on the basis of which I have reasoned in all my writings, and which I have developed in this last one [*Émile*] with as much clarity as I was able, is that man is naturally good, loving justice and order; that there is absolutely no original perversity in the human heart, and that the first movements of nature are always right.
Letter to Christophe de Beaumont, trans. N. J. H. Dent, *Oeuvres*, IV, p. 935

4 Let us set down as an incontestable maxim that the first movements of nature are always right. There is no original perversity in the human heart. There is not a single vice to be found in it of which it cannot be said how and whence it entered. The sole passion natural to man is *amour-de-soi* . . .
Émile, or On Education, trans. Allan Bloom, p. 92

5 . . . social man lives constantly outside himself, and only knows how to live in the opinion of others, so that he seems to receive the consciousness of his own existence merely from the judgment of others concerning him . . . everything being reduced to appearances, there is but art and mummery in even honour, friendship, virtue and often vice itself, of which we at length learn the secret of boasting; . . . in short . . . always asking others what we are, and never daring to ask ourselves, . . . we have nothing to show for ourselves but a frivolous and deceitful appearance, honour without virtue, reason without wisdom, and pleasure without happiness.
A Discourse on the Origin of Inequality, trans. G. D. H. Cole, rev. J. H. Brumfitt and J. C. Hall, p. 104

6 The first man who, having enclosed a piece of land, thought of saying 'This is mine' and found people simple enough to believe him, was the true founder of civil society. How many crimes, wars, murders; how

much misery and horror the human race would have been spared if someone had pulled up the stakes and filled in the ditch and cried out to his fellow men: 'Beware of listening to this impostor. You are lost if you forget that the fruits of the earth belong to everyone and that the earth itself belongs to no one!'

A Discourse on [the Origin of] Inequality, trans. Maurice Cranston, p. 109

Each one began to consider the rest, and to wish to be considered in turn; and thus a value came to be attached to public esteem. Whoever sang or danced best, whoever was the handsomest, the strongest, the most dexterous, or the most eloquent, came to be of most consideration; and this was the first step towards inequality and at the same time towards vice. From these first distinctions arose on the one side vanity and contempt and on the other shame and envy . . .

A Discourse on the Origin of Inequality, trans. G. D. H. Cole, rev. J. H. Brumfitt and J. C. Hall, p. 81

7

All ran headlong to their chains, in hopes of securing their liberty; for they had just wit enough to perceive the advantages of political institutions, without experience enough to enable them to foresee the dangers . . . Such was, or may well have been, the origin of society and law, which bound new fetters on the poor, and gave new powers to the rich; which irretrievably destroyed natural liberty, eternally fixed the law of property and inequality, converted clever usurpation into unalterable right, and, for the advantage of a few ambitious individuals, subjected all mankind to perpetual labour, slavery and wretchedness.

A Discourse on the Origin of Inequality, trans. G. D. H. Cole, rev. J. H. Brumfitt and J. C. Hall, p. 89

8

There is only one law which by its nature requires unanimous assent. This is the social pact: for the civil association is the most voluntary act in the world; every man having been born free and master of himself, no one else may under any pretext whatever subject him without his consent. To assert that the son of a slave is born a slave is to assert that he is not born a man.

If, then, there are opposing voices at the time when the social pact is made, this opposition does not invalidate the contract; it merely excludes the dissentients; they are foreigners among the citizens. After the state is instituted, residence implies consent: to inhabit the territory is to submit to the sovereign.

The Social Contract, trans. Maurice Cranston, p. 152

9

Finally, since each man gives himself to all, he gives himself to no one; and since there is no associate over whom he does not gain the same rights as others gain over him, each man recovers the equivalent of

10

everything he loses, and in the bargain he acquires more power to preserve what he has.

If, then, we eliminate from the social pact everything that is not essential to it, we find it comes down to this: 'Each one of us puts into the community his person and all his powers under the supreme direction of the general will; and as a body, we incorporate every member as an indivisible part of the whole.'

The Social Contract, trans. Maurice Cranston, p. 61

11 Yet it may be asked how a man can be at once free and forced to conform to wills which are not his own. How can the opposing minority be both free and subject to laws to which they have not consented?

I answer that the question is badly formulated. The citizen consents to all the laws, even to those that are passed against his will, and even to those which punish him when he dares to break any one of them. The constant will of all the members of the state is the general will; it is through it that they are citizens and free. When a law is proposed in the people's assembly, what is asked of them is not precisely whether they approve of the proposition or reject it, but whether it is in conformity with the general will which is theirs; each by giving his vote gives his opinion on this question, and the counting of votes yields a declaration of the general will. When, therefore, the opinion contrary to my own prevails, this proves only that I have made a mistake, and that what I believed to be the general will was not so. If my particular opinion had prevailed against the general will, I should have done something other than what I had willed, and then I should not have been free.

This presupposes, it is true, that all the characteristics of the general will are still to be found in the majority; when these cease to be there, no matter what position men adopt, there is no longer any freedom.

The Social Contract, trans. Maurice Cranston, p. 153

12 Distributive justice would still be opposed to the strict equality of the state of nature, even if it were practicable in civil society, and as all members of the state owe it services proportionate to their talents and their strength, the citizens in turn ought to be honoured and favoured in proportion to their services.

Second Discourse, trans. Maurice Cranston, p. 48

13 A child cries from birth; the first part of his childhood is spent crying. At one time we bustle about, we caress him in order to pacify him; at another, we threaten him, we strike him in order to make him keep quiet. Either we do what pleases him, or we exact from him what pleases us. Either we submit to his whims, or we submit him to ours. No middle ground, he must give orders or receive them. Thus his first ideas are those

of domination and servitude. Before knowing how to speak, he commands; before being able to act, he obeys.
Émile, or On Education, trans. Allan Bloom, p. 48

The strictness of the relative duties of the two sexes is not and cannot be   14
the same. When woman complains on this score about unjust man-made inequality, she is wrong. This inequality is not a human institution – or, at least, it is the work not of prejudice but of reason. It is up to the sex that nature has charged with the bearing of children to be responsible for them to the other sex. . . . Women, you say, do not always produce children? No, but their proper purpose is to produce them.
Émile, or On Education, trans. Allan Bloom, p. 361

Everything that characterizes the fair sex ought to be respected as   15
established by nature. You constantly say, 'Women have this or that failing which we do not have.' Your pride deceives you. They would be failings for you; they are their good qualities. . . . All the faculties common to the two sexes are not equally distributed between them; but taken together, they balance out. . . .

The quest for abstract and speculative truths, principles, and axioms in the sciences, for everything that tends to generalize ideas, is not within the competence of women. . . . Regarding what is not immediately connected with their duties, all the reflections of women ought to be directed to the study of men or to the pleasing kinds of knowledge that have only taste as their aim . . .
Émile, or On Education, trans. Allan Bloom, p. 363

BERTRAND RUSSELL (1872–1970)

For my part, I believe that, partly by means of study of syntax, we can   1
arrive at considerable knowledge concerning the structure of the world.
An Inquiry into Meaning and Truth, p. 347

Every philosophical problem, when it is subjected to the necessary   2
analysis and justification, is found either to be not really philosophical at all, or else to be, in the sense in which we are using the word, logical.
Our Knowledge of the External World, p. 42

In a logically perfect language, there will be one word and no more for   3
every simple object, and everything that is not simple will be expressed by a combination of words, by a combination derived, of course, from the words for the simple things that enter in, one word for each simple component.
'The Philosophy of Logical Atomism', *Logic and Knowledge*, p. 197

4 To understand a name you must be acquainted with the particular of which it is the name.
'The Philosophy of Logical Atomism', p. 205

5 The reason that I call my doctrine *logical* atomism is because the atoms that I wish to arrive at as the sort of last residue in analysis are logical atoms and not physical atoms. Some of them will be what I call 'particulars' – such things as little patches of colour or sounds, momentary things – and some of them will be predicates or relations and so on.
'The Philosophy of Logical Atomism', p. 179

6 I think one might describe philosophical logic, the philosophical portion of logic which is the portion I am concerned with in these lectures . . ., as an inventory, or if you like a more humble word, a 'zoo', containing all the different forms that facts may have.
'The Philosophy of Logical Atomism', p. 216

7 The supreme maxim in scientific philosophizing is this: *Wherever possible, logical constructions are to be substituted for inferred entities.*
Mysticism and Logic, p. 115

8 When you have taken account of all the feelings roused by Napoleon in writers and readers of history, you have not touched the actual man; but in the case of Hamlet you have come to the end of him. If no one thought about Hamlet, there would be nothing left of him; if no one had thought about Napoleon, he would soon have seen to it that someone did. The sense of reality is vital in logic, and whoever juggles with it by pretending that Hamlet has another kind of reality is doing a disservice to thought. A robust sense of reality is very necessary in framing a correct analysis of propositions about unicorns, golden mountains, round squares, and other such pseudo-objects.
Introduction to Mathematical Philosophy, p. 169

9 By the law of the excluded middle, either 'A is B' or 'A is not B' must be true. Hence either 'the present King of France is bald' or 'the present King of France is not bald' must be true. Yet if we enumerated the things that are bald, and then the things that are not bald, we should not find the present King of France in either list. Hegelians, who love a synthesis, will probably conclude that he wears a wig.
'On Denoting', *Logic and Knowledge*, p. 48

10 When we say, 'George IV wished to know whether Scott was the author of *Waverley*', we normally mean 'George IV wished to know whether one and only one man wrote *Waverley* and Scott was that man'; but we

may also mean: 'One and only one man wrote *Waverley* and George IV wished to know whether Scott was that man'.
'On Denoting', p. 52

Every proposition which we can understand must be composed wholly of   **11**
constituents with which we are acquainted.
The Problems of Philosophy, p. 32

I will illustrate the utility [of the philosophy of logical analysis] by a brief   **12**
explanation of what is called the theory of descriptions. By a 'description'
I mean a phrase such as 'The present President of the United States', in
which a person or thing is designated, not by name, but by some property
which is supposed or known to be peculiar to him or it. Such phrases had
given a lot of trouble. Suppose I say 'The golden mountain does not
exist', and suppose you ask 'What is it that does not exist?' It would seem
that, if I say 'it is the golden mountain', I am attributing some sort of
existence to it. Obviously I am not making the same statement as if I said,
'The round square does not exist.' This seemed to imply that the golden
mountain is one thing and the round square another, although neither
exists. The theory of descriptions was designed to meet this and other
difficulties.

According to this theory, when a statement containing a phrase of the
form 'the so-and-so' is rightly analysed, the phrase 'the so-and-so'
disappears. For example, take the statement 'Scott was the author of
Waverley'. The theory interprets this statement as saying: 'One and only
one man wrote *Waverley*, and that man was Scott.' Or, more fully:
'There is an entity c such that the statement "x wrote *Waverley*" is true if
and only if x is c and false otherwise: moreover c is Scott.'

The first part of this, before the word 'moreover', is defined as
meaning: 'The author of *Waverley* exists (or existed or will exist).' Thus
'The golden mountain does not exist' means: 'There is no entity c such
that "x is golden and mountainous" is true when x is c, but not
otherwise.'

With this definition the puzzle as to what is meant when we say 'The
golden mountain does not exist' disappears.

'Existence', according to this theory, can only be asserted of
descriptions. We can say 'The author of *Waverley* exists', but to say
'Scott exists' is bad grammar, or rather bad syntax. This clears up two
millennia of muddle-headedness about 'existence', beginning with Plato's
Theaetetus.
A History of Western Philosophy, p. 785

Understanding words does not consist in knowing their dictionary   **13**
definitions, or in being able to specify the objects to which they are

appropriate. . . . Understanding language is more like understanding cricket: it is a matter of habits, acquired in oneself and rightly presumed in others. To say that a word has meaning is not to say that those who use the word correctly have ever thought out what the meaning is. . . . The relation of a word to its meaning is of the nature of a causal law governing our use of the word and our actions when we hear it used. There is no more reason why a person who uses a word correctly should be able to tell what it means than there is why a planet which is moving correctly should know Kepler's laws.
The Analysis of Mind, p. 197

14 The process of sound philosophizing, to my mind, consists mainly in passing from those obvious, vague, ambiguous things, that we feel quite sure of, to something precise, clear, definite, which by reflection and analysis we find is involved in the vague thing that we start from, and is, so to speak, the real truth of which that vague thing is a sort of shadow.
'The Philosophy of Logical Atomism', *Logic and Knowledge*, p. 179

15 I once received a letter from an eminent logician, Mrs Christine Ladd Franklin, saying that she was a solipsist, and was surprised that there were no others. Coming from a logician, this surprise surprised me.
Human Knowledge: Its Scope and Limits, p. 196

16 'Neutral Monism' – as opposed to idealistic monism and materialistic monism – is the theory that the things commonly regarded as mental and the things commonly regarded as physical do not differ in respect of any intrinsic property possessed by the one set and not by the other, but differ only in respect of arrangement and context. The theory may be illustrated by comparison with a postal directory, in which the same names appear twice over, once in alphabetical and once in geographical order . . .
'On the Nature of Acquaintance', *Logic and Knowledge*, p. 139

17 . . . there is absolutely nothing that is seen by two minds simultaneously. When we say that two people see the same thing, we always find that, owing to difference of point of view, there are differences, however slight, between their immediate sensible objects. (I am here assuming the validity of testimony . . .)
Our Knowledge of the External World, p. 95

18 If I see the sun and it makes me blink, what I see is not 93,000,000 miles and eight minutes away, but is causally (and therefore spatio-temporally) intermediate between the light-waves striking the eye and the consequent blinking.
Human Knowledge: Its Scope and Limits, p. 220

Indeed, such inadequacies as we have seemed to find in empiricism have 19
been discovered by strict adherence to a doctrine by which empiricist
philosophy has been inspired: that all human knowledge is uncertain,
inexact, and partial. To this doctrine we have not found any limitation
whatever.
Human Knowledge: Its Scope and Limits, p. 527

In every writer on philosophy there is a concealed metaphysic, usually 20
unconscious; even if his subject is metaphysics, he is almost certain to
have an uncritically believed system which underlies his specific
arguments.
'Dewey's New Logic', *The Philosophy of John Dewey*, ed. P. A. Schilpp

The law of gravitation will illustrate what occurs in any exact science. . . . 21
Certain differential equations can be found, which hold at every instant
for every particle of the system. . . . But there is nothing that could be
properly called 'cause' and nothing that could be properly called 'effect'
in such a system.
Mysticism and Logic, p. 194

[Inductive] principles of inference . . . certainly cannot be logically 22
deduced from facts of experience. Either, therefore we know something
independently of experience, or science is moonshine.
Human Knowledge: Its Scope and Limits, p. 524

The observer, when he seems to himself to be observing a stone, *is really,* 23
if physics is to be believed, observing the effects of the stone upon
himself. Thus science seems to be at war with itself. . . . Naive realism
leads to physics, and physics, if true, shows naive realism to be false.
Therefore naive realism, if true, is false; therefore it is false.
An Inquiry into Meaning and Truth, p. 14

I conclude that, while it is true that science cannot decide questions of 24
value, that is because they cannot be intellectually decided at all, and lie
outside the realm of truth and falsehood. Whatever knowledge is
attainable, must be attained by scientific methods; and what science
cannot discover, mankind cannot know.
Religion and Science, p. 243

Pure mathematics consists entirely of assertions to the effect that, if such 25
and such a proposition is true of *anything*, then such and such another
proposition is true of that thing. . . . Thus mathematics may be defined as
the subject in which we never know what we are talking about, nor
whether what we are saying is true. People who have been puzzled by the
beginnings of mathematics will, I hope, find comfort in this definition.
Mysticism and Logic, p. 59

26   All pure mathematics – Arithmetic, Analysis, and Geometry – is built up by combinations of the primitive ideas of logic, and its propositions are deduced from the general axioms of logic, such as the syllogism and the other rules of inference. And this is no longer a dream or an aspiration. On the contrary, over the greater and more difficult part of the domain of mathematics, it has been already accomplished; in the few remaining cases, there is no special difficulty, and it is now being rapidly achieved. Philosophers have disputed for ages whether such deduction was possible; mathematicians have sat down and made the deduction. For the philosophers there is now nothing left but graceful acknowledgements.
Mysticism and Logic, p. 60

27   Mathematics has ceased to seem to me non-human in its subject matter. I have come to believe, though very reluctantly, that it consists of tautologies. I fear that, to a mind of sufficient intellectual power, the whole of mathematics would appear trivial, as trivial as the statement that a four-footed animal is an animal. I think that the timelessness of mathematics has none of the sublimity that it once seemed to me to have, but consists merely in the fact that the pure mathematician is not talking about time. I cannot any longer find any mystical satisfaction in the contemplation of mathematical truth.
My Philosophical Development, p. 157

28   It was Whitehead who was the serpent in this paradise of Mediterranean clarity. He said to me once 'You think the world is what it seems like in fair weather at noon-day. I think it is what it seems like in the early morning when one first wakes from deep sleep.' I thought his remark horrid, but could not see how to prove that my bias was better than his. At last he showed me how to apply the technique of mathematical logic to his vague and higgledy-piggledy world, and dress it up in Sunday clothes that the mathematician could view without being shocked.
Portraits from Memory, p. 41

29   The method of Cartesian doubt, which appealed to me when I was young and may still serve as a tool in the work of logical dissection, no longer seems to me to have fundamental validity. Universal scepticism cannot be refuted, but also cannot be accepted. I have come to accept the facts of sense and the broad truth of science as things which the philosopher should take as data, since though their truth is not quite certain, it has a higher degree of probability than anything likely to be achieved in philosophical speculation.
My Philosophical Development, p. 207

30   Ever since I was engaged on *Principia Mathematica*, I have had a certain method of which at first I was scarcely conscious, but which has

gradually become more explicit in my thinking. The method consists in an attempt to build a bridge between the world of sense and the world of science. I accept both as, in broad outline, not to be questioned. As in making a tunnel through an Alpine mountain, work must proceed from both ends in the hope that at last the labour will be crowned by a meeting in the middle.
My Philosophical Development, p. 205

I say quite deliberately that the Christian religion, as organized in its   31
Churches, has been and still is the principal enemy of moral progress in the world.
Why I Am Not A Christian, p. 15

And God smiled; and when he saw that Man had become perfect in   32
renunciation and worship, he sent another sun through the sky, which crashed into Man's sun; and all returned again to nebula.
  ' "Yes", he murmured, "it was a good play; I will have it performed again." '
Mysticism and Logic, p. 47

Racism not only confuses the historical origins of the Vietnam war; it   33
also provokes a barbarous, chauvinist outcry when American pilots who have bombed hospitals, schools, dykes and civilian centres are accused of committing war crimes. It is only the racist underpinning of the American world-view which allows the US press, the Senate and many public figures to remain absolutely silent when 'Vietcong' prisoners are summarily shot; yet at the same time these bodies demand the levelling of North Vietnamese cities if the pilots are brought to trial for their crimes.
War Crimes in Vietnam, p. 1

Since power over human beings is shown in making them do what they   34
would rather not do, the man who is actuated by love of power is more apt to inflict pain than to permit pleasure.
'Nobel Prize Acceptance Speech', *Human Society in Ethics and Politics*

The British are distinguished among the nations of modern Europe, on   35
the one hand by the excellence of their philosophers, and on the other hand by their contempt for philosophy. In both respects they show their wisdom.
Unpopular Essays, p. 11

GILBERT RYLE (1900–1976)

'Know' is a capacity verb, and a capacity verb of that special sort that is   1
used for signifying that the person described can bring things off, or get things right. 'Believe', on the other hand, is a tendency verb and one

which does not connote that anything is brought off or got right. 'Belief' can be qualified by such adjectives as 'obstinate', 'wavering', 'unswerving', 'unconquerable', 'stupid', 'fanatical', 'whole-hearted', 'intermittent', 'passionate', and 'childlike', adjectives some or all of which are also appropriate to such nouns as 'trust', 'loyalty', 'bent', 'aversion', 'hope', 'habit', 'zeal', and 'addiction'. Beliefs, like habits, can be inveterate, slipped into and given up; like partisanships, devotions, and hopes they can be blind and obsessing; like aversions and phobias they can be unacknowledged; like fashions and tastes they can be contagious; like loyalties and animosities they can be induced by tricks. A person can be urged or entreated not to believe things, and he may try, with or without success, to cease to do so. Sometimes a person says truly 'I cannot help believing so and so'. But none of these dictions, or their negatives, are applicable to knowing, since to know is to be equipped to get something right and not to tend to act or react in certain manners.

Roughly, 'believe' is of the same family as motive words, where 'know' is of the same family as skill words; so we ask how a person knows this, but only why a person believes that, as we ask how a person ties a clove-hitch, but why he wants to tie a clove-hitch or why he always ties granny-knots. Skills have methods, where habits and inclinations have sources. Similarly, we ask what makes people believe or dread things but not what makes them know or achieve things.

The Concept of Mind, p. 128

2   Overt intelligent performances are not clues to the workings of minds; they are those workings. Boswell described Johnson's mind when he described how he wrote, talked, ate, fidgeted and fumed. His description was, of course, incomplete, since there were notoriously some thoughts which Johnson kept carefully to himself and there must have been many dreams, daydreams and silent babblings which only Johnson could have recorded and only a James Joyce would wish him to have recorded.

The Concept of Mind, p. 57

3   When two terms belong to the same category, it is proper to construct conjunctive propositions embodying them. Thus a purchaser may say that he bought a left-hand glove and a right-hand glove, but not that he bought a left-hand glove, a right-hand glove and a pair of gloves. 'She came home in a flood of tears and a sedan-chair' is a well-known joke based on the absurdity of conjoining terms of different types. It would have been equally ridiculous to construct the disjunction 'She came home either in a flood of tears or else in a sedan-chair'. Now the dogma of the Ghost in the Machine does just this. It maintains that there exist both bodies and minds; that there occur physical processes and mental processes; that there are mechanical causes of corporeal movements and

mental causes of corporeal movements. I shall argue that these and other analogous conjunctions are absurd; but, it must be noticed, the argument will not show that either of the illegitimately conjoined propositions is absurd in itself. I am not, for example, denying that there occur mental processes. Doing long division is a mental process and so is making a joke. But I am saying that the phrase 'there occur mental processes' does not mean the same sort of thing as 'there occur physical processes', and, therefore, that it makes no sense to conjoin or disjoin the two.
The Concept of Mind, p. 23

Such in outline is the official theory. I shall often speak of it, with **4** deliberate abusiveness, as 'the dogma of the Ghost in the Machine'. I hope to prove that it is entirely false, and false not in detail but in principle. It is not merely an assemblage of particular mistakes. It is one big mistake and a mistake of a special kind. It is, namely, a category-mistake. It represents the facts of mental life as if they belonged to one logical type or category (or range of types or categories), when they actually belong to another. The dogma is therefore a philosopher's myth. In attempting to explode the myth I shall probably be taken to be denying well-known facts about the mental life of human beings, and my plea that I aim at doing nothing more than rectify the logic of mental-conduct concepts will probably be disallowed as mere subterfuge.
The Concept of Mind, p. 17

S

𝕊𝕊𝕊𝕊𝕊𝕊

GEORGE SANTAYANA (1863–1952)

1   Evidently the governing principle in seeds is no soul in [the] modern sense, no thinking moral being; it is a mysterious habit in matter. Whether this total habit is reducible to minor habits of matter, prevalent in the world at large, is the question debated between mechanical and vitalist psychologists; but it is a stupid controversy. The smallest unit of mechanism is an event as vital, as groundless, and as creative as it is possible for an event to be; it summons fresh essences into existence . . . On the human scale of observation it is the larger habits of living beings that are most easily observed; and the principle of these habits, transmitted by a seed, I call the Psyche: it is either a complex of more minute habits of matter, or a mastering rhythm imposed upon them by the habit of the species. Many Greek philosophers taught that the Psyche was material; and even Plato, although of course his Psyche might eventually take to thinking, regarded it as primarily a principle of motion, growth, and unconscious government; so that the associations of the word Psyche are not repugnant, as are those of the word soul, to the meaning I wish to give it: that habit in matter which forms the human body and the human mind.
Soliloquies in England and Later Soliloquies, p. 220

2   A bodily feat, like nutrition or reproduction, is celebrated by a festival in the mind, and consciousness is a sort of ritual, solemnising, by prayer, jubilation, or mourning, the chief episodes in the body's fortunes.
Reason in Common Sense, p. 213

3   The notion that there is and can be but one time, and that half of it is always intrinsically past and the other half always intrinsically future, belongs to the normal pathology of an animal mind: it marks the egoistical outlook of an active being endowed with imagination. Such a being will project the moral contrast produced by his momentary absorption in action upon the conditions and history of that action, and

394

upon the universe at large. A perspective of hope and one of reminiscence divide for him a specious eternity; and for him the dramatic centre of existence, though always a different point in physical time, will always be precisely in himself.
Realms of Being, p. 253

The psyche is a natural fact, the fact that many organisms can nourish 4 and reproduce themselves, and on occasion can feel and think. This is not merely a question of the use of words; it is a *deliberate refusal to admit the possibility of any mental machinery.*
Realms of Being, p. 332

Intuition is in some sense always a synthesis, even when the datum is an 5 inarticulate feeling, like a scent or a pain . . . Yet the word synthesis is highly ambiguous and misleading, like other Kantian terms that have become indispensable . . . A synthesis may be said to have occurred, but not in consciousness. Consciousness gives the result of that synthesis.
Realms of Being, p. 651

Sometimes, as in deep thought, no image of one's own body figures at all 6 in intuition. *Here* then means whatever point in imagined space is the centre of attention. *Here* may be the word on the page which I have reached in reading: or if my attention has passed from the words to the images awakened by them in my fancy, *here* may be Dante's Purgatorio, rising solitary out of a glassy sea and lifting its clear-cut terraces in perfect circles, up to the fragrant wood at the summit, whence souls grown too pure for a mild happiness pass into the flame of heaven. *Here* is then at the antipodes of Jerusalem and Calvary. . . . But now, perhaps, someone knocks at my door and disturbs my reverie. *Here* is now, if still a purgatory, a purgatory of a very different sort; it is this room in this town where my body finds itself. I look out of the window, and now *here* is Paris; I notice on my table Baedeker's guidebooks and the *Indicateur des chemins de fer*, and I consider how easily *here* may be transferred to quite another geographical place. As to the *here* of a moment ago, it is not only not here, but it is nowhere. It belongs to Dante's imaginary world. It is a theme from the symphony of essence.
Realms of Being, p. 246

The dead past? . . . There is no moment in the whole course of nature 7 (unless there be a first and a last moment) which is not both future and past for an infinity of other moments. In itself, by virtue of its emergence in a world of change, each moment is unstably present, or in the act of elapsing; and by virtue of its position in the order of generation, both pastness and futurity pervade it eternally. . . . Futurity and pastness, the reproach of being not yet and being no longer, fall upon it from different

quarters like lights of different colours, and these same colours, like the red light and the green light of a ship, it itself carries and spreads in opposite directions. And these shafts cross one another with a sort of correspondence in contradiction: the moments which any moment calls past call it future, and those which it calls future call it past.
Realms of Being, p. 264

8 It would not be a rational ambition to wish to multiply the population of China by two, or that of America by twenty, after ascertaining that life there contained an overplus of pleasure. To weed a garden, however, would be rational, though the weeds and their interests would have to be sacrificed in the process. Utilitarianism took up false ground when it made right conduct terminate in miscellaneous pleasures and pains, as if in their isolation they constituted all that morality had to consider, and as if respect offered to them, somehow in proportion to their quantity, were the true conscience. The true conscience is rather an integrated natural will, chastened by clear knowledge of what it pursues and may attain. What morality has to consider is the form of life, not its quantity.
Reason in Science, p. 260

9 As William James put it, in his picturesque manner, if at the last day all creation was shouting hallelujah and there remained one cockroach with an unrequited love, *that* would spoil the universal harmony. . . . The existence of any evil anywhere at any time absolutely ruins a total optimism.
Character and Opinion in the United States, p. 107

10 Opinions are true or false by repeating or contradicting some part of the truth about the facts which they envisage; and this truth about the facts is the standard comprehensive description of them – something in the realm of essence, but more than the essence of any fact present within the limits of time and space which that fact occupies; for a comprehensive description includes also all the radiations of that fact – I mean, all that perspective of the world of facts and of the realm of essence which is obtained by taking this fact as a centre and viewing everything else only in relation with it. The truth about any fact is therefore infinitely extended, although it grows thinner, so to speak, as you travel from it to further and further facts, or to less and less relevant ideas. It is the splash any fact makes, or the penumbra it spreads, by dropping through the realm of essence. Evidently no opinion can embrace it all, or identify itself with it; nor can it be identified with the facts to which it relates, since they are in flux, and it is eternal.
Scepticism and Animal Faith, p. 267

Empiricism used to mean reliance on the past; now apparently **11**
[according to logical positivism] all empirical truth regards only the
future, since truth is said to arise by the verification of some presumption.
Presumptions about the past can evidently never be verified; at best they
may be corroborated by fresh presumptions about the past, equally
dependent for their truth on a verification which in the nature of the case
is impossible. At this point the truly courageous empiricist will say that
the real past only means the ideas of the past which we shall form in the
future. Consistency is a jewel; and, as in the case of other jewels, we may
marvel at the price some people will pay for it. In any case, we are led to
this curious result: that radical empiricism ought to deny that any idea of
the past can be true at all.
Character and Opinion in the United States, p. 160

To call Berkeley a stepping-stone between Locke and Hume is like calling **12**
an upright obelisk a stepping-stone between two sphinxes that may be
crouching to the right and the left of it.
Animal Faith and Spiritual Life, p. 103

It is a great advantage for a philosophy to be substantially true. **13**
Obiter Scripta

JEAN-PAUL SARTRE (1905–1980)

What do we mean by saying that existence precedes essence? We mean **1**
that man first of all exists, encounters himself, surges up in the world –
and defines himself afterwards. . . . there is no human nature, because
there is no God to have a conception of it. . . . Man is nothing else but
what he makes of himself . . .
Existentialism and Humanism, trans. P. Mairet, p. 28

. . . it is necessary that we *make ourselves* what we are. **2**
 . . . The waiter in the café can not be immediately a café waiter in the
sense that this inkwell *is* an inkwell, or the glass is a glass. . . . It is
precisely this person *who I have to be* (if I am the waiter in question) and
who I am not. It is not that I do not wish to be this person or that I want
this person to be different. But rather there is no common measure
between his being and mine. It is a 'representation' for others and for
myself, which means that I can be he only in *representation*. But if I
represent myself as him, I am not he; I am separated from him as the
object from the subject, separated by *nothing*, but this nothing isolates
me from him. I can only play at *being* him. . . . What I attempt to realize
is a being-in-itself of the café waiter.
Being and Nothingness, trans. Hazel E. Barnes, p. 59

3   . . . I am the self which I will be, in the mode of not being it.
Being and Nothingness, trans. Hazel E. Barnes, p. 32

4   I have an appointment with Pierre at four o'clock. I arrive at the café a quarter of an hour late. Pierre is always punctual. Will he have waited for me? I look at the room, the patrons, and I say, 'He is not here'. . . . This does not mean that I discover his absence in some precise spot in the establishment. In fact Pierre is absent from the *whole* café; his absence fixes the café in its evanescence; the café remains *ground*. . . . Only it makes itself ground for a determined figure; it carries the figure everywhere in front of it, presents the figure everywhere to me. This figure which slips constantly between my look and the solid, real objects of the café is precisely a perpetual disappearance; it is Pierre raising himself as nothingness on the ground of the nihilation of the café. . . . my expectation has caused the absence of Pierre *to happen* as a real event concerning this café. . . . Pierre absent haunts this café . . .
Being and Nothingness, trans. Hazel E. Barnes, p. 9

5   Nothingness is not, Nothingness 'is made-to-be' . . . *The being by which Nothingness comes to the world must be its own Nothingness.*
Being and Nothingness, trans. Hazel E. Barnes, p. 23

6   To use Heidegger's expression, the world and outside of that – *nothing.* . . . This *nothing* is human reality itself as the radical negation by means of which the world is revealed. . . . human reality is that which causes *there to be* nothing outside of being.
Being and Nothingness, trans. Hazel E. Barnes, p. 181

7   Human reality is its own surpassing toward what it lacks; it surpasses itself toward the particular being which it would be if it were what it is. . . . Concretely, each *for-itself* is a lack of a certain coincidence with itself. This means that it is haunted by the presence of that with which it should coincide in order to be *itself*.
Being and Nothingness, trans. Hazel E. Barnes, p. 89

8   . . . picture an ass drawing behind him a cart. He attempts to get hold of a carrot which has been fastened at the end of a stick which in turn has been tied to the shaft of the cart. Every effort on the part of the ass to seize the carrot results in advancing the whole apparatus. . . . Thus we run after a possible which our very running causes to appear, . . . which thereby is by definition out of reach. We run toward ourselves and we are – due to this very fact – the being which can not be reunited with itself.
Being and Nothingness, trans. Hazel E. Barnes, p. 202

9   We can see the use which bad faith can make of these judgments which all aim at establishing that I am not what I am. If I were only what I *am*, I

could, for example, seriously consider an adverse criticism which someone makes of me, question myself scrupulously, and perhaps be compelled to recognize the truth in it. But thanks to transcendence, I am not subject to all that I am.

. . . the ambiguity necessary for bad faith comes from the fact that I affirm here that I *am* my transcendence in the mode of being of a thing.
Being and Nothingness, trans. Hazel E. Barnes, p. 57

In bad faith human reality is constituted as a being which is what it is not   **10** and which is not what it is[.] Let us take an example. A homosexual . . . has an obscure but strong feeling that a homosexual is not a homosexual as this table is a table or as this red-haired man is red-haired. . . . He would be right actually if he understood the phrase 'I am not a paederast' in the sense of 'I am not what I am.' . . . But instead he slides surreptitiously towards a different connotation of the word 'being'. He understands 'not being' in the sense of 'not-being-in-itself'. He lays claim to 'not being a paederast' in the sense in which this table is not an inkwell. He is in bad faith.

But the champion of sincerity . . . demands of the guilty one that he constitute himself as a thing ['a homosexual'], precisely in order no longer to treat him as a thing. And this contradiction is constitutive of the demand of sincerity.

. . . This explains the truth recognized by all that one can fall into bad faith through being sincere. . . .

In the final analysis the goal of sincerity and the goal of bad faith are not so different.
Being and Nothingness, trans. Hazel E. Barnes, p. 63

The For-itself, in fact, is nothing but the pure nihilation of the In-itself; it   **11** is like a hole of being at the heart of Being.
Being and Nothingness, trans. Hazel E. Barnes, p. 617

The point of view of pure knowledge is contradictory; there is only the   **12** point of view of engaged knowledge. This amounts to saying that knowledge and action are only two abstract aspects of an original, concrete relation. . . .

Perception is naturally surpassed toward action; better yet, it can be revealed only in and through projects of action. The world is revealed as an 'always future hollow', for we are always future to ourselves.
Being and Nothingness, trans. Hazel E. Barnes, p. 308

Far from the body being first *for us* and revealing things to us, it is the   **13** instrumental-things which in their original appearance indicate our body

to us. The body is not a screen between things and ourselves; . . . it is at once *a point of view and a point of departure* . . .
Being and Nothingness, trans. Hazel E. Barnes, p. 325

14 It is undeniable that pain contains information about itself; it is impossible to confuse pain in the eyes with pain in the finger or the stomach. Nevertheless pain is totally void of intentionality. . . . Pain *is precisely the eyes* in so far as consciousness 'exists them'. . . . But pain-consciousness is a project toward a further consciousness which would be empty of all pain; that is, to a consciousness whose contexture, whose being-there would be not painful. This *lateral* escape, this wrenching away from self which characterizes pain-consciousness does not for all that constitute pain as a psychic object. It is a non-thetic project of the For-itself; we apprehend it only through the world.
Being and Nothingness, trans. Hazel E. Barnes, p. 332

15 There is no more first a consciousness which receives *subsequently* the affect 'pleasure' like water which one stains, than there is first a pleasure (unconscious or psychological) which receives subsequently the quality of 'conscious' like a pencil of light rays.
Being and Nothingness, trans. Hazel E. Barnes, p. xxx

16 Consciousness . . . is total emptiness (since the entire world is outside it) . . .
Being and Nothingness, trans. Hazel E. Barnes, p. xxxii

17 Desire therefore does not *come to* consciousness as heat *comes to* the piece of iron which I hold near the flame. Consciousness chooses itself as desire.
Being and Nothingness, trans. Hazel E. Barnes, p. 391

18 An emotion . . . is a transformation of the world. When the paths before us become too difficult, or when we cannot see our way, we can no longer put up with such an exacting and difficult world. All ways are barred and nevertheless we must act. So then we try to change the world; that is, to live it as though the relations between things and their potentialities were not governed by deterministic processes but by magic.
Sketch for a Theory of the Emotions, trans. P. Mairet, p. 63

19 No emotional apprehension of an object as frightening, irritating, saddening, etc. can arise except against the background of a complete alteration of the world. For an object to appear *formidable*, indeed, it must be realized as an immediate and magical presence *confronting* the consciousness. For example, this face that I see ten yards away behind the window must be lived as an immediate, present threat to myself. . . . The window is no longer grasped as 'that which would first have to be

opened', it is grasped simply as the *frame* of the frightful visage. And in a general way, areas form themselves around me out of which the horrible makes itself felt. For the horrible is *not possible* in the deterministic world of the usable.
Sketch for a Theory of the Emotions, trans. P. Mairet, p. 88

... the yellow of the lemon is not a subjective mode of apprehending the lemon; it *is* the lemon. And it is not true either that the object X appears as the empty form which holds together disparate qualities. In fact the lemon is extended throughout its qualities, and each of its qualities is extended throughout each of the others. It is the sourness of the lemon which is yellow, it is the yellow of the lemon which is sour. We eat the color of a cake, and ... if I poke my finger into a jar of jam, the sticky coldness of that jam is the revelation to my fingers of its sugary taste. The fluidity, the tepidity, the bluish color, the undulating restlessness of the water in a pool are given at one stroke, each quality through the others; and it is this total interpenetration which we call the *this*. . . . Quality is *the whole of being* revealing itself within the limits of the 'there is'. It is not the 'outside' of being . . .
Being and Nothingness, trans. Hazel E. Barnes, p. 186 — 20

No factual state whatever it may be (the political and economic structure of society, the psychological 'state', etc.) is capable by itself of motivating any act whatsoever. . . . No factual state can determine consciousness to apprehend it as a *négatité* or as a lack. . . . In fact in so far as consciousness is 'invested' by being, in so far as it simply suffers what is, it must be included in being. It is the organized form – worker-finding-his-suffering-natural – which must be surmounted and denied in order for it to be able to form the object of a revealing contemplation. This means evidently that it is by a pure wrenching away from himself and the world that the worker can posit his suffering as unbearable suffering and consequently can *make of it the motive* for his revolutionary action.
Being and Nothingness, trans. Hazel E. Barnes, p. 435 — 21

... in this world where I engage myself, my acts cause values to spring up like partridges. — 22
Being and Nothingness, trans. Hazel E. Barnes, p. 38

Value derives its being from its exigency and not its exigency from its being. . . . On the contrary, it can be revealed only to an active freedom which makes it exist as value by the sole fact of recognizing it as such. It follows that my freedom is the unique foundation of values and that *nothing*, absolutely nothing, justifies me in adopting this or that particular value, this or that particular scale of values. — 23
Being and Nothingness, trans. Hazel E. Barnes, p. 34

24 ... there exist concretely alarm clocks, signboards, tax forms, policemen, so many guard rails against anguish. But as soon as the enterprise is held at a distance from me, as soon as I am referred to myself because I must await myself in the future, then I discover myself suddenly as the one who gives its meaning to the alarm clock, the one who by a signboard forbids himself to walk on a flower bed or on the lawn, the one from whom the boss's order borrows its urgency, the one who decides the interest of the book which he is writing, the one finally who makes the values exist in order to determine his action by their demands. I emerge alone and in anguish confronting the unique and original project which constitutes my being; all the barriers, all the guard rails collapse, nihilated by the consciousness of my freedom. I do not have nor can I have recourse to any value against the fact that it is I who sustain values in being. Nothing can ensure me against myself, cut off from the world and from my essence by this nothingness which I *am*. I have to realize the meaning of the world and of my essence; I make my decision concerning them – without justification and without excuse.

Being and Nothingness, trans. Hazel E. Barnes, p. 39

25 ... man is condemned to be free.

Existentialism and Humanism, trans. P. Mairet, p. 34

26 And without formulating anything clearly, I understood that I had found the key to Existence, the key to my Nausea, to my own life. In fact, all that I was able to grasp afterwards comes down to this fundamental absurdity. . . . The world of explanations and reasons is not that of existence. . . .

The essential thing is contingency. I mean that, by definition, existence is not necessity. To exist is simply *to be there*; what exists appears, lets itself be *encountered*, but you can never *deduce* it. There are people, I believe, who have understood that. Only they have tried to overcome this contingency by inventing a necessary causal being. But no necessary being can explain existence: contingency is not an illusion, an appearance which can be dissipated; it is absolute, and consequently perfect gratuitousness. Everything is gratuitous, that park, this town, and myself. When you realize that, it turns your stomach over and everything starts floating about . . .

Nausea, trans. Robert Baldick, p. 393

27 Slime is the revenge of the In-itself. . . . A sugary-sliminess is the ideal of the slimy; it symbolizes the sugary death of the For-itself (like that of the wasp which sinks into the jam and drowns in it). But at the same time the . . . sucking of the slimy which I feel on my hands outlines a kind of continuity of the slimy substance in myself. . . . [Slime] transcends all

distinctions between psychic and physical, between the brute existent and the meanings of the world; it is a possible meaning of being.
Being and Nothingness, trans. Hazel E. Barnes, p. 609

... all human activities are equivalent. ... Thus it amounts to the same 28
thing whether one gets drunk alone or is a leader of nations. If one of these activities takes precedence over the other, this will not be because of its real goal but because of the degree of consciousness which it possesses of its ideal goal ...
Being and Nothingness, trans. Hazel E. Barnes, p. 627

The necessity of perpetually choosing myself is one with the pursued- 29
pursuit which I am. ... my freedom eats away my freedom.
Being and Nothingness, trans. Hazel E. Barnes, p. 479

... a voluntary deliberation is always a deception. How can I evaluate 30
causes and motives on which I myself confer their value before all deliberation and by the very choice which I make of myself? The illusion here stems from the fact that we endeavor to take causes and motives for entirely transcendent things which I balance in my hands like weights and which possess a weight as a permanent property. Yet on the other hand we try to view them as contents of consciousness, and this is self-contradictory. Actually causes and motives have only the weight which my project – i.e., the free production of the end and of the known act to be realized – confers upon them. When I deliberate, the chips are down. ... When the will intervenes, the decision is taken, and it has no other value than that of making the announcement.
Being and Nothingness, trans. Hazel E. Barnes, p. 450

... every action, no matter how trivial, is not the simple effect of the 31
prior psychic state and does not result from a linear determinism but rather is integrated as a secondary structure in global structures and finally in the totality which I am.
Being and Nothingness, trans. Hazel E. Barnes, p. 459

It is impossible seriously to consider the feeling of inferiority without 32
determining it in terms of the future and of my possibilities. Even assertions such as 'I am ugly', 'I am stupid', etc. are by nature anticipations. We are not dealing here with the pure establishment of my ugliness but with the apprehension of the coefficient of adversity which is ·presented by women or by society to my enterprises. And this can be discovered only through and in the choice of these enterprises. Thus the inferiority complex is a free and global project of myself as inferior before others ...
Being and Nothingness, trans. Hazel E. Barnes, p. 459

33 Perpetually absent to my body, to my acts, I am despite myself that 'divine absence' of which Valéry speaks. I cannot say either that I *am* here or that I *am* not here, in the sense that we say 'that box of matches *is* on the table'; this would be to confuse my 'being-in-the-world' with a 'being-in-the-midst-of-the-world'. . . . On all sides I escape being and yet – I am.
Being and Nothingness, trans. Hazel E. Barnes, p. 60

34 Thus this relation which I call 'being-seen-by-another', far from being merely one of the relations signified by the word *man*, represents an irreducible fact which can not be deduced either from the essence of the Other-as-object, or from my being-as-subject. . . .

Let us imagine that moved by jealousy, curiosity, or vice I have just glued my ear to the door and looked through a keyhole. I am alone and on the level of a non-thetic self-consciousness. This means first of all that . . . I am a pure consciousness of things. . . . Behind that door a spectacle is presented as 'to be seen', a conversation as 'to be heard'.

. . . But all of a sudden I hear footsteps in the hall. Someone is looking at me! What does this mean?

. . . First of all, I now exist as *myself* for my unreflective consciousness. It is this irruption of the self which has been most often described: I see *myself* because *somebody* sees me.
Being and Nothingness, trans. Hazel E. Barnes, p. 257

35 The *Other's look* as the necessary condition of my objectivity is the destruction of all objectivity for me. The Other's look touches me across the world and is not only a transformation of myself but a total metamorphosis of the *world* . . . [it] denies my distances from objects and unfolds its own distances. . . .

At the same time I experience the Other's infinite freedom. . . . In fact my wrenching away from myself and the upsurge of the Other's freedom are one; I can feel them and live them only as an ensemble . . .
Being and Nothingness, trans. Hazel E. Barnes, p. 269

36 The Other *looks* at me and as such he holds the secret of my being, he knows what I *am*. Thus the profound meaning of my being is outside of me, imprisoned in an absence. The Other has the advantage over me.
Being and Nothingness, trans. Hazel E. Barnes, p. 363

37 Hell is other people.
In Camera

38 . . . the Other escapes me. I should like to act upon his freedom, to appropriate it, or at least, to make the Other's freedom recognize my freedom. But this freedom is death; it is no longer absolutely *in the world*

in which I encounter the Other-as-object, for his characteristic is to be transcendent to the world. To be sure, I can *grasp* the Other, grab hold of him, knock him down. . . . But everything happens as if I wished to get hold of a man who runs away and leaves only his coat in my hands. It is the coat, it is the outer shell which I possess. . . . I can make the Other beg for mercy or ask my pardon, but I shall always be ignorant of what this submission means for and in the Other's freedom.
Being and Nothingness, trans. Hazel E. Barnes, p. 393

Desire is an attempt to strip the body of its movements as of its clothing **39** and to make it exist as pure flesh; it is an attempt to *incarnate* the Other's body. . . . But, someone will object, was the Other not already incarnated? To be precise, *no*. The Other's flesh did not exist explicitly for me since I grasped the Other's body in situation; neither did it exist for her since she transcended it toward her possibilities and toward the object. The caress causes the Other to be born as flesh for me and for herself.
Being and Nothingness, trans. Hazel E. Barnes, p. 389

Desire is an attitude aiming at enchantment. Since I can grasp the Other **40** only in his objective facticity, the problem is to ensnare his freedom within this facticity. It is necessary that he be 'caught' in it as the cream is caught up by a person skimming milk. So the Other's For-itself must come to play on the surface of his body, and be extended all through his body; and by touching this body I should finally touch the Other's free subjectivity. This is the true meaning of the word *possession*. It is certain that I want to *possess* the Other's body, but I want to possess it in so far as it is itself a 'possessed', that is, in so far as the Other's consciousness is identified with his body. Such is the impossible ideal of desire: to possess the Other's transcendence as pure transcendence and at the same time as *body*.
Being and Nothingness, trans. Hazel E. Barnes, p. 394

A philosophy is first of all a particular way in which the 'rising' class **41** becomes conscious of itself. . . . Every philosophy is practical, even the one which at first appears to be the most contemplative. Its method is a social and political weapon.
Search for a Method, trans. Hazel E. Barnes, p. 3

F. W. J. SCHELLING (1775–1854)

The eternal, timeless act of self-consciousness which we call *self* is that **1** which gives all things existence.
System of Transcendental Idealism, trans. Peter Heath, p. 32

2 The first question which can be legitimately asked of a philosophy of history is without doubt this: since, if everything that is, is posited for everyone only through his own consciousness, the whole of past history too can be posited for everyone only through his own consciousness, how is a history conceivable at all?
System of Transcendental Idealism, Werke, ed. K. Schelling, III, p. 590, trans. M. Inwood

3 All knowledge is founded upon the coincidence of an objective with a subjective.
System of Transcendental Idealism, p. 555, trans. M. Inwood

4 We have an earlier revelation than any written one – nature. It contains archetypes which no one has yet interpreted.
Philosophical Inquiries into the Nature of Human Freedom, trans. James Gutmann, p. 98

5 It is only by the fact that there are intelligences outside me that the world becomes objective for me at all.
System of Transcendental Idealism, p. 555, trans. M. Inwood

6 Nature-philosophy and transcendental philosophy have divided into the two directions possible to philosophy, and if *all* philosophy must go about *either* to make an intelligence out of nature, *or* a nature out of intelligence, then transcendental philosophy, which has the latter task, is thus *the other necessary basic science of philosophy*.
System of Transcendental Idealism, trans. Peter Heath, p. 7

7 If we think of history as a play in which everyone involved plays his part quite freely and as he pleases, a rational development of this muddled drama is conceivable only if there be a single spirit who speaks in everyone.
System of Transcendental Idealism, trans. Peter Heath, p. 210

8 All antitheses disappear with respect to the Absolute.
Philosophical Inquiries into the Nature of Human Freedom, trans. James Gutmann, p. 91

9 The *absolute* intelligence, which has absolute rather than empirical eternity . . . is everything that is, and was, and will be.
System of Transcendental Idealism, trans. Peter Heath, p. 119

10 The absolute acts through each single intelligence, whose action is thus *itself* absolute, and to that extent neither free nor unfree, but both at once, *absolutely* free, and for that very reason also necessary.
System of Transcendental Idealism, trans. Peter Heath, p. 210

Inner necessity is itself freedom; man's being is essentially *his own deed*. **11**
Necessity and freedom interpenetrate as one being which appears as the
one or the other only as regarded from various aspects; in itself it is
freedom, but formally regarded, necessity.
Philosophical Inquiries into the Nature of Human Freedom, trans. James
Gutmann, p. 63

Philosophy attains, indeed, to the highest, but it brings to this summit **12**
only, so to say, the fraction of a man. Art brings *the whole man*, as he is,
to that point, namely to a knowledge of the highest.
System of Transcendental Idealism, trans. Peter Heath, p. 233

It is a poor objection to a philosopher that he is unintelligible. **13**
On the History of Modern Philosophy: Munich Lectures, Werke, X, p. 163

FRIEDRICH VON SCHLEGEL (1772–1829)

It's equally fatal for the mind to have a system and to have none. It will **1**
simply have to decide to combine the two.
'Athenaeum Fragments', *Friedrich Schlegel's Lucinde and the Fragments*, trans.
Peter Firchow, p. 167

Some things philosophy must assume for the present and forever, and it **2**
may do so because it must.
'Athenaeum Fragments', trans. Peter Firchow, p. 172

Principles are to life what instructions written by the cabinet are for the **3**
general in battle.
'Athenaeum Fragments', trans. Peter Firchow, p. 171

Publishing is to thinking as the maternity ward is to the first kiss. **4**
'Athenaeum Fragments', trans. Peter Firchow, p. 169

As yet every great philosopher has explained his predecessors – often **5**
quite unintentionally – in such a way that it seemed that before him they
had been entirely misunderstood.
'Athenaeum Fragments', trans. Peter Firchow, p. 172

At the words 'his philosophy, my philosophy', one is always reminded of **6**
that line in [Lessing's] *Nathan* [*the Wise*]: 'Who owns God? What kind
of God is that who belongs to a man?'
'Athenaeum Fragments', trans. Peter Firchow, p. 173

The fact that one can annihilate a philosophy . . . or that one can prove **7**
that a philosophy annihilates itself is of little consequence. If it's really
philosophy, then, like a phoenix, it will always rise again from its own
ashes.
'Athenaeum Fragments', trans. Peter Firchow, p. 173

FRIEDRICH SCHLEIERMACHER (1768–1834)

Knowing the world means knowing that one doesn't signify much in it, means believing that no philosophical dream can be realized in it, and means hoping that it will never be otherwise, or at best only somewhat flimsier.

'Athenaeum Fragments', *Friedrich Schlegel's Lucinde and the Fragments*, p. 217

MORITZ SCHLICK (1882–1936)

1 In order, therefore, to find the meaning of a proposition, we have to transform it by introduction of successive definitions, until finally only such words appear in it as can no longer be defined, but whose meanings can only be indicated directly. The criterion for the truth or falsity of the proposition then consists in this, that under specific conditions (stated in the definitions) certain data are, or are not, present. Once this is established, I have established everything that the proposition was talking about, and hence I know its meaning. If I am *not* capable, in principle, of verifying a proposition, that is, if I have absolutely no knowledge of how I should go about it, what I would have to do, in order to ascertain its truth or falsity, then I obviously have no idea at all of what the proposition is actually saying. . . . To state the circumstances under which a proposition is true is *the same* as stating its meaning, and nothing else.

'Positivism and Realism', *Philosophical Papers*, ed. H. Mulder and B. van der Velde-Schlick, II, p. 264

2 . . . every statement has a meaning only insofar as it can be verified; it only *signifies* what is verified and absolutely *nothing* beyond this. Were someone to maintain that it contains more, he would have to be able to say what this more is, and for this he must again say what in the world would be different if he was wrong; but he can say nothing of the kind, for by previous assumption all observable differences have already been utilized in the verification.

'Positivism and Realism', p. 266

3 But now how about science? When it speaks of the external world, does it, unlike daily life, mean something other than things such as houses and trees? It seems to me that this is by no means the case. For atoms and electric fields, or whatever else the physicist may speak of, are precisely what houses and trees consist of, according to his teaching; the one must therefore be real in the same sense as the other. The objectivity of mountains and clouds is just exactly the same as that of protons and energies; the latter stand in no greater contrast to the 'subjectivity' of feelings, say, or hallucinations, than do the former. We have long

convinced ourselves, in fact, that the existence of even the most subtle of the 'invisible' things postulated by the scientist is verified, in principle, in exactly the same way as the reality of a tree or a star.
'Positivism and Realism', p. 278

. . . the so-called problem of the freedom of the will . . . has long since 4
been settled by the efforts of certain sensible persons . . . Hence it is really one of the greatest scandals of philosophy that again and again so much paper and printer's ink is devoted to this matter, to say nothing of the expenditure of thought, which could have been applied to more important problems (assuming that it would have sufficed for these).
Problems of Ethics, trans. David Rynin, p. 143

ARTHUR SCHOPENHAUER (1788–1860)

In endless space countless luminous spheres, round each of which some 1
dozen smaller illuminated ones revolve, hot at the core and covered over with a hard cold crust; on this crust a mouldy film has produced living and knowing beings: this is empirical truth, the real, the world. Yet for a being who thinks, it is a precarious position to stand on one of those numberless spheres freely floating in boundless space, without knowing whence or whither, and to be only one of innumerable similar beings that throng, press, and toil, restlessly and rapidly arising and passing away in beginningless and endless time. Here there is nothing permanent but matter alone, and the recurrence of the same varied organic forms by means of certain ways and channels that inevitably exist as they do. All that empirical science can teach is only the more precise nature and rule of these events. But at last the philosophy of modern times, especially through Berkeley and Kant, has called to mind that all this in the first instance is only *phenomenon of the brain*, and is encumbered by so many great and different *subjective* conditions that its supposed absolute reality vanishes, and leaves room for an entirely different world-order that lies at the root of that phenomenon, in other words, is related to it as is the thing-in-itself to the mere appearance.

'The world is my representation' is, like the axioms of Euclid, a proposition which everyone must recognize as true as soon as he understands it, although it is not a proposition that everyone understands as soon as he hears it. To have brought this proposition to consciousness and to have connected it with the problem of the relation of the ideal to the real, in other words, of the world in the head to the world outside the head, constitutes, together with the problem of moral freedom, the distinctive characteristic of the philosophy of the moderns. For only after men had tried their hand for thousands of years at merely *objective* philosophizing did they discover that, among the many things that make

409

the world so puzzling and precarious, the first and foremost is that, however immeasurable and massive it may be, its existence hangs nevertheless on a single thread; and this thread is the actual consciousness in which it exists.

The World as Will and Representation, trans. E. F. J. Payne, II, p. 3

2 'The world is my representation': this is a truth valid with reference to every living and knowing being, although man alone can bring it into reflective, abstract consciousness. If he really does so, philosophical discernment has dawned on him. It then becomes clear and certain to him that he does not know a sun and an earth, but only an eye that sees a sun, a hand that feels an earth; that the world around him is there only as representation, in other words, only in reference to another thing, namely that which represents, and this is himself.

The World as Will and Representation, trans. E. F. J. Payne, I, p. 3

3 Even the most practised logician, if he notices that in a particular case he concludes otherwise than as stated by the rule, will always look for a mistake in the rule rather than in the conclusion he actually draws. To seek to make practical use of logic would therefore mean to seek to derive with unspeakable trouble from universal rules what is immediately known to us with the greatest certainty in the particular case. It is just as if a man were to consult mechanics with regard to his movements, or physiology with regard to his digestion; and one who has learnt logic for practical purposes is like a man who should seek to train a beaver to build its lodge.

The World as Will and Representation, trans. E. F. J. Payne, I, p. 46

4 In fact, the meaning that I am looking for of the world that stands before me simply as my representation, or the transition from it as mere representation of the knowing subject to whatever it may be besides this, could never be found if the investigator himself were nothing more than the purely knowing subject (a winged cherub without a body). But he himself is rooted in that world; and thus he finds himself in it as an *individual*, in other words, his knowledge, which is the conditional supporter of the whole world as representation, is nevertheless given entirely through the medium of a body, and the affections of this body. . . . To the subject of knowing, who appears as an individual only through his identity with the body, this body is given in two entirely different ways. It is given in intelligent perception as representation, as an object among objects, liable to the laws of these objects. But it is also given in quite a different way, namely as what is known immediately to everyone, and is denoted by the word *will*. Every true act of his will is also at once and inevitably a movement of his body; he cannot actually will the act

without at the same time being aware that it appears as a movement of the body. The act of will and the action of the body are not two different states objectively known, connected by the bond of causality; they do not stand in the relation of cause and effect, but are one and the same thing, though given in two entirely different ways, first quite directly, and then in perception for the understanding. The action of the body is nothing but the act of will objectified, i.e., translated into perception.
The World as Will and Representation, trans. E. F. J. Payne, I, p. 99

The concept of *will* is of all possible concepts the only one that has its 5 origin *not* in the phenomenon, *not* in the mere representation of perception, but which comes from within, and proceeds from the most immediate consciousness of everyone. In this consciousness each one knows and at the same time is himself his own individuality according to its nature immediately, without any form, even the form of subject and object, for here knower and known coincide.
The World as Will and Representation, trans. E. F. J. Payne, I, p. 112

. . . the inner nature of his own phenomenon, which manifests itself to 6 him as representation both through his actions and through the permanent substratum of these his body, is his *will*. . . . The reader who with me has gained this conviction will find that of itself it will become the key to the knowledge of the innermost being of the whole of nature, since he now transfers it to all those phenomena that are given to him, not like his own phenomenon both in direct and in indirect knowledge, but in the latter solely, and hence merely in a one-sided way, as *representation* alone. . . . Only the *will* is *thing-in-itself*; as such it is not representation at all, but *toto genere* different therefrom. It is that of which all representation, all object, is the phenomenon, the visibility, the *objectivity*. It is the innermost essence, the kernel, of every particular thing and also of the whole. It appears in every blindly acting force of nature, and also in the deliberate conduct of man, and the great difference between the two concerns only the degree of the manifestation, not the inner nature of what is manifested.
The World as Will and Representation, trans. E. F. J. Payne, I, p. 109

But now, what kind of knowledge is it that considers what continues to 7 exist outside and independently of all relations, but which alone is really essential to the world, the true content of its phenomena, that which is subject to no change, and is therefore known with equal truth for all time, in a word, the *Ideas* that are the immediate and adequate objectivity of the thing-in-itself, of the will? It is *art*, the work of genius. It repeats the eternal Ideas apprehended through pure contemplation, the essential and abiding element in all the phenomena of the world.

According to the material in which it repeats, it is sculpture, painting, poetry, or music. Its only source is knowledge of the Ideas; its sole aim is communication of this knowledge. Whilst science, following the restless and unstable stream of the fourfold forms of reasons or grounds and consequents, is with every end it attains again and again directed farther, and can never find an ultimate goal or complete satisfaction, any more than by running we can reach the point where the clouds touch the horizon; art, on the contrary, is everywhere at its goal. For it plucks the object of its contemplation from the stream of the world's course, and holds it isolated before it. This particular thing, which in that stream was an infinitesimal part, becomes for art a representative of the whole, an equivalent of the infinitely many in space and time. It therefore pauses at this particular thing; it stops the wheel of time . . .

The World as Will and Representation, trans. E. F. J. Payne, I, p. 184

8   No attained object of willing can give a satisfaction that lasts and no longer declines; but it is always like the alms thrown to a beggar, which reprieves him today so that his misery may be prolonged till tomorrow. Therefore, so long as our consciousness is filled by our will, so long as we are given up to the throng of desires with its constant hopes and fears, so long as we are the subject of willing, we never obtain lasting happiness or peace. . . .

When, however, an external cause or inward disposition suddenly raises us out of the endless stream of willing, and snatches knowledge from the thraldom of the will, the attention is now no longer directed to the motives of willing, but comprehends things free from their relation to the will. Thus it considers things without interest, without subjectivity, purely objectively; it is entirely given up to them in so far as they are merely representations, and not motives. Then all at once the peace, always sought but always escaping us on that first path of willing, comes to us of its own accord, and all is well with us. It is the painless state, prized by Epicurus as the highest good and as the state of the gods; for that moment we are delivered from the miserable pressure of the will. We celebrate the Sabbath of the penal servitude of willing; the wheel of Ixion stands still.

The World as Will and Representation, trans. E. F. J. Payne, I, p. 196

9   Nature in turbulent and tempestuous motion; semi-darkness through threatening black thunder-clouds; immense, bare, overhanging cliffs shutting out the view by their interlacing; rushing, foaming masses of water; complete desert; the wail of the wind sweeping through the ravines. Our dependence, our struggle with hostile nature, our will that is broken in this, now appear clearly before our eyes. Yet as long as

personal affliction does not gain the upper hand, but we remain in aesthetic contemplation, the pure subject of knowing gazes through this struggle of nature, through this picture of the broken will, and comprehends calmly, unshaken and unconcerned, the Ideas in those very objects that are threatening and terrible to the will. In this contrast is to be found the feeling of the sublime.

The World as Will and Representation, trans. E. F. J. Payne, I, p. 204

All satisfaction, or what is commonly called happiness, is really and essentially always *negative* only, and never positive. It is not a gratification which comes to us originally and of itself, but it must always be the satisfaction of a wish. For desire, that is to say, want, is the precedent condition of every pleasure; but with the satisfaction, the desire and therefore the pleasure cease; and so the satisfaction or gratification can never be more than deliverance from a pain, from a want. **10**

The World as Will and Representation, trans. E. F. J. Payne, I, p. 319

What we see in poetry we find again in music, in the melodies of which we again recognize the universally expressed, innermost story of the will conscious of itself, the most secret living, longing, suffering, and enjoying, the ebb and flow of the human heart. Melody is always a deviation from the keynote through a thousand crotchety wanderings up to the most painful discord. After this, it at last finds the keynote again, which expresses the satisfaction and composure of the will, but with which nothing more can then be done, and the continuation of which would be only a wearisome and meaningless monotony corresponding to boredom. **11**

The World as Will and Representation, trans. E. F. J. Payne, I, p. 321

I cannot here withhold the statement that *optimism*, where it is not merely the thoughtless talk of those who harbour nothing but words under their shallow foreheads, seems to me to be not merely an absurd, but also a really *wicked*, way of thinking, a bitter mockery of the unspeakable sufferings of mankind. **12**

The World as Will and Representation, trans. E. F. J. Payne, I, p. 326

Of course the world does not exhibit itself to knowledge which has sprung from the will to serve it, and which comes to the individual as such in the same way as it finally discloses itself to the inquirer, namely as the objectivity of the one and only will-to-live, which he himself is. On the contrary, the eyes of the uncultured individual are clouded, as the Indians say, by the veil of Maya. To him is revealed not the thing-in-itself, but only the phenomenon in time and space . . . **13**

The World as Will and Representation, trans. E. F. J. Payne, I, p. 352

14 According to the true nature of things, everyone has all the sufferings of the world as his own; indeed, he has to look upon all merely possible sufferings as actual for him, so long as he is the firm and constant will-to-live, in other words, affirms life with all his strength. For the knowledge that sees through the *principium individuationis*, a happy life in time, given by chance or won from it by shrewdness, amid the sufferings of innumerable others, is only a beggar's dream, in which he is a king, but from which he must awake, in order to realize that only a fleeting illusion had separated him from the suffering of his life.
The World as Will and Representation, trans. E. F. J. Payne, I, p. 353

15 Far from being denial of the will, suicide is a phenomenon of the will's strong affirmation. For denial has its essential nature in the fact that the pleasures of life, not its sorrows, are shunned. The suicide wills life, and is dissatisfied merely with the conditions on which it has come to him. Therefore he gives up by no means the will-to-live, but merely life, since he destroys the individual phenomenon.
The World as Will and Representation, trans. E. F. J. Payne, I, p. 398

16 Kant's proposition: 'The *I think* must accompany all our representations', is insufficient; for the 'I' is an unknown quantity, in other words, it is itself a mystery and a secret. What gives unity and sequence to consciousness, since, by pervading all the representations of consciousness, it is its substratum, its permanent supporter, cannot itself be conditioned by consciousness, and therefore cannot be a representation. On the contrary, it must be the *prius* of consciousness, and the root of the tree of which consciousness is the fruit. This, I say, is the *will*; it alone is unalterable and absolutely identical, and has brought forth consciousness for its own ends. It is therefore the will that gives it unity and holds all its representations and ideas together, accompanying them, as it were, like a continuous ground-bass. Without it the intellect would have no more unity of consciousness than has a mirror, in which now one thing now another presents itself in succession, or at most only as much as a convex mirror has, whose rays converge at an imaginary point behind its surface.
The World as Will and Representation, trans. E. F. J. Payne, II, p. 139

17 The way in which this *vanity* of all objects of the will makes itself known and comprehensible to the intellect that is rooted in the individual is primarily *time*. It is the form by whose means that vanity of things appears as their transitoriness, since by virtue of this all our pleasures and enjoyments come to nought in our hands, and afterwards we ask in astonishment where they have remained. Hence that vanity itself is the only *objective* element of time, in other words, that which corresponds to it in the inner nature of things, and so that of which it is the expression.
The World as Will and Representation, trans. E. F. J. Payne, II, p. 574

He who is capable of thinking a little more deeply will soon perceive that 18 human desires cannot begin to be sinful simply at that point at which, in their chance encounters with one another, they occasion harm and evil; but that, if this is what they bring about, they must be originally and in their essence sinful and reprehensible, and the entire will to live itself reprehensible. All the cruelty and torment of which the world is full is in fact merely the necessary result of the totality of the forms under which the will to live is objectified, and thus merely a commentary on the affirmation of the will to live. That our existence itself implies guilt is proved by the fact of death.

Essays and Aphorisms, trans. R. J. Hollingdale, p. 63

Yet music speaks not of things but of pure weal and woe, which are the 19 only realities for the *will*: that is why it speaks so much to the heart, while it has nothing to say *directly* to the head and it is a misuse of it to demand that it should do so, as happens in all *pictorial* music . . .

Essays and Aphorisms, trans. R. J. Hollingdale, p. 162

Among people untrained in philosophy – which includes all who have 20 not studied the philosophy of Kant, that is to say most foreigners – and no less among many present-day physicians, etc., in Germany who are content to philosophize on the basis of their catechism, there still exists the old, fundamentally false antithesis between *mind and matter*. . . . If you suppose the existence of a *mind* in the human head, as a *deus ex machina*, then, as already remarked, you are bound to concede a mind to every stone. If, on the other hand, your dead and purely passive *matter* can, as weight, exert itself, or as electricity attract, repel and give off sparks, then it can also, as grey-matter, think. In short: all ostensible mind can be attributed to matter, but all matter can likewise be attributed to mind; from which it follows that the antithesis is a false one.

Essays and Aphorisms, trans. R. J. Hollingdale, p. 212

Why, despite all our mirrors, do we never really know what we look like, 21 and consequently cannot picture ourselves in imagination, as we can everyone else we know?

The reason is undoubtedly in part the fact that when we look at ourselves in a mirror we always do so with a direct and unmoving gaze, whereby the play of the eyes, which is so meaningful and in fact the actual characteristic of our gaze, is in great part lost. With this physical impossibility, however, there seems to go an analogous ethical impossibility. The condition under which *objective* comprehension of something perceived is possible is *alienation* from that which is perceived; but when we see our own reflection in a mirror we are unable to take an alienated view of it, because this view depends ultimately on moral egoism, with its

profound feeling of *not me*: so that when we see our own reflection our egoism whispers to us a precautionary 'This is not not-me, but me', which has the effect of a *noli me tangere* and prevents any purely objective comprehension.
Essays and Aphorisms, trans. R. J. Hollingdale, p. 171

JOHN R. SEARLE (*b.* 1932)

1   The reason that no computer program can ever be a mind is simply that a computer program is only syntactical, and minds are more than syntactical. Minds are semantical, in the sense that they have more than a formal structure, they have a content.

To illustrate this point I have designed a certain thought-experiment. Imagine that . . . you are locked in a room, and in this room are several baskets full of Chinese symbols. Imagine that you (like me) do not understand a word of Chinese, but that you are given a rule book in English for manipulating these Chinese symbols. The rules specify the manipulations of the symbols purely formally, in terms of their syntax, not their semantics. So the rule might say: 'Take a squiggle-squiggle sign out of basket number one and put it next to a squoggle-squoggle sign from basket number two.' Now suppose that some other Chinese symbols are passed into the room, and that you are given further rules for passing back Chinese symbols out of the room. Suppose that unknown to you the symbols passed into the room are called 'questions' by the people outside the room, and the symbols you pass back out of the room are called 'answers to the questions'. Suppose, furthermore, that the programmers are so good at designing the programs and that you are so good at manipulating the symbols, that very soon your answers are indistinguishable from those of a native Chinese speaker. There you are locked in your room shuffling your Chinese symbols and passing out Chinese symbols in response to incoming Chinese symbols. . . .

Now the point of the story is simply this: by virtue of implementing a formal computer program from the point of view of an outside observer, you behave exactly as if you understood Chinese, but all the same you don't understand a word of Chinese. . . . Understanding a language, or indeed, having mental states at all, involves more than just having a bunch of formal symbols. It involves having an interpretation, or a meaning attached to those symbols.
Minds, Brains and Science, p. 31

2   Unless you believe that the mind is separable from the brain both conceptually and empirically – dualism in a strong form – you cannot hope to reproduce the mental by writing and running programs since

416

programs must be independent of brains or any other particular forms of instantiation. . . .

'Could a machine think?' My own view is that *only* a machine could think, and indeed only very special kinds of machines, namely brains and machines that had the same causal powers as brains. And that is the main reason strong AI has had little to tell us about thinking, since it has nothing to tell us about machines. By its own definition, it is about programs, and programs are not machines. Whatever else intentionality is, it is a biological phenomenon, and it is as likely to be as causally dependent on the specific biochemistry of its origins as lactation, photosynthesis, or any other biological phenomena.
'Minds, Brains and Programs', *The Philosophy of Artificial Intelligence*, ed. M. Boden, p. 86

It is often said that one cannot derive an 'ought' from an 'is'. This thesis 3 . . . comes from a famous passage in Hume's *Treatise*. . . . Put in more contemporary terminology, no set of *descriptive* statements can entail an *evaluative* statement without the addition of at least one evaluative premise. To believe otherwise is to commit what has been called the naturalistic fallacy.

I shall attempt to demonstrate a counterexample to this thesis. . . . Consider the following series of statements:

(1) Jones uttered the words 'I hereby promise to pay you, Smith, five dollars.'
(2) Jones promised to pay Smith five dollars.
(3) Jones placed himself under (undertook) an obligation to pay Smith five dollars.
(4) Jones is under an obligation to pay Smith five dollars.
(5) Jones ought to pay Smith five dollars.

I shall argue concerning this list that the relation between any statement and its successor, while not in every case one of 'entailment', is nonetheless not just a contingent relation; and the additional statements necessary to make the relationship one of entailment do not need to involve any evaluative statements, moral principles, or anything of the sort.
'How to Derive on "Ought" from an "Is" ', *Philosophical Review* (1964), p. 101

A marriage ceremony, a baseball game, a trial, and a legislative action 4 involve a variety of physical movements, states, and raw feels, but a specification of one of these events only in such terms is not so far a specification of it as a marriage ceremony, a baseball game, a trial, or a legislative action. . . . Such facts as are recorded in my above group of statements I propose to call *institutional facts*. They are indeed facts; but their

existence, unlike the existence of brute facts, presupposes the existence of certain human institutions.
Speech Acts, p. 51

5 . . . the illusion of limitless uses of language is engendered by an enormous unclarity of what constitutes the criteria for delimiting one language game or use of language from another. If we adopt illocutionary point as the basic notion on which to classify uses of language, then there are a rather limited number of basic things we do with language: we tell people how things are, we try to get them to do things, we commit ourselves to doing things, we express our feelings and attitudes and we bring about changes through our utterances. Often, we do more than one of these at once in the same utterance.
Expression and Meaning, p. 29

6 So deeply embedded in our whole mode of sensibility are certain metaphorical associations that we tend to think there *must* be a similarity or even that the association itself is a form of similarity. Thus, we feel inclined to say that the passage of time *just is like* spacial movement, but when we say this we forget that 'passage' is only yet another spacial metaphor for time and that the bald assertion of similarity, with no specification of the respective similarity, is without content.
Expression and Meaning, p. 99

WILFRED SELLARS (1912–1989)

1 According to VB [Verbal Behaviourism], thinking 'that -p', where this means 'having the thought occur to one that -p', has as its *primary* sense *saying* 'p'; and a *secondary* sense in which it stands for a short term proximate propensity to say 'p'. Propensities tend to be actualised (a logical point about the term); when they are not, we speak of them as, for example, 'blocked'. The VB I am constructing sees the relevant inhibiting factor which blocks a saying that -p as that of not being in a thinking-out-loud frame of mind.
'Meaning as Functional Classification', *Synthèse* (1974), p. 418

2 . . . the world we have been constructing is one in which every basic state of affairs is expressed by the use of verbs and adverbs. The idea has fascinating implications. . . . There are no *objects* . . . the world is an on going tissue of goings on.
'Foundations for a Metaphysics of Pure Process', *Monist* (1981), p. 56

3 The crucial issue then is this: can we define, in the framework of neurophysiology, states which are sufficiently analogous in their *intrinsic* character to sensations to make identification plausible? The answer

seems clearly to be 'no'. . . . The trouble is . . . that the feature which we referred to as 'ultimate homogeneity' and which characterises the perceptible qualities of things, e.g. their colour, seems to be essentially lacking in the domain of the definable states of nerves and their interactions. Putting it crudely, colour expanses in the manifest world consist of regions which are themselves colour expanses, and these consist in their turn of regions which are colour expanses, and so on; whereas the state of the group of neurons, though it has regions which are also states of groups of neurons, has ultimate regions which are *not* states of groups of neurons but rather states of single neurons.
Science, Perception and Reality, p. 35

. . . there are various forms taken by the myth of the given . . . but they all   4
have in common the idea that the awareness of certain *sorts* – and by 'sorts' I have in mind, in the first instance, determinate sense repeatables – is a primordial, non-problematic feature of 'immediate experience'.
Science, Perception and Reality, p. 157

For the philosopher is confronted not by one complex many-dimensional   5
picture, the unity of which, such as it is, he must come to appreciate, but by *two* pictures of essentially the same order of complexity, each of which purports to be a complete picture of man-in-the-world, and which, after separate scrutiny, he must fuse into one vision. Let me refer to these two perspectives, respectively, as the *manifest* and the *scientific* images of man-in-the-world. . . . The 'manifest' image of man-in-the-world . . . is, first, the framework in terms of which man came to be aware of himself as man-in-the-world . . . first encountered himself . . . [while] what I have referred to as the 'scientific' image of man-in-the-world and contrasted with the 'manifest' image, might better be called the 'postulational' or 'theoretical' image.
Science, Perception and Reality, p. 4

SEXTUS EMPIRICUS (*fl.* late 2nd century)

Those who investigate any subject are likely either to make a discovery or   1
to deny the possibility of discovery and agree that nothing can be apprehended or else to persist in their investigations. That, no doubt, is why of those who undertake philosophical investigations some say that they have discovered the truth, others deny the possibility of apprehending it, and others are still pursuing their investigations. Those who are properly called dogmatists – such as the Aristotelians and the Epicureans and the Stoics and others – think they have discovered the truth; Clitomachus and Carneades and other Academic philosophers have said

that the truth cannot be apprehended; and the sceptics persist in their investigations.
Outlines of Pyrrhonism, quoted in J. E. Annas and J. Barnes, *Modes of Scepticism*, p. 1

2   The eighth [sceptical] mode is the one deriving from relativity, by which we infer that, since everything is relative, we shall suspend judgement as to what things are independently and in their nature. It should be recognised that here (as elsewhere) we use 'is' instead of 'appears', implicitly saying: everything appears relative.
Outlines of Pyrrhonism, quoted in *Modes of Scepticism*, p. 128

3   Scepticism is an ability which sets up antitheses among appearances and judgments in any way whatever: by scepticism, on account of the 'equal weight' which characterizes opposing states of affairs and arguments, we arrive first at 'suspension of judgment', and second at 'freedom from disturbance'.
Outlines of Pyrrhonism, quoted in A. A. Long, *Hellenistic Philosophy*, p. 75

ANTHONY ASHLEY COOPER, Earl of SHAFTESBURY (1671–1713)

1   Nor is there less Evidence in what has been said, of *the united Structure and Fabrick of the Mind*, and of those Passions which constitute *the Temper*, or Soul; and on which its Happiness or Misery so immediately depend. It has been shewn, That in *this Constitution*, the impairing of any one Part must instantly tend to the disorder and ruin of other Parts, and of the Whole it-self; thro' the necessary *Connexion* and *Balance* of the Affections: That those very Passions thro' which Men are vitious, are of themselves a Torment and Disease . . .
An Inquiry concerning Virtue or Merit, s. 65

2   There is no real love of virtue without the knowledge of public good.
An Inquiry concerning Virtue or Merit, quoted in *Encyclopedia of Philosophy*, VII, p. 430

3   . . . let us carry *Scepticism* ever so far, let us doubt, if we can, of every thing about us; we cannot doubt of what passes *within ourselves*. Our Passions and Affections are known to us. *They* are certain, whatever the *Objects* may be, on which they are employ'd. Nor is it of any concern to our Argument, how these exterior Objects stand; whether they are Realitys, or mere Illusions; whether we wake or dream. For *ill Dreams* will be equally disturbing. And a good *Dream*, if Life be nothing else, will be easily and happily pass'd. In this Dream of Life, therefore, our Demonstrations have the same force; our *Balance* and *Œconomy* hold good, and our Obligation to VIRTUE is is every respect the same.
An Inquiry concerning Virtue or Merit, s. 64

SYDNEY SHOEMAKER (b. 1921)

There is noncriterial knowledge of the identity (or persistence) of 1
persons, namely that expressed in memory statements. So far as I can see,
there is no noncriterial knowledge of the identity of such things as
hurricanes. If all knowledge of personal identity were noncriterial,
personal identity could be said to be indefinable . . . This is of course not
the case. However, it is not merely an accidental fact that there is
noncriterial knowledge of personal identity; rather, it is essential and
central to the notion of a person that there be such knowledge. For
something to lack altogether the ability to have this kind of knowledge of
itself would be for it to lack a kind of memory the possession of which
seems essential to being a person, namely the ability to remember
particular events and actions in the past. And if, for the idea . . . that ϕ's
are substances if and only if all 'direct' knowledge of the identity of ϕ's is
noncriterial, we substitute the idea that ϕ's are substances if and only if it
is essential to the concept of a ϕ that there be noncriterial knowledge of
the identity of ϕ's, then we can give sense to (and, using this as our
criterion of substantiality, make true) the assertion that persons are
substances while hurricanes are not.
Self Knowledge and Self Identity, p. 258

There is, I think, a tendency to find the use 'as subject' of 'I' mysterious 2
and to think that it is perhaps not reference at all, because it cannot be
assimilated to other sorts of reference, e.g., to the use 'as object' of 'I' or
to demonstrative reference, the latter being taken as paradigms of
unproblematic reference. This tendency ought not to survive the
realization that these other sorts of reference are possible only because
this sort of self-reference, that involving the use 'as subject' of 'I', is
possible. There is an important sense in which each person's system of
reference has that person himself as its anchoring point, and it is
important for an understanding of the notion of reference, and also for
an understanding of the notion of the mental, that we understand why
and how this is so.
Identity, Cause and Mind, p. 18

To hold that it is logically possible (or, worse, nomologically possible) 3
that a state lacking qualitative character should be functionally identical
to a state having qualitative character is to make qualitative character
irrelevant both to what we can take ourselves to know in knowing about
the mental states of others and also to what we can take ourselves to
know in knowing about our own mental states.
Identity, Cause and Mind, p. 189

421

HENRY SIDGWICK (1838–1900)

1 ... the doctrine that Universal Happiness is the ultimate *standard* must not be understood to imply that Universal Benevolence is the only right or always best *motive* of action ... it is not necessary that the end which gives the criterion of rightness should always be the end at which we consciously aim: and if experience shows that the general happiness will be more satisfactorily attained if men frequently act from other motives than pure universal philanthropy, it is obvious that these other motives are reasonably to be preferred on Utilitarian principles.
Methods of Ethics, p. 413

2 From the point of view, indeed, of abstract philosophy, I do not see why the Egoistic principle should pass unchallenged any more than the Universalistic. . . . If the Utilitarian has to answer the question 'Why should I sacrifice my own happiness for the greater happiness of another?' it must surely be admissible to ask the Egoist, 'Why should I sacrifice a present pleasure for a greater one in the future? Why should I concern myself about my own future feelings any more than about the feelings of other persons?'
Methods of Ethics, p. 418

3 Common-sense morality is really only adapted for ordinary men in ordinary circumstances – although it may still be expedient that these ordinary persons should regard it as absolutely and universally prescribed, since any other view of it may dangerously weaken its hold over their minds.
Methods of Ethics, p. 466

4 ... the Utilitarian conclusion, carefully stated, would seem to be this; that the opinion that secrecy may render an action right which would not otherwise be so should itself be kept comparatively secret; and similarly it seems expedient that the doctrine that esoteric morality is expedient should itself be kept esoteric. . . . thus a Utilitarian may reasonably desire, on Utilitarian principles, that some of his conclusions should be rejected by mankind generally . . .
Methods of Ethics, p. 490

5 I think that in most cases when a man yields to temptation, judging that it is 'no use trying to resist', he judges in semi-conscious self-sophistication, due to the influence of appetite or passion disturbing the process of reasoning. I do not doubt that this self-sophistication is likely to take a Determinist form in the mind of one who has adopted Determinism as a speculative opinion: but I see no reason for thinking that a Libertarian is not in equal danger of self-sophistication, though in his case it will take a

different form. E.g. where a Determinist would reason 'I certainly shall take my usual glass of brandy tonight, so there is no use resolving not to take it', the Libertarian's reasoning would be 'I mean to leave off that brandy, but it will be just as easy to leave it off tomorrow as today; I will therefore have one more glass, and leave it off tomorrow.'
Methods of Ethics, p. 67

... we must be careful not to confound intensity of *pleasure* with   6
intensity of *sensation*: as a pleasant feeling may be strong and absorbing, and yet not so pleasant as another that is more subtle and delicate.
Methods of Ethics, p. 94

... my feelings next year should be just as important to me as my feelings   7
next minute, if only I could make an equally sure forecast of them. Indeed this equal and impartial concern for all parts of one's conscious life is perhaps the most prominent element in the common notion of the *rational* – as opposed to the merely *impulsive* – pursuit of pleasure.
Methods of Ethics, p. 124

However subtly we state in general terms the objective relations of   8
elements in a delightful work of art, on which its delight seems to depend, we must always feel that it would be possible to produce out of similar elements a work corresponding to our general description which would give no delight at all.
Methods of Ethics, p. 190

Kant seems to have held that all particular rules of duty can be deduced   9
from the fundamental rule 'Act as if the maxim of thy action were to become by thy will a universal law of nature.' But this appears to me an error analogous to that of supposing that Formal Logic supplies a complete criterion of truth.
Methods of Ethics, p. 209

Since we do not positively blame a man for remaining celibate ... it is   10
difficult to show why we should condemn – in its bearing on the individual's emotional perfection solely – the imperfect development afforded by merely sensual relations.
Methods of Ethics, p. 359

The Utilitarian must repudiate altogether that temper of rebellion against   11
the established morality, as something purely external and conventional, into which the reflective mind is always apt to fall when it is first convinced that the established rules are not intrinsically reasonable. He must, of course, also repudiate as superstitious that awe of it as an absolute or Divine Code which Intuitional moralists inculcate. Still, he will naturally contemplate it with reverence and wonder, as a marvellous

product of nature, the result of long centuries of growth, showing in many parts the same fine adaptation of means to complex exigencies as the most elaborate structures of physical organisms exhibit . . .
Methods of Ethics, p. 475

12   Grant that the Ego is merely a system of coherent phenomena, that the permanent identical 'I' is not a fact but a fiction, as Hume and his followers maintain; why, then, should one part of the series of feelings into which the Ego is resolved be concerned with another part of the same series, any more than with any other series?
Methods of Ethics, p. 419

13   But it seems that most persons are only capable of strong affections towards a few human beings in certain close relations, especially the domestic: and that if these were suppressed, what they would feel towards their fellow-creatures generally would be, as Aristotle says, 'but a water kindness' and a very feeble counterpoise to self-love: so that such specialised affections as the present organisation of society normally produces afford the best means of developing in most persons a more extended benevolence, to the degree to which they are capable of feeling it.
Methods of Ethics, p. 434

PETER SINGER (*b.* 1946)

1   . . . when in the 1850s the call for women's rights was raised in the United States, a remarkable black feminist named Sojourner Truth made the same point in more robust terms at a feminist convention:

> They talk about this thing in the head; what do they call it? ['Intellect', whispered someone nearby.] That's it. What's that got to do with women's rights or Negroes' rights? If my cup won't hold but a pint and yours holds a quart, wouldn't you be mean not to let me have my little half-measure full?

It is on this basis that the case against racism and the case against sexism must both ultimately rest; and it is in accordance with this principle that the attitude that we may call 'speciesism', by analogy with racism, must also be condemned. Speciesism – the word is not an attractive one, but I can think of no better term – is a prejudice or attitude of bias in favor of the interests of members of one's own species and against those of members of other species.
Animal Liberation, p. 6

2   In misguided attempts to refute the arguments of this book, some philosophers have gone to much trouble developing arguments to show

that animals do not have rights. They have claimed that to have rights a being must be autonomous, or must be a member of a community, or must have the ability to respect the rights of others, or must possess a sense of justice. These claims are irrelevant to the case for Animal Liberation. . . .

If a being suffers there can be no moral justification for refusing to take that suffering into consideration. No matter what the nature of the being, the principle of equality requires that its suffering be counted equally with the like suffering – insofar as rough comparisons can be made – of any other being.
Animal Liberation, p. 8

MICHAEL SLOTE (*b.* 1941)

But if love and friendship are weaknesses, they are *basic* human   1
weaknesses: by which I mean that they are weaknesses so endemic to our nature that if one seeks, as the Stoics urge, to avoid being subject to them, one is likely to get oneself into a worse position than one would be in if one simply accepted the weakness in oneself. The tendency towards, the need for, the various affections of love and friendship may be basic weaknesses in this sense because if one attempts to be utterly free of them, one will simply cover up one's needs and feelings and in the process give them free rein for subterranean mischief and eventual destructive effect within one's life.
Goods and Virtues, p. 134

. . . it seem[s] natural and appropriate to feel both admiration and a sense   2
of repelling coldness about Gauguin's, or Churchill's, single-mindedness, and someone who has such a mixed reaction to that single-mindedness may actually see it better than those who reject either element of the compound. Thus . . . we have found what may properly be called admirable immorality.
Goods and Virtues, p. 107

Earlier in this century and possibly as a result of lingering Victorian, and   3
more generally Christian, high-mindedness, the selflessness of common-sense morality went largely unnoticed and entirely uncriticized. But in recent years many philosophers have advocated a healthy self-assertive-ness on the part of moral agents. And . . . a climate of opinion has . . . been created in which it is easier to make and perhaps to sympathize with the broader defense of virtue ethics.
Identity, Character and Morality, p. 446

Consider, again, how the optimizer appears to others. Will not his   4
tendency to eke out the most or best he can in every situation strike

someone who witnesses or hears about it as lacking in self-sufficiency? Will not the optimizer appear needy and grasping and his persistent efforts a form, practically, of desperation, by contrast with the satisficer who accepts the good enough when he gets it?
Beyond Optimizing, p. 43

J. J. C. SMART (*b.* 1920)

1 This characteristic inconclusiveness of philosophical argument is a fact familiar to all philosophers. If they were to take it seriously more of them would be favourably disposed to my conception of philosophy as in part depending on merely plausible considerations. If a philosopher keeps on patching up his theory we may try to persuade him that his way of talking is becoming more and more baroque and is ill-fitting to our scientific knowledge. The libertarian philosopher of free-will may, if he is ingenious enough, render himself immune to our logical arguments, but only at the cost of great artificiality in his theory, and at the price of bringing in a great discontinuity in the story of animal evolution. Just where in the line of evolution, the primates, or sub-men, or early men, does this 'soul', or power of free choice in the libertarian sense, become superadded to man as he appears in the usual biological story?
Philosophy and Scientific Realism, p. 13

2 The first argument against the identification of experiences and brain processes can be put as follows: Aristotle, or for that matter an illiterate peasant, can report his images and aches and pains, and yet nevertheless may not know that the brain has anything to do with thinking. (Aristotle thought that the brain was an organ for cooling the blood.) Therefore what Aristotle or the peasant reports cannot *be* a brain process, though it can, of course, be something which is (unknown to Aristotle or the peasant) causally connected with a brain process.

The reply to this argument is simply this: when I say that experiences are brain processes I am asserting this *as a matter of fact*. I am not asserting that 'brain process' is part of what we *mean* by 'experience'. . . . I am, however, suggesting . . . that it may be the true nature of our inner experiences, as revealed by science, to be brain processes, just as to be a motion of electric charges is the true nature of lightning, what lightning really is.
Philosophy and Scientific Realism, p. 92

3 I should . . . like to make it clear that by 'lightning' I mean the publicly observable physical object lightning, not a visual sense datum. The sense datum, or rather the having of the sense datum, may well on my view be a correlate of the electric discharge. For on my view the having of the

sense datum is the brain process that is *caused* by the lightning. But the physical object lightning *is* the electric discharge, and is not just a correlate of it.
Philosophy and Scientific Realism, p. 93

The extreme utilitarian regards moral rules as rules of thumb and as   4
sociological facts that have to be taken into account when deciding what to do, just as facts of any other sort have to be taken into account. But in themselves they do not justify any action.
'Ethics', *Essays Metaphysical and Moral*, p. 264

No, I am not happy to draw the conclusion that McCloskey quite rightly   5
says that the utilitarian must draw. But neither am I happy with the anti-utilitarian conclusion. For if a case really *did* arise in which injustice was the lesser of two evils (in terms of human happiness and misery), then the anti-utilitarian conclusion is a very unpalatable one too, namely that in some circumstances one must choose the greater misery, perhaps the *very much* greater misery, such as that of hundreds of people suffering painful deaths.
J. J. C. Smart and Bernard Williams, *Utilitarianism: For and Against*, p. 72

Utilitarianism is concerned with maximisation of expected utility, and is   6
not concerned with distribution of utility. One unit of pleasure in Jones and five units in McTavish is neither better nor worse than three in Jones and three in McTavish. A utilitarian has to think of people rather as buckets into which happiness can be poured. (The analogy is imperfect, because buckets cannot have negative amounts of liquid, whereas people can be positively unhappy.) Indeed, properly speaking, utilitarianism, as I conceive it, should be universalistic: the happiness of non-human animals, and of extra-terrestrial beings too, should we have any dealing with or effects on them, should count equally. Of course sentient beings can have varying capacities for pleasure: I doubt whether a lizard is really conscious, while sheep almost certainly are. The buckets can vary in size. In practice the very small buckets will not affect our calculations, but medium sized ones will.
'Utilitarianism and Punishment', Conference, Jerusalem, 1988

What sort of chemical process could lead to the springing into existence   7
of something non-physical? No enzyme can catalyse the production of a spook!
'Materialism', *Essays Metaphysical and Moral*, p. 211

ADAM SMITH (1723–1790)

By preferring the support of domestic to that of foreign industry, he [the owner of capital] intends only his own security; and by directing that industry in such a manner as its produce may be of greatest value, he intends only his own gain, and he is in this, as in many other cases, led by an invisible hand to promote an end which was no part of his intention. Nor is it always the worse for society that it was no part of it. By pursuing his own interest he frequently promotes that of the society more effectively than when he really intends to promote it. I have never known much good done by those who affected to trade for the public good.

The Wealth of Nations (Everyman edn), II, p. 400

SOCRATES (c.470 BC – 399 BC)

1 The unexamined life is not worth living.
Plato, *Apology*, 38A

2 The wisest is he who realizes, like Socrates, that in respect of wisdom he is worthless.
Plato, *Apology*, 23B

3 No one does wrong willingly.
Plato, *Protagoras*, 345D

4 [on looking at an expensive shop] How many things I can do without!
Diogenes Laertius, *Lives of the Eminent Philosophers*, II, 25

5 The first philosophers met together and dedicated in the temple of Apollo the first fruits of their wisdom, the famous inscriptions 'know thyself' and 'nothing too much'.
Plato, *Protagoras*, 343B

6 SOCRATES: And should we not desire to have our own minds in the best state possible?
HIPPIAS: Yes.
SOC.: And will our minds be better if they do wrong and make mistakes voluntarily or involuntarily?
HIP.: O, Socrates, it would be a monstrous thing to say that those who do wrong voluntarily are better than those who do wrong involuntarily!
SOC.: And yet that appears to be the only inference.
Plato, *Hippias Minor*, 375C

7 One ought not to return a wrong or an injury to any person, whatever the provocation.
Plato, *Crito*, 49C

8 Socrates is guilty of corrupting the minds of the youth and of believing in deities of his own invention instead of gods recognized by the city.
Plato, *Apology* (The charge against Socrates), 24B

[On his death bed] The coldness was spreading about as far as his waist   9
when Socrates uncovered his face – for he had covered it up – and said
(they were his last words): 'Crito, we ought to offer a cock to Asclepius.
See to it, and don't forget.'
Plato, *Phaedo*, trans. W. K. C. Guthrie, 118A

BENEDICT SPINOZA (1632–1677)

This is the end I aim at: to acquire knowledge of the union of mind with   1
the whole of nature. . . . To do this it is necessary first to understand as
much of nature as suffices for acquiring such knowledge, and second to
form a society of the kind which permits as many as possible to acquire
such knowledge. Third, attention must be paid to moral philosophy. . . .
Fourthly, because health is no small means to achieving this end, the
whole of medicine must be worked out. And fifthly . . . because it is
possible to gain more free time and convenience in life, mechanics is in no
way to be despised.
The Emendation of the Intellect, trans. E. Curley, *Collected Works*, I, p. 11

Just as men in the beginning were able to make the easiest things with the   2
tools they were born with . . . so the intellect by its inborn power makes
intellectual tools for itself, by which it acquires other powers for other
intellectual works.
The Emendation of the Intellect, trans. E. Curley, p. 17

By 'cause of itself' I understand that whose essence involves existence, or   3
that whose nature cannot be understood except as existing.
Ethics, trans. E. Curley, Pt. I, def. 1, p. 408

By 'substance' I understand that which is in itself and is conceived   4
through itself.
Ethics, trans. E. Curley, Pt. I, def. 3, p. 408

That thing is called 'free' which exists from the necessity of its being, and   5
is determined to act by itself alone.
Ethics, trans. E. Curley, Pt. I, def. 7, p. 408

Since being able to exist is a power, it follows that the more reality   6
belongs to the nature of a thing, the more power it has of itself to exist.
Therefore an absolutely infinite being, or God, has of himself an
absolutely infinite power of existing. For that reason he exists absolutely.
Ethics, trans. E. Curley, Pt. I, prop. 11, p. 418

Except God, no substance can be or be conceived.   7
Ethics, trans. E. Curley, Pt. I, prop. 14, p. 420

8   God is the cause of all things, which are in him.
    Ethics, trans. E. Curley, Pt. I, prop. 18, p. 428

9   In nature there is nothing contingent, but all things have been determined
    from the necessity of the divine nature to exist and produce an effect in a
    certain way.
    Ethics, trans. E. Curley, Pt. I, prop. 29, p. 433

10 By *natura naturans* we must understand what is in itself and is conceived
    through itself . . . i.e. God in so far as he is considered a free cause.
    Ethics, trans. E. Curley, Pt. I, prop. 29, p. 433

11 By *natura naturata* I understand whatever follows from the necessity of
    God's nature.
    Ethics, trans. E. Curley, Pt. I, prop. 29, p. 433

12 The will cannot be called a free cause, but only a necessary one.
    Ethics, trans. E. Curley, Pt. I, prop. 32, p. 433

13 I have explained God's nature and properties: that he exists necessarily;
    that he is unique; that he is and acts from the necessity of his nature
    alone; that (and how) he is the free cause of all things; that all things are
    in God and so depend on him that without him they can neither be nor be
    conceived; and finally that all things have been predetermined by God,
    not from freedom of the will or absolute good pleasure, but from God's
    absolute nature or infinite power.
    Ethics, trans. E. Curley, Pt. I, appendix, p. 439

14 Mind and body are one and the same individual which is conceived now
    under the attribute of thought, and now under the attribute of extension.
    Ethics, trans. E. Curley, Pt. II, prop. 21, p. 467

15 Thinking substance and extended substance are one and the same
    substance which is now comprehended under this attribute, now under
    that. . . . Therefore whether we conceive nature under the attribute of
    extension or under the attribute of thought, or any other attribute, we
    shall find one and the same order or one and the same connection of
    causes.
    Ethics, trans. E. Curley, Pt. II, prop. 7, p. 451

16 The human mind is part of the infinite intellect of God. Therefore, when
    we say the human mind perceives this or that, we are saying nothing but
    that God, not insofar as he is infinite, but insofar as he is explained
    through the nature of the human mind . . . has this or that idea.
    Ethics, trans. E. Curley, Pt. II, prop. 11, p. 456

Men are deceived if they think themselves free, an opinion which consists 17 only in this, that they are conscious of their actions and ignorant of the causes by which they are determined.
Ethics, trans. E. Curley, Pt. II, prop. 35, p. 473

He who has a true idea at the same time knows he has a true idea, and 18 cannot doubt the truth of the thing. . . . As the light makes both itself and the darkness plain, so truth is the standard both of itself and of the false.
Ethics, trans. E. Curley, Pt. II, prop. 43, p. 479

It is the nature of reason to perceive things under a certain species of 19 eternity.
Ethics, trans. E. Curley, Pt. II, prop. 44, p. 481

The striving by which each thing strives to persevere in its being is 20 nothing but the actual essence of the thing.
Ethics, trans. E. Curley, Pt. III, prop. 7, p. 409

That eternal and infinite being we call God or nature acts from the same 21 necessity from which he exists.
Ethics, trans. E. Curley, Pt. IV, Preface, p. 544

Human power is very limited and infinitely surpassed by the power of 22 external causes. . . . Nevertheless we shall bear calmly what happens to us against our advantage if we are conscious first that we have done our duty, second that the power we have could not have stretched to the point where we could have avoided those ills, and third that we are part of the whole of nature, whose order we follow.
Ethics, trans. E. Curley, Pt. IV, appendix, p. 593

Clear and distinct knowledge, especially the third kind of knowledge 23 whose foundation is the knowledge of God himself, can accomplish much against the affects. Insofar as the affects are passions, such knowledge brings it about . . . that they constitute the smallest part of the mind. And then it begets a love towards a thing which is immutable and eternal.
Ethics, trans. E. Curley, Pt. V, prop. 21, p. 606

The mind's intellectual love of God is part of the infinite love by which 24 God loves himself.
Ethics, trans. E. Curley, Pt. V, prop. 36, p. 612

Love is nothing else but pleasure accompanied by the idea of an external 25 cause: hate is nothing else but pain accompanied by the idea of an external cause.
Ethics, trans. R. H. W. Elwes, quoted in W. Lyons, *Emotion*, p. 38

26 They narrated their miracles, trying to show that the God whom they worshipped arranged the whole of nature for their benefit; this idea was so pleasing that men go on this day imagining miracles so that they may believe themselves God's favorites. . . . Yet nature cannot be contravened, but preserves a fixed and immutable order.
Tractatus Theologico-Politicus, ch. 6, *Spinoza Opera*, III, p. 82

27 The ultimate aim of Government is not to rule or restrain by fear, not to exact obedience, but on the contrary, to free every man from fear, that he may live in all possible security; in other words to strengthen his natural right to exist and work without injury to himself and others. The object of government is not to change men from rational beings into puppets, but to enable them to develop their minds and bodies in security, and to employ their reason unshackled. . . . The true aim of Government is liberty.
Tractatus Theologico-Politicus, ch. 20, III, p. 241

TIMOTHY SPRIGGE (*b.* 1932)

1 I suggest that 'pCFq' ['If p had been the case, then q would have been'] means 'P is not the case but among all logically possible but non-actual universes there is one which includes p and q, and which is more similar to the actual universe than any logically possible universe which includes p and not-q'.
Facts, Words and Beliefs, p. 283

2 One is wondering about the consciousness which an object possesses whenever one wonders what it must be like being that object. Concerning an object deemed non-conscious one cannot thus wonder. To wonder what it is like being an object is to concern oneself with a question different from any scientific or practical question about the observable properties or behaviour of that object or about the mechanisms which underlie such properties or behaviour. . . . Thus consciousness is that which one characterises when one tries to answer the question what it is or might be like to *be* a certain object in a certain situation.
'Final Causes', *Aristotelian Society Suppl. Vol.* (1971), p. 167

3 However, I believe it is built into the very nature of our separate individualities that, in thinking of an experience as someone else's rather than mine, I think of it as not having quite the same intense reality as it would if it were mine. We can recognize this in a kind of notional way, but one who could really bring home to himself the illusion involved would be ceasing to be a separate person in the ordinary way at all. . . . Adoption of a utilitarian ethic turns largely on the kind of partial correction of that illusion which we can make on the basis of abstract reasoning. . . .

Not that . . . constant total sensitivity to the welfare of all others, so far as it might be known, is either a desirable or a possible state for human beings.
The Rational Foundations of Ethics, p. 180

Thus a virtuous character is a form of the good as it were attempting to   4
impose itself on the flux of consciousness and on the world around it.
The Rational Foundations of Ethics, p. 244

If this is correct, all that is contained in a single divine consciousness   5
within which an inconceivably vast number of streams of finite experience interact and interweave. When the lower level streams of experience which correspond to the basic items postulated in physics enter into appropriately complex relations with each other they form aggregates (and aggregates of aggregates) which are what living things are in themselves, and which underpin the emergence of the streams of consciousness of animals and men. Within such streams of consciousness, more particularly the human, a not self aspect, which is primarily the physical world as it is for us, confronts a self aspect, and serves as its representation of the system of interweaving streams of experience in the midst of which it exists and with which it must interact appropriately in order to survive, communicate with other similar selves, and realize its personal essence as fully as it can.
The Rational Foundations of Ethics, p. 263

Monism . . . bids us recognize that what looks forth from another's eyes,   6
what feels itself in the writhing of a worm, what perhaps throbs with felt if dim emotion within an electron, is really that very thing which, when speaking through my lips, calls itself 'I'.
The Vindication of Absolute Idealism, p. 274

I shall claim that every conception of a physical reality as such is the   7
conception of it as in some sense or other what on reflection we must classify as phenomenal, and that corresponding to every phenomenal thing there is a noumenon or thing in itself, or alternatively that whatever has a physical, and therefore phenomenal, character also has a noumenal character. I shall then argue that this noumenal backing or being of the phenomenal can be known as somehow psychical, or constituted of or included in what is such.
The Vindication of Absolute Idealism, p. 39

433

CHARLES L. STEVENSON (1908–1979)

1 It [the non-cognitive view] maintains that although a speaker normally uses 'X is yellow' to express his belief about X, he normally uses 'X is good' to express something else, namely his approval of X. It adds that 'good', being a term of praise, usually commends X to others and thus tends to evoke their approval as well. And it makes similar remarks about 'right', 'duty', and so on.
Facts and Values, p. 79

2 My methodological conclusions center less on my conception of meaning than on my conceptions of agreement and disagreement. If the solution of normative issues requires agreement in attitude, if the relation between attitudes and beliefs is causal and possibly subject to individual differences, and if rational methods can effect agreement in attitude only through the indirect means of altering beliefs, then the essential features of my analysis remain intact. There will be important questions, of course, regarding the degree to which agreement in attitude is *in fact* secured by non-rational methods, and whether it *ought* to be; but these questions will not affect my discussion of the various *possibilities* of securing ethical agreement, with which the methodological part of my analysis is concerned.
Facts and Values, p. 170

3 In revealing the scope and variety of justifying reasons, then, the so-called non-cognitive view implies nothing that is paradoxical. And if it makes no attempt to say which R[eason]s will justify a given E[valuation], that is only because, having shown that such an inquiry reduplicates an evaluative inquiry, it is careful not to go beyond its limited aims. As a non-normative theory of norms, its business is not to make value judgments but only to survey and clarify them.
Facts and Values, p. 90

THE STOICS (*c.*300 BC – *c.*100 AD)

1 Prior events are causes of those following them, and in this manner all things are bound together with one another, and thus nothing happens in the world such that something else is not entirely a consequence of it and attached to it as cause. . . . From everything that happens something else follows depending on it by necessity as cause.
Quoted in A. A. Long, *Hellenistic Philosophy*, p. 164

2 The Stoics say that man differs from irrational animals because of internal speech not uttered speech, for crows and parrots and jays utter articulate sounds. Nor does he differ from other creatures in virtue of

simple impressions – for they too receive these – but in virtue of impressions created by inference and combination. This amounts to man's possessing an idea of 'connexion', and he grasps the concept of signal because of this. For signal itself is of the following form: 'If this, then that'. Therefore the existence of signal follows from the nature and constitution of man.
Sextus Empiricus, *Adversus Mathematicis*, trans. R. G. Bury, II, p. 382

P. F. STRAWSON (*b.* 1919)

Agreement among experts in the special sciences and in exact scholarship 1
may reasonably be hoped for and gradually attained. But philosophy, which takes human thought in general as its field, is not thus conveniently confined; and truth in philosophy, though not to be despaired of, is so complex and many-sided, so multi-faced, that any individual philosopher's work, if it is to have any unity and coherence, must at best emphasize some aspects of the truth, to the neglect of others which may strike another philosopher with greater force. Hence the appearance of endemic disagreement in the subject is something to be expected rather than deplored; and it is no matter for wonder that the individual philosopher's views are more likely than those of the scientist or exact scholar to reflect in part his individual taste and temperament.
Skepticism and Naturalism: Some Varieties, p. vii

The concept of a person is logically prior to that of an individual 2
consciousness. The concept of a person is not to be analysed as that of an animated body or of an embodied anima.
Individuals: An Essay in Descriptive Metaphysics, p. 103

. . . it is a necessary condition of one's ascribing states of consciousness, 3
experiences, to oneself, in the way one does, that one should also ascribe them, or be prepared to ascribe them, to others who are not oneself. This means not less than it says. It means, for example, that the ascribing phrases are used in just the same sense when the subject is another as when the subject is oneself. . . .

The main point here is a purely logical one: the idea of a predicate is correlative with that of a *range* of distinguishable individuals of which the predicate can be significantly, though not necessarily truly, affirmed.
Individuals: An Essay in Descriptive Metaphysics, p. 99

There is Platonistic zeal as well as nominalistic zeal. But zeal of either 4
kind is out of place. If we fully understand the analogies which underlie the structure of our language, we shall not be made, in either way, their zealous dupes.
Individuals: An Essay in Descriptive Metaphysics, p. 234

5 What will be the attitude of one who experiences sympathy with a variety of conflicting ideals of life? It seems that he will be most at home in a liberal society, in a society in which there are variant moral environments but in which no ideal endeavours to engross, and determine the character of, the common morality. . . . He will simply welcome the ethical diversity which the society makes possible, and in proportion as he values that diversity he will note that he is the natural, though perhaps the sympathetic, enemy of all those whose single intense vision of the ends of life drives them to try to make the requirements of the ideal coextensive with those of common social morality.
'Social Morality and Individual Ideal', *Freedom and Resentment*, p. 44

6 We must not suppose that the nature of reality is exhausted by the kinds of knowledge which we have of it.
The Bounds of Sense, p. 267

7 Those very things which from one standpoint we conceive as phenomenally propertied we conceive from another as constituted in a way which can only be described in what are, from the phenomenal point of view, abstract terms. 'This smooth, green, leather table-top', we say, 'is, considered scientifically, nothing but a congeries of electric charges widely separated and in rapid motion.' Thus we combine the two standpoints in a single sentence. The standpoint of commonsense realism, not explicitly signalled as such, is reflected in the sentence's grammatical subject phrase, of which the words are employed in no esoteric sense. The standpoint of physical science, explicitly signalled as such, is reflected in the predicate. Once relativity of description to standpoint is recognised, the sentence is seen to contain no contradiction; and if it contains no contradiction, the problem of identification is solved.
'Perception and its Objects', *Perception and Identity*, ed. G. F. Macdonald, p. 59

8 . . . the participant reactive attitudes are essentially natural human reactions to the good or ill will or indifference of others towards us, as displayed in *their* attitudes and actions. The question we have to ask is: what effect would, or should, the acceptance of the truth of a general thesis of determinism have upon these reactive attitudes? More specifically, would, or should, the acceptance of the truth of the thesis lead to the decay or the repudiation of all such attitudes? Would, or should, it mean the end of gratitude, resentment, and forgiveness; of all reciprocated adult loves; of all the essentially *personal* antagonisms?
Studies in the Philosophy of Thought and Action, ed. P. F. Strawson, p. 80

9 It might be said that all this leaves the real question unanswered. . . . It is a question about what it would be *rational* to do if determinism were

true, a question about the rational justification of ordinary inter-personal attitudes in general. To this I shall reply, first, that such a question could seem real only to one who had utterly failed to grasp the purport of the preceding answer, the fact of our natural human commitment to ordinary inter-personal attitudes. This commitment is part of the general framework of human life, not something that can come up for review as particular cases can come up for review within this general framework. And I shall reply, second, that if we could imagine what we cannot have, viz. a choice in this matter, then we could choose rationally only in the light of an assessment of the gains and losses to human life, its enrichment or impoverishment; and the truth or falsity of a general thesis of determinism would not bear on the rationality of *this* choice.
Studies in the Philosophy of Thought and Action, p. 83

BARRY STROUD (*b.* 1935)

Could it be that I am now dreaming? Not only does the right answer   1
seem to me to be 'Yes' but, more importantly, it seems to me that the possibility continues to make sense even if I go on to imagine that no one on the face of the earth or anywhere else could ever know that I *am* dreaming because they too could never know whether they were awake or dreaming. Adding the further thought that the truth about my state is unknown or even unknowable to everyone does not seem to me to affect the possibility I originally tried to imagine at all. Of course, I might be wrong about this, but how is one to tell?
The Significance of Philosophical Scepticism, p. 270

David Hume is generally considered to be a purely negative philosopher   2
– the arch sceptic whose primary aim and achievement was to reduce the theories of his empiricist predecessors to the absurdity that was implicitly contained in them all along. . . . No doubt some passages in Hume, taken alone, might support this line of interpretation, but it is an extreme and unfortunate distortion of what he actually wrote. Not only is it mistaken; it would make Hume much less interesting and important for us as a philosopher than he actually is.

Hume is a philosopher of human nature. He puts forth a new theory or vision of man, and one that he thinks differs significantly from those of his predecessors. It is a bold and simple theory, and is much more an expression of the unbounded optimism of the enlightenment than of the clever negativism of a man at the end of his intellectual rope.
Hume, p. 1

E. STUMP (*b.* 1947) and N. KRETZMANN (*b.* 1928)

It is just because no event can be past with respect to an eternal entity that an eternal entity cannot alter a *past* event. An omnipotent, omniscient, eternal entity can affect temporal events, but it can affect events only as they are actually occurring. As for a past event, the time at which it was actually occurring is the time at which it is present to such an entity; and so the battle of Waterloo is present to God, and God can affect the battle. Suppose that he does so. God can bring it about that Napoleon wins, though we know that he does not do so, because whatever God does at Waterloo is over and done with as we see it. So God cannot alter the past, but he can alter the course of the battle of Waterloo.
'Eternity', *Journal of Philosophy* (1981), p. 453

RICHARD SWINBURNE (*b.* 1934)

1 I . . . suggest the following understanding of omniscience. . . . *P* is omniscient if he knows about everything except those future states and their consequences which are not necessitated by anything in the past; and if he knows that he does not know about those future states. If there is any future state which is not physically necessitated by goings-on in the past or present, then, of logical necessity, no person can now know that it will happen – without the possibility of error. There may of course not be any such future state. In that case any person omniscient on this account would be omniscient on the earlier account also. But if there are men who have free will, as many theists have claimed, there will be at some time such future states. And further if God has free will, as almost all theists have claimed, there will be at some time such future states. Omniscience in the earlier sense is not compatible with God's freedom, but omniscience in this sense is compatible. A being may be perfectly free and know everything – except which free choices he will make and what will result from the choices which he will make.
The Coherence of Theism, p. 175

2 My claim . . . is that although the predictive power of theism is quite low, and so too is its prior probability, nevertheless its overall probability is well away from 1 or 0 because the prior probability of the evidence is very low indeed.
The Existence of God, p. 289

T

𝔊𝔊𝔊𝔊𝔊

ALFRED TARSKI (1902–1983)

Let us start with a concrete example. Consider the sentence '*snow is* 1
white'. We ask the question under what conditions this sentence is true or
false. It seems clear that if we base ourselves on the classical conception
of truth, we shall say that the sentence is true if snow is white, and that it
is false if snow is not white. Thus, if the definition of truth is to conform
to our conception, it must imply the following equivalence:

  The sentence 'snow is white' is true if, and only if, snow is white.
'The Semantic Conception of Truth', *Readings in Philosophical Analysis*, ed. H.
Feigl and W. Sellars, p. 54

We shall now generalize the procedure which we have applied above. Let 2
us consider an arbitrary sentence; we shall replace it by the letter '*p*'. We
form the name of this sentence and we replace it by another letter, say
'*X*'. We ask now what is the logical relation between the two sentences
'*X is true*' and '*p*'. It is clear that from the point of view of our basic
conception of truth these sentences are equivalent. In other words, the
following equivalence holds:

  (T)   *X is true if, and only if, p.*

We shall call any such equivalence (with '*p*' replaced by any sentence of
the language to which the word '*true*' refers, and '*X*' replaced by a name
of this sentence) an '*equivalence of the form* (T)'. . . .

  It should be emphasized that neither the expression (T) itself (which is
not a sentence, but only a schema of a sentence) nor any particular
instance of the form (T) can be regarded as a definition of truth. We can
only say that every equivalence of the form (T) obtained by replacing '*p*'
by a particular sentence, and '*X*' by a name of this sentence, may be
considered a partial definition of truth, which explains wherein the truth
of this one individual sentence consists. The general definition has to be,
in a certain sense, a logical conjunction of all these partial definitions.
'The Semantic Conception of Truth', p. 55

THALES (*c.*626–*c.*546 BC)

Most of the first philosophers thought that principles in the form of matter were the only principles of all things: for the original source of all existing things, that from which a thing first comes-into-being and into which it is finally destroyed, the substance persisting but changing in its qualities, this they declare is the element and first principle of existing things. . . . Thales, the founder of this type of philosophy, says that the first principle is water.

Aristotle, *Metaphysics*, 983B

JUDITH JARVIS THOMSON (*b.* 1929)

1 A newly fertilized ovum, a newly implanted clump of cells, is no more a person than an acorn is an oak tree. . . . Opponents of abortion commonly spend most of their time establishing that the fetus is a person, and hardly any time explaining the step from there to the impermissibility of abortion. . . .

I propose then, that we grant that the fetus is a person from the moment of conception. How does the argument go from here? Something like this, I take it. Every person has a right to life. So the fetus has a right to life. No doubt the mother has a right to decide what shall happen in and to her body; everyone would grant that. But surely a person's right to life is stronger and more stringent than the mother's right to decide what happens in and to her body, and so outweighs it. So the fetus may not be killed; an abortion may not be performed.

It sounds plausible. But now let me ask you to imagine this. You wake up in the morning and find yourself back to back in bed with an unconscious violinist. A famous unconscious violinist. He has been found to have a fatal kidney ailment, and the Society of Music Lovers has canvassed all the available medical records and found that you alone have the right blood type to help. They have therefore kidnapped you, and last night the violinist's circulatory system was plugged into yours, so that your kidneys can be used to extract poisons from his blood as well as your own. The director of the hospital now tells you, 'Look, we're sorry the Society of Music Lovers did this to you – we would never have permitted it if we had known. But still, they did it, and the violinist now is plugged into you. To unplug you would be to kill him. But never mind, it's only for nine months. By then he will have recovered from his ailment, and can safely be unplugged from you.' Is it morally incumbent on you to accede to this situation? No doubt it would be very nice of you if you did, a great kindness. But do you *have* to accede to it? What if it were not nine months, but nine years? Or longer still?

'A Defense of Abortion', *Philosophy and Public Affairs* (1971), p. 48

I am arguing only that having a right to life does not guarantee having   2
either a right to be given the use of or a right to be allowed continued use
of another person's body – even if one needs it for life itself. So the right
to life will not serve the opponents of abortion in the very simple and
clear way in which they seem to have thought it would. . . .

Opponents of abortion have been so concerned to make out the
independence of the fetus, in order to establish that it has a right to life,
just as its mother does, that they have tended to overlook the possible
support they might gain from making out that the fetus is *dependent* on
the mother, in order to establish that she has a special kind of
responsibility for it, a responsibility that gives it rights against her which
are not possessed by any independent person – such as an ailing violinist
who is a stranger to her.
'A Defense of Abortion', p. 56

. . . in no state in this country is any man compelled by law to be even a   3
Minimally Decent Samaritan to any person. . . . By contrast, in most
states in this country women are compelled by law to be not merely
Minimally Decent Samaritans, but Good Samaritans to unborn persons
inside them. This doesn't by itself settle anything one way or the other,
because it may well be argued that there should be laws in this country –
as there are in many European countries – compelling at least Minimally
Decent Samaritanism. But it does show that there is a gross injustice in
the existing state of the law. And it shows also that the groups currently
working against liberalization of abortion laws, in fact working toward
having it declared unconstitutional for a state to permit abortion, had
better start working for the adoption of Good Samaritan laws generally,
or earn the charge that they are acting in bad faith.

I should think, myself, that Minimally Decent Samaritan laws would
be one thing, Good Samaritan laws quite another, and in fact highly
improper.
'A Defense of Abortion', p. 64

THRASYMACHUS (c.400–c.340 BC)

I say that justice is nothing other than the interest of the stronger.
Plato, *The Republic*, 338E

LEO TOLSTOI (1828–1910)

To evoke in oneself a feeling one has once experienced, and having
evoked it in oneself, then, by means of movements, lines, colours, sounds,
or forms expressed in words, so to transmit that feeling that others may
experience the same feeling – this is the activity of art.

Art is a human activity, consisting in this, that one man consciously, by means of certain external signs, hands on to others feelings he has lived through, and that other people are infected by these feelings, and also experience them.

'What is Art?', *What is Art? and Essays on Art*, trans. Aylmer Maude, p. 123

CATHARINE TROTTER (COCKBURN) (1679–1749)

1 . . . it will follow, that the nature of man, and of the good of society, are *to us* the reason and rule of moral good and evil; and there is no danger of their being less immutable on this foundation than any other, whilst man continues a *rational and sociable creature* . . . nor will this foundation make it the less sacred, since it cannot be doubted, that it is originally the will of God, whilst we own him the author of that nature, of which this law is a consequence.

'A Defence of Mr. Locke's Essay of Human Understanding', *Works*, I, p. 58

2 . . . even granting the author [Rutherford] . . . his main principle, 'That every man's own happiness is the ultimate end, which nature and reason teach him to pursue', why may not nature and reason teach him, too, to have some desire to see others happy as well as himself, or give him some delight in doing what seems fit and right, if these things do not interfere with his own happiness? . . . Why may he not, with the pursuit of that end, join some other pursuits not inconsistent with it, instead of transforming every benevolent affection, every moral view, into self-interest? This surely neither does honour to religion, nor justice to human nature.

'Remarks upon the Principles and Reasoning of Dr. Rutherford's Essay on the Nature and Obligations of Virtue', *Works*, II, p. 8

U

ⓢⓢⓢⓢⓢⓢ

MIGUEL DE UNAMUNO (1864–1936)

Descartes . . . arrives at the *cogito ergo sum*, which St Augustine had 1
already anticipated; but the *ego* implicit in this enthymeme, *ego cogito,*
ergo ego sum, is an unreal – that is, an ideal – *ego* or I, and its *sum*, its
existence, something unreal also. 'I think, therefore I am' can only mean
'I think, therefore I am a thinker'; the being of the 'I am', which is
deduced from 'I think', is merely a knowing; that being is knowledge, but
not life. And the primary reality is not that I think, but that I live, for
those also live who do not think.
The Tragic Sense of Life, trans. J. E. C. Flitch, p. 35

Hegel made famous his aphorism that all the rational is real and all the 2
real rational; but there are many of us who, unconvinced by Hegel,
continue to believe that the real, the really real, is irrational, that reason
builds upon irrationalities. Hegel, a great framer of definitions, attempted
with definitions to reconstruct the universe, like that artillery sergeant
who said that a cannon was made by taking a hole and enclosing it with
steel.
The Tragic Sense of Life, p. 5

To say that everything is God, and that when we die we return to God, or 3
more accurately, continue in Him, avails our longing nothing; for if this
indeed be so, then we were in God before we were born, and if when we
die we return to where we were before being born, then the human soul,
the individual consciousness, is perishable.
The Tragic Sense of Life, p. 88

. . . this personal and affective starting-point of all philosophy and all 4
religion is the tragic sense of life.
The Tragic Sense of Life, p. 37

V

𝔊𝔊𝔊𝔊𝔊𝔊

B. C. VAN FRAASSEN (*b.* 1941)

1 The success of current scientific theories is no miracle. It is not even surprising to the scientific (Darwinist) mind. For any scientific theory is born into a life of fierce competition, a jungle red in tooth and claw. Only the successful theories survive – the ones which *in fact* latched on to the actual regularities in nature.
The Scientific Image, p. 40

2 Do the concepts of the Trinity, the soul, haeccity, universals, prime matter, and potentiality baffle you? They pale beside the unimaginable otherness of closed space-times, event-horizons, EPR correlations, and bootstrap models. Let realists and antirealists alike bracket their epistemic and ontic commitments and contribute to the understanding of these conceptual enigmas. But, thereafter, how could anyone who does not say *credo ut intelligam* be baffled by a desire to limit belief to what can at least in principle be disclosed in experience? Or, more to the point, by the idea that acceptance in science does not require belief in truth beyond those limits?
The Images of Science, ed. P. M. Churchland and C. A. Hooker, p. 258

GIAMBATTISTA VICO (1668–1744)

1 In Latin, *verum* [the true] and *factum* [what is made] are interchangeable or, in the language of the Schools, convertible terms. . . . Moreover, the word *cogitare* [to think] was used where we, in the vernacular, use *pensare* [to think] and *andar raccogliendo* [to collect]. . . .

. . . just as divine truth is what God orders and produces as He comes to know it, so human truth is what man arranges and makes as he knows it. In this way knowledge is cognition of the genus or mode by which a thing is made, and by means of which, as the mind comes to know the mode, because it arranges the elements, it makes the thing. Divine truth is

444

solid because God grasps all things; human truth is two-dimensional because man grasps the externals of things.

On the Ancient Wisdom of the Italians taken from the Origins of the Latin Language, Vico: Selected Works, trans. Leon Pompa, p. 51

Given these opinions of the ancient philosophers of Italy about the true, and the distinction between what is begotten and what is made which obtains in our religion, . . . we can return to the origin of the branches of human knowledge and, finally, can obtain a criterion for recognising the true. God knows all things because He contains within Himself the elements from which He synthesises them, whereas man strives to know them by analysis. Thus human knowledge is a kind of dissection of the works of nature.

On the Ancient Wisdom of the Italians taken from the Origins of the Latin Language, trans. Leon Pompa, p. 53

From what has been said so far, it is possible to conclude with certainty that the criterion and rule of the true is to have made it. Accordingly, our clear and distinct idea of the mind cannot be a criterion of the mind itself, still less of other truths. For while the mind perceives itself it does not make itself, and because it does not make itself it does not know the genus or mode by which it perceives itself.

On the Ancient Wisdom of the Italians taken from the Origins of the Latin Language, trans. Leon Pompa, p. 55

When, therefore, man sets out to investigate the nature of things, he eventually realises both that it is impossible to achieve his goal, because he does not contain within himself the elements by virtue of which composite things exist, and that this is a consequence of limitations of his own mind, since everything exists outside himself.

On the Ancient Wisdom of the Italians taken from the Origins of the Latin Language, trans. Leon Pompa, p. 54

It is noteworthy that in all languages the greater part of expressions concerning inanimate things are created by metaphors drawn from the human body and its parts and from the human senses and passions. For example, 'head' for summit or beginning; . . . 'mouth' . . . for every [sort of] hole. . . . And there are innumerable others to be collected in all languages. All this follows from the axiom that 'when man is ignorant he makes himself the measure of the universe', since, in the examples brought forward, he has made of himself an entire universe. For, as rational metaphysics teaches that *homo intelligendo fit omnia* [man becomes everything through understanding], so this imaginative metaphysics shows that *homo non intelligendo fit omnia* [man becomes everything through failing to understand]; and there is perhaps more truth in the latter than in the former, for by understanding things man unfolds his mind and comprehends things, but by failing to understand he makes these things of himself and, in transforming himself into them, he becomes the world.

The Third New Science, Vico: Selected Writings, trans. Leon Pompa, p. 223

6 Legislation considers man as he is, in order to create of him good practices in human society: as, from violence, avarice and ambition, which are the three vices prevalent throughout the whole of mankind, it creates the army, commerce and the court, and thus the strength, wealth and wisdom of states; and from these three great vices, which would certainly destroy the human species on earth, it creates civil happiness.

This axiom proves that divine providence exists and that it is a divine legislative mind which, from the passions of men concerned only for their own personal advantage, in pursuit of which they would live as wild beasts in solitude, has created the civil orders through which they may live in a human society.

The Third New Science, trans. Leon Pompa, p. 161

FRANÇOIS-MARIE AROUET DE VOLTAIRE (1694–1778)

1 It would be very singular that all nature and all the stars should obey eternal laws, and that there should be one little animal five feet tall which, despite these laws, could always act as suited its own caprice. It would act by chance, and we know that chance is nothing. We have invented this word to express the known effect of any unknown cause.

Le philosophe ignorant, Oeuvres, XXXI, p. 85

2 . . . liberty can no more belong to the will than can color and movement.

What is the meaning of this phrase 'to be free'? It means 'to be able', or else it has no meaning. To say that the will 'can' is as ridiculous at bottom as to say that the will is yellow or blue, round or square. Will is wish, and liberty is power. . . . Nothing happens or can happen without a reason, a cause; so there must be one for your wish. What is it? It is [for example] the agreeable idea of going on horseback, which presents itself in your brain as the dominant idea, the determinant idea. But, you will say, can I not resist an idea which dominates me? No, for what would be the cause of your resistance? None. Your will could 'resist' only by obeying a still more despotic idea.

Now you receive all your ideas; therefore you receive your 'wish', you 'wish' by necessity. . . .

Will, therefore, is not a faculty that can be called free.

Dictionnaire Philosophique, trans. H. Woolf

We learn to see just as we learn to speak and read. . . . The quick and 3
almost uniform judgments which all our minds form at a certain age with
regard to distances, magnitudes, and positions make us think that we
need only open our eyes in order to see things as we actually do perceive
them. This is an illusion. . . . If all men spoke the same language, we
should always be inclined to believe that there is a necessary connection
between words and ideas. But all men speak the same language with
respect to the imagination. Nature says to all: when you have seen colors
for a certain length of time, your imagination will represent to you in the
same manner the bodies to which these colors seem to belong. The
prompt and involuntary judgment which you will form, will be useful to
you in the course of your life.
Éléments de la philosophie de Newton, Pt. II, Ch. 7, *Oeuvres*, XXX, p. 147

I agree with Locke that there is really no innate idea; it clearly follows 4
that there is no proposition of morality innate in our soul; but from the
fact that we were not born with beards, does it follow that we were not
born, we inhabitants of this continent, to be bearded at a certain age? We
are not born with the strength to walk, but whoever is born with two feet
will some day walk. Similarly, no one is born with the idea that it is
necessary to be just; but God has so formed the organs of man that all at
a certain age agree to this truth.
Letter to Crown Prince Frederick, October 1737, *Oeuvres*, L, p. 138

Even though that which in one region is called virtue, is precisely that 5
which in another is called vice, even though most rules regarding good
and bad are as variable as the languages one speaks and the clothing one
wears; yet it seems to me, nevertheless, certain that there are natural laws
with respect to which human beings in all parts of the world must agree. .
. . To be sure, God did not say to man: 'Here you have laws from my lips
according to which I desire you to govern yourselves'; but He did the
same thing with man that He did with many other animals. He gave to
bees a powerful instinct by virtue of which they work together and gain
their sustenance, and He endowed man with certain inalienable feelings;
and these are the eternal bonds and the first laws of human society.
Traité de métaphysique, *Oeuvres*, XXI, p. 65

I want my attorney, my tailor, my servants, even my wife to believe in 6
God, and I think that then I shall be robbed and cuckolded less often.
Dictionnaire philosophique

FRIEDRICH VON HÜGEL (1852–1925)

Now doubtless not only Luther but Kant also intended thus to find
certainty concerning God within their own souls, and so to escape that

lapse into doubt and self-delusion which they considered to attach to all seeking of such assurance in social traditions and external proofs and practices. Yet the modern idealist philosophy, as first clearly formulated (between Luther's time and the time of Kant) by Descartes in his fundamental principle, was so eager to make sure of this kind of interiority and sincerity that it started, not from the concrete fact, viz., a mind thinking *something*, and from the analysis of this ultimate trinity in unity (the subject, the thinking, and the object), but from that pure abstraction – thinking, or thought, or a thinking of a thought; and, from this unreal starting point, this philosophy strove to reach that now quite problematical thing, the object.

Essays and Addresses on the Philosophy of Religion: First Series, p. 186

W

𝕨𝕨𝕨𝕨𝕨

G. J. WARNOCK (b. 1923)   1

Resources are limited; knowledge, skills, information, and intelligence
are limited; people are often not rational, either in the management of
their own affairs or in the adjustment of their own affairs in relation to
others. Then, finally, they are vulnerable to others, and dependent on
others, and yet inevitably often in competition with others; and, human
sympathies being limited, they may often neither get nor give help that is
needed, may not manage to co-operate for common ends, and may be
constantly liable to frustration or positive injury from directly hostile
interference by other persons. Thus it comes about that – as Hobbes of
course most memorably insisted – there is in what may be called the
human predicament a certain 'natural' tendency for things to go very
badly . . .
The Object of Morality, p. 23

Now, the general suggestion that (guardedly) I wish to put up for   2
consideration is this: that the 'general object' of morality, appreciation of
which may enable us to *understand* the basis of moral evaluation, is to
contribute to betterment – or non-deterioration – of the human
predicament, primarily and essentially by seeking to countervail 'limited
sympathies' and their potentially most damaging effects. It is the proper
business of morality . . . to expand our sympathies, or, better, to reduce
the liability to damage inherent in their natural tendency to be narrowly
restricted.
The Object of Morality, p. 26

MARY WARNOCK (b. 1924)

One of the consequences of treating ethics as the analysis of ethical   1
language is, as I have suggested earlier, that it leads to the increasing
triviality of the subject. This is not a general criticism of linguistic
analysis, but only of this method applied to ethics. In ethics, alone among
the branches of philosophical study, the subject matter is not so much the

449

categories which we use to describe or to learn about the world, as our own impact upon the world, our relation to other people and our attitude to our situation and our life. . . . Evaluating is not the distinctive function of moral agents either. Deliberating, wishing, hating, loving, choosing; these are things which characterize us as people, and therefore as moral agents, and these are the things to which the emotive theory and its later developments paid insufficient attention.

One aspect of this trivializing of the subject is the refusal of moral philosophers in England to commit themselves to any moral opinions. They have for the most part fallen in happily with the positivist distinction between moral philosophers, who analyse the logic of moral discourse, and moralists, who practise it. . . . It would be generally agreed that some opinions might be outrageous, and some principles harmful, but where we get our principles and opinions from, how we should decide between them, and what would be an example of a good one – these things they will not tell us, for to do so would be actually to express a moral opinion. . . .

But I believe that the most boring days are over.
Ethics Since 1900 (2nd edition), p. 144

2   One common effect of the truly Existentialist writer is to provoke in his readers the exasperated desire to rewrite what he says in plain language, and to show that it doesn't after all amount to more than a platitude.
Existentialist Ethics, p. 16

3   If choosing freely for oneself is the highest value, the free choice to wear red socks is as valuable as the free choice to murder one's father or sacrifice oneself for one's friend. Such a belief is ridiculous.
Existentialist Ethics, p. 54

4   . . . we do not choose to prefer pleasure to pain. Despite Sartre's arguments, we may well deny that we at any rate always choose what to feel, or how to react emotionally to the world. . . . the extreme subjectivism and the extreme libertarianism of the existentialists seem equally unacceptable.
Existentialist Ethics, p. 55

5   . . . without *some* element of objectivity, without *any* criterion for preferring one scheme of values to another, except the criterion of what looks most attractive to oneself, there cannot in fact be any morality at all . . .
Existentialist Ethics, p. 56

MAX WEBER (1864–1920)

1   An ideal type is formed by the one-sided accentuation of one or more points of view and by the synthesis of a great many diffuse, discrete, more

or less present and occasionally absent concrete individual phenomena, which are arranged according to those one-sidedly emphasized viewpoints into a unified analytical construct. In its conceptual purity, this mental construct cannot be found empirically anywhere in reality. It is a utopia.
'The Ideal Type', *Sociological Perspectives*, ed. K. Thompson and J. Tunstall, p. 63

Not every type of contact of human beings has a social character; this is   2 rather confined to cases where the actor's behaviour is meaningfully orientated to that of others. For example, a mere collision of two cyclists may be compared to a natural event. On the other hand, their attempt to avoid hitting each other, or whatever insults, blows, or friendly discussion might follow the collision, would constitute 'social action'.
Economy and Society: An Outline of Interpretive Sociology, ed. G. Roth and C. Wittich, p. 23

... the *summum bonum* of this [modern capitalist] ethic, the earning of   3 more and more money, combined with the strict avoidance of all spontaneous enjoyment of life ... is thought of so purely as an end in itself, that from the point of view of the happiness of, or utility to, the single individual, it appears entirely transcendental and absolutely irrational. Man is dominated by the making of money, by acquisition as the ultimate purpose of his life. Economic acquisition is no longer subordinated to man as the means for the satisfaction of his material needs. This reversal of what we should call the natural relationship, so irrational from a naive point of view, is evidently as definitely a leading principle of capitalism as it is foreign to all peoples not under capitalist influence.
The Protestant Ethic and the Spirit of Capitalism, trans. T. Parsons, p. 53

Since ascetism undertook to remodel the world and to work out its ideals   4 in the world, material goods have gained an increasing and finally an inexorable power over the lives of men as at no previous period in history. To-day the spirit of religious ascetism – whether finally, who knows? – has escaped from the cage. But victorious capitalism, since it rests on mechanical foundations, needs its support no longer.
The Protestant Ethic and the Spirit of Capitalism, trans. T. Parsons, p. 181

SIMONE WEIL (1909–1943)

Anybody who is in our vicinity exercises a certain power over us by his   1 very presence, and a power that belongs to him alone, that is, the power of halting, repressing, modifying each movement that our body sketches out. If we step aside for a passer-by on the road, it is not the same thing as stepping aside to avoid a billboard; alone in our rooms, we get up, walk about, sit down again quite differently from the way we do when we have a visitor.

'The Iliad', *Simone Weil: an Anthology*, ed. S. Miles, p. 187

2 . . . only obstacles set a rule or a limit for human action. These are the only realities with which it comes into contact. Matter imposes obstacles according to its own mechanisms. A man is capable of imposing obstacles by virtue of a power to refuse which he sometimes possesses, and sometimes not. When he does not possess it, he constitutes no obstacle, and hence no limit either. From the point of view of the action and agent he simply does not exist.

Whenever there is action thought reaches right through to a goal. If there were no obstacles the goal would be attained the moment it was conceived. . . . Anything within the field of action which does not constitute an obstacle – as, for instance, men deprived of the power to refuse – is transparent for thought in the way completely clear glass is for sight. It has no power to stop, just as our eyes have no power to see the glass.

Someone who does not see a pane of glass is not aware of not seeing it. Someone else who, being in a different position, does see it, is not aware that the other person does not see it.

When our will finds expression externally to us, through action carried out by others, we do not spend our time or our power of attention on investigating whether they have consented to this. . . . the result is that action is defiled by sacrilege. For human consent is something sacred.

'Are We Singing for Justice?', *Écrits de Londres*, trans. Marina Barabas

MORRIS WEITZ (1916–1981)

'Art', itself, is an open concept. New conditions (cases) have constantly arisen and will undoubtedly constantly arise; new art forms, new movements will emerge, which will demand decisions on the part of those interested, usually professional critics, as to whether the concept should be extended or not. . . . 'It's not a sculpture, it's a mobile'.

'The Role of Theory in Aesthetics', *A Modern Book of Esthetics*, ed. M. Rader, p. 438

WILLIAM WHEWELL (1794–1866)

1 The principles which constituted the triumph of the preceding stages of the science may appear to be subverted and ejected by the later discoveries, but in fact they are (so far as they were true) taken up into the subsequent doctrines and included in them. They continue to be an

essential part of the science. The earlier truths are not expelled but absorbed, not contradicted but extended; and the history of each science, which may thus appear like a succession of revolutions, is, in reality, a series of developments.
History of the Inductive Sciences, I, p. 7

. . . there is a mask of theory over the whole face of nature . . .　　2
The Philosophy of the Inductive Sciences, I, p. 24

. . . we may do something in tracing the process by which such [scientific]　3 discoveries are made. . . . We may observe that these . . . are not improperly described as happy *guesses*; and that guesses, in these as in other instances, imply various suppositions made, of which some one turns out to be the right one. We may, in such cases, conceive the discoverer as inventing and trying many conjectures, till he finds one which answers the purpose of combining the scattered facts into a single rule.
The Philosophy of the Inductive Sciences, II, p. 206

But if it be an advantage for the discoverer of truth that he be ingenious　4 and fertile in inventing hypotheses which may connect with the phenomena of nature, it is indispensably requisite that he be diligent and careful in comparing his hypotheses with the facts, and ready to abandon his invention as soon as it appears that it does not agree with the course of actual occurrences.
The Philosophy of the Inductive Sciences, II, p. 221

ALFRED NORTH WHITEHEAD (1861–1947)

The seventeenth century had finally produced a scheme of scientific　1 thought, . . . yielding on the one hand *matter* with its *simple location* in space and time, on the other hand *mind*, perceiving, suffering, reasoning, but not interfering . . .

Thereby, modern philosophy has been ruined. It has oscillated in a complex manner between three extremes. There are the dualists, who accept matter and mind as on an equal basis, and the two varieties of monists, those who put mind inside matter, and those who put matter inside mind. But this juggling with abstractions can never overcome the inherent confusion introduced by the ascription of *misplaced concreteness* to the scientific scheme of the seventeenth century.
Science and the Modern World, A Whitehead Anthology, ed. F. Northrop and M. Gross, p. 413

We find ourselves in a buzzing world, amid a democracy of fellow　2 creatures; whereas, under some disguise or other, orthodox philosophy

can only introduce us to solitary substances, each enjoying an illusory experience. . . . The 'particular' is thus conceived as being just its individual self with no necessary relevance to any other particular. . . . In fact if we allow for degrees of relevance, and for negligible relevance, we must say that every actual entity is present in every other actual entity.
Process and Reality, p. 79

3 The reformed subjectivist principle adopted by the philosophy of organism is merely an alternative statement of the principle of relativity. This principle states that it belongs to the nature of a 'being' that it is a potential for every 'becoming'. . . . Process is the becoming of experience.
Process and Reality, p. 243

4 . . . for Kant the process whereby there is experience is a process from subjectivity to apparent objectivity. The philosophy of organism inverts this analysis, and explains the process as proceeding from objectivity to subjectivity, namely, from the objectivity, whereby the external world is a datum, to the subjectivity, whereby there is one individual experience.
Process and Reality, p. 236

5 The ontological principle as here defined, constitutes the first step in the description of the universe as a solidarity of many actual entities. Each actual entity is conceived as an act of experience arising out of data. It is a process of 'feeling' the many data, so as to absorb them into the unity of one individual 'satisfaction'. . . . Feelings are variously specialized operations, effecting a transition into subjectivity. An actual entity is a process, and is not describable in terms of the morphology of a 'stuff'.
Process and Reality, p. 40

6 Opposed elements stand to each other in mutual requirement. In their unity, they inhibit or contrast. God and the World stand to each other in this opposed requirement. God is the infinite ground of all mentality, the unity of vision seeking physical multiplicity. The World is the multiplicity of finites, actualities seeking a perfected unity. Neither God, nor the World, reaches static completion. Both are in the grip of the ultimately metaphysical ground, the creative advance into novelty. Either of them, God and the World, is the instrument of novelty for the other.
Process and Reality, p. 244

7 According to Bradley, the ultimate subject of every judgement is the one ultimate substance, the absolute. In the philosophy of organism . . . Bradley's doctrine of actuality is simply inverted. The final actuality is the particular process with its particular attainment of satisfaction. The actuality of the universe is merely derivative from its solidarity in each actual entity.
Process and Reality, p. 304

... perception in its primary form is consciousness of the causal efficacy 8
of the external world by reason of which the percipient is a concrescence
from a definitely constituted datum. The vector character of the datum is
this causal efficacy.

Thus perception, in this primary sense, is perception of the settled
world in the past as constituted by its feeling-tones, and as efficacious by
reason of those feeling-tones. Perception, in this sense of the term, will be
called 'perception in the mode of causal efficacy'. . . . [It] is not that sort
of perception which has received chief attention in the philosophical
tradition. Philosophers have disdained the information about the
universe obtained through their visceral feelings, and have concentrated
on visual feelings.
Process and Reality, p. 120

The body is that portion of nature with which each moment of human 9
experience intimately cooperates. There is an inflow and outflow of
factors between the bodily actuality and the human experience, so that
each shares in the existence of the other. The human body provides our
closest experience of the interplay of actualities in nature.
Modes of Thought, p. 157

I find myself as essentially a unity of emotions, enjoyments, hopes, fears, 10
regrets, valuations of alternatives, decisions – all of them subjective
reactions to the environment as active in my nature. My unity – which is
Descartes' '*I am*' – is my process of shaping this welter of material into a
consistent pattern of feelings. The individual enjoyment is what I am in
my role a natural activity, as I shape the activities of the environment
into a new creation, which is myself at this moment, and yet, as being
myself, it is a continuation of the antecedent world.
Modes of Thought, p. 228

It is a profoundly erroneous truism . . . that we should cultivate the habit 11
of thinking what we are doing. The precise opposite is the case.
Civilisation advances by extending the number of important operations
which we can perform without thinking about them. Operations of
thought are like cavalry charges in a battle – they are strictly limited in
number, they require fresh horses, and must only be made at decisive
moments.
Introduction to Mathematics, p. 61

An analysis of the paradoxes to be avoided shows that they all result 12
from a certain kind of vicious circle. The vicious circles in question arise
from supposing that a collection of objects may contain members which
can only be defined by means of the collection as a whole. Thus, for
example, the collection of *propositions* will be supposed to contain a

proposition stating that 'all propositions are either true or false'. It would seem, however, that such a statement could not be legitimate unless 'all propositions' referred to some already definite collection which it cannot do if new propositions are created by statements about 'all propositions'. We shall, therefore, have to say that statements about 'all propositions' are meaningless. . . .

The principle which enables us to avoid illegitimate totalities may be stated as follows: 'Whatever involves *all* of a collection must not be one of the collection'; or, conversely: 'If, provided a certain collection had a total, it would have members only definable in terms of that total, then the said collection has no total.' We shall call this the 'vicious-circle principle' . . .
Alfred North Whitehead and Bertrand Russell, Principia Mathematica, p. 37

13 Philosophy is akin to poetry, and both of them seek to express that ultimate good sense which we term civilization. In each there is reference to form beyond the direct meanings of words. Poetry allies itself to metre, philosophy to mathematic pattern.
Modes of Thought, p. 237

DAVID WIGGINS (*b.* 1933)

1 . . . our claim was only that what sortal concepts we bring to bear upon experience determines what we can find there – just as the size and mesh of a net determine, not what fish are in the sea, but which ones we shall catch. The thesis is that the concepts under which experience is articulated and things are singled out determine the persistence conditions of what is singled only because such concepts determine *what* is singled out.
Sameness and Substance, p. 141

2 I shall . . . claim to uncover the possibility that philosophy has put happiness in the place that should have been occupied in moral philosophy by meaning. This is a purely theoretical claim, but if it is correct, it is not without consequences; and if (as some say) weariness and dissatisfaction have issued from the direct pursuit of happiness as such, then it is not without all explanatory power.
Needs, Values, Truth, p. 88

3 . . . the *prima facie* appearance is that a matter that is anthropocentric may be either more objective or less objective, or (at the limit) *merely* subjective. This is how things will appear until we have an argument to prove rigorously the mutual coincidence of independently plausible accounts of the anthropocentric/non-anthropocentric distinction, the

non-objective/objective distinction, and the subjective/non-subjective distinction.

A similar observation needs to be entered about all the other distinctions that are in the offing here – the distinctions between the neutral and the committed, the neutral and the biased, the descriptive and the prescriptive, the descriptive and the evaluative, the quantifiable and the unquantifiable, the absolute and the relative, the scientific and the unscientific, the not essentially contestable and the essentially contestable, the verifiable or falsifiable and the neither verifiable nor falsifiable, the factual and the normative. . . . In common parlance, and in sociology and economics . . . these distinctions are used almost interchangeably. But they are different. Each of these contrasts has its own rationale. An account of all of them would be a contribution not only to philosophy but to life.
Needs, Values, Truth, p. 101

The larger the obstacles nature or other people put in our way, and the   4
more truly hopeless the prospect, the less point most of us will feel anything has. 'Where there is no hope, there is no endeavour' as Samuel Johnson observed. In the end point is partly dependent on expectation of outcome; and expectation is dependent on past outcomes. So point is not necessarily independent of outcome.
Needs, Values, Truth, p. 98

A social morality cannot, of course, give any particular person a   5
guaranteed title to wealth, health, happiness, or security from ordinary misfortune. But equally it must not be such as to threaten anyone who is to be bound by it that it will bring upon him or any other individual participant, as if gratuitously, the misfortune of having his vital interests simply sacrificed for the sake of some larger public good. What sustains and regulates or adjusts a social morality, and what rebuts objections to it, must be something intelligible to all its individual participants, in human (never mind archangelic or ideal observer) terms. It must engage with the passions of those who are to live by it, or at the very least not *dis*engage with those passions.
'Claims of Need', *Morality and Objectivity*, ed. T. Honderich, p. 171

OSCAR WILDE (1854–1900)

To the critic the work of art is simply a suggestion for a new work of his   1
own, that need not necessarily bear any obvious resemblance to the thing it criticises.
Intentions, p. 146

2 Where, if not from the Impressionists, do we get those wonderful brown fogs that come creeping down our streets, blurring the gas-lamps and changing the houses into monstrous shadows? . . . The extraordinary change that has taken place in the climate of London during the last ten years is entirely due to a particular school of Art. . . . For what is Nature? Nature is no great mother who has borne us. She is our creation. It is in our brain that she quickens to life. Things are because we see them, and what we see, and how we see it, depends on the Arts that have influenced us. To look at a thing is very different from seeing a thing. One does not see anything until one sees its beauty. Then, and then only, does it come into existence.
The Decay of Lying, Collected Writings, ed. I. Murray, p. 232

3 No great artist ever sees things as they really are. If he did he would cease to be an artist.
The Decay of Lying, p. 235

4 After playing Chopin, I feel as if I had been weeping over sins that I had never committed, and mourning over tragedies that were not my own. Music always seems to me to produce that effect. It creates for one a past of which one has been ignorant, and fills one with a sense of sorrows that have been hidden from one's tears. I can fancy a man who had led a perfectly commonplace life, hearing by chance some curious piece of music, and suddenly discovering that his soul, without his being conscious of it, had passed through terrible experiences, and known fearful joys, or wild romantic loves, or great renunciations.
The Critic as Artist, p. 243

5 The truth is rarely pure and never simple. Modern life would be very tedious if it were either, and modern literature a complete impossibility!
The Importance of Being Earnest, p. 485

6 Education is an admirable thing, but it is well to remember from time to time that nothing that is worth knowing can be taught.
The Critic as Artist, p. 248

7 A sentimentalist is simply one who desires to have the luxury of an emotion without paying for it.
De Profundis

WILLIAM of OCKHAM (c.1285–1349)

1 [A sign is] anything which, when grasped, makes something else to come to mind, though what is brought to mind is not in the mind for the first time but is actually in the mind after being known dispositionally.
Summa Logicae, Opera Philosophica, I, p. 8

That no universal is a substance existing outside the mind can be   2
evidently proved.
Summa Logicae, Opera Philosophica, I, p. 50

Plurality should not be posited unnecessarily.   3
Scriptum in Librum Primum Sententiarum, Opera Theologica, I, p. 74

WILLIAM OF SHERWOOD (1200/10–1266/71)

Linguistic science has three parts, grammar, which teaches us to speak
correctly, rhetoric, which teaches us to speak ornately, and logic, which
teaches us to speak truly.
Introductiones in Logicam, ed. M. Grabmann

BERNARD WILLIAMS (*b.* 1929)

. . . it is not a contingent fact that I cannot bring it about, just like that,   1
that I believe something, as it is a contingent fact that I cannot bring it
about, just like that, that I'm blushing. Why is this? One reason is
connected with the characteristic of beliefs that they aim at truth. If I
could acquire a belief at will, I could acquire it whether it was true or not;
moreover I would know that I could acquire it whether it was true or not.
If in full consciousness I could will to acquire a 'belief' irrespective of its
truth, it is unclear that before the event I could seriously think of it as a
belief, i.e. as something purporting to represent reality.
'Deciding to Believe', *Problems of the Self*, p. 148

Anyone who believed that personalities could be identified without   2
reference to bodies might be expected to make sense of the idea of bodily
interchange. . . . Suppose a magician is hired to perform the old trick of
making the emperor and the peasant become each other. He gets the
emperor and the peasant in one room, with the emperor on his throne
and the peasant in the corner, and then casts the spell. What will count as
success? Clearly not that after the smoke has cleared the old emperor
should be in the corner and the old peasant on the throne. That would be
a rather boring trick. The requirement is presumably that the emperor's
body, with the peasant's personality, should be on the throne, and the
peasant's body with the emperor's personality, in the corner. What does
this mean? In particular, what has happened to the voices? The voice
presumably ought to count as a bodily function; yet how would the
peasant's gruff blasphemies be uttered in the emperor's cultivated tones,
or the emperor's witticisms in the peasant's growl? A similar point holds
for the features; the emperor's body might include the sort of face that

459

just *could not* express the peasant's morose suspiciousness, the peasant's a face no expression of which could be taken for one of fastidious arrogance. These 'could's are not just empirical – such expressions on these features might be unthinkable.

'Personal Identity and Individuation', *Problems of the Self*, p. 11

3 Immortality, or a state without death, would be meaningless, I shall suggest; so, in a sense, death gives the meaning to life.

'The Makropulos Case', *Problems of the Self*, p. 82

4 Moral conflicts are neither systematically avoidable, nor all soluble without remainder.

'Ethical Consistency', *Problems of the Self*, p. 179

5 This is not at all to say that the alternative to consequentialism is that one has to accept that there are some actions which one should always do, or again some which one should never do, *whatever the consequences*: this is a much stronger position than any involved, as I have defined the issues, in the denial of consequentialism. All that is involved, on the present account, in the denial of consequentialism, is that with respect to some type of action, there are some situations in which that would be the right thing to do, even though the state of affairs produced by one's doing that would be worse than some other state of affairs accessible to one.

J. J. C. Smart and Bernard Williams, *Utilitarianism: For and Against*, p. 90

6 It is because consequentialism attaches value ultimately to states of affairs, and its concern is with what states of affairs the world contains, that it essentially involves the notion of *negative responsibility*: that if I am ever responsible for anything, then I must be just as much responsible for things that I allow or fail to prevent, as I am for things that I myself, in the more everyday restricted sense, bring about.

J. J. C. Smart and Bernard Williams, *Utilitarianism: For and Against*, p. 95

7 It is absurd to demand of such a man, when the sums come in from the utility network which the projects of others have in part determined, that he should just step aside from his own project and decision and acknowledge the decision which utilitarian calculation requires. It is to alienate him in a real sense from his actions and the source of his actions in his own convictions. It is to make him into a channel between the input of everyone's projects, including his own, and an output of optimific decision; but this is to neglect the extent to which *his* actions and *his* decisions have to be seen as the actions and decisions which flow from the projects and attitudes with which he is most closely identified. It is thus, in the most literal sense, an attack on his integrity.

J. J. C. Smart and Bernard Williams, *Utilitarianism: For and Against*, p. 116

The trouble with religious morality comes not from morality's being 8
inescapably pure, but from religion's being incurably unintelligible.
Morality: An Introduction to Ethics, p. 96

There are indeed areas in which the 'inculcation of principles' is an 9
appropriate phrase for the business of moral education: truth-telling, for
example, and the sphere of justice. But more broadly, as Aristotle
perceived, we are concerned with something not so aptly called the
inculcation of principles, but rather the education of the emotions.
'Morality and the Emotions', *Problems of the Self*, p. 225

. . . surely *this* is a justification on behalf of the rescuer, that the person he 10
chose to rescue was his wife? It depends on how much weight is carried
by 'justification': the consideration that it was his wife is certainly, for
instance, an explanation which should silence comment. But something
more ambitious than this is usually intended, essentially involving the
idea that moral principle can legitimate his preference, yielding the
conclusion that in situations of this kind it is at least all right (morally
permissible) to save one's wife. . . . But this construction provides the
agent with one thought too many: it might have been hoped by some (for
instance, by his wife) that his motivating thought, fully spelled out,
would be the thought that it was his wife, not that it was his wife and that
in situations of this kind it is permissible to save one's wife.
'Persons, Character and Morality', *The Identities of Persons*, ed. A. O. Rorty

The choice can only be whether animals benefit from our practices or are 11
harmed by them. This is why speciesism is falsely modeled on racism and
sexism, which really are prejudices. To suppose that there is an
ineliminable white or male understanding of the world, and to think that
the only choice is whether blacks or women should benefit from 'our'
(white, male) practices or be harmed by them: this is already to be
prejudiced. But in the case of human relations to animals, the analogues
to such thoughts are simply correct.
Ethics and the Limits of Philosophy, p. 118

EDGAR WILSON (*b.* 1938)

The *myth myth* is the view that monarchy alone expresses something
deep and mythic in human nature that is indispensable to a cohesive and
stable society.
The Myth of British Monarchy, p. 4

LUDWIG WITTGENSTEIN (1889–1951)

The correct method in philosophy would really be the following: to say 1
nothing except what can be said, i.e. propositions of natural science – i.e.

461

something that has nothing to do with philosophy – and then, whenever someone else wanted to say something metaphysical, to demonstrate to him that he had failed to give a meaning to certain signs in his propositions. . . . ·

My propositions serve as elucidations in the following way: anyone who understands me eventually recognizes them as nonsensical, when he has used them – as steps – to climb up beyond them. (He must, so to speak, throw away the ladder after he has climbed up it.)

He must transcend these propositions, and then he will see the world aright.

What we cannot speak about we must pass over in silence.

Tractatus Logico-Philosophicus, trans. D. F. Pears and B. F. McGuinness, 6.53–7

2   . . . I used to believe . . . that it is the task of logical analysis to discover the elementary propositions. I wrote, We are unable to specify the form of elementary propositions. . . . Yet I did think that the elementary propositions could be specified at a later date. Only in recent years have I broken away from that mistake. At the time I wrote in a manuscript of my book (this is not printed in the *Tractatus*), The answers to philosophical questions must never be surprising. In philosophy you cannot discover anything. I myself, however, had not clearly enough understood this and offended against it.

Friedrich Waismann, *Wittgenstein and the Vienna Circle*, p. 182

3   It was true to say that our considerations could not be scientific ones. . . . The problems are solved, not by giving new information, but by arranging what we have always known. Philosophy is a battle against the bewitchment of our intelligence by means of language.

Philosophical Investigations, trans. G. E. M. Anscombe, I, §109

4   All testing, all confirmation and disconfirmation of a hypothesis takes place already within a system. And this system is not a more or less arbitrary and doubtful point of departure for all our arguments: no, it belongs to the essence of what we call an argument. The system is not so much the point of departure, as the element in which arguments have their life.

On Certainty, trans. Denis Paul and G. E. M. Anscombe, §105

5   . . . can it even be said: Everything speaks for, and nothing against the table's still being there when no one sees it? For what does speak for it?

But if anyone were to doubt it, how would his doubt come out in practice? And couldn't we peacefully leave him to doubt it, since it makes no difference at all? . . .

Doesn't one need grounds for doubt?
On Certainty, trans. Denis Paul and G. E. M. Anscombe, §§119–21

I should like to say: Moore does not *know* what he asserts he knows, but   6
it stands fast for him, as also for me; regarding it as absolutely solid is
part of our *method* of doubt and enquiry.
On Certainty, trans. Denis Paul and G. E. M. Anscombe, §151

Essence is expressed by grammar.   7
   Consider: 'The only correlate in language to an intrinsic necessity is an
arbitrary rule. It is the only thing which one can milk out of this intrinsic
necessity into a proposition.'
   Grammar tells what kind of object anything is. (Theology as
grammar.)
Philosophical Investigations, trans. G. E. M. Anscombe, I, §371

'So you are saying that human agreement decides what is true and what is   8
false?' – It is what human beings *say* that is true and false; and they agree
in the *language* they use. That is not agreement in opinions but in form of
life.
   If language is to be a means of communication there must be
agreement not only in definitions but also (queer as this may sound) in
judgments.
Philosophical Investigations, trans. G. E. M. Anscombe, I, §241

I want to regard man here as an animal; as a primitive being to which one   9
grants instinct but not ratiocination. As a creature in a primitive state.
Any logic good enough for a primitive means of communication needs no
apology from us. Language did not emerge from some kind of
ratiocination.
On Certainty, trans. Denis Paul and G. E. M. Anscombe, §475

Here the term 'language-*game*' is meant to bring into prominence the fact   10
that the *speaking* of language is part of an activity, or of a form of life.
Philosophical Investigations, trans. G. E. M. Anscombe, I, §23

If a lion could talk, we could not understand him.   11
Philosophical Investigations, trans. G. E. M. Anscombe, II, xi, p. 223

Someone coming into a strange country will sometimes learn the   12
language of the inhabitants from ostensive definitions that they give him;
and he will often have to *guess* the meaning of these definitions; and will
guess sometimes right, sometimes wrong.
   And now, I think, we can say: Augustine describes the learning of
human language as if the child came into a strange country and did not

understand the language of the country; that is, as if it already had a language, only not this one.
Philosophical Investigations, trans. G. E. M. Anscombe, I, §32

13 . . . a great deal of stage-setting in the language is presupposed if the mere act of naming is to make sense.
Philosophical Investigations, trans. G. E. M. Anscombe, I, §257

14 To repeat – naming is something like attaching a label to a thing. One can say that this is preparatory to the use of a word. But *what* is it a preparation *for*?
Philosophical Investigations, trans. G. E. M. Anscombe, I, §26

15 We are tempted to think that the action of language consists of two parts; an inorganic part, the handling of signs, and an organic part, which we may call understanding these signs, meaning them, interpreting them, thinking. These latter activities seem to take place in a queer kind of medium, the mind; and the mechanism of the mind, the nature of which, it seems, we don't quite understand, can bring about effects which no material mechanism could. . . .

In fact, as soon as you think of replacing the mental image by, say, a painted one, and as soon as the image thereby loses its occult character, it ceases to seem to impart any life to the sentence at all.
The Blue and Brown Books, pp. 3, 5

16 . . . the *kind* of thing that you would suggest is that he imagined something yellow when he *understood* the order, and then chose a ball according to his image. To see that this is not *necessary* remember that I could have given him the order, 'Imagine a yellow patch'. Would you still be inclined to assume that he first imagines a yellow patch, just *understanding* my order, and then imagines a yellow patch to match the first? (Now I don't say that this is not possible. Only, putting it in this way immediately shows you that it need not happen. This, by the way, illustrates the method of philosophy.)
The Blue and Brown Books, p. 12

17 'I set the brake up by connecting up rod and lever.' – Yes, given the whole of the rest of the mechanism. Only in conjunction with that is it a brake-lever, and separated from its support it is not even a lever; it may be anything, or nothing.
Philosophical Investigations, trans. G. E. M. Anscombe, I, §6

18 Every sign *by itself* seems dead. *What* gives it life? – In use it is *alive*. Is life breathed into it there? – Or is the *use* its life?
Philosophical Investigations, trans. G. E. M. Anscombe, I, §432

For a *large* class of cases – though not for all – in which we employ the 19
word 'meaning' it can be defined thus: the meaning of a word is its use in
the language.
Philosophical Investigations, trans. G. E. M. Anscombe, I, §43

... philosophical problems arise when language *goes on holiday.* 20
Philosophical Investigations, trans. G. E. M. Anscombe, I, §38

Think of the tools in a tool-box: there is a hammer, pliers, a saw, a screw- 21
driver, a rule, a glue-pot, glue, nails and screws. – The functions of words
are as diverse as the functions of these objects.
Philosophical Investigations, trans. G. E. M. Anscombe, I, §11

For someone might object against me: 'You take the easy way out! You 22
talk about all sorts of language-games, but have nowhere said what the
essence of a language-game, and hence of language, is ...'
   And this is true. – Instead of producing something common to all that
we call language, I am saying that these phenomena have no one thing in
common which makes us use the same word for all, – but that they are
related to one another in many different ways. ...
   Consider for example the proceedings that we call 'games'. I mean
board-games, card-games, ball-games, Olympic games, and so on. What
is common to them all? – Don't say: 'There *must* be something common,
or they would not be called "games"' – but *look and see* whether there is
anything common to all. – For if you look at them you will not see
something that is common to *all*, but similarities, relationships, and a
whole series of them at that. ...
   I can think of no better expression to characterize these similarities
than 'family resemblances'; for the various resemblances between
members of a family: build, features, colour of eyes, gait, temperament,
etc., etc., overlap and criss-cross in the same way. – And I shall say:
'games' form a family.
Philosophical Investigations, trans. G. E. M. Anscombe, I, §§65–7

Our craving for generality has another main source: our preoccupation 23
with the method of science. ... I want to say here that it can never be our
job to reduce anything to anything, or to explain anything. Philosophy
really *is* 'purely descriptive'. (Think of such questions as 'Are there sense
data?' and ask: What method is there of determining this? Introspection?)
The Blue and Brown Books, p. 18

We feel as if we had to *penetrate* phenomena: our investigation, however, 24
is directed not towards phenomena, but, as one might say, towards the
'possibilities' of phenomena. We remind ourselves, that is to say, of the
kind of statement that we make about phenomena.
Philosophical Investigations, trans. G. E. M. Anscombe, I, §90

25   When we do philosophy we are like savages, primitive people, who hear the expressions of civilized men, put a false interpretation on them, and then draw the queerest conclusions from it.
Philosophical Investigations, trans. G. E. M. Anscombe, I, §194

26   The expression 'The rule meant him to follow up 100 by 101' makes it appear that this rule, as it was meant, *foreshadowed* all the transitions which were to be made according to it. But the assumption of a shadow of a transition does not get us any further, because it does not bridge the gulf between it and the real transition. If the mere words of the rule could not anticipate a future transition, no more could any mental act accompanying these words.
The Blue and Brown Books, p. 142

27   Your idea, then, is that you know the application of the rule of the series quite apart from remembering actual applications to particular numbers. And you will perhaps say: 'Of course! For the series is infinite and the bit of it that I can have developed finite.'
     But what does this knowledge consist in?
Philosophical Investigations, trans. G. E. M. Anscombe, I, §§147–8

28   For just where one says 'But don't you *see* . . .?' the rule is no use, it is what is explained, not what does the explaining.
     'He grasps the rule intuitively.' – But why the rule? Why not how he is to continue?
Zettel, §§302–3

29   When someone says the word 'cube' to me, for example, I know what it means. But can the whole *use* of the word come before my mind, when I *understand* it in this way?
     Well, but on the other hand isn't the meaning of the word also determined by this use? And can these ways of determining meaning conflict? Can what we grasp *in a flash* accord with a use, fit or fail to fit it? . . .
     What really comes before our mind when we *understand* a word? – Isn't it something like a picture? Can't it *be* a picture?
     Well, suppose that a picture does come before your mind when you hear the word 'cube', say the drawing of a cube. In what sense can this picture fit or fail to fit a use of the word 'cube'? – Perhaps you say: 'It's quite simple; – if that picture occurs to me and I point to a triangular prism for instance, and say it is a cube, then this use of the word doesn't fit the picture.' – But doesn't it fit? I have purposely so chosen the example that it is quite easy to imagine a *method of projection* according to which the picture does fit after all.

The picture of the cube did indeed *suggest* a certain use to us, but it was possible for me to use it differently.

Then what sort of mistake did I make; was it what we should like to express by saying: I should have thought the picture forced a particular use on me? How could I think that? What *did* I think? Is there such a thing as a picture, or something like a picture, that forces a particular application on us; so that my mistake lay in confusing one picture with another? . . . our 'belief that the picture forced a particular application upon us' consisted in the fact that only the one case and no other occurred to us. . . .

What is essential is to see that the same thing can come before our minds when we hear the word and the application still be different. Has it the *same* meaning both times? I think we shall say not.

Philosophical Investigations, trans. G. E. M. Anscombe, I, §§139–40

The expression of the experience is: 'Now I'm seeing it as a pyramid;   30 now as a square with its diagonals.' ⊠ Now, what is the 'it' which I see now this way, now that? Is it the drawing? . . .

I cannot say 'A new interpretation keeps on striking me'. Indeed it does; but it also incorporates itself straight away in what is seen. There keeps on striking me a new aspect of the drawing – which I see remains the same. It is as if a new garment kept being put on it, and as if all the same each garment was the same as the other.

Remarks on the Philosophy of Psychology, I, §§31, 33

Should I say: 'The picture-rabbit and the picture-duck look just the   31 same'?! Something militates against that – But can't I say: they look just the same, namely like this – and now I produce the ambiguous drawing. (The draft of water, the draft of a treaty.) But if I now wanted to offer reasons against this way of putting things – what would I have to say? That one sees the picture differently each time, if it is now a duck and now a rabbit . . . ? . . .

What has been said, if it is said that anyone who sees the drawing now as a rabbit now as a duck has quite different visual experiences? . . . What is the description of what I see? (This doesn't mean only: In what words am I to describe what I see? – but also 'What does a description of what I see look like? What am I to call by that name?')

Remarks on the Philosophy of Psychology, I, §§75, 80, 89

32 'Now he's seeing it like *this*', 'now like *that*' would only be said of someone *capable* of making certain applications of the figure quite freely. . . .

Do I really see something different each time, or do I only interpret what I see in a different way? I am inclined to say the former. To interpret is to think, to do something; seeing is a state.

. . . When we interpret we form hypotheses, which may prove false. – 'I am seeing this figure as a —' can be verified as little as (or in the same sense as) 'I am seeing bright red'. So there is a similarity in the use of 'seeing' in the two contexts. . . .

We find certain things about seeing puzzling, because we do not find the whole business of seeing puzzling enough.

Philosophical Investigations, trans. G. E. M. Anscombe, II, pp. 208, 212

33 An aspect is subject to the will. If something appears blue to me, I cannot see it red, and it makes no sense to say 'See it red'; whereas it does make sense to say 'See it as —'.

Remarks on the Philosophy of Psychology, I, §899

34 At these words I form this image. How can I *justify* this?

Has anyone shewn me the image of the colour blue and told me that *this* is the image of blue?

What is the meaning of the words: '*This* image'? How does one point to an image? How does one point twice to the same image?

Philosophical Investigations, trans. G. E. M. Anscombe, I, §382

35 I want to keep a diary about the recurrence of a certain sensation. To this end I associate it with the sign 'S' and write this sign in a calendar for every day on which I have the sensation. – I will remark first of all that a definition of the sign cannot be formulated. – But still I can give myself a kind of ostensive definition. – How? Can I point to the sensation? Not in the ordinary sense. But I speak, or write the sign down, and at the same time I concentrate my attention on the sensation – and so, as it were, point to it inwardly. – But what is this ceremony for? for that is all it seems to be! – . . . Well, . . . I impress on myself the connexion between the sign and the sensation. – But 'I impress it on myself' can only mean: this process brings it about that I remember the connexion *right* in the future. But in the present case I have no criterion of correctness. One would like to say: whatever is going to seem right to me is right. And that only means that here we can't talk about 'right'.

Philosophical Investigations, trans. G. E. M. Anscombe, I, §258

36 If I say of myself that it is only from my own case that I know what the word 'pain' means – must I not say the same of other people too? And how can I generalize the *one* case so irresponsibly?

Now someone tells me that *he* knows what pain is only from his own case! – Suppose everyone had a box with something in it: we call it a 'beetle'. No one can look into anyone else's box, and everyone says he knows what a beetle is only by looking at *his* beetle. – Here it would be quite possible for everyone to have something different in his box. One might even imagine such a thing constantly changing. – But suppose the word 'beetle' had a use in these people's language? – If so it would not be used as the name of a thing. The thing in the box has no place in the language-game at all; not even as a *something*: for the box might even be empty. – No, one can 'divide through' by the thing in the box; it cancels out, whatever it is.

That is to say: if we construe the grammar of the expression of sensation on the model of 'object and designation' the object drops out of consideration as irrelevant.

Philosophical Investigations, trans. G. E. M. Anscombe, I, §293

It shews a fundamental misunderstanding, if I am inclined to study the headache I have now in order to get clear about the philosophical problem of sensation. 37

Philosophical Investigations, trans. G. E. M. Anscombe, I, §314

You learned the *concept* 'pain' when you learned language. 38

Philosophical Investigations, trans. G. E. M. Anscombe, I, §384

Why can't my right hand give my left hand money? – My right hand can 39 put it into my left hand. My right hand can write a deed of gift and my left hand a receipt. – But the further practical consequences would not be those of a gift. . . . we shall ask: 'Well, and what of it?' And the same could be asked if a person had given himself a private definition of a word; I mean, if he has said the word to himself and at the same time has directed his attention to a sensation.

Philosophical Investigations, trans. G. E. M. Anscombe, I, §268

. . . words are connected with the primitive, the natural, expressions of 40 the sensation and used in their place. A child has hurt himself and he cries; and then adults talk to him and teach him exclamations and, later, sentences. They teach the child new pain-behaviour.

'So you are saying that the word "pain" really means crying?' – On the contrary: the verbal expression of pain replaces crying and does not describe it.

Philosophical Investigations, trans. G. E. M. Anscombe, I, §244

'But you will surely admit that there is a difference between pain- 41 behaviour accompanied by pain and pain-behaviour without any pain?' – Admit it? What greater difference could there be? – 'And yet you again and again reach the conclusion that the sensation itself is a *nothing.*' – Not at all. It is not a *something,* but not a *nothing* either! The conclusion was only that a nothing would serve just as well as a something about which nothing could be said. We have only rejected the grammar which tries to force itself on us here.

The paradox disappears only if we make a radical break with the idea that language always functions in one way, always serves the same purpose: to convey thoughts – which may be about houses, pains, good and evil, or anything else you please.

Philosophical Investigations, trans. G. E. M. Anscombe, I, §304

42 'But "joy" surely designates an inward thing.' No. 'Joy' designates nothing at all. Neither any inward nor any outward thing.
Zettel, §487

43 I have been trying in all this to remove the temptation to think that there '*must* be' what is called a mental process of thinking, hoping, wishing, believing, etc., independent of the process of expressing a thought, a hope, a wish, etc.
The Blue and Brown Books, p. 41

44 We say, 'surely the thought is *something*; it is not nothing'; and all one can answer to this is, that the word 'thought' has its *use,* which is of a totally different kind from the use of the word 'sentence'.
The Blue and Brown Books, p. 7

45 How does the philosophical problem about mental processes and states and about behaviourism arise? – The first step is the one that altogether escapes notice. We talk of processes and states and leave their nature undecided. Sometime perhaps we shall know more about them – we think. But that is just what commits us to a particular way of looking at the matter. For we have a definite concept of what it means to learn to know a process better. (The decisive movement in the conjuring trick has been made, and it was the very one that we thought quite innocent.) – And now the analogy which was to make us understand our thoughts falls to pieces. So we have to deny the yet uncomprehended process in the yet unexplored medium. And now it looks as if we had denied mental processes. And naturally we don't want to deny them.
Philosophical Investigations, trans. G. E. M. Anscombe, I, §308

46 In what sense can the physiological processes be said to correspond to thoughts, and in what sense can we be said to get the thoughts from the observation of the brain?

I suppose we imagine the correspondence to have been verified experimentally. Let us imagine such an experiment crudely. It consists in

looking at the brain while the subject thinks . . . assuming that the subject is at the same time the experimenter, who is looking at his own brain, say by means of a mirror. . . . The subject-experimenter is observing a correlation of two phenomena. One of them he, perhaps, calls the *thought*. This may consist of a train of images, organic sensations, or on the other hand of a train of the various visual, tactual and muscular experiences which he has in writing or speaking a sentence. – The other experience is one of seeing his brain work. Both these phenomena could correctly be called 'expressions of thought'; and the question 'where is the thought itself?' had better, in order to prevent confusion, be rejected as nonsensical.
The Blue and Brown Books, p. 7

The prejudice in favour of psycho-physical parallellism is also a fruit of the primitive conception of grammar. For when one admits a causality between psychological phenomena, which is not mediated physiologically, one fancies that in doing so one is making an admission of the existence of a soul *alongside* the body, a ghostly mental nature.
Remarks on the Philosophy of Psychology, I, §906

47

What is your aim in philosophy? – To shew the fly the way out of the fly-bottle.
Philosophical Investigations, trans. G. E. M. Anscombe, I, §309

48

Now when in the solipsistic way . . . I point before me saying, 'this is what's really seen', although I make the gesture of pointing, I don't point to one thing as opposed to another.
 . . . I robbed the pointing of its sense by inseparably connecting that which points and that to which it points. I constructed a clock with all its wheels, etc., and in the end fastened the dial to the pointer and made it go round with it. And in this way the solipsist's 'Only this is really seen' reminds us of a tautology.
The Blue and Brown Books, p. 71

49

There is no such thing as the subject that thinks or entertains ideas.
 If I wrote a book called *The World as I found it*, I should have to include a report on my body, and should have to say which parts were subordinate to my will, and which were not, etc., this being a method of isolating the subject, or rather of showing that in an important sense there is no subject; for it alone could *not* be mentioned in that book. –
 The subject does not belong to the world: rather, it is a limit of the world.
Tractatus Logico-Philosophicus, trans. D. F. Pears and B. F. McGuinness, 5.631–3

50

51 We feel then that in the cases in which 'I' is used as subject, we don't use it because we recognize a particular person by his bodily characteristics; and this creates the illusion that we use this word to refer to something bodiless, which, however, has its seat in our body. In fact *this* seems to be the real ego, the one 'of which it was said, 'Cogito, ergo sum'. – 'Is there then no mind, but only a body?' Answer: The word 'mind' has meaning, i.e., it has a use in our language; but saying this doesn't yet say what kind of use we make of it.
The Blue and Brown Books, p. 69

52 The word 'I' does not refer to a possessor in sentences about having an experience, unlike its use in 'I have a cigar'. We could have a language from which 'I' is omitted from sentences describing a personal experience. Instead of saying 'I think' or 'I have an ache' one might say 'It thinks' (like 'It rains'), and in place of 'I have an ache', 'There is an ache here'.
Lectures, Cambridge 1932–5, ed. A. Ambrose, p. 21

53 I can see – but not at all clearly – a connection between the problem of solipsism or idealism and the problem of the way a sentence signifies. Is it perhaps like this – the I is replaced by the sentence and the relation between the I and reality is replaced by the relation between the sentence and reality?
The Big Typescript (unpublished), quoted in David Pears, *The False Prison: A Study of the Development of Wittgenstein's Philosophy*, p. 269

54 The sense of the world must lie outside the world. In the world everything is as it is, and everything happens as it does happen: *in* it no value exists – and if it did exist, it would have no value.
Tractatus Logico-Philosophicus, trans. D. F. Pears and B. F. McGuinness, 6.41

ROBERT PAUL WOLFF (*b.* 1933)

1 Men are no better than children if they not only accept the rule of others from force of necessity, but embrace it willingly and forfeit their duty unceasingly to weigh the merits of the actions which they perform. When I place myself in the hands of another, and permit him to determine the principles by which I shall guide my behavior, I repudiate the freedom and reason which give me dignity. I am then guilty of what Kant might have called the sin of willful heteronomy.

There would appear to be no alternative but to embrace the doctrine of anarchism and categorically deny *any* claim to legitimate authority by one man over another. Yet I confess myself unhappy with the conclusion that I must simply leave off the search for legitimate collective authority.
In Defense of Anarchism, p. 72

Pluralist democracy, with its virtue, tolerance, constitutes the highest 2
stage in the political development of industrial capitalism. It transcends
the crude 'limitations' of early individualistic liberalism and makes a
place for the communitarian features of social life, as well as for the
interest-group politics which emerged as a domesticated version of the
class struggle. Pluralism is humane, benevolent, accommodating, and far
more responsive to the evils of social injustice than either the egoistic
liberalism or the traditionalistic conservatism from which it grew. But
pluralism is fatally blind to the evils which afflict the entire body politic,
and as a theory of society it obstructs consideration of precisely the sorts
of thoroughgoing social revisions which may be needed to remedy those
evils.
'Beyond Tolerance', *A Critique of Pure Tolerance*, p. 60

Only extreme economic decentralization could permit the sort of 3
voluntary economic coordination consistent with the ideals of anarchism
and affluence. At the present time, of course, such decentralization would
produce economic chaos, but if we possessed a cheap, local source of
power and an advanced technology of small-scale production, and if we
were in addition willing to accept a high level of economic waste, we
might be able to break the American economy down into regional and
subregional units of manageable size. The exchanges between the units
would be inefficient and costly – very large inventory levels, inelasticities
of supply and demand, considerable waste, and so forth. But in return for
this price, men would have increasing freedom to act autonomously. In
effect, such a society would enable all men to be autonomous agents,
whereas in our present society, the relatively few autonomous men are –
as it were – parasitic upon the obedient, authority-respecting masses.
In Defense of Anarchism, p. 81

RICHARD WOLLHEIM (*b.* 1923)

What then is the appeal of Monism, when it is presented in this severe 1
form, divorced from practical considerations and unqualified by any
compensating principle? The true answer to this question must lie deep in
the recesses of the human mind, and it would be presumptuous to claim
any certain possession of it. At the same time there can fairly be said to be
a powerful, indeed an irresistible, analogy between the metaphysical
attachment to the idea of an undivided Reality and the desire to establish
'whole objects' which is of such crucial importance in infantile
development.
F. H. Bradley, p. 278

Richard Wollheim

2 The simplest way of putting the matter, which is not to be taken as a metaphysical claim, is this: there are persons, they exist; persons lead lives, they live; and as a result, in consequence – in consequence, that is, of the way they do it – there are lives, of which those who lead them may, for instance, be proud, or feel ashamed. So there is a thing, and there is a process, and there is a product. . . . The process, which is the leading of a life, occurs in, though not necessarily inside, the person, and it issues in his life. The life is his life, uniquely his, but others are not excluded from it. Others, leading their lives, lives that are uniquely theirs, may nevertheless participate in his, just as he, unless he is an unsung autochthonous stylite, will participate in theirs. . . .

The central claim of these lectures is the fundamental status of the process.
The Thread of Life, p. 2

3 When the mind is passive, thoughts are conceived of as effecting an entry into it, from the outside: on occasions, when the thoughts are obsessional, doing so with the use of force. There is something or somewhere that they enter. And when the mind is active, the presumption would be – though the presumption here is fainter – that it is in this same place that the thoughts arise or are generated.

I foresee two immediate objections. The first would be that I have taken what is no more than a sustained metaphor as though it were, or were intended as, a literal description. . . . the argument as it stands is tendentious. For it assumes that we have a clear distinction between what is metaphorical and what is not: which we do not have.
On Art and the Mind: Essays and Lectures, p. 35

4 Which brings me to the one general point of a positive kind that I have to make about representation: and that is, that to see something as a representation is intrinsically bound up with, and even in its highest reaches is merely an elaboration or extension of, the way in which, when the black paint is applied to white canvas, we can see the black on the white, or behind the white, or level with it.
On Art and the Mind: Essays and Lectures, p. 27

5 In the mature expression of Wittgenstein's philosophy, the phrase 'form of life' (*Lebensform*) makes a frequent appearance. Art is, in Wittgenstein's sense, a form of life.
Art and its Objects, p. 104

6 I now think that representational seeing should be understood as involving, and therefore best elucidated through, not seeing-as, but another phenomenon closely related to it, which I call 'seeing-in'. Where previously I would have said that representational seeing is a matter of

seeing x (= the medium or representation) as y (= the object, or what is represented), I would now say that it is, for the same values of the variables, a matter of seeing y in x.
Art and its Objects, p. 209

If I am looking at x, and x is a particular, I can see a woman in x, and I   7
can also see in x that a woman is reading a love-letter: but, whereas I can see x as a woman, I cannot see x as that a woman is reading a love-letter.
Art and its Objects, p. 210

The story of Ur-painting begins like this: An agent — he is as yet no artist   8
— holding a charged instrument places himself next to a support and deposits marks. That is all there is to it: he deposits marks. And by saying that that is all there is to it, I mean that that is the total privileged description: that is *the* description under which the action is intentional. The thought of the mark enjoys a monopoly in the agent's head when it comes to the guidance of his action. Though there may well be other thoughts floating around there.
Painting as an Art

MARY WOLLSTONECRAFT (1759–1797)

The association of our ideas is either habitual or instantaneous; and the   1
latter mode seems rather to depend on the original temperature of the mind than on the will. When the ideas, and matters of fact, are once taken in, they lie by for use, till some fortuitous circumstance makes the information dart into the mind with illustrative force, that has been received at very different periods of our lives. Like the lightning's flash are many recollections; one idea assimilating and explaining another, with astonishing rapidity. . . . Over those instantaneous associations we have little power; for when the mind is once enlarged by excursive flights, or profound reflection, the raw materials will, in some degree, arrange themselves.
Vindication of the Rights of Woman, ed. M. Brody, p. 219

A kind of mysterious instinct is *supposed* to reside in the soul, that   2
instantaneously discerns truth, without the tedious labour of ratiocination. This instinct, for I know not what other name to give it, has been termed *common sense*, and more frequently *sensibility*; and, by a kind of *indefeasible* right, it has been *supposed*, for rights of this kind are not easily proved, to reign paramount over the other faculties of the mind, and to be an authority from which there is no appeal. . . . It is to this instinct, without doubt, that you [Burke] allude, when you talk of the 'moral constitution of the heart.' . . . Sacred be the feelings of the heart! concentred in a glowing flame, they become the sun of life; and, without

his invigorating impregnation, reason would probably lie in helpless inactivity, and never bring forth her only legitimate offspring – virtue. But to prove that virtue is really an acquisition of the individual, and not the blind impulse of unerring instinct, the bastard vice has often been begotten by the same father.

In what respect are we superior to the brute creation, if intellect is not allowed to be the guide of passion? Brutes hope and fear, love and hate; but, without a capacity to improve, a power of turning these passions to good or evil, they neither acquire virtue nor wisdom. – Why? Because the Creator has not given them reason.

A Vindication of the Rights of Men, Works, ed. J. Todd and M. Butler, V, p. 30

3 We ought to beware of confounding mechanical instinctive sensations with emotions that reason deepens, and justly terms the feelings of *humanity.* This word discriminates the active exertions of virtue from the vague declamation of sensibility.

A Vindication of the Rights of Men

4 To account for, and excuse the tyranny of man, many ingenious arguments have been brought forward to prove, that the two sexes, in the acquirement of virtue, ought to aim at attaining a very different character: or, to speak explicitly, women are not allowed to have sufficient strength of mind to acquire what really deserves the name of virtue. Yet it should seem, allowing them to have souls, that there is but one way appointed by Providence to lead *mankind* to either virtue or happiness.

Vindication of the Rights of Woman, p. 100

5 In fact, it is a farce to call any being virtuous whose virtues do not result from the exercise of its own reason. This was Rousseau's opinion respecting men. I extend it to women. . . . Still the regal homage which they receive is so intoxicating, that till the manners of the times are changed, and formed on more reasonable principles, it may be impossible to convince them that the illegitimate power, which they obtain, by degrading themselves, is a curse, and that they must return to nature and equality, if they wish to secure the placid satisfaction that unsophisticated affections impart. But for this epoch we must wait – wait, perhaps, till kings and nobles, enlightened by reason, and, preferring the real dignity of man to childish state, throw off their gaudy hereditary trappings: and if then women do not resign the arbitrary power of beauty – they will prove that they have *less* mind than man.

Vindication of the Rights of Woman, p. 103

6 Men and women must be educated, in a great degree, by the opinions and manners of the society they live in. In every age there has been a stream of popular opinion that has carried all before it, and given a family

character, as it were, to the century. It may then fairly be inferred, that, till society be differently constituted, much cannot be expected from education.
Vindication of the Rights of Woman, p. 102

ALLEN W. WOOD (*b.* 1942)

Whenever we pronounce condescendingly on what history has shown us about the fate of Marx's thought, we speak as if we ourselves, our own collective life and history, were something already settled, over and done with, as if we had long ago already come to terms with all of humanity's possible futures. The history of Marx's thought will remain unfinished as long as revolutionary possibilities still live for us and Marx's thought is still their principal source.
Marx: Selections, Introduction, p. 18

CRISPIN WRIGHT (*b.* 1942)

. . . we have, it appears, radically to revise our whole conception of 1
meaning: there is no property of a statement which, irrespective of how we react or whether we ever get the chance to do so, combines with the character of the relevant non-linguistic facts to determine correct use of that statement. What constitutes correct use of the statement in particular circumstances always needs a contribution from *us*, from our dispositions to react and judge, in short from our nature. Where we cannot give that contribution, if only for external, trivial-seeming reasons like lack of facility or shortness of time, what constitutes correct use is therefore so far indeterminate.
'Strict Finitism', *Realism, Meaning and Truth*, p. 150

. . . there can be no philosophical science of ontology, no well-founded 2
attempt to see past our categories of expression and glimpse the way in which the world is truly furnished.
Frege's Conception of Numbers as Objects, p. 51

It follows that necessity is not purely recognitional, that attributions of 3
necessity are not genuine assertions, and that there is an element of decision involved in accepting any proof as a proof. We take a step, that is to say, not required of us by correct understanding of the concepts involved and correct apprehension of the proof's mechanics. Not that there need be any sense of freedom or consciousness of a decision; the step is one which we are *trained* to take as much as any other.
Wittgenstein on the Foundations of Mathematics, p. 459

JOHN WYCLIF (c.1320–1384)

[N]either the possibility nor the fact of assigning a term can cause extramental things to resemble each other more or less. The specific resemblance or difference between things is based essentially on the constituents of the things and not on signs. The predication or predicability of signs is not the reason for the resemblance of extramental things; it is the other way round . . .

On Universals, trans. A. Kenny, p. 9

X

XENOPHANES (c.570 BC–c.475 BC)

But if cattle and horses or lions had hands, or were able to draw with   1
their hands and do the works that men can do, horses would draw the
forms of the gods like horses, and cattle like cattle, and they would make
their bodies such as they each had themselves.
G. S. Kirk, J. E. Raven and M. Schofield, *The Pre-Socratic Philosophers*, p. 168

No man knows, or ever will know, the truth about the gods and about   2
everything I speak of: for even if one chanced to say the complete truth,
nevertheless one would not know it.
The Pre-Socratic Philosophers, p. 179

Z

𝕾𝕾𝕾𝕾𝕾

ZENO (*c.*490–430 BC)

1 The first [argument] asserts the non-existence of motion on the ground that that which is in locomotion must arrive at the half-way stage before it arrives at the goal. . . .
Aristotle, *Physics*, 239B 11

2 The second is the so-called *Achilles*, and it amounts to this, that in a race the quickest runner can never overtake the slowest, since the pursuer must first reach the point whence the pursued started, so that the slower must always hold a lead.
Aristotle, *Physics*, 239B 20

3 The third amounts to this, that the flying arrow is at rest. This result follows when one assumes that time is made up of moments.
Aristotle, *Physics*, 239B 30

GLOSSARY

᠖᠖᠖᠖᠖᠖

abduction A type of creative or speculative inference spoken of by Peirce, but few others, and distinguished from ordinary deductive and inductive inference.

Absolute, the The ultimate, all-embracing, unconditioned reality, postulated by certain idealist metaphysicians, and understood to have something like the explanatory power of God. Seemingly organic and conscious, though impersonal, it was also conceived as a diversity-in-unity. It generates, contains, and transmutes into a higher synthesis the fragmentariness, diversity and contradictions of finite existence (Bradley 6–8; Hegel 1, 15–25, 28; Schelling 1, 3, 8–10). *See* IDEALISM.

abstract idea In the theories of seventeenth- and eighteenth-century philosophers, best regarded as a concept. It features in some forms of solution to the problem of universals. Ideas were conceived as mental images essential to thought, and it seemed that an abstract idea, for example of a man, must somehow contain the diversity, yet prune away the discrepancies, of particular ideas of individual men, so as to provide a generalized picture of a man – the essential man. So Locke thought, but Berkeley, also a conceptualist, vehemently argued against him (Locke 7; Berkeley 3). *See* IDEA, UNIVERSAL.

analytic and synthetic statements An analytic statement is one in which the predicate is covertly 'contained in' the subject, or a statement true by virtue of the meaning of its terms, or a tautology. In contrast, a synthetic statement is such that the predicate does provide new information, which could not be obtained by analysing the subject. Kant formulated the distinction in the first way above, and superimposed it on the *a priori*/*a posteriori* distinction. All analytic statements are *a priori*, but, according to Kant, there can also be synthetic *a priori* statements (Kant 4–12). Empiricists claim that any proposition alleged to be synthetic *a priori* is either analytic, because a matter of the definitions of terms (in mathematics and logic), or really derived from

481

experience, or (in ethics) a disguised prescription or command. Quine and other philosophers have questioned the analytic–synthetic distinction (Quine 4). *See* A PRIORI, A POSTERIORI.

anomalous monism *See* MONISM.

antecedent In a conditional statement, one of the form 'If p, then q', p is the antecedent (or protasis) and q is the consequent (or apodosis).

antinomy The contradiction of two statements or principles, each of which rests on premises of equal strength. Kant, in 'The Antinomy of Pure Reason', argues that to hold either that the world is finite, or that it is infinite, leads to a self-contradictory conclusion. He therefore concludes that the only solution is to say that reality is outside space and time (Kant 32).

anti-realism View that truths are not independent of observers and their reflections, or, in a weaker form, that our knowledge of reality is theory- or language-dependent. Related to COHERENCE THEORY OF TRUTH. *See also* REALISM.

apodosis *See* ANTECEDENT.

a priori, a posteriori 'Prior to' and 'after' experience; a distinction between types of proposition, argument, knowledge, etc. An *a priori* proposition can be known to be true or false without reference to experience, although experience is necessary to coming to understand its terms. An *a posteriori* proposition can be known to be true or false only by reference to how, as a matter of contingent fact, things have been, are or will be (Frege 4). Empiricists and rationalists are divided over how far our concepts precede experience or are derived from it, whether we are born with innate ideas or the mind is a *tabula rasa*. *See* ANALYTIC AND SYNTHETIC STATEMENTS, EMPIRICISM, RATIONALISM, TRANSCENDENTAL IDEALISM.

behaviourism Doctrine, or policy, of reducing mental concepts to publicly observable behaviour, once attractive to psychologists. Among its numerous problems are (a) specifying the behaviour which is to be identified as a mental state, which attempt generally leads to circularity; (b) accounting for the fact that mental states have causal interactions with one another. (c) It may also be thought, against behaviourism, that a desire, emotion or other mental state exists at all, and in the specific character it has, only by virtue of a whole background ramification of dispositions, beliefs, emotions, sensations, etc. – that is, other mental states.

cognitivism The view that moral statements are capable of being true or false or have factual content. It is opposed to non-cognitivism, according to which moral statements can only be overt or disguised commands, or else expressions of approval or disapproval, because there are no moral facts (Mackie 5; McDowell 1, 3).

coherence theory of truth Theory which in one form asserts that 'true' means 'coheres with all true statements'. Thus a statement or belief is true, or nearer the truth, if it coheres with a wider system of statements than any other contending statement (Bradley 9). More metaphysical versions of the coherence theory hold that the Absolute is the all-inclusive truth from which all other truths derive their being, and from which they can be logically deduced. The coherence theory is opposed to, among others, the correspondence theory of truth. This asserts that 'true' means 'corresponds to the facts', and has problems in explaining the nature of the correspondence. The semantic theory of truth (Tarski 1, 2) is said to be a version of the correspondence theory. *See* Absolute, the.

compatibilism The claim that the proposition that our actions are determined or subject to causation does not conflict with the proposition that they are free (Honderich 2, 3).

concept Sometimes, an idea – of any degree of concreteness or abstraction – used in abstract thinking. (Thus 'to have a concept of x' is to be able to recognize, mentally envisage, or know the meaning of, x.) Sometimes, 'concept' is used for any generic or class term which enables the mind to distinguish one thing from another. In Platonism, concepts are regarded as universals, and as entities of some sort. In conceptualism, on the other hand, universals are regarded as concepts, usually with the sense of mental standard. 'Concept' is one of the oldest, most equivocal philosophical terms, and it is variously, often technically, used by different philosophers.

conditional *See* Antecedent.

consequentialism A group of theories, of which utilitarianism is one, which hold that the rightness or goodness, wrongness or badness, of an action is to be assessed in terms of its expected consequences.

constructivism A view that mathematical entities are constructed by us, as opposed to existing or being true independently of our apprehension of them (Heyting).

contingency The property of not having to exist, or occur or be true, as contrasted with necessary existence, occurrence or truth.

correspondence theory of truth *See* COHERENCE THEORY OF TRUTH.

counterfactual A conditional statement with a false antecedent, or interpreted as entailing or presupposing that its antecedent is false.

covering-law theory Theory representing scientific explanation as a matter of finding a law which covers the phenomenon to be explained – the law, together with a statement of initial conditions, entails the phenomenon to be explained.

Dasein The German term is translated as 'being there', and is applied, by Heidegger and his followers, to the specifically human mode of being-in-the-world. This involves awareness of one's unique purposiveness and potential, and a tendency to forfeit this through inauthenticity. 'Dasein' is used differently by different existentialist thinkers, and is sometimes used less technically for humanly meaningful existence.

deconstruction A strategy, adopted by post-structuralists such as Derrida, to demonstrate that metaphysical, epistemological, ethical and logical systems have been constructed on the basis of conceptual oppositions (for example transcendental/empirical, universal/particular, internal/external, good/evil), and that the privileged term within each binary set is constituted by the antithesis it suppresses, and is haunted by it, which renders its privileged status untenable. Deconstructionists oppose structuralism as much as they oppose other philosophical systems. *See* POST-STRUCTURALISM, STRUCTURALISM.

determinism Theory that all events are effects and therefore necessitated. Applied to human actions, this seems to deny free will and perhaps all significant freedom.

dialectic The Greek term refers to a 'method or art of conversation or debate'. 'Dialectic' is variously and often technically used by different philosophers, but with a common kernel – the idea of a process of interplay between two or more somehow contradictory entities which culminates in some sort of resolution in which the contradiction is surmounted and progressed beyond. Plato used 'dialectic' in its literal sense (his philosophizing was conducted as a debate), and also metaphorically, for example for the relationship between the universal and its particulars, and the way we come to perceive this. Hegel tended to conflate the laws that govern reasoning with those applying to history and the universe as a whole. For him, progress in each consisted of a necessary movement from thesis to antithesis and then to a synthesis (Hegel 17–19). The dialectical materialism of Marx and Engels (Engels 1) was a reframing of the Hegelian dialectic.

distributive justice That part of justice, whether legal or moral, concerning itself with the fair distribution of benefits and burdens.

dogmatism Since Kant the term has often been used philosophically for the assumption, by such philosophers as Leibniz, that metaphysics can answer questions about the origin of the universe, the existence of God, the soul's immortality, and the whole nature of reality, purely on the basis of *a priori* reasoning.

dualism In philosophy, usually the view that mind and body are separate substances. Although something like it must be immemorial, it is attributed to Descartes, who is generally held responsible for ushering in the intractable mind–body problem. The view faces the difficulty that an objective account of reality seems to omit the subjective viewpoint which locates each of us at an experiential centre of the world. Science is centreless, and an individual's mental states are of dubious physical location, though he or she can be considered to be non-inferentially and indubitably aware of them, as one cannot be of the physical entities one perceives. Also any form of dualism faces the problem of what exactly 'the mental' is, and of how two totally different (mental and physical) substances can causally interact. Descartes' interactionist solution to the latter problem involved scientifically absurd notions about interaction in the pineal gland. Other dualist solutions to the mind–body relation are psychophysical parallelism and occasionalism (Leibniz 21; Malebranche 1, 2; Geulincx 1, 2) and epiphenomenalism. Monist solutions, whether materialist or idealist, are counter-intuitive. *See* MONISM.

ek-stase Heidegger's term for the subject's active transcendence in relation to the world. *See* TRANSCENDENCE.

empiricism A family of theories to the effect that experience, mainly sensory – rather than reason or innate ideas, as claimed by rationalists – is the source of knowledge. Radical empiricism, which limits our knowledge strictly to the contents of our experience, issues in scepticism about even our most ordinary claims to knowledge. *See* RATIONALISM.

en-soi A term, translated as 'in-itself', used by existentialists for the self-enclosed, subject-to-determination mode of existence which things or animals have. This is opposed to the self-transcending, self-determining type of being (*pour-soi*, 'for-itself') possessed by humans. Merleau-Ponty uses '*en-soi*' as a collective noun for nature-as-distinct-from-humanity. What Sartre calls 'bad faith', Heidegger 'inauthenticity', is our tendency to pretend, or act as if, we had the thing-like essence of

485

the *en-soi*, and were part of the law-governed natural world, in an attempt to escape the anguishing constraints of being free and the arduous responsibility for choice which this imposes (Sartre 1–3, 5–11, 33). *See* IMMANENCE, TRANSCENDENCE.

entelechy   In Aristotle, essence, realization as against potentiality, or the principle of life. He calls the soul the entelechy of the body. The term has been variously used since.

enthymeme   Argument in which a premise, or interim deductions, are not explicitly stated, for example 'Socrates is a man, so Socrates is mortal'.

entification   The procedure of taking something, perhaps the mind, to be an entity or thing.

epiphenomenalism   A proposed solution to the mind–body problem which regards mental phenomena as epiphenomena – by-products, themselves without effects, of physical processes. Consciousness is thus an effect of the body but does not causally interact with it. *See* DUALISM.

epistemology   A branch of philosophy which investigates the nature, origin, scope, structure, types, methods and validity of knowledge. To say that a philosophical investigation or whatever is 'epistemological' is to say that its starting-point is the problem of how, or indeed whether, we can know a specific thing or fact, or reality in general. Such an investigation does not presuppose that we *can* know, as do some types of metaphysics.

excluded middle [third]**, principle of**   Either *p* is true or *p* is not true – one or the other is the case. It is one of the 'laws of thought', often considered to be an ineluctable and fundamental presupposition of reasoning and to describe the nature of reality.

existentialism   A philosophy or attitude, opposed to dogma and system, starting out from the philosopher's own specific situation in life, abandoning the objective for the individual's standpoint. Its concern is not just the 'individual' in the sense used by many philosophers – the generalized-human mind – but the individual as the unique, idiosyncratic, free entity engaged in living. Existentialism is said variously to have originated with Pascal, Kierkegaard, Nietzsche and others.

externalism   In Burge and others, the doctrine that mental events, say a thought about arthritis, are somehow dependent, perhaps dependent for their existence, on events external to the person, say the established meaning of 'arthritis' in English, rather than on neural or brain events.

The dependency is not the ordinarily assumed one involving education, sense experience, etc. (Burge 1–3; Putnam 1).

external world The world as it becomes for the philosopher whose starting-point is the contents of his or her own perceiving consciousness, and who is then faced with the problem of scepticism – that is, doubt about the separate existence of a reality outside the mind.

facticity A term puzzlingly used by Sartre. Ordinarily 'facticité' means artificiality, falseness, superficiality, as against naturalness. But Sartre's translator, Hazel Barnes, regards it as at least partly conveying 'the for-itself's necessary connection with the in-itself, hence with the world and its own past'. Sartre also seems to use 'facticity', however, in the sense of embodied thingness, or of the mistaken sense of oneself as purely an embodied being rather than as transcendent and free.

finalism Sometimes, the theory that purpose is present in all events of the physical order, and that they have a teleological character.

first cause One of Aquinas's arguments for the existence of God is that the chain of causes and effects had to have started somewhere.

folk psychology The corpus of beliefs and assumptions having to do with beliefs, desires, intentions and the like, which we all use to understand and predict human behaviour. The term is used, generally disparagingly, by certain physicalist philosophers as if this corpus of beliefs were merely an inadequate theory. Keen to have a seamless scientific picture of the world and ourselves, and to fit what seems the unaccommodated mental into it, they claim that our psychological terminology is ultimately dispensable, and may, or will, be supplanted by a new and superior – neuroscientific – theory (Churchland; Fodor 1, 2; Putnam 6). *See* DUALISM.

for-itself *See* EN-SOI.

form The term that is used to translate the ancient Greek 'eidos', also interpreted as 'idea'. In both Plato and Aristotle, the form makes an object what it is. For Aristotle it usually exists in combination with matter; for Plato, it is in some sense a timeless essence or universal that exists independently of objects which instantiate it or minds which apprehend it. Plato has various alternative theories of the Forms, but overall they are the explanation of the visible world and the required starting-point for knowledge, as well as for a kind of mysticism.

functionalism A purported solution to the problem of the nature of mentality or consciousness which claims that the essential or defining feature of any type of mental state is the causal or logical relations it has to (a) environmental effects on the body, (b) other inner states, and (c) bodily behaviour. What makes a mental state the mental state it is, is its having a certain causal or logical role in the life of the organism. A computer's varied activities can similarly be described in terms of its programme (Putnam 2). Functionalism has the consequence that the mental can in principle be instantiated in any type of material, and hence it may seem to make the mental yet more ethereal and other-worldly than do scorned dualistic accounts. Also among its problems are the fact that it fails to account for the phenomenology of mental states – what they feel like – and for their intentionality (Fodor 3). There is also Searle's famous Chinese room objection (Searle 1).

hen Greek for 'one'. The ultimate reality, the unity that includes everything and is not included in anything.

homunculus Some accounts of mental processes are, usually disparagingly, said to postulate a 'little man' or group of 'little men' *inside* the brain to perform functions or feel sensations, since mere physical processes cannot be said to act or feel. The enlistment of homunculi is sometimes acknowledged, sometimes tacit. It may seem to lead to an infinite regress, however, since they are after all persons within persons (Dennett 2–5).

idea (1) In Plato, used interchangeably with form. (2) Descartes gave 'idea' a new sense, making it into something subjective – 'whatever the mind directly perceives'. It became a technical term, with varying usages in different philosophers of the seventeenth century and later. *See* ABSTRACT IDEA, FORM, IMPRESSION.

idealism A range of theories which hold that all reality is in nature mental or spiritual. Starting with their own mental contents as objects of certain knowledge, some idealists claim that the external world exists only as ideas in the mind, or is in varying degrees dependent on the mind. Others, who may or may not take an epistemological starting-point, hold that reality is not dependent on the human mind, but is ultimately a mental substance or a World Mind (Bradley, Hegel). Since the so-called death of metaphysics, few philosophers have been metaphysical idealists. Though many still take immediate experience as the initial certainty, their ensuing anxiety about perception/reality discrepancies does not lead them to characteristic idealist conclusions. Some have embraced what is related to it, phenomenalism. *See* ABSOLUTE, THE; PHENOMENALISM, REALISM.

ideality The term is sometimes used for the condition or character of being mental.

iff 'If and only if'. Thus 'p iff q' means the second is a sufficient and also a necessary condition of the first.

immanence (1) The term is sometimes used to describe the state of being embedded in the world rather than transcendent. In existentialist philosophy, the state of being immanent has negative connotations of thinghood and lack of freedom. (2) For Kant, the immanent is the experiential in contrast with the non-experiential and transcendent. (3) As used for example of God, the term means what is present as opposed to absent. *See* TRANSCENDENCE.

impression For Hume, the mind is struck by impressions, related to what later philosophers called sense-data, sensations, emotions, etc., and from these are derived fainter, less forceful copies, the ideas which occur in thought and reasoning. He was attempting to remedy Locke's overworking of 'idea', which failed to distinguish perception from thought, understanding, belief, etc.

individual Whatever can be individuated, that is, distinguished and enumerated, or made the referent of a thought or sentence. The term is sometimes used interchangeably with 'particular'.

induction Method of reasoning by which a general law, and hence further particulars, are inferred from observed particular instances, perhaps many of them. From observations of the sun rising on many mornings, we conclude that it will continue to rise. The problem of induction, posed by Hume, is the problem of what if anything justifies us in making this sort of move, which seems indispensable for both scientific theory and everyday life. There seems no logical or necessary connection between the premise or evidence and the conclusion.

intentional inexistence According to a doctrine of the scholastics, objects of thought, whether or not they are also said to exist in reality outside the mind, have intentional inexistence. This is a mode of being which is considered to be short of actuality but more than nothingness. In most versions of the doctrine, it lasts for just the length of time in which the intentional object is thought about or imagined. Purged of its ontological commitments, the theory might be said to persist in contemporary philosophies of language and mind. *See* INTENTIONALITY.

intentionality A term occurs intentionally in a true statement or illustrates the fact of intentionality, as is commonly said, if substituting another term for it – a term which refers to the same thing – makes the statement false (for example 'Carol believes that Cicero was an orator', if Carol does not know that Cicero was the man also called Tully, becomes false if 'Cicero' is replaced by 'Tully'). Thus the fact of intentionality is taken to distinguish statements about the mental (Chisholm). 'Intentionality' is also used more generally in connection with the relation of aboutness or directedness which characterizes all or many mental events.

intuition An item of belief or knowledge, either of a proposition or an object, that is uninferred or immediate. In Kant, intuitions, which he counterposes to concepts, are the starting-point of knowledge. He thought that intuitions could be *a priori* (for example our ideas of space and time) as well as sensory. 'Intuition' is also used for a conviction, presumed to be generally held, which is a ground of or guide to our philosophical reasoning. There are differing views on how far intuitions in this sense should be catered for.

intuitionism In mathematics, intuitionism is a form of constructivism.

language game The expression is used by Wittgenstein to emphasize that language is not merely or even mainly a matter of naming and referring to objects, but has a series of overlapping, non-homogeneous functions – and also that language is a series of interwoven activities which initially arose from our primitive human animality and are 'forms of life' (Wittgenstein 22, 8, 9, 10, 11, 13). Followers and detractors of Wittgenstein alike have tended to use 'language game' in the sense of 'area or type of discourse', scientific, religious, or whatever.

law of excluded middle *See* EXCLUDED MIDDLE, PRINCIPLE OF.

libertarianism (1) View, opposed to determinism, that our choices and actions are not – or not entirely – governed by necessitating causal laws. It also denies that actions are random and asserts our responsibility for them. (2) All-out political, social and economic liberalism, rejecting many ordinarily accepted constraints on personal liberty. *See* DETERMINISM.

logical positivism Doctrine promulgated by the Vienna Circle of the 1920s and 1930s, which, influenced by Humean empiricism, aimed at purging language and belief of anything not a matter of logical necessity, or not, at least in principle, verifiable by sense experience. Its proponents (Ayer, Carnap, Schlick) attempted to formulate successfully the verification or verifiability principle of meaning – utterances which are neither tautologies, definitions, or statements in logic or mathematics, nor empirically verifiable, are meaningless or without truth-values. Thus metaphysics was held to be rubbish, ethics a matter of emotive attitudes and utterances. One problem was the principle itself – is *it* either empirically verifiable or analytic?

logos The Greek term is used for 'speech', 'word', 'thought', 'meaning', 'the underlying reason why a thing is what it is'. In Heraclitus, it is the immanent principle of rationality, pattern and identity underlying the constant flux. For the Stoics, it was the cosmic principle of order in the universe (God) and the active principle of reason in humans enabling them to understand the universe's rational purpose, perceive how to conduct their lives so as to conform with nature, and cultivate an acceptance of all that happens, in full awareness that it is fated (Stoics).

meaning *See* REFERENCE.

meta- The Greek term is used for 'after', 'beyond' and 'over and above'. In philosophical usage, the expression obtained by prefixing 'meta' to the name of some body of knowledge or practice ('metaethics', 'metalanguage', etc.) is used for a description, analysis or examination of the original body of knowledge or practice.

metaphysics A central though sometimes disparaged part of Western philosophy since the ancient Greeks, often the attempt to characterize reality as a whole, instead of, as in the various special sciences, particular parts or aspects of it. 'Metaphysics' was the name given to what Aristotle wrote after his *Physics*. To his original subject matter ('being as such') subsequent metaphysicians have added the appearance/reality preoccupation. 'Metaphysics' is also used for a set of more limited inquiries, for example into the nature of causation or time.

mind–body problem *See* DUALISM, EPIPHENOMENALISM, MONISM.

monism Theories about several subject-matters to the effect that only one thing, or one kind of thing, exists in each. Materialism thus claims that all that exists is material, idealism that all that exists is somehow mental, dual-aspect theory, or neutral monism, that there is a common substance of which matter and mind are phenomenal modifications. Monism with respect to the mind–body or mind–brain problem is to the effect that the mind is material. Davidson's *anomalous monism* holds that all mental events are physical events but that there are no laws for explaining or predicting mental events.

naive realism View, ascribed to the plain man, that we have direct perception of things, unmediated by sense data.

naturalism Term used for a range of views holding that whatever exists or happens is part of 'nature' and thus is ultimately accessible to scientific explanation, and that other forms of explanation are false or redundant.

natural language   A language that has evolved naturally and is spoken by relatively large groups of people, as opposed to artificial languages which are specifically designed, for example for computers or for an area of research.

natural laws   (1) Scientific laws. (2) The term is also used traditionally for laws of another character. Natural law theories, which originated in ancient Greek philosophy, are said to hold that there are laws which are both prescriptive, perhaps somehow moral, and also descriptive or scientific. The nature and reality of such laws has been much disputed.

natural rights   Rights or liberties derived from natural rather than positive laws – seemingly a kind of moral rights. That they exist is disputed (Bentham 7).

necessary and sufficient conditions   A necessary condition for something is one without which the thing would not exist or occur. Oxygen is a necessary condition for fire. A sufficient condition for something is one such that, if it does occur, the thing also occurs. Oxygen is but part of the sufficient condition for fire. Necessary and sufficient conditions, however, may also be logical or conceptual rather than nomic or physical.

nomic   Concerning or involving laws of nature or scientific laws.

nominalism   The view that only particulars are real, and that universals have no existence independently of being thought, being mere names applied to particulars on the basis of resemblance. *See* Universal.

nomological *See* Nomic.

non-cognitivism *See* Cognitivism.

non-intentionality *See* Intentionality.

noumenon   According to Kant, the 'thing-in-itself', the unknowable source of experience, which can only be inferred from, and postulated to account for, the actual experience of phenomena.

nous   Term derived from the Greek for 'mind', 'reason', 'intellect'. In Anaxagoras and other Pre-Socratics, Aristotle, Plato and the Stoics, the cosmic mind that renders the universe rational and intelligible, and, while all-pervading, is distinct from it (Anaxagoras 2; Aristotle; Plato 32, 34, 35, 40). It is also employed for human as well as cosmic reason. Aristotle used '*nous*' for intellect as distinct from sense perception

(Aristotle 9), and Plato used it for the rational principle in the soul that makes it immortal (Plato 10, 11, 18, 34).

ontology That part of metaphysics (though sometimes the term is used interchangeably with 'metaphysics') concerned with the study of being, of the nature or status of all that exists. The question is raised of whether material objects, minds, numbers, facts, universals, etc., all 'are' in the same sense and to the same degree.

optimific The optimific action or policy is the one likely to produce the greatest total of happiness or satisfaction.

ostensive definition Definition by pointing to, or otherwise indicating, a specimen, instance, or sample of a thing. Wittgenstein, who was sceptical about it, describes it as the 'private baptism of an object' when giving it a name.

particular A member of a class, as opposed to the property (universal) which defines the class. All particulars are individuals, but not vice versa.

phenomenalism The view that all we directly know or are aware of in perception is phenomena or sense-data: and opposed to the common-sense realism which takes us to be directly aware of material objects. In some forms, phenomenalism holds that material-object statements are equivalent to, or mean no more than, sense-data statements (Mill 25). In other forms, it includes an inference to the existence of unperceived material objects. It is related to idealism.

phenomenology Philosophical enquiry which concentrates on phenomena, the objects of immediate experience. Husserl (Brentano's pupil) advocated the suspension of all presuppositions, beliefs and categories: the world is to be 'bracketed' off, so that phenomenology can 'intuit the essences' of phenomena – invariant features or structures of objects, consciousness, etc. Phenomenological investigation resembles conceptual analysis: Husserl's aim was to extend the scope of the *a priori* to the entire field of experience. Phenomenology led, via Husserl's pupil Heidegger, to the study of being and to existentialism. Meaning and practice vary according to phenomenologist (Husserl 2, 3; Heidegger 18, 19; Merleau-Ponty 1–4; Jaspers 1, 3).

phenomenon An object or occurrence as it appears to the senses, sometimes used in contradistinction to a reality which the appearance is of. Kant distinguishes phenomena from noumena, the unknowable 'things-in-themselves'.

physicalism Doctrine that there is nothing but physical entities, forces, etc., or that ultimately physical laws explain everything. It is often used in a more limited sense for theories which reduce the mind to the brain.

physis Nature, what exists outside humankind; sometimes used to include human nature. The term was variously used by the Pre-Socratics, Plato and Aristotle in the context of problems about what is natural or real as opposed to man-made and illusory, and about what the intrinsic essence of things is in the midst of change and becoming.

pineal gland The gland at the base of the brain which, according to Descartes, is the location of mind–body interaction.

Platonism Philosophy or series of philosophies discontinuously developed from Plato's, chiefly in Greece immediately after his death, but also under Plotinus in the second century and in the early Middle Ages. Platonism in its various forms tended to ignore much of Plato's theory and tone in favour of the doctrine of the Forms in its more mystical aspects. Via Augustine, it had a great influence on early Christianity. In a modern usage, 'Platonism' has come to mean theories postulating the self-subsistent reality of abstract objects, for example universals, or of logical, mental, propositional and mathematical objects. It is, in this sense, synonymous with REALISM as applied to universals.

pluralism Doctrine that there is not one ultimate substance (as in monism), or two ultimate substances (as in dualism), but many.

positive law Law of a state or society as opposed to natural or scientific law.

positivism Philosophical position, traceable to Francis Bacon but more explicitly developed by Auguste Comte, that all genuine knowledge is based on sense experience and extended by means of systematic experiment and law-formulation, and is therefore contained within the bounds of science.

post hoc ergo propter hoc 'After this, therefore on account of this'. Fallacy in reasoning that confuses 'happening before' with 'causing'.

post-structuralism A movement, begun in the 1970s, largely associated with Derrida, which challenged structuralism, rejecting its binary oppositions and scientific pretensions in favour of claims for the irreducible excesses of language. *See* DECONSTRUCTION.

pragmatism Originally a theory of meaning developed by Peirce, to the effect that to understand a sentence's meaning is to understand all the practical effects in our experience that its truth could have. It was developed into a theory of truth by William James and others: a belief is true if it works, or if it produces fruitful results (James 1–4).

presentation Anything directly present to a knowing mind, for example sense-data, images of memory and imagination, emotional states.

prima facie On first appearance. The term is often used to indicate that something – an obligation, a right, evidence – has a presumptive force that will hold unless defeated by a superior consideration.

primary and secondary qualities Primary qualities are those such as size, shape, motion/rest, number and solidity which belong to things irrespective of their being observed. Secondary qualities are those such as colour, taste, sound and smell which are merely modes in which things happen to appear to us, and not, in the form we perceive them, in the objects themselves. The distinction was first conceived by Democritus (Democritus 1, 3), named by the seventeenth-century chemist Robert Boyle and elaborated by Locke (Locke 3).

private language A language whose privacy is not that of a code or secret language grafted onto the speaker's usual form of communication, but the privacy of total incommunicability because it is entirely compounded of his or her own self-determined ostensive definitions. Argument about the possibility and nature of private language is relevant not only to the philosophy of language but to the philosophy of mind and in particular our talk of mental events (Wittgenstein 35–40; Ayer 8).

projectivism Metaethical theory which is subjectivist in that it rejects belief in mind-independent moral facts, and asserts that such 'facts' are a projection of our own sentiments, but which is also quasi-realist.

protasis *See* ANTECEDENT.

quale (pl. qualia) Term often used for the 'feel' or felt nature of mental events or experience.

quantifier A symbol in formal logic which indicates that what is in question is all of a class of things, or some, or none. The universal quantifier is read as 'For any x, or all x, . . .'. The existential quantifier is read as 'There exists at least one thing such that . . .'.

quiddity The essence or 'whatness' of a thing. The term was used in scholastic arguments about the essential differences between things. In modern English, it refers to trivial hair-splitting or a quibble.

rationalism The view that reason rather than experience is the only or main source of knowledge, and hence that we have innate ideas, that is concepts that pre-exist or shape our first encounters with the world.

realism A range of views that things exist independently of being thought or observed. In scholastic philosophy, the view (opposed to nominalism and conceptualism) that universals have a real objective existence; in modern philosophy, the view (contrasted with idealism, anti-realism) that material objects exist externally to us, independently of our sense experience.

reductio ad absurdum Method of arguing which refutes a proposition by showing that something absurd or contradictory follows from it.

reductionism [reductivism] Any doctrine which attempts completely to translate one type of concept into another type, supposedly simpler, more basic or with better empirical confirmation. Hence a doctrine which reduces one type of event or thing to another. To reduce a psychological to a physiological theory is to show that the latter can in principle yield all the results of the former.

reference What a term stands for or names, or the relation between the term and the thing. Referential theories of meaning have taken the meaning of a term to be what it stands for or names, or to be the relation between the word and its referent. Original versions of the theory quickly ran into difficulties (Frege 1). Wittgenstein and others have given a richer account of meaning and language, and taken reference to be but one feature of language, something which requires a ramified background (linguistic, conventional, social, etc.) to be possible at all.

reification Taking something to be a thing. Usually thought of as the mistake of taking an abstraction, relation, convention or artificial construction to be other than it is.

satisfice To aim to get results sufficient but not necessarily the best possible.

scepticism Doctrine, more or less general, which denies that knowledge can be had of a subject-matter, usually reality as a whole. A general scepticism was maintained by Pyrrho, a lesser scepticism penetratingly and exhaustively argued by Hume.

scholasticism System and style of philosophy practised in the Middle Ages, roughly from the ninth to the sixteenth century. It was subsequently disparaged, especially by the Renaissance thinkers who immediately followed it, as prone to sterile logic-chopping, ponderous artificialization of language, and excessive deference to authority. In fact, important work was done in logic, and in connection with meaning and universals. But the Church's authoritarianism, and the failure to divide religion from philosophy, meant that the many brilliant scholastics (such as Abelard, Boethius, Aquinas and Ockham) were hampered by uneasily having, as the eleventh-century Damian put it, to make philosophy handmaid to theology.

scientism The view or attitude that natural science is the only method for obtaining knowledge, and that other inquiry is inferior.

secondary qualities *See* PRIMARY AND SECONDARY QUALITIES.

semiology Branch of linguistics concerned with signs and their applications. It has come to be the investigation of surface events of language to discover the concealed signifying systems underlying them.

sense-data Objects of which one is said to be directly aware in sense-perception, as distinct from material objects themselves. The arguments from illusion, and from the relativity and causality of perception, suggest that immediate perception is impossible. However, belief in sense-data leads to the problem of the relation between them and material objects. Further, if all we are aware of is sense-data, how can we have knowledge of reality? *See* PHENOMENALISM.

signifier Saussure, the early twentieth-century philologist who first developed structural linguistics and the study of signs, conceived of a sign as the union of a signifier – a form by which to convey meaning – and a signified – the idea to be conveyed.

solipsism An extreme form of scepticism or idealism, the position that only I can be taken to exist, since I cannot really know that anyone or anything else does. Epistemological or methodological solipsism is any system or doctrine which takes the contents of the individual mind as a starting-point, for instance in cognitive science (Fodor 5).

sortal concept A concept which involves a principle for distinguishing, reidentifying and counting particulars. The term associated with the concept is a basic classifying term which applies to an object throughout its existence. Cow and chair are sortals, blue and snow are not.

structuralism Basically the view that an entity is what it is by virtue of its participation in an underlying structure. Influenced by Marx and Freud, such structuralists as Barthes, Althusser, Lacan, Foucault and Lévi-Strauss elaborated doctrines which take persons as determined by hidden forces, whether social or psychological. Linking Marxism and psychoanalysis to Saussure's structural linguistics, they engaged in exposing the hidden structures which, they said, lie behind surface meanings in language, behaviour, culture and psychology, and create and control us. It is not we, apparently, who speak language – it speaks us. Structuralists and their movement influenced literature, linguistics, history, sociology and other fields, were involved in lengthy disputes with humanists and existentialists, whose gospel of self-creation they challenged, and were themselves challenged in turn by Derrida and the deconstructionists.

subjectivism Range of theories holding that knowledge or value is dependent upon and relative to the experiencing individual, and has no independent objective reality.

subsistent Having being or existence, often less than full-blooded, three-dimensional existence. The term is applied to dubious entities such as universals, numbers, relations, values, God, etc., and sometimes to non-existent things referred to or imagined.

substance (1) An ultimate subject of predications, which cannot be predicated in turn of any subject. (2) In Aristotle, either a particular concrete object, or the form or essence which makes a substance, in sense (1), the thing it is. (3) Substratum, or what has independent existence, in contrast to properties, accidents and relations, which it underlies, and which belong to or depend on it. (4) That which is sought when philosophers investigate the primary being of things.

summum bonum The greatest good, sometimes understood as sought by all. The concept was introduced into ethics by Aristotle and taken up by Aquinas.

superstructure For Marx, non-economic social institutions such as religion, ethical values, etc. are an edifice thrown up by the material conditions of human life. The superstructure serves to stabilize the existing economic structure, but can also become the arena of conflict in periods of profound economic change (Marx 18, 19, 22, 23; Cohen 1–3; Engels 1, 4).

supervenience By one definition, a family of events, say mental events, supervenes on another family of events, say neural events, if the following is true: if a given neural event is accompanied by a certain mental event – say of mental sort A – then any identical neural event will also be accompanied by a mental event of sort A, and any change in a mental event will be accompanied by a change in a neural event. Supervenience is thus conducive to physicalist conclusions about the mind without being reductivist in a strong sense.

syllogism A traditional argument pattern, with two premises and a conclusion, in which the premises are so related to the conclusion that they necessarily imply it (for example 'All men are mortal; Socrates is a man; therefore, Socrates is mortal').

synthetic statement *See* ANALYTIC AND SYNTHETIC STATEMENTS.

techne The Greek term denotes 'art', 'skill', 'technique', 'system of making or doing something'. It is used by Aristotle in contrast to *physis*, to distinguish anything deliberately created by humans from the natural order of things.

teleology Doctrine that the world, a thing or an activity is to be explained in terms of its purpose or end. It is sometimes bound up with the idea that the world, and the creatures in it, have a function, and thus have been designed, usually by God.

thing-in-itself *See* NOUMENON.

transcendence The term has been borrowed from discourse about God. (1) In idealism, the state of being outside or independent of the world. (2) In some existentialism (for example Sartre and de Beauvoir), the state of being not fully identified with or instantiated in oneself, which enables some sort of freedom, *from* determinism and *for* self-determination, and the ability to 'project' oneself into the future. (3) In Jaspers, 'the source and the goal, both of which lie in God and out of whose depths alone we really become authentically human', or one of the two modes of the Being that surrounds us, of which 'one aspect of our essence constitutes an infinitesimal part'.

transcendental (1) Beyond experience. (2) In Kant, what is presupposed by and necessary to experience, established by a transcendental argument. (3) Outside or somehow free of the world. *See* IMMANENCE, TRANSCENDENCE.

transcendental argument (1) An argument which purports to establish a proposition by showing that if it were false it would not even be possible to discuss it. (2) An argument which proceeds, from a proposition or body of knowledge assumed to be true, to a conclusion about what conditions must be fulfilled in order for it to be true. Transcendental arguments were most famously used by Kant in his transcendental idealism.

transcendental idealism Kant's theory that although reality exists independently, how it appears to us is determined by the structure of the human mind. Space, time, causation, etc., are *a priori* conditions of experience, 'transcendentally' necessary if we are to have the knowledge we actually have. How things-in-themselves are we shall never know. Even of ourselves we know only the empirical self rather than the transcendental self which synthesizes experience (Kant 5–14, 23, 27–30).

truth conditions   The conditions under which a proposition is or would be true.

truth values   Traditionally, a proposition's truth value is either its being true or its being false. But there are also three-valued logics using 'true', 'false' and 'undetermined'.

universal   The property possessed by all particulars of a certain type, for example blueness, cat-ness, beauty. The problem of universals, sometimes considered the central problem of metaphysics, and initiated by Plato, is about the ontological status of these general properties, and what our experience of them involves. To say that we recognize red things as red because they all have the common property of being red merely re-states, and does not explain, the fact that it is possible to use 'red'. Platonism or realism, the view that universals exist independently of human awareness, faces problems about their spatio-temporal location, exact nature, and relation to their instances. Conceptualism, the view that universals exist in the mind, is for several reasons as problematic. The resemblance theory, which depends on similarities between particulars, seems to be a disguised form of realism, since resemblance is itself a universal. *See* NOMINALISM.

universalizability   The principle that a moral judgement about a particular action commits one to a universal judgement about all like actions in like circumstances. The term was coined by Hare, but originally propounded in Kant's categorical imperative (Kant 88). The trouble is, what is to count as 'like actions' and 'like circumstances'?

utilitarianism [utility]   The type of consequentialist doctrine which holds that the right action is the one reasonably judged likely to produce the greatest total of happiness or satisfaction (Bentham 1, 2). Act utilitarianism considers the happiness-producing consequences of each individual action. Rule utilitarianism considers the happiness-producing consequences of acting according to general rules, usually the sort of moral rules that already exist (Smart 4).

value   For the use of the term in logic, *See* VARIABLE.

variable   Symbol, usually 'x', used in logic to stand as place-holder for any one of a set of things or notions. It 'ranges over' the members of the set, which are its 'values'.

verificationism The view that a non-analytic proposition is a candidate for meaning or truth only if sense-experience could in principle decide its truth. *See* LOGICAL POSITIVISM.

virtue ethics Ethical theories which concentrate on goodness taken as the possession and cultivation of virtues – as against goodness taken as having to do with the consequences of actions, or the fulfilment of duties, or as acting from the right motives. Foot and MacIntyre are virtue ethicists.

vitalism Belief that what distinguishes living from non-living things is the presence within living things of a vital force or principle different from other forces in the universe. The force is taken to impart powers which no inanimate body could possess (Bergson 7, 8; Santayana 1).

INDEX

𝔊𝔊𝔊𝔊𝔊𝔊

All quotations by a given philosopher have been numbered in the text in a single sequence for ease of reference. These numbers are shown as superscripts after each page reference. Where there is more than one philosopher represented on a page, a shortened form of the name is also given in superscript.

Index

slavery (*cont'd*)
  justice of 17[18]
  slave morality 322[36]
  wage-slavery 250[Len]
sleep
  and thoughts 262[15]
Smith, Adam 290[21]
social contract 76[2], 183[2,3], 184[6],
    199[43], 368[Row 1], 369[2–4], 383[8–10]
socialism 287[9], 328[3]
socialism, Marxian 232[Key]
social science 96[Cond 1], 338[Pass 2]
society 2[1], 6[4], 23[Ast 2], 40[7], 64[Bos 1],
    64[2], 95[8,9], 116[4], 117[Did 1],
    121[DwoR 1,2], 147[10], 159[3], 166[Hart 1],
    172[23], 180[34], 180[Held], 199[43], 240[3],
    264[22–4], 276[7], 283[2], 289[19], 291[24],
    308[2], 339[5], 346[11], 368[Raw 1], 382[5],
    420[Sha 2], 442[1], 447[5], 476[6]
  and conflict 162[6]
  conservative view of 76[2], 77[4,6]
  economic superstructure of 126[4]
  liberal view of 307[26]
  Marxist view of 126[5], 127[7–10],
    163[5], 237[Kola 1], 287[11], 289[18], 291[23]
  and morality 121[4], 122[6]
  social control 3[7]
  social physics 94[4]
  see also social contract; sociology
sociology 120[1]
Socrates 16[11], 428[8], 429[9]
solipsism *def.* 84[9]; 137[5], 204[1], 282[5],
    300[24–27], 330[1], 388[15], 471[49], 472[53]
Sophocles 275[3]
sorts *def.* 419[4]
soul *def.* 21[39]; 13[20], 14[21], 15[3], 21[39],
    67[17], 110[10], 115[36], 162[6], 168[8],
    182[8,9], 220[10], 244[Lam 1], 248[8],
    250[20,21], 256[2], 297[14], 321[26], 346[11],
    347[13], 348[18], 353[33], 354[34], 355[Plo 2],
    367[3], 394[1], 426[1], 471[47]
  analogy with
    commonwealth 195[23]
  and I/first person 330[4]
  immortality of 346[12]
  limits of 182[8]
  and matter 248[6]
  nature of 21[38], 346[10]
  and self 330[5]
  soul-self 28[1]
space 7[And 2], 72[1], 220[9], 227[71], 260[5],

    308[Min]
spirit 50[4], 57[12], 65[6], 96[Conw1], 97[2,3],
    166[Heg 1], 169[12], 171[17], 172[20,23],
    173[24], 174[28], 226[61,62], 258[16], 259[4],
    471[47]
spiritualism
  and feminism 240[2]
Stalin, Joseph 376[5]
state 17[15,17], 126[6], 127[7], 278[1]
  conservative view of 77[6]
  minimal 237[Kola 1], 327[Noz 1]
  as power-relationship 141[6,7]
  and social contract 183[1,2], 186[14],
    383[9]
  total-authoritarian 2[1], 283[2]
  withering away of 14[1], 127[8,9],
    237[Kola 1], 288[15]
statements 363[3]
  analytic 361[5], 364[4]
  empirically testable 361[5]
  synthetic 364[4]
state of nature 184[4–6], 185[7], 264[23,24],
    269[2]
Stich, Stephen 362[6]
stillness 235[22]
stoicism 425[1]
'strong man' *see under* man (generic)
structuralism 37[7], 38[8], 106[2,4]
  deep and surface structure 86[1]
  signification 36[1], 36[Bar 2], 107[6], 243[5]
  see also deconstruction
stupefaction 3[6–8]
stupidity 220[15]
subject 40[10], 41[15], 240[5], 242[2], 319[15],
    410[4], 421[2], 427[5], 447[Von], 471[50]
  existential 50[4]
  knowing subject 378[2]
  as limit of world 471[50]
subjectivism 37[6], 71[2], 91[2], 104[7], 167[2],
    169[10], 180[33,35], 204[1], 253[7], 258[16],
    286[7], 291[24], 294[Mer 1], 406[2], 454[3–5],
    455[10]
subjectivity 134[10], 145[2], 206[7], 212[19],
    220[9], 232[1], 234[13,14], 265[2], 314[1],
    318[8], 322[31], 406[3], 456[3]
  and arithmetic 144[5]
  intersubjectivity 299[22], 300[24,27]
  of phenomena 314[2]
  and representation 220[13]
  and truth 232[2]
  as truth 232[2], 233[5]